FIGHTING TERROR AFTER NAPOLEON

How Europe Became Secure after 1815

BEATRICE DE GRAAF

Utrecht University, The Netherlands

CAMBRIDGE
UNIVERSITY PRESS

CAMBRIDGE
UNIVERSITY PRESS

University Printing House, Cambridge CB2 8BS, United Kingdom

One Liberty Plaza, 20th Floor, New York, NY 10006, USA

477 Williamstown Road, Port Melbourne, VIC 3207, Australia

314–321, 3rd Floor, Plot 3, Splendor Forum, Jasola District Centre,
New Delhi – 110025, India

79 Anson Road, #06–04/06, Singapore 079906

Cambridge University Press is part of the University of Cambridge.

It furthers the University's mission by disseminating knowledge in the pursuit of
education, learning, and research at the highest international levels of excellence.

www.cambridge.org
Information on this title: www.cambridge.org/9781108842068
DOI: 10.1017/9781108895873

© Beatrice de Graaf 2020

This is a translated and updated publication of *Tegen de terreur: Hoe Europa veilig werd na Napoleon*,
written in Dutch by Beatrice de Graaf and published by Prometheus in 2018 (ISBN 9789035144583)

First published in English by Cambridge University Press in 2020

Printed in the United Kingdom by TJ International Ltd, Padstow Cornwall

A catalogue record for this publication is available from the British Library.

Library of Congress Cataloging-in-Publication Data
Names: Graaf, Beatrice de, author.
Title: Fighting terror after Napoleon : how Europe became secure after 1815 / Beatrice de Graaf,
Universiteit Utrecht, Netherlands.
Other titles: How Europe became secure after 1815
Description: Cambridge ; New York : Cambridge University Press, [2020] | Includes bibliographical
references and index.
Identifiers: LCCN 2020027278 (print) | LCCN 2020027279 (ebook) | ISBN 9781108842068 (hardback) |
ISBN 9781108895873 (ebook)
Subjects: LCSH: Europe – History – 1815–1848. | Napoleonic Wars, 1800–1815 – Peace. | Allied Council
of Ministers – History. | Terrorism – Prevention – Europe – History – 19th century. | Internal security –
Europe – History – 19th century. | National security – Europe – History – 19th century. | Europe –
Foreign relations – 19th century.
Classification: LCC D383 .G675 2020 (print) | LCC D383 (ebook) | DDC 940.2/82–dc23
LC record available at https://lccn.loc.gov/2020027278
LC ebook record available at https://lccn.loc.gov/2020027279

ISBN 978-1-108-84206-8 Hardback

CONTENTS

FIGURES

MAPS

TABLES

ACKNOWLEDGEMENTS

A journey into the nineteenth century requires suitable luggage, especially if one is a child of the twentieth century and departs from the twenty-first. People did things differently two hundred years ago. The international language was French, everything was written by hand, in Germany still in the oftentimes hardly legible *Kurrentschrift*. What complicates matters even more is the fact that the historical people I encountered were not even from the nineteenth century, but came from the eighteenth century – an era of pompadoured wigs that seems even more distant in time and customs. How should we then begin to understand what a politician, general or diplomat meant when talking about the balance of power, about peace or security?

I have been able to follow through with this voyage back in time and space and make sense of these historical encounters only thanks to my group of travel companions. My European Research Council group – Constantin Ardeleanu, Susanne Keesman, Wouter Klem, Erik de Lange, Melle Lyklema, Ozan Ozavci, Joep Schenk, Jossie van Til – accompanied me along the winding paths, through the mists of the immediate post-1815 years, and helped me avoid pitfalls and dead alleys.[1] Our group's student assistants were also indispensable; without them I would still be wandering about: Yannick Balk, Annelotte Janse, Hannah Joosse, Paul Kardoulakis, Eva van de Kimmenade, Nicolette Moors and Celine Mureau, with Yannick and Celine being of essential help during the final stretch. The NWO Blueprints group in Utrecht – Clemens van den Berg, Trineke Palm, Peter-Ben Smit and Jorrit Steehouder – and the GIB/ Conflict section in our History Department provided support and inspiration throughout. In between, the students of my MA tutorial on 1815 – Carla, Daan, Leone, Merit, Rob, Tim and Yannick – were a great audience for finding and testing the main arguments. I am grateful to Ozan, Wouter and Erik for helping me find my way through various archives, to Yannick for the beautiful images, to Erik Goosmann for the elegant maps and to Carla Spiegel and Myrthe van Groningen for the fine-tuning of the English edition.

---

[1] The research leading to these results also received funding from the ERC under the European Union's Seventh Framework Programme (FP/2007-2013) / ERC Grant Agreement n.615313.

Inspiration and insight into the timescapes and temporalities of the early nineteenth century came from Chris Clark, Christine Haynes, Mark Jarrett, Lotte Jensen, Matthijs Lok, Niek van Sas, Glenda Sluga and Brian Vick. Eckart Conze's support, his ideas on historicizing security and presence in Utrecht in 2017 were essential to this project. Susan Legêne helped me understand the nexus between the Concert of Europe and Empire. Without Mieke Canneman-van Leeuwen I would not have been able to decipher the crucial texts in the *Kurrentschrift*; I am very grateful for her patient help. Christoph Baumgartner, Guido de Bruin, Eckart Conze, Lotte Jensen, John Kok, Kees Noorda, Maarten van Riel and Maarten Wildervanck read and provided valuable comments.

Essential for a journey into uncharted territory – here, the winding trail of the Allied Council – were the archives and their guardians, the archivists, who were so very friendly everywhere. Stijn Lybeert at the Oudenaarde City Archives, Philip Schofield from the Bentham Papers in London and Christian Schwarzbach from the Secret State Archives Prussian Cultural Heritage Foundation in Berlin deserve a special reference for their patient and lengthy answers to my manifold requests.

The journey also went via Cambridge, through the charming gates of St Catherine's, where Chris Clark and Hans van de Ven invited me as visiting fellow to work on this project, and enjoy the lively discussions there and within the History Faculty. Colin Higgins, Andrew McKenzie-McHarg, Rachel Hoffman, Matthew Champion and Mary-Ann Middelkoop were perfect sparring partners.

At the end of the tour the book came in sight, first the Dutch one, but only thanks to the encouraging words of Joost Dankers, Marieke van Oostrom and Mai Spijkers, who advised me to make this story accessible to a broader audience. For the English version, I owe so much to Michael Watson, who encouraged me to write this history years ago. John Kok was of invaluable assistance in providing me with the English translation of the first Dutch draft, which I could then complement and adapt into the current, final one, but only with the help of Ruth Boyes at Cambridge University Press and Jane Burkowski.

Roland and the children descended with me into underground mines and fortresses, helped me to navigate the Wellington Barrier and were always willing to listen to my endless stories of distant battles, Napoleon, Wellington or those marvellous radical women in Brussels. I am grateful for their companionship throughout this adventure. The story of this journey is also theirs.

~

Prologue

Though seemingly intangible, a continent's degree of security can be measured by the anxieties of a lone traveller wandering its roads. It all begins with the question of whether the roads are safe. Are they passable, maintained and marked well? Much of the European Union's progress towards an ever closer union runs along interlinked road works, the growing availability of Italian coffee in roadside cafes and the increasingly standardized fares for gas station toilets. The number of toll gates may be on the rise again, but highway robbers have rarely been sighted in the last few decades. This process of an increasing European integration of safety and security on the roads has had its precursors in previous eras. In fact, the first real instantiation of intercontinental safe and secure travel manifested itself as early as two centuries ago, at the end of the Napoleonic Wars. A highly engaging and at times stupefying account of such a journey through Europe was offered by an American first-lady-to-be: Louisa Adams, spouse of the US ambassador to Russia (and later president), John Quincy Adams. It has recently been marvellously recounted by Michael O'Brien. After all, nothing illustrates the state of a continent's security so well as the safe passage of a lone lady on the road.

On 12 February 1815, 40-year-old Louisa Adams (Fig. 0.1), a daughter of the British nobility, set out from her home in St Petersburg to join her husband in Paris. In a solitary carriage, she slowly hobbled over the icy roads of a continent that was in the process of being liberated by Allied troops. With her 7-year-old son, two maid servants and a veteran soldier attendant for company she travelled via Riga towards Tilsit (present-day Sovjetsk, just to the north-east of Kaliningrad). There, she saw 'houses half burnt, a very thin population; women unprotected; and that dreary look of forlorn desertion, which sheds its gloom around all the objects, announcing devastation and despair'.[1]

In those days, Europe was far from an ideal place for touristic travel. Journeying was a cumbersome endeavour, and whatever tourism existed was an elite affair. It is therefore all the more remarkable that, from the early

[1] M. O'Brien, *Mrs. Adams in Winter. A Journey in the Last Days of Napoleon* (New York: Farrar, Straus and Giroux, 2010), 124.

Figure 0.1 Louisa Adams (Mrs John Quincy Adams), 1852. (Universal History Archive/UIG/Bridgeman Images)

nineteenth century, women were increasingly found on the roads without their husbands or masters, which points not only to (civil and female) emancipation but also improved road security.

At Tilsit, Louisa saw the looks of a continent that had been subject to more than twenty years of warfare and devastation. Yet this devastation was only part of the war's legacy. Armed conflicts cause chaos and upheaval, but campaigns also bring in their wake better infrastructure, improved roads and new means of communication. And if these means of communication and transport are not destroyed afterwards, by the victors, or in a strategy of scorched earth, then they will also serve the post-war generations in peacetime. In this respect, Napoleon's mass troop movements – while using the old network of postal routes that dated back to Roman times – led to new roads, with better paving, lined by semaphores (optical telegraph systems), checked by road patrols and overseen through the inspection of standardized passports.

Although the scars of war were visible and at some points still bleeding, the roads Louisa Adams travelled – via Riga, Königsberg, Berlin, Frankfurt am Main and Strasbourg to Paris – were passable, and often paved. When approaching Berlin, Louisa Adams noticed something remarkable: 'To my utter astonishment I heard nothing but the praises of the gallantry of Napoleon, and his Officers.' Inhabitants assured her that she would 'travel over the most beautiful road in the world, which had been completed by his order'.[2]

Notwithstanding these logistic improvements, Louisa was still astonished by the huge differences in morals and customs of the areas she passed through. The weights, measures and units of length sometimes changed every few kilometres. To her relief, communication (in French) and payment (in Dutch ducats, or via banknotes that were issued by a network of international bankers) were internationalized enough to keep insurmountable obstacles out of her way.[3]

While still in the German lands, and quite unexpectedly, Louisa and her companions got mired up in troop formations that roamed the roads. These troops were gathering themselves for the final battle against Napoleon – who had escaped from Elba and landed in the south of France in early March 1815. The Allies quickly appropriated the roads to France and turned them to their own interest, using them for the remobilization towards Waterloo, and, from then on, issued joint standardized passports of their own making. This also affected Louisa, since, with her British nationality and diplomatic status as an ambassador's wife, she was able to quickly acquire Prussian and Russian letters of safe conduct. Allied cooperation translated into the quick accepting and issuing of passports. Hence, with her Allied passports in hand, Louisa easily passed through the fifty-one postal controls that she met with prior to approaching the border with France.

In the end, it took Louisa Adams forty days to travel from St Petersburg to Paris, arriving on 23 March. (Today the trip takes three and a half hours by plane or about thirty hours by car.) She did not arrive in a state of guaranteed peace yet, but Europe was almost there. There still were unsettling encounters with foraging Prussian, Russian and marauding French soldiers in the last leg of her journey. Still, the continent Louisa Adams travelled through was preparing for decades of peace, after years of 'total war'.[4] After the years of insecurity and confusion, a new age of industrial and commercial growth was about to set in, holding the promise of an end to the population's

---

[2] O'Brien, *Mrs. Adams in Winter*, 134–5.

[3] Ibid., 53–4; M. Broers, *The Napoleonic Empire in Italy, 1796–1814. Cultural Imperialism in a European Context?* (Basingstoke: Palgrave Macmillan, 2005), 213–24.

[4] D. Bell, *The First Total War. Napoleon's Europe and the Birth of Warfare as We Know It* (London: Bloomsbury, 2007); A. Forrest, K. Hagemann and J. Rendall, 'Nations in Arms, People at War', in Forrest, Hagemann and Rendall (eds.), *Soldiers, Citizens and Civilians. Experiences and Perceptions of the Revolutionary and Napoleonic Wars, 1790–1820* (Basingstoke: Palgrave Macmillan, 2009), 1–19.

destitution. Demobilization would take another couple of months after the final battles were fought in June 1815. But forests that were once ridden with veterans, deserters and vagabonds became gradually pacified. More road patrols and the introduction of new omnibus systems made the continent increasingly accessible for travellers.

Louisa Adams was one of the first ladies that travelled (nearly) alone to reap the fruits of peace – including good coach inns and passable coffee. Others like her would soon follow suit. Tourist guides came into vogue only a couple of years later, and spas were attracting more and more travellers from all corners of the continent. After the tectonic shocks of the French Revolution and the Napoleonic Wars, the currents of tumultuous times could finally quieten down, and travellers, farmers and citizens alike could start to profit from the newly created state of security.

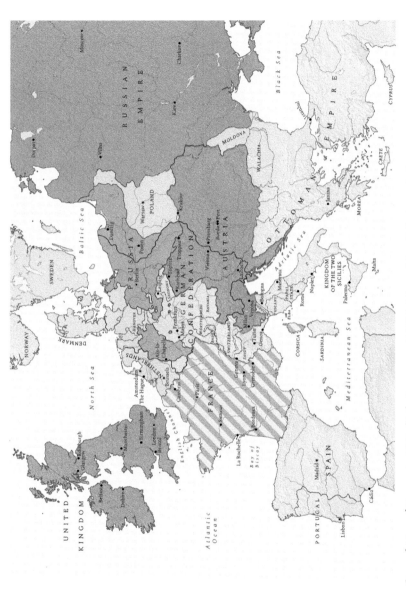

Map 0.1 General Map of Europe in 1815. (Erik Goosmann © 2020, Mappa Mundi Cartography)

Map 0.2 The Allied occupation of France, July–December 1815. (Erik Goosmann © 2020, Mappa Mundi Cartography)

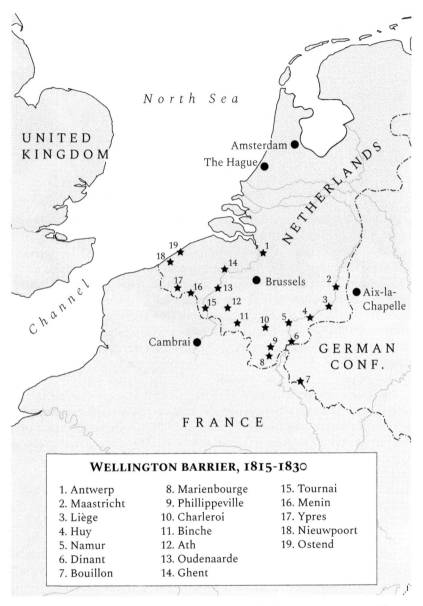

Map 0.3 Map of the Wellington Barrier, 1815–30. (Erik Goosmann © 2020, Mappa Mundi Cartography)

1

Introduction

Napoleon's Frustration

What Sort of Peace?

Following Napoleon's refusal to accept the favourable conditions offered him
by the Allies after his defeat at the Battle of Leipzig in October 1813, Napoleon
is said to have sighed: 'I'm tired of this old Europe! I refuse to rule over
a withered empire!'[1] After 1815 the imperial dream of a united Europe
under one military ruler came to an end. In its stead came something different:
changes that did not revert back to the fragmented world of the *ancien régime*,
but that expanded on a fateful sense of solidarity that the European powers
nolens volens had been subjected to during the Napoleonic Wars. That over
twenty-year-long period of insecurity and unstable alliances gave rise to a new
community linked by the fear of terror and violence on the one hand, and the
dream of peace and repose on the other.

Napoleon's reference to that 'old, withered Europe' expressed his lack of
comprehension and frustration with the leading princes and ministers who
had allowed him to play them off against each other multiple times, but who
had still got the better of him. What he found even more difficult to fathom was
why the victors of 1815 did not pick up where he left off and stretch their sway
over Europe in their turn. He simply could not comprehend why the head of
the largest and most successful contingent of allied troops in history, the Duke
of Wellington, submitted himself after the glorious victory at Waterloo to the
authority of a government official, the British foreign secretary Robert Stewart,
Viscount Castlereagh (1769–1822), instead of ascending to the throne in
France, or anywhere else for that matter: 'Can it be possible that the modern
Marlborough has linked himself in the train of Castlereagh, and yoked his
victories to the turpitude of a political mountebank? It is inconceivable!'[2] What
were they, Wellington and Castlereagh, thinking? 'What sort of peace has

---

[1] According to Frances Lady Shelley, in R. Edgcumbe (ed.), *The Diary of Frances Lady Shelley, 1787–1817* (London: John Murray, 1912), 57.
[2] Emmanuel, comte de Las Cases(ed.), *Memorial de Sainte Hélène. Journal of the Private Life and Conversations of the Emperor Napoleon at Saint Helena*, vol. 4 (London: Colburn, 1823), 221.

England concluded? Lord Castlereagh had the whole Continent at his disposal, and yet what advantage, what indemnity, has he secured to his own country? He has signed just such a peace as he would have signed had he been conquered.'[3]

Indeed, what sort of peace was this, a peace that had to be enforced with the blood of so many casualties and battles? It was certainly not the quiet of the churchyard, with a new hegemonic power stepping up to claim the now empty imperial throne. Every European power was acutely wary of any other power aspiring to hegemony again. What united them was their abhorrence of the 'iron sceptre' of (French) domination on the one hand and revolutionary terror on the other. That infernal chaos – of revolutionary and Napoleonic warfare – had to be prevented from recurring ever again. The question was how.

This book unpacks a rather forgotten story out of the mothballs of European history: the story of the first collective European fight against terror in peace-time. This fight can be considered a unique and innovative security experiment, that for a variety of reasons only lasted a couple of years and only partially succeeded. This first experiment in collective and institutionalized security management foreshadowed the future European system of mutual security as we know it today. Waging peace can be as complex as waging war, if only because post-war peace objectives may present far larger challenges for a coalition to pursue than fighting a joint enemy. This exceptional period of transition – from concluding a war to consolidating a new order – presents us with a setting and a stage on which very remarkable, well-known and lesser-known figures of military, political, diplomatic or administrative distinction engaged each other in something unheard of.

An (Anti-)Revolutionary Security Experiment

In 1815, the four great powers of Europe – the United Kingdom, Prussia, Austria and Russia (Fig. 1.1) – embarked on a unique experiment: the implementation of a collective security system, via the creation of an Allied Council, and by the leverage of an Allied Army of Occupation.[4] The French

---

[3] Emmanuel, comte de Las Cases (ed.), *Memoirs of the Life, Exile, and Conversations of the Emperor Napoleon*, vol. 3 (London: Colburn, 1836), 251. See also: Las Cases, *Memorial de Sainte Hélène*, vol. 3, 82. John Bew cites this slightly differently: J. Bew, *Castlereagh. A Life* (Oxford: Oxford University Press, 2012), 408.

[4] From July to the end of November 1815, the Council consisted of the European great powers' princes and principal foreign ministers themselves. From December 1815 their diplomats took over. Yet differences in rank and stature did exist and continued to do so. Some diplomats were titled 'ambassador', while others were referred to as 'minister'. The title of minister was often confusing, since it had different meanings in different countries; it could be a junior position, a honorary function, or a full-fledged cabinet position, such as a Secretary of State.

Figure 1.1   The Allied entry into Paris, 31 March 1814. By Thomas Sutherland, 1815. (Heritage Images)

Revolutionary and Napoleonic Wars had achieved something unprecedented. Not only had they forged the European states together into a wartime alliance against the Bonapartist *Grande Armée*. But even after the conclusion of the armistice and the first peace treaty, the *Grande Peur* that survived after all these years of warfare pushed the powers closer together than ever before.[5] The philosopher Immanuel Kant had speculated on the possibilities of world peace; pundits and publicists had designed blueprints for a post-war federation of European states. But these plans had never reached the baize-covered tables of Europe's diplomats and ministers. The Vienna Congress, convening from September 1814 until June 1815, consolidated the existing wartime alliance and deliberated on the new, post-war peace order. However, contrary to received wisdom, rather than the Vienna Final Act, it was two other treaties that were to be concluded a couple of months later that contained and cemented the real revolutionary requisites for this new post-war security system: the Treaty of the Quadruple Alliance and the Second Treaty of Paris,

---

[5] By 'grande peur' Lefebvre meant the fear and chaos in the years of the French Revolution. These primal anxieties constantly loomed in the years thereafter, including after 1815. See G. Lefebvre, *La Grande Peur de 1789. Suivi de Les foules révolutionnaires* (Paris: Armand Collin, 1932).

both signed on 20 November 1815. When the lights of the Vienna spectacle went out and the princes and their diplomats left, the peace in Europe had not been secured at all. Napoleon had to be fought and beaten once again, after his staggering return in March 1815. The post-Napoleonic security of Europe only found its real shape and framework through the consistent efforts of the ministers of the four great powers, who – after Waterloo – came together in Paris to monitor and enforce the execution of the treaties and encompassing agreements. Only thus, via the persistence of this Allied Council in waging their security efforts in peacetime, could the double-headed serpent of revolution and despotic hegemony be tamed and domesticated.

The innovative part of this anti-revolutionary security system was fourfold. First of all, the ministers of the four great powers introduced a new reading of that classic principle, the 'balance of power'. Well known in European international relations, it was reinterpreted in the early nineteenth century and renovated to match the challenges of the new international system – not by reverting back to the unstable alliance of the *ancien régime* of the 1740–89 period, when the so-called balance was highly volatile, unpredictable and transient and aggressive, both towards weaker states and each other, but in a novel, more structured and institutionalized way.

Secondly, the victors of 1815 established an Allied Council, the so-called Paris Conference, or Ministerial and later Ambassadorial Conference, to enable the day-to-day deliberation on and management of the post-war peace and security arrangements. Castlereagh (and Wellington) fondly referred to this council as the 'Allied Machine'.[6] Herein lay the most far-reaching and revolutionary aspect of the peace arrangements – a revolutionary aspect that remained rather unnoticed at the time, and even thereafter, but in practice transformed the European scene of interstate relations into a new system of collective security. Rather than leaving the stage, the generals, princes and their ministers did not go home, but remained in place to translate their fight against terror into new and continuous practices of security management. The great advantage of such an administrative body was its novel and relatively informal format. The participants were not obliged to engage in complicated formalities and protocol that normally characterized official congresses, stately and royal get-togethers, nor did they need to invest in receptions, balls and other pomp and circumstance. The protocols of the Paris Conference, moreover, were understood as binding international law. Once they were accepted and agreed upon, the Allied courts would have to sign up to these commitments and translate the Paris stipulations into national law. Mostly, the foreign minister of the country that hosted such a ministerial or

---

[6] Castlereagh to Wellington, 13 May 1816, cited in N. van Sas, *Onze natuurlijkste bondgenoot. Nederland, Engeland en Europa, 1713–1831* (Groningen: Wolters-Noordhoff, 1985), 122.

ambassadorial conference would chair the meetings. During the nineteenth century, many more conferences would follow suit.[7] Yet this one, the Parisian conference, as the first of its kind, was not presided over by the French, but the British ministers. First Castlereagh, later Wellington and Charles Stuart.

The third novel dimension of this post-war security system was the invention and implementation of a series of standardized and centrally conceived security practices in peacetime. The participating ministers and diplomats in the Paris Conference – in the main council as well in the subordinated committees – discussed, developed and disseminated new, professional and institutionalized governmental practices geared towards engendering stability and security.[8] Tedious and bureaucratic as that may sound, the invention and proscription of passport regulations, a joint Allied security service and military police and border controls contributed to an emergent European security culture that made itself felt throughout the continent (as Louisa Adams, the travelling wife of diplomat John Quincy Adams, experienced not to her detriment). These collective exertions in the security field also included substantial military efforts. Together, the Allied powers instigated an immense project for the construction of fortresses along the borders of France. Conceived as the material foundation for the newly re-established balance of power, or perhaps better put, for the balance of deterrence, this project was initiated by the Allied Council, executed under supervision of the British generals, most notably Wellington (Fig. 1.2), with assistance from Dutch and German experts, and financed predominantly through the French reparation funds.

Rather than working towards a restoration, these immediate post-war years saw a gigantesque, unheard of (and soon to be dissolved) attempt to join forces in the fight against terror. Obviously, such a system could only be enforced. Hence, the Allied Council's crucial leverage was the Allied Army of Occupation – the fourth novelty of the post-war system. Between 1740 and 1815, warfare had been directed towards expansion, and the balance of power had hinged on land-grabbing battles amongst the five great powers – wars in these decades were often waged to partition specific countries or solve succession disputes (Austria, Prussia or Poland). In 1815, the Allied powers opted for another solution. They decided to leave the troops in France after the Battle of Waterloo, in June 1815, and not repatriate them for the time being. Prussian thirst for revenge aside, the other victors had no intention of cutting up the country or dividing the invaded provinces. An overwhelming total of 1.2 million troops remained deployed in France, occupying at first two thirds of the French territories, to be scaled back, but still leaving a substantial

---

[7] H. Blomeyer-Bartenstein, 'Conferences of Ambassadors', in Y. Zhou (ed.), *Encyclopedia of Public International Law* (Amsterdam: Elsevier, 1984), 48–9.

[8] See C. Bayly, *The Birth of the Modern World 1780–1914. Global Connections and Comparisons* (Oxford: Blackwell, 2004), 49, 51, 62.

Figure 1.2   Arthur Wellesley, Duke of Wellington. Portrait by Thomas Lawrence, 1815/16. (Apsley House, London/Heritage Images)

number behind from early 1816 until late 1818. The Allied courts appointed the Duke of Wellington as supreme commander of this army of occupation, which was from the beginning conceived as a temporary occupation, in order to guarantee France's compliance with the stipulations of the peace treaties that needed to be concluded. With his authority and his ultimate allied force, the Paris Conference's leverage was assured.

After twenty-six years of unprecedented revolutionary upheavals and endless fighting, with the unspeakable consequences of invasion, occupation, exploitation and suppression of their countries in mind, the victorious powers craved stability. The revolutionary changes that Napoleon had pushed through in the wake of his armies had left them pining for peace and quiet. At the same time, the position of France in Europe made it necessary to invite the country back into the circle of great powers in the long run – a stable balance of power without France was hardly imaginable strategically. Given this conundrum, a new settlement, and a dynamic one, involving a temporizing of France's position, needed to be designed. And indeed, where Napoleon had tried and overplayed his hand, the anti-Napoleonic coalition exited the long, winding wars not only as victors but also as custodians and managers of a new system of unified rule. With the threat of war and revolutionary terror still looming large,

ONTMOETING VAN DE GENERAALS WELLINGTON EN BLUCHER, NA DEN GEËINDIGDEN SLAG VAN WATERLOO, BIJ DE HOEVE: LA BELLE ALLIANCE.

Figure 1.3   Meeting between Blücher and Wellington after the Battle of Waterloo, 1815. By Reinier Vinkeles, 1815/16. This image illustrates the so-called 'horseback diplomacy'. (Rijksmuseum, Amsterdam)

the necessity to combat these threats together kept the coalition united after 1815. At least in these very first post-war years (far more than ever accounted for) the 'horseback diplomacy' (Fig. 1.3), the battle-hardened solidarity and the shocking experiences of the emperor's return had ripened hearts and minds for a new type of peace.[9] The vagaries of fate ushered in a multilaterally discussed, arranged and secured peace that we may interpret as the birth of the first modern system of collective security in Europe: a system that in the numerous nationalist and patriotic historiographic accounts that were produced throughout the nineteenth century has found little acknowledgement. Long before commercial interest and economic considerations about scale and

---

[9] Cf. J. Paulmann, *Pomp und Politik. Monarchenbegegnungen in Europa zwischen Ancien Régime und Erstem Weltkrieg* (Paderborn: F. Schöningh, 2000), 131. See also J. Mitzen, *Power in Concert. The Nineteenth-Century Origins of Global Governance* (Chicago: University of Chicago Press, 2013).

productivity dictated and inspired the project of European integration, the common denominator behind this first impulse for a unification of Europe in norms and institutions was the collective fight against terror.

A New History of Terror and Security

This first experiment in European collective security management, in the form of the Paris Conference, has been almost completely lost in oblivion.[10] The reasons for this oblivion are not illogical. The Allied Council convened behind the scenes and did not last long: it dissolved in 1818. The council had completed its main task: to mitigate the threat of war and terror and to design and consolidate a system of deterrence. France was less of a threat in 1818, and the surrounding countries had regained much of their stability. The council could have lasted longer but was downscaled to the level of an ambassadorial (and less effective) conference for reasons of diverging national interests and domestic power changes. Purely coincidental developments, such as the early demise of some of its main agents, precipitated this dissolution of Allied unity.

Moreover, those historians who worked themselves up into a professionalized guild and academic discipline in the nineteenth century predominantly concerned themselves with the historiography of their own nations and national peculiarities. In the wake of the rising power of national movements, they became the heralds of the newly (re)discovered or created national identity. As chroniclers of a supposed European unity and collaboration, they would have stood little chance of making a name for themselves at home. The history of terror and security as a collective, European history therefore remains to be written. This book makes a first start in presenting, assembling and interpreting the protocols of this first collective European undertaking – the Allied Council – as they have been painstakingly collected and contextualized from various archives in European capitals.

The story of this Allied Council, this Paris Conference, is not merely presented as an organizational or institutional history, but is embedded and historicized within the context of considerations, emotions and sentiments as experienced and voiced by the main protagonists and contemporaries that made up this council – or became the object of its manifold activities. Terror and security are highly contested concepts and can only be correctly understood within the web of meanings, emotions and associations that were

---

[10] Niek van Sas, Reiner Marcowitz and Matthias Schulz mention the Allied Conference in passing, thus kindling my interest. Cf. (Van) Sas, *Onze natuurlijkste bondgenoot*, 126–7; R. Marcowitz, *Grossmacht auf Bewährung. Die Interdependenz französischer Innen- und Aussenpolitik und ihre Auswirkungen auf Frankreichs Stellung im europäischen Konzert 1814/15–1851/52* (Stuttgart: Thorbecke, 2001), 48; M. Schulz, *Normen und Praxis. Das Europäische Konzert der Großmächte als Sicherheitsrat, 1815–1860* (Munich: Oldenbourg, 2009), 63–4.

attributed to them at the time. From a distance of over two centuries, the salience of the French Revolution and Napoleonic Wars stands out as deeply incisive in the development of national and European identities. Those years of turmoil and distress ushered in a new European notion of common destiny – albeit a notion that was predominantly fostered by the European elites and that echoed their concerns and sentiments. These elites, the princes and their entourage, had come to realize that they depended on each other in the joint fight against the double-headed terror of revolution and despotism. Their populaces were equally aware of having entered into a new era of transition. Old monarchs returned; new ones equally stepped out of the shadows of their previous marginal dynasties and pedigrees. Historical privileges of the nobility and clergy were not completely, or only haphazardly restored; confiscated properties and territories were not returned. Neither were the manifold achievements of the Napoleonic rulers in centralized and professionalized governance turned back. A volatile and confusing combination of a desire for normalcy and an end to war and deprivation on the one hand, and the still floating hope for (gradual) change and reform on the other, kept the European continent on alert in 1815. Subsistence crises further deepened the feelings of distress and social unrest in countries that were already suffering from the complicated transition from wartime to peace economies.[11] The discussions, decisions and statements regarding terror and security within the Allied Council should therefore also be read as an expression of the collective sentiments of that time – conflicting and incompatible as they oftentimes seemed.[12] Security is never only a category of governance, management or physical protection, but always also an expression of desire and sentiment. To approach these sentiments, and the way they were channelled by the Allied Council, this book's narrative is enriched with the accounts of individual travellers, women, diplomats and ordinary citizens that commented upon the coming of this new European system of peace and security.

Finally, a junction is established between security in Europe and beyond the continent. The security threats envisaged and confronted by the Allied Council did not only manifest themselves in and around France, or at other vulnerable places in Europe where crises had not subsided after 1815. They also raised their radical heads in the colonies and on the open waters. Timewise, the great powers' efforts to implement a collective security system in Europe coincided with the process of colonizing and stepping up imperial efforts outside Europe. What is more, these internal European and external imperial security efforts

---

[11] See R. Evans, *The Pursuit of Power. Europe, 1815–1914* (New York: Penguin, 2016), 9–11.

[12] I refer here to a chapter, 'Literature Review: Emotions in Global Politics', in the forthcoming PhD thesis of Lotje van Uhm, preliminary title: The Moving Dead. The Politics of Mourning, Dead Bodies, and Violent Conflict. See also E. Hutchinson and R. Bleiker, 'Theorizing Emotions in World Politics', *International Theory*, 6:3 (2014), 491–514.

underwent a process of cross-pollination: what happened in France was translated into lessons learned elsewhere in Europe, or in the colonies. And vice versa: imperialist and hierarchical notions on security, the division into categories, the political sorting of groups and countries, gleaned while governing intercontinental empires, was implemented at home as well. The security managers of 1815 were not only highly innovative, but elitist and imperialist in the way they developed new methods and techniques of inclusion and exclusion, blacklisting and espionage. They shared their best practices and deployed their best professional agents and experts in trimming the new collective system of security in and beyond Europe. A brief elaboration on these four aspects – the historiographical deficiency in addressing the Allied Council, the need for historicizing security, the importance of applying a cultural and emotional approach, and the imperialist nature of this post-war order – is called for, and will be offered below.

A Forgotten History Reconstructed from Forgotten Archives

The bicentennial commemorations of the Congress of Vienna have produced a wealth of new publications on that Congress.[13] From these manifold studies, it transpires that the Congress did not only concern itself with the protection of the status quo, nor was it merely the platform on which a restoration of the *ancien régime* order was contemplated. The Congress demonstrated a spirit of renewal and reform: new norms and institutions in international relations, international and constitutional law were created – to which an increasing number of states subscribed voluntarily.[14] These novel studies seem to uphold the findings in the pioneering work of Paul Schroeder from 1994.[15] Where some still interpret the international relationships in the years around 1815 from the perspective of power realism and bellicism,[16] many experts have

[13] Including B. Vick, *The Congress of Vienna. Power and Politics after Napoleon* (Cambridge, MA: Harvard University Press, 2014); W. Gruner, *Der Wiener Kongress 1814/15* (Stuttgart: Reclam, 2014); R. Stauber, *Der Wiener Kongress* (Vienna: Böhlau, 2014); M. Jarrett, *The Congress of Vienna and its Legacy. War and Great Power Diplomacy after Napoleon* (London: I. B. Tauris, 2013). Next to these more academic monographs some other tomes have been published that are more focused on the storytelling aspect and that stand out more by their richness and readability than their source analysis, the main example here being A. Zamoyski, *Rites of Peace. The Fall of Napoleon and the Congress of Vienna* (London: Harper Collins, 2007).

[14] Cf. J. Dülffer, M. Kröger and H. Wippich (eds.), *Vermiedene Kriege. Deeskalation von Konflikten der Grossmächte zwischen Krimkrieg und Erstem Weltkrieg (1856–1914)* (Munich: Oldenbourg, 1997). See especially Schulz, *Normen und Praxis*.

[15] P. Schroeder, *The Transformation of European Politics, 1763–1848* (Oxford: Clarendon, 1994).

[16] Predominantly H. Kissinger, *Diplomacy* (New York: Simon & Schuster, 1994), 78–102. For a rich and nuanced work in this vein, see J. Leonhard, *Bellizismus und Nation.*

come to approach matters from the constructivist–institutionalist angle and underline the role of norms and institutions in the international arena, and the importance of multilateralism and joint deliberation.[17] The Congress was not merely about protecting the status quo, it was an attempt to design a dynamical order, geared to produce 'repose and tranquillity' in times of change and turmoil.[18] How should the *Pax Europeana* be waged in the future? What treaties and arrangements were called for to enable gradual reform and improvement?[19]

Significant questions remained, however. Neither Schroeder nor Ikenberry (who, from a political scientist perspective, also pondered on the post-war collective security system)[20] elaborated on how exactly that stable order after 1815 was put together, consolidated and operated in the following years. Ikenberry's main concern was to develop and defend a more schematic take on the institutionalization of post-war power systems, while Schroeder, because his eye was on the entire period from the 1760s to the 1840s, gave scant attention to the years immediately after 1815. In addition, for both scholars, any kind of long-term international cooperation was ultimately merely a matter of strategic considerations and cost–benefit analyses. They left little room for the more principle and sometimes even moral and spiritual weight that those around the table in 1815 gave to their collective security ambitions.[21] In reconstructing the deliberations of the Allied Council, the tentative and hesitant attempts to create such a post-war security system – and to make it function over time – will be fleshed out, as well as the underlying moral values and emotional beliefs attached to this emerging order.

Kriegsdeutung und Nationsbestimmung in Europa und den Vereinigten Staaten 1750–1914 (Munich: Oldenbourg, 2008).

[17] Schulz, Normen und Praxis; W. Pyta (ed.), *Das europäische Mächtekonzert. Friedens- und Sicherheitspolitik vom Wiener Kongress 1815 bis zum Krimkrieg 1853* (Cologne: Böhlau, 2009); E. Conze, 'Abschied von Staat und Politik? Überlegungen zur Geschichte der internationalen Politik', in U. Lappenküper and G. Müller (eds.), *Geschichte der internationalen Beziehungen. Erneuerung und Erweiterung einer historischen Disziplin* (Cologne: Böhlau, 2004), 14–43.

[18] J. Klüber (ed.), *Acten des Wiener Congresses in den Jahren 1814 und 1815*, 9 vols. (Erlangen: Palm & Enke, 1815–35), here: *Acten*, vol. 2 (1817), 530–7. 'Repose' or 'tranquillity' were Metternich's favourite words. See Metternich to Franz Georg, 8 June 1815, Metternich family papers. Rodinný archive Metternissky. Acta Clementina, Correspondance politique Autriche. Cart 49, vol. 5. Státní ústřední archiv, Prague (SUA). Cf. Schulz, *Normen und Praxis*, 74, 559 n. 90.

[19] Schroeder, *The Transformation of European Politics*; E. Kraehe, *Metternich's German Policy*, vol. 2: *The Congress of Vienna, 1814–1815* (Princeton, NJ: Princeton University Press, 1983), 3–17.

[20] G. J. Ikenberry, *After Victory. Institutions, Strategic Restraint and the Rebuilding of Order after Major Wars* (Princeton/Oxford: Princeton University Press, 2001), 80, 82.

[21] Lucien Frary makes a similar point: L. J. Frary, *Russia and the Making of Modern Greek Identity, 1821–1844* (Oxford: Oxford University Press, 2015), 3.

The main source for this study are the records of the Allied Council, formally called the Paris Conference of Ministers (later also Ambassadors), including the subcommittees attached to it. These records have never been properly investigated before and were retrieved from various archives in Europe, including London, Berlin, Nantes, Vienna, Paris and Amsterdam. They had been quite mistakenly neglected, since this council tasked itself with the supervision of the execution of seminal aspects of the Vienna Congress's Final Act, was invoked to negotiate the Second Treaty of Paris and acted as the interstate control council (and inter-court communication centre) to oversee the deployment of the Allied Army of Occupation in France, as well as being a platform for Quadruple Alliance communications. The Paris Conference decided on borders, arrearages, debts and reparations, on returning looted artworks and on matters pertaining to property rights – not only with respect to France but also regarding the rest of Europe and beyond. It was, in short, the bedrock to the European post-war security system.

The council also deliberated on legal, constitutional and police matters, such as whether European-wide censorship or gag orders on the press needed to be implemented. The records of the council are supplemented by correspondence, often even published in print form, between the diplomats involved and other key figures, like Metternich, Castlereagh, Wellington and Alexander I, as well as with eyewitness reports and journals, inasmuch as they could be retrieved. On the activities of the occupying forces and the repayment of debts a number of specialized studies and papers have been published.[22] A number of articles in French, from the nineteenth and early twentieth centuries, deal with the military occupation from a local or regional perspective.[23]

---

[22] See T. Veve, *The Duke of Wellington and the British Army of Occupation in France, 1815–1818* (Westport, CT: Greenwood Press, 1992); Veve, 'Wellington and the Army of Occupation in France, 1815–1818', *The International History Review*, 11: 1 (1989), 98–108; P. Mansel, 'Wellington and the French Restoration', *The International History Review*, 11:1 (1989), 76–83; E. Kraehe, 'Wellington and the Reconstruction of the Allied Armies during the Hundred Days', *The International History Review*, 11:1 (1989), 84–97; V. Wacker, *Die alliierte Besetzung Frankreichs in den Jahren 1814 bis 1818* (Hamburg: Kovac, 2001). Christine Haynes addresses the feelings and reactions of the French population during the occupation: C. Haynes, 'Making Peace: The Allied Occupation of France, 1815–1818', in A. Forrest, K. Hagemann and M. Rowe (eds.), *War, Demobilization and Memory. The Legacy of War in the Era of Atlantic Revolutions* (Basingstoke: Palgrave Macmillan, 2016), 51–67; C. Haynes, *Our Friends the Enemies. The Occupation of France after Napoleon* (Cambridge, MA: Harvard University Press, 2018); J. Hantraye, *Les Cosaques aux Champs-Élysées. l'occupation de la France après la chute de Napoléon* (Paris: Belin, 2005).

[23] R. André, *L'Occupation de la France par les Alliées en 1815 (Juillet–Novembre)* (Paris: Boccard, 1924); M. Béguin, 'Les Prussiens à Evreux en 1815', *Revue Catholique de Normandie*, 31 (1922), 122–7; F. Dutacq, 'L'occupation autrichienne à Lyon en 1815', *Revue des Études Napoléoniennes*, 43 (1936), 270–91; H. Houssaye, *1814* (Paris: Perrin, 1888); Houssaye, *1815. La première restauration, le retour de l'île d'Elbe, les cent jours*

Notwithstanding these insightful publications, the broader security–political and intellectual–cultural framework of the post-war European 'Allied Machine' has, however, never been investigated properly.

Parallels with the Allied Control Council in Berlin after 1945 come to mind. That council oversaw the denazification, democratization, decartelization and demilitarization of a defeated Germany, but soon fell apart into a communist and a liberal–capitalist camp.[24] Another obvious point of comparison would be the committees charged with implementing the peace treaties with Germany, Hungary and the Ottoman Empire after 1918, and the conditions for reparations, the occupation of parts of Germany and the division of the Austro-Hungarian Empire that they imposed on these vanquished powers.[25] Other points for comparison may be provided by the League of Nations' attempts to design the governance of previous Ottoman provinces in the Middle East, or the former German colonies in Africa and the Pacific region.[26] Even the creation of the European Economic Community or the aborted plans for the European Defence Community in the 1950s are material for comparison. Although some after 1918 have sought to draw lessons from experiences booked during and after the Congress of Vienna, the effect and results of the Allied Council between 1815 and 1818 have yet to be plumbed as a possible blueprint for or counterpoint to later occupation statutes or defence communities: something this book will also seek to do.

In order to comprehend the breadth and the depth of the history of collective security, due attention is given to the physical security measures adopted by the Council. These measures materialized not just in the paperwork of treaties or the bayonets of the occupation army, but also in the brick and mortar of physical barriers and fortresses. The Allied Council's deliberations repeatedly reverted back to the creation of a so-called *Boulevard de l'Europe* – the largest and most lasting project undertaken by the Allied ministers. This metaphor both indicated the importance the victorious courts

(Paris: Perrin, 1893); Houssaye, *1815. La seconde abdication – la terreur blanche* (Paris: Perrin, 1905); C. Lefèvre, 'Le département de l'Aisne et l'invasion de 1815 d'après les lettres contemporaines inédites', *Bulletin de la Société historique et académique de Haute-Picardie*, 18 (1847), 42–81; P. Rain, *L'Europe et la restauration des Bourbons 1814–1818* (Paris: Perrin, 1908).

[24] N. Naimark, *The Russians in Germany. A History of the Soviet Zone of Occupation, 1945–1949* (London/Cambridge, MA: Belknap Press, 1997); W. Benz, *Potsdam 1945. Besatzungsherrschaft und Neuaufbau im Vier-Zonen-Deutschland* (Munich: DTV, 2012); G. Mai, *Der Alliierte Kontrollrat in Deutschland 1945–1948. Alliierte Einheit – deutsche Teilung?* (Munich: Oldenbourg, 1995).

[25] See C. Webster, *The Congress of Vienna, 1814–1815* (Oxford: Oxford University Press, 1918), especially the conclusion, 145–8. For 1918, see also M. Macmillan, *Peacemakers. The Paris Conference of 1919 and its Attempt to End War* (London: John Murray, 2001).

[26] S. Pedersen, *The Guardians. The League of Nations and the Crisis of Empire* (Oxford: Oxford University Press, 2015), 403.

attributed to the erection of a series of fortresses throughout Europe, in order to contain France and deter her from new military adventures, and the pivotal position the council had in mind for the Low Countries within this new collective security system. For the 'Wellington Barrier', as the band of fortresses came to be known, stretching from the North Sea coast along the French northern frontier as far as the German city of Mainz, was to be erected on Dutch territories. The United Kingdom of the Netherlands, at one point off-handedly described by Metternich as the 'lapdog' of the European powers, would therefore become the main theatre of and even one of the main actors in these security plans. The Netherlands comes off rather poorly in the historiography of the European Concert. Aside from a few standard works in Dutch – particularly and in fact exclusively the work of Van Sas – little attention has been given to the crucial role of the Low Countries in the post-war security system. But ever since the French Revolution, the Netherlands – whether it was the Batavian Republic, the Kingdom of Holland or the United Kingdom of the Netherlands (including Belgium) – in its 'special relation' with Britain, had a significant role to play in the strategic plans for the post-war order.[27] Not only were the Netherlands, after Prussia, the second largest stakeholder in the French arrear payments. But the Netherlands were also key to the new system of collective security: In March 1815, the Allied powers enabled the Sovereign Prince Willem to proclaim himself King Willem I and become the head of a kingdom that was literally given the task of bolstering Fortress Europe by building this first collective European defensive work, the Wellington Barrier. The history of the Wellington Barrier and the *Boulevard de l'Europe* has never been properly understood for what it was: one of the vital pillars under the new European security architecture.[28] Although most of the archives in the twenty fortified Belgian cities along this barrier were destroyed in the First or Second World War, the archives in the city of Oudenaarde do still contain very extensive – and completely unused – records from this time period. They contain unique material about the aftermath of the wars for liberation, the impact of the Battle of Waterloo and especially about the

---

[27] (Van) Sas, *Onze natuurlijkste bondgenoot*; J. Boogman, *Nederland en de Duitse Bond 1815–1851*, 2 vols. (Groningen/Jakarta: J. B. Wolders, 1955); J. van Zanten, *Schielijk, Winzucht, Zwaarhoofd en Bedaard. Politieke Discussie en Oppositievorming 1813–1840* (Amsterdam: Boom, 2004); M. Lok, *Windvanen. Napoleontische Bestuurders in de Nederlandse en Franse Restauratie (1813–1820)* (Amsterdam: Bert Bakker, 2009); cf. also B. de Graaf, 'Nederland en de collectieve veiligheid', in J. Pekelder, R. Raben and M. Segers (eds.), *De wereld volgens Nederland. Nederlandse buitenlandse politiek in historisch perspectief* (Amsterdam: Boom, 2015), 42–58. See also K. Härter, 'Security and Cross-Border Political Crime: The Formation of Transnational Security Regimes in 18th and 19th Century Europe', *Historical Social Research*, 38:1 (2013), 96–106; H. Reiter, *Politisches Asyl im 19. Jahrhundert. Die deutschen politischen Flüchtlinge des Vormärz und der Revolution von 1848/49 in Europa und den USA* (Berlin: Duncker & Humblot, 1992).

[28] See W. Uitterhoeve, *Cornelis Kraijenhoff 1758–1840. Een loopbaan onder vijf regeervormen* (Nijmegen: Vantilt, 2009).

internationally monitored building of the Wellington Barrier and the presence of Allied occupation forces nearby; sources also include the voices of some of the ordinary citizens of the Belgian provinces, who had to deal with billeting, unpaid debts, receivables and about 120,000 soldiers passing through in a few months' time.

Historicizing Security

An appeal is called for here, to not immediately disqualify the ideas and blueprints on security that resurfaced around 1815 as authoritarian and restorative. Oftentimes epitaphs such as 'conservative', 'romantic' or 'reactionary' are applied to people like the Austrian chancellor and foreign minister Klemens von Metternich, the Irish philosopher and politician Edmund Burke, or Friedrich Gentz, the secretary and nigh *spiritus rector* of the Congress of Vienna. These categories, however, were mostly devised later by early twentieth-century historians such as Meinecke, Mannheim and Schmitt. Contemporaries did not see them, or themselves, that way at all. Gentz, for example, a student of Immanuel Kant, considered himself a liberal.[29] Tsar Alexander and Metternich were considered quite liberal by compatriots and diplomats alike in the ambition they unfolded to advocate new constitutions for France and Poland, and political reforms in France. Yet in a good deal of (older) historiography this period is often discussed under the category 'restoration'. The doyen of the history of Europe during and after Napoleon, Michael Broers, speaks explicitly about 'the men of the Restoration'.[30] Many popular books continue to describe the Congress of Vienna and the resulting Concert of Europe as a 'system of illiberal oppression',[31] as anachronistic and unjustified as this generalized qualification may be.

---

[29] For the historiography of thinkers who are portrayed as conservative (especially Burke and Gentz), see F. Meinecke, *Weltbürgertum und Nationalstaat. Studien zur Genesis des deutschen Nationalstaates* (Munich: Oldenbourg, 1907); Meinecke, *Die Idee der Staatsräson in der neueren Geschichte* (Munich: Oldenbourg, 1925); Meinecke, *Die Entstehung des Historismus* (Munich: Oldenbourg, 1936); K. Mannheim, 'Das konservative Denken: Soziologische Beiträge zum Werden des politischen-historischen Denkens in Deutschland', *Archiv für Sozialwissenschaft und Sozialpolitik*, 57:1 (1927), 68–142; C. Schmitt, *Politische Romantik* (Berlin: Duncker & Humblot, 1919). With thanks to Jonathan Green, who recently defended his PhD dissertation on this topic in Cambridge, see J. Green, Edmund Burke's German Readers at the End of Enlightenment, 1790–1815 (unpublished PhD thesis, University of Cambridge, 2017). See also Green, '*Fiat iustitia, pereat mundus*: Immanuel Kant, Friedrich Gentz, and the Possibility of Prudential Enlightenment', *Modern Intellectual History*, 14:1 (2017), 35–65.
[30] M. Broers, *Europe after Napoleon. Revolution, Reaction and Romanticism, 1814–1848* (Manchester/New York: Manchester University Press, 1996), 3, 19–20.
[31] Zamoyski, *Rites of Peace*, 168.

In our current era of the 'War on Terror', some recognition is needed for the undoubtedly alarmist manner in which European monarchs and ministers dealt with opposing voices and the lingering threat of revolution and terror. With Europe still shaking from the revolutionary earthquake, administrative tolerance for (alleged) sedition and conspiracy was hard to come by in 1815. Virtually every country maintained a network of spies and informants to keep their eye out for those kinds of plots. For instance, the Dutch King Willem I, without batting an eye, took over most of the informants and agents of his predecessor, Louis Napoleon.[32] Still, it is going too far to dismiss the post-war security system as a closed bastion of despotism. The majority of the populations of the liberated countries, and even large parts of the French populace, were initially relieved and grateful towards the Allied generals for having defeated Napoleon and tamed the spirit of chaos and revolution. The European security order was indeed an imperialist project (as will become clear), but more idealist, reformist and moral motives also lay at the bottom of these plans – motives that were recognized and shared by many citizens in France and beyond.

It is therefore high time to 'historicize' notions such as balance of power and security, implying that these notions need to be contextualized and embedded in the sentiments, interpretations and associations attributed to them at the time.[33] More often than not, political scientists and historians alike tend to define the concept of security either in far too normative a fashion, in the moral vernacular of their own times, on the basis of presentist aversions and sympathies. Or, on the other hand, they inadvertently cast this contested concept in much too generalized, seemingly objectified and quantitative terms. Both readings overlook the importance of contemporary interpretations of seemingly similar semantic concepts.[34] Eckart Conze, Martti Koskenniemi and Matthias Schulz, in his pioneering work *Normen und Praxis*, have already laid an important foundation for such a historicizing approach to security, international relations and international law.[35] So, too, David Reynolds shows late in his book *Summits* that a communicative and cultural, but also very detailed historical approach to international high-level meetings between state

---

[32] Cf. (Van) Zanten, *Schielijk*, 104. See also Lok, *Windvanen*.

[33] E. Conze, '"Securitization": Gegenwartsdiagnose oder historischer Analysenzatz?', *Geschichte und Gesellschaft*, 38:3 (2012), 453–67; B. de Graaf and C. Zwierlein, 'Historicizing Security: Entering the Conspiracy Dispositive', *Historical Social Research*, 38:1 (2013), 46–64.

[34] With a great exception to this rule in the seminal text by W. Conze, 'Sicherheit, Schutz', in Conze, et al. (eds), *Geschichtliche Grundbegriffe*, vol. 5 (Stuttgart: Klett-Cotta, 1984), 831–62.

[35] E. Conze, *Geschichte der Sicherheit. Entwicklung – Themen – Perspektiven* (Göttingen: Vandenhoeck & Ruprecht, 2018); M. Koskenniemi, *The Gentle Civilizer of Nations. The Rise and Fall of International Law, 1870–1960* (Cambridge: Cambridge University Press, 2004).

leaders, diplomats and their entourage can garner new insights on how security was understood at the time.[36] When peace is the absence of war, then security is the dynamic operationalization and protection of this state of peace over time. Again, it needs to be understood that the concept 'security' is not to be read here with its post-Second World War connotations in mind – as the policy field of intelligence and security agencies and national security councils. For our purposes and in this context, security is a concept that needs to be placed and historicized in time itself, when it had not yet been institutionalized into narrowly defined bureaucratic units of domestic, foreign, legal or economic security. In 1815, security could include all of these aspects at the same time, both international and national, 'moral' and military, and was used in a similarly broad vein.

Therefore, to avoid the pitfalls of anachronistic interpretations and present-ist normative evaluations, the notion of a European security culture is introduced here.[37] As will transpire, the emergence of such a culture was an open and contested process, propelled by the community of diplomats, publicists and politicians who together thought about and reflected on their (purported) shared interests and imagined threats. These 'men of 1815' developed a shared political and emotional vocabulary, and derived from that a series of political, juridical, financial, administrative and military practices. These three elements – the security community, their shared vocabulary and the political and administrative actions that followed from these (including the reactions and protestations) – will allow us to give detailed historical clout to the abstract category of security. This definition and application of the notion of a European security culture helps us both to abstain from ventriloquism – making historical figures voice our present-day normative security concerns – and from resorting to excessively statist, non-dynamical and abstract categories.[38]

---

[36] D. Reynolds, *Summits. Six Meetings That Shaped the Twentieth Century* (London: Allen Lane, 2007).

[37] See M. de Goede, *European Security Culture. Preemption and Precaution in European Security* (Amsterdam: Vossius Press, 2011). See also M. Williams, *Culture and Security. Symbolic Power and the Politics of International Security* (London: Routledge, 2007); P. Katzenstein (ed.), *The Culture of National Security. Norms and Identity in World Politics* (New York: Columbia University Press, 1996); and recently especially Conze, *Geschichte der Sicherheit*, 71–81. Culture should be read not in the narrow, literary or artistic sense, but as the sum of norms, values, practices, perceptions and institutions in a society in a given time and space. For a study on the literature and cultural interpretation of 1815 in the said narrow sense, see L. Jensen, *Celebrating Peace. The Emergence of Dutch Identity, 1648–1815* (Nijmegen: Vantilt, 2017), 163–82.

[38] See also B. Stollberg-Rilinger, 'State and Political History in a Culturalist Perspective', in A. Flüchter and S. Richter (eds.), *Structures on the Move* (Berlin: Springer, 2012), 43–58.

An Imagined and Sensed European Security Community

The old, shrivelled Europe seemed to have shed its skin and, though still recognizable, emerged in a new form from the ashes of the Napoleonic fire-brand. As the French Revolution had unleashed ideas on human rights, freedom and solidarity into world history, Napoleon had with his wars and occupations let loose an enormous range of transformations in politics, state and society and accelerated ongoing ones. The emperor had willed an 'inner Empire' into existence, consisting of comparable and synchronized institutions, such as codes of laws, judicial courts, systems of registration and identification, land registries and fiscal systems.[39] The revolutionary and Napoleonic transformations had already done away with many of the 'withered' institutions the emperor had lamented so much. However, the real push towards new post-war transformations came from the fight against exactly this revolutionary and Bonapartist terror. Post-war notions about peace and security were designed and ordained from above, by the new and returning royals and their ministers. But they were also conceived and disseminated within the societies of Europe, produced by experiences, emotions and impressions of so many citizens who lived through the chaos and turmoil of the Revolutionary and Napoleonic Wars and suffered their part.[40]

The post-war European security culture, therefore, can be understood as part of an 'imagined security community'. Although Benedict Anderson has set up a monument for the invention of nationalism, his concept can in many ways also be applied to the continent of Europe as a whole, and in particular to the network of elites that during and after the Napoleonic Wars tried to construct a stable framework for collective security.[41] Anderson applied his concept to a community of peoples who could not possibly know each other personally, but nevertheless experienced a sense of solidarity. These individual citizens shared a common notion of belonging to the same imagined nation, and translated this feeling of belonging together into symbols, traditions and practices of patriotism or nationalism – a process that underwent an acceleration in the nineteenth century, according to Anderson. His claims may *mutatis mutandis* also be attributed to the community of European states and their elites, with their shared sense of common destiny and responsibility in 1815 – and common abhorrence of war and terror.

---

[39] M. Broers, *Europe under Napoleon 1799–1815* (London: Arnold, 1996). On 'inner empire', see Broers, *The Napoleonic Empire in Italy, 1796–1814. Cultural Imperialism in a European Context?* (Basingstoke: Palgrave Macmillan, 2005), 213–74.

[40] Cf. for the power of ideas in this transitional period: L. Hunt, 'The French Revolution in Global Context', in D. Armitage and S. Subrahmanyam (eds.), *The Age of Revolutions in Global Context, c.1760–1840* (Basingstoke: Macmillan Education, 2010), 31–2.

[41] B. Anderson, *Imagined Communities. Reflections on the Origin and Spread of Nations* (revised ed., London/New York: Verso, 2006 [1983]), 2.

Here as well, this European security community became palpable in collectively expressed, diverging and oftentimes conflicting sentiments, statements and artefacts (such as monuments). Emotions do not only indicate a state of psychological being, inasmuch as they can empirically be verified in letters, statements and writings; they should also be read as social and cultural practices of understanding and communication. Emotions vary through time and space; some are enlarged, others repressed in specific cultural and social settings. Fear for loss of honour, anger directed at monarchical repression or Bonapartist despotism were recurring themes in public discourse across the continent in the early nineteenth century. Without aiming to write a history of emotions of 1815, some of the insights produced by the recent 'emotional turn in history' will be gratefully applied here. The discourse on terror and security in 1815 cannot be understood without identifying the emotional juxtapositions that it employed explicitly or implicitly: the contradistinction between passion and reason, for example, or between jealousy and moderation – with 'emotional', 'hysterical' or 'jealous' intended as disqualifications. Specific sentiments – relief, fear of revolution – were, moreover, wilfully channelled to mobilize the European security community into giving consent or legitimacy to certain administrative interventions. 'The passions of the masses are not irrational,' as one researcher quipped, 'they are political'.[42]

The great unifier that brought the diverging community of European states and elites together was the overriding fear of terror. This primordial fear fuelled and shaped the cultural climate of the immediate post-war order. It consisted of the dual nightmare of, on the one hand, the terror of the French Revolution: the unleashed chaos and violence, the decapitation of princes and noblemen, the upending of existing social structures, the expropriation of estates and clerical properties and the ensuing dynamics of ongoing war and despotism. That was the other part of the nightmare: the rise to power of the people's tribune and warmonger Bonaparte with his Grande Armée, unleashing military invasions, revolutionary changes, usurpations, occupations, war reparations, and looting and pillaging wherever he went. Especially the last years of Napoleonic rule had aggravated this collective fear of terror. In the perception of contemporaries in 1815, terror was not a narrowly defined criminal paragraph (such a paragraph did not exist), but a continuum ranging from revolution to invasions, expropriations and despotism. Terror comprised a whole range of fluctuating threats and enemies. The Allied Council spoke about 'revolutionaries', 'Jacobins', 'radicals', 'republicans', *terroristes* or

---

[42] J. Lang, 'New Histories of Emotion', *History & Theory*, 57:1 (2018), 104–20, here: 120. See also S. Ahmed, *The Cultural Politics of Emotion* (Edinburgh: Edinburgh University Press, 2004); R. Leys, 'The Turn to Affect: A Critique', *Critical Enquiry*, 37:3 (2011), 434–72; N. Eustace et al., 'AHR Conversation: The Historical Study of Emotions', *American Historical Review*, 117:5 (2012), 1487–531.

'Bonapartists' – categories that were not well defined or judicially circumscribed, but mostly lumped together in a vague and general pejorative manner. 'Terror' was in this context read as a 'set of concrete facts'; it was the 'product of a political culture', an 'emotion'.[43] More than 300,000 people, including the French king and queen, had fallen victim to a small group of radicals coming from the middle classes, in conjunction with the *sans culottes*. The continuous slaughter, the judicial avarice, the persecution of nobility and clergy alike, the ruthless transformation of society and the military crusade spreading the gospel of the Revolution through the world had given way to the rise of Napoleon's military dictatorship and unbridled aggression. This whole threat complex was surmised under the hellish header 'war and terror'. The post-war European security community had to relate itself to this double-headed monster. Contrary to Zamoyski's account, the fear of terror cannot therefore be discarded merely as a 'phantom' fear, or a ploy wielded by conservative statesmen to push their political agendas.[44] Especially during these first, transitional and forgotten years, the revolutionary and Napoleonic period left real marks and scars, and continued to do so, be it in more or less violent plots hatched by supporters of the revolutionary or Bonapartist causes, or by their adversaries. Sentiments of collective fear, the dread of losing house and property, of being expelled from the society of respectable citizens once again, were the real and strong undercurrents that kept the Allied ministers' diverging deliberations together for at least this transitional period.

The remarkable thing about this community was that its participants, from high to low, were in many ways 'joined at the hip' for years. Castlereagh, Alexander I, the Prussian King Friedrich Wilhelm III, Wellington, and their ambassadors and diplomats were away from home for at least a year. Tsar Alexander was in Europe from October 1813 through September 1815; Castlereagh left London on 28 December 1813 and remained on the continent, except for two short trips back home, until the end of November 1815, albeit much to the increasing chagrin of parliament. The physical presence of government leaders during the lengthy negotiations on peace and security from 1813 on reflects a sense of how much value was attached to these ongoing discussions, and of how much the physical absence of these leaders and their ministers was deemed in their homeland to be in the interest of national security. In that light, this period of high-profile, well-documented and, for that time, widely reported-on series of consultations almost qualified as a modern form of 'summitry', understood as the frequent, high-level meetings of state leaders and ministers enabled by plane travel and televised to the

---

[43] Cf. R. Schechter, *A Genealogy of Terror in Eighteenth-Century France* (Chicago/London: University of Chicago Press, 2018), 31–2.
[44] Cf. A. Zamoyski, *Phantom Terror. The Threat of Revolution and the Repression of Liberty 1789–1848* (London: Harper Collins, 2015).

public. Obviously, 1815 was still an era far away from twentieth-century plane diplomacy, but the number of congresses, which had been few and little in the four previous centuries, increased rapidly in the nineteenth. Statesmen continued to spend protracted periods in each other's capitals, with their deliberations reported on extensively in the newspapers and periodicals of the day; reviewing contemporary journals reveals that the 'news sky' was already quite global.[45]

Such common notions on terror and security, and the overriding need to combat such extremities, were not only shared amongst the elites. Most of the citizens of Europe, especially those who read newspapers and feuilletons, had to adjust themselves to new ideas on power, law, peace and security. The dawn of the European peace after 1814 shone over a wide array of post-revolutionary states and traditional dynasties. Some states boasted their newly gained autonomy and sovereignty; here and there a first glimpse of nationalism and patriotism surfaced, as in Prussia and the German lands, or in Poland for example. The new state of peace was, however, also celebrated by citizens who realized that peace and security were obtained only through Allied cooperation – a reckoning that at least in the first immediate post-war years was cogent and strong. The rise of nationalism in the early nineteenth century cannot therefore be set apart from the development of a transnational sense of security and the need for cooperation.[46] The sentiments as expressed just below the surface of the international elites will therefore be traced, and the stories narrated by lower-level experts, diplomats, professionals, bankers, policemen, journalists and ordinary citizens within this transitional time frame will be excavated as well.[47] Where they are available, this book also draws on travelogues and diaries kept by women – a specific apt and useful category for mapping the cultural climate of those years. It was common usage for noblewomen to report on their experiences and sentiments in their diaries, writing as much on their personal sense of well-being as on the state of the roads, the dangers ahead and the ways of the land, as Louisa Adams did.[48]

Through the high-level meetings, in Paris, at the British embassy where the Allied Council convened, or in all those other places where experts and

---

[45] See for a detailed press analysis Vick, *The Congress of Vienna*, 99–111. On summitry see Reynolds, *Summits*, 11–36.

[46] F. Lyons, *Internationalism in Europe, 1815-1914* (Leiden: Sythoff, 1963); M. Mazower, *Governing the World. The History of an Idea* (London: Penguin, 2012). See also L. Richardson, 'The Concert of Europe and Security Management in the Nineteenth Century', in H. Haftendorn, R. Keohane and C. Wallander (eds.), *Imperfect Unions. Security Institutions over Time and Space* (Oxford: Oxford University Press, 1999), 48–80.

[47] See also Conze, 'Abschied von Staat und Politik?', 41–2.

[48] See Lang, 'New Histories of Emotion', 107. See also, for example, E. Bohls, *Women Travel Writers and the Language of Aesthetics, 1716-1818* (Cambridge: Cambridge University Press, 1995), 230–45.

professionals from various nations combined forces to rebuild the post-war order, a circulation of new ideas, notions, emotions and concepts originated. Old notions were reinterpreted and given new meanings, such as the principle of the balance of power.[49] The leading statesmen and diplomats of the day were united in their collective digestion of those treatises, notions and ideas coming from the Enlightenment – they had all read their Voltaire, had been educated with Montesquieu, Diderot and the *Encyclopédie* and were open to gradual and moderate reforms.[50] Ministers and experts enjoyed the same novels and writings, for example those by Sir Walter Scott (of whom Castlereagh was a friend), Johann Wolfgang von Goethe or Madame de Staël.[51] They started to emulate each other's manners and clothing, something described by Bayly as the spread of 'uniformities', for example in the standardization and transfer of certain 'bodily practices'. The European nobility and wealthy citizenry started to sport portable watches, adjusted their times, visited each other's city palaces and developed a type of modern European court culture. When Lady Castlereagh joined her husband in Vienna, she was ridiculed because of her outdated clothing, which made her seem at odds with the sophisticated Viennese society.[52]

This European security community developed a specific vernacular to identify danger and insecurity, something that came close to a veritable 'emotional vocabulary'. The Allied ministers extensively debated on the level of someone's or some country's state of 'jealousy', 'irrationality' or 'unreasonableness'. They also discussed the definition of 'piracy', 'terror' and *terroristes*. Who merited the epitaph 'radical', 'Bonapartist' or 'Jacobin', and when and how should these identifications translate into administrative practice? The Congress of Vienna had produced a series of detailed regulations and stipulations on commercial matters, navigation on the Rhine, the status of diplomatic representatives and the metrics of power and influence (in square kilometres, in economic profits or in the number of 'souls'). These processes of juridification – increased centralized and legal regulation[53] – continued after 1815 and

---

[49] Cf. R. Keohane, *After Hegemony. Cooperation and Discord in the World Political Economy* (Princeton: Princeton University Press, 1984), 244–5; Mitzen, *Power in Concert*. See also D. Armitage, 'Globalizing Jeremy Bentham', *History of Political Thought*, 32:1 (2011), 63–82; Armitage, *Foundations of Modern International Thought* (Cambridge, MA: Harvard University Press, 2004).

[50] Cf. N. Hampson, *A Cultural History of the Enlightenment* (New York: Pantheon, 1968), 128–61.

[51] See B. de Graaf, 'Bringing Sense and Sensibility to the Continent: Vienna 1815 Revisited', *Journal of Modern European History*, 13:4 (2015), 447–57.

[52] Bayly, *The Birth of the Modern World*, 49, 51, 65; Zamoyski, *Rites of Peace*, 344–5.

[53] Defined here as 'the spread of rule-guided action or the expectation of lawful conduct'; see L. Blichner and A. Molander, 'Mapping Juridification', *European Law Journal*, 14:1 (2008), 36–54, here: 36. See also M. Vec, 'Verrechtlichung internationaler Streitbeilegung im 19. und 20. Jahrhundert?', in S. Dauchy and M. Vec (eds.), *Les conflits entre peuples* (Baden-Baden: Nomos, 2011), 1–21.

brought about an alignment of the participating countries at least on sectoral levels – sometimes even pitching them against their own postulated national interests, as when the riparian states of the Rhine held each other accountable in lowering or abandoning toll tariffs altogether. This European security community, with its emotional vocabulary of security, reason and moderation, hence affected real, incremental or more substantial transformations and created its own *acquis communautaire*.

This course of juridification was intrinsically connected to the phenomenon of securitization: the process of putting something on the security agenda, of framing and presenting an issue as threat or endangered interest.[54] From 1815 onwards, this process, which captivated the Allied ministers present in Paris alike, was markedly Janus-faced in the dissemination of power and protection across the continent. With their interventions, the Allied ministers did initiate a dissemination of new standards and practices of security, order and predictability, especially in those first post-war years. This dissemination, however, was explicitly lopsided: it operated through processes of inclusion and exclusion. Some persons and parties profited far more from the new security system than others, who were crushed beneath its weight and fell prey to its repressive effects – a process of securitization that intensified once the openness of these first years was over, and a more repressive turn set in.

An Imperial Situation

One of the seminal questions of this book touches upon the highly elusive and slippery notion of 'success' of the Allied Council's machinations. Did the Allied ministers in Paris succeed in bringing about an effective state of peace and security in Europe, and if yes, how did they manage to achieve this? The post-war years may have witnessed the above-mentioned unique experiment in collective security management, but what did this experiment yield, and for whom? As it turned out, the 'Allied Machine' was a highly exclusive and hierarchical gathering of gentlemen, representing a commonly understood alignment of first-, second- and third-rank powers. The Sixth and Seventh Coalition had been assembled from a range of Allied powers. In Vienna, all of these powers and more dispatched their envoys to the deliberations. The Final Act of Vienna was the first general peace concluded as a multilateral treaty, and could be considered a type of 'constitutional order for Europe'.[55] This order was, however, highly exclusive – Christian,

---

[54] See Conze, 'Securitization'; B. Buzan, O. Waever and J. de Wilde, *Security. A New Framework for Analysis* (Boulder, CO: Lynne Riener, 1998), 23–9.

[55] M. Schulz, 'The Construction of a Culture of Peace in Post-Napoleonic Europe: Peace through Equilibrium, Law and New Forms of Communicative Interaction', *Journal of Modern European History*, 13:4 (2015), 464–74, 465.

European, and 'civilized' in its character. The Ottoman Empire was, for example, squarely placed outside this order.[56]

The Paris Conference was, if possible, an even more imperial set. With their far-reaching interventions, the Allied ministers waged peace and managed collective security. But they did so in governing over the heads and on the backs of smaller nations, minorities, specific factions and regions. With their centralizing and imperial policies, they managed to tame the terror in France in the short run, but sowed the seeds of discord and discontent for the near future, not just in France, but also elsewhere in Europe and beyond. Many a minister or general that convened on a daily basis in Paris to ponder France's and Europe's destiny had made his career in the colonies. What they had learned and achieved in India, Crimea or the newly colonized Prussian lands in the east, they put into practice in Europe in turn: the colonizing of hearts and minds, the implementation of new institutions and the administration of indigenous populations. This also indicated a policy of identifying those considered radical, seditious, revolutionary, or simply 'immoderate' or 'jealous', be it individual citizens or countries, cities or minorities in Europe or far beyond, in the Americas. Enlightened theories on modern governance and management, on security and the common good went hand in glove with authoritarian, imperialist and exclusive attitudes.

The trend of decoupling colonial issues from European questions at the Congress of Vienna, as demanded and enforced by the British representatives at the time, has continued in the past two hundred years of historiography. While initial approaches towards an 'integrated historiography' have been made, for example with Bayly's masterpiece *The Birth of the Modern World*, no book as of yet has investigated the nexus between the European security system and international relations on the one hand and the history of imperialism and colonialism in the nineteenth century on the other.[57] Some experts on the history of empire and colonialism have pointed out that imperial logics were relevant to the process of creating the European states system of the nineteenth century. But this era is still mostly characterized as an ascending line of 'interempire competition' from 1815 to the outbreak of the First World War.[58]

---

[56] The Ottoman Empire was invited, but did not want to attend because it felt it was not being treated as a full-fledged first- or second-rank power. See E. Ingram, 'Bellicism as Boomerang: The Eastern Question during the Vienna System', in P. Krüger and P. Schroeder (eds.), *The Transformation of European Politics, 1763–1848'. Episode or Model in Modern History?* (Münster, 2002), 202–25, here: 210–11, 216. See for more details below, at footnote 109.

[57] Bayly, The Birth of the Modern World; J. Osterhammel, *The Transformation of the World. A Global History of the Nineteenth Century* (Princeton: Princeton University Press, 2014).

[58] J. Burbank and F. Cooper, *Empires in World History. Power and the Politics of Difference* (Princeton: Princeton University Press, 2010), 331.

Naturally, competition between consolidated, emerging and declining empires stood out. But there were equal attempts to cooperate, and to converge the different imperial strategies. These attempts were inspired not just by 'strategies of disinterest',[59] or alleged love of peace, but also by the wish to assist other countries in living their imperial dream and receiving support for one's own colonial adventures in turn, or the wish to embark on joined inter-imperial projects. Security proved to be a single, outstanding unifying principle in bringing together the empires in their quests for power and consolidation. Inter-imperial ambitions started in France, in colonizing the unruly hearts and minds together, or along the Rhine, where the first inter-empire security regimes were established to protect navigation and free trade, but they also spread to the Mediterranean, North Africa and the New World, where, for example, piracy and rebellion in the Americas provided a common threat to foil. Security provided joint instances and techniques 'to exercise power, inflict rules and generate violence not only for the purposes of actual conquest but also with regard to conducting civilizing missions',[60] be it on the land, on the seas or in border regions. The European security culture cannot, therefore, be dissected into an inner and outer one. The fight against terror started in the heart of the European continent, in France, but the above-mentioned spread of 'uniformities' went far beyond the continent.

This empire–security nexus, therefore, needs to be pondered by starting with one of its very beginnings: the Allied occupation in France. These years of collective occupation immediately following the Congress of Vienna, more often than not left out of the textbooks, were formative for the making of this new, European, collective and imperial security culture. The essential character-istic of colonization, or of the colonial situation, is that it entails a situation of 'coercive incorporation' of one or more entities into an expansionist other.[61] Such a state of affairs may lead to the rise of an 'informal empire' – a phenomenon that Barton defines as 'a relationship in which a national or regional imperial elite intentionally or unintentionally exercises a dominant influence over the elite formation, identities and conditions of exchange of the subjected elite in another nation or region with none of the formal structures of empire'.[62]

---

[59] See Williams, *Culture and Security*, 43.

[60] V. Barth and R. Cvetkovski, 'Introduction. Encounters of Empires: Methodological Approaches', in Barth and Cvetkovski (eds.), *Imperial Cooperation and Transfer, 1870–1930. Empires and Encounters* (London: Bloomsbury, 2015), 3–34, here: 30. See also J. MacKenzie, 'European Imperialism: A Zone of Cooperation Rather than Competition?', in Barth and Cvetkovski (eds.), *Imperial Cooperation and Transfer*, 35–56, here: 39–40.

[61] F. Cooper, *Colonialism in Question. Theory, Knowledge, History* (Los Angeles: University of California Press, 2005), 26–7.

[62] G. Barton, *Informal Empire and the Rise of One World Culture* (Basingstoke: Palgrave Macmillan, 2014), 14.

In the light of this, the occupation of France between 1815 and 1818 can be seen as a transitory, 'imperial situation', where the indigenous population was subjugated to Allied rule. The four great powers directing the European Concert set up the occupation and the management of collective security on the basis of shared notions of hierarchy and inequality amongst the states and populaces of Europe. Those who had carried the day during the Napoleonic Wars felt perfectly entitled and justified to subjugate states and peoples – Poland, Saxony, parts of Italy, the Belgian provinces – to their rule, and to exclude others from the dividends of peace. Although a temporary military occupation cannot be fully equated to a colonial situation,[63] the Allied ministers were wholly convinced of their superiority and responsibility vis-à-vis the restoration of peace and security in France, in the novel states of secondary rank and power, or even in the rest of Europe for that matter. Their shared 'imperial idiom' was just as powerful, and even more influential, than the nationalistic and patriotic strains that sounded here and there already at that time.[64]

Thus, a new inter-imperial security community emerged, its centre situated in France, where protagonists from far-away capitals lorded over French elites, created a kind of informal empire and applied experiences gained at their previous colonial posts. In sum, the history of the new beginnings of the European states system in 1815 cannot be understood without accounting for the way the Allied Council functioned as a platform on which imperial experiences, convictions and attitudes circulated.

A Journey through Time

This book tells the story of these forgotten years – this window of threats, opportunities and reforms – by following the workings of the Allied Council, that unique security experiment conducted in the footsteps of the Allied forces and their entourage from 1813 onwards. From all directions, commanders, generals, princes and their diplomats headed to Paris. There they remained until late 1818, with some ambassadors continuing their deployment until 1823. Several persons will be followed on their journey, with the Duke of Wellington standing out as the embodiment of the new security order. He was considered, and attacked, as *l'homme de l'Europe*, in his command of the Allied Army of Occupation and presidency over the Allied Council. With his military and strategic talents, diplomatic skills and British pounds, he kept the Allied ministers together and managed to hold the French King Louis XVIII on board as well, while overseeing the execution of sometimes quite harsh occupation

---

[63] J. Osterhammel, *Colonialism. A Theoretical Overview* (Princeton: Wiener, 1997), 3, 10, definition on 16–17.
[64] Burbank and Cooper, *Empires in World History*, 245.

measures. Wherever Wellington went, he was assured attention from admirers and supplicants, causing hubbub among his equally numerous critics. The Allied ministers' and generals' visibility and performances inevitably also provided a screen for the projection of the vehement protests caused by the pervasive security interventions.

Chapter 2 explains how the Allied ministers arrived in Paris, what they brought with them in lessons learned and experiences, and how the Allied experiment unfolded along an unpredictable journey full of surprising turns. During this trajectory, unwinding from early 1813 until June 1815, the many imperial ambitions frequently clashed. All sorts of ideas about revenge, retribution, mercy and providence played out, and were entertained by the protagonists of the day: Tsar Alexander, Metternich, Castlereagh and the Prussian general Blücher. The Allied partners deliberated and compromised, with the management of security being very much a case of leadership and charisma, as demonstrated by the ascent of Wellington within the community of ministers.

Chapter 3 outlines the cultural climate of those days in 1815, as a range of diverging and oftentimes conflicting sentiments. Napoleon was defeated, leaving many of his supporters disillusioned and alienated, and trying to flee the country. Elsewhere, many more felt liberated and free to pick up their trade again after the continental blockade had been lifted. A new emotional vocabulary of peace, security and order was wrought, with old concepts being redressed and adjusted to the new state of affairs. The peace of 1815 was not just a realignment of power, it was as much an idea, a principle, filled with new meanings, emotions and collective sentiments. To repair the 'break in time',[65] and restore peace, repose and order – such desires were common throughout society, but they were translated into a range of different sentiments and voiced in a variety of collective emotions.

Chapter 4 describes how the Allied Council set out to fulfil its tasks and negotiated the Paris Peace Treaty. The Allied infrastructure was now in place and the 'machine' turned on. The council provided a platform for a well-structured and closely knit conference diplomacy, calibrating inputs from the various courts and parliaments, and supported by military force. This chapter unpacks how pervasively, and how equivocally at the same time, this imperial peace was waged and gained traction. The defeated French did not easily subjugate themselves to these attempts at Allied colonialism. The fight against terror was as much a project of converging Allied cooperation as one that started to expose underlying tensions and differences. Allied ministers and diplomats clashed on how heavily France should be punished, how draconian the reparation payments were to be, how much of the looted artwork needed to

---

[65] See R. Jones, '1816 and the Resumption of "Ordinary History"', *Journal for Modern European History*, 14:1 (2016), 119–44.

be returned, and how much of a say the other, second-rank powers would have in the matter.

Chapters 5 and 6 deal with the police-related, political side of security – the most controversial dimension of the Allied occupation efforts. How inclusive or exclusive was the European security community to be? What would set boundaries to the newly achieved freedoms? It did not take long before the management of international peace turned inward. All sorts of spectres of revolutionary, Bonapartist or patriotic rebellion were invoked and a specific Allied security service established to coordinate the joint fight against terror. Real or perceived attacks against representatives of the Allied force were discovered and thwarted – not just in France, but also beyond its borders.

Security came with a price, and would cost France a lot. Chapter 7 reconstructs how the Allied occupation was secured financially. Security without justice was a possibility, but without funding, altogether unthinkable. Financial security had to be invented and purchased with the help of the emerging international European financial markets. The Allied Council was therefore also very much a capitalist machine, linking political and military security to financial securities. The greatest common effort that brought the Allied powers and France together was the conception and realization of a huge sum of reparation payments. With the help of European bankers, financiers, and investors from France, Britain, the German lands and the Netherlands, France was able to procure immense loans to relieve its debts and meet the treaty conditions in 1818. The new peace and security – materialized in the fortresses, settlement of debts, maintenance of the army of occupation – was paid for with these loans. The French treasury administered the loans, and paid them, but the European powers, with their army of occupation, acted as guarantors.

The evacuation of the Allied Army of Occupation in late 1818 was directly dependent on the completion of the Wellington Barrier along the French northern frontier. Chapter 8 retells its conception, execution and functioning. The fortresses were the most concrete and physical pillar under the new security architecture. They were as such explicitly mentioned and circumscribed in a secret protocol to the Congress of Aix-la-Chapelle Final Act, signed in November 1818. At the eponymous congress, France was invited to accede to the ring of first-rank powers again. The gathered princes and the ministers of the Quadruple Alliance announced the Allied army's departure and the completion of the Allied Council's tasks. With that meeting, this first experiment in inter-imperial European security management came to a temporary end. Chapter 9, however, continues with a reconstruction of the aborted attempt to expand the Allied Council's military interventions to South America.

The threat of revolutionary terror and Bonapartist military aggression seemed to have been mitigated and domesticated in France, but now appeared to raise its ugly head again beyond France, elsewhere in Europe and even beyond the continent. The spectre of the resurrection of terror outside France increasingly captivated the European powers – as did the strenuous relation with representatives of that new, upcoming power of the United States, which most Allied ministers wanted to keep outside the Concert of Europe. On this, Napoleon had made some shrewd observations. At St Helena, he cynically quipped about that old Europe, which did not realize that his 'favoured country [the United States] grew rich by our follies'. Out of dissatisfaction with the regimes of the restoration, according to the former emperor, many highly educated artisans and students left for the New World. The European powers did not realize they were fighting a rearguard action in trying to keep Washington at bay while clinging on to colonial rule in South America. Europe had to acknowledge, Napoleon allegedly and quite hypocritically declared, that 'their emancipation [of the colonies] was inevitable; that when children had attained the size of their fathers, it was difficult to retain them long in a state of obedience'. In the tenth, concluding chapter, the balance of Europe's fight against terror will be drawn, and Napoleon's judgements on Europe's rearguard actions will be evaluated.[66]

---

[66] Las Cases (ed.), *Memorial de Sainte Hélène*, vol. 1 (London: Colburn, 1823), 63.

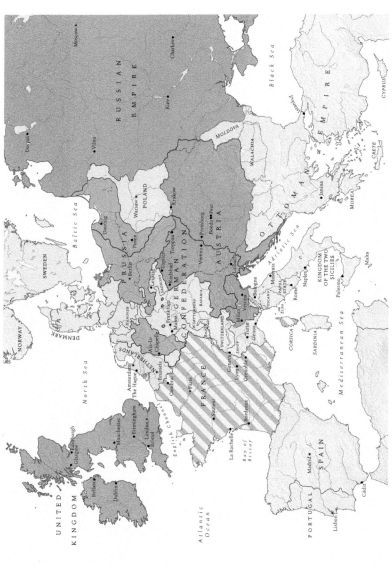

Map 1.1 General map of Europe in 1815. Together, the dark-coloured countries form the Allied Council. The shaded country is occupied France. Some of the light-coloured countries were coalition partners of the Quadruple Alliance, but did not count as 'first-rank powers'. (Erik Goosmann © 2020, Mappa Mundi Cartography)

2

Providence in Paris

'What is to be Done Now?'

On the afternoon of 19 October 1813, the 37-year-old Baron Karl von Müffling (Fig. 2.1) stood on Leipzig's market square. It was strewn with the bodies of the dead and wounded, and for a moment he just did not know what to do next. As staff officer of General Field Marshal Gebhard Leberecht von Blücher, he had, since 16 October, together with the Allied powers, defied Napoleon's Grande Armée for three days. He had endured the fierce confrontations with the troops of the French marshal Marmont north of Leipzig and was now, together with the Bohemian (Austrian, Russian and Prussian) troops, Silesian (Russian and Prussian) troops and Northern Army (Prussian, Russian and Swedish troops), in the heart of the conquered city to celebrate their decisive victory over the emperor. A week later, in a report to the newspapers, Müffling spoke of a *Völkerschlacht* – of the slaughtering of nations. He wanted to underscore the fact that so outrageously many armed forces had been in on the march. Later this name was taken as an expression of the number of different countries that had sent troops into battle – 'The Battle of Nations'. But back in 1813 Müffling's choice of words was intended to express to his contemporaries how massive the mobilization (and slaughter) had been.[1] On that October afternoon, what was most amazing was what a terrible massacre it had been. The market square was strewn with innumerable stretchers, casualties, dead and wounded; in the coming days, along the road to the west, along which the remnants of Napoleon's army had fled, many more corpses would be found. Of the approximately 600,000 soldiers involved, 92,000 did not live to tell of it. Priscilla Fane – Lady Burghersh, a diplomat's wife who accompanied him and the British Allies – stumbled to find the words:

---

[1] Cf. Müffling's report, 'Fortsetzung der Nachrichten von der deutschen Schlacht: Bericht von der Schlesischen Armee. Leipzig, den 19. Oktober', in *Der Preussische Correspondent*, no. 119, 25 October 1813, 1–3. See also J. Knaack, 'Wie die "Völkerschlacht" bei Leipzig 1813 zu ihren Namen kam', in S. Dietzsch and A. Ludwig (eds.), *Achim von Arnim und sein Kreis* (Berlin/New York: De Gruyter, 2010), 269–78.

Figure 2.1 Karl von Müffling, Prussian general. By F. J. L. Sebbers, before 1837. (©
SLUB / Deutsche Fotothek / Rapp, Günter)

> No language can describe the horrible devastation these French have left
> behind them, and without seeing it no one can form an idea of the country
> through which such a retreat has been theirs. Every bridge blown up, every
> village burnt or pulled down, fields completely devastated, orchards all
> turned up, and we traced their bivouaques all along by every horror you
> can conceive. None of the country people will bury them or their horses, so
> there they remain lying all over the fields and roads, with millions of crows
> feasting – we passed quantities, bones of all kinds, hats, shoes, epaulettes,
> a surprising quantity of rags and linens – every kind of honour.[2]

Müffling had little time for such sentiments; he recalled especially how he
stood there with his comrades, and asked himself: 'What is to be done now?'
But the officers soon pulled themselves together: '"Continue", we replied,
"what we have begun; crush the power of the tyrant, and conclude the peace
only in Paris."'[3] The cavalry, in the wake of the turbulent Blücher, were soon
chasing after the French in the direction of the Rhine.

---

[2] R. Weigall (ed.), *The Letters of Lady Burghersh (afterwards Countess of Westmorland).
From Germany and France during the campaign of 1813–14* (London: John Murray, 1893),
66–7.

[3] C. von Müffling (ed.), *The Memoirs of Baron von Müffling. A Prussian Officer in the
Napoleonic Wars* (London: Greenhill, 1997), 90–1.

Uncertainty about the future and the best shape and direction of the Allied peace was the common thread during the history of the wars of liberation in 1813–15. The Allies' erratic route, balancing shakily with one eye on a post-Napoleonic, peaceful future and the other on the conflicting interests within their own camp, took a crucial turn in 1813. But after Leipzig a long ordeal ensued prior to the Allies finally arriving in Paris through the Porte Saint-Martin. In 1813 the Allies could still not at all agree that they would march on the French capital, let alone that they would pitch their tents there for a longer period. All kinds of ideas were circulating, but consensus among the four major powers regarding the post-war period was hard to come by. The route from Leipzig to Paris was indirect and rather chaotic. Numerous side paths were taken or considered before hostilities ceased, and a final ceasefire agreement – the Convention of Saint-Cloud – was signed in the French capital on 3 July 1815.

As Metternich's biographer Wolfram Siemann has accurately pointed out, the peace of 1815 can only be studied as a whole series of interactions and contingencies.[4] Outlining that erratic route, filled as it was with unexpected interactions, shows how their thinking about peace took shape. The Prussian drive for organizing a centralized administration of Allied affairs brought about the notion of an Allied occupation. Because that was the most salient outcome of this Allied campaign: how the four Allied courts came up with the idea of a joint occupation of France, by means of a multinational army of occupation, a veritable Allied ministerial council and accompanying administrative agencies. Before this outcome was realized, however, all kinds of different imperial ambitions and ideas about grace, revenge, retribution and providence clashed and needed to become reconciled during that process.

A 'Noble' Project

After Napoleon's defeat in Moscow in December 1812, the Prussians, Russians and Austrians signed a mutual peace accord, determined to keep the emperor from ever playing them off against each other again. Owing in many ways to the efforts of Metternich (Fig. 2.2) as Austrian chancellor to forge the Allies together around his vision for restoring the balance of power, that determination – to no longer settle for a partial peace, but to pursue the French emperor into his own capital – took on more concrete form after June 1813.

That month the parties of the Sixth Coalition met in the town of Reichenbach and agreed to declare war jointly on Napoleon (Russia and Prussia had done so already in March), pledging not to break the alliance unilaterally should Napoleon try to seduce any of them with individual peace accords. Russia's ambition and Britain's gold were decisive: in Reichenbach, Castlereagh

---

[4] W. Siemann, *Metternich. Stratege und Visionär* (Munich: C. H. Beck, 2016), 447.

Figure 2.2   Klemens von Metternich, Chancellor of Austria. Portrait by Thomas
Lawrence, *c.*1816. (Royal Collection Trust / © Her Majesty Queen Elizabeth II 2019)

promised the Prussians 666,666 pounds sterling if they would keep 80,000
troops at the ready, and 1,333,334 pounds to Russia for maintaining a force
of 160,000 men.[5] The Allies further agreed to keep fighting to the bitter end,
and not to stop until the complete defeat of the French forces was an accomplished fact. On 19 August, Austria, in an extensive war manifesto composed by
Gentz, also formally joined the alliance; and with that the Coalition was born.[6]

    According to the hard-boiled revolutionary Jeanbon Saint-André, the
prefect of Mainz, 'the whole of Europe was now mobilized against
France'. Quite nervously he observed how 'this ancient civilization' had
now 'surrounded and enclosed us in a ring of iron' – inadvertently echoing
Napoleon's complaint about this 'old Europe'.[7] With his 'holistic, centrally

---

[5] See the Treaties of Reichenbach in I. Clare (ed.),*Library of Universal History*, vol. 7
  (New York: Peale & Hill, 1897), 2707.
[6] Schroeder, *The Transformation of European Politics*, 472–3; Siemann, *Metternich*, 420–1.
[7] Cited in A. Beugnot (ed.), *Mémoires du Comte Beugnot, Ancién Ministre (1783–1815)*
  (Paris: Dentu, 1868), 16–17; G. Kirmse, *Der Musterpräfekt vom Donnersberg. Das Leben
  des Jeanbon St. André und dessen geschichtlicher Hintergrund* (Simmern: Pandion, 1998).

driven imperial project',[8] and his despotic fantasies, Napoleon had achieved the opposite: a Europe united against his rule. But what exactly did these unified European opponents understand victory to entail? Pushing France back to the borders of 1792? Completely eliminating the Grand Armée? Or getting rid of Napoleon himself? All the while, Metternich still remained in secret bilateral negotiations with Napoleon.[9] After the Battle of Leipzig, neither the Prussian king nor the Austrian emperor were convinced that the French army had to be chased all the way into Paris.

According to Metternich, a total victory over France would distort the balance of power between Russia and France and give the tsarist presence too much leeway. His aim in war was to restore the 'equilibrium' – not to create a new situation of unilateral hegemony on the part of one of the great powers.[10] No one in Napoleon's camp gave much thought to that possibility either. Even in August, when the generals Vandamme, Oudinot and MacDonald had been defeated and taken prisoner, Napoleon's minister Beugnot, who had assisted the emperor during the campaign in Germany, was more worried about the ornamental garden he was having refurbished for himself in Düsseldorf and the nightingales that nested in its elms and well-cut yews than about seeing to supplies for French troops. After the battle at Leipzig had been lost, he thought the war would be over once the French were driven back to the Rhine; 'no one would ever dream of pursuing them any further than that',[11] let alone that an 'invasion [of France] from abroad' would ever end well for the Allies.[12]

Things turned out differently. Pushed on by Alexander's Cossacks, the Allies were in position on the French border in December 1813, two months after the Battle of Leipzig. Although some of France's troops continued to occupy a few German fortifications on into the spring of 1814, the emperor and most of his troops had been driven out of Germany and the Rhine Confederation was abolished.[13] The final negotiations with Napoleon stranded on his refusal to settle for anything less than the 'natural' boundaries of France – the Rhine, the Alps and the Pyrenees.

On 1 December, in Frankfort, the Allies declared that they were not waging war on France, but against the hegemonic ambitions of the emperor. With

---

[8] Broers, *The Napoleonic Empire in Italy*, 5. See also D. Lieven, 'International Relations in the Napoleonic Era: The Long View', in J. Hartley, P. Keenan and D. Lieven (eds.), *Russia and the Napoleonic Wars* (Basingstoke: Palgrave Macmillan, 2015), 12–27, here: 14–17.

[9] Schulz, *Normen und Praxis*, 54–5; Siemann, *Metternich*, 394–414, 440–53.

[10] C. J. Esdaile, *Napoleon's Wars. An International History, 1803–1815* (London: Allen Lane, 2007), 504; Siemann, *Metternich*, 409–10; M. Price, *Napoleon. The End of Glory* (New York: Oxford University Press, 2014), 83–5.

[11] Beugnot, *Mémoires du Comte Beugnot*, 27, 42–3.

[12] F.-R. Chateaubriand, *Mémoires d'outre-tombe*, vol. 2 (Paris: Brodard & Taupin, 1973 [1849]), 242.

[13] See H. Helmert and H.-J. Uszeck, *Der Befreiungskrieg 1813/4. Militärischer Verlauf* (Berlin: Militärverlag der DDR, 1968).

a view to the European balance of power, France did not have to fear being wiped off of the map; even though she was to lose her emperor, she would be allowed to retain her borders of 1792. The choice of words in the declaration clearly reflected Metternich's earlier statements and indicate in no uncertain terms what the Allies considered to be an honest and decent distribution of power, a 'just equilibrium' that would guarantee happiness for everyone:

> The allied sovereigns desire that France should be great, strong and happy, because the great and strong French power is one of the fundamental bases of the social edifice. They desire that France should be happy, that French commerce should rise again, and that the arts, those blessings of peace, should flourish again, because a great people cannot be tranquil except in as far as it is happy. The powers confirm to the French Empire an extent of territory which France never knew under its kings, because a valiant nation should not lose rank for having in its turn experienced reverse in an obstinate and bloody conflict, in which it has fought with its usual daring.
>
> But the powers also wish to be free, happy and tranquil. They desire a state of peace which, by a wise distribution of power and a just equilibrium, may preserve henceforth their peoples from the innumerable calamities which for the past twenty years have weighed upon Europe.
>
> The allied powers will not lay aside their arms without having attained that great and beneficent result, that noble object of their efforts. They will not lay aside their arms until the political condition of Europe shall be again consolidated, until immutable principles shall have resumed their rights over vain pretensions, until the sanctity of treaties shall have finally assured a real peace for Europe. Frankfort, December 1, 1813.[14]

Unlike Napoleon, the Allies clearly indicated that they were pursuing a 'noble' project and did not consider France a conquered land. A post-war order needed to be drawn up that provided what Metternich had described earlier as a 'restoration of a fair balance between the powers'.[15]

From Old to New Imperial Ambitions

Metternich's ideas for the new order fit well with those of his British colleague Castlereagh. In April 1813, Castlereagh had dusted off an old blueprint from 1805 and sent it on to the British ambassador in Moscow, Lord Cathcart, with the request to gauge what Tsar Alexander thought about 'so masterly an

---

[14] 'The Frankfort Declaration', 1 December 1813, in Foreign Office (ed.), *British and Foreign State Papers, 1812–1814*, vol. 1 (London: Ridgway, 1842), 911.

[15] See also the Preamble to the Treaty of Teplitz, 9 September 1813, in G. de Martens (ed.), *Nouveau recueil de traités des puissances et états de l'Europe. Depuis 1808 jusqu'à présent*, vol. 3 (Göttingen: Dieterich, 1818), 295.

outline for the restoration of Europe' (more on this in Chapter 3).[16] This memorandum on the 'Deliverance and Security of Europe' had been drawn up by the British prime minister William Pitt the Younger in a letter to the tsar in 1805, and was now being excavated again.[17] It was a highly ambitious, strategic note, based on the principle that larger power inequalities ('projects of Aggrandizement and Ambition') should be restrained – indicating that both France and Russia needed to be contained. From the British perspective, such a European territorial balance of power could only be realized in a sustainable fashion with the North Sea ports 'free' and in the hands of associated powers. An independent and stable Dutch state should therefore be created, with a strong, fortified border, acting as a military *Boulevard de l'Europe* and offering protection and deterrence vis-à-vis future French aggression. Britain would appropriate the role of 'balancer' itself, in order to give 'Solidity and Permanence to the System', and hence secure British hegemony on the seas and in the colonies. Free access to the Scheldt and Tagus estuaries was required to enable free trade to and from Europe again; the myriad protectionist measures had been highly detrimental to British export, which after the loss of the American colonies and the lifting of the continental blockade would be well served with a novel European impulse.[18]

In December 1813, the main war objectives in the Pitt-Plan had been achieved: the Netherlands and Spain had been liberated, they had re-established their independence and, thanks to the British, the original dynasties had returned to the throne. So too, the French colonies and trading posts in Africa, the Caribbean and India had been (re)conquered, the continental blockade along the coast of France and its (former) allies lifted and the Portuguese and Belgian ports along the Tagus and Scheldt opened and freed. The territory of Hanover, now 25 per cent larger in size, had also been returned (and in 1814 elevated to a kingdom in personal union with the British crown). The British and Austrian signatories of the Frankfort Declaration had hoped that Napoleon would abandon his old imperial ambitions and agree to a joint solution and partition of the continent; in short, that he would as yet concede, and allow Britannia once again to rule the waves.

The commanders of the Silesian army were, strategically speaking, not that far-sighted. Driven by revenge, pride and above all by tactical ambitions, Field Marshal Blücher and his chief of staff Gneisenau were eager to march on Paris

---

[16] Castlereagh to Cathcart, 8 April 1813, in C. W. Vane (ed.), *Correspondence, Despatches, and Other Papers of Viscount Castlereagh*, vol. 8 (London: Shoberl, 1851), 356–7.

[17] William Pitt, in a letter to the Russian ambassador in London (hereafter: 'the Pitt-Plan'), in T. C. Hansard (ed.), *The Parliamentary Debates from the Year 1803 to the Present Time*, vol. 31 (London: Hansard, 1815), 177–82.

[18] Ibid., 182. Cf. M. Mandelbaum, *The Fate of Nations: The Search for National Security in the Nineteenth and Twentieth Centuries* (Cambridge: Cambridge University Press, 1988), 18–19.

and to humiliate the emperor in the very heart of his empire. With the publicity-driven *Tugendbund* (the 'League of Virtue', a secret political society in Prussia) breathing down their necks, they wanted to deliver on securing war booty and garnering compensation for the immense losses tied to the German war efforts. The Prussian ambitions were especially focused on expanding Prussia's own powerbase within the states of the former German Empire, also in order to improve its own position in relation to Austria.[19]

The Russian Tsar Alexander (Fig. 2.3) had yet another perspective. He had received the British Memorandum and was giving it sympathetic

Figure 2.3   Tsar Alexander I of Russia. Portrait by Thomas Lawrence, *c.*1814–18. (Royal Collection Trust / © Her Majesty Queen Elizabeth II 2019)

[19]   See T. Crepon, *Leberecht von Blücher. Leben und Kämpfe. Biografie* (Berlin: Neues Leben, 1988); R. Parkinson, *The Hussar General. The Life of Blücher, the Man of Waterloo* (London: Peter Davies, 1975); H. Otto, *Gneisenau. Preussens unbequemer Patriot. Biographie* (Bonn: Keil, 1979).

consideration, but his own main goal was not to rest until Napoleon, that scourge of world peace, was eliminated for good. With the emperor still on the throne and the real risk that a new crop of recruits for the Grand Armée would again be called up, things would never quiet down. Napoleon would indeed levy up another 300,000 young conscripts in January 1814 (of whom 175,000 would turn up). Nothing in Napoleon's actions even alluded to scaled-back ambitions or an openness for compromise.[20] Moreover, Alexander hoped that a victory in Paris would reinforce his own imperialist claim; by incorporating Poland into a kind of alliance, or possibly directly into his realm, he would be able to extend Russia's influence into Europe. The Russian navy, in addition only to that of Britain, emerged virtually intact from the Napoleonic Wars, and dominated the Baltic and Caspian seas. Both in the Balkans and the Ottoman Empire as well as on the continent, in the capitals of the West, Alexander wanted to show that Russia was on the rise as a great European power.[21] That is why he did not let up on the reluctant Austrian commander Schwarzenberg until he hesitantly agreed to continue his march, right into Paris.[22] As a result, between 21 December 1813 and 1 January, the coalition forces – while not united in their ultimate goals – crossed the Rhine together between Koblenz and Basel.[23]

At the same time, Castlereagh, accompanied by his wife, sailed through the thick fog from Britain to the Netherlands, arriving on 7 January, marking the beginning of the first time that a British foreign secretary would stay abroad for so long. As a line of defence between Britain and France and as a springboard to the continent, including the free port of Antwerp, the Netherlands was crucial to the British efforts to restore the balance of power. Castlereagh talked pointedly with Crown Prince Willem Frederik, who had just returned on 29 November 1813, about what the Dutch role in the new inter-imperial Europe would be: the Kingdom of the Netherlands would have 'to serve as a boulevard for the independence and tranquillity of Europe'[24] – the crux of the Pitt-Plan – and to that end would be allowed to annex the Belgian regions into the prior territory of the Dutch Republic. Redrawing borders, reforming state

[20] Houssaye, *1814*, 8–10.
[21] See Burbank and Cooper, *Empires in World History*, 333; D. Lieven,*Russia against Napoleon. The Battle for Europe, 1807 to 1814* (London: Allen Lane, 2009).
[22] V. M. Bezotosnyi, 'Factions and In-Fighting among Russian Generals in the 1812 Era', in Hartley, Keenan and Lieven (eds.), *Russia and the Napoleonic Wars*, 106–18, here: 117.
[23] See also Dorothea Lieven, wife of the Russian ambassador, to her brother, Alexander von Benckendorff, the Russian general who at that point was fighting French troops in the Netherlands. Letter of Dorothea to Alexander, 27 December 1813, in Lionel G. Robinson (ed.), *Letters of Dorothea, Princess Lieven, during her Residence in London, 1812–1834* (London/New York: Longmans, Green and Co., 1902), 8–9.
[24] This according to Crown Prince Willem (later King Willem I) to Castlereagh, in H. Colenbrander (ed.), *Gedenkstukken der algemeene geschiedenis van Nederland van 1795 tot 1840*, vol. 6.3 (The Hague: Martinus Nijhoff, 1912), 1876–8.

institutions and supporting 'second-tier' powers like the Netherlands militarily and financially were all part of the new imperialist plans for Europe.[25]

On 18 January, after an arduous trek through snow and ice, Castlereagh arrived at the Allied headquarters in Basel, where he made Metternich's acquaintance for the first time. They hit it off well and soon concurred with each other's views about what the future balance of power should look like. 'He has everything,' wrote Metternich with delight, 'affability, wisdom, moderation. He agrees with me in every way, and I have the conviction from him to be equally well-suited. We hold our own against the asininity of a certain personage [the tsar], and I am no longer anxious over his plans.' Metternich was particularly pleased that he had found an ally in Castlereagh regarding his plans for the post-war European balance of power, and that he had been able to convince the British minister that Russia's military advance and its increasing influence in Europe was in no way a cause for concern.[26] The Concert of Europe was playing, but not in tune yet.

Prussian Administrative Colonialism

From January 1814 onwards, the Allied troops closed in on Paris from the east and the north. Napoleon himself rejected any and all of the latest diplomatic overtures, binding the Allies together even further.[27] In practice this meant that, once they crossed the Rhine, the Allied powers had to agree on the administration and military occupation of the French provinces, as well as on what to do with the goods they found or appropriated there. And what were the plans for the long run? In most textbooks on the emergence of the Concert of Europe and the Vienna Congress, this level of practical decision-making has often been glossed over. But here the crucial strategic considerations converged: how would the Allied powers translate their cooperation 'on the ground'? It was very clear already in early 1814 that the Allied forces would be deployed in France for a longer period, and would not be demobilized straight away. Peace negotiations had to be carried out, treaties concluded. In attendance at these formal negotiations, commanders and officials on the spot took the initiative.

The Prussians marching into France in the wake of the Silesian army knew how to set up administrative rule in the newly liberated provinces. Masters at bureaucratic modernization, they had created an Allied Central Administration (ACA) after the Battle of Leipzig. On 15 January 1814, the

---

[25] See especially (Van) Sas, *Onze natuurlijkste bondgenoot*, 35–55. See also B. de Graaf, 'Second-tier Diplomacy: Hans von Gagern and William I in their Quest for an Alternative European Order, 1813–1818', *Journal of Modern European History*, 12:4 (2014), 546–66.

[26] Bew, *Castlereagh*, 332–8.

[27] Castlereagh to Liverpool, 6 February 1814, cited in Bew, *Castlereagh*, 341, 343. See also Schulz, *Normen und Praxis*, 56.

Allies, then still in Basel, agreed that the ACA would decide on the organizational details of the occupation behind the front as it advanced into France. The ACA had laid out the arrangements between the countries of the Sixth Coalition regarding troops, finances and information-gathering and would extend its rule in France now as well. That was a crucial turning point: the conquered lands were not completely rendered to the mercy – in practice, to the revenge and retribution – of army generals on the march, but subjugated to a specific civil administration in the occupied territories.[28] This seminal decision was inspired by healthy mutual distrust, coupled with a drive for bureaucratic control: no single army unit was to profit unilaterally from an Allied victory. The conquered lands were not to be looted and pillaged at random, but needed to be put under civilized Allied control and guardianship. Such an arrangement would provide better and more structural financial rewards.

According to the historian Brian Vick, the European peacemakers were driven by 'eurocentrist enlightenment ideas on the post-war order'. The executives of this order were enlightened autocrats, inspired by current liberal notions on citizenship and the 'commercial society'.[29] What stood out here, however, were the Prussian bureaucrats making the greatest leaps in creating a modern, centralized order. In Prussia, a new academic discipline had emerged, the *Kameralistik*, that considered the state apparatus a 'machinery', to be assembled with an eye for detail and operational logics. This conception of the state as a machine had gained traction in the eighteenth century. Oftentimes, this metaphor was applied in reference to mechanical clockwork, and around 1813 it may have been associated with automatic spinning devices or steam engines as well. In any case, the new professional bureaucrats of the early nineteenth century happily appropriated the discourse to indicate a rational, logical relation between means, ends and outcomes of a specific policy or administrative programme. Inasmuch as the authorities in charge were to conceive of a sound plan, a *systema*, and allocate appropriate means and measures to it, this would then 'automatically' – following the logic of an automated machine – bring about the desired results.[30] These modern interpretations of state rule and administration were applied by the Prussian professionals in their own provinces, but also tested in the newly colonized areas in the east. Rulers and administrators assembled the machinery of the

---

[28] Cf. P. von Kielmansegg, *Stein und die Zentralverwaltung 1813/1814* (Stuttgart: Kohlhammer, 1964).

[29] B. Vick, 'Power, Humanitarianism, and the Global Liberal Order: Abolition and the Barbary Corsairs in the Vienna Congress System', *The International History Review*, 40:4 (2018), 939–60, here: 951–2.

[30] See B. Stollberg-Rilinger, *Der Staat als Maschine. Zur politischen Metaphorik des absoluten Fürstenstaats* (Berlin: Duncker & Humblot, 1986); see also Stollberg-Rilinger, *Maria Theresia. Die Kaiserin in ihrer Zeit. Eine Biografie* (Munich: C. H. Beck, 2017), 178–84.

state, turned it on, and would observe its automated course of action. These new, professional insights went with them to Paris, were they were applied to create and fine-tune the Allied administration.

The head of this new European and Allied administrative apparatus, the ACA, was the Prussian reformer and minister Baron Heinrich Friedrich Karl vom Stein. Born in Nassau in 1757 into the family of a *Reichsritter*, Stein had quickly made a name for himself as an extremely conscientious and efficient bureaucrat. He was tireless in his efforts to modernize agriculture and the mining and shipping industries in the Rhine provinces, was responsible for the construction of roads and canals and travelled to Britain to study the Industrial Revolution. Stein was appointed as the administrator for the western Prussian provinces, and between 1802 and 1804, living in Münster, shepherded the process of secularizing church properties and incorporating them into the Prussian state. He was a proponent of collective management, federal associations and local autonomy and participation, also manifesting liberal tendencies, for example by involving the civil registry in administration and governance. In addition to being a dynamic and future-oriented public servant, Stein was, however, primarily a German patriot. With his Prussian bureaucratic and colonizing zeal, he advocated the creation of a stronger German nation. After the ignominious defeats of 1806 and the Treaty of Tilsit in 1807, he insisted on major reforms within the antiquated, autocratic Prussian state and military apparatus. Along with the Prussian Lieutenant General Gebhard Leberecht von Blücher, who governed the province of Westphalia from Münster and whom Stein shared an office with, he urged Friedrich Wilhelm III incessantly to take up arms against Napoleon and to defend the honour of Prussia. Friedrich Wilhelm, however, resented the headstrong and hardly diplomatic moves of his minister. Napoleon, who initially – but wrongly so – took Stein to be a liberal and pro-French ally, became so annoyed with his patriotic opposition that he declared Stein to be an enemy of France and issued an order that he be executed. Stein escaped and chose instead to become a consultant in the service of Tsar Alexander. He returned to Germany at the end of 1812 in the wake of the Russian troops' march behind the retreating Grand Armée.

Upon his return, Stein went straight back to work, nominally still in the service of the tsar, but in fact operating as a Prussian patriot in everything he did. As head of the Central Administrative Authority, he dealt with money, weapons and soldiers for the coalition troops; he also took over the administration of Saxony and the former Napoleonic duchies of Berg, Westphalia and Frankfurt. Even more of a fanatic than before, he tried to realize his former ideals: to strengthen Prussia and reposition it as a power with respect to Austria so as together to resurrect the old empire from the ashes – also with an eye to extending Prussia's holdings at the expense of 'liberated' German states, and preferably also via incorporating a part of France. Although Stein did have his supporters, like Justus Gruner, the former chief of the Berlin police and linchpin of a large spy network, who was to assume an important task in Paris in 1815, the 'emperor of Germany', as Stein was mockingly referred to, did not have enough support for his ambitious plans. Stein wanted too much at the same time and rubbed key figures up the wrong way. His attempts to incorporate states of the Confederation of the Rhine met with opposition from Austria and the middle and southern German states, not to mention states in the Confederation of the Rhine.

The Prussian king was himself too hesitant and passive, and not very much inclined to support his far too dynamic super bureaucrat (who, by the way, just like his master, is lacking any serious up-to-date international biography). When Stein crossed into France with his ACA, he had to abandon his own strategic and political ambitions for Germany and align himself more with the joint Allied headquarters, in offering administrative and executive support to the advancing troops there. While somewhat disappointed, he adjusted himself to his new tasks. Again, he proved himself a modern and highly innovative administrator. At short notice he set up a system of uniform rule and management in the 'liberated' French provinces, including the apportioning of resources, taxes and the care of the troops, coupled with the centralized supervision of the police and the courts. In this, he cooperated closely with his colleague Gruner, who was already setting up a similar system in the liberated Grand Duchy of Berg – now in Prussian hands. The revolutionary strike in all this was the fact that Stein, commissioned by the Sixth Coalition, was building a functioning 'machine' of Allied security management, designed as a veritable multinational, even supranational project.[31]

The 57-year-old Stein was the one who placed the Belgian provinces, liberated in February 1814, under Allied administration (they would formally fall to the new Kingdom of the Netherlands only in September 1815).[32] In France, his greatest challenge was to ensure that the Allied powers would benefit equally from the occupation. Caring for the troops and appropriating the funds needed to that end were top priorities. But so was seeing to it that no one power outdid another when it came to, say, appropriating French tax revenues. Accounts receivable for money, dry goods, food, housing and

---

[31] T. Nipperdey, *Deutsche Geschichte 1800–1866. Bürgerwelt und starker Staat* (Munich: C. H. Beck, 1998), 87–90; W. Hubatsch, *Die Stein-Hardenbergschen Reformen* (Darmstadt: Wissenschaftliche Buchgesellschaft, 1977), 197–9; W. Ribhegge, *Preußen im Westen. Kampf um den Parlamentarismus in Rheinland und Westphalen, 1789–1947* (Münster: Aschendorff Verlag, 2008), 46–8.

[32] See the reports in 'Vorübergehende Verwaltung Belgiens durch die alliierte Mächte', April 1814–October 1816, Geheimes Staatsarchiv Preussischer Kulturbesitz, Berlin (GStA PK) III. Haubtabteilung (HA) Ministerium des auswärtigen Angelegenheiten (MdA) I. no. 891; 'Administration von Belgien nach der Besetzung durch die alliierten Truppen', February–August 1814, GStA PK, III. HA I. no. 1238.

clothing had to be distributed and allocated proportionally. The Prussians, wanting to broaden their claims westward, hoped that the possibility of discussing 'acquisitions' and a permanent realignment of the French border remained on the table. (This proved to be the case for the Duchy of Berg, which went to the Hohenzollerns after the Congress of Vienna.)[33] Facilitating the occupation was easier said than done, because Stein's organization first had to see to it that its civil governors, who were jointly appointed by the Allies, obtained the authority called for in the conquered French territories. Up until that time, these were being managed by the military commanders who had moved into those areas with their troops and continued to make the most of their military prerogatives. They were hardly inclined to hand over authority or share privileges with their civilian counterparts. Still just as crass as he was honest and principled, as always, Stein took his job seriously and chose (with the consent of the Allied heads of state) a civil and collegial governance structure for the occupied territories, consisting of Allied and French representatives alike. For example, he appointed a committee consisting of two French representatives and one representative from each of the Allied powers to calculate the revenues from direct and indirect taxation together and to see to their redistribution.[34] The generals were not partial to such civil deliberations; they needed supplies for their troops straight away. They would and could not account for administrative, let alone French, considerations. The Bavarian field marshal Karl Philipp von Wrede, for example, refused to transfer the departments of Haut-Rhin and Vosges, which he had conquered, to Stein's Central Administration. So too, the commander of the Prussian–Silesian Army, Blücher, his chief of staff Gneisenau and quartermaster Müffling were not at all inclined to transfer their authority over the general government of Lothringen (which they had conquered and occupied with their troops themselves) to the Russian diplomat Count Alopeus, as had been agreed in Basel.[35]

Stein's Faltering Machine

The irony of Stein's conscientious sense of duty was that he ended up working at cross purposes with his old compatriot, the Prussian general Blücher, who was still committed to a course of diehard German patriotism. Before Stein was able to arrange for the management of occupied territories based on his detailed and calibrated allocation of ways and means, Blücher preferred to

---

[33] Wacker, *Die alliierte Besetzung*, 43–4.

[34] The Stein Plan: see notations on pages 1–22, in preparation for the meeting of 23 April 1814, 'Besetzung von Frankreich und den noch nicht vertheilten deutschen Territorien', March–June 1814, GStA PK, III. HA I. no. 862.

[35] Kielmansegg, *Stein und die Zentralverwaltung 1813/1814*, 22–97; Wacker, *Die alliierte Besetzung*, 43–5, 56–8.

proceed himself with the appropriation of tobacco, spirits, municipal funds and other supplies for his troops. Likewise, an increasingly frustrated Alopeus complained to Stein that, as governor of Lothringen (Lorraine), he got the impression that the Prussian commanders preferred not to receive their orders from 'a foreigner'.[36] Only when the Austrian general Schwarzenberg, commander of the imperial Austrian army, issued a general order that all military units had to act in accordance with Stein's civil administration, and were only allowed to appropriate finances and goods to meet pressing and immediate needs, did the Prussian troops agree to comply. It took Stein's insisting, before Blücher passed the order on to his troops; but he could not keep himself from simply deleting the passage banning soliciting (financial) contributions from conquered French municipalities.[37]

Administering civil matters was further complicated by the fact that Stein, in part owing to a lack of Allied personnel, urged the Allied governors to make use of local French intendants and supervisors. But those who had not already fled elsewhere, usually leaving their posts unmanned, were seldom inclined to cooperate without protest. So too, many of the locals had few qualms about engaging in outright obstruction and sabotage.[38] One consequence of these conflicts was that the tax revenue and other administrative fees usually collected by the civil authorities seldom came anywhere close to meeting what was expected or what necessity called for. Only the *département* of Meurthe (part of the general government of Lothringen) could be managed in accordance with the agreements made in Basel, and produced sufficient tax revenues.[39] That was probably also due to the agile Russian diplomat Alopeus's steady hand in the matter (as someone who attached great importance to rebuilding the 'old institutions'), and to, as he saw it, the 'brave people' who had never renounced their allegiance to the House of Bourbon, its return being that of 'the legitimate princes, who alone could put an end to the maladies of France'. Alopeus was also shrewd enough to appoint a Frenchman of some stature, the Baron de Chambray, as head of the Maréchaussée in order to re-establish public order and security.[40] Alopeus's reasonably effective engagement of resident agencies and elites was, however, quite an isolated case.

Stein's intentions were further thwarted by finance minister Von Bülow, who informed the interim government in Paris that it had a right to a compensatory claim of 169.8 million French francs. Bülow explained to his

[36] Alopeus to Stein, 10 February 1814, GStA PK, I. HA Rep. 92. Nachlass (Nl.) Eichhorn, no. 22; Wacker, *Die alliierte Besetzung*, 46–7.

[37] See Wacker, *Die alliierte Besetzung*, 46–8.

[38] See Houssaye, *1814*, 55–9, 271–2, 406–11.

[39] Wacker, *Die alliierte Besetzung*, 45–54. The department of Meurthe generated 1.65 million francs, half of what the Austrian provinces produced; Alopeus to Stein, 13 March 1814, GStA PK, I. HA Rep. 92. Nl. Eichhorn, no. 22.

[40] Letter of Alopeus, 15 May 1814, GStA PK, I. HA Rep. 92. Nl. Eichhorn, no. 22.

colleague Jacques Claude Beugnot (whom Talleyrand had appointed as minister of the interior in April 1814) that given the havoc wreaked by the French forces in German countries, and in view of the sacrifices that the German people and their troops had made, this was simply a matter of victor's justice. Moreover, German public opinion was breathing down the necks of the Prussian state and army leaders, calling for revenge and retribution. Stein added weight to the Prussian claim by announcing that the Prussian troops would not be withdrawing from France until the French had paid their taxes and settled the compensatory claims.[41] With this, the military occupation behind the front had degenerated into structural extortion – not quite how Stein had envisaged his Central Administration, as a well-oiled machine and beacon of good governance.

Both the British and the Russian ministers, however, rejected the excessive claims made by the Prussians. They were satisfied with 25 million francs in compensation,[42] and saw Stein's administrative overtures regarding the liberated and occupied regions as merely a temporary solution. Metternich did not want to saddle the new French government with undue financial burdens either, nor to subject them to a prolonged occupation or a reduction beyond the borders of 1792 (minus the Saar basin and Savoy, which France had annexed in 1789–92). Moreover, Castlereagh, Wellington – who was advancing from Spain into southern France – and British prime minister Liverpool increasingly saw merit in 'returning' France to the Bourbon dynasty. Should Napoleon make way for the Bourbons, they even promised the French an immediate ceasefire – and with that an end to the occupation. Such a restoration would help a legitimate government establish itself; France would no longer be anyone's subject, allowing it to take its place among the other great powers in supporting a stable balance of power and making further armed conflict superfluous. General Schwarzenberg, speaking on behalf of Austria, agreed. Because Napoleon was married to Marie-Louise, a daughter of the Austrian emperor, a regency in the name of her young son Napoleon II was another option for Austria. Chancellor Metternich, however, realized that, with the bottom of the Austrian treasury pretty much in sight, he could better settle on a straightforward peace with a Bourbon rather than commit to endless negotiations or await new adventures with Napoleon or his family. Tsar Alexander, however, did not have a very high opinion of Louis XVIII and was open to his return only if the French themselves really wanted him back;

---

[41] Report of a meeting of Beugnot, minister of finance, with his colleague Bülow, 13 May 1814, Archives du ministère des Affaires étrangères (AMAE), Mémoires et Documents, France – Fonds 'Bourbon', vol. 646, cited in Wacker, *Die alliierte Besetzung*, 78.

[42] Wacker, *Die alliierte Besetzung*, 43–79.

otherwise, he could also live with Sweden's Crown Prince (and former French general) Bernadotte in the Tuileries Palace.[43]

The French Lily Flies Again

On 9 March 1814, the Sixth Coalition had further advanced on Paris. On that day, the kings and emperors and their ministers concluded an official alliance treaty in Chaumont, 200 km east of the capital. With this treaty, they expressed their mutual war aims as concretely as possible, and outlined their intentions with France. Their alliance was created 'for the salutary purpose of putting an end to the miseries of Europe, of securing its future repose, by re-establishing a just balance of Power', they solemnly declared.[44] In practice this meant: that the four Allies would each keep 150,000 troops in the field to enforce France's accession to the conditions of peace based on the borders of 1792; that the Netherlands, including the Belgian provinces, would be entrusted to the House of Orange; that Switzerland would remain independent; that Italy would be divided into independent states; that the Bourbons would return to the throne in Spain; and that the German states would unify themselves in a federative bond. The signatories also pledged to extend their joint defensive alliance against French aggression for the next twenty years in what was, in effect, a multilateral solidarity pact obliging them to assist each other in this regard as the need arose. In addition, Castlereagh made a decisive contribution to the alliance in promising a British subsidy of 5 million pounds sterling to the Allied war chest.[45] Although it was not literally laid down in the treaty, but only discussed verbally on 19 March (because the Allies officially held to the line that it was up to the French to decide), the suggestion was that such a lasting peace could only be concluded with a representative of the Bourbon family, preferably with Louis XVIII himself. The tenure of the Bonaparte clan was over.[46]

Once the treaty had been signed, Castlereagh proudly wrote to his prime minister: 'I send you my Treaty, which I hope you will approve. It has been signed at a whist table, and the signatories agreed that "never were the stakes so high at any former party".' Castlereagh underscored the treaty's strategic value

---

[43] Regarding the discussion among the Allies about the return of the Bourbons, see A. von Ilsemann, *Die Politik Frankreichs auf dem Wiener Kongress. Talleyrands aussenpolitische Strategien zwischen Erster und Zweiter Restauration* (Hamburg: Krämer, 1996), 41–59.

[44] Treaty of Chaumont, dated 1 March 1814 and actually signed on 9 March, see Foreign Office (ed.), *British and Foreign State Papers, 1812–1816*, vol. 1, part 1 (London: Ridgway, 1841), 121–9.

[45] Schroeder, *The Transformation of European Politics*, 501–4; Schulz, *Normen und Praxis*, 56–7.

[46] For an overview of this period see further: Wacker, *Die alliierte Besetzung*, 30–7; Von Ilsemann, *Die Politik Frankreichs*, 41–53.

for all of Europe: 'not only as a systematic pledge of preserving concert amongst the leading Powers, but as a refuge under which all the minor states, especially those on the Rhine, may look forward to find their security upon the Return of Peace, relieved from the necessity of seeking a compromise with France'.[47] In other words, the treaty curtailed Stein's grand ambitions for Prussia considerably. His Civil Administration was to be dissolved and the sovereignty of the lands within the borders of 1792 would be returned to France eventually. The white Lily of the Bourbons would fly again. Where Britain's 'informal empire' in India did nothing but grow during the Napoleonic period, and was further enriched by new acquisitions in 1814 and 1815, Prussia saw its annexation plans in the east (Poland and Saxony) and in the west (subjugating states in the Confederation of the Rhine and parts of the left bank of the Rhine) repeatedly thwarted. In spring 1814, the Allied machine was distinctly less Prussian.

The Grace of Tsar Alexander

The British were the paymasters of the alliance, but Tsar Alexander was the one who made the decisions on the future of France during this critical period. He was the one who had the wit to appoint Stein and Alopeus to oversee the coalition's management and who was urging Schwarzenberg and King Friedrich Wilhelm III to advance to Paris. It was his idea, in March 1814, to chase Napoleon southwards, but simultaneously attack Paris with the brunt of the Allied forces. 'Europe is lucky in having her destinies left in the hands of Alexander', as Dorothea, Princess Lieven, wife to the Russian ambassador in London, fawned to her brother, General Alexander von Benckendorff.[48]

Alexander's attitude towards the defeated France was as decisive for the post-war peace order of 1814 as it was surprising. Against French terror, he positioned Russian magnanimity and even reconciliation. At the turn of the year 1814, on the evening before the Russian troops crossed the Rhine, Tsar Alexander sent them off with a fiery and almost messianic message: 'Warriors! Your valor has led you from the banks of the Oka to the banks of the Rhine', he commenced his homily:

> The wrath of God has burst on our enemies ... Let us not imitate them; forget what they have done to us. Let us carry into France, not resentment and vengeance, but a hand held out in peace. The glory of the Russian is to vanquish the enemy that attacks him, and to treat the disarmed enemy as

---

[47] Castlereagh to Liverpool, 10 March 1814, The National Archives, Kew (TNA), Foreign Office (FO) 92/3. See also Bew, *Castlereagh*, 346.
[48] Letter of Dorothea Lieven to Alexander Benckendorff, 6 April 1813, in Robinson (ed.), *Letters of Dorothea*, 2–3.

> a brother. Our revered faith teaches us, by the very mouth of God, to love
> our enemies, to do good to those who hate us.

He moreover ordered his generals to watch out that the Russian honour
remained 'spotless'.[49]

On 31 March, 'Divine Providence' – as Alexander believed – provided what
he had been yearning for. The man who had cried over the smoking ruins of
Moscow now drew loud cheers as he entered the French capital, flanked by the
Prussian king and General Schwarzenberg (on behalf of the Austrian
emperor). The tsar wore his Chevaliers Gardé general's uniform, rode his
grey horse Mars and was escorted by the exotic Cossack Life-Guards on their
small, fast horses.[50] The capital's key was ceremonially handed over to the tsar
by Talleyrand. And with that the French were delivered over to the mercy of
the Russian tsar. 'These damaging war sentiments!' Beugnot sighed, 'this
deplorable madness for conquest!' 'We've run all the way to Moscow, only to
provoke the cossacks and draw them to the banks of the Seine.'[51] In Moscow,
however, Alexander had sworn at the time that, when his empire was saved, he
would defeat his enemies and, out of Christian gratitude, would even forgive
them. Even though Napoleon had invaded his kingdom and set his cities
ablaze, Alexander wanted to be a conqueror who would have Paris fall at his
feet – and show it his grace. Inspired and exalted, and without waiting for his
Allied partners, he issued a statement declaring the banishment of Napoleon
and his family and the installation of a new, legitimate government for France,
based on a new liberal constitution.[52] For the 'happiness of Europe', the
declaration held, it was essential that France should become 'great and strong'
again.[53]

That same day, in the Capitulation Treaty of 30 March (signed on 31March,
at two o'clock in the morning), Article VIII announced that the capital would
be 'recommended to the generosity of the high powers'.[54] The tsar understood
this to mean that he would see to it that the city and its residents were protected

---

[49] Cited in M.-P. Rey, *Alexander I. The Tsar Who Defeated Napoleon* (Illinois: NIU Press, 2012), 264.

[50] As recalled by the Russian general and aide-de-camp of the tsar: A. Mikhailofsky-Danilefsky, *History of the Campaign in France in the Year 1814* (London: Smith, Elder and Co., 1839), 383–90; Bew, *Castlereagh*, 349.

[51] Beugnot, *Mémoires du Comte Beugnot*, 96.

[52] See, for example, in letters of Pozzo di Borgo to Nesselrode, 23 May/6 June 1814; 11/23 May 1815, in C. Pozzo di Borgo (ed.), *Correspondance diplomatique du comte Pozzo di Borgo, ambassadeur de Russie en France, et du comte de Nesselrode (1814–1818)*, vol. 1 (Paris: Calmann Lévy, 1890), 2–3, 134–5.

[53] Cited in Rey, *Alexander I*, 268–9. See also Tsar Alexander, 'Declaration of his majesty, the emperor of Russia', 31 March 1814, *The Monthly Magazine; or British Register*, 37:1 (London: R. Phillips, [1 May] 1814), 366.

[54] Cited in Houssaye, *1814*, 537 n. 1; P. Giraud (ed.), *Campagne de Paris, en 1814, précédée d'un coup-d'oeil sur celle de 1813* (Paris: Chez les Marchands de Nouveautés, 1814), 58.

as much as possible, also against predators and vengeful soldiers. The tsar would also see to it that troops were not billeted in private homes, that the majority of them were stationed outside the city and that the gendarmerie and National Guard did not have to be disbanded.[55] 'His majesty, the emperor Alexander gives his guarantee for the safety of persons and properties', the surprised and somewhat relieved prefects of the Seine told the people of Paris.[56]

The French writer, diplomat and Romantic Bourbon supporter François-René Chateaubriand did not know what to make of it all. He was almost at loss for words in the face of so much benevolence and goodwill: 'I felt my exasperation grow against the man whose glory had reduced us to this shame.'[57] The population of Paris was especially relieved that, after ceaseless war efforts and repeated calls for sons and fathers to enlist, the fighting was finally over. The joyous shouts that reverberated through the streets of Paris in March and April, 'Vive Alexandre, vivent les alliés', must also be seen in that light. The French were sick of war, and regarded Alexander as the apostle who was bringing them the peace for which they longed.[58]

Child of the Enlightenment

To understand the imprint the Russian tsar left on the post-war plans for collective security, Alexander's intellectual and political trajectory needs to be retraced. Historical accounts often depict Tsar Alexander I as a reactionary despot who wanted more than anything that Europe after all of the revolutionary turmoil should once again be ruled by authoritarian monarchs.[59] Fellow rulers, such as Castlereagh and Metternich, substantially contributed to this reactionary and backward image with denigrating remarks.[60] Yet it is too simple to dismiss Alexander as a religiously derailed autocrat. After all, he was doing exactly what Castlereagh had suggested: thinking about the overall context of European peace – it is just that his doing so turned out to be much more religious and grandiose than the British had anticipated.[61] His grandiloquent declarations should be historicized rather than discarded. During these

---

[55] 'Alliierte Dispositionen in Sachen Truppenkantonierungen in Frankreich', 10 April 1814, GStA PK, III. HA I. no. 862.
[56] Houssaye, 1814, 549–672, here: 569.
[57] Chateaubriand, Mémoires d'outre-tombe, vol. 2, 251. English translation offered in Rey, Alexander I, 268.
[58] Cf. T. McNally, 'Das Russlandbild in der Publizistik Frankreichs zwischen 1814 und 1843', Forschungen zur osteuropäischen Geschichte, 6 (1958), 82–170, here: 90–5; Wacker, Die alliierte Besetzung, 79–94; Houssaye, 1814, 561–72.
[59] See especially P. Menger, Die Heilige Allianz. Religion und Politik bei Alexander I. (1801–1825) (Stuttgart: Steiner, 2014).
[60] Cited in Bew, Castlereagh, 410–11.
[61] Ibid.

years, Alexander was driven by a unique combination of unexpectedly liberal ideas, an extraordinary sense of responsibility and a robust sense of mission. His ambition was to continue the work of his grandmother – to elevate the Russian nation and position it on the international map. There was once again a tsar on the throne who, in the line of Peter the Great and Catherine the Great, laid claim to a role for himself in European politics, who also thought and lived like a European and entertained great plans for the continent's peace and prosperity.[62]

According to his biographer, Marie-Pierre Rey, Alexander was a child of the Enlightenment, a prodigal optimist, raised by his extremely progressive Swiss tutor Frédéric-César de La Harpe and groomed for the job by an ambitious grandmother, Catherine the Great. His mother was a tall German princess who did much for charitable organizations; his father, Tsar Paul I, was a paranoid tyrant who was murdered by a court camarilla in 1801. Alexander was probably aware of a conspiracy against his father, but was nonetheless surprised by his murder and felt guilt and remorse about this turn of events for the rest of his life. But the 23-year-old heir to the throne courageously set about to put his own ideals into practice, to further modernize Russia and to colonize and make the newly annexed territories in the Caucasus and in Crimea productive. But Russia's realities frustrated and quashed almost all of his plans for reform. Sometimes his own messianic, Russian Orthodox ideas about the infallibility and sanctity of his calling dulled his grasp of what was politically feasible. The 15-year-old poetic genius Pushkin praised him as a 'fiery angel' in 1814 in a poem in which Alexander as the Archangel Michael defeats the Napoleonic beast – an appealing image to both the tsar and his upright subjects.[63] Yet, Alexander was a tormented soul. The fact that he was indirectly complicit in the murder of his father and sat almost every day at the same table with the perpetrator slowly but surely began to take its toll. This enlightened Russian tsar, a bundle of contradictions, was sucked into the Napoleonic Wars unprepared, and witnessed how, against all odds, the French emperor was done in by the Russian winter. In Moscow's flames Alexander found a confirmation of his divine calling: 'Since that time, I have become another man; to the deliverance of Europe from ruin, I owe my own salvation and my deliverance.'[64]

---

[62] See for example Alexander's exalted letter with plans for a 'new order' of 'total security' to Castlereagh, 21 March/2 April 1816, or his invitation to the other Christian monarchs of Europe to join the Holy Alliance: 'Reskript Alexander I', 22 March/3 April 1816, in Ministerstvo inostrannykh del CCCP (ed.), *Vneshniaia politika Rossii XIX i nachala XX veka: dokumenty Rossiiskogo Ministerstva inostrannykh del, 1815–1830*, vol. 1 (Moscow: Izdatelstvo politicheskoy literatury, 1974), 108–11, 113–15.

[63] A. Pushkin, 'Bova' (1814), cited in L. Melnikova, 'Orthodox Russia against "Godless" France: The Russian Church and the "Holy War" of 1812', in Hartley, Keenan and Lieven (eds.), *Russia and the Napoleonic Wars*, 179–95, here: 191.

[64] Cited in Rey, *Alexander I*, 256.

Alexander's words to the people of Paris bespeak a unique combination of political ambition and heartfelt piety. He, too, had imperial aspirations, but these were, as far as extending Russia's sphere of influence and territory, directed for the most part towards Poland. As for Europe as a whole, he saw himself as *spiritus rector* of a new just order. Divine providence, belief in a morally legitimate balance of power, enlightened self-interest and a liberal preference for a distribution of power – all of these were evident in his concern for France.[65] It rested on him to restore these ideas to the throne of France again. He therefore decided upon a far-reaching intervention in encouraging the French Senate to restore the monarchy as the only legitimate form of government – but coupling it to a constitution. With this, he quite surprised the other Allies, who could only agree. Even Metternich – certainly not someone known to stand ready with compliments – was impressed by Alexander's poise in Paris. 'I found the emperor of Russia's views very reasonable', he wrote to his own regent Franz I after arriving in Paris. 'He talks much less nonsense than I would have believed.'[66]

Castlereagh, who due to circumstances had been detained with Metternich and Hardenberg in Dijon until 7 April, arriving with him in Paris three days later, concurred with Alexander's ideas on a new constitution but was less pleased with his magnanimity regarding the French people. Alexander had given away too much, and negotiated a far too lenient peace settlement. The tsar had promised Napoleon sovereignty over Elba, an island off the coast of Tuscany, as a place of exile, and that he could retain his title of emperor. Castlereagh found Elba altogether too risky; he would sooner have seen Napoleon much further away. But there was nothing more to do about that; during those first few days, the tsar was in charge in Paris.[67]

Putting Up With the Tsar

In 1814, as in 1945, the commander whose troops were the first to enter the capital of the defeated opponent would also rule the roost after the capitulation. Not the Prussian generals, the British or the Austrians, but Alexander was the man on the spot (Fig. 2.4).

On 6 April, Napoleon abdicated as emperor, and on 23 April, the Allies signed an armistice with France. They promised to hand over the government and administration of the occupied territories to the French authorities. As of 1 June, the Allied forces would leave the country altogether. The Prussian commanders were not very pleased, but had to cede this point to joint British–Austrian–Russian pressure. One of the few bright spots for the Prussians was the discovery

[65] Beugnot, *Mémoires du Comte Beugnot*, 143–4.
[66] Rey, *Alexander I*, 269.
[67] Bew, *Castlereagh*, 355.

Figure 2.4   The Russian army, under the command of Tsar Alexander, rides into Paris,
1814. Artist unknown, 1815. (Niday Picture Library / Alamy)

of the Berlin Quadriga – a bronze rendering of the Roman peace goddess Victoria
(which, incidentally, was modelled on the image of the mother of King Willem I,
Wilhelmina of Prussia) in a chariot drawn by a team of four horses. Napoleon
had had this sculpture removed from the top of the Brandenburg Gate in 1806
and had it transported to Paris in crates. Legend has it that a Frenchwoman told
the Prussians where the images were hidden (and was later executed for doing
so). On 21 April, General von Pfuel sent the statue back to Berlin, where the
precious cargo arrived in June. In August, the restored gate was unveiled.[68]

At that time, the Senate had recalled Louis XVIII from his British exile. Because,
as Talleyrand (who through intercession of the British ministers was reinstated as
minister) put it: for Europe, the return of the Bourbons in the Tuileries was the
only guarantee for a lasting peace. A stable peace order could only rest on a clear
principle: legitimacy. 'And there was only one such principle: Louis XVIII; the only
legitimate king of France.'[69] Not everyone was entirely pleased with this outcome.
According to Beugnot, who became the interim government's minister of the
interior on 3 April 1814, it was, besides general relief, especially anxiety and
confusion that prevailed in France. Would the Allies soon leave the occupied
territories? 'The [French] authorities were paralysed by uncertainty, anxiety and

---

[68] Cf. Z. Pöthe, *Perikles in Preussen. Die Politik Friedrich Wilhelms II. im Spiegel des
Brandenburger Tores* (Berlin: epubli, 2014).

[69] Comte de Broglie (ed.), *Charles-Maurice de Talleyrand-Périgord. Mémoires du prince de
Talleyrand, 1809–1815*, vol. 2 (Paris: Calman Lévy, 1891–2), 156, 165.

trembling with emotions invoked by the great dread that prevailed.'[70] Officials such as Beugnot, who, under Napoleon, had ruled the occupied territories, were indeed fully aware of what the French could expect. However, they first of all picked up where they had left off in France. Beugnot, for example, made work of having all of the horse carcasses and the bodies along the streets and in the fields removed before the stench and risk of infection (e.g. from typhus) got too strong.[71]

For the time being, the Allies commanded the day. Alexander appointed the Prussian general Osten-Sacken – he had been the first to retake a large French city (Nancy) – as the governor of Paris, along with three local subordinate commanders (Goltz, Herzogenberg and Rochechouart, a French *émigré* in Russia's service) to assist Sacken. Most of the troops set up camp outside the city; only a select few elite units were given permission to take up quarters within the city.[72] Besides Paris, the Allies actually only occupied a small part of France – only those areas 'liberated' by the Allied armies during their march on Paris. The occupied area was marked by a line behind which the French army was to remain, and where the French themselves retained all of the administrative duties. That line ran along the western border of the governorates of Ardennes, Meuse, Aube, Yvonne, via de Saône-et-Loire to Rhône-Isère, which meant that Bar-le-Duc, Dijon, Lyons and Grenoble fell under the auspices of the Allies.[73] The tactless Sacken was not very popular as governor, but in practice he proved to be quite accommodating both to the Parisians and to the new Bourbon regime. He allowed the gendarmerie and the National Guard their autonomy, as promised by Alexander, and Sacken also worked well with the Parisian police. He also saw to it that royalists and even ultra-royalists had a place in the city's new administration.[74]

Tsar Alexander initially planned on settling down in the Elysée, but on Talleyrand's advice, he came to stay in the foreign minister's palace on the Rue Saint-Florentin. That set the tone. The tsar considered himself a guest, and kept his soldiers tightly in check. On pain of flogging or even death the tsar forbade his troops to plunder. During Holy Week, around Easter (for Russian Orthodox believers, the central liturgical celebration), his men were not allowed to indulge in amusements or pleasures. The occupying forces interfered little if at all with local administrative details; the French were given a free hand, also financially, in those matters. The tsar was himself particularly keen to participate in symbolic acts of reconciliation that helped spread the new

[70] Beugnot, *Mémoires du Comte Beugnot*, 106–7.
[71] Ibid., 110.
[72] Rey, *Alexander I*, 267–8.
[73] Müffling, *The Memoirs*, 99–100.
[74] Audiffret-Pasquier (ed.),*Mémoires du Chancelier Pasquier. Révolution – Consulat – Empire*, vol. 1, part 2, 1812–1814 (Paris: Plon, 1893–4), 274–6; Wacker, *Die alliierte Besetzung*, 81–3.

culture of brotherly love and peace. He also promptly released 1,500 French prisoners of war. On 10 April, Alexander organized a public service of thanks-giving at the Place de la Concorde in order to underscore his ecumenical desire for peace. At the spot where Louis XVI was beheaded the *Te Deum* was sung and a prayer service was jointly conducted by Russian Orthodox and Roman Catholic priests. The tsar also made a point of visiting Empress Josephine frequently, as well as her daughter Hortense, the wife of then-outlawed Louis Bonaparte, the former king of the Netherlands, and of advocating for her and her children.[75] So much compassion and generosity shown to a Napoléonide from a 'new prince' confused Hortense. 'Their only support left is an enemy', an emotional Hortense noted when Alexander came to see her personally and even took her two young children (cousins of Napoleon) on his lap.[76]

To Louis XVIII, this demonstration of goodwill and magnanimity by these 'generous Russian enemies' was all the more vexing.[77] How could a member of the obscure Romanov line rule the roost in the capital of the eternal Bourbon dynasty? After more than twenty years in exile, and having moved from the Netherlands to Russia, Warsaw, Sweden and lastly to Britain, Louis Stanislas Xavier, Count of Provence and brother of the beheaded Louis XVI, was finally invited to assume the crown. But a severe attack of gout in January 1814 had put the rather obese king-to-be in a wheelchair. He did not arrive in Paris until 3 May, albeit in an open carriage pulled by eight white horses and accompanied by the thunder of cannons and pealing church bells.[78] But all the *Te Deums* could not undo the fact that in the meantime Tsar Alexander had already positioned himself on the throne – not literally, but near enough.

A Moderate, Enlightened Peace

For the most part, the king had Alexander to thank – and with him the British – for how very favourable the provisions of the First Treaty of Paris of 30 May 1814 proved to be. France retained the borders of 1792, including Avignon, large parts of Savoy and Mulhouse; it did not have to return stolen artworks (only archives, documents and the Quadriga); almost all of its colonies, except for Tobago, St Lucia and Malta, were given back to it, and in the person of Talleyrand it could take part in the Congress of Vienna, where the remaining questions would be dealt with. So too, the Allied troops pulled up camp directly,

[75] Le prince Napoléon (ed.), *Mémoires de la Reine Hortense publiés par le prince Napoléon. Avec notes de Jean Hanoteau*, vol. 2 (Paris: Plon, 1927), 203, 211–22; L. Cochelet, *Mémoires sur la Reine Hortense et la Famille Impériale* (Paris: Ollendorf, 1907), 70–89.

[76] Le prince Napoléon (ed.), *Mémoires de la Reine Hortense*, vol. 2, 221.

[77] Cochelet, *Mémoires*, 89.

[78] P. Mansel, *Louis XVIII* (Thrupp: Sutton, 1999), 147; Houssaye, *1815. La première restau-ration*, 1–2.

and the final vestige of the occupied armistice was dismantled, the tents in the Bois de Boulogne rolled up and billeting brought to an end.

But there was another side to these matters. Alexander, as an 'internal colonizer', harboured grand designs for a liberal post-war order in Europe. He had wanted to impose reforms on the Russians by force and had commissioned the drafting of a new constitution for Poland and a new code of criminal and civil law for Russia.[79] The erudite royalist Chateaubriand saw the irony here: 'the head of two supreme authorities, doubly autocratic by sword and by religion, he alone of all the sovereigns of Europe had understood that France at the age of civilization it had reached could only be governed thanks to a free constitution'.[80] In the end, the Bourbon monarch reluctantly revised the constitution that he had drafted, making it more liberal – although less so than the text that the Senate had already drawn up in April; the final text, the *Charte Constitutionnelle*, was adopted on 4 June 1814.[81]

This Charter was an important instrument in the fight against terror. It was a compromise between the Napoleonic codes, the achievements of the Revolution, the Senate version of April and Louis's own desire to include something about the divine origin of the monarchy. It contained pureblood liberal stipulations on religious toleration, freedom of the press, equality before the law, the abolition of conscription, due process of law and amnesty for all political crimes before 1814. British influence was clearly evident in the design for a contractual, constitutional government tempered through the appointment of a Chamber of (elected) Deputies and a Chamber of (appointed) Peers.[82] At the same time, ultra-royalists and Louis himself did add a passage that made it very clear that it was not the people who chose the king, but that it was the king who, called by the grace of God, gifted a charter to his people. Louis also underscored that he wanted 'to renew the chain of time': he talked about the nineteenth year of his reign, implicitly erasing the history of the Revolution and the Empire. The term 'Charter' – proposed by Beugnot, a member of the committee that drafted the constitution – also implied that this was not a contract between the people and the king, but a concession by the king that he was granting to the people.[83] The king, moreover, had both executive and legislative powers, 'the person of the king was inviolable' and the ministers were not accountable to the parliament but to him. For the moment, this was a great leap of progress, but in the months that followed, the royalists

[79] See Rey, *Alexander I*, 214–15; for Alexander's visit to London, see 274.
[80] Ibid., 275–6.
[81] See Mansel, *Louis XVIII*, 175–80; M. Price, *The Perilous Crown. France between Revolutions* (Basingstoke: Palgrave Macmillan, 2009), 52–5.
[82] B. Goujon,*Monarchies postrévolutionnaires 1814–1848. Histoire de la France contemporaine* (Paris: Seuil, 2012), 51.
[83] Lok, *Windvanen*, 58.

would hurry a number of laws through that would substantially abridge many of those constitutional and civil liberties.[84]

For Castlereagh, the British paymaster of the new order, the principle of tempering and containing authoritarian power was a welcome innovation. Yet, Europe had seen enough political earthquakes and tectonic changes. It was now time for temporizing and consolidating; the greatest danger, according to Castlereagh, lurked in changes that were too extreme and too rapid:

> It is impossible not to perceive a great moral change coming in Europe, and that the principles of freedom are in full operation. The danger is, that the transition may be too sudden to ripen into anything likely to make the world better or happier. We have new constitutions launched in France, Spain, Holland and Sicily. Let us see the result before we encourage further attempts. The attempts may be made, and we must abide the consequences; but I am sure it is better to retard than accelerate the operation of this most hazardous principle which is abroad.[85]

Coming from totally different directions, using a highly dissimilar political vocabulary, Castlereagh and Alexander found each other in 1814. Together, they tried to navigate between the Scylla of reactionary radicalism and the Charybdis of revolutionary haste. Metternich could also familiarize himself with this vision for France's future and its place in the new European order: liberalization, yes, but not too much and not too fast.

France lacked a tactical captain on the bridge. Louis XVIII initially tried half-heartedly to maintain a balance between the past and the present, between the years of revolution, war and France's glory on the one hand, and the restoration of the old regime on the other. But it soon became clear that he had no control over his reactionary brother, the Comte d'Artois, and the many *émigrés* who were hastening home – and perhaps did not want that either. The ultra-royalists were out for revenge and retribution; they wanted to turn back the clock, including the restoration of the power of the clergy and a reversal of past expropriations. Rather than committing to a balanced, moderate and enlightened peace within a European perspective, they advocated an inward-

---

[84] Cf. G. de Bertier de Sauvigny, *The Bourbon Restoration* (Philadelphia: University of Pennsylvania Press, 1966), 39–72; F. B. Artz, 'The Electoral System in France during the Bourbon Restoration, 1815–30', *The Journal of Modern History*, 1: 2 (1929), 205–18; S. Rials, 'Essai sur le concept de monarchie limitée (autour de la charte de 1814)', in *Révolution et contre-révolution au 19ème siècle* (Paris: Albatros, 1987), 119–25; P. Mansel, 'From Exile to the Throne: The Europeanization of Louis XVIII', in Mansel and T. Riotte (eds.), *Monarchy and Exile. The Politics of Legitimacy from Marie de Médicis to Wilhelm II* (Basingstoke: Palgrave Macmillan, 2011), 181–213. For extensive details, see F. Démier, *La France sous la Restauration (1814–1830)* (Paris: Gallimard, 2012); E. de Waresquiel and B. Yvert, *Histoire de la Restauration (1814–1830). Naissance de la France moderne* (Paris: Perrin, 1996).

[85] Bew, *Castlereagh*, 358–9.

facing restoration of France's royalist and Roman Catholic glory days. Neither Stein's occupation nor Alexander's generosity had made much of an impression on what was near to the heart of the French royalists. They were as open to being colonized as they were to being Europeanized. The new notion of collective security still needed to foreground itself in France.

A New Conception of Security

Security 'turns its eye towards the future',[86] wrote British philosopher Jeremy Bentham around 1800.[87] In his standard work *The Principles of the Civil Code* he underscored the importance of a predictive and precautionary security policy – in fact, a kind of risk management. Equality and prosperity were also basic desirables, but 'among these objects of the law, security is the only one which necessarily embraces the future: subsistence, abundance, equality, may be regarded for a moment only; but security implies extension in point of time, with respect to all the benefits to which it is applied. Security is therefore the principal object.'[88] Security depended on the 'care taken to save from disturbance the current of expectation', Bentham wrote in flowery prose, some years before the 'disturbance' of the French Revolution. That event gave his insights some credit and after 1815 his works became increasingly popular.[89]

Bentham's claim here, with which David Hume would agree, deviated from thinkers like Hugo Grotius, John Locke and Samuel Pufendorf, who saw security, expressed in a system of laws and regulations, as a consequence, reflection or outworking of the 'state of nature'. According to John Locke, a good government had to ensure that existing social institutions and interactions were set in their place and protected. The pre-social state, with its natural law framework, simply had to be rewritten into positive law. Hobbes was somewhat more pessimist and considered the state of nature a chaotic, anarchist situation, in which the state was required to intervene proactively. Bentham and Hume were somewhere in between. They rejected the idea that the modern state and society had their origin in an existing community of law

---

[86] J. Bentham, comments (unpublished, incomplete manuscript), Manuscripts, University College Library, London, box 61, 47. With thanks to Philip Schofield. See also P. J. Kelly, *Utilitarianism and Distributive Justice. Jeremy Bentham and the Civil Law* (Oxford: Clarendon Press, 1990), 77.

[87] See Bentham, 'An Introduction to the Principles of Morals and Legislation', in J. Burns and H. Hart (eds.), *The Collected works of Jeremy Bentham* (Oxford: Oxford University Press, 1996), 11–33.

[88] Kelly, *Utilitarianism*, 77.

[89] Bentham, comments (unpublished, incomplete manuscript), Manuscripts, University College Library, London, box 32, 1; see also box 100, 167; F. Rosen, 'Bentham and Mill on Liberty and Justice', in G. Feaver and F. Rosen (eds.), *Lives, Liberties and the Public Good* (Basingstoke: Macmillan, 1987), 121–38.

and reason. That so-called primordial state had not been all that harmonious at all. The modern state had to make at least a modicum of effort to keep human nature within its banks. But this nature had not been completely out of bounds. Authorities had to design and execute their rule in interaction with existing conventions, in close deliberation with their citizens and with an eye on the principle of utility, and the promotion of the 'greatest happiness'. At the same time, they needed to leave some space for improvement and change. Just as the human condition called out for the corset of security and justice, so too the international community needed the constraints of treaties and mutual obligations, to see to it that one state could no longer trump another.[90]

Bentham's thoughts in many respects perfectly reflect the transition from the era of economic *laissez-faire,* mercantilism and the cabinet wars of the eighteenth century to the bureaucratized nineteenth century, which saw states simultaneously launching national centralizing efforts and initiating large-scale economic, foreign and military interventions.[91] He was also a thinker who was widely read and respected by the pioneers of the post-war security system. When Russia's Tsar Alexander I visited London in 1814, his close friend and adviser Adam Czartoryski was dispatched to seek Bentham out deliberately. His arrival at Bentham's address in York Street, with an impressive entourage of mounted Cossacks and a train of attendants, caused quite a stir. The tsar used Bentham as a sounding board in order to talk through the nature of the new peace and security measures, presenting himself as a supporter of liberal reforms and negotiating with the philosopher regarding an assignment to write a criminal codebook for the Russian state and a constitution for Poland. That constitution needed to be 'balanced', 'reasonable' and 'useful' for the general interest and well-being – the tsar's favourite emotional and political vernacular of the time. French and British politicians equally lined up to exchange with Bentham.[92]

The emergence of this new reading of security offered a direct interlinking of domestic reforms and constitutional securities for the citizens at home on the one hand and international peace and stability on the other hand. It channelled experiences from the past and translated those into attempts to prevent the horrors of war and terror in the future. Countries with 'sensible' governments and fair constitutions would less likely resort to military aggression and

---

[90] Kelly, *Utilitarianism*, 81–2.
[91] Kelly, *Utilitarianism*, 132.
[92] See also Rey, *Alexander I*, 214–15. For correspondence between Bentham and Alexander, see e.g. J. Bentham, *The Correspondence. January 1809 to December 1816*, nr. 2319, Bentham to Alexander, June 1815 (Aet. 67), S. Conway (ed.), *The Collected Works of Jeremy Bentham. The Correspondence of Jeremy Bentham*, vol. 8 (Oxford: Oxford University Press, 1988); P. Schofield and J. Harris, 'Editorial Introduction', in Schofield and Harris (eds.), *'Legislator of the World'. Writings on Codification, Law, and Education* (Oxford: Oxford University Press, 1998), xxi–xxiii.

invasion – or so Tsar Alexander and the other Allied ministers reckoned. The implementation of new laws and charters, and the development of a mutual system of peace and security, therefore, was also considered an instrument of risk management, to prevent and constrain future conflicts and unrest. This project was centre stage in the deliberations of the ministers, sovereigns and their experts in Vienna, the following autumn.

Outlining the New Order: The Congress of Vienna

In early June the Allied sovereigns left the French capital, and the victors' caravan headed off to London for a series of banquets, parties and celebrations. Louis 'The Desired' had to fend for himself with his new government. Prior to September 1814, when the Congress of Vienna began, things in France were devoted to domestic recovery and the process of reclaiming dynastic power. No large-scale purges took place, but there were extensive layoffs. More than 300,000 of the 500,000 troops in the Grande Armée were sent home, and the officers that remained were put on half pay. Given the negative balance in the treasury and large debts to be paid, Baron Louis, the minister of finance, decided not to disburse the benefits promised to Napoleon and his family in the Treaty of Fontainebleau. The promise to forgive and forget the past was itself soon forgotten. Returning émigrés and Catholic clerics demanded and had many of their privileges, and sometimes even lands, returned to them. The mood was nonetheless grim. The discontent and humiliation experienced by the French people would prove fertile ground for the return of the emperor less than a year later.[93]

Amid that growing discontent, Talleyrand, with his almost unequalled diplomatic talents, had gone to Vienna to stake out and reclaim France's influence. Tomes have been published about the Congress of Vienna.[94] From September 1814 until March 1815 (officially: June) the powers negotiated and deliberated on the design for the post-war peace order. The congress was especially geared towards redrawing or confirming the European borders after the termination of the Napoleonic Wars and liberation of conquered lands. Other issues, however, were discussed as well: navigation on the Rhine, questions on standardizing statistics (calculating population sizes and national revenues), the necessity of new constitutions, the neutrality of Switzerland and the policy towards Jewish minorities. Through the great powers' representatives, smaller European partners could have their say as well. The Congress was presided over by Metternich. Officially, eight powers were in charge: Austria, Russia, Great Britain, Prussia, France, Spain, Portugal and Sweden. In practice,

---

[93] Cf. Houssaye, *1815. La première restauration*, 14–70; Bertier de Sauvigny, *The Bourbon Restoration*, 73–84.

[94] See the literature references in the Introduction.

the four Allied powers took the lead. In the manifold subcommittees, however, second- and third-rank powers could join in and contribute as well.[95]

The Congress was, moreover, framed by spectacular balls, parties, dinners, musical performances and, notably, the accompanying amorous entanglements. In historiography, Vienna is almost always considered the end station for the Allied route towards a new European order, and as the bedrock under the Concert of Europe. That is, however, not quite correct; Vienna was a crucial way station, but it was neither the start nor the finish of the Allied deliberations on the post-war order that started in early 1813 and continued in the wake of the advancing troops. In Vienna, the great powers agreed in principle on borders, spheres of influence and procedures, rules and standards to guarantee and manage these agreements in a sustainable way. The work was, however, not done at all in March 1815. Only in late November 1815 did the great powers manage to translate these general orientations into concrete financial, territorial and military stipulations. In the meantime, the system would wobble and positions would shift quite considerably.

The agreements in Vienna marked a combination of historically motivated security considerations and forward-looking innovations. The random force of Napoleon's lust for conquest was banished, and a new balance of power outlined based on objectified standards for accounting its units. A Statistical Committee provided a detailed review on square kilometres and 'souls' per country. The titles and legal status of ambassadors, plenipotentiaries and diplomats were standardized throughout Europe. In diplomatic meetings and settings, not the right of the strongest, but the alphabet was to dictate the placement of participants in an assembly. In some cases, historical, dynastic claims were recognized. The House of Orange and many German and Habsburg princes in Italy were 'restored' and could govern again; the size of their territories and their titles could, however, very well have been adapted to the new circumstances. Yet, in other cases, the Vienna negotiators indiscriminately cut kingdoms into pieces, such as Poland and Saxony, and Denmark was forced to cede Norway to Sweden. The Burgundian Netherlands was bequeathed to the Netherlands, to create an enlarged and allegedly more viable United Kingdom of the Netherlands along France's northern border. In return, Austria expanded its sphere of influence southwards with the annexation of Lombardy and Venice. France was reduced to its 'natural borders', that is, to the borders of 1792. Consequently, talking about restoration, or a reverting to the *status quo ante* of the *ancien régime*, is to gloss over these incisive transformations of the European order.

---

[95] P. Schroeder, 'Did the Vienna Settlement Rest on a Balance of Power?', *The American Historical Review*, 97:3 (1992), 683–706, here: 688.

Perhaps the most innovative agreement and one of the key pieces of the Vienna negotiations was the creation of the German Confederation. That federation, described by Metternich as an intermediate system, was conceived to arrange and regroup the states within the former territory of the Holy Roman Empire (dissolved by Napoleon in 1806), and to settle the competitions between the two largest hegemonic German states, Austria and Prussia. Austria and Prussia both acceded to the federation, but only concerning their areas formerly part of the Holy Roman Empire. The areas outside that territory would not fall under the federation's jurisdiction. The German Confederation was given a constitution, but not considered an autonomous, sovereign state, and hence, was no party to the Concert of Europe. It was a federation, formed to protect and guarantee the independence and security of the middle and smaller German states. For Austria and Prussia, it was a vehicle to settle their reciprocal balance of power and an instrument for managing risk in the heart of Europe.[96]

Vienna's order was hence more than merely a redistribution of power and influence between Britain and Russia, as Schroeder has it. It was a collective security system *in statu nascendi* that would develop its own dynamics.[97] With an endless series of maps, statistics and tables, the Statistical Commission supplied objectively verifiable material for further negotiations and realloca-tions in the years to come. The Rhine, for centuries a disputed and contested thoroughfare and front line, was subjected to the authority of the newly erected Central Commission for Navigation on the Rhine, which would serve as a platform to contain the heated debates about tolls, free navigation and other navigation-related issues that were to follow. In such committees and talks, envoys and exports dispatched by smaller powers and principalities would be granted participation too – another novel aspect of the post-war order. Thanks to Castlereagh, for example, the Netherlands contributed to the Statistical Committee, through its representative, the imperial knight and special royal emissary (of Willem I), Hans Christoph von Gagern.[98]

The overriding significance of the Congress was, however, embedded within the decision not to go home immediately, but to devise new forms and means by which to continue this type of multilateral 'conference diplomacy' in peacetime, and thus to work towards a repetitive system of collective security management.[99]

---

[96] See, for example, also: W. Gruner, *Grossbritannien, der Deutsche Bund und die Struktur des europäischen Friedens im frühen 19. Jahrhundert. Studien zu den britisch-deutschen Beziehungen in einer Periode des Umbruchs 1812–1820* (Munich: Eigenverlag, 1979), 204, 270–95; Gruner, *Der Wiener Kongress 1814/15* (Stuttgart: Reclam, 2014), 193–212; Gruner, *Der Deutsche Bund 1815–1866* (Munich: C. H. Beck, 2012), 13–28.

[97] See Richardson, 'The Concert of Europe', 48–79. And extensively: Schulz, *Normen und Praxis*, 35–72.

[98] (De) Graaf, 'Second-tier Diplomacy', 246–66.

[99] B. de Graaf, 'The Allied Machine: The Conference of Ministers in Paris and the Management of Security'; B. Vick, 'The London Ambassador's Conferences and

A Springboard to Inter-Imperial Enterprise

While underscoring all the novel and innovative decisions and institutions that were created, it should be noted that what was being outlined in Vienna was highly imperialist. It could be argued that this was exactly one of the key dimensions of the Congress: its relaunch and convergence of the European imperial ambitions. The Vienna Congress, and the Paris Treaties a couple of months later, only set the table for the resumption and high aspirations of Europe's overseas ambitions in the decades that followed. According to the historian Edward Ingram, the Vienna order laid the basis for the 'export of bellicism' to the periphery – in other words, for an ongoing nationalistic or imperialistic competition between the European powers outside the continent.[100] But that is not what is indicated here. In Vienna, the imperial powers agreed (sometimes through gritted teeth) that they would not only tolerate each other's imperial ambitions, but would at the same time be willing to assist each other.

Already during the negotiations surrounding the First Treaty of Paris in May 1814, the other Allies granted Castlereagh support for the British claim to a lasting incorporation of a few key colonies that had previously belonged to France and the Netherlands.[101] Precisely because the other countries agreed to exclude further talks about the (re)allocation of colonies from the Vienna negotiations, the British were able to continue their imperial expansion in the outer European world. The French colonies of Malta, Mauritius and Tobago and the Dutch possessions of the Cape of Good Hope and Ceylon remained in British hands permanently – as seminal 'stepping stones' on the route to India. Britain thus increased its lead over the other European powers, in terms of imperial and expansive ambitions, in 1815. With its superior maritime forces, financial credit, colonial empire (despite her losses in North America) and commercial expertise, Britain had become the leading power in Europe.[102] According to Friedrich Gentz,

> England appeared in Vienna with all the glamour which she owed to her immense successes, to the eminent part which she had played in the Coalition, to her limitless influence, to a solid basis of prosperity and

---

Beyond: Abolition, Barbary Corsairs and Multilateral Security in the Congress of Vienna System', both in B. de Graaf, I. de Haan and B. Vick (eds.) *Securing Europe after Napoleon. 1815 and the New European Security Culture* (Cambridge: Cambridge University Press, 2019), 130–49; 114–29.

[100] Ingram, 'Bellicism as Boomerang'.

[101] Castlereagh to Liverpool, 19 April 1814, Vane (ed.), *Correspondence*, vol. 9, 474.

[102] For numbers regarding correlations between the relative economic presence of the major powers in 1800 and 1820, see Ikenberry, *After Victory*, 85–6; see also Bayly, *The Birth of the Modern World*, 128–9.

power such as no other country has acquired in our days – in fact to the respect and fear which she inspired and which affected her relations with all the other Governments. And echoing Napoleon's exclamation of disbelief regarding the reluctant and peacemaking attitude of Castlereagh and Wellington: 'Profiting by this, England could have imposed her will on Europe.'[103]

Austria, too, was given free hand for its imperial ambitions in Italy. After having rid him of the burdensome Belgian provinces, the other Allied ministers gave Metternich free rein to bring the unruly Italian regions under Habsburg control, and by setting up new police and administrative institutions, further 'colonize' the area. Tsar Alexander realized his mother's ambitions by binding Poland, through a so-called autonomous administration, to Russia's sphere of influence by not putting the Polish patriot Adam Czartoryski in charge of the Congress Kingdom, but appointing Grand Duke Constantin Pavlovich, his own brother, as its first viceroy. Prussia probably got the short end of the stick when it came to Saxony (because it grudgingly had to settle for annexing only two fifths of the Saxon territory), but, in taking possession of the Rhineland and creating the German Confederation, was nonetheless able to lay the groundwork for a steady expansion of power and the 'internal colonization' of a Northern German Empire.[104]

This imperial community rested on the principle of excluding other states that were deemed inferior. By banning the Ottoman Empire from their negotiations, the four major powers were emphasizing Europe's identity as a community of 'civilized' and 'Christian' nations. In so doing, they implicitly considered the Ottoman Empire and its provinces as hunting grounds for joint imperial ambitions in the (very) near future, such as the Spanish–Dutch–Russian–British interventions against the Barbary pirates in 1815–16.[105] The Porte did indeed receive informal invitations by Austrian and British agents to send observers, and Yanko Mavroyeni, the Ottoman resident in Vienna, was given assurances as to the 'integrity' of the Ottoman Empire.[106] But no formal guarantees or show of diplomatic respect were issued.[107] Out of frustration because Ottoman agents were only granted observing status and did not receive formal permission, and because the Porte was even less considered a first-rank power – he decided not to participate at all.[108] The new Vienna

[103] Cited in H. Nicholson, *The Congress of Vienna. A Study in Allied Unity, 1812–1822* (New York: Grove Press, 2001 [1946]), 128.
[104] For a clear overview of all agreements and rearrangements, see Jarrett, *The Congress of Vienna and its Legacy*.
[105] Ingram, 'Bellicism as Boomerang', 210–11, 216.
[106] Note of the Ottoman Chargé d'Affaires, 16 February 1815, TNA, FO 139/26, fp. 36–9.
[107] Liston to Wellington, 25 March 1815, TNA, FO 139/26, fp. 40–3.
[108] Fikret Adanır holds that the Porte did not receive an invitation, but that cannot be correct; see F. Adanır, 'Turkey's Entry into the Concert of Europe', *European Review*,

order may have been constitutional and enlightened, but it was also a highly imperial one, and served as a springboard for the expansive ambitions of the greater powers towards the outer European world.

The result, the Final Act of the Vienna Congress, with its numerous related bilateral agreements and sub-treaties, was simultaneously a crucial way station and blueprint for colonizing the European continent – and beyond. This imperial security community was immediately put to the test. The great aggressor himself, Napoleon, disrupted the Viennese envoys' breakfast and final negotiations in early March 1815. The eagle had taken flight, only to land again in southern France on 1 March. News reached the Allied ministers in the early hours of 7 March. Napoleon's escape from Elba, his successful march on Paris and the ignominious flight of Louis XVIII to Ghent seemed to put a bomb under the Vienna plans (Fig. 2.5). The Hundred Days that followed, nevertheless, did more for the solidarity and sustainability of the Allied coalition than all of their negotiations prior to that point. Napoleon's return gave to the still relatively fluid agreements a sense of fixed resolve that transformed the European project from ideals on paper to a truly inter-imperial edifice. On 25 March 1815, the Allies renewed and confirmed the Quadruple Alliance and declared Napoleon to be a firebrand and a danger to the peace of Europe and the world.

Mutual Security

The monarchs, ministers and diplomats in Vienna – thanks in part to Talleyrand's ingenious talents – had almost forgotten that they had gathered to erect a barrier against the two-headed (French) monster of revolution and aggression. But on 7 March they were rudely awakened from their diplomatic inebriation. On 25 March 1815, they agreed to a plan for 'mutual security'. This plan did not stem from Kantian idealism, but was born from the need of the moment, Napoleon's return to France and the advance of his army towards Paris. Britain, Austria, Prussia and Russia signed a series of bilateral treaties that bound them together in defence of the 'safety of Europe'. They confirmed the content of the treaties of Chaumont (13 March 1814), Paris (30 May 1814) and the provisional agreements made in Vienna, but went a significant step further than in 1814. Back then, Tsar Alexander quite unconditionally and

13:3 (2005), 395–417, here: 402. See for the invitation: Liston to the Sublime Porte, 13 July 1814, Başbakanlık Osmanlı Arşivleri (BOA), TS.MA.e 243/16/1; see also A. C. Paşa, *Tārīh-i Cevdet*, vol. 10 (Istanbul, 1858), 175–6. Thanks to Ozan Ozavci for discovering and translating this source. See for further correspondence and meetings between Yanko Efendi and Castlereagh, Wellington and Metternich: Stürmer to Testa, 9 February 1815, BOA HAT. 286/17183; Yanko Efendi, 27 February 1815, BOA HAT. 961/41197 M; Yanko Efendi to Bab-i Ali, 3 March/February 1815, BOA HAT. 960/41184 U; Yanko Efendi to Bab-i Ali, 20 November 1815, BOA HAT. 953/40926.

(a)

(b)

Figure 2.5 (a) 'The Congress dissolved before the cake was cut up', cartoon about the return of Napoleon. By George Cruikshank, 1815. (b) Detail showing a card entitled 'A Plan for the Security of Europe', which is trampled on by Napoleon. (© The Trustees of the British Museum)

generously had left the implementation and enforcement of the treaties and their provisions to Louis XVIII and his government. But he cared little for these commitments. The assurances made to Napoleon and his family in the Treaty of Fontainebleau had in no way been met. He had not seen one centime of the agreed-upon allowance – a willful default that Napoleon in his statement upon arriving in France on 1 March 1815 mentioned as one of his reasons for having returned to France.[109] Against this backdrop, the Allied ministers now decided to wage peace differently.

---

[109] See T. Morris, *Recollections of Military Service in 1813, 1814, and 1815, through Germany, Holland and France* (London: Madden, 1845), 116–24, as well as F. McLynn, *Napoleon. A Biography* (London: Pimlico, 1998), 604.

This meant, first of all, that 'the common enemy' (Napoleon) must be irreversibly defeated. Article I of the Treaty of 25 March reads:

> For this purpose they engage ... to direct, in common and with one accord, should the case require it, all their efforts against him, and against all those who should already have joined his faction, or shall hereafter join it, in order to force him to desist from his projects, and to render him unable to disturb in future the tranquillity of Europe, and the general peace under the protection of which the rights, the liberty, and independence of nations had been recently placed and secured.

In Article II they indicated what that 'common action' would look like: the 'High Contracting Parties' would 'keep constantly in the field, each, a force of 150,000 men complete' (one tenth of whom were to be cavalry), plus 'a just proportion of artillery, not reckoning garrisons'.[110] But unlike in 1814, when the lack of any uniform or central command and control leadership almost resulted in Napoleon being able to play one armed force against the other, the Allied forces would this time 'actively and jointly [employ these resources] against the common enemy'. The most far-reaching and revolutionary stipulation was that the Allied powers would only lay down their arms and demobilize their armies once their final objective had been attained. That goal was this time more than the military defeat of Napoleon; all of the provisions of the treaties of Chaumont and Paris were to be consistently implemented this time. To this end, France, once defeated, would be dealing with a peacetime occupation by the Allies that would guarantee and enforce compliance with these treaties.[111]

The notion of 'collective security' is usually linked to the League of Nations, the United Nations or NATO in the twentieth century. According to the political scientist Hans Morgenthau, one should only talk of collective security when assembling and maintaining a strong military force against a potential aggressor is a real possibility; when the nations involved have shared beliefs about what counts as a potential and dangerous threat; and when the participating parties are in a position to put conflicts amongst themselves temporarily to the side.[112] A. F. K. Organski adds, among other things, that the cumulative power of these Allies must have what it takes to overpower the might of the aggressor, and that the members of the coalition must have an equal degree of

---

[110] The actual numbers vary. Morris, for example, reports: 300,000 for Austria, 225,000 for Russia, 336,000 for Prussia, 150,000 for the smaller states (with 60,000 of these coming from Bavaria), 50,000 for the Netherlands and 150,000 for Britain. Morris, *Recollections*, 125.

[111] Foreign Office (ed.), *British and Foreign State Papers 1814–1815*, vol. 2 (London: Ridgway, 1839), 443–50.

[112] Cf. H. Morgenthau, *Politics among Nations. The Struggle for Power and Peace* (New York: McGraw-Hill, 1992 [1948]), 198, 208, 290–1.

autonomy and say-so in the decision to deploy forces.[113] Even though the
cooperative defence and security efforts of the Allies in 1815 meets these
criteria completely, hardly any mention is made of them either in the literature
on collective security or in the growing historiographical discussions about
international occupation regimes. For political scientists, the immediate
months and years after the Congress of Vienna are still empirically uncharted
territory. Most historical studies, on the other hand, wear themselves thin in
dramatic descriptions of the Congress of Vienna or the Battle of Waterloo, and
have to catch their breath in order to pick up the thread again with the next test
of the Congress System in Aix-la-Chapelle in 1818, or with the uprisings in
Naples and Greece.[114] In French studies about the restoration period, the focus
is understandably on the House of Bourbon or on the internal parliamentary
squabbling going on at the time. Historical literature on international relations
in the nineteenth century was for a long time quite fragmented and partitioned
along national lines. The broader context of the Allied cooperation and the
integration of that regime of collective security in the larger scheme of
European peace is given far less attention.[115]

The Treaty of 25 March was nonetheless a prelude to a bona fide occupational regime that added momentum to the 1814–15 European system of
collective security by introducing explicitly modern vernacular on 'mutual
security', and even more so by fully acting on it. The remarkable aspect of
this regime was that the principle of the balance of power, after the drama of
the Hundred Days, was enforced by joint Allied military power during peacetime. Its precise form, though, still needed to be fleshed out, and that
depended – just as with more recent occupation regimes – directly on the
course of the military advancements preceding it and on the relationships
between the Allies themselves. Norman Naimark, in his authoritative work
The Russians in Germany, about the Allied occupation of Germany, wrote:
'Soviet planning for postwar Germany during the "Great Fatherland War" of
1941–1945 depended on the fortunes of the battlefield and the vicissitudes of
relations among the Allies.'[116] The same was equally true a hundred and fifty
years earlier. Beginning in 1813, the communal stages in the victory over
Napoleon, up to the entry into Paris, determined the nature of the occupation
regime.

What took shape happened in four stages: the brief occupation of 1814 was
the first phase, a foreshadowing of and administrative dry run for the regime of
1815. In drawing up the statutes for the occupation in 1815, the politicians

---

[113] See for more: A. Organski, *World Politics* (New York: Knopf, 1958).
[114] Schulz does briefly mention the Allied Council in *Normen und Praxis*, 63.
[115] Veve discusses the British military strategy; Wacker zooms in on the details of the
  occupation from a Prussian perspective. See literature references in the Introduction.
[116] Naimark, *The Russians in Germany*, 9.

referred explicitly to the shortcomings of that first – far too brief and far too liberal – peace accord of March–May 1814. The second phase began with the news of Napoleon's landing and ran through to the Battle of Waterloo. In this phase everything was focused on recruiting troops and forging them into a military machine. After the victories of Quatre Bras and Waterloo, the Paris capitulation and the second abdication of the emperor, the third phase began. All of the heads of state agreed that European cooperation should be anchored in an occupation regime that was treaty-based and put into effect administratively. This phase culminated in the Second Treaty of Paris on 20 November 1815 and the adjacent treaties regarding the military occupation and the payment of debts. During the fourth and final stage, the armistice occupation was translated into a peacetime occupation, supervised by the Allied Council of Ministers and Ambassadors. With the Treaty of the Quadruple Alliance of 20 November 1815, that occupation regime was embedded in a system of collective security that was formally tasked to last until 1820, but would be aborted in 1818 in practice.

In March 1815, however, things were not that far developed yet. Faced with the renewed menace of Napoleonic rule, the alliance was re-established and a European security vocabulary was developed that spoke of 'common enemies', a 'fight against terror' and a 'mutual security system'. At the same time, the powers reverted to their default positions as well and expressed diverging sentiments regarding the new war aims. Prussia demanded revenge and retribution; Britain and Austria insisted on restoring the balance of power; the small German states – stirred up by Talleyrand – continued to appeal to international law; Alexander had got what he wanted with Poland and expressed himself in increasingly exalted terms. With all his insistence on forgiveness and magnanimity, he was, however, particularly struck by the French population's ingratitude and incensed about the cowardly flight of Louis XVIII. Not only did Napoleon have to be defeated (again), these diverging positions and sentiments had to be reconciled and brought back together (again).

Wellington in the Saddle

During the reprise of the capture of Paris in 1815, Alexander took a back seat with Austria. The guarantor of the European 'balance' was now not primarily the tsar, but the British foreign secretary Castlereagh, assisted by Britain's commander-in-chief, the Duke of Wellington. Wellington's troops were flanked by Prussian forces led by Blücher, the other hero of Waterloo. But, for military and financial reasons that everyone found convincing, the British were in the lead.

'Balancing' was not only an act that required strategic insight; it also implied adopting an attitude of compromise and moderation. Creating and maintaining a balance of power was furthermore an investment with financial consequences. Balancing cost money, and more than a token amount. Already when drafting the collective security Treaty of 25 March 1815, the other powers indicated that they could possibly commit to the agreed-upon number of troops in theory, but that they would not be in a position to actually deliver the same without additional financial support. So, in order to guarantee these 'sinews of war', the British parliament approved an increase in the tax on income and underwrote a huge loan. In so doing, the British government was able to generate some 5 million pounds sterling to bolster the efforts of the Austrian, Russian, Prussian and other treasury-poor partners.[117] The newly crafted European imperial peace was also paid for in large part with monies arising from newly exploited colonial acquisitions, such as in India.

Requests for assistance went through the Duke of Wellington, the new star on the European stage. After Napoleon and Alexander, the nod to hold sway over European politics went to Arthur Wellesley (1769–1852), who was the same age as Napoleon. According to his biographer Rory Muir, Wellington was 'a very British hero'. His 'larger than life' personage was the recipient of all kinds of attacks as well as decorations over the course of the nineteenth century and far beyond. Cast in political cartoons with a large hooked nose, Wellington, who would govern the country as an extremely conservative prime minister (1828–30 and 1834), was a beloved whipping boy, also for liberal, progressive and radical publicists. From 1815 on, he (along with Castlereagh) was targeted as an advocate of restoration and repression in critical, liberal magazines like *The Examiner*.[118] Although only a minority was taken by the ultra-critical portrayal of Wellington in Britain, it was a high-profile minority, and Cruikshank's caricatures found a receptive audience far beyond the British Isles.[119]

Wellington himself suffered at times under that image, which came to tower high above someone who on the outside seemed live in such a Spartan way. As he explained to a friend, 'I am the Duke of Wellington, and *bon gré mal gré* must do as the Duke of Wellington doth.'[120] Beyond these rich stories, anecdotes and bon mots attributed to the laconic general, his complex career and influential role in the policy-making and administration of post-war Europe have been somewhat forgotten. His role in the design and execution of the occupation in France, and, even more important, within the Allied Council of Ministers, has not been properly investigated before.

---

[117] See Morris, *Recollections*, 125.

[118] One caricature by George Cruikshank, 'The Afterpiece to the Tragedy of Waterloo – or Madame Françoise & her managers!!!', 9 November 1815, is discussed in Chapter 4.

[119] R. Muir, *Wellington. Waterloo and the Fortunes of Peace, 1814–1852* (New Haven/London: Yale University Press, 2015), 2. See also R. Patten, *George Cruikshank's Life, Times and Art*, 2 vols. (London: Lutterworth Press, 1996).

[120] Cited in Muir, *Wellington. Waterloo and the Fortunes of Peace*, xi.

A Long School of Learning

No one would ever have thought that Arthur Wellesley was to become both a British and a European hero; certainly not his mother or his teachers. 'Could do better', reads one of his year-end school reports, to be followed the next year by 'Couldn't do any worse.'[121] Arthur was the third of five surviving sons of the Earl of Mornington, part of an aristocratic Protestant Anglo-Irish family from Dublin. When his father died in 1871 – Arthur was twelve at the time – he left few assets and many debts behind, such that his mother was forced to move to Brussels in 1785. Arthur, who felt very lonely at the prestigious boarding school Eton, was delighted that he could now finish his schooling at the French Royal Academy of Equitation in Angers. With the musical talents of his father, who had purchased and played the first grand piano to be found in Britain, Arthur was actually planning on making his career as a violinist. But when the brother of his intended bride, the well-to-do Kitty Pakenham, daughter of Lord Longford, rejected his proposal to marry her because of his meagre circumstances and uncertain prospects, he burnt his violin and enlisted in the army.[122]

Thanks to Arthur's oldest and wealthier brother Richard, he made a new start, first as a major and then lieutenant colonel.[123] In the meantime, he also became an MP in the Irish House of Commons; he would gradually come to master this fairly unique threesome of policy, governance and military service. Between 1793 and 1795 he underwent his baptism by fire during an unfortunate campaign in Flanders against the French. Arthur stood his ground at the Battle of Boxtel, defended the front along the Waal River, but returned defeated to Britain in 1795. His laconic comment about this tour of duty, years later, was: 'At least I learned what not to do, and that is always a valuable lesson.'[124] After 1796, when he went to India as a colonel, he had more success. Backed since their father's death by his brother Richard, now Lord Mornington, who was appointed governor general of India in 1798, Arthur made the most of every opportunity that came his way. Thanks to careful logistical planning and clearly increasing insights, he defeated the equally

---

[121] These reports are exhibited in the display cases of Apsley House, London (Private Archive Wellington). For more information about Arthur's youth, see R. Muir, *Wellington. The Path to Victory, 1769-1814* (New Haven/London: Yale University Press, 2013), 6–11.

[122] Muir, Wellington. The Path to Victory, 27–9; E. Pakenham, *Tom, Ned and Kitty. An Intimate Portrait of an Irish Family* (Phoenix: W&N, 2008).

[123] In those times, well-to-do families bought an officer's rank for their sons; see J. Cookson, 'Regimental Worlds: Interpreting the Experience of British Soldiers during the Napoleonic Wars', in Forrest, Hagemann and Rendall (eds.), *Soldiers*, 23–42, here: 27–30.

[124] R. Holmes, *Wellington. The Iron Duke* (New York: Harper Collins, 2003), 32; Muir, *Wellington. The Path to Victory*, 31–7.

poetic and murderous Tipu, Sultan of Mysore and Seringapatam, himself became governor of that region and advanced the East India Company's presence with British conquests in the Indian interior. In 1805, he returned enriched to Britain with his rather thriftless and ostentatious brother, a fortune of 42,000 pounds and an even greater wealth of experience. He had also adopted a unique style: white trousers, dark jacket, few frills in comparison with more heavily decorated and colourful colleagues. But above all, he had learned in India how crucial a good combination of military insight and administrative skills was. He had grown from a tactically creative and tenacious commander into a political strategist and capable governor who was able to pair military victories with creating and consolidating the stable administration and management of conquered territories. That was how he, as a major general, colonized the interior of India: with loyal commanders, the regular supply of grain, a widespread network of spies and scouts, good lines of communication and the incorporation of indigenous administrators (who, based on their informed and established position, were better able to impose and collect taxes). Only with the help of a stable and durable administration could Britain's colonial and imperial interests remain well served into the future – an administrative experience that he would put into practice in France, after 1815.[125]

While garnering these insights, Arthur Wellesley also seems to have wanted to theoretically understand and substantiate them. He had taken an impressive collection of books and writings with him to India, which he also annotated along the way: books about the languages, grammar and culture of India, writings by John Locke, Adam Smith, Jeremy Bentham and William Blackstone's *Commentaries on the Laws of England*.[126] Against the backdrop of Napoleon's seizing power in Egypt and the Mediterranean and his military assistance to Tipu Sultan, in India Wellesley came to realize (more than his brother) that British colonial expansion also needed to be directed towards winning the hearts and minds of the people, and to creating a stable government that was assured of sufficient support. That is perhaps why he dared present himself as both a legislator and reformer.

As governor of Seringapatam, he not only strengthened its garrisons and built barracks for his troops, he also issued a long series of executive orders to facilitate Islamic and Hindu courts of law and took care to ensure that

---

[125] See, for example, Arthur Wellesley to Henry Wellesley, 24 January 1804, 'Report on the outcome of the battle near Assaye and the treaties signed there', in J. Gurwood (ed.), *The Dispatches of Field Marshal the Duke of Wellington, K. G. during his Various Campaigns in India, Denmark, Portugal, Spain, the Low Countries and France* (hereafter: *WD*), vol. 3 (London: John Murray, 1837), 1–9; cf. Holmes, *Wellington*, 87; J. Severn, *Architects of Empire. The Duke of Wellington and his Brothers* (Oklahoma City: University of Oklahoma Press, 2007).

[126] Muir, *Wellington. The Path to Victory*, 46.

indigenous communities and their religions were treated with respect. He even devoted himself to assuring the right of the friendly sultan to retain his harem (*zenana*). To see to order, justice and the common weal (preferably by incorporating local administrators) is how Wellesley summarized his service to the British Empire, which is also why – certainly given his sincere intentions – he did not cower at rebellion or shy away from brutally quashing insurrections.[127] With Pitt's India Act of 1784 in the back of his mind, which put an end to the East India Company's acquisitional desires and subjected it to the political directions and control of the government, he was no supporter of unbridled expansion and needless incursions into enemy terrain.[128] In later years, Wellesley would further cultivate his pragmatic views about the pitfalls and possibilities of both military interventions and imperialist expansionism, implementing these views with caution again in Spain and then during the occupation of France.[129]

Back in Britain, the ambitious major general, now Sir Arthur – having been made a member of the Order of the Bath in August 1804 – again asked (this time, in writing) for Kitty's hand. The bride-to-be did not accept immediately, but requested that her old flame first stop by in person before committing himself. A long illness had quenched her vivacity and charm and she was only a pale shadow of her former self. Indeed, he is said to have commented in shock to his brother, 'She has grown ugly, by Jove!'[130] But he remained faithful to his first love and the couple was joined in matrimony in 1806 by Wellesley's clergyman, his brother Gerald, after which they remained unhappily married for many years. Despite a brief interlude as a Tory MP in England and then as chief secretary in Ireland – a weighty position that was often seen as precursor to a cabinet position – his interests were with the army, and in 1808 a number of expeditions to Germany, Denmark and Portugal followed.[131]

Wellington on the European Theatre

Wellington acquired an indelible status as celebrated hero and public figure based on the way in which he had comported himself during the Spanish War of Independence. His many letters and suggested improvements regarding command and control, the need for more support at sea and stricter discipline as well as a tremendous amount of diplomatic tact, earned him a reputation,

---

[127] Ibid., 88–92.
[128] See P. Marshall, *Problems of Empire. Britain and India, 1757–1813*, vol. 2 (London: Routledge, 2001 [1968]), 43; see also Wellington to Munro, 20 August 1800, in *WD*, vol. 1, 168–70.
[129] Cf. Muir, *Wellington. The Path to Victory*, 164–6.
[130] As reported by Lady Shelley, in R. Edgcumbe (ed.), *The Diary of Frances Lady Shelley, 1818–1873* (New York: Scribner's, 1913), 407.
[131] Muir, *Wellington. The Path to Victory*, 172–4.

both in the eyes of Lord Castlereagh (then minister of war) and the British public, as well as among the Spanish and Portuguese allies. He soon became the marshal general of the British forces in Portugal, and then of the allied forces on the entire Iberian Peninsula. A crushing series of victories followed. After Talavera, Arthur was ennobled as Viscount Wellington of Talavera and of Wellington, as well as Baron Douro of Wellesley. The viscount became an earl, then a marquess and finally, after winning the Battle of Vittoria in 1813 and Toulouse in 1814, a duke. Beethoven immortalized Wellington's victories in his 15-minute-long fireworks concert, *Wellingtons Sieg oder die Schlacht bei Vittoria*, including the sound of musket rifles and artillery.

Wellington's fame resounded throughout Europe, not only in the media and the courts of sovereigns, but also among military peers. Baron Karl von Müffling, who would later become his Prussian liaison officer during the final campaign against Napoleon, was quite impressed with Wellington's grip on and control over his troops.[132] Yet, Wellington was also, often correctly, considered arrogant. Still, it was widely accepted that the duke was at ease in military, diplomatic and political affairs. Moreover, unlike Alexander, he was able to receive and deal with criticism and opposing viewpoints, and had learned – the hard way – to take the sharp edge of the press, and parliamentary attacks on the home front, into account. He was an obvious and committed conservative, an imperialist at heart, but expressed his convictions in a moderate and pragmatic manner – at least he did so during his years in Europe.

While Alexander, marching from the east, arrived in Paris with the Allied troops in March 1814, Wellington was still embroiled in heavy fighting with General Soult in the south of France. The war was not over for him until 10 April in Toulouse. Soon thereafter, on 21 April, Charles Stuart brought him a letter from Paris, asking that he become the British ambassador to the liberated capital. He arrived there on 4 May, where he heard for the first that he had been made a duke the day before. He met Alexander and Metternich (who felt that Wellington was 'Austrian in his soul'), but could not stay long. One of the first acts of King Ferdinand of Spain, who had been freed by the French, had been to abolish the constitution, including the freedom of the press, and he had begun to incarcerate all of the liberals. Castlereagh and Wellington were afraid that the country, which with great difficulty had just been liberated, would again become a powder keg of revolution and civil war. So Wellington immediately left again for Spain in May to convince Ferdinand to adopt a new, liberal constitution – in which he only succeeded partially, in putting heavy financial pressure on the Spanish court. During these two weeks he developed an equal loathing of the unbridled absolutist vanity of Ferdinand's supporters and of the radical ideological rigidity of the *liberales*.

---

[132] Müffling, *The Memoirs*, 213–14.

His own preference for a moderate executive, tolerance and rule-of-law-based government was seriously strengthened while in Spain.[133]

After a festive summer in London, full of tributes and celebrations, and after an extended stay in the Netherlands to provide the young kingdom with moral, but also military-strategic support and advice, Wellington returned to Paris on 22 August 1814. This first stay in Paris, in the fall and winter of 1814–15, was not entirely successful. There were so many rumours about attacks on the duke's life that prime minister Liverpool wanted to recall him and send him to America to bring the peace negotiations there to a successful conclusion. For the French, even though he spoke flawless French, Wellington's presence, along with that of his clutch of British adherents, was a daily reminder of their military humiliation. It pained them all the more that Louis XVIII was so taken by Wellington and his British friends that he often seemed to prefer wearing the symbol of the Order of the Garter rather than his French decorations.[134] In Talleyrand, Wellington moreover found a daunting diplomatic opponent, one who did everything he could to play the one great power off against the others.[135] In February 1815, Wellington left for Vienna to take Castlereagh's place as negotiator. Upon arriving, he immediately made a deep impression; according to Metternich, the whole room fell silent when the hero of Vittoria entered the ballroom. But the return of Napoleon undoubtedly catapulted Wellington even more into the forefront, putting him centre stage in the apotheosis of the Bonapartist drama.

A few days after Napoleon's arrival in France it was clear that his advance was not about to be thwarted. On 14 March, the popular Marshal Ney, who had shortly before then found favour with Louis XVIII, returned once again to the ranks of his former leader. Soult was sacked for fear of possible treason, and on 20 March Louis XVIII fled like a thief in the night to Ghent. By eight o'clock that same evening, Napoleon was once again ensconced in the Tuileries. For the Allies, there was work to be done; the proposed contingents of the joint forces had to be activated. Wellington was put in charge. There was no other option. Blücher, temperamental as he was, had as little tact as he had political friends. He was furthermore in no position – and the same held for Schwarzenberg – to access the financial resources that were available to Wellington as representative of the British treasury. Alexander, who on a number of unfortunate occasions, and much to the consternation of the generals, had tried to manoeuvre himself into the position of commander, did toy briefly with the idea that he would be able to fill the role of commander-in-chief. Fortunately, he let this cup pass him by when he noticed that

[133] Muir, *Wellington. Waterloo and the Fortunes of Peace*, 6–9.
[134] Ibid., 15–17.
[135] E. de Waresquiel, *Talleyrand. Le prince immobile* (Paris: Fayard, 2003), 463–78, 483–9; Ilsemann, *Die Politik Frankreichs*, 319–38. See also Castlereagh to Wellington, 25 October 1814, Vane (ed.), *Correspondence*, vol. 10, 173–5.

the reaction of the other Allies was hardly a positive one. On paper, then, every-thing was settled; but the reality of battle-ready brigades of joint forces on Vienna's doorstep was at the time nothing more than a projection. The Austrians had promised 150,000 men, who would come up from Italy; Bavaria, Württemberg and Baden formed the army of the Upper Rhine, which would be augmented with Austrian reserves, to bring their numbers up to 200,000. A third contingent would be stationed in the Netherlands, consisting of British, Dutch and Hanoverian troops, plus the Prussian corps from Kleist. In addition, 200,000 Russian soldiers would be stationed in Würzburg as the central reserve.[136]

Here, as in 1814, the Allied administrative machine needed to be assembled quickly. Wellington immediately set to work to get the promised troop quotas actually under arms. He hastily corresponded with all of the participants, throwing money and promises around left and right in order to ensure the readiness of the troops.[137] The duke left Vienna on 29 March in order to set up the headquarters of his troops in Brussels, arriving there on 4 April. On 11 April, he formally took command of the Allied Army that was in the process of assembling. One momentary hitch was the stubborn behaviour of King Willem I, who in early May still refused to cede the supreme command of the Dutch troops to Wellington – something that eventually happened under duress. All of Europe was again on the move. Troops from the Netherlands, Belgium, Nassau and parts of Germany gathered from the north and the east in the vicinity of Brussels. The new kingdoms were able and now wanted to show what they were worth and fight for their independence in the face of the looming Napoleonic shadow. King Willem I, on 16 March, made use of the shocking news to announce the unification of the Netherlands with Belgium and the formation of the Kingdom of the Netherlands, with him as its king. In the Netherlands and the liberated German states, the troops were cheered and waved off with song and poetry.[138] Russian troops, Polish and Prussian, flocked to Heilbronn, where Blücher gathered his troops. In Austria and Italy, a front was built along the western border of France, which also served to keep an eye on King Joachim Murat in Naples. In Paris, Napoleon was himself preparing for the fight. In the Balkans, however, few paid heed to what was happening in France; on 23 April the Serbian rebellion against Turkey broke out – a harbinger of future Balkan wars with which the imperial powers would have to deal later.

The story of the battles of Ligny, Waterloo and Wavre is well known and exhaustively reported. In early May, Wellington was still bemoaning the disastrous

---

[136] Muir, *Wellington. Waterloo and the Fortunes of Peace*, 22–4.

[137] Correspondence, Wellington to Foreign Office, as well as to the plenipotentiaries of Württemberg, Bavaria, Hanover and Baden with the offer to provide subsidies for their armies, April–May 1815, TNA, FO 92/15.

[138] See the communications and declarations of Willem I, March 1815 in Hessisches Staatsarchiv Darmstadt (HStD), Familienarchiv der Freiherrn Von Gagern, no. O11, no. B32, no. B104.

disarray of his army. Regarding the British army, he remarked, 'I have got an infamous army, very weak and ill equipped and a very inexperienced staff.' He had even less to say about the Dutch–Belgian troops: 'the troops in that quarter are not of the best description'. He preferred working with the British–Portuguese brigades that he had himself crafted into a well-oiled machine during the previous years.[139] Eventually, Wellington had about 110,000 soldiers under his wing, including some 40,000 British troops, plus the king's German Legion, Hanoverian, Dutch–Belgian, Nassau troops and a cohort from Braunschweig.[140] With that international melange of troops, Wellington and Blücher won the Battle of Waterloo (Fig. 2.6). 'Soldiers!', the Dutch Prince Frederick (brother of the hereditary prince, and son of Willem I), who had performed deftly on the battlefield, called out, 'The war has ended … United with the Allied armies, Europe's freedom and the independence of its nations is owing in part to your bravery and courage.'[141]

Figure 2.6 *The Battle of Waterloo.* To the left lies the Dutch Crown Prince, the later King Willem II, wounded on a stretcher. In the centre stands the Duke of Wellington. Painting by J. W. Pieneman, 1824. (Rijksmuseum, Amsterdam)

---

[139] Muir, *Wellington. Waterloo and the Fortunes of Peace*, 29, 31.
[140] Ibid., 33.
[141] Reprinted in W. Wüppermann, *De vorming van het Nederlandsche leger na de omwenteling van 1813 en het aandeel van dat leger aan den veldtocht van 1815* (Breda: KMA, 1900), 185.

Despite the controversy as to the quality and the part played by the various brigades and commanders in the battle, Wellington's status as the Prince of Waterloo was undisputed. 'He fought the hardest', his own soldiers claimed.[142] But the other generals too, General Bülow, Field Marshal Blücher and the Prince of Orange (Prince Willem, later King Willem II), initially readily agreed as well and showered him with titles, gifts, tableware, medals, inlaid snuffboxes and portraits of themselves.[143] Carl von Clausewitz, in 1815 still a young and unknown officer (who had registered with the Prussian army at the age of twelve in 1792 by falsifying his age), fought in the battles of Ligny (16 June) and Wavre (18–19 June) under Blücher. He attributed the victory at Waterloo – notwithstanding all his critical comments about the tactical blunders made by commanders on both sides – in part to the vast and overwhelming superiority of the Allied numbers. Thanks to Wellington's perseverance, an immense army had indeed been gathered under a reasonably functioning central command. According to Clausewitz, the victory was also due to the 'great energy of the pursuit' after the Battle of Waterloo itself. Unlike in previous confrontations, the conquerors did not disengage themselves at the border, but had pursued their opponent right into their capital. This time Napoleon's army was completely defeated and destroyed: a conclusion on which Clausewitz would ground his theory about total war and the necessity of carrying out the complete destruction of the enemy.[144]

In June 1815, Wellington was the man of the hour. This meant that he, together with Castlereagh, could also define and implement what the peace would look like. That form was closely related to what he, as supreme commander and administrator, had learned in the colonies, in Spain and at home, in parliament: success on the battlefield depended on political and financial backing from one's own polis, on support from the populace and elites back at home, a clear military strategy (including clear end goals) and centralized control and command as well as constantly monitoring quality improvement and drilling the troops. Wellington took all of these lessons with him when setting up the occupation regime. He sorely needed these diplomatic experiences, because tensions with Prussia soon led to renewed irritations.

[142] Muir, *Wellington. Waterloo and the Fortunes of Peace*, 80–1.
[143] These can all be admired in Apsley House, including portraits of the monarchs of the coalition, a portrait of a young Prince of Orange and a depiction of Willem I that looks nothing like him.
[144] C. von Clausewitz, 'Feldzug von 1815 in Frankreik', in P. Hofschroër (trans. and ed.), *On Wellington. A Critique of Waterloo* (Norman: University of Oklahoma Press, 2010), 173–5.

Prussia in the Revanche

On the eve of the decisive battles with Napoleon, Blücher, Stein and Friedrich Wilhelm III tried to make the most of those preparations by creating a better military basis for an increased Prussian influence in Germany down the road. Ever since the humiliation of Prussia in 1806, the leaders of this aspiring German state felt heavily aggrieved and wronged by their allies. At the Congress of Vienna, they had been apportioned only two fifths of Saxony (and had not realized yet how valuable the compensations with the Rhineland and Westphalia in commercial and industrial terms would turn out to be). They were not even considered for receiving reparations from France in 1814 and felt that they had been insufficiently rewarded for their part in the war effort. Their immense losses, Napoleon's scorched-earth tactics and the war effort in general had brought the Prussian state to the brink of bankruptcy. France needed to bleed. Blücher's requisition demands were ten times higher this time. At the same time, the Prussian leaders had devised a plan to increase Prussia's presence within the German Confederation by building on the military integration of the troops from the smaller German states – principalities that, from the perspective of Prussia, had struck far too high a tone in Vienna.[145] With that, the mobilization of troops in the spring of 1815 also became a competition over enhanced control over these smaller states. Attempts on the part of the smaller German states, the so-called middle powers, to offer a kind of 'third Germany' counterbalance to Prussia and Austria, and looking in that regard to Britain – and later, even to France – for support, were indicative of the battle that would break out in the coming years within the German Confederation.[146]

Requests for supporting and funding the recruiting were a powerful means, also for the British, of allotting balance in central Europe. That explains the extraordinarily generous willingness of Wellington to grant virtually every request from the smaller German states, and in so doing to keep Prussia at bay. Wellington had the money and was more than happy to dispense grants and pledges (some of which would later come to haunt him)[147] in order to ensure a balanced allotment of troops throughout the continent and to preclude the Prussians from swallowing up the German Confederation. Smaller

---

[145] For the background of Prussian ideas about the German Confederation in 1814–15, see Gruner, *Grossbritannien*, 312–22.

[146] See Ilsemann, *Die Politik Frankreichs*, 169–214; H. von Gagern, *Mein Antheil an der Politik*, vol. 2: *Nach Napoleons Fall. Der Congress zu Wien* (Stuttgart/Tübingen: Cotta, 1826), 36–7, 69–122; W. Gruner, 'Frankreich in der europäischen Ordnung des 19. Jahrhunderts', in Gruner and K.-J. Müller (eds.), *Über Frankreich nach Europa: Frankreich in Geschichte und Gegenwart* (Hamburg: Krämer, 1996), 201–74, here: 211–15.

[147] See Wellington's correspondence with Denmark and the German states, August–October 1815, TNA, FO 92/15.

states within the federation literally begged the British to care for their armies financially, and not let them succumb to Blücher's greed.[148]

After three endless days of fighting, from 16 June at Ligny until late into 18 June near Waterloo, the battle was over. As dusk fell, around nine o'clock in the evening, the two commanders, Blücher and Wellington, met and saluted each other as victors. The war was, however, not over yet. Napoleon, with the troops he had remaining (70,000), including veterans (17,000) and the National Guard (30,000), continued to counter with fierce resistance from Paris and its environs.[149] This time, the Prussian troops were bound and determined not to let the Russians (or Wellington, for that matter) trump them as they had in 1814. Blücher did everything he could possibly do to arrive in Paris before Wellington, and there to make his move. That is why Wellington, who saw the storm brewing, issued a decree as he was entering France on 20 June that his soldiers were to treat the ordinary people of France well – 'as citizens of a country of the coalition powers' – so as to avoid further escalation and uprisings.[150] That military strategy had also served him well in India and on the Iberian Peninsula. The Staff Corps of Cavalry, Britain's first standing military police corps, formed during his years in Spain, saw to its implementation.[151] They tracked down a cohort of Dutch–Belgian troops, for example, that was deep into plundering. Its leaders were arrested and sent back to The Hague with a letter in their pocket for King Willem I.[152] But curbing the Prussian troops proved to be more difficult. They considered their second triumphal march through France as the ultimate opportunity to take revenge for the ongoing bloodshed and destruction that the Napoleonic armies had wrought in German territories.[153]

The Prussian thirst for revenge also expressed itself in a controversy on the question of what should be done with Napoleon. Immediately after Waterloo, during the race with Napoleon and troops to Paris, Blücher – via Müffling – let Wellington know that he was on the heels of the emperor. Müffling recalls: 'I received from him [Blücher] instructions to inform the Duke of Wellington, that as the Congress of Vienna had declared Napoleon outlawed, it was his intention to have him shot whenever he caught him.' But Blücher and Gneisenau still had enough sense and respect to want to know, again via Müffling, what the duke was thinking: 'But he desired, at the same time, to

[148] See Wellington's correspondence with the German states, April–May 1815, TNA, FO 92/15; Muir, *Wellington. Waterloo and the Fortunes of Peace*, 28–9.

[149] W. Siborne, *The Waterloo Campaign, 1815* (Westminster: Constable, 1895), 716–17.

[150] C. H. Gifford, *History of the Wars Occasioned by the French Revolution, from the Commencement of Hostilities in 1792, to the End of 1816. Embracing a Complete History of the Revolution*, vol. 2 (London: Lewis, 1817), 1493–4.

[151] Muir, *Wellington. Waterloo and the Fortunes of Peace*, 84.

[152] Siborne, *The Waterloo Campaign*, 703; Morris, *Recollections*, 168.

[153] Gifford, *History of the Wars*, 1494.

know what were the duke's views on this subject, for should he entertain the same as himself, he wished to act in concert with him.'[154] Wellington was quite shocked about this austere lack of sportsmanship and immediately tried to convince Blücher that this was in no way what they were after. The declaration in Vienna, that Napoleon was an outlaw and to be considered the 'common enemy', 'was never meant to incite to the assassination of Napoleon'. Military honour and decorum do not allow for that. Moreover, as Wellington explained to Müffling (who needed no convincing), 'as far as his [the duke's] own position and that of the Field-Marshal with respect to Napoleon were concerned, it appeared to him that, since the battle they had won, they were become much too conspicuous personages to justify such a transaction in the eyes of Europe'. 'Such an act', according to Wellington, 'would hand down our names to history stained by a crime, and posterity would say of us, that we did not deserve to be the conquerors of Napoleon; the more so as such a deed is now quite useless, and can have no object'.[155] From this remarkable declaration it follows how deeply aware Wellington was of the importance of reputation and image in the eyes of the public – on top of real victories. 'Power and authority cannot endure without collective imaginations and ascriptions.' As Thomas Hobbes had it already in *Leviathan* (a book Wellington had read), 'The reputation of power is power.'[156]

The Prussian response deserves extended mention, because General Gneisenau – unlike Blücher – understood very well what Wellington meant. But he confronted the British imperial attitudes with Prussia's views about law and justice:

> When the Duke of Wellington declares himself against the execution of Bonaparte, he thinks and acts in the matter as a Briton. Great Britain is under weightier obligation to no mortal man than to this very villain; for by the occurrences whereof he is the author, her greatness, prosperity, and wealth, have attained their present elevation. The English are the masters of the seas, and have no longer to fear any rivalry, either in this dominion or the commerce of the world.
>
> It is quite otherwise with us Prussians. We have been impoverished by him. Our nobility will never be able to right itself again.
>
> Ought we not, then, to consider ourselves the tools of that Providence which has given us such a victory for the ends of eternal justice? Does not the death of the Duc d'Enghien call for such a vengeance? Shall we not draw upon ourselves the reproaches of the people of Prussia, Russia, Spain, and Portugal [the other signatories at Vienna], if we leave

---

[154] Gneisenau to Müffling, two letters on 27 June; and another on 29 June 1815. Reprinted in Müffling, *The Memoirs*, 272–4.

[155] Müffling, *The Memoirs*, 252–3.

[156] T. Hobbes, *Leviathan* (London/New York: Routledge, 2008 [1651]), 55; See also Stollberg-Rilinger, 'State and Political History in a Culturalist Perspective', 44, 47.

unperformed the duty that devolves upon us? But be it so! – If others will assume a theatrical magnanimity, I shall not set myself against it. We act thus from esteem for the Duke and – weakness. (signed: Count von Gneisenau, 29 June 1815, Senlis.)[157]

In other words, why should Prussian rights be made subordinate to British imperial claims? The British had what they wanted, but for Prussia vindictive revenge was the only way to restore the European balance of power. 'Eternal justice' demanded it; 'Providence' – appealed to here again, as by Alexander – required it. Prussia saw nothing in theatrical benevolence. They also laid claim to their share of the balance of power; for the British had already collected their booty. But given their grudging respect for Wellington, Blücher and Gneisenau were forced to retract and swallow their demands.

The Bond of Peace

On the morning of 3 July 1815, Major General Müffling crossed the Seine. The British troops of Wellington had established a bridge over the river at Argenteuil, re-establishing the lines of communication with Blücher's forces, who had reached Paris earlier and in the early morning were still engaged in the final throes of heavy fighting with General Dominique Vandamme. A few hours later the French troops surrendered, and the Battle of Issy was over. Müffling was there, and enjoyed the view he had from the Palace of Saint-Cloud over the Seine valley. There on the slopes of Hauts-de-Seine, 5 km west of Paris, the Bonapartes had turned a seventeenth-century chateau of Marie Antoinette into a beautiful family palace. While taking the place, Prussian soldiers discovered Altdorfer's painting of Alexander the Great in Napoleon's bathroom. This time, the palace functioned as an Allied headquarters, where they issued their demand for a ceasefire.[158]

The difference from the previous invasion into France and following military occupation was immense. In contrast to the length and intensity of the series of battles and sieges that were needed in 1813–14, this campaign was settled in three weeks. As Clausewitz observed: the French were hit in their heart. The enemy had not only been pushed back, it was in shreds. The destruction of troops and equipment was total.[159] The same was true of the last morsel of French political autonomy, which actually only existed on paper. The French provisional government under Joseph Fouché had to comply with the dictates of Saint-Cloud. Once again, Paris had to bow to the Allies' superiority – but this time much deeper than the previous year. Another major difference from 1814 was that this time no Allied sovereign called the shots on

---

[157] Müffling, *The Memoirs*, 275.
[158] Gifford, *History of the Wars*, 1505–6; Müffling, *The Memoirs*, 251–5.
[159] Clausewitz, *On Wellington*, 173–5.

his own. The Allied powers really acted in concert via a unified military command that was this time backed by a joint political council.

The main and most outstanding difference was, however, the decision to keep the Allied alliance in place for much longer than before. Instead of Stein's (far too) complicated civil occupation administration, in which various military, civil, central and regional jurisdictions either ran parallel to or at cross purposes with each other, this time a single administrator held the reins of the Allies' occupation regime; and that was Wellington. One sixth of France had been occupied between April and June 1814. In 1815, two thirds of France was in Allied hands. In July, there were 1.2 million Allied soldiers within its borders. The occupation was to enforce and ensure that France would pay the reparations and enact the stipulations to which it had been subjected; in short, it was to provide the Allies with what they felt entitled to: money, territory, submission and the guarantee of peace.

In 1813, after the Battle of Leipzig, Müffling could never have imagined that he, as Blücher's representative (along with the British signatory Colonel Felton Hervey-Bathurst, Wellington's adjutant), would be signing the Convention of Saint-Cloud along with the French government. That agreement was the first step in the harnessing of an occupation regime. The Allies stipulated that the French army had to leave the capital and pull back beyond the Loire. They repeatedly expressed their awareness and recognition of the local French authorities, and promised an amnesty for soldiers who had let Napoleon entice them in March to follow his ambitions. In Articles XI and XII, they also confirmed that they would respect public and private property (but not military stockpiles).[160] These articles were worded so loosely that especially the passages about the intended 'respect' for French citizens, for property rights and for those who followed Napoleon during the Hundred Days misled the French populace, and would also lead to serious misunderstandings and bickering among the Allies themselves. It was not at all clear what Article X meant, judicially, in promising that amnesty would be granted to everyone who had been a supporter of Napoleon. Would amnesty imply immunity from being purged or prosecuted? Were the Allies the ones who would safeguard and execute this convention? Did it apply only during the period of the occupation, or afterwards as well? Would the French retain their forts and garrisons, or possibly lose some of their territory? Respect for French property could mean that the expropriation of 'the goods of the nation' (*biens nationaux* – properties previously seized from the church and royalists, etc.) would be protected against the claims of returning *émigrés*. However, some French

---

[160] See W. Maxwell, G. Wright and Alexander (eds.), *Leben und Feldzüge des Herzogs von Wellington. Mit Benutzung der übrigen neuesten englischen Quellen deutsch bearbeitet von F. Bauer*, vol. 6 (Quedlingburg/Leipzig: Basse, 1844), 15–18. See also Siborne, *The Waterloo Campaign*, 753–6; Gifford, *History of the Wars*, 1506.

officials took this promise to mean that all of the works of arts and other things that Napoleon had plundered could be retained, and that the Allies would themselves have to pay for their billeting and other necessities. The answers to these questions defined the shape and impact of the occupation regime in France.

The vagaries of war and the velocity with which the Allied forces defeated the Grande Armée and marched on Paris meant that the Prussian and German troops had the better part of the north and the east in hand. The Austrians controlled the south and the east. The British and the Russians had to make do with a slightly smaller area in the north.[161] Nonetheless, after Waterloo, it was Wellington who made the crucial decisions. He was still the commander of the Allied forces. But also at the political level and in questions of civil adminis-tration, his voice made the difference. He moreover enjoyed the quite hard-to-come-by respect of Louis XVIII. Blücher and Gneisenau, who, with Wellington, had the most military prestige, forfeited much of their goodwill among the French people, as well as among Allied diplomats, because of the repulsive manner in which the Prussian troops behaved. Even the Prussian king was ashamed of his men and let Blücher know that in no uncertain terms when he joined up with the troops in July: 'While on the road, he had encountered so much disorder and laggards, that it was a disgrace to the Prussian arms and a display of a pervasive lack of discipline.'[162]

Contrary to 1814, the Allied alliance of 1815 did not have a Prussian general or Russian tsar at the helm, but a British duke in the saddle. A pragmatist, British-imperial interpretation of the new collective security system would – with Austrian consent – trump the Prussian thirst for revenge and the tsarist inclination to generosity.[163] As Wellington wrote to Castlereagh on 11 August 1815: 'These measures will not only give us, during the period of occupation, all the military security which could be expected from the perma-nent cession [of territory], but, if carried into execution in the spirit in which they are conceived, they are in themselves the bond of peace.'[164] The decision to install a joint Allied occupation in France in peacetime was a very practical but also highly strategical choice. The 'bond of peace' held not only for the security of France, but for all of Europe.

---

[161] Wacker, *Die alliierte Besetzung*, 116–46; W. Petonke, *Der Konflikt zwischen Preussens Staats- und Heeresleitung während der Okkupation in Frankreich, Juli bis November 1815* (Greifswald: Adler, 1906), 1–54.

[162] Cited in Petonke, *Der Konflikt*, 7.

[163] R. Bullen, 'France and Europe 1815–1848: The Problems of Defeat and Recovery', in A. Sked (ed.), *Europe's Balance of Power, 1815–1848* (London: Macmillan, 1979), 134.

[164] Wellington to Castlereagh, 11 August 1815, in *WD*, vol. 12, 596–600. See also Haynes, 'Making Peace: The Allied Occupation of France', in Forrest, Hagemann and Rendall (eds.), *Soldiers*, 51–67.

That Allied sense of communality and solidarity, paid for with their blood, masked a whole series of deeper-lying tensions and incongruities. These would show their face in July already, when details for the military and political administration of the occupation began to be laid out and the powers in the Allied Council met with each other almost every day to discuss the Allies' mandate. The core of these tensions could be traced back to differences of opinion regarding how best to give form to a new balance of power, and to the question of what the subjugation of France should look like. What terror needed to be tamed, and how should the 'Allied machine' be assembled this time? And, at least as important: how would the people of France respond to this Allied rule?

3

Balancing in a Climate of Distress

Wine and *Gleichgewicht*

In July 1814, in preparation for the Congress of Vienna, Hans von Gagern wrote his wife to send him various crates of the best bottles of Rheingau wine.[1] Gagern was a German nobleman of highly respectable lineage, a *Reichsritter*, who had served as chief minister to the Duke of Nasssau-Weilburg and had been a close adviser to Wilhelmina of Prussia, wife to Dutch Stadholder Willem V and the late Friedrich the Great's favourite niece. In March 1813, the Dutch Prince Willem, Wilhelmina's son and heir to the Orange territories, asked Gagern to become his plenipotentiary and envoy on the continent, in preparing for the Sixth Coalition. Gagern was a well-known and seasoned diplomat, had defended the interests of the House of Nassau before, in Paris, Vienna and Warsaw, and also enjoyed good relations with Prussian chancellor Stein. Wilhelmina saw an old, loyal family friend in Gagern, someone who could guarantee and defend the relation between the House of Orange and the German states, including Prussia – and could help to restore Dutch independence vis-à-vis the powers of Europe.[2] Gagern gladly accepted, and after months of organizing troops, managing the Nassau provinces and plotting in the wake of the withdrawing French troops, he found himself indeed at the service of the soon-to-be-crowned king of the Netherlands, Willem of Orange.[3] But this still needed to be negotiated with the great powers. Therefore, the Sovereign Prince, as he had proclaimed himself in December 1813, dispatched his loyal envoy to Vienna.

---

[1] Gagern's wine supply had survived the French looting and pillaging during the Napoleonic Wars; see H. von Gagern, *Mein Antheil an der Politik*, vol. 1: *Unter Napoleons Herrschaft* (Stuttgart/Tübingen: Cotta, 1823), 66; cf. H. Rössler, *Zwischen Revolution und Reaktion. Ein Lebensbild des Reichsfreiherrn Hans Christoph von Gagern 1766–1852* (Göttingen: Musterschmidt, 1958), 151. See also (De) Graaf, 'Second-tier Diplomacy', 546–66.

[2] Willem to Gagern, Breslau, 20 March 1813; Berlin, 27 March 1813, HStD, no. O11 and no. B32. The 20 March letter is also printed in Colenbrander (ed.), *Gedenkstukken*, vol. 6.3, 1865.

[3] Gagern to Fritz, Breslau, 30 March 1813, in H. von Gagern, *Das Leben des Generals Friedrich von Gagern*, vol. 1 (Leipzig/Heidelberg: C. F. Winter, 1856), 83.

93

Gagern found a spacious and decent apartment on the Unteren Bräunerstrasse (no. 1196), only a few metres from the Hofburg. The quarters had belonged to a princess, Pauline von Kurland, and were luxuriously equipped, with a kitchen, stables for four horses, two rooms for Gagern and his secretary, space for four servants, and a reception and dining hall. His wife, Charlotte, sent him her cooking maid (a specialist in *Dampfnudeln*) and Gagern himself hired an additional chef de cuisine from Paris and ordered more wine and liquor from Amsterdam and Paris. Staffed and equipped like this, Gagern opened his diplomatic overtures to convince the gathered European envoys and princes of his and King Willem I's version of a new European order.[4] Not in the least in doubt about his skills – he described himself as being in full possession of 'Höflichkeit, Gastfreyheit, Eleganz, Weltkenntniss und Verstand'[5] – Gagern set out with one overarching aim: to support the creation of a stable balance-of-power system in which smaller countries, such as the German principalities and the Netherlands, would be respected as well. In one of his voluminous and widely disseminated memoirs he wrote:

> Nothing hindered me from taking a direct or indirect part in all European and German matters. . . . the events had been so extreme, the pressure so unbearable, the dominance [of the French] so decisive and abusive, the humiliations so severe that it was uplifting for the soul to restore inter-national public law, balance of power, reason and order; to save the best from the past, . . . to denounce violence, arbitrary rule or command and hence, on level paths, secure the peace.[6]

The whole purpose of the Congress of Vienna was, according to Gagern, to abandon the 'right of the strongest' in international relations and replace it with 'real law' and *Gleichgewicht*, a true balance of power.[7] Indeed, with this idea – that comprised both political and moral connotations – the years of transition opened, and led to the institutionalization of a new system for mutual security. This new system came to rest on a re-engineered balance-of-power principle, but it was to function more as a machine than as a body, and it would be assembled as a hierarchical and exclusive arrangement rather than as an egalitarian and inclusive one, as Gagern soon came to realize. Against the backdrop of the prevailing unrest, the victors of 1815 wanted to put in place something that could prevent the troubled heritage of the Revolution or the Hundred Days from bearing fruit again. The year 1815 saw the dawn of a new era, but it was not an era of trust and *élan*, so much as one that tried to make the

---

[4] Cf. Gagern, *Mein Antheil an der Politik*, vol. 2: *Nach Napoleons Fall. Der Congress zu Wien* (Stuttgart/Tübingen: Cotta, 1826), 19–20. Rössler, *Zwischen Revolution und Reaktion*, 151.
[5] Rössler, *Zwischen Revolution und Reaktion*, 141.
[6] Gagern, *Mein Antheil an der Politik*, vol. 2, 6. Translation by the author.
[7] Ibid., 347.

best of both worlds, combining the vigour of strong monarchs assuming old and new thrones, the well-tried bureaucratic means of control implemented during the Napoleonic years, and some of the privileges and enlightened moderation of the pre-revolutionary times. Before turning to the inauguration of the Allied Machine in July 1815 in Chapter 4, this chapter investigates the intellectual baggage that the 'men of 1815' brought with them to Paris and Vienna, most notably their ideas on the balance of power. This more impressionistic chapter will conclude by painting the cultural, political and meteorological climate of distress in some broad lines and rather sober hues – since this was the canvas on which all the peace and security dreams and ambitions of the power brokers of 1815 were projected.

A New Reading of an Old Concept

After the second victory on the battlefields of Flanders came the challenge of waging peace at the diplomatic front lines in Paris. Vienna had already staked out the coordinates of this new order, by redrawing borders, dividing the spoils of war and solving the struggle over Poland and Saxony (to their detriment and the great powers' advantage). Although these major power struggles over territories and borders between Austria, Prussia and Russia were now over, and Britain had equally won the day by managing to keep the colonies and the outer European world out of the negotiations in Vienna, the concrete design for the new peace order to be established on the European continent was still an unsolved question. Different perspectives and principles to underpin this new order vied for dominance. While discussing the post-war order, the European political discourse of 1815 abounded with reflections on *repos* and *tranquillité* where public order and security were concerned. But 'God's providence' was an equally popular concept, often quoted to attribute legitimacy to border adjustments or territorial compensations. For others, an invocation of 'the law of nations' did the job.

Whichever principle of peace and security was invoked, it was inevitably juxtaposed with the threat of 'terror', indicating both the terror of possible new revolutions and the rise of new (or old) despots. That was indeed something on which everyone could agree: that it was necessary to fight terror, and to rein in 'instincts', 'passions' and 'jealousies', with notions of 'moderation'.[8] Right after the Battle of Waterloo, while patriotic poems and passionate hymns were still resounding, official Allied security vocabulary abounded with this fervour for moderation. The ministers underscored 'the urgent necessity of putting a brake to those principles subversive to the social order upon which Buonaparte had based his usurpation', as Metternich

---

[8] See I. de Haan and M. Lok (eds.), *The Politics of Moderation in Modern European History* (Basingstoke: Palgrave Macmillan, 2019).

phrased it.[9] In that he echoed Castlereagh's warning regarding the manifold unrests that broke out after the defeat of Napoleon: 'It is not insurrection we now want in Italy or elsewhere ... we want disciplined force under sovereigns we can trust.'[10]

A key concept channelling this political vocabulary on which all victors could agree was provided with the notion – linked to 'moderation' – of the 'balance of power', *das Gleichgewicht der Kräfte*, or *l'équilibre*. This concept has in the literature too often indiscriminately been seen as an objective description, as a quantitative calculation of raw materials, manpower and simply resources; a concept that also – since its first use by contemporaries in the seventeenth and eighteenth centuries – has been uncritically reiterated by scholars too often. Experts and scholars in the field of International Relations in particular – including Henry Kissinger, and his many epigones – have appropriated the concept without questioning it, reduced it to a process for managing power differences and tailored it to their own quite abstract interpretations – turning it into a far too narrowly rational, calculated and strategic activity.[11] Historians have fallen short in similar ways. Paul Schroeder sees 'the balance of power' and the Concert of Europe too starkly as a tool of crisis management and power distribution; for example, in summarizing the treaties of 1814 and 1815 as 'pacts of restraint (*pacta de contrahendo*)'.[12] At the same time, he maintains that the balance-of-power idea is a far too competitive, conflict-centred, eighteenth-century notion that no longer applies to the situation in 1815. According to Schroeder, it is better to talk about the transformation of the state of anarchy into a stable balance, a political 'equilibrium', owing to the fact that the two hegemonic powers Britain and Russia opted to anchor their mutual respect for each other's spheres of influence in 1813.[13] Others have suggested doing away with the obfuscated concept of balance of power altogether.[14]

---

[9] Metternich, 'Austrian Memoir', cited in Jarrett, *The Congress of Vienna and its Legacy*, 165. See also Jones, '1816', 124–6.

[10] Cited in R. Holland, *Blue-Water Empire. The British in the Mediterranean since 1800* (London: Allen Lane, 2012), 26–7.

[11] Kissinger, *Diplomacy*, 78–102. See also M. Zürn, *Interessen und Institutionen in der internationalen Politik. Grundlegung und Anwendungen des situationsstrukturellen Ansatzes* (Opladen: Leske & Budrich, 1992); Keohane, *After Hegemony*. See also H. Müller, 'Internationale Beziehungen als kommunikatives Handeln: Zur Kritik der utilitaristischen Handlungstheorien', *Zeitschrift für Internationale Beziehungen*, 1:1 (1994), 15–44; Ikenberry, *After Victory*, 11–13.

[12] P. Schroeder, 'Alliances, 1815–1945: Weapons of Power and Tools of Management', in K. Knorr (ed.), *Historical Dimensions of National Security Problems* (Lawrence: University Press of Kansas, 1976), 227–62; Schroeder, 'Did the Vienna Settlement Rest on a Balance of Power?', 683–706; E. Kraehe, 'A Bipolar Balance of Power', *American Historical Review*, 97:3 (1992), 707–15.

[13] Schroeder, *The Transformation of European Politics*, vii, 482, 803.

[14] See for example Gruner, 'Frankreich in der europäischen Ordnung des 19. Jahrhunderts', 201–2. See also Gruner, 'Was There a Reformed Balance of Power System or Cooperative

To delete a concept after, or because, it has been deconstructed by political scientists is as unhelpful as it is ahistorical. Schroeder's distinction between 'balance' and 'equilibrium' would moreover not have made any impression on an early nineteenth-century reader, since the *Encyclopaedia Britannica*'s entry on 'mechanica' in those years used the phrases 'balance' and 'in equilibrio' interchangeably.[15] Already in 1953, the political scientist Ernst B. Haas complained that historians as well as his colleagues were remiss in continually confusing the sense of the balance concept as a description, as an analytic concept, as propaganda and as ideology.[16] He maintained that one needs to realize that 'balance' is a fleeting concept, one that is conceived of differently depending on the historical period, and that must always be understood and read as a cultural and ideological, time-dependent construct.[17] Both historians and political scientists have neglected the historical situatedness and fluidity of the 'balance of power' concept for too long. In the early nineteenth century it was simultaneously a moral imperative and a description of the desired state of international relations. 'Balance of power' was not a neutral term. It was rather the key to and the cornerstone of the quite normative security idiom of the day. The balance of power was a metaphor, on which notions of peace, tranquillity and harmony were projected, and thereby one that served not just as a principle of politics but also as an expression of a collective sentiment – and the thread that stitched the fabric of the newly woven European community of statesmen and diplomats together.

'A Bridle upon the Strong'

From the start of the first coalition wars against Napoleon, the 'balance of power' was the thread that connected the Allies' discussions about post-war security in Europe and beyond. But it was not a neologism. The term was in use long before, by collaborating Italian city-states during the latter half of the fifteenth century for example. It resurfaced again after the great wars of the seventeenth century, and was used to describe the new system for sovereign state interaction after 1648, the 'Westphalian State System'. After the Peace of Utrecht in 1713, where the hegemonic ambitions of Louis XIV were condemned and the equal status of victor and vanquished under international

---

Great Power Hegemony?', *American Historical Review*, 97:3 (1992), 725–32; Gruner (ed.), *Gleichgewicht in Geschichte und Gegenwart* (Hamburg: Krämer, 1989).

[15] 'Mechanics', in *Encyclopaedia Britannica*, vol. 14, 349–92, here: 356.

[16] Despite his highly meticulous and informative article, Wight fell into the same trap; see M. Wight, 'The Balance of Power and International Order', in M. Brands, N. van Sas and B. Tromp (eds.), *De veiligheid van Europa. Aspecten van de ontwikkeling van het Europese statenstelsel* (Rijswijk: Universitaire Pers Rotterdam, 1991), 1–25.

[17] E. Haas, 'The Balance of Power: Prescription, Concept, or Propaganda?', *World Politics*, 5:4 (1953), 442–77.

law was agreed upon, the balance-of-power concept gained increasingly pro-minent importance. Eighteenth-century philosophers like Christian Wolff, Emer de Vattel and Samuel Pufendorf, building on the work of Hugo Grotius, coupled the political and descriptive balance-of-power principle to the legal norms of international law, hence casting it in a more normative light and conveying a moral perspective on international relations as well.[18] But the decades between 1740 and 1790 still saw a highly volatile, unstable system of five great powers, competing with each other to dominate the continent, arranging mutual treaties and balance-of-power arrangements in times of war to shift alliances straight after concluding the first armistice.

It was only during the last years of the Napoleonic Wars of conquest that balance-of-power thinking became slowly inverted: it rose to become the key concept for all of the anti-Napoleonic coalition's plans and initiatives to create stability and permanence for the system – instead of a scheme for new con-quest. In fact, it turned out to be the preferred guiding principle for the development of a system of collective security.[19] This transformation from the balance of power as a warring principle towards a pacifying tool and an institution in peacetime can be discerned in the 'coffee-table books' of those days, the encyclopaedia and 'conversation-lexicons', where it was a trending topic around 1815. Following on the entry on the 'mechanical balance', the *Brockhaus Enzyklopädie* of 1815 defined the political balance of power as 'the principle of the reciprocal preservation of freedom and independence in the European system of states by means of preventing the ascendency and preten-sions of a single power among them'. 'Cultivated states' strove to reinstate this ideal system; one that the *Brockhaus* simply projected back into the distant past of the Greek city-states, but which now the despotism of the French Revolution had brought to naught. Opposite the benefits gained from larger and smaller states respecting each other in a system of alliances and reciprocal solidarity – second- and third-rank states are also mentioned as being part of this system – stood the threat of that one state, the usurper, which would choose might over right and pay no heed to any sense of balance at all. Although the *Brockhaus*'s 1815 picture of this threat is quite obfuscated, it does point directly to the French Revolution and to the French state itself, which since the time of Louis XIV had been driven by the tendency towards hegemony.[20] Interestingly, this German description of the *System des Gleichgewichts*, as the pre-revolutionary *Idealzustand* of states of differing sizes working together

---

[18] See W. Rech, *Enemies of Mankind. Vattel's Theory of Collective Security* (Leiden/Boston: Martinus Nijhoff, 2013).

[19] H. Duchhardt, *Gleichgewicht der Kräfte, Convenance, Europäisches Konzert. Friedenskongresse und Friedensschlüsse vom Zeitalter Ludwigs XIV. bis zum Wiener Kongreß* (Darmstadt: Wissenschaftliche Buchgesellschaft, 1976), 68–76.

[20] 'Gleichgewicht (politisches)', in F. Brockhaus (ed.), *Conversations-Lexicon*, vol. 4 (Leipzig/Altenburg: Brockhaus, 1815), 276–7.

on the basis of laws and treaties that was torn asunder in 1789, clearly lacks any historical support. It was more of a projection, more of an imagined reality, than a political stock-taking – and very much breathing the anti-French sentiments *en vogue* in the German lands.

In the *Encyclopaedia Britannica* entry on the 'Balance of Power' that was written between 1815 and 1824, we find a similar argument, neatly conveying the intricate connection between fact, imagination and feelings. The *Britannica* entry begins, in a very modern way, by acknowledging the sponginess of the concept:

> Among states, a most important object of foreign policy, intimately connected with the general peace and independence of nations; but which some have strangely treated as altogether chimerical, and others as strangely represented as having led only to pernicious results.[21]

Meanwhile, the nineteenth century had dawned and the balance-of-power principle had demonstrated its pacifying effect in international politics: 'It is far more generally admitted, however, to have a real foundation in the principles of intercourse and union among states, and to have exercised a great and beneficial influence on the affairs of modern Europe.' The *Britannica* did not mean to suggest that the power of states in relation to each other had to be 'equalized'. Balance-thinking had a different purpose, namely to create a structure of overall security amongst the states.[22]

Balancing was, therefore, no longer an argument to initiate wars, but an instrument to establish a system of collective security with an eye to taming an uncertain future. It was a way of 'coping with change', of engaging, in Metternich's words, 'the urgent necessity of putting a brake to those principles subversive to the social order upon which Buonaparte had based his usurpation'.[23] That system was formed by a community of united sovereignties that at all times could provide a counterweight to aggressive powers. That counterbalance was afforded by 'the union of powers' as well as by the foresight with which treaties of assistance were concluded. Thinking in terms of balance had become, in a very modern sense, security thinking – an instrument of precaution and anticipatory risk management.[24] This amounted to nothing less than postulating the right to a pre-emptive strike, although the *Britannica*

---

[21] 'Balance of Power', in *Encyclopaedia Britannica*, vol. 4 (Edinburgh: Black, 1842), 308–13, here: 308. This seventh edition is rather rare, but can be found in the Rare Manuscripts Room of the Cambridge University Library. The 'balance of power' entry was first included in the 'supplement' that was written between 1815 and 1824. In other words, this entry was composed shortly after the war and is older than the 1842 publication date.

[22] 'Balance of Power', in *Encyclopaedia Britannica*, vol. 4, 308–9.

[23] Metternich, 'Austrian Memoir', cited in Jarrett, *The Congress of Vienna and its Legacy*, 165.

[24] 'Balance of Power', in *Encyclopaedia Britannica*, vol. 4, 308–9.

gave this interventionist reading an Ovidian twist by referring to an 'Obsta principiis' – the right to resist the beginnings.[25] It was a kind of early-warning system: such is the general tendency of the system; and however it may have occasionally failed to prevent outrages, it cannot be doubted that it has proved a formidable barrier against conquest, and a rampart of defence to the weaker states.[26] And in an even more beautiful flower of speech: 'the system founded on the balance of power ... was a bridle upon the strong, and a bulwark to the weak'.[27]

At the same time, the *Britannica* also did its best (by citing, for example, Grotius, Pufendorf and Vattel) to indicate that individual states could of course grow in wealth, size and influence without that automatically meaning that other states would derive the right to interfere with that increase in assets and power. The question sooner had to do with the grounds legitimating the right to (threaten to) intervene, and with how to determine under which circumstances such an intervention would be appropriate. Thus, balance-thinking was transformed into a kind of doctrine of 'just security', but one that would only work when continuously applied.[28] To be effective, the balance principle required uniform attention and oversight. Only then, when a 'number of considerable states' promoted 'a regular intercourse among them', would it be possible to 'develop and systematize this great principle of national security'.[29] The *Britannica*'s fantastically optimistic interpretation of the results of the Vienna Congress and the Congress System ended with an even rosier paean, apparently attempting to rival the emotional vocabulary and lyrical prose of Sir Walter Scott:

> The evil passions which give rise to ambitious attacks, like all other evil passions, will be more apt to be indulged, the less exposed they are to opposition or restraint. And it cannot be questioned, that in proportion as the maxims of this system are vigilantly and steadily pursued, there will be less inducement, because less prospect of success for ambitious undertakings.[30]

Between the lines, however, even the *Britannica* has to admit: balance of power in 1815 was of course also a bureaucratic process of adding and taking away 'souls' and territories and rearranging the map of Europe, as practised during the Congress of Vienna. Yet, it was also a highly normative, even sentimental approach to the post-war order – a reading that came to fruition especially after the second defeat of Napoleon in June 1815. From 1815 onwards, the

---

[25] Ibid.
[26] Ibid., 311.
[27] Ibid., 312.
[28] Ibid., 309.
[29] Ibid., 310.
[30] Ibid., 311.

balance of power was applied as an instrument to 'colonize' the evil passions and aggressive ambitions of the previous epoch. In this, this reading directly speaks to Walter Scott's popular story of the young Englishman Edward Waverley, who, after his Romantic love for the beautiful Scottish rebel Flora and his brash adventure in the Scottish Highlands, comes to his senses in the arms of the quite proper and, above all, English Miss Rose Bradwardine.[31] Scott published his novel anonymously in 1814, but that he was the author was soon an open secret. As noted earlier, Scott travelled to Europe in August 1815 and remained there for some time, in the company of high-standing 'tourists' and diplomats, including Castlereagh and Wellington.[32] His book became a bestseller across Europe, not least because it was a veiled condemnation of 'those passions common to men in all stages of society ... which have alike agitated the human heart, whether it throbbed under the steel corset of the fifteenth century, the brocaded coat of the eighteenth, or the blue frock and white dimity waistcoat of the present day'.[33] We can also refer to the ongoing success of the 1811 novel *Sense and Sensibility* by Jane Austen, whose own brother fought against Napoleon. Although Austen's novels, unlike those of Scott, are devoid of any war or rumours of war,[34] her works too are pervaded by the implicit appeal to reason, a tranquillity of mind and good sense.[35]

'Balance' was both the expression of the emotional spirit of the times and a preferred moral policy, in which power, at least on paper, in treaties and in speeches, was reconciled with justice and legitimacy, with moderation and restraint. As Gagern had envisaged it, it was the opposite of power politics and the right of the strongest, and it was a new thread that had to be spun out of old pieces.[36] It was a moral category that was at odds with the despotism, radicalism and terror of the previous period. Remarkably, even the power-realist *par excellence* Henry Kissinger could not gloss over the moral dimension of the 1815 order: 'the new international order came to be created with a sufficient awareness of the connection between power and morality; between security and legitimacy'.[37] The new order of the day articulated itself in terms of peace,

[31] W. Scott, *Waverley; or, 'Tis Sixty Years Since* (London: Penguin, 2011 [1814]).

[32] J. Lockhart, *Memoirs of the Life of Sir Walter Scott*, vol. 3 (Edinburgh, 1837), 346–72; J. Scott, *Journal of a Tour to Waterloo and Paris, in Company with Walter Scott in 1815* (London: Saunders, 1842); Bew, *Castlereagh*, 403–4; M. Pittock (ed.), *The Reception of Sir Walter Scott in Europe* (London: Continuum, 2006).

[33] Scott, *Waverley*, 5–6.

[34] Austen wrote: 'Let other pens dwell on guilt and misery.' J. Austen, *Mansfield Park* (New York: Penguin, 2003 [1814]), 428.

[35] L. Prescott, 'Voices in Britain during the Napoleonic Wars: Jane Austen', *Jane Austen Studies Center*, paper 1 (2009), via: https://commons.pacificu.edu/jasc/1 (last viewed: 7 April 2019).

[36] Gagern, *Mein Antheil an der Politik*, vol. 2, 194.

[37] See H. Kissinger, *A World Restored. The Politics of Conservatism in a Revolutionary Age* (New York: Grosset and Dunlap, 1964), 317–18.

order, reason and balance. These were the new key terms in the emotional vocabulary of security in Europe. That said, security policies early in the nineteenth century had a very bourgeois hue to them – more *Biedermeier* than *Vormärz*.

Important to note here is the fact that the invocation of balance and moderation did not contrast with the more hierarchical power politics of the great powers, but precisely legitimized these. It foreshadowed the implementation and enforcement of a clear hierarchical stratification of producers and receivers within this collective security community. An intrinsic part of this sense of decency and morality within Europe and between the cultivated European states themselves, moreover, was that it had a different face when turned towards the non-European and colonial world. The junction of moderation and balance, therefore, soon revealed itself to be a tool of imperial, and often also imperious power politics as well, both on the domestic front and abroad.[38]

A Hierarchical Principle

The revival of the balance-of-power discourse, and the revised sense of what it implied, was due in large part to political leaders and pundits from the United Kingdom and Austria, who – their Enlightenment educations notwithstanding – gave it a distinctive imperial imprint. It is important for the workings of the Allied Council, its successes and limitations, to gain a better understanding of this dual, ambivalent character: moderate *and* imperial, as follows from two seminal texts that precisely underscored this reading of the balance-of-power genealogy.

In 1806 Friedrich von Gentz published a comprehensive study on the need for Europe to once again model its politics on the balance of power – the same year that the Holy Roman Empire was dissolved and confined to history. Gentz, the son of a Prussian civil servant's family from Breslau, later became the secretary of the Congress of Vienna and Chancellor Metternich's right-hand man. He was a jurist with ambitions equally loftily intellectual and pecuniary and had studied under Immanuel Kant in Königsberg. He spoke with authority and wielded a sharp pen. For Gentz it was all about conserving the power of the Habsburg Empire by consolidating a political balance on the continent that would be expressed through mutual respect between dynasties and states for each other's territorial spheres of influence. That mutual respect was an expression of the propriety of a civilized and ideal community of states,

---

[38] See for a discussion of 'moderation' in the French Restoration regime: A. Craiutu, *A Virtue for Courageous Minds. Moderation in French Political Thought, 1748–1830* (Princeton/Oxford: Princeton University Press, 2012); Craiutu, *Le Centre introuvable. La pensée politique des doctrinaires sous la Restauration* (Paris: Plon, 2006).

as stated by Gentz's mentor Immanuel Kant in his essay on 'Eternal Peace' (*Zum ewigen Frieden*, 1795). Gentz, however, went one step further than Kant. He coupled that respect to a reciprocal pledge to monitor and enforce the balance of power. Such an ideal community was an illusion, according to Gentz; sanctions, or at least a credible threat of sanctions, were necessary to keep the peace.[39]

Similar thoughts, though from a British imperial perspective, had already emerged in the United Kingdom. Gentz's 1806 thesis was an echo of the so-called 'Pitt-Plan'. This memorandum about 'security and deliverance in Europe' was composed by the British prime minister William Pitt the Younger for the Russian tsar in 1805. Castlereagh took it out of the drawer and presented it to the British parliament for consideration in 1815.[40] This British interpretation of the balance idea traded in the precarious alliance politics and the mercantilism of the eighteenth century for a sustainable project of reciprocal security guarantees and economic interdependency in peacetime. It also assumed that significant disparities amongst the powers in Europe ('any projects of Aggrandizement and Ambition') should be avoided, and that both France and Russia had to be kept in check.

The British memorandum and Gentz's study complemented each other perfectly. Together, they may be considered as the blueprint for the post-war balance-of-power system.[41] In both plans the balance-of-power principle was applied on various levels: not only on the level of the European state system, but also in relation to the German Confederation, and the balance between smaller and larger German states. It was, moreover, also projected on to the desired state of internal affairs, where the power of the sovereigns should be mediated and even constrained by wise constitutions and independent court systems. At the same time, and quite ambivalently, both the Austrian and British blueprints had a quite hierarchical character and were clearly imbued with an 'imperial idiom' regarding the community of European states in relation to each other. Both Gentz and Pitt, and later Castlereagh, drew a sharp distinction between the decision-makers – 'the four great military Powers' – and the subordinate 'second-class' states (like Spain, Portugal, a number of German and Italian states, Switzerland and the Netherlands). The third category, the 'separate petty sovereignties', could best disappear from the map of Europe altogether and not be restored as independent states,

---

[39] F. von Gentz, *Fragments upon the Balance of Power in Europe* (trans. London: Baldwin, 1806); Gentz, 'Über de Pradt's Gemälde von Europa nach dem Kongress von Aachen', *Wiener Jahrbüchern der Literatur*, 5 (1819), 279–318, also in G. Schlesier (ed.), *Schriften von Friedrich Gentz. Ein Denkmal* (Mannheim: Hoff, 1838), 88–156.

[40] William Pitt, in a letter to the Russian Ambassador at London, January 19, 1805 (The 'Pitt-Plan'), in Hansard (ed.), *The Parliamentary Debates*, vol. 31, 177–82.

[41] Duchhardt, *Gleichgewicht der Kräfte*, 68–76, 137. See also Jarrett, *The Congress of Vienna and its Legacy*, 39–42; (Van) Sas, *Onze natuurlijkste bondgenoot*, 41.

since they would only arouse the expansive appetite of the larger states. Their claims – 'either of justice or liberality' – could therefore not be vouchsafed.[42]

This hierarchical reading of the balance-of-power principle was not limited to Austrian or British intellectuals or politicians, but also surfaced in the Prussian discussions on the German Confederation.[43] The Prussian scholar and diplomat Wilhelm von Humboldt, for example, developed an extensive theory regarding the political and moral need to put an end to the territorial fragmentation (*Kleinstaaterei*) within Germany and to grant Prussia, in contrast to Austria, a stronger role in the German Confederation that was to come into effect in 1815. As would become readily apparent around the negotiating tables in Vienna, the 'law of nations', or what was referred to at the time as 'public international law', did not hold for everyone and everything equally.[44]

Gentz, Humboldt and Pitt thus tied the norms of justice, balance and legitimacy in international relations to the great powers' privilege. That had always been the case in the past, but this connection was now compounded by theoretical treatises on the necessity of guaranteeing not just an ideal, but also an effective system of collective security. That system hinged on the internal ranking and subordination of states and empires on the continent. This hierarchical principle for the states of Europe amongst each other, however, also bore on their ambitions towards the non-European world. By invoking peace, security, 'public law' and the like, the 'balancers' implied their superiority vis-à-vis other political systems, both in time and space. In claiming the correct reading of a *juste équilibre*, other ideas could be discarded as too unstable, weak or despotic. The new balance-of-power dogma served Europe well, according to the victors of 1815, but it would not serve all states and peoples equally. This was something Gagern also lamented on when he complained that the balance principle was appropriated by the four powers in Vienna, who used assumed *Oberherrschaft* 'to lay down the law to the others' – for example in carving up Poland and Saxony, incorporating the Rhineland, and securing a condominium of the victorious powers over all others.[45]

---

[42] The 'Pitt-Plan', in Hansard (ed.), *The Parliamentary Debates*, 179–80.

[43] For an overview of these discussions, see W. Gruner, *Grossbritannien, der Deutsche Bund und die Struktur des europäischen Friedens im frühen 19. Jahrhundert. Studien zu den britisch-deutschen Beziehungen in einer Periode des Umbruchs, 1812–1820*. Habilitationsschrift. (Munich: Ludwig Maximilian Universität, 1979).

[44] W. von Humboldt, 'Über die Behandlung der Angelegenheiten des Deutschen Bundes durch Preußen', 30 September 1816, in A. Flitner and K. Giel (eds.), *Wilhelm von Humboldt. Werke in fünf Bänden*, vol. 4 (Darmstadt, 1969), 347–417. See also S. Kaehler, *Wilhelm v. Humboldt und der Staat. Ein Beitrag zur Geschichte deutscher Lebensgestaltung um 1800* (Göttingen: Vandenhoeck & Ruprecht, 1963), 324–8.

[45] Gagern, *Mein Antheil an der Politik*, vol. 2, 347.

Body or Machine?

In 1815, the balance-of-power principle embodied the collective desire for order, peace and stability, but it was still more of a metaphor than a concrete policy plan. Moreover, anyone who seriously studies international relations in the nineteenth century cannot but conclude that there was no factual balance. Power inequalities were cherished, and great powers pushed and shoved the borders of smaller principalities and states as they saw fit. The key question therefore still remains, as to what contemporaries exactly understood by it, and what they intended to achieve. How would the victors translate this principle into a blueprint for a concrete new order, with encompassing treaties and institutions?

The next step was indeed for all the princes, diplomats and their bureaucrats involved in the Allied Council to find a common ground in discussing the nature and format of the envisaged new order. Was the balance of power something that cast the international system of states in the mould of a 'body', as a community of entities that were mutually and organically connected to each other – as in the old federative nature of the Holy Roman Empire? Or did the balance idea rather fit the notion of that same states system as a machine, assembled in a modern, technocratic way – more like a modern, centralized monarchy? That choice of imagery mattered. Some saw the state as a 'living being', as a 'moral body, which has a most finely tuned harmony and proportion in all of its parts and an equally necessary coherence that only a natural body could ever have'. Accordingly, the community of states as a whole was also perceived as a coherent organism.[46] This same metaphor was clearly echoed by Immanuel Kant, who explained in 1784 that it is only logical that individual states will eventually merge into a *grossen Staatscörper* (a 'vast system of states').[47] In 1794, Kant expanded on his reflections regarding such an organic, spontaneously unfolding world constitution in his *Zum ewigen Frieden*.

These organic and quite uncomplicated ideas on the development of a body of states, resting on a similar organic and divinely ordained society of orders, were shattered first by the wars of the second half of the eighteenth century, and then definitively by the terror of the French Revolution. After that it was no longer Kant, with his idealism, but his pupil Gentz, along with Metternich and the British 'balancers', who came to dominate the discourse. For them, the balance of power had to be conceived of in terms of 'machines' that needed a masterly and forceful hand to put them into operation.[48] That imagery was

---

[46] See for example the Saxon freelance writer and political economist Johann Heinrich Gottlob von Justi, *Natur und Wesen der Staaten als die Quelle aller Regierungswissenschaften und Gesetze* (Aalen: Scientia, 1969 [1771]), 52–6, 274.

[47] I. Kant, 'Idee zu einer allgemeinen Geschichte in weltbürgerlicher Absicht', in *Kants Werke, Akademie-Ausgabe*, vol. 8 (Berlin: Georg Reimer, 1912 [1784]), 28.

[48] See, for example, the various entries under 'Mechanik und Statik' in *Brockhaus*, or the entries on 'balance' and 'equilibrium' in the *Encyclopaedia Britannica* or the

not new either; such rational, calculative metaphors had been used in the late eighteenth century as well, when chemists such as Lavoisier and Cavendish developed their theories based on ultra-precise measurements, made by different types of balances designed specifically for their research (Fig. 3.1). With

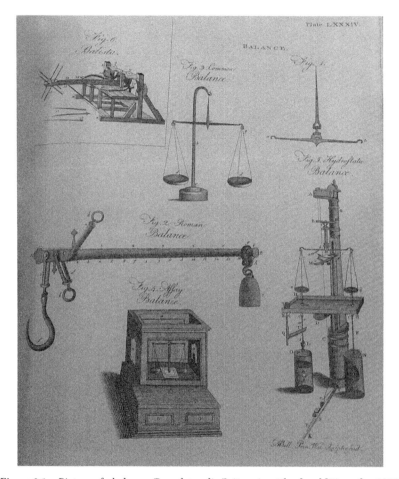

Figure 3.1   Picture of a balance, *Encyclopaedia Britannica*, 4th ed., addition after 1815. Source location: Cambridge University Library. (Photo owned by the author)

Grand dictionnaire encyclopédique Larousse. Cf. S. Manhart, *In den Feldern des Wissens. Studiengang, Fach und disziplinäre Semantik in den Geschichts- und Staatswissenschaften (1780–1860)* (Würzburg: Köningshausen & Neumann, 2011), 382–90. Gentz uses the word 'machine' a number of times when referring to the political system of states: 'Über de Pradt's Gemälde von Europa nach dem Kongress von Aachen', 95, 100, 112, 180.

such precision instruments, 'quantitative facts' came to dominate over unfounded philosophical premises and presumptions. According to a triumphant Lavoisier, balancing theories could be applied to anything, even the economy. Should the balance of trade not rather be assessed and calculated by casting currency circulation as a hydrostatic problem?[49]

If so, why not also try to calculate the level of peace in a community of states in this way? Of course, state communities were not spontaneously inclined towards peace, as a setup in a physics lab would automatically revert to a natural balance. The states system was not a natural body; it was more similar to a machine: technicians were needed to tinker and tamper in order to make the system operate according to the political laws of balancing forces. As a matter of fact, both metaphors – of body and mechanism – were still in vogue in 1815. However, in both cases the challenge was to find the right constitution and combination of forces and counter-forces to keep the whole in balance and its motion in check. The unit of calculating the right balance within the framework of the states system was power, or force, that needed to be equalized with counterpoise. Within the more traditional imagery of a body, the balance was created by arranging princes, sovereigns, dynasties and existing privileges in a legitimate, hierarchical order in relation to each other. Gagern and others seemed to favour exactly this: the return of a prerevolutionary, rather loosely knit 'body' of estates, and a return of the medieval *Kreise*, a federation of sovereign princes, or even a resuscitating of the old Holy Roman Empire, rather than centralized and modern monarchies.[50]

Metternich also stressed the fact that the states system was a society: 'Politics', Metternich wrote,

> is the science of the vital interests of States, in its widest meaning. Since however, an isolated state no longer exists and is found only in the annals of the heathen world ... we must always view the Society of States as the essential condition of the modern world.

However, in his version of a society, the axioms that made this system work rested more on modern, technocratic views, operating through the imagery of machines, countervailing forces, and instruments of intervention, than on the unpredictable heuristic of patient deliberation between a bunch of petty princes and smaller states. These were no fit for the modern forces of revolution and revolting masses. As Metternich, with his fascination for the astronomical clocks, astrolabes and other scientific instruments he amused himself with, was prone to see it: the balance of power could and should only be considered and applied as a cosmic principle, dictating a repression of the

---

[49] See B. Bensaude-Vincent, 'The Balance: Between Chemistry and Politics', *The Eighteenth Century*, 33:3 (1992), 217–37, here: 228–9.
[50] Gagern even asked Franz Joseph to take back the imperial crown of the Holy Roman Empire. See (De) Graaf, 'Second-tier Diplomacy'.

chaos caused by the Revolution in order for the pendulum of this machine to swing again to a stable and capable centre of power.[51]

In 1815, ideas on how to operate the 'bridle upon the strong' diverged substantially. Would it be the countervailing power of the conqueror, the invocation of Providence and the insistence upon moral and religious laws, rather than civil liberties? Or would it be the more modern way, as applied in the Statistical Committee in Vienna, by calculating the number of 'souls' and square kilometres? And should the machine rather be controlled by the checks and balances of a just constitution, basic law or *Charte* than by royal prerogative? Collective, or 'mutual security', as it was called, was a concept as intensively discussed as it was judicially pristine. Although much had been written in the eighteenth century about the 'law of nations', and legal positivism had found its way into international law, much still had to be filled in. A legal framework for the right of occupation did not exist yet, and the laws of war were hardly codified. That is why it mattered how the new instruments of maintaining a European balance of power were described. The imagery of the machine legitimated and translated into different measures than the moral normative metaphor of the body would – as will transpire in Chapter 4, where the makeup of the Allied Council will be discussed.

A Climate of Distress

The inclination of the 'men of 1815' towards balancing, wanting to bring the 'machine' in order again, with the pendulum swing back to a stable centre, can only be understood by situating it in the deeply felt confusion and insecurity of the immediate post-1815 years.[52] The reinterpretation and revamping of that principle, and its translation into a real system of collective security, with Allied Council and Army of Occupation, was both a political response to the revolutionary and Napoleonic wars and an attempt to meet the demands for moral and emotional orientation after the bewilderment and perturbation that still persisted in 1815. At the same time, the gradual transformation of a general balancing principle into an institutionalized, hierarchical and even imperialist order – rather than into a more organic body or federation of loosely knit and equal fiefdoms – also can only be understood by pointing to the shaky peace, the troublesome heritage of revolution and Napoleonic hegemony and large levels of suffering and distress that still loomed large over Europe. The victors of 1815 saw this all too well, and were therefore all the

---

[51] Cited in H. Nicolson, *The Congress of Vienna. A Study in Allied Unity, 1812–1822* (London: Constable, 1946), 39.
[52] Parts of the following paragraphs are drawn from (De) Graaf, 'Bringing Sense and Sensibility'.

more preoccupied with restoring public peace and tranquillity as soon as possible, lest new riots and revolts should break out.

Indeed, the devastation and despair were momentous, both in terms of human suffering and loss of life. The Napoleonic Wars had cost about 4 million men and boys their lives – in Europe alone; another million had been killed in the colonies. Still more were scarred for life by injuries and trauma, not to mention the socio-economic devastation and financial crisis in which the continent had landed.[53] Although the battles of 1790–1815 had not been bloodier and more gruesome than the battles during the Seven Years' War, historian David Bell nonetheless speaks of a 'total war'.[54] Estimates of civil casualties range between 0.75 and 3 million; in the Tyrol, Spain, Italy, Russia and France irregular bands of armed rebels and citizens fought along-side conscripted soldiers. Even in Britain, which had not been occupied or plagued by battles, the effects of the war were fully visible. More than a million men had been called to action, a fourth of whom were the heads of families; 315,000 of these soldiers died. If they did not return as invalids, then they left countless numbers of dismayed and impoverished family members behind.[55] The Netherlands, after the introduction of conscription, with its population of about 2 million, called up 28,000 men between 1810 and 1813. Of these, 70 per cent never returned. In the departments of the Rhine, 80,000 recruits were called up between 1802 and 1813, the equivalent of 30 per cent of the able-bodied male population.[56] These wars still belonged to the 'age of men', when wars were waged with infantry and cavalry. The 'age of machines and technology', with its industrial capacities to destroy, had not dawned yet, but that did not make the socio-economic, military and especially human wages of war any less catastrophic or total.[57] More than half of all the casualties and victims, moreover, fell in the last three years of the wars, when the scale of armies and battlefields went up considerably, impregnating the citizens of Europe with vivid memories of death and destruction after the war was over in 1815.[58]

Moreover, the economic and financial state of most of the countries in Europe was equally devastating. The wars had upended economies, revenues and financial budgets. In France alone, the 462 million francs for military

---

[53] Cf. Esdaile, *Napoleon's Wars*; G. Rothenberg, *The Art of Warfare in the Age of Napoleon* (Bloomington: Indiana University Press, 1977), 81 and Appendices I and II, 247–55.

[54] Bell, *The First Total War*.

[55] P. Lin, 'Caring for the Nation's Families', in Forrest, Hagemann and Rendall (eds.), *Soldiers*, 99–117, here: 100.

[56] H. Carl, 'Religion and the Experience of War: A Comparative Approach to Belgium, the Netherlands and the Rhineland', in Forrest, Hagemann and Rendall (eds.), *Soldiers*, 222–42, here: 230. See also J. Smets, *Les Pays Rhénans (1794–1814). Le comportement des Rhénans face à l'occupation français* (Bern: Peter Lang, 1997), 460–1.

[57] A. Forrest, K. Hagemann and J. Rendall, 'Nations in Arms, People at War', in Forrest, Hagemann and Rendall (eds.), *Soldiers*, 1–19.

[58] See Rothenberg, *The Art of Warfare in the Age of Napoleon*, Appendix I, 247–53.

expenditures in 1807 had risen to 817 million francs in 1813. To squeeze those sums out of the populace, tax rates and duties were immensely increased, and a financial system for loans and credit was created. The war machine of the Grande Armée had devoured 1,660,000 French soldiers.[59] The wars were, however, especially paid for on the backs of the countries that Napoleon invaded. The troops were billeted; Prussia, for example, after its defeat near Jena had to pay 311 million francs for the maintenance of the French military. The Habsburg Empire had to pay up as well; and in countries like Italy and the Low Countries (between 1806 and 1810, after which the Kingdom of Holland was entirely incorporated into the French Empire) about one half of their taxes went straight to Paris.[60] The Russian Empire was also hit hard. While on the march, the Grande Armée largely lived off of the land of the countries they traversed, and when retreating from Moscow left a swathe of scorched earth behind them. During the Napoleonic Wars nearly 1.6 million Russians were called up for service in the army. In 1812 alone three levies were issued, resulting in about twenty recruits for every five hundred reporting.[61] Napoleon's army lost 380,000 of its 680,000 soldiers during the Russian campaign of 1812 (100,000 were captured, and only 27,000 reached the other side of the Berezina River), but Russia too lost more than 210,000 men.[62]

During the final years of the war, population growth ground to a halt, or even contracted slightly in the cities. In Amsterdam, children were abandoned almost daily by mothers who could no longer support their families, gangs of children roamed the city in search of food and when the call went out for new conscripts riots increased.[63] Trade on the coasts had been disrupted by the Continental System and the loss of overseas markets had robbed the continent of sales and raw materials. The city-state of Hamburg, once among the richest commercial seaports on the continent, was virtually bankrupt. There was hardly a ship to be seen on its main waterway, the River Elbe. French customs patrols brought trade in Hamburg, and everywhere else along the coasts of Europe, to a standstill. As one German citizen reported, 'Everyone, even those

---

[59] N. Petiteau, 'Survivors of War: French Soldiers and Veterans of the Napoleonic Armies', in Forrest, Hagemann and Rendall (eds.), *Soldiers*, 43–58, here: 45.

[60] P. Kennedy, *The Rise and Fall of the Great Powers. Economic Change and Military Conflict from 1500 to 2000* (New York: Random House, 1989), 132–3; S. Schama, 'The Exigencies of War and the Politics of Taxation in the Netherlands 1795–1810', in J. de Winter (ed.), *War and Economic Development. Essays in Memory of David Joslin* (Cambridge: Cambridge University Press, 1975), 103–37, here: 111, 117, 128; or see the oft-cited G. Brunn, *Europe and the French Imperium, 1799–1814* (New York: Harper, 1938).

[61] J. Hartley, 'Patriotism in the Provinces in 1812. Volunteers and Donations', in Hartley, Keenan and Lieven (eds.), *Russia and the Napoleonic Wars*, 148–62, here: 148.

[62] Cf. Lieven, *Russia against Napoleon*.

[63] See J. Joor, *De Adelaar en het Lam. Onrust, opruiing en onwilligheid in Nederland ten tijde van het Koninkrijk Holland en de Inlijving bij het Franse Keizerrijk (1806–1813)* (Amsterdam: De Bataafsche Leeuw, 2000).

who do not hear the resounding drums of war, feel themselves oppressed, half numb, hopeless, and reduced to desperation.'[64] The war had reached the home front, certainly when Napoleon jacked up the economic sanctions in those final years after 1810. Even large-scale smuggling and trade on the black market could not compensate for the mounting malaise and rise in unemployment. In 1811 about 17,000 of the 100,000 inhabitants of Hamburg depended on handouts.[65]

Against this backdrop, the ethos of the lives of those living in the countryside and cities of Europe after being liberated from the Napoleonic carousel of ever more taxes, imposed billeting and still more sons that had to be sacrificed to his military dreams, as sketched above, gains relief. This helps us to understand the immense relief and joy that broke out when, of all things, the wildest of packs from the east, the Russian Cossacks, advanced towards and entered Dutch cities to pitch their exotic encampments there in the market squares and streets: a joy commemorated in paintings, in street names (there are at least ten streets named Cossack Way throughout the Netherlands) and an annual holiday to honour the Cossacks' liberation (celebrated in Utrecht right up to 1913).[66] At the same time, in other places the suffering and devastation caused by the wars also explain the concerns of the elites and their fear for new uprisings, and bread riots turning into political revolts.

Death indeed continued to take its toll on a daily basis, whether harnessed or like an assassin. The last major battles of Leipzig and Waterloo, being the largest conflagrations but by no means the only ones, claimed the lives of 100,000 of the 600,000 soldiers gathered at Leipzig and 65,000 of the 200,000 men in uniform at Waterloo.[67] Owing to hunger, the cold and sharply deteriorating hygiene in German cities and on and around the battlefields of the westward-moving front, typhus began to rage, probably brought by the Napoleonic army retreating from Russia. About 2 million people succumbed to the plague: 250,000 in Germany, 20,000 in East Prussia alone, as well as many of those still living in cities like Dresden, Leipzig, Würzburg and Mainz

[64] J. Reimarus, *Klagen der Völker des Continents von Europa die Handelssperre betreffend. Ihren Fürsten dargestellt* (Hamburg, 1809), 12. Also cited in K. Aaslestad, 'War without Battles. Civilian Experiences of Economic Warfare during the Napoleonic Era in Hamburg', in Forrest, Hagemann and Rendall (eds.), *Soldiers*, 118–36, here: 119.

[65] Aaslestad, 'War without Battles', 127.

[66] C. van de Graft, 'Kozakkendag te Utrecht', *Maandblad van Oud-Utrecht*, 41:4 (1968), 37–9; R. de Bruin, 'Regenten en revolutionairen (1747–1851)', in Van de Graft et al. (eds.), *'Een paradijs vol weelde'. Geschiedenis van de stad Utrecht* (Utrecht, 2000), 315–73, here: 350–3. See also the famous painting by P. G. van Os, *De aankomst van de kozakken in Utrecht, 1813* (1816, now in the Central Museum, Utrecht).

[67] See D. Smith, *The Napoleonic Wars Data Book. Actions and Losses in Personnel, Colours, Standards and Artillery, 1792–1815* (London: Greenhill, 1998); A. Barbero, *The Battle. A New History of Waterloo* (London: Atlantic Books, 2013), 160.

after the battles and sieges.[68] Between 1816 and 1819, 16 to 37 per cent of those who became infected in central and western Europe died because of it. The epidemic also marched into the centre of Paris, claiming victims as late as 1820 – including the Austrian field marshal General Schwarzenberg and the aforementioned prefect of Mainz, Jeanbon Saint-André.[69] Plagues spread to the outermost edges of Europe and beyond, flourishing in the midst of the massive displacement of inhabitants and the lowered standards of living; between 1813 and 1816, approximately 70,000 residents of the Danubian Principalities – the area around the mouth of the Danube on the Black Sea, which was sandwiched between the Russian, Habsburg and Ottoman empires – fell prey to the bubonic plague.[70] The sick and inflected were quarantined only after 1815, once the military campaigns had ended, and the medical infra-structure – which until then consisted of emergency military hospitals – could be rebuilt, thanks to donations and fundraising efforts.[71]

Things were not quieter straight away on the main roads and byways once the Grande Armée and other armies were demobilized after June 1815. Some 500,000 hastily mobilized French military men were discharged, and only around 100,000 remained. Russia, Prussia and Austria did keep their standing conscription-based armies intact, but sent the militias home.[72] Countless displaced persons streamed back to their country. From March 1814 onwards,

---

[68] Cf. M. Vasold, 'The Epidemic Typhus of 1813/14 in the Area of Lower Franconia', *Würzburger Medizinhistorische Mitteilungen*, 23 (2004), 217–32.

[69] R. Bray, *Armies of Pestilence. The Impact of Diseases on History* (Cambridge: James Clarke, 2004), 146–7.

[70] C. Giurescu, *Istoria românilor* ['A History of the Romanians'], vol. 3: *De la moartea lui Mihai Viteazul la sfârșitul epocei fanariote (1601-1821)* ['From the death of Michael the Brave to the end of the Phanariot Age'] (Bucharest: Editura All, 1944), 330–1; V. Urechia, 'Din domnia lui Ioan Caragea. Avenire la tron. Mișcări contra grecilor. Finanțe, 1812–1818' ['From Caradja's reign: his enthronement; movements against the Greeks; finances, 1812–1818'], *Analele Academiei Române*, 22:2 (1900), 177; S. Ionescu, *Bucureștii în vremea fanarioților* ['Bucharest in Phanariot times'] (Cluj-Napoca: Dacia, 1974), 284; P. Cernovodeanu and N. Edroiu (eds.), *Istoria românilor* ['History of the Romanians'], vol. 6: *Românii în epoca clasică și epoca luminilor* ['The Romanians in the Classical Age and during the Enlightenment'] (Bucharest: Editura Enciclopedică, 2002), 495.

[71] K. Hagemann, '"Unimaginable Horror and Misery": The Battle of Leipzig in October 1813 in Civilian Experience and Perception', in Forrest, Hagemann and Rendall (eds.), *Soldiers*, 157–78, here: 170.

[72] See J. Leighton, 'The Experience of Demobilization: War Veterans in the Central European Armies and Societies after 1815', in Forrest, Hagemann and Rowe (eds.), *War*, 68–83; J. Hartley, 'War, Economy and Utopianism: Russia after the Napoleonic Era', in Forrest, Hagemann and Rowe (eds.), *War*, 84–99; G. Craig, *Politics of the Prussian Army, 1640-1945* (Oxford: Clarendon Press, 1955), 60–9; C. Macartney, *The Habsburg Empire 1790-1918* (London: Faber & Faber, 1969), 203–4; D. Davidson, C. Haynes and J. Heuer, 'Ending War: Revisiting the Aftermath of the Napoleonic Wars', *Journal of Military History*, 80 (2016), 11–30; Y. Guerrin, *La France après Napoleon. Invasions et occupations 1814-1818* (Paris: L'Harmattan, 2014).

the roads through Europe bustled with coming and going deserters, discharged soldiers, liberated prisoners of war and lagging disabled, wounded or sick veterans. French and Spanish prisoners returned from Russia, Germans from France, Italians from Sweden and Austria, Dutch from the hospitals in Prussia.[73] Many soldiers were disorientated by the loss of the camaraderie and sense of purpose that the army had offered them. My unit was 'my military family', sighed one captain; and another soldier, Victor Dupuy, lamented nostalgically his sense of companionship: 'Nothing binds us together like the dangers we have shared, like the happiness and the sorrow we have felt as a group.'[74] The 1.2 million Allied troops in France were also reduced after the summer of 1815 to a standing army of occupation of 150,000 men. So the swarm of veterans, merchants, couriers and orphaned youth was still not settling down. Refugees and displaced children roamed the cities and streets, and angry rumours of an emperor geared up to return hung in the air. Given all that, the summer of 1815 did not see a *Stunde Null* or *tabula rasa*, but confusion, uncertainty and all kinds of contradictory expectations and imaginations.

The years from 1815 to 1817 were also years in which new economic crises erupted. The overproduction of the wartime period induced sharp price falls after the termination of the war.[75] Crop failures led to famine and rebellions in many areas during the icy winters of 1815/16 and 1816/17. Save Britain, the Netherlands and Switzerland, two thirds of the national populations of the countries of Europe were involved in agriculture. Increases in taxes and financial reforms could hardly alleviate the immediate pressure on the national treasuries.[76] Almost all countries were compelled to raise yet further loans and had to cut down the social and economic relief programmes that were so dearly needed. The spectre of social unrest, once again marrying political protest and revolutionary upheaval, was raised throughout the continent and beyond. Extraordinary volcanic activity between the years 1811 and 1818 was responsible for calamitous weather; especially in 1816/17, subsistence crises and famine extended over extensive regions in the Western world.[77]

An oft-cited theme in art and culture that captured how portentous and yet fascinating these new days were was the eruption of Mount Tambora on the island of Sumbawa in the Dutch East Indies (present-day Indonesia) in April 1815, which in the months that followed threw the seasons seriously

---

[73] See reports on returned prisoners of war, the sick and wounded in GStA PK, III. HA I. no. 931–49.

[74] Dupuy, 'Souvenirs', cited in Petiteau, 'Survivors of War', 47.

[75] Cf. W. Abel, *Landwirtschaftspolitik* (Wiesbaden: Springer Fachmedien, 1950), 74–5.

[76] Cf. J. Cardosa (ed.), *Paying for the Liberal State. The Rise of Public Finance in 19th Century Europe* (Cambridge: Cambridge University Press, 2010).

[77] Cf. J. Post, *The Last Great Subsistence Crisis in the Western World* (Baltimore/London: Johns Hopkins University Press, 1977), xii–xiii.

out of whack. The eruption propelled gigantic streams of volcanic ash and sulphur dioxide more than 40 km high, deep into the stratosphere. Winds carried these gases and fine ash particles around the globe, and disrupted standard weather patterns in many parts of the world, especially in America and Europe. The enormous ash cloud first passed over North America, causing deep snowfalls in the north-east the next year.[78] Europe, too, became shrouded in a dark cloud of ash and smog, which led to incessant rainfall and failed harvests, and to a mood of doom among some poets as well as the superstitious.[79] A British newspaper reported:

> The foreign papers continue to inform us of the damage done by storms of hail and thunder, in almost every part of Europe. Whole districts have been ravaged and laid waste, houses have been blown down, the labours of the husbandman destroyed, rivers have burst their banks, and inundated vast tracts.[80]

The effects were evident elsewhere in Europe as well. Germany called it *Das Hungerjahr*, Switzerland referred to *L'Année de la misère*. Newspapers reported, 'There is no longer any hope for agriculture. The calamity appears almost general; all travellers assert that it is experienced in Turkey, Hungary, Italy, Germany, and throughout all the East of Europe.' Crop failures meant inadequate food supplies, and famine sparked off riots in many places in Europe.[81]

The volcanic aerosol veil also affected the light of the sun, which looked much redder, bigger and brighter; but its radiant heat was far less powerful, and did not melt much of the snow that fell that summer. Poets, like Byron in his apocalyptic fantasy poem 'Darkness', were greatly inspired by these oddities: 'I had a dream, which was not all a dream. / The bright sun was extinguish'd, and the stars / Did wander darkling in the eternal space, / Rayless, and pathless ... '.[82] The British painter J. M. W. Turner captured powerfully evocative images of this natural drama in a series of etchings in mezzotint depicting wild sunsets and showers. Turner sketched the Valley of Chamonix, the setting for an almost supernatural storm in which ice floes crash and shatter against each other: the same kind of storms that the British Frances Winckley, Lady Shelley and company had to go through while on the

---

[78] Post, *The Last Great Subsistence Crisis*, 26.
[79] See Jones, '1816', 119–42; C. Skeen, 'The Year without a Summer: A Historical View', *Journal of the Early Republic*, 1:1 (1981), 51–67.
[80] *Caledonian Mercury*, 25 July 1816.
[81] *Morning Chronicle*, 24 July 1816; see also G. D'Arcy Wood, *Tambora: The Eruption that Changed the World* (Princeton: Princeton University Press, 2014); W. Klingaman and N. Klingaman, *The Year without a Summer. 1816 and the Volcano That Darkened the World and Changed History* (New York: St. Martin's Press, 2013).
[82] Byron, 'Darkness', July 1816.

continent, visiting, amongst others, their friend the Duke of Wellington.[83] Lady Shelley kept a diary while travelling through Europe in 1815 and 1816 and lyrically described her journey through the Alps:

> As we were returning along the direct road to Chamonix, the sun sud-denly broke through the clouds, and quickly dispersed the dense vapours which had shrouded Mont Blanc. It was, for me, a moment of ecstasy; and the beauty of the spectacle was enhanced by occasional cloud-drifts which passed swiftly over the summit of the dome – for a moment veiling, in order to increase, the splendour of its reappearance.[84]

The beauty was contrasted by the failed crops, damaged roads and bridges, and the abject poverty of the Swiss – 'they are all beggars', concluded Lady Shelley.[85]

The question was, could these beggars be contained, or would economic distress and social unrest translate into political upheaval again? Most con-temporary statesmen dreaded as much. Gagern warned the Frankfurt Diet that the manifold migrations caused by the economic distress posed a threat to the internal security of Germany, and that the famine and despair of these classes would end in 'embitterment of the people', and perhaps new uprisings.[86] Against this fear, the 'men of 1815' tried to come up with a new system of collective security, both directed towards the Concert of Europe as a whole, and towards their own domestic societies.

Experiencing Transition Together

Given this climate of distress, a careless slide back in time, to the life of yesteryear, was out of the question.[87] 'This old Europe thought it was only fighting France; she didn't realize that a new century was on the march', quipped the always astute Chateaubriand. Although the Europe of those days had no option but to counter revolution and Bonaparte's despotism, it was reborn in the process. 'When the revolutionary war broke out, the sovereigns

---

[83] See E. Ling and A. Marquis, '1816: Prints by Turner, Goya and Cornelius', Department of Paintings, Drawings and Prints (The Fitzwilliam Museum, University of Cambridge, 2016), via: www.fitzmuseum.cam.ac.uk/sites/default/files/1816.pdf (last viewed: 12 March 2019). See also the paintings by J. M. W. Turner, *The Source of the Arveyron in the Valley of Chamonix, Savoy*, January 1816, as well as *Tenth Plague of Egypt*, January 1816, both in The Fitzwilliam Museum (Cambridge).

[84] Edgcumbe (ed.), *The Diary of Frances Lady Shelley, 1787–1817*, 242–3.

[85] Ibid., 232.

[86] Gagern, *Mein Antheil an der Politik*, vol. 3: *Der Bundestag* (Stuttgart and Tübingen: Cotta, 1830), 150.

[87] See R. Koselleck, '"Erfahrungsraum" und "Erwartungshorizont": Zwei historische Kategorien', in Koselleck, *Vergangene Zukunft. Zur Semantik geschichtlicher Zeiten* (Frankfurt, 1989), 349–75.

did not understand it: they saw a revolt, but should have seen nations in transformation, the end of former things and the beginning of a new world.'[88] The transition of 1815–18 was, however, a combination of old and new. On the one hand, contemporaries experienced almost physically how a new day had dawned.[89] On the other hand, many people, like the Austrian chancellor Metternich, would have preferred to go back to how things had been, to the 'ordinary history' of the *ancien régime*, to a time that unhurriedly ticked by, without too many startling events. King Louis XVIII, provisionally restored to the throne in 1814, was on the same page; as he put it in the new French *Charte* of 1814: 'Striving thus to re-forge links with the past, which certain tragic divergences had interrupted, we have erased from our memory, just as we wish one could erase from history itself, all the evils which afflicted the country during our absence.'[90] This imagery was obviously just as catchy as misleading; the chain of time had not been broken; its pace had accelerated enormously. For, as one discouraged royalist put it, Napoleon, the great accelerator, 'did in twenty days what Louis XVI had been unable to do in twenty years'.[91] No one could reverse by decree the huge upheavals that occurred during the French Revolution and the Napoleonic Wars. Too many had indeed very much embraced the rapid changes and new horizons that came with the French Revolution.[92]

A sense of new times on the move, of breaking with the days of yore, was pervasively present. According to some historians, the rise of collective sentimentalism coincided with the transition from the Enlightenment to the post-Napoleonic era. William Reddy believes that after that, extravagant 'performances of emotion' became routine among the educated elite.[93] Reddy's observations tie in with Georg Lukács's argument in *The Historical Novel* (1937), in which Lukács couples the emergence of a new, historical consciousness to the rise and fall of Napoleon, suggesting that with that, history became

---

[88] Chateaubriand, *Mémoires d'outre-tombe*, vol. 2, 39.

[89] See Jones, '1816'.

[90] *Charte Constitutionelle*, Préambule, 4 June 1814. Cited and translated by S. Carpenter, *Aesthetics of Fraudulence in Nineteenth-Century France. Frauds, Hoaxes, and Counterfeits* (Aldershot: Ashgate, 2009), 73–4.

[91] A. Galland, *Du Retour des Bourbons en France et du Gouvernement Paternel de Louis XVIII* (Paris, 1815), 8.

[92] H. Williams, *Letters on the Events Which Have Passed in France since the Restoration in 1815* (London: Baldwin, 1819), 3. Also cited in Jones, '1816', 121.

[93] W. Reddy, *The Navigation of Feeling. A Framework for the History of Emotions* (Cambridge: Cambridge University Press, 2001), 155ff. For the 'emotional turn in history' see further U. Frevert, *Emotions in History. Lost and Found* (New York: Central European University Press, 2011); Frevert et al. (eds.), *Emotional Lexicons. Continuity and Change in the Vocabulary of Feeling 1700–2000*. (Oxford: Oxford University Press, 2014); J. Plamper, *Geschichte und Gefühl. Grundlagen der Emotionsgeschichte* (Munich: Siedler, 2012). See also Eustace et al., '*AHR* Conversation'.

'a *mass experience*, and moreover on a European scale'. The succession of wars and upheavals between 1789 and 1815 'makes their historical character far more visible than would be the case in isolated, individual instances'.[94] The American historian Lynn Hunt goes a step further and maintains that this shared experience, as well as the epistolary novels that appeared during this period, 'helped spread the practices of autonomy and empathy'.[95] Individuals far away recognized each others' experiences and adventures and started putting this recognition on paper, translating these collective experiences into political pamphlets, novels and poems.

Following the 'emotional turn in history', specific emotions and individual sentiments were being translated into broader, shared emotional norms and attitudes. Thus, cultivated emotional communities gave shape to the political realm, while, in turn, political power may also be interpreted as an expression of a collectively shared emotional culture.[96] From this perspective, the 'sentiment of 1815' combined experience of war weariness, shock over the Hundred Days, mistrust and polarization between Bonapartists, liberals and those opposed to a restoration on the one hand and, on the other, those pining for exactly that, a return to the privileges lost. But all factions shared a sense of acceleration and a break in time. Their desires and longings were at times cast in nationalist or patriotic paintings and poems, sometimes also translated into a shared European imagining and a European vocabulary of peace and security. Representations and reports on the last Napoleonic battles, such as those composed by the novelist Walter Scott, were in great demand across the continent.[97] A broad readership found comfort and recognition in his historical novels after all the perils they had gone through. As Lukács saw it, such novels helped readers to begin 'to comprehend their own existence as something historically conditioned', and to see their daily lives as belonging to a larger history and picture – as shrill and contrasting as these pictures may have been.[98]

Against this heartfelt shock to the European moral and political system, the 'men of 1815' were groping their way towards a new stability – a balance that

---

[94] G. Lukács, *The Historical Novel* (trans. H. and S. Mitchell, Lincoln: University of Nebraska Press, 1962), 23.

[95] L. Hunt, *Inventing Human Rights. A History* (New York: Norton, 2007), 32.

[96] See for example: E. van Rythoven, 'Learning to Feel, Learning to Fear? Emotions, Imaginaries, and Limits in the Politics of Securitization', *Security Dialogue*, 46:5 (2015), 458–75; T. Michel, 'Time to Get Emotional: Phronetic Reflections on the Concept of Trust in International Relations', *European Journal of International Relations*, 19:4 (2013), 869–90.

[97] For example, W. Scott, *Paul's Letters to his Kinsfolk* (Edinburgh: Ballantyne, 1816). See also N. van Sas, 'From Waterloo Field to Bruges-La-Morte: Historical Imagination in the Nineteenth Century', in H. Dunthorne and M. Wintle (eds.), *The Historical Imagination in Nineteenth-Century Britain and the Low Countries* (Leiden/Boston: Brill, 2013), 19–41.

[98] Lukács, *The Historical Novel*, 24.

needed to be performed, experienced and seen across the continent. That is why they staged their victories in all kinds of cultural performances and celebrations, shaped their monarchies, played the balance-of-power card, compounded their hierarchical outlook and thus tried to calm the tides of time – as will be expanded on below.

Staging Victory

For the 'men of 1815', the picture they liked best portrayed a banquet of kings and sovereigns, returning to their rightful, hereditary and legitimate thrones – hailed home by their grateful populaces. And in fact, it has indeed been recounted how the three Allied rulers who defeated Napoleon – Tsar Alexander of Russia, King Friedrich Wilhelm III of Prussia and Emperor Franz I of Austria – were received on 25 September 1814 as the 'blessed' bestowers and 'angels' of peace.[99] Gratitude was expressed in musical renderings of homage and joy that spread across borders and could be heard in all the capitals of Europe.[100] Beethoven had already pulled out all the stops in his orchestral work *Wellingtons Sieg oder die Schlacht bei Vittoria*, first performed in Vienna in December 1813: a deafening musical tribute, with 'Rule Britannia' and 'God Save the King' (and even 'For He's a Jolly Good Fellow') woven into it, in honour of the Duke of Wellington, commemorating his June 1813 defeat of Joseph Bonaparte in Spain.[101] Anton Diabelli's 'tone portrait' *The 18th of October* was performed in Vienna in 1814, on the occasion of the first anniversary of the Battle of Leipzig; other composers followed suit.[102] The musical event of the season in St Petersburg was the anniversary of the French invasion, which they referred to as the Patriotic War of 1812. The Invalid Concert celebrated the entry of Russian troops into Paris at the end of the Napoleonic Wars. The militaristic concert, with martial symphonies, regimental marches and a rendition of 'God Save the King', was meant to 'support those Russian Invalids ... who, with their blood, redeemed *the freedom of Europe*'.[103] The reference to Allied solidarity and a common European destiny shone through in these early post-war years, before nationalism and patriotism glossed over these more international reminiscences.

With momentous gatherings, celebrations and processions, ceremonial troop inspections and commemorations of Allied battles the kings, emperors and their entourage purposefully mobilized and staged such expressions of

[99] *Friedensblätter*, 40:1 (October 1814), 166, cited in Vick, *The Congress of Vienna*, 25.
[100] See Jensen, *Celebrating Peace*, 163–82.
[101] L. van Beethoven, *Wellingtons Sieg oder die Schlacht bei Vittoria*, op. 91, completed in October 1813, premiered in Vienna on 8 December 1813.
[102] Vick, *The Congress of Vienna*, 15.
[103] Cited in L. Sargeant, *Harmony and Discord. Music and the Transformation of Russian Cultural Life* (Oxford: Oxford University Press, 2011), 30–1. Emphasis added.

gratitude for their victory and return. Inspections of the troops, ceremonial tributes and commemorative exercises were wonderful occasions where inhabitants of the region (irrespective of whether these parades took place in Paris, Leipzig, Austerlitz or Vienna), high-ranking guests, their armed forces and an international travelling circus of sutlers, memorabilia vendors, musicians, composers, diplomats and their ladies found each other participating in a common experience.[104] A unique example of this was the commemoration of the Battle of Waterloo. Lady Shelley and her husband were not the only ones to jump straight into a coach and travel off to the mainland intent on visiting the hero of Waterloo, Wellington, and hearing from him personally the stories he had to tell. Countless tourists flocked to Belgium in order to get a tour of the still corpse-strewn fields near Quatre-Bras and Waterloo, 15 km south of Brussels.[105] Walter Scott, too, crossed the Channel in August 1815, in a rush to see the battlefield with his own eyes. His poem 'The Field of Waterloo' was published in October 1815 and sold well; his travel notes and accounts were published a year later in his *Paul's Letters to his Kinsfolk*.[106] This recollection of the horrors of the battlefield, which is then contrasted with the sound cause and calm determination of the Allied generals, as well as with the peace and quiet that followed, is also reflected in the paintings of J. M. W. Turner, and the historical representations of many other painters who committed the ravages of Waterloo to canvas.[107]

Even in France – the country that had little reason to be thankful and that would still have to cope with an extended period of humiliation and occupation following years of exhausting wars – there was initially some talk of joy and gratitude. According to the French historian Henry Houssaye, who published a series of detailed accounts of the years 1814 and 1815 between 1888 and 1899, public spirit was deeply shaken, but the royalists, supporters of the Bourbon dynasty, did express some initial support for the Allies who reinstated Louis XVIII to the throne. The Allied forces were not the enemy; they were the liberators. At least, that was the collective sentiment the French king himself tried to stir up. In March and April 1814, the king proclaimed, 'Frenchmen . . .

---

[104] For more about the anniversary celebrations of the Battle of Leipzig, the Battle of the Nations, in October 1814, see e.g. Vick, *The Congress of Vienna*, 47–8, 67.

[105] Edgcumbe (ed.), *The Diary of Frances Lady Shelley, 1787–1817*, 167–75.

[106] W. Scott, 'The Field of Waterloo; A Poem'. First printed by James Ballantyne and Co. for Archibald Constable and Co. (Edinburgh); and Longman, Hurst, Rees, Orme and Brown, and John Murray (London), 1815. For critics of Scott, see Marquess of Anglesey (ed.), *The Capel Letters. Being the Correspondence of Lady Caroline Capel and her Daughters with the Dowager Countess of Uxbridge from Brussels and Switzerland 1814–1817* (London: Jonathan Cape, 1955), 150. See also C. Kennedy, 'From the Ballroom to the Battlefield. British Women and Waterloo', in Forrest, Hagemann and Rendall (eds.), *Soldiers*, 137–56, here: 143.

[107] For example J. M. W. Turner, *The Field of Waterloo*, unveiled at the Royal Academy in 1818.

receive these generous allies as friends, open to them the gates of your towns, forestall the violence which a criminal and useless resistance cannot fail to draw down upon you, and let their entrance into France be welcomed with joy.'[108] Of course, this was more make-do than an expression of heartfelt sentiments within the court elites, since most (ultra-)royalists preferred that the Allies should leave post-haste.

In the cultural imagination, national heroism in these early post-war years still went hand in glove with references to Europe and to the joint struggle against Napoleon. In 1817, on one of the Blackdown Hills overlooking Wellington, in Somerset county, the first stone was laid for an enormous (53 m tall) obelisk to honour the victory at Waterloo. The inscriptions at the base express 'Gratitude and Admiration' for the Duke of Wellington, whose accomplishments were seen as Olympian in nature, honouring his efforts both within Europe and beyond. His work as colonizer in India was celebrated right along with his victory over Napoleon: 'India protected', 'Spain and Portugal rescued', 'Republican tyranny subdued', 'The Netherlands saved, and Europe delivered'.[109] A similar monument was erected in Dublin, this one being 62 m tall (thereby breaking European records), once again noting praise for Wellington's efforts on Europe's behalf:

> Asia and Europe, sav'd by thee, proclaim
> Invincible in war thy deathless name,
> Now round thy brow the civic oak we twine,
> That every earthly glory may be thine.[110]

That intertwining of national pride and service to Europe is found elsewhere as well: for example, already in 1813, when King Willem I (the Sovereign Prince), just after arriving in the Netherlands in December 1813, thanked the Russian tsar for his part in restoring Dutch sovereignty 'in the midst of other independent European nations'.[111] Similar words are inscribed on the national monument dedicated to the restoration of Dutch independence in 1813, which was erected in The Hague in 1869 by order of King Willem III (Willem I's grandson). On the north side of the sturdy square pedestal, which is crowned with the triumphant Dutch Maiden, the three men who helped found the kingdom and organize Willem's return are rendered in bronze; on the east and

---

[108] 'Proclamation du roi aux Francais, Louis-Joseph de Bourbon, prince de Condé aux Français', cited in Houssaye, *1814*, 20–1. Houssaye, *Napoleon and the Campaign of 1814* (trans. R. McClintock, London: Hugh Rees, 1914), 17.

[109] Muir, *Wellington: Waterloo and the Fortunes of Peace*, 470; 'The Wellington Monument of Somerset', *Bath Chronicle and Weekly Gazette*, 20 January 1853.

[110] Muir, *Wellington: Waterloo and the Fortunes of Peace*, 470; P. Garnett, 'The Wellington Testimonial', *Dublin Historical Record*, 13:2 (1952), 48–61.

[111] Letters from Willem I to Tsar Alexander, reproduced in A. van der Zwaan, 'Holland is vrij. Dankzij Rusland', *Thema Tijdschrift*, 4:4 (2013), 44–7; A. Aalders, *Met gevelde lans en losse teugel. Kozakken in Nederland, 1813–1814* (Bedum: Egbert Forsten, 2002).

west sides are two female figures; above the female figure representing History
there is a quote attributed to one of those three founding fathers, Gijsbert Karel
van Hogendorp, which may be loosely translated: 'The fatherland has once
again returned to the rank and file of European peoples.'[112] Europe did indeed
play a role in the imagination and cultural vocabulary of liberation; in 1815, the
popular poetess Petronella Moens published a heroic ode entitled 'On
Napoleon Bonaparte's Entering Paris'.[113] In it she calls up the spectre of the
return of the 'monster':

> Terror intoxicates my soul. A fearful and terrible darkness,
> Oh Providence! has totally engulfed your steps.
> Peoples' guardian angels rejoiced, wreathed in the rays of the morning;
> But now of a sudden it is night and calamity's thunder roars.
> Millions of lives, through which the common weal had begun to grow;
> Millions of lives, for which the source of joy was flowing,
> Are now paralysed by grief or undone by death –
> And the life of an executioner, who fixes himself on corpses,
> For whom hellish compunction long spoiled all his pleasure,
> That life burns on and smothers Europe's peace.

The poet then encourages fathers, sons, women and 'Dutch virgins' to support
the war effort, but not before making an urgent appeal to the crowned heads of
Europe:

> Oh come, come you who have been crowned by God!
> Come! Avenge the people's right to be redeemed!
> Plait in those renewed laurels of war
> Europe's lush green olive branches.
> All your triumphing was in vain,
> When the predator's eagles are set to rise again,
> Then God's chorales sang your fame,
> Crowned with rays of light, for naught; –
> Then *Moscow* burned for nothing![114]

---

[112] See K. Schulten, *Plein 1813. Het Nationaal Monument in Den Haag* (The Hague: Hega Offset, 2013).

[113] See L. Jensen, 'A poem by Petronella Moens: "Bij het intrekken van Napoleon Buonaparte in Parijs"', via: www.100days.eu/items/show/61 (last viewed: 13 April 2019); L. Jensen, 'De hand van broederschap toegereikt: Nederlandse identiteiten en identiteitsbesef in 1815', in F. Judo and S. van de Perre (eds.), *Belg of Bataaf. De wording van het Verenigd Koninkrijk der Nederlanden* (Antwerp: Polis, 2015), 79–101.

[114] P. Moens, *Bij het intrekken van Napoleon Buonaparte in Parijs* (Utrecht: Zimmerman, 1815). (The eagles, here, refer to the decorative ones atop the standards of the Grande Armée.) See, as well, the poem 'Vaderlander', *Strijd! Voor God! Den Koning! En het Vaderland* (Amsterdam, 1815).

In the poems that appeared during or after Napoleon's final Hundred Days, as well as in the many literary depictions of the Battle of Waterloo, the emphasis fell on the 'peace of Europe' in contrast to the bloodthirstiness and chaos of the 'monster' who marched with eagles and subjected peoples. In the emotional vocabulary of the post-war years, these references return time and again: abhorrence for both the revolutionary chaos and Napoleon's despotism, the joy and relief that peace and the end of the war brought, praise for one's own national heroes and the recognition of European solidarity and the results of Allied unanimity.[115]

Shaping Post-War Monarchy

The political currency of the balance-of-power system in 1815 was, in fact, monarchical power. The Concert of Europe rested on the monarchy as the foundation of order. Already in November 1813, with the Battle of Leipzig just behind them and the Dutch revolting to regain their independence, Castlereagh had expressed his preference for a resurrection of the Orange rule in the Netherlands. Because, as Dutch Prince Willem transmitted the British strategy towards restructuring the European map to Gagern, post-war rule needed to be 'more monarchical' than before.[116]

The new European peace rested on a series of crowned heads who, given the constraint of the circumstances, rallied together behind the new order. They were the pillars of the balance of power.[117] That monarchical enthusiasm was not so much inspired by a desire to return to the days of the *ancien régime*. The ruling elites did not particularly wanted the old order back, but they craved new forms of governance that would, better than the traditional ones, sustain security and protect the continent against new outbursts of war and revolution. The monarchy had to see to that – a new form of government that was, for many countries, not a return to pre-Napoleonic federative relationships, but one that promised a more central and uniform system. In 1813–15, the Netherlands, Norway, Hanover, Lombardy–Venetia, Sardinia–Piedmont, the Two Sicilies and Congress Poland entered a monarchist period (again), with Belgium and Greece joining this list in 1830–2. In addition, Switzerland, the German Confederation and the Netherlands each adopted a new constitution,

---

[115] Cf. (De) Graaf, 'Bringing Sense and Sensibility'; C. Nübel, 'Auf der Suche nach Stabilität: 1813 und die Restauration der Monarchie im europäischen Vergleich', in B. Aschmann and T. Stamm-Kuhlmann (eds.), *1813 im Europäische Kontext* (Stuttgart: Steiner, 2015), 163–86.

[116] Letter from Willem I to Hans von Gagern, his plenipotentiary at the headquarters of the Allied forces, 2 November 1813, HStD, no. O11 and no. B32. See also (De) Graaf, 'Second-tier Diplomacy'.

[117] Cf. V. Sellin, *Gewalt und Legitimität. Die europäische Monarchie im Zeitalter der Revolutionen* (Munich: Oldenbourg, 2011).

and France a constitutional charter. For the Netherlands – which in the British plans for the continent was to play a crucial role – this was a remarkable development, since the country had from 1648 onwards always been a republic, headed by stadtholders rather than by monarchs. This advocacy for a new constitutional order, whether or not crowned by a king or emperor, caught on in the colonies of Spain, Portugal and France as well. At the Congress of Chilpancingo (September–November 1813), Mexico declared independence from Spain, ratified a national constitution and, after a number of wars between royalists and insurgents, even appointed an emperor in 1821.[118] These tendencies also spilled over into the principalities of the Danube, under Ottoman rule, where the rulers initiated a series of centralizing reforms. So too, John George Caradja, governor (*hospodar*) of the Danubian Principalities, saw wisdom in implementing a code of law in 1818, which was a combination of the Napoleonic *Code Civil* and local legal traditions, in order to strengthen his princely reign.[119]

This upsurge of monarchical enthusiasm, more or less embedded in refor-mulated constitutions, was part of the blueprint for a new balance of power that, when it came to power and security, could draw on standing laws, (redefined) constitutions and tradition. It was not only the restoration of new and old monarchies, but also the reciprocal intertwining of those dynasties that pointed to a joint European need to have the balance of power be supported by power (coming from the monarchies) as well as authority and law (constitu-tions and books of law). The fraternization among and increased communica-tion between the European dynasties, thanks in part to the 'horseback diplomacy' that arose during the wars that the Allies fought, has been under-scored in much of the literature of late.[120] Those ties were perpetuated after 1815 in treaties and subsequent marriages. (The Dutch Crown Prince, later King Willem II was to wed the British crown Princess Charlotte, but married Anna Pavlovna, sister of Alexander I, instead; Willem's father, Willem I, was married to the sister of the Prussian King Friedrich Wilhelm III; the afore-mentioned Charlotte became the spouse of the German Prince Leopold, who would become the king of Belgium in 1830; etc.) The royalty of 1815 realized only too well that they owed their new or reinstated position to each other. That

---

[118] See M. Costeloe, *Response to Revolution. Imperial Spain and the Spanish American Revolutions, 1810–1840* (Cambridge: Cambridge University Press, 1986); J. Chasteen, *Americanos. Latin America's Struggle for Independence* (Oxford: Oxford University Press, 2008).

[119] A. Oțetea, *Fuga lui Caragea* ['The flight of Caradja'], in *Omagiu lui P. Constantinescu-Iași. cu prilejul împlinirii a 70 de ani* ['Tribute to P. Constantinescu-Iași on the occasion of his 70th birthday'] (Bucharest: Editura Academiei Republicii Populare Romîne, 1965); W. Wilkinson, *An Account of the Principalities of Wallachia and Moldavia with Various Political Observations Relating to Them* (London: Longman, 1820).

[120] Paulmann, *Pomp und Politik*. See also Mitzen, *Power in Concert*.

was especially true for the smaller and middle-sized, younger realms; 'older' empires were more on the granting than on the receiving end. But they were all more than happy to let themselves be depicted and immortalized in group portraits. They appeared together at major parades and troop inspections, they bestowed military honours on each other, and in so doing created a European language of artefacts and art objects that underscored their common destiny and salutary effect in the cause of all European nations.

Once the last weapons had been mothballed, these new kings and princes were sung a *Te Deum* by the people in almost every capital city in Europe, whether that was a version composed by Haydn, Mozart or Lully. Chorales and the *Te Deum*'s *Salvum fac populum tuum, Domine* ('Save Thy people, O Lord') echoed through the churches and cathedrals of Vienna, Brussels,[121] London, Madrid and Buenos Aires, but also in smaller towns, like Oudenaarde in Belgium – all to the greater honour and glory of God, but above all as praise to their God-given monarchs.[122] Artists like Penning, Wilkie and Canova were commissioned to immortalize these new rulers as seen at the scene of their victory, and as thus having contributed to the cause of Europe's liberation. After 1815, a king did not really count if the most famous sculptor of the day, the Italian Antonio Canova, had not (yet) sculpted his noble features in marble.[123] In his dining room at Apsley House, Wellington fashioned a veritable royal 'who's who', with portraits of Willem I, Louis XVIII, Friedrich Wilhelm III and other European kings hanging on the walls of what today is known as the Waterloo Gallery, looking down on a lavishly bedecked table that could seat more than eighty guests. The annual 18 June banquet that he hosted for the first time in 1820, celebrating the Battle of Waterloo, continued on until his death in 1852.

With these old and new monarchs, security reigned, and respectability – at least that was the image that these sovereigns aimed to convey. The new rulers were not about to flaunt the exaggerated pomp of a Napoleon or to stoop to power-mongering or whimsy. They posed as fathers of their peoples, as patresfamilias, by also literally surrounding themselves with their relatives on portraits and at ceremonies, and by embracing the bourgeois virtues of loyalty, moderation and domesticity (even though it was more for show than

---

[121] See 'Te Deum in de Sint-Michiel-en Sint-Goedelekerk'. Print series of the inauguration of Willem I as king of the Netherlands in Brussels in 1815. J. Gibèle and P. Leroy, 1815, The Hague, Koninklijke Verzamelingen.

[122] See the announcements of the church service in 1814 en 1815, City Archive Oudenaerde (SAO); P. Ortemberg, 'El tedeum en el ritual político: Usos y sentidos de un dispositivo de pactos en la América española y en la revolucion de Mayo', *Anuario del Instituto de Historia Argentina*, 10 (2010), 199–226.

[123] Cf. K. Eustace, '"Questa scabrosa missione": Canova in Paris and London in 1815', in Eustace (ed.), *Canova Ideal Heads* (Oxford: Ashmolean Museum, 1997), 9–38.

actually sincere).[124] Citizens of these old and new kingdoms were invited to project their own desires for public contentment, peace and tranquillity onto the royal family.[125] Early nineteenth-century sentiments of patriotism should not, therefore, be confused with the surge of popular nationalism in later decades. In the newly created Kingdom of the Netherlands during 1813–15, national elation was related to the end of the war and the restoration of a stable form of government.[126] Motives for feelings of relief also included the return of an – allegedly – benevolent and compassionate king, as opposed to that emperor without mercy, Napoleon.[127] In Ghent, the city's fourteenth-century belfry spewed fire once again when the Prince of Orange passed through; so too, church bells pealed in every self-respecting city on the birth-day of one of the princes or princesses.

Incumbent royalty joined the efforts of those (re)ascending to the throne by casting themselves in such familiar representations. Even Tsar Alexander I, for all of his grandiloquent manners and sense of grandeur, made clear that he was a fatherly reformer, and very approachable – as demonstrated by his inclina-tion to stoop down to pat a child, for example.[128] Friedrich Wilhelm III of Prussia, too, tried to present his weak government as 'fatherly': something that worked reasonably well during the initially enthusiastic years after the 'wars of liberation', as the Napoleonic Wars were referred to in the German lands, but that became increasingly difficult with the course of increased repression that he charted after 1817.[129] Friedrich's Bourbon colleague, Louis XVIII, was more successful, presenting himself, for example in his *Charte Constitutionelle*, as a benevolent paterfamilias who wanted to cover the terror of the past with the cloak of oblivion:

> Happy to find ourselves once more in the bosom of our great family, we can only respond to the love of which we have received so many

[124] Cf. M. Lok and N. Scholz, 'The Return of the Loving Father: Masculinity, Legitimacy and the French and Dutch Restoration Monarchies (1813-1815)', *BMGN-Low Countries Historical Review*, 127:1 (2012), 19–44.

[125] See J. van der Palm, *Geschied- en redekunstig gedenkschrift van Nederlands herstelling in den jare 1813* (Amsterdam, 1816), 156–7.

[126] H. te Velde, *Over het begrijpen van 1813 tweehonderd jaar later* (The Hague: National Archives, 2013), 34–8. See also L. Jensen and B. Verheijen, 'De betekenis van 1813 voor het gewone volk: Oranje boven!', *Thema Tijdschrift*, 4:4 (2013), 10–11; L. Jensen, *Verzet tegen Napoleon* (Nijmegen: Vantilt, 2013).

[127] Cf. Lok and Scholz, 'The Return of the Loving Father', 31, 33; M. Grever, 'Van Landsvader tot moeder des vaderlands: Oranje, gender en Nederland', *Groniek*, 158/9 (2002), 131–45.

[128] He also took good care of his illegitimate children. Rey, *Alexander I*, 132–3, 270–74; A. McConnell, 'Alexander I's Hundred Days: The Politics of a Paternalist Reformer', *Slavic Review*, 28:3 (1969), 373–93.

[129] See, for example, *Allgemeine Zeitung*, 27 February 1816, 232; cf. J. Luh, *Der kurze Traum de Freiheit. Preussen nach Napoleon* (Munich: Siedler, 2015).

testimonials by uttering words of peace and consolation. The dearest wish of our heart is that all Frenchmen should live as brothers, and that no bitter memory should ever disturb the security that must follow the solemn decree that we grant to them today.[130]

This text was clearly intended also to speak to that part of France that did not belong to the royalist camp and lamented the loss of their emperor. Enthusiasm in France for the monarchy was, in addition, a double-edged sword: in its ultra-royalist form it would push the king from the frying pan into the fire. After 1814, the French political landscape was divided amongst three officially tolerated groups: the ultra-royalists, the constitutional-moderate royalists and the liberals. But Louis XVIII still tried to reconcile them with each other and with the new situation by proposing a *gouvernement paternel*.[131] That motto – of the king as benevolent father of the family attending to its harmony and happiness – was quickly incorporated into the cultural imagery of France. Many poets and novelists put mothers in the limelight, who thanked their king for the end of the war; for example, in 'La Bonne Mère', from December 1815: 'mes enfants, je vous conservai; Louis nous a délivré de la conscription' ('my children, I preserved you; Louis has freed us from conscription').[132] A tangential advantage of focusing on mothers, and on gratitude for the king, was that the defeat (and hence emasculation) of French men was, in so doing, sidestepped. In the light of all of that homely and familial imagery, the Duke of Wellington remained quite sceptical. The only government in Europe that could truly own the epithet 'really paternal government' was Austria's, he contended, having a soft spot for Austria's Emperor Franz I.[133]

Indeed, from a perspective of centralized, modern bureaucratic rule, the monarchy was the most adequate form of government. From the vantage point of legitimacy, however, one of the pet principles of conservative pundits and politicians, monarchical rulers had a serious problem to face. The global wars of the revolutionary and Napoleonic era had undermined their legitimacy fundamentally, not just in Europe but elsewhere too. The Revolution had

---

[130] *Charte Constitutionelle*, Préambule, 4 June 1814.

[131] See, for example, *Collection des Discours du Trône. Seconde édition* (Paris: Boucher, 1826), 13; M. Maurin, *À la gloire de l'auguste famille des Bourbons, épître à Louis XVIII, roi de France et de Navarre suivie de Ode sur la misère* (Dijon: Carion, 1814). Not everyone accepted that suggestion; see, for example, the bitter critique by the royalist Antoine Galland of Louis's proposed 'paternal government' in Galland, *Du Retour des Bourbons en France*, 19–22.

[132] 'La Bonne Mère', 2 December 1815, cited in J. Heuer, '"No More Fears, No More Tears"? Gender, Emotion and the Aftermath of the Napoleonic Wars in France', *Gender & History*, 282:2 (2016), 438–60, here: 450 n. 71.

[133] According to Lady Shelley, Edgcumbe (ed.), *The Diary of Frances Lady Shelley, 1787–1817*, 114.

brought an end to enlightened despotism everywhere, and even in the places where it lingered – in Southern Europe, Latin America or Russia – the idea of reform and constitutionalism could not be put back in the bottle. Even in those countries the state apparatus had been centralized, the power of the aristocracy over state affairs had been reduced and in Prussia for example serfdom had been abolished. Alexander had introduced a constitution to the Grand Duchy of Warsaw and had improved the educational system. The list of irreversible changes to the old dynastical system are countless. To the eternal dismay of the returning French *émigrés* and their fellow ultra-conservative compatriots elsewhere, the registration of births, marriages and deaths had been assigned to secular authorities and would not revert back to the church, whereas religious power and privileges had been further reduced by, for example, the introduction of civil marriage and divorce and education. This could all be summed up by the observation that with all the pomp and circumstance surrounding their victories, 'the basis of sovereignty had shifted perceptibly from individuals and families to nations and states'. The international treaties of the *ancien régime* were considered invalid upon the demise of a sovereign; after 1815 treaties were no longer concluded between princes and sovereigns, but between states: 'The prince or ruler became, in effect, the executor of national or state sovereignty guaranteed by international agreement with the virtual force of law.'[134]

Indeed, almost all of the newly restored sovereigns that were so keen on flaunting their crowns in front of the cheering masses in 1815 had to adapt to a more restraining environment and political context. As a condition for Louis XVIII's allegedly paternal and benign monarchy to flourish, the Allied powers were adamant about binding it by a constitution, and not completely renouncing the liberal gains of the Revolution and the Empire.[135] Their order was still absolute (since most kings could dissolve their assemblies, whereas they could not even introduce a budget of their own), but it was now unavoidably tempered by legislatures, bicameral systems or representative assemblies. Without general support and without a willingness to make concessions to the people, royal rule and the European balance of power would not be stable. Even in the most absolutist of monarchies, such as Austria, Prussia and the Kingdom of Naples, rulers were apprehensive about *l'esprit public* as well as publicists and pamphleteers. However much Louis XVIII wanted to dismiss the Revolution and the Napoleonic period as a 'nightmare' and to pick up the old thread again, he could not help but align himself with a number of crucial transformations.[136] Michael Broers distinguishes three types of regimes in this

---

[134] Evans, *The Pursuit of Power*, 15–23, 28. See also J. Sperber, *Revolutionary Europe, 1780–1850* (London/New York: Routledge, 2017 [2000]), 236–72.

[135] See for example the insistence of Pozzo di Borgo on a liberal constitution: Pozzo to Nesselrode, 11/23 May 1815, in Pozzo (ed.), *Correspondance*, vol. 2, 134–41.

[136] Cf. M. Lok, '"Renouer la chaîne des temps" ou "repartir à zéro"? Passé, présent, futur en France et aux Pays-Bas (1814–1815)', *Revue d'histoire du XIXe siècle*, 49 (2014), 79–92 ;

connection: monarchies that allowed themselves to be bound by some sort of constitution and legislature (the Netherlands, France and Baden), monarchies that embraced the reforms and administrative centralization introduced during the Napoleonic era, but refused to be constrained by a constitution (Prussia and Austria) and kingdoms that radically rejected all of the accomplishments of the revolutionary and Napoleonic period and literally wanted to turn back the clock (Spain and Piedmont–Sardinia).[137] But even there, more than ever before 1789, the power of royalty was increasingly tied perhaps not to the binding practice, but at least to the notion or principle of constitutional order that floated over the market. Legitimacy required more than simply an appeal to the divine principles of providence and hereditary succession.

Owing to their diplomats, the new trend of monarchical rule was explicitly linked to the principle of the European balance of power. Diplomatic praxis around 1815 was clearly not a matter of unilaterally conveying the wishes issued from the throne back home and voicing national interests without listening to other interests at stake. A new generation of professional administrators and highly cosmopolitan diplomats had emerged and was running international affairs. Beginning in 1813, their gathering round negotiating tables, copious dinners, whist-playing and endless conversations began to create an *esprit de corps* that was defining a new Europe. Behind the scenes of monarchical restoration, a new caste of European officials and envoys was rising to the occasion of negotiating armistices and treaties – that increasingly nudged their monarchs into contributing to this newly emerging European security arrangement.

Playing the Balance-of-Power Card

All lofty poems and sentiments aside, the 'secondary' states and principalities knew that they could only move forward by accepting, embracing and appropriating the great powers' system. Many therefore immediately jumped to the occasion and integrated the balance-of-power principle into their diplomatic discourse. In countries such as Spain, Portugal, the Netherlands, Bavaria and Hanover for example, the notion of the European balance of power was inserted immediately into foreign policy arguments.

Dutch diplomats, for example, tried to mobilize Spain and Britain to support a joint expedition against the Barbary corsairs off the North African coast in this fashion. After the collective peace of Europe had been confirmed, the predatory practices of the Barbary pirates began increasingly to work on Europe's nerves. Their attacks – taking crew and passengers captive without

---

see also Lok, *Windvanen*, 55–60; E. de Waresquiel, *L'histoire à rebrousse-poil. Les élites, la Restauration, la Révolution* (Paris : Fayard, 2005), 60.
[137] Broers, *Europe after Napoleon*, 13.

reprieve and enslaving them or demanding that ransom be paid – and the blackmail that power lords in Algiers, Tunis and Tripoli used with prowess were considered an unacceptable affront to peace and civilization.[138] After the Dey of Algiers and his fleet captured Danish, Swedish and Dutch ships during the summer of 1815, that was the last straw for Hendrik Fagel, the Dutch ambassador in London. In emotional language, he tried to convince Castlereagh to intervene – while appropriating the British minister's own vernacular. Given the peace on the continent, were not, so he argued, the 'depredations' of the Barbary rovers particularly 'insufferable'? Since the balance of power on the continent had now been restored, thanks to British sacrifices, should it not be a responsibility of the Allied powers to fight this Barbary terror in the Mediterranean and pacify that region as well?[139]

Attempts to rally Spanish support for such an Allied intervention were equally cast in balancing metaphors. The Dutch ambassador in Madrid, Hugo Baron van Zuylen van Nijevelt, explained to his Spanish partners that this was precisely an excellent opportunity to jointly bolster the European balance. His country supported the British initiative, 'for the sake of commerce and colonies', as well as with an eye to 'tranquility', rest and peace on the continent. It was, after all, as the British and Dutch admirals Exmouth and Van de Cappellen expressed it later, a collaborative 'act in the Cause of Humanity'.[140] Moreover, Van Zuylen van Nijevelt added, again from the perspective of the balance of power, the smaller powers urgently needed Britain to provide a counterbalance to Russia's efforts to expand its sphere of influence in and around the Mediterranean. Only a multilateral force would be able to contain individual aggression, or even a conflagration between European powers.[141] As an envoy from a smaller country, and as a satellite of Britain, Van Zuylen understood what would best serve the interests of the Netherlands: the risk of a Russian show of power along the coast of Africa could only be contained by the countervailing presence of another great power. In other words, thinking in terms of a European balance of power was also picked up by smaller, non-imperial powers.

---

[138] E. de Lange, Menacing Tides. Piracy, Security and Imperialism in the Nineteenth-Century Mediterranean (unpublished PhD thesis, Utrecht University, 2019); D. Panzac, Barbary Corsairs. The End of a Legend, 1800–1820 (Leiden: Brill, 2005); M. Kempe, Fluch der Weltmeere. Piraterie, Völkerrecht und Internationale Beziehungen (Frankfurt: Campus, 2010), 286; Vick, The Congress of Vienna, 194, 217.

[139] Fagel to Castlereagh, 9 November 1815, TNA, FO 37/84. With thanks to Erik de Lange. See also Fagel to Van Nagell, two years later, on 18 February 1817, National Archive, The Hague (NL-HaNA), 2.05.44, inv. no. 59.

[140] 'Exchange between Van Capellen and Exmouth', Bay of Gibraltar, 10 August 1816, NL-HaNA, 2.05.44, inv. no. 59.

[141] Cf. Van Zuylen to Van Nagell, Madrid, 26 August 1816, NL-HaNA, 'Dutch Envoy in Spain, Letters to Foreign Affairs, July 1816–December 1817', no. 2.05.46, inv. no. 16; (Van) Sas, Onze natuurlijkste bondgenoot.

In another strategically important corner of Europe, the Balkans and the Danube Delta also knew what was 'on', and embraced the balance vocabulary. Friedrich von Gentz had been, with the full knowledge of Metternich, deliberately busy in those parts teaching the *hospodars* (governors), who, in the name of the Ottomans, governed the Romanian principalities in relative autonomy, about the benefits of balance-thinking – in a manner entirely favourable to Austria, of course. Gentz, who always seemed short of money, sold his lessons and reports regarding the state of international relationships and movements in the European capitals for a pretty penny.[142] John George Caradja (1754–1844), who had been appointed *hospodar* by Sultan Mahmud II in 1812, invested a small fortune in Gentz's efforts and learned much. On the one hand, Gentz's reports helped him to appease those in the High Porte in Istanbul. On the other hand, he suggested to the Austrians that the *hospodars* would do everything they could to avoid a new Russian occupation or a Russian–Turkish war. For Gentz, it was equally important to learn from Caradja whether or not the Russians were in fact expanding their sphere of influence along the Danube.[143] Caradja played along for a while, but in 1815 took the safest way out when it appeared that the prestige of Russia, which in the Balkans was seen to have been the major factor in Napoleon's defeat, had increased enormously. As it stood, Caradja knew that Alexander was a proponent of peace, but he did not know how long the tsar would continue to respect the lines of the territorial balance of power drawn up in Vienna. However, when Alexander came to question his convictions about the prospect of peace and no longer excluded the possibility of military action, Caradja had seen enough. He was not about to adopt a wait-and-see attitude regarding the potential after-effects in the Balkans and the principalities of that tilting of the balance of power. The *hospodar* emptied his principality's treasury and left with his family for Austrian-ruled Transylvania.[144]

Across the width of the continent and beyond, the idea and principle of balance-thinking was expressly adopted. For reasons of cunning, or given

---

[142] P. Sweet, *Friedrich von Gentz. Defender of the Old Order* (Madison: University of Wisconsin Press, 1935), 283; A. Prokesch-Osten (ed.), *Dépêches inédites du Chevalier de Gentz aux Hospodars de Valachie pour servir à l'histoire de la politique européenne (1813 à 1828)*, vol. 1 (Paris: Plon, 1876). With thanks to Constantin Ardeleanu.

[143] See e.g. Gentz to Caradja, 16 January 1817, in Prokesch-Osten (ed.), *Dépêches inédites*, 277.

[144] Cf. C. von Klinkowström (ed.), *Aus der alten Registratur der Staatskanzlei. Briefe politischen Inhalts von und an Friedrich von Gentz aus den Jahren 1799–1827* (Vienna: Wilhelm Braumüller, 1870), 118–48; Oțetea, 'Fuga lui Caragea', 386; A. Pippidi, 'Jean Caradja et ses amis de Genève', printed in Pippidi, *Hommes et idées du sud-est européen à l'aube de l'âge moderne* (Bucharest: Editura Academiei Republicii Socialiste România, 1980), 295–314; Pippidi, 'Notules phanariotes, II, Encore Jean Caradja à Genève', *Ho Eranistes*, 17 (1981), 74–85; Wilkinson, *An Account of the Principalities of Wallachia and Moldavia*, 122–3.

a shared sense of morality, it became part of the ideological undercarriage in the caravan of the four great powers. Of course, one should not presume that ignorance and indifference prevailed amongst the general public regarding the new European peace plan. Newspaper-reading citizens were aware of which treaties were being considered and which were adopted. Crowds in London, Vienna and Paris let their presence be felt with their applause and cheering for visiting Allied sovereigns and their entourage during processions, parades and marches. But their war-wearied existential relief upon the end of the war was more often than not behind their enthusiasm, rather than any genuine interest in this new phase of European integration. Given their more or less fear-filled expectations, they were more inclined to feel out the situation. Those both inside and outside France who were inclined to value Europe's efforts in this regard expressed themselves for the most part indirectly, via praise and accolades for their own sovereigns, who, despite everything, had done their part so well in the midst of the other monarchs and princes.[145]

For most of the peoples of Europe, the concerns and theories of the imperial powers were of little consequence. Their delight with the peace soon gave way to the order of the day. In the Netherlands, the 's Gravenhaagsche Courant tried to stir the interest of citizens in the European treaties. On 8 June 1814 it published the text of the Treaty of Paris, together with an announcement that a 'general congress', to be held in Vienna, would further work out questions relating to peace and security in Europe. In the same edition, the poetry society 'Kunstliefde spaart geen vlijt' ('Love of Art Spares No Diligence') announced a competition for the best poem on the theme 'The Peace of 1814',[146] and, a year later, on the theme 'Europe's General Peace restored'. There were few submissions.[147] Creative energy and enthusiasm were apparently hard to come by when it came to inspired responses to Europe's general peace and security. The new order was symbolized in stone and on canvas, and diplomats knew their way with the balancing discourse, but the project of European cooperation had yet to stir the average citizen's involvement much at all.

An Exclusive Club

This was indeed the major flaw in this system of post-war peace. The entire balance-of-power construct, as written up in the treaties, was in spite of everything the project of an elite men's club that deliberated and decided these matters in private. In that, the new imperial order differed little from

---

[145] See e.g. Beugnot, *Mémoires*, 106–8.
[146] *'s Gravenhaagsche Courant*, 8 June 1814. With thanks to Ronald Gonsalves.
[147] *Rotterdamsche Courant*, 7 March 1815, 5 November 1816.

Napoleon's elitist project; the French Empire, too, was most appreciated by top-ranking officials, directors and the new nobility.[148] After 1815, it was once again a small group of power brokers that determined what the future was to look like: stable, monarchical and with room for only gradual and limited reforms. They controlled the networks of undercover agents and spies and had a monopoly on information, on the basis of which they determined who or what the threats were that were rising or waning on the horizon or in their worst nightmares. They were the ones who levelled the sanctions: fines, gag orders, exile and persecution, imprisonment or execution – or sometimes grace. Even in countries where the parliament's words carried (some) weight, as in the Dutch States General, the British Commons and the French Chamber of Peers, these were aristocratic peers and wealthy gentlemen who differed with each other about the length of the list of suspects. For the critics, who saw how the Revolution's lists of human rights were removed from the statutes, this restorative system smacked too much of nepotism and the repression of the *ancien régime*.

Becoming a member of this club of decision makers was almost impossible; even with a peerage or age-old lineage in hand, the criteria for inclusion lacked transparency. The size of the country, army and treasury, as well as the proper pedigree of the gentleman in question certainly influenced the level of one's access to the system. In the governing assemblies in the Netherlands and in Britain, the liberals were in the opposition and had little more say-so than the power of the word. Starting in 1815, frustrated and embittered *émigrés*, patriots, republicans and Bonapartists began to congregate in places like Poland's Krakow and Belgium's Brussels; as we will see in the next chapter, their sharp retorts tore the post-war order and balance-of-power plans to shreds. In Russia, the 'children of 1812' – the new generation of writers, poets and even officers (including Pushkin) – became bitter about how, after the great liberation from the French oppressor, the shutters in Russia were slowly being closed. Despite Alexander's liberal lobby in Paris, control and censorship in the heart of the tsarist realm were actually on the rise after 1812. Dissatisfaction with the new restorative order, in which monarchs and tsars tried to force the spirit of reform back into the bottle, gave rise to an escalation of all kinds of secret societies and clandestine conspiracies (like the *Soiuz spaseniia* – 'Union of Salvation'), which maintained contact with like-minded folks throughout Europe.[149] In one of the Western European countries where the freedom of the press was greater, the critical-radical British weekly *The Examiner* opened a direct assault on the Allies' ideas regarding the new

---

[148] Napoleon's 'inner empire' was 'elitist'. See D. Lieven, 'Introduction', in Hartley, Keenan and Lieven (eds.), *Russia and the Napoleonic Wars*, 1–11, here: 3.

[149] See A. Tosi, *Waiting for Pushkin. Russian Fiction in the Reign of Alexander I (1801–1825)* (Amsterdam/New York: Rodopi, 2006), 28–30.

order. It was particularly unpalatable 'for the lovers of liberty', *The Examiner* fumed in November 1815, that the 'Allied Sovereigns did not perform their promises . . . of gratitude and deliverance to all the people of Europe'. Norway, Saxony, Poland and Italy were cited as cases in point. With 'all the overbearing pretensions of Might versus Right', the Allies denied these peoples their rights again, and subjected them to the yoke of a repressive government, just as Napoleon had done.[150] Liberal and radical media outlets poured a constant stream of criticism on the crowned heads of Europe. In Brussels and Paris, *Le Nain jaune* ('The Yellow Dwarf') and other satirical political journals included repeated exposés of the restored Bourbon regime, ridiculed the Prussian, Russian and Austrian sovereigns, and made fun of the Dutch King Willem I.[151]

The most sand thrown in the gears of the Allied machine came from the French government and people themselves. Initially, resignation and apathy characterized the majority of the French population. 'There is no more spirit left in France', the Duke of Vicence wrote in February 1813. The marshal of France under Napoleon, General Édouard Mortier, concurred: 'The inertia is the same everywhere.' According to the sub-prefect of Vervins, the people had become 'indolent' and 'cowardly': 'They are without emulation or energy, and do not realize the disgrace of being invaded.'[152] But in many parts of the country during the invasions of 1814 and 1815, rebellion and resistance were the topic of the day; many of the French would hear nothing of their being tamed by or subservient to the dictates of the Allies. After the second invasion or 'liberation' of France in the latter half of June 1815, the people's mood was, where that was possible, even more desolate, and polarized further in the months to come. Cheers and chiming church towers in the northern and southern parts of the country contrasted with sullen looks from Bonapartist soldiers and peasants in Brittany. Protestants in the south clashed with royalists; public lynching and outbreaks of violence between supporters of various parties throughout the entire country were all part of the order of the day. The king and his retinue of (ultra-)royalists were quite probably thankful, but even that gave way to sentiments of entitlement and vengefulness pretty quickly. But gratitude is not the right term to describe the emotional climate in France at the end of June; schizophrenic, disorientated and vindictive sooner come to mind.[153] France's emotional state was probably best expressed by the poet Casimir Delavigne, who, upon hearing of the battle lost at Waterloo, mourned the sadness of his country in his *Messéniennes* (an instant classic). The poet connected its grief and sorrow with its pugnacity. He called on the French

---

[150] 'Gloomy State of Things in France. No. XI. Continued. Doctrine of Divine Right', *The Examiner*, 25 November 1815, 753–5.
[151] See (Van) Sas, *Onze natuurlijkste bodgenoot*, 125–36.
[152] Cited in Houssaye, *1814*, 16; Houssaye, *Napoleon*, 13.
[153] Houssaye, *1815. La seconde abdication*, 148–67.

people, in the face of the Allies' victory, to put away what divided them and to form a united front around the king:

> France! France! Awake, with one indignant mind!
> With newborn hosts the throne's dread precinct bind!
> Disarmed, divided, conquerors o'er us stand;
> Present the olive, but the sword in hand.[154]

A striking example of this conundrum is presented by the responses of the French public intellectual Germaine de Staël. Madame de Staël, as she was commonly referred to, was the daughter of Jacques Necker, the famous Swiss banker and finance minister under Louis XVI. Her mother, Suzanne Curchod, hosted one of the most celebrated salons in Paris, which Germaine eventually took over from her. Given her spirited pen, it was not long before she found herself at odds with Napoleon, who banished her from Paris. Though periodically pursued by Napoleon, occasioning various stays throughout Europe, torn by her longing for her homeland, but too proud to distance herself from her freedom-loving, liberal ideas, she returned to her smitten fatherland to defend it with tooth and nail.[155] What bothered her most was that the Allied victors, who had come to liberate France, now subjugated the country to a situation of military occupation, thereby reining in their only newfound freedom. Shortly before her death, she aimed her poisonous pen at Wellington. How could this British liberator allow those hundred and fifty thousand 'foreigners' to defile her homeland? 'Mon coeur vraiment françois ne peut pas supporter la présence des troupes étrangères – représentez vous des françois campés dans hyde park!'[156] Wellington, who according to De Staël not only had to play 'victor' but was also beholden to present himself as 'liberator', felt sufficiently addressed by this influential voice to write her an elaborate letter in reply to justify himself. He went to great lengths to reconcile himself to her and visited her almost daily on her deathbed in July 1817.[157] But to no avail – as long as France remained occupied, and 'the influence of the stranger' persisted, the voice of the critics only grew louder.[158]

[154] C. Delavigne, 'Première Messénienne sur la Bataille de Waterloo', in Delavigne, *Trois Messéniennes* (Paris: Ladvocat, 1822), 3–9.
[155] G. Sluga, 'Women, Diplomacy and International Politics, before and after the Congress of Vienna', in Sluga and C. James (eds.), *Women, Diplomacy and International Politics since 1500* (London: Routledge, 2015); Sluga, 'Madame de Staël and the Transformation of European Politics, 1812–1817', *International History Review*, 37: 1 (2015), 142–66.
[156] De Staël to Wellington, February 1816, printed in V. de Pange (ed.), *Madame de Staël et le duc de Wellington. Correspondance inédite 1815–1817* (Paris: Gallimard, 1967), 54.
[157] (De) Pange, *Madame de Staël et le duc de Wellington*, 130–1.
[158] Wellington to de Staël, 14 December 1816, Ibid., 100–1.

Calming the Tides of Time

This more impressionistic chapter has sought to distil the vibrancy of the period after the Napoleonic Wars so as to make plain the transitional and entirely novel and open nature of these first post-war years. There was no turning back to the *ancien régime*. Neither did the populaces, sovereigns and diplomats want to return to the whimsical arbitrariness of the alliances and absolutist *systema* that previously defined world politics. They yearned for peace, normalcy and moderation and for the tide of time to calm down. Citizens longed for an end to the 'savage barbarity of war', as Louisa Adams put it when recalling the sickening sight of the 'immense quantity of bones' while travelling along the road from Eisenach to Frankfurt, where the great battles had been fought.[159] These feelings and their emotional vocabulary, which were shared and understood throughout the continent, reaching even to the colonies, cradled the birth of the imagined European security community. Gratitude, monarchical enthusiasm and a sense of sharing a common European fate and future bound the sovereigns, the diplomats and their entourages and the majority of the populace together. A future of peace – surpassing borders and languages – had begun to capture the imagination.

Key to this hope was the manner in which peace and security could be made certain for not only the near but also the distant future. All of the powers agreed that the only way to institute a dynamic system of collective security was to create a new balance of power, one that would define both foreign and certainly domestic policies. Power had to be tempered by justice; territorially, politically, militarily and also morally. This new collective security logic was first operationalized with the occupation of France by Allied forces, but it in fact affected all of Europe. Even Napoleon understood the trend of the time when he ventured to cast himself as a peacemaker upon his return in March 1815. But that anti-war sentiment could come to expression in a variety of ways: in the preference for 'no more revolution!', in a rejection of tyrants and despotism, by embracing new liberal principles on liberty and constitutionalism, or in reverting back to repression and conservatism instead. This new post-war community of states could moreover be thought of as an organism and body, or as a modern-day machine. Most remarkably: there was no fixed and permanent solution present in 1815; the future was open, the expectations manifold and variegated.

That open future was, however, defined and framed by past experiences of threat and danger and common notions about the right norms, values and attitudes. The security community, which had to agree on these matters, was extremely elitist in its constitution. The role of the great powers had been enhanced in 1815, with lesser powers such as Sweden or Spain, which had still played a part in Vienna in 1814, now to be excluded from the Allied Conference in Paris. Gagern

---

[159] O'Brien, *Mrs. Adams in Winter*, 196.

was amongst the more polite and traditional envoys to notice this transformation. He had urged his sovereign, Prince Willem of Orange, to 'stand up for the security and interests of the smaller powers' and encouraged him to 'enter the larger European system'.[160] But to no avail; as Metternich confided to Gagern, smaller countries could find a place within this system, but only as the 'lapdog' of the greater powers.[161] A growing group of radicals, liberals and other more patriotic contenders took an even more contrarian stance against the great power order, inciting, in turn, within the bosom of these state bureaucracies and amongst the great power elites renewed anxieties about the resurfacing of revolutionary threats. The inclination to see the germ of revolution in every form of democratic protest or 'liberal' opposition was widespread. This was the case not only in Vienna's absolutist State Chancellery. Even in so-called liberal Britain, ideas on civil rights were considered premature or even suspect.[162]

Thus, the new order rested on a highly ambivalent principle: a balance of power, on the domestic front and within the international system, but dictated by the great powers, predominantly by Britain. This explains the highly positive British under-standing of the 1815 system, also in later years. As British prime minister William Gladstone remarked in 1879 about the peacemakers of 1815:

> to keep the Powers of Europe in union together [was crucial] . . . Because by keeping all in union together you neutralise and fetter and bind up the selfish aims of each. I am not here to flatter either England or any of them. They have selfish aims, as, unfortunately, we in late years have too sadly shown that we too have had selfish aims; but then common action is fatal to selfish aims.[163]

Gladstone's views echoed the mantra that Castlereagh constantly repeated; here in a letter to his prime minister, Lord Liverpool, in August 1815, after the Battle of Waterloo: 'it is not our business to collect trophies, but to try . . . [to] bring back the world to peaceful habits'.[164] Foreign secretary Austen Chamberlain in the run-up to the Conference of Locarno in 1925 also heaped praise on the balancers of 1815: 'Britain's part now is the same as in 1815 and *mutatis mutandis* Castlereagh's policy is the right one today.'[165] Of course,

---

[160] Gagern to Willem I, report III, 26 November 1814; Willem I to Gagern, 14 December 1814, NL-HaNA (State Secretariat of the Cabinet 1813–40), 2.02.01, inv. no. 6356; cf. correspondence between Willem I and Gagern, HStD, no. O11 and no. B24.

[161] Gagern, *Mein Antheil and der Politik*, vol. 2, 118–19.

[162] Cf. R. Stites, *The Four Horsemen. Riding to Liberty in Post-Napoleonic Europe* (Oxford: Oxford University Press, 2015); B. Hilton, *A Mad, Bad and Dangerous People? England 1783–1846* (Oxford: Oxford University Press, 2006).

[163] W. Gladstone, 'Speech at West Calder', 27 November 1879, in Gladstone, *Political Speeches in Scotland, November–December 1879* (Edinburgh: Elliott, 1880), 115–16.

[164] Cited in Bew, *Castlereagh*, 407. See also P. Schroeder, 'A Mild Rejoinder', *The American Historical Review*, 97:3 (1992), 733–5.

[165] Cited in P. Cohrs, *The Unfinished Peace after World War I. America, Britain and the Stabilisation of Europe, 1919–1932* (Cambridge: Cambridge University Press, 2008), 217.

balancing served British interests at that time: 'Great Britain stands forth again as the moderator and peace maker of the new Europe created by the Great War.'[166]

It also explains why the balance-of-power rhetoric and the alleged moderation of the 'men of 1815' came to be discredited in later years. In 1918, US president Woodrow Wilson had condemned the congress system as a series of 'covenants of selfishness and compromise'.[167] For Wilson, the balance of power was a device to promote the egotistical, colonial and imperialist power politics of the great powers vis-à-vis their populations, and with respect to minorities and smaller states – just as Justi had foreseen in his eighteenth-century critique, or Martineau in the early nineteenth century. However, the way it has been reduced to a narrow category of 'hard' power politics, or even repressive *Realpolitik*, does not entirely do justice to its early nineteenth-century connotations. The 1815 colouring of this concept in more benign terms and its juxtaposition with the ruthless despotism and hegemonic aspirations of the Napoleonic age served the emergence of a European system of crisis and security management in this initial transition period – something that got lost in the fog of time.

In 1815 the new great power system simultaneously sparked critique *and* fanned expectations. All over Europe, inscriptions on monuments, treaties and letters of safe passage invoked the new *Pax Europeana* as realized by the Allied forces. From far and wide, from France and the countries it had rampaged over, economic, financial and political representatives came forward, searching for redress and relief, filing their claims and complaints with the Allied rulers. On this quicksand of high expectations and lingering frustrations, the Allied powers tried to build their new system of collective security. For the officials and experts, the work to drive piles in this tricky ground was about to start in July 1815.

---

[166] Cited in Z. Steiner, *The Lights That Failed. European International History, 1919–1933* (Oxford: Oxford University Press, 2005), 403. Thanks to Eva Maria Werner.

[167] See Wilson's speech to the Congress of the United States (State of the Union), 4 December 1917. H. Doc No. 65–468, U.S. Cong. Serial Set vol. 7443, LCCN: https://lccn.loc.gov/92643101 (last viewed: 14 March 2010). See also F. Freksa, *A Peace Congress of Intrigue (Vienna, 1815). A Vivid, Intimate Account of the Congress of Vienna Composed of the Personal Memoirs of its Important Participants* (New York: Century, 1919).

4

'A Moderate Occupation'

Eternal Hatred

In 1815, little remained of the age-old stately walled royal park just west of the French capital, the Bois de Boulogne, which Louis XVI had reopened to the public a few years before. Its eight gates gave access to an oak grove where the illustrious kings of France, beginning with Dogebert in the seventh century, had hunted deer and bears. Henry VI had planted 15,000 mulberry trees, and extended the park across some 845 hectares. But in 1815 those gates framed a dismal panorama. In 1814 the forest had been commandeered in its entirety by 40,000 Allied troops after their first successful conquest of Paris, and now they had set up camp there once again. A scene painted in pleasant pastels from 1815 records how the soldiers' white conical tents filled the entire grove: men of the mainly British contingent strolling up and down the lanes, with or without a lady on their arm, bending to examine the wares of female souvenir-sellers (Fig. 4.1).

In reality, the forest soon looked more like a moonscape. Most of the trees were chopped down within a month, and the spot where the very first manned balloon flight had taken place in 1783 was nothing more than a grazed plain.[1] As for the many shaded artificial ponds throughout the park, only a few stinking quagmires remained.[2]

The French ego suffered more than simply property damage. After having defeated Napoleon and conquered Paris, British and Prussian troops turned to tangible expressions of French grandeur. They scoured the city in search of the many plundered works of art from all over Europe and North Africa that had been hauled to the imperial capital – to take them home with them when they left. The British sergeant Thomas Morris witnessed such a Prussian–British removal project and got an undiluted taste of the French people's disgust – for they firmly believed that these plundered goods quite rightfully belonged to France:

---

[1] Morris, *Recollections*, 254–5.
[2] P. de Moncan, *Les jardins du baron Haussmann* (Paris: Les Éditions du Mécène, 2007), 57–8.

Figure 4.1   Encampment of the British army in the Bois de Boulogne, Paris, 1815. By Matthew Dubourg, 1817. (Heritage Images)

> I had an opportunity of witnessing the removal of the celebrated Group of Horses, of which Napoleon had despoiled the Venetians, and which were now about to be restored. The Horses, which had been placed over the entrance to the palace, were, with much difficulty and labour, lowered into small waggons or cars, under a strong guard of British and Prussians. The Parisians, who had assembled in considerable numbers, looked on in gloomy silence; and when the last Horse was safely deposited, one of Napoleon's old veteran's exclaimed, 'Now, I have nothing left to give my children, but my eternal hatred of the English!' 'And that', said an English gentleman, who was standing by, and understood the language; 'that will do your children no good, and England no harm.'[3]

In 1815, Paris was a hub for Allied activities. Collective peace was cast as a project of Allied occupation. Allied ministries and their entourage confiscated the palaces and city mansions of the French elite. From Paris and beyond they also set themselves the task of defusing the French spirit of revolt and revolution, for the second time, but this time with far more dedication. The established Allied platform, the Allied Council, functioned as the delivery room for increased Allied cooperation in Europe. At the same time it proved to be the forum where underlying disagreements and diverging sentiments were exposed

---

[3] Morris, *Recollections*, 257–8.

and handled. This joint Allied project of subjugating an unruly population – not in India or the Crimea, but in France – was from the outset as controversial as it was modern. At the same time, it was a highly open and contingent endeavour. No one knew what form this imperial peace would take, how invasive and ambivalent it would be and whether the defeated opponent would allow itself to be colonized so easily. The transformative nature of this occupation period, not just in its effects in France, but for the whole of Europe, becomes apparent when one follows the footsteps of the 'men of 1815' and their Allied Council during the first months after the Battle of Waterloo, up until and including the conclusion of the Second Treaty of Paris in November 1815.

A Very Modern Regime of Occupation

Before entering into the details of the Allied Council, a slightly anachronistic comparison with previous and future post-war situations is in order, to highlight the innovative nature of the occupation regime of 1815. The peace of 1815 rested on an unconditional surrender, but was not a matter of total subjection. In 1815 a maxim still held that came to be abandoned in the course of the nineteenth century: that not destroying the vanquished enemy entirely was good for the balance of Europe. 'The war of 1815 is not a war of conquest', Metternich urged his Prussian counterpart Hardenberg in a memorandum dated 6 August of that year. For the Allies, 'the double aim' of the war was 'bringing down the usurpation of Napoléon Bonaparte' on the one hand, and installing a government in France that would guarantee repose and order for both France and the remainder of Europe on the other.[4] A state like France could not just be wiped off the map; Napoleon had made plain what kind of chaos obliterating states would produce.[5] Destroying France would only create a new vacuum of power, and no one knew who would jump in to fill that void. But unlike in 1814, the victors in 1815 realized that something more than simply formulating courteously worded reciprocal obligations was called for. The paperwork of treaties was not enough; something more was necessary to enforce the peace. That is what the cutting-edge discussions in Paris between June and September 1815 were all about. The eventual outcome of these discussions (recounted below) was a temporary occupation of France, which was meant to secure peace in Europe and to enforce the domestic transition within the country. That was a novel element. The Allied powers entered the territory of the conquered country, temporarily assumed the seat of power, put

---

[4] Metternich, Memorandum to Hardenberg, 6 August 1815, GStA PK, III. HA I. no. 1461, 75.
[5] A. Osiander, *The States System of Europe, 1640–1990. Peacemaking and the Conditions of International Stability* (London: Oxford University Press, 1994), 121; M. Anderson, 'Eighteenth-Century Theories of Balance of Power', in R. Hatton and M. Anderson (eds.), *Studies in Diplomatic History. Essays in Memory of David Bayne Horn* (London: Archon Books, 1970), 183–98.

an occupational force in place and created a European condominium over France (Map 4.1) – all of which seems more like 1945 than 1713 (the end of the War of the Spanish Succession) or 1918.[6]

Comparing the activities of the American, British and Soviet occupations authorities, joined later by the French, as well as the underlying blueprints for the defeated and post-war Nazi Germany, does have its limits, obviously. Napoleon was no Hitler, even though a fierce debate still rages regarding how best to evaluate the Corsican emperor's moral and historical repute.[7] The magnitude of human annihilation and the extensive destruction of infrastructure, the moral abyss of the Holocaust and the blind hatred that were unleashed by the Nazi regime put a heavy if not unbearable burden on the rehabilitation and reconstruction after 1945. An equivalent to the highly wrought and deep metaphysical debates on an alleged collective guilt for Germany and its inhabitants was lacking in 1815.[8] There were no accusations of crimes against humanity or a call for the need of a war crimes tribunal in 1815. References to Napoleon as a 'common enemy' and a general condemnation of the 'terror' of the revolutionary and Napoleonic wars in the post-war treaties are as close as it comes. But these did not come near the abysmal moral or judicial vituperations of 1945.

The configuration of geopolitical relations in Europe in 1945 was entirely different from 1815 as well. The 'Concert of Europe' had met its demise with the First World War; the *Pax Britannica* had long given way to a *Pax Americana*. Already during the initial tentative talks among the most important Allied players regarding the post-war peace a very clear dividing line emerged. The Allied powers, meeting in Tehran two years prior to the end of the Second World War, talked for the first time about what a post-war peace would look like for Germany and for Europe. They represented two diametrically opposed ideologies: a capitalist, liberal model versus a communist, collectivist one. Soviet leader Stalin cemented this rift when he suggested dividing Germany into spheres of influence. Such a divide was absent in 1815; not even the diffuse, cultural distinction between the 'Tatar' power of Russia and 'the West' or that between the conservative powers of the Holy

---

[6] Naimark, *The Russians in Germany*; Benz, *Potsdam 1945*; Mai, *Der alliierte Kontrollrat in Deutschland*.

[7] See for example the contributions in the catalogue of the eponymous exhibition: B. Savoy (ed.) *Napoleon und Europa. Traum und Trauma. Kunst- und Ausstellungshalle der Bundesrepublik Deutschland, Bonn, 17. Dezember 2010 bis 25. April 2011* (Munich, 2010). See also N. Petiteau, *Napoleon, de la mythologie à l'histoire* (Paris: Seuil, 1999); A. Jourdan, *Mythes et légendes de Napoléon. Un destin d'exception, entre rêve et réalité* (Toulouse: Privat, 2004); P. Gueniffey, *Bonaparte, 1769–1802* (Paris: Gallimard, 2013); J. Boudon, *Napoléon expliqué à mes enfants* (Paris: Seuil, 2009).

[8] K. Jaspers, *Die Schuldfrage* (Heidelberg: Schneider, 1946); Jaspers, *The Question of German Guilt* (New York: Fordham University Press, 1965).

Map 4.1 The Allied occupation of France, July–December 1815. The shaded areas show which of the four great powers occupied which zone. (Erik Goosmann © 2020, Mappa Mundi Cartography)

Alliance (Russia, Austria, Prussia) and the liberal nations of the north-west (Britain, the Netherlands, to some extent France) seem to matter much in the first post-war deliberations. Nor did such differences translate into distinct administrative ideologies or occupation cultures.

Moreover, in contrast to 1945, democratic states were obviously not part of the picture in 1815. Indeed, unlike in the twentieth century, the nineteenth century knew nothing about codifying occupational regimes; laws, formal agreements, conventions or international law regarding the stipulations of an occupational regime were quite simply lacking. These would only arrive in 1907. In 1815, authoritarian-ruled, imperial powers called the shots and together negotiated a collective security system. No democratic values and international human rights undergirded this system[9] – these things were still far beyond the horizon of political understanding.

Nor was the total overthrow and unconditional surrender of the conquered state on the agenda in 1815. The victors had no interest in undermining the administrative sovereignty of the country in question or entirely divesting it of its power. By contrast, the absence of an internal coup or domestic insurgency in Hitler's Germany and the determination of the National Socialist regime and its people to keep fighting to the bitter end prompted the Allies' desire to deal the death blow to its administration. In 1943, in Casablanca, the Allies agreed to pursue unconditional surrender, occupy Germany completely and demilitarize it entirely. In Potsdam, in 1945, these plans were developed into a comprehensive programme, later described as the '4 Ds' (demilitarization, denazification, decartelization and democratization), that would, once translated into practice, lead to countless confrontations and conflicts on the ground. An Allied Council, consisting of the supreme commanders of the Allied Armed Forces, met monthly to oversee the occupation, but with the subdivision of the country and the capital city of Berlin into four occupational sectors, this was an increasingly arduous undertaking. Moreover, despite some autonomy for local German administrations, Germany as an independent state no longer existed.[10]

Things were very different in 1815. France simply carried on as an autonomous state. Local, provincial and national administrators carried out their duties in the name of the new king, and implemented measures and decisions that bore the royal seal as required by the government and the Chamber of Deputies, which was elected in August 1815. They did, nonetheless, have to share that administrative autonomy with the Allies' civil council and the occupational military command, which was responsible for the care and management of the troops stationed throughout two thirds of the country, and about which the French themselves had no say.[11] This occupational

---

[9] See, for example, for a diachronic comparison: Ikenberry, *After Victory*, 5–7, 29.

[10] See Mai, *Der alliierte Kontrollrat in Deutschland*. See also C. Erlichman and C. Knowles, 'Introduction: Reframing Occupation as a System of Rule', in Erlichman and Knowles (eds.), *Transforming Occupation in the Western Zones of Germany: Politics, Everyday Life and Social Interactions, 1945–55* (London: Bloomsbury, 2018), 3–24.

[11] See the stipulations in the Military Convention annexed to the Treaty of Paris, 20 November 1815, in particular, Article IV, in Foreign Office (ed.), *British and Foreign State Papers, 1815–1816*, vol. 3 (London: Ridgway, 1838), 280–1, 315–39.

regime was hence far more hybrid than the one in 1945; it was a mixture of national sovereignty and international guardianship.

That said, there were also significant parallels. The greatest similarity – and the difference from the Versailles system after 1918 – was clearly the overwhelming presence of foreign troops stationed within the borders of the conquered nation. Defeat was translated into subjection and visible humiliation. France had to deal with billeting soldiers, their parades and exercises and the initial occupation of two thirds of its territory (Fig. 4.1). That was somewhat similar to the more than 20 per cent of the German Democratic Republic (GDR) that served as training grounds and tactical bases for Soviet troops, and the initial US and British military presence in West Germany. The 'occupational guarantee' loomed large over all France's political and administrative decisions, as it did in Germany after 1945. The troops guaranteed that France would stay the course that the Allies imposed upon her. Their presence enforced the repayment of debts, the implementation of reforms, the reparations and the return of stolen artworks.

The early nineteenth-century occupation also involved a mandated governmental and even ideological transformation that was aimed at defusing Bonapartist sympathies by re-establishing the Bourbons on the throne, introducing a constitution and combating and (partially) purging radical and revolutionary elements. These purifications of 1815 were by far not so systematically executed or morally legitimized as in 1945, but egged on by the Allied powers, the French king did order the compilation of lists of supporters of the Bonapartist or revolutionary regime to be executed or exiled, and some heads did indeed roll.

Against this diachronical backdrop, the Allied Council and the occupation regime that was created in 1815 was both highly innovative and complex, and had to deal with wide-ranging resistance, from within France, but also from diverging views and ideas amongst the Allies themselves.

Indirect Rule

By mid-July 1815 an entirely new situation saw the light of day. The European powers found themselves in the heart of a vanquished France and had no plans of leaving anytime soon. The circumstances called for circumspect governance and close deliberations to avoid the mistakes of 1814. The first, very brief military occupation of France in 1814 served as a blueprint, but the commanders and ministers of 1815 could also draw from their experiences in colonial administration. Wellington, who had served as a general in India, had learned from his own brother amongst others that it was more convenient and advantageous not to sit on the throne himself, but to employ his advice and influence as the 'whisper behind the throne'. Richelieu, who would assume Talleyrand's place as prime minister in September, had been appointed by

Catherine the Great, Tsar Alexander's grandmother, to be the governor of Odessa, present-day Ukraine.[12] He had helped Crimea to flourish prosperously, introducing a functional governance structure, trade, modern industry, western laws and regulations and education. He had especially impressed himself on the people with his campaign against corruption and his advocacy for integrity of the law and just governance. Justus von Gruner, who would be appointed head of an Allied secret service in July, had been an official in the Prussian colonial administration to exploit the territories of eastern Germany. Thereafter, he had been appointed to design and set up a central police force in Berlin, over which he presided until 1812, and joined Stein at the Allied Central Administration (see Chapter 2), governing the liberated Rhenish provinces after 1813. Colonial rule obviously differs from military occupation in terms of intended duration and final objective. Colonial rule has an eye on the permanent exploitation of the conquered lands, and on their incorporation into an imperial system. These differences, however, may only be distinguished clearly in retrospect. For the indigenous people involved, the intentions of the invaders – as occupational force or as colonizers – were not always neatly delineated. Neither did the occupiers themselves have a clear outcome in mind. For all parties involved, the occupation was often a rather chaotic and unpredictable affair, sparking unrest and anxieties. In this situation, where concrete instructions or detailed blueprints were often lacking, we may understand Wellington and his colleagues as 'men on the spot',[13] who brought their current skills and previous experience to fruition. They applied what they were used to, what they were capable of and what they understood as good governance.[14]

This immediately transpired from Wellington's initiative to swiftly engage tested and legitimate 'indigenous' French officials and apply his favourite form of 'indirect rule'. When the provisional government of France, under the leadership of Joseph Fouché, offered Wellington and Blücher a suspension of hostilities on behalf of Napoleon II on 24 June, the Allies dismissed the proposal out of hand. They 'could not consider [Napoleon's 22 June] abdication of usurped power in favour of his son, and his handing over the government provisionally to five persons, named by himself, to be that description of security which the allies had in view'.[15] Liberal supporters of Louis Philippe II

[12] E. de Waresquiel, *Le Duc de Richelieu, 1766–1822. Un sentimental en politique* (Paris: Perrin, 1990), 106–204; P. Herlihy, *Odessa. A History, 1794–1914* (Cambridge, MA: Harvard University Press, 1986), 21–48.

[13] See R. Long (ed.), *The Man on the Spot. Essays on British Empire History* (Westport, CT: Greenwood Press, 1995). See for a similar situation in 1945: Naimark, *The Russians in Germany*, 465.

[14] For example M. Crowder, 'Indirect Rule: French and British Style', *Africa. Journal of the International African Institute*, 34:3 (1964), 197–205.

[15] Wellington to Bathurst, 25 June 1815, in *WD*, vol. 8 (London: John Murray, 1838), 167–8.

tried to push the Duke of Orléans' candidacy through via the tsar. But Wellington was not all interested in those kinds of exotic adventures; he preferred the restoration of the Bourbon King Louis XVIII. Wellington did not think very highly of this Bourbon successor, who had not been particularly successful the first time around. As a pragmatist, he was, however, convinced that this course of action offered the most likely guarantee for the Allied plans for 'mutual security' in Europe. Of all the other pretenders to the throne, Louis XVIII seemed to be the most reliable and pliable partner. Wellington acknowledged to Lord Bathurst, the British minister of war, that it was obviously not up to him to decide upon the French domestic reconstruction, but he nevertheless voiced a clear opinion:

> I conceived the best security for Europe was the restoration of the King, and that the establishment of any other government than the King's in France must inevitably lead to new and endless wars.[16]

The Allied occupation regime, according to Wellington, needed to align itself with the 'native rulers' of France, as he had done earlier in India and Spain. He was supported in this by the British government, which during the campaign in Spain and Portugal had maintained a tight network of secret agents in Europe who were to explore the possibilities of putting legitimate royalty (back) on the empty thrones: Ferdinand VII in Spain (including a plan to liberate the still-captive ruler, kept under guard since 1808 by Napoleon at the Château de Valençay), Willem in the Netherlands and a Bourbon in France.[17] Moreover, the cousin of the king, Louis Antoine (son of Louis Philippe), Duke of Angoulême, along with his troops, had already liberated major parts of southern France, and established special commissioners in Bordeaux, Marseilles and Toulouse in the name of Louis XVIII. In that light, Wellington's personal preference for Louis XVIII was not only politically motivated, but was also a question of military strategy. Restoring the Bourbon monarchy to the oldest brother was the best option militarily, in the short term (with southern France liberated, expelling the Duke of Angoulême would not have been prudent) as well as the long term.

It was not altogether certain that Wellington would succeed with this form of indirect rule. Alexander had yet to weigh in on the matter. Blücher, too, avoided any contact with the French king; as long as France was in an interregnum, Prussian troops could roam and pillage as they saw fit. Metternich was not opposed to restoring the Bourbon monarchy, but did point to the provisions of the Congress of Vienna, namely, that the Allies had only taken up arms in order to defeat Napoleon. Choosing a new form of

---

[16] Wellington to Bathurst, 2 July 1815, in *WD*, vol. 8, 188–93: here 190.
[17] E. Sparrow, *Secret Service. British Agents in France 1792–1815* (Woodbridge: Boydell Press, 1999), 369–413; see 386–9 on the abduction plan.

government had to be left to the French people themselves, for only then would the new government enjoy legitimacy (and stability).[18] From his headquarters in Cateau-Cambrésis Wellington therefore prepared, with some of his characteristic shrewdness, the return of Louis XVIII.

On 20 June, he presented his Allied colleagues with a fait accompli and declared publicly that His Majesty the King of France was an ally of the great powers. The same day, he informed Louis XVIII that it was time to leave Ghent with the Duke of Berry, the commander of the small royal army, and return to France.[19] Louis left the next day and travelling via Brussels and in northern France was welcomed with cheers. On the morning of 24 June, Wellington asked his Prussian liaison officer Müffling to ride out with him. Müffling tried to worm his way out of the invitation with the excuse that he did not have a horse with him, but Wellington had already had one of his horses saddled for him. The Russian ambassador to Paris, Carlo Andrea Pozzo di Borgo, was similarly induced to ride out with them. Together they constituted a veritable Allied committee that welcomed the king that same evening in the Allied military headquarters in Cateau-Cambrésis. As Müffling, who could not hide his irritated admiration for Wellington's knack, recorded later: 'Wellington had obtained his object, when it was reported in the newspapers that the duke had gone to meet the King, riding between a Russian and a Prussian general.'[20] Wellington moreover now made Louis XVIII – contrary to the king's own preference – appoint Talleyrand as prime minister and, a few days later, Fouché as minister of police.[21] Assisted by Talleyrand and minister of state Beugnot, and on the insistent advice of Wellington, the king furthermore once more declared his loyalty to the *Charte Constitutionelle*.[22] Louis XVIII was definitely not a 'puppet king' of the Allies, but Wellington had made sure that the king felt obliged to him for the coming period and would indeed take – with some exceptions – Wellington's advice to heart.

---

[18] Houssaye, *1815. La seconde abdication*, 126–8; A. Wellesley (ed.) *Supplementary Despatches and Memoranda of Field Marshal Arthur Wellesley, 1st Duke of Wellington* (hereafter: *WSD*), vol. 10 (London: John Murray, 1871), 585, 630; see also Wacker, *Die allierte Besetzung*, 96.

[19] Houssaye, *1815. La seconde abdication*, 129, 134–5. The letter reached the king on 21 June; see Wellington to Clarke, 20 June 1815, in *WD*, vol. 12, 492.

[20] Müffling, *The Memoirs*, 253–4.

[21] See E. de Waresquiel, *Fouché. Les silences de la pieuvre* (Paris: Fayard, 2014), 572–93; H. Houssaye, 'Le retour du Roi en 1815', *Revue des Deux Mondes*, 5:24 (1904), 481–509; here 487–92.

[22] Houssaye, *1815. La seconde abdication*, 143–5. See Stuart to Wellington, Cambrai, 28, 29, 30 June 1815, *WSD*, vol. 10, 614, 625, 633.

Blücher's Revenge

By the end of June, the British occupiers had preselected 'Louis the Desired' to ascend the refurbished throne in Paris. The provisional government under Fouché formally ruled the country, King Louis waited in Neuilly for further developments, and the Allies stood outside the gates of the city. Around Paris, in the eastern border region, French commanders were, however, still violently resisting Allied advances and were not about to give up their strongholds. Moreover, among the Allies themselves different opinions prevailed as to how the occupation and the administration should be set up: with or without taking former regicides and Bonapartists to account? With or without revenge, territorial indemnities and retaliation? And how long would they remain in the country – until the Second Peace Treaty of Paris was concluded in November, or even extending their stay until all treaty stipulations were met? Negotiations started right from the beginning, passionate and persistent.

Again, the Prussians advocated a total surrender and bleeding out of France. After winning the Battle at Waterloo, the Prussian troops had given their last energies to reach Paris first. They pushed forward, plundering and ransacking as they went, and after a series of final significant battles near Ligny, just outside Paris, they approached the capital city, arriving from the south-west. After the Battle of Issy on 2 and 3 July, and the subsequent capitulation, General Gebhard Leberecht von Blücher, also nicknamed 'Marshal Forwards', entered the gates of the city. There he focused all his aggression on the Pont d'Iéna; as an ultimate act of redress and revenge, Blücher wanted to see the bridge destroyed – his memorial for that infamous battle lost. Napoleon had the bridge built between 1808 and 1814, connecting the Champ de Mars's extended green space in front of the École Militaire with the other bank of the Seine. The bridge was named after the triumphant battle against the Prussians near Jena and Auerstedt in October 1806. Blücher, as cavalry general, was directly involved in that dramatic defeat, carrying out a series of desperate charges against the French troops, but to no avail. However, together with Scharnhorst, he had managed to keep thirty-four cannons from the French, which won him legendary status. The Prussian armies nonetheless suffered a crushing defeat. Now, nine years later, Blücher entered the city as supreme commander of the Prussian troops and cherished one burning passion: to erase that scandalous blemish from the Prussian banner by blowing up the bridge. He had been kept from doing so in 1814, during 'the first peace of Paris', by Tsar Alexander's magnanimous posture. But this time he was the first to arrive in Paris, before Wellington, and could settle the scales. The very day he arrived in Paris, 7 July, Blücher instructed his sappers to plant explosives and blow up the bridge.[23]

---

[23] See Wacker, *Die alliierte Besetzung*, 125.

From that moment on, however, history's recollection begins to fragment and unveils how open and contingent not only this story, but also its writing into historiography was. Every country has its own nationalist rendering of this seminal transition from a *sortie de guerre* towards a settled peace. First, the French historians. According to the doyen of French restoration historiography Guillaume de Bertier de Sauvigny – who in turn relies on Talleyrand's memoirs[24] – it was the king himself who intervened. Having recently returned from his exile in Ghent on 8 July, King Louis heard about Blücher's malevolent intentions and informed the Prussians that they would have to blow him into the sky as well, since he would go and seat his Royal Person on the bridge himself.[25] The French historian Emmanuel de Waresquiel, however, sees the former minister of foreign affairs Charles-Maurice de Talleyrand-Périgord as the bridge's guardian angel. According to Waresquiel, Talleyrand, who had been appointed to lead the government on 9 July, was able to pull the fuse by immediately issuing a statute that reverted the names of all public buildings and monuments to what they had been as of 1 January 1790. Pont d'Iéna was renamed Pont de l'École Militaire and in due time the imperial eagles were removed.[26] In short, for the French historians, it was pretty much an exclusively French affair, conducted by leading French officials, such as Talleyrand, Fouché, Richelieu and the king himself. France was unequivocally saved by French interference, and in the French collective memory, Blücher was referred to, if at all, as a name for a mad dog.

British historiography, however, has a different story to tell. Andrew Roberts, Rory Muir, John Bew and other British historians believe that it was really the Duke of Wellington who saved the bridge and the French honour. After he caught wind of Blücher's plans, Wellington ordered his soldiers immediately to stand guard at the bridge to ensure that the Prussian army engineers could not get anywhere near it.[27] In various British novels and works of non-fiction, from Thackeray's *Vaniety Fair* to Scott's novels and Waterloo reports to Lady Shelley's memoirs, the British spirit of generosity and moderation is proudly mentioned. The *Pax Britannica* brought peace to Europe and protected its cultural heritage. In these retellings, Wellington is the pre-eminent sportsmanlike hero, who taught the Prussians and French a few things about 'fair play'.

Finally, there is also a Russian retelling of the story. Here, in a weak echo of the British version, Tsar Alexander is championed as the true saviour of the bridge. However, for Russian historiography the second peace of Paris and the

---

[24] See Comte de Broglie (ed.), *Mémoires du Prince de Talleyrand*, vol. 3, 236–40.
[25] Bertier de Sauvigny, *The Bourbon Restoration*, 120.
[26] Waresquiel, *Talleyrand*, 509.
[27] A. Roberts, *Wellington and Napoleon. The Long Duel* (London: Weidenfeld and Nicolson, 2003), 182–98.

subsequent occupation of 1815 were less relevant than the occupation of 1814, when the tsar ruled the roost in the French capital and made an indelible impression on French and European public opinion. In her biography of Alexander, Rey spends twenty pages on 1814 and only half a page on 1815.[28]

From the archives, a far more complex image emerges: rescuing the bridge was a truly polyphonous, and somewhat awkward, European intervention. What exactly happened, according to the sources? On 7 July, the day the Prussian troops entered Paris, Blücher indeed ordered the commander of the First Army Corps, General Zieten, to have the bridge destroyed by his sappers. According to Blücher, this was not an act of pointless cruelty, but a move that was legitimized by 'eternal justice' and 'Providence'. Using the same moral argument between 27 and 29 June, he and his chief of staff Gneisenau had tried to convince Wellington to allow them to execute Napoleon. Since that attempt at getting justice had been frustrated, Blücher and Gneisenau were now determined to stand firm. According to Blücher, the Capitulation Treaty of 3 July legitimized his action, given that Article XI on the protection of 'public properties' did not hold for 'those related to war'. The Pont d'Iéna, the Pont d'Austerlitz, the Arc de Triomphe du Carrousel and de l'Étoile and the Column of the Grande Armée were, according to Blücher, symbols of French military hubris and might therefore, quite legally, be destroyed. And so, the Prussian sappers set out, with gunpowder in tow, to undermine the bridge.

Talleyrand heard about what was happening from his spies that same day or night, and sent a letter of protest to Blücher on 9 July.[29] Fouché, too, did his best to convince the Allies that destroying the bridge did not comply with the Capitulation Treaty of 3 July.[30] Blücher's reaction came the next day. In his illegible and ungrammatical scrawl he replied: 'die brüke wird gesprengt und ich wünsche Herrn Tallieran setze sich vorher drauff ('The bridge will be blown up, and I would that Mr Talleyrand sit down on it').[31] The reported willingness to be blown up with the bridge – 'on me fera sauter si l' on veut' – that was attributed to Louis XVIII was taken from a letter from the king to Talleyrand. But that letter was not printed until 15 July (i.e. days after the event), and probably came from Beugnot's quiver. The idea that the obese French monarch had personally positioned himself on the bridge was thus more a romanticized *ex post facto* rendering of what had transpired.[32] Anyhow, *si non è vero, e ben trovato*. In any case, on 9 July, Blücher still stuck to his plan (Fig. 4.2).

[28] Rey, *Alexander I*, 268–78, 287; A. Mikhailovsky-Danilevsky, *Memuary. Memoirs on the Campaign of 1813* (St Petersburg: RNB, 2001 [1834]), 45–8.
[29] Houssaye, *1815. La seconde abdication*, 337–41.
[30] See Waresquiel, *Fouché*, 604, 743 n. 11.
[31] Letter of Blücher, GStA PK, IV. HA Rep. 15A, Preussische Armee, no. 64.
[32] Waresquiel, *Talleyrand*, 509, 715 n. 1. Houssaye found it likely that the letter from Louis to Talleyrand was written on 8 July, but admitted that the letter only appeared in Talleyrand's memoirs later on. Houssaye, 'Le retour du Roi en 1815', 503–4 n. 14.

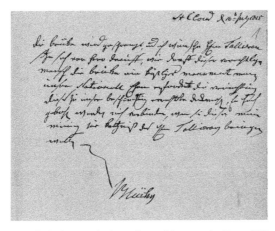

Figure 4.2   Letter of Blücher, with the order to blow up the Pont d'Iéna, 9 July 1815. (GStA, IV. HA, Rep 15 A, No. 64)

In the meantime, Wellington too started to interfere. On the night of 8 July, he wrote Blücher a letter protesting against his plans. On 9 July in the morning, Castlereagh and the duke visited Saint-Cloud, a country place west of Paris, where Blücher had set up his headquarters. Unsure whether they had persuaded him, Wellington sent him another letter later that day, imploring the Prussian general – 'mein lieber Fürst' – to at least postpone his actions pending further consultation with the Allies. The bridge was a French monument, and such aggression would not sit well with the people: 'The destruction of the bridge of Jena is highly disagreeable to the King and to the people, and may occasion disturbance in the city.'[33] At the same time, Wellington, thinking it better to be safe than sorry, had several British sentries posted to guard the bridge. This did not put off Blücher's Prussians from starting to put gunpowder into one of the four supporting piers, however. In 1838, this still disturbed Wellington: 'In spite of all I could do', the duke recounted in a conversation with the Earl of Stanhope, 'he did make the attempt, even while I believe my sentinel was standing at one end of the bridge.' The Prussians, however, had a lot to learn about working with gunpowder. Their attempt failed miserably, the duke gloated:

> But the Prussians had no experience in blowing up bridges. We, who had blown up so many in Spain, could have done it in five minutes. The Prussians made a hole in one of the pillars, but their powder blew out instead of up, and I believe hurt some of their own people.'[34]

[33] Wellington to Blücher, 9 July 1815, in *WD*, vol. 12, 552–3.
[34] 'Blücher and the Bridge of Jena', *The Spectator*, 12 September 1914; P. Stanhope, *Notes of Conversations with the Duke of Wellington, 1831–1851* (New York: Longmans, 1888), 119.

Indeed, one of the Prussian soldiers ended up in the Seine.

But the sappers did not give up, and started on the next pier. They were busy at it when the Prussian King Friedrich Wilhelm III arrived in the city and heard from Wellington and his own staff what was going on. He could not help but agree with the British objections. Together with Wellington's Prussian liaison Karl von Müffling and Friedrich Wilhelm von Bülow, they tried to convince Blücher to leave the bridge alone and to retract his order. Bülow tried to persuade Blücher, as had Wellington, to abandon his course, because then the Prussian nation would 'appear greater and nobler'.[35] But even the king did not have a handle on his general. 'It is about the honour of the Prussian army', Blücher stubbornly countered, and to make amends for the Napoleonic troops' violation of the grave of Friedrich II.[36] Gneisenau defended their actions the next day in front of the Prussian chancellor Hardenberg by explaining to him how 'the destruction of the Jena bridge for us is nothing short of a national duty. Public opinion has already complained about this with us the last time and I do not dare to ignore that voice and thus attract public and military discontent.' Would not the British nation have been equally galvanized if their troops had not blown up that bridge in Washington that reminded them of the lost Battle at Saratoga? He and Blücher were fully justified in acting this out.[37] It was not just about his and Blücher's own personal sentiments and feelings of revenge, but a matter pertaining to the German nation and its pride as such. Public opinion demanded retribution, according to Gneisenau.

Only when Tsar Alexander got involved, having arrived along with the Prussian king and the Austrian emperor on the evening of 10 July, did Blücher retrench.[38] According to Houssaye, the tsar also stood ready to sacrifice his life for the bridge: 'J'irai de ma personne me placer sur le pont et je verrai si l'on aura l'audace de le faire sauter' – 'we'll see if he's got the audacity to blow it up!' Although the words of Louis and/or Talleyrand have probably been put into the tsar's mouth, Alexander's determination tipped the scales.[39] He once again assured the French that the monuments in its capital would be protected. Eyeing this amount of Allied superiority, Blücher conceded. Talleyrand and Louis immediately saw to it that the name of the bridge over the Seine was changed to the more general, reconciliatory Pont des Invalides; and at the tsar's suggestion the Pont d'Austerlitz was renamed the

---

[35] Cited in Wacker, *Die alliierte Besetzung*, 126.
[36] Also, see Blücher's letter of 10 July, GStA PK, IV. HA Rep. 15, no. 64.
[37] At Saratoga, the British suffered a crushing defeat against the Americans. Here, Gneisenau compares the lost battle at Jena to the British defeat against the American troops. See Gneisenau to Hardenberg, 9 July 1815, GStA PK, IV. HA, Nl. Gneisenau, no. 452.
[38] *Journal de Paris*, 12 July 1815, no. 193, 1.
[39] Houssaye, *1815. La seconde abdication*, 341 n. 1.

Pont du Jardin-du-Roi.[40] The chiselled imperial eagles were, however, left intact and the damage caused by the half-baked effort to destroy the bridge was quickly repaired, at a cost of 12,000 francs.[41]

Blücher, aggrieved as he was, refused to move to the city along with the other generals and ministers. He withdrew to Saint-Cloud, just outside the city, so as to avoid the bridge. But it did not do him much good. While showing off for a few ladies in Paris, 'poor old Blücher' (*dixit* Wellington) fell from his horse and took a blow to the head. After that he was quite confused, believing that he was pregnant – by a French soldier – with an elephant. He left France in November 1815, returning to Germany, where he was warmly received and admired, only to die a short time later, in 1819.[42]

What is interesting about this example of multiperspectivity is the clash of nationalist readings of the French restoration. As Bertier de Sauvigny, and later Waresquiel, see things, the courage and cunning of Talleyrand and the good grace of the Bourbon king helped France back to a peaceful state. Bertier juxtaposes King Louis's willingness to 'sacrifice' himself for the bridge with the brutish behaviour of the Prussians, who abused their right as victors. Wellington himself tried to steer a middle course and in later life distinguished between Blücher, whom he saw as the evil genius, on the one hand, and the generals Müffling and Gneisenau on the other hand, whom he considered less rancorous. His British biographers subsequently abandoned all nuance and lifted only Wellington up to the pantheon of very British heroes who saved the day for the French. This multi-archival reconstruction, however, shows that the rescue of the bridge came from an awkward but nevertheless joint Allied effort. Wellington, Castlereagh, the tsar and the Prussian king together managed to force Blücher to spare the bridge – with Louis XVIII, Talleyrand and Fouché indeed being quick-witted enough to swiftly change its name.

This bridge episode provides a window on some initial basic differences in conviction among the Allies, as well as within the Prussian camp. The incident made it painfully clear that the Prussian government had a problem with its

[40] Fifteen years later, these changes in name were again reversed. Today's Pont des Invalides, just south of the Grand Palais, dates from 1878. The Pont d'Iéna still exists, connecting the Eiffel Tower on the Left Bank with the Trocadéro district on the Right Bank. Its chiselled imperial eagles were replaced in 1852 when Napoleon III ascended the throne of the Second Empire. See A. and W. Galignani, *Galignani's New Paris Guide for 1880* (Paris: Galignani Library, 1880 [1827]), 98; Veve, *The Duke of Wellington and the British Army of Occupation in France*, 69–70; J. Dulaure, *Histoire civile, physique et morale de Paris*, vol. 9 (Paris: Baudouin Frères, 1825), 204.

[41] D. King, *Vienna 1814. How the Conquerors of Napoleon Made Love, War, and Peace at the Congress of Vienna* (New York: Crown Publishing, 2008), 412–13.

[42] Houssaye, *1815. La seconde abdication*, 342 n. 2; Stanhope, *Conversations with Wellington*, 119–20. Blücher's delusion about being pregnant with an elephant has also been tied to his depression after the campaigns of 1806: Parkinson, *The Hussar General*, 82. But it was apparently an *idée fixe* of Blücher's, 247–51.

military. The patriotic Prussian generals Blücher and Gneisenau, radical *Tugendbund* activists of the first hour,[43] knew only one master, their national pride. By unifying the forces of moderation, however, it proved possible to keep Prussia just enough in line to allow a tone of reconciliation to carry the day. French quick thinking, moreover, helped to consolidate this peaceful outcome. This incident marked the beginning of the jointly assumed custody of France, when the Allied Council commenced its work and, with this episode, had at least staked out one principle: not unilateral conquest and revenge, but something else was to characterize the Allied presence in France.

A Prussian in Paris

How much the British, especially Wellington, did leave nothing to chance, followed from the fact that in anticipation of the definitive peace treaty and the joint Allied negotiations the Prince of Waterloo swiftly appointed the Prussian general Karl von Müffling as military governor of Paris. In doing so, Wellington resolved two challenges simultaneously: with Müffling he would be able to mould local administrators to his liking, and keep the Prussians on a short leash. Micromanagement would remain a feature of Allied rule (and cause of French contestation) until the very end of the occupation.

For five months, from the armistice, the Convention of Saint-Cloud, in early July to the formal withdrawal from Paris and the shift to the occupation of the country in peacetime after November 1815, the 40-year-old Müffling was formally in charge of the French capital.[44] Raised a son of low nobility, Philipp Friedrich Karl Ferdinand Freiherr von Müffling (1775–1851) was commissioned as a lance corporal (*Gefreiterkorporal*) in 1788 and, seeing steady promotions during the many coalition wars, was promoted in 1813 for his brave performance in Leipzig to general major in the Prussian army. Müffling was a typical Prussian officer: sober, extremely loyal, a lover of cartography and geodetics, traditional, but also vain and somewhat conceited.[45] After Paris fell the first time, he was awarded the *Pour le Mérite*, with oak leaves, and was appointed as chief of staff for the Russian general Barclay de Tolly before being assigned the same role for the Prussian general Count Kleist. After the beginning of the last coalition campaign in March 1815, Müffling served as liaison in Wellington's headquarters between the British commander and his own chief commander, Blücher. From the dead- and wounded-strewn market square in Leipzig to military governor of the French capital, this corporal had come a long way.

[43] See e.g. P. Stettiner, *Der Tugendbund* (Koningsberg: Koch, 1904).
[44] Wacker makes a distinction between occupation in wartime, a ceasefire occupation and occupation in peacetime. See Wacker, *Die alliierte Besetzung*, 2–3, 17.
[45] M. Lehmann, *Scharnhorst*, vol. 2 (Leipzig: Hirzel, 1887), 600; Müffling, *The Memoirs*, vi.

When Müffling's superior, the Prussian chief of staff Gneisenau, delegated him as liaison to Wellington's headquarters, he advised his protégé to be on his guard:

> for that by his relations with India, and his transactions with the deceitful Nabobs [local Indian rulers], this distinguished general had so accustomed himself to duplicity, that he had at last become such a master in the art as even to outwit the Nabobs themselves.[46]

Wellington did indeed take Müffling for a ride, as noted above, making him complicit in his strategy of creating a fait accompli with respect to Louis XVIII's return to France. Nevertheless, they got along well. And Wellington urged Blücher and Gneisenau to agree that Müffling would be the new military commander of Paris until the sovereigns had arrived and an official peace agreement had been signed. Müffling was absolutely delighted with the appointment, and considered it as 'proof of his confidence, which I valued more highly than the Commander's Cross of the Bath, which he [Wellington] presented to me by order of the Prince Regent'.[47]

Müffling thus became responsible for the organization of the first stage of the occupation, the temporary military control of Paris that would last until a peace treaty was concluded. His main task was to restore peace and order in the capital, and facilitate and control all movements to, through and from Paris – commercial traffic, military communications, civil travel and postal services alike. Wellington had instructed him to put French local governance under surveillance, but at the same time respect the French local administrators. The Allies had declared, after all, on 4 December 1813, that they had come to fight Napoleon and to liberate the rest of France, not to subjugate it.[48] Müffling took this ambivalent instruction to heart. He divided the city into two halves, to the left and the right of the Seine. He appointed a British colonel to keep watch over the six *Mairies* (municipal arrondissements or boroughs) on the right, and a Prussian colonel with the same responsibility for the left bank. Hence, the Allies would be able to monitor the enforcement of the military order of the occupation forces, to regulate the procurement of food and the billeting of troops and to address complaints from both the French and the Allied forces. As in 1814, the public administration, and even the police, secret police and gendarmerie, remained in the hands of the French authorities. The Paris prefect of police was Élie Decazes, a royalist who would soon make his career as a favourite and minister of Louis XVIII. Wellington and his 20,000 men made camp in the Bois de Boulogne; he kept the rest of his troops outside the city, except for one detachment on the Champs Elysées. Blücher did

---

[46] Müffling, *The Memoirs*, 212.
[47] Ibid., 255–6.
[48] See Guerrin, *La France après Napoléon*.

quarter his infantrymen from the First Army Corps in the centre of the city (although he himself remained at Saint-Cloud). The Champs Elysées detachment and the Prussian infantrymen were both under Müffling's jurisdiction. The combination of restoring normal order, enforcing military discipline amongst the Allied soldiers and controlling the French administrators soon became a huge headache for him.[49]

The local French authorities were not all that compliant and did not easily subject themselves to Allied rule. Immediately after Müffling had been appointed, prefect Decazes came to explain to him that under no circumstances could Parisians start to report their guests for the night to the Allies; such a requirement – as issued by Müffling – infringed on their inalienable right, 'a very ancient prerogative of the city of Paris'. The immediate disarmament of the suburbs, and in particular the evacuation of the Fort of Vincennes, was also impossible, according to Decazes. If the Allies were to insist on this, he implicitly threatened the Prussian governor, this could spark a general uprising against the troops. It would, moreover, be far better to leave the execution of Allied orders to him, Decazes. Soon enough, the good-hearted Müffling caved in, after which many of the Allied measures were simply watered down or stalled altogether.[50] Another prefect, Count Chabrol, was equally clever in defusing the Allies' actions. Müffling had issued orders to erect barricades at crucial crossings and to set up blockhouses with *embrasures* – small bunkers – at key intersections, so that his troops could easily keep main roads open with guns and muskets. Yet the charming and flattering Chabrol talked him out of it.[51] Provided he was treated with all due respect, and mollified with reasonable arguments, the pompous general could easily be won over.

Fouché, as minister of police, likewise repeatedly led Müffling down the garden path, as his diplomatic skills did not keep pace with his vigour. On 5 July, Wellington had indicated that, unlike in 1814, wearing tricolour cockades was strictly forbidden. Flags were to be white, the colour of the French lily and the Bourbon dynasty. The tricolour had fallen into disrepute, as it represented revolution and Bonapartist rebelliousness. Nevertheless, the next day Marshal André Masséna instructed the French National Guard to wear the tricolour – probably at Fouché's urging.[52] For some reason, Müffling could be convinced that the cockades would not matter much and could either be tricolour or white. Of course, immediate rows and skirmishes on the Paris streets were the direct consequence, upon which Müffling, now thoroughly agitated, announced that his troops would not hesitate to fire on riotous gatherings. This order was subsequently seized upon by Fouché, who – never

---

[49] Müffling, *The Memoirs*, 256–7.
[50] Ibid., 258–9.
[51] Ibid., 260.
[52] Waresquiel, *Fouché*, 584–5.

the one to skirt an opportunity to fan the fire – coolly published Müffling's spontaneous order in the newspapers.[53]

The Allied Council was not happy with Müffling's blundering. On 12 July, during its inaugural session, the Council discussed the complaints lodged by Talleyrand and General Desolles, his minister of justice, concerning Müffling's regulations for Paris. To the French officials, the Prussian governor was undermining the stability of the newly appointed royal government. The Council realized that Müffling's actions were a direct consequence of the ambivalent Allied orders. To the French, they pointed out that when Müffling issued his decrees, the king was not yet in town and the general situation was still unclear. Now that the king was back, the tricolour cockade should of course be banned.[54] Müffling remained caught between all fires: the Allied ministers, who kept sending their orders, the French officials, who on all sides tried to wriggle around him, and the citizens of Paris, who were very hard to rein in at all. The prefects were working overtime; caricatures of Louis XVIII, Wellington and the other Allied sovereigns appeared in newspapers and journals,[55] a pig with a white lily was led through the streets, the tricolour was still seen everywhere and shouts of 'Vive l'empereur, à bas le roi!' went up from the street corners. Müffling had learned his lesson and meted out increasingly stiff sanctions. Two-week sentences were handed out to those caught singing *La Marseillaise*. But that did not bring more security either. Soldiers from the king's retinue were advised not to walk about on their own, and to wear the military uniform of the Maison du Roi only while on duty within the king's household. The risk was real; in July the body of a murdered Allied soldier was fished from the Seine. 'We are getting into a very critical state', Wellington wrote to Castlereagh, 'and you may depend upon it that, if one shot is fired in Paris, the whole country will rise in arms against us.'[56] Lady Shelley, who with her husband had followed Wellington to the continent and had temporarily found residence in Paris, expressed her worries: 'Every morning we hear of riots having occurred in the gardens of the Tuileries during the night. The rioters throw stones at the women, and sabre those men who refuse to cry "Vive le Roi". I think that matters look very bad.'[57] On 24 July, Müffling stipulated that in the event of insurgency or crisis, three cannon shots would

[53] Ibid., 604.
[54] See the appendices to the protocols of 12 July 1815; the letters of Talleyrand, Desolles, and the note to Müffling, GStA PK, III. HA, no. 1464.
[55] See, for example, R. Goldstein, *Censorship of Political Caricature in Nineteenth-Century France* (Kent, OH: Kent State University Press, 1989), 99–102.
[56] Houssaye, *1815. La seconde abdication*, 346–8; Wellington to Castlereagh, 14 July 1815, in *WD*, vol. 12 558; Wellington to Nesselrode, 18 July 1815, in *WD*, vol. 12, 563–4; Müffling's regulations, 24 July 1815, *WSD*, vol. 11, 53–4.
[57] Edgcumbe (ed.), *The Diary of Frances Lady Shelley, 1787–1817*, 130.

be the sign that all Allied troops were to report immediately to their camps and that the residents of Paris were to leave the streets straight away.

It did not come to such an emergency; the presence of the thousands of Allied soldiers was enough of a deterrent to even the most fiery Parisian protesters, who were not inclined to start a war all over again, but simply seized every opportunity to manipulate and obstruct, for example by playing the Allies off against each other. Especially Tsar Alexander was very open to any complaint or protestation voiced by the French citizens, hence undermining Müffling's authority. Moreover, when Müffling, for example, issued a decree to apprehend all male relatives of Napoleon, Joseph Bonaparte found refuge in the city palace of the Swedish ambassador (he was married to the sister of Bernadotte's wife). Upon hearing about this rumour in the Allied Council, Tsar Alexander openly enquired with the Swedish ambassador whether that was indeed the case – thereby warning Joseph off, who escaped abroad via passports handed out to him by the Russians. 'I did not spare the Emperor Alexander the embarrassment of a circumstantial verbal report of this flight', an offended Müffling noted with some bitterness.[58]

At the end of his somewhat turbulent term of service as governor of Paris, with the conclusion of the Second Peace Treaty on 20 November 1815, Müffling was granted an audience with Louis. Müffling, who was not in the least impressed with this French favour, used the opportunity to give Louis a piece of advice. He put in a good word for prefect Decazes, reporting extensively on his good qualities. After that:

> I described to him the influence which the unfeeling rule of Napoleon had had on the impressionable French, and how all his [Louis's] endeavours to attach them to himself by moral and religious means would turn out unsuccessful, unless he combined these with a cold measured strictness, to which Napoleon had accustomed them, and without which his power would break against the wild unruly state of the people.

The king, at first, listened with rapt attention, and then, according to Müffling, burst into tears, at which point Müffling retired to another room, leaving Louis alone with his sorrow.[59]

Unfazed by the listed incidents, Müffling looked back with satisfaction on this spell as governor and entertained high impressions of his impact. He had not quite noticed how, as a right-wing, upright Prussian baron – used to the predictable and staid bureaucracy of Germany – he had been a bit of a square peg in the gently rounded hole of the Parisian culture of intrigue and bonvivantism. In contrast to his predecessor during the first occupation, Osten-Sacken, he did not have the time of day for the decadent bounty of food and

[58] Müffling, *The Memoirs*, 269–70.
[59] Ibid., 271–2.

wine that came his way from the city during those first days: 'I instantly sent it all back again, with the remark, that as a Prussian general I had my own cook and field-kitchen.' He also sent home straight away the rent-monies due to him (by 'ancient custom') as governor (2,000 francs daily) for the gambling houses in Paris, as bounty to the Prussian general state treasury.[60] Self-assuredly, but quite correctly, Müffling remarked:

> During the whole time of my government I lived exclusively for my duty, and quite secluded from social life, as much because I had no time for its enjoyments, as because I deemed it expedient from prudential reasons. On principle, I never took the slightest notice of all the threatening letters and anonymous reports of plots on my life.[61]

In other words, Müffling had made his mark as regent of Paris, but only to underscore the fragility of the kind of indirect rule the Allies were trying to impose on the occupied territories. The military occupation of Paris had merely been the start; a full-fledged peacetime occupation had now to be rolled out by the Allied Council for the whole of France.

The 'Allied Machine'

While Müffling was trying to bring some Prussian order into French bureaucracy, his superiors were busy filling the administrative vacuum at the national level. Wellington's impatience in pushing Louis forward was not a stubbornly dashing exploit; his preference for the prompt proclamation of Allied support for the Bourbon option was part of Britain's plans for a post-war order for France and Europe as a whole. Although no explicit legal paragraphs were drawn up or cited, as would be the case with occupation regimes in the twentieth century, some reference was certainly made to general principles of international law. The Allied ministers invoked the treaties of Chaumont and Paris from 1814, and the Allies' declaration of mutual security of March 1815, in which the great powers had agreed to jointly defend the 'balance of power' and 'European security' – co-signed by Louis XVIII. The Prussians also gave their own spin on its legitimacy by referring to 'the Allied right' that ensued from the 'great sacrifices' that their troops had made for the peace of Europe. According to Hardenberg this was clearly not a mundane 'right of conquest', but a right deriving from the agreed-upon stipulations in the treaties of Paris and Vienna.[62]

---

[60] Ibid., *The Memoirs*, 260–1. See also J. von Gruner, 'Müffling und Gruner', *Deutsche Zeitschrift für Geschichtswissenschaft*, 11:1 (1894), 364–8. See also Chapter 5 of this book. Chancellor Hardenberg allowed Müffling to keep 100 of the 2,000 francs daily for 'table money'.

[61] Müffling, *The Memoirs*, 262.

[62] [Hardenberg], 'Etat des Négociations actuelles entre les Puissances Alliées & la France', 16–28 July 1815, GStA PK, III. HA I. no. 1461, 55.

Metternich immediately corrected the Prussian argument: it was not a matter of *conquêtes* (conquest) or *Siegerjustiz* (victor's justice) at all, but about restoring law and order.[63] With these invocations of international public law, Blücher's and Gneisenau's archaic Providence, imploring thirst for revenge, was now theoretically sidelined. The occupation regime was, however, still only staked out in very broad lines.

Practically speaking, the Allies fell back on their previous experiences, gained both in colonial situations (indirect rule) and with Stein's and Osten-Sacken's administrative practices of 1814. For example, Müffling was advised by the Allied Council to study further how Osten-Sacken had done things the last time the Allies occupied Paris.[64] Stein's Central Department, however, proved to be more a case of how not to do things. According to the Allied ministers, Stein had been far too directive in his approach. They therefore declined to appoint a supranational administrator and would bear equal responsibility for the decisions made. This, they would do as a council consisting of representatives of the four courts, thereby preventing any form of *Alleingänge* – having especially the Prussians in mind.[65]

On this note, the 'political machine' of Friedrich Gentz was set in motion.[66] The machine consisted of various components. The Allied Administration Council – initially referred to by the Germans as the *General-Armee-Kommission*, and later also as the *Vereinigtes Ministerium der alliierten Armeen* – immediately took up its business upon entering Paris.[67] As in 1814, it comprised representatives of the four major powers, but now without an executive director. The four envoys had to process the requests of the Allied governors regarding care for the troops, and discuss these with their French counterpart, the Requisition Committee.[68] These discussions focused on mundane, but highly essential affairs. At the beginning of August a treaty was drawn up in which the Allies discussed with the French how many bales of linen and cloth the French had to provide for the Allied troops. After fighting so many battles, the troops stood in need of food, clothing, equipment, medical care and materials; and the French had to provide these things – as was agreed upon. Blücher, in particular, initially focused on immediate demands, such as the urgent need to replace the troops' rags with new uniforms, and threatened

---

[63] Metternich, Memorandum, 6 August 1815, sent to Hardenberg, GStA PK, III. HA I. no. 1461, 75.

[64] Memorandum, Allied Council, protocol of 12 July 1815, GStA PK, III. HA I. no. 1464.

[65] See Wacker, *Die alliierte Besetzung*.

[66] Gentz, 'Über de Pradt's Gemälde von Europa', 295.

[67] See Wacker, *Die alliierte Besetzung*, 105.

[68] See the folder 'Devis et soumissions de fournitures de commerçants pour les armées alliées', 12 August–3 September 1815, in 'Commission des Requisitions', 'Commission des Requisitions, Procès Verbaux et correspondances, 1815'. Centre des Archives diplomatiques de Nantes (CAdN), no. 8ACN/1, no. 8ACN/6, no. 8ACN/7[8].

to confiscate it all by himself when the Allied Administration would not provide for his needs. Delays and non-delivered goods came with a fine, and were penalized with direct confiscations.[69]

Notwithstanding these strict stipulations, the Administrative Council was clearly an improvement for the French population compared to the brazen confiscation practices that the Prussian troops had used to stock their shelves in the territories they had occupied. Blücher had blatantly allowed municipal treasuries to be looted, and local goods seized.[70] Field Marshal Wellington had to keep reminding the generals that Louis and the royal government were their formal allies now; even though that might seem counterintuitive to the troops, it was an important principle of Allied rule. The fight against terror and the efforts to stabilize France could not be won without the French government and population.[71]

The Administrative Council, however, was merely an executive agency charged with seeing to adequate supplies for the occupational forces. The real political decisions and negotiations were made by the Allied Council itself, drawing its legitimacy from the above-mentioned treaties. This international body was installed once the military Capitulation Treaty was signed on 3 July 1815 and was to remain in the French capital for the time of the occupation and take an active part in managing the peace. The Allied leaders – especially Metternich and Castlereagh – very much adhered to the principle that none of the occupying powers should operate in isolation, but that all decisions, following 'discussion and deliberation', should be taken jointly and consistently, based on 'common and uniform principles'. Thus, for negotiating possible and anticipated differences, the council would serve as a forum of daily deliberation.[72]

The *Conférence des Ministres Alliés*, or Allied Council,[73] as it was often referred to, declared its formal creation on 12 July and constituted a veritable novelty in history; it was in fact an alliance organization and a strategic military council in one. It convened daily until December 1815, and thereafter two or three times a week.[74] The Council originally consisted of Vienna's main players: Chancellor Prince Klemens von Metternich, for Austria; minister of

---

[69] 'Articles arrêtés entre M. l'Intendant Général des armées & les Commissaires de S. M. T. C. sur le mode d'exécution pour l'entretien, l'habillement & l'équipement des troupes', 15 August 1815, GStA PK, III. HA I. no. 1461.
[70] Protocol of 14 July 1815; see the memorandum attached from Talleyrand, GStA PK, III. HA I. no. 1464.
[71] Wacker, *Die alliierte Besetzung*, 115.
[72] Protocol of 12 July 1815, GStA PK, III. HA I. no. 1464.
[73] Strictly speaking, it was no council, but a diplomatic conference, since executive authority lay with the governments and cabinets, not with the Allied ministers in Paris. Yet, in practice, the ministers assumed quite a great amount of executive leeway.
[74] Cf. (De) Graaf, 'The Allied Machine'.

foreign affairs, Robert Stewart, Viscount Castlereagh, for Britain; ambassador Friedrich Wilhelm von Humboldt, Chancellor Prince Karl August von Hardenberg and General Neidhardt von Gneisenau for Prussia; and Count Carlo Andrea Pozzo di Borgo and Count Karl von Nesselrode for Russia. Minister Prince Charles-Maurice de Talleyrand, and his successor after 20 September, Armand-Émmanuel du Plessis, Duke of Richelieu, were summoned to join the Council (and to receive orders from them) as the need arose. The members knew each other well, having literally weathered the anti-Napoleonic campaigns together, following the trail of the troops to their headquarters on horseback.[75] They had, moreover, spent time with each other extensively in the corridors and chambers of the Viennese palaces.

Important strategic decisions would be centrally conveyed to France, which was only allowed to represent itself in the observing role of its prime minister, who in July was still Talleyrand. The Council would convene promptly at eleven o'clock in the British embassy (Hôtel de Charost), the former palace and 'love nest' of Pauline Borghese on the Rue du Faubourg Saint-Honoré, where *méthodiquement* all the issues pertaining to security in France, as well as throughout Europe (and later, even regarding territories overseas), were discussed and arranged. A secretary would work up the protocols and send them out. These protocols summarized the discussions, recorded the joint decisions reached, and counted as binding international law to all the courts of Europe. Communication with the French government was to occur via joint Allied memoranda, signed by each of the four ministers. The ministers also agreed to communicate in French and have standardized monetary and measurement units in their accounts.[76]

The Allied Council was assisted by another important subcommittee, alongside the administrative body mentioned above. All questions regarding the army of occupation and issues regarding demilitarization were to be dealt with by the Military Committee, which was installed on 13 July. Müffling's Paris administration now fell to this committee as well. It consisted of the Allied commanders of the Seventh Coalition – Schwarzenberg, Gneisenau, Wolkonsky, Radetzky, Wrede and Wellington – under the leadership of the last. The Military Committee also took care of all issues relating to *haute police* (national security and intelligence services), military-strategic issues and military requisitions. An *Alliierte Verbündetenpolizei* (Allied secret police) would be added by decree on 22 July. Other, regular police matters remained in the hands of French officials and the royal government.[77] Matters relating to security, politics and the care of the troops would first be dealt with in the

---

[75] Müffling, *The Memoirs*, 219.
[76] Protocol of 12 and 13 July 1815, GStA PK, III. HA I. no. 1464. Citation from annex 6, protocol of 13 July.
[77] Protocol of 13 July, GStA PK, III. HA I. no. 1464.

subcommittees and only delegated to the Council when they transcended the competences of the individual commanders. Wellington was pleased with this construction: 'la machine sera aussi bien montée qu'il est possible dans les circonstances du moment'.[78]

'Principles of Salutary Precaution'

The Council was a powerful machine that cranked out printed memos, advice and instructions for distribution among the French. It was also a machine that ran primarily on British oil, not only because Wellington had come to assume such a crucial role in all matters of practical military, political and police affairs, but also because the British were initially basically paying for the troops. That is why all agreed to convene the Council at the British embassy, a highly symbolic and significant gesture. Alexander was far less active; missives from the Russians for the Council were few and far between. Metternich concentrated primarily on the fight against 'armed Jacobinism' and on tracking down revolutionaries and Bonapartists.[79] The Prussians stubbornly and single-mindedly clung to the reparations question. Thus, Castlereagh and Wellington could prop themselves up as honest brokers for the new peace and security order. They did indeed develop a series of strategic blueprints not only for the future of France, but for Europe as a whole.

In a 'memorandum', the first major document discussed by the Council that 13 July, Castlereagh articulated a series of 'principles of salutary precaution' that was to hold as a blueprint for the Allied objectives; for 'the Allies are now for the second time at Paris, and they owe it to their own People as well as to France, not to be obliged to return a third time'. Based on 'circumspection', in line with 'their own interest' given their task as 'Concert of Europe', and on the basis of treaties current at the time, Castlereagh narrowed it down to four principles: demilitarize, de-Bonapartize, stabilize and a fourth principle that was not explicitly articulated here, namely, indemnify and organize the collection of reparations, but that was already considered as generally accepted (and had already been in effect from the get-go). These four principles were to dictate the contact and dealings with the 'political state of France', composed of '1st. The King. 2nd. The Nation. 3rd. The Army and the active Conspirators'.[80] That third party was the most dangerous, according to the Council, because the army had been 'the source of all evil that had prompted the invasion of France'.[81] That is

---

[78] Wellington, Memorandum for the Allied Council, 'Réponses aux questions à discuter', protocol of 20 July 1815, GStA PK, III. HA I. no. 1464.

[79] Cf. (De) Graaf, 'The Allied Machine', 140.

[80] Castlereagh, Memorandum, 13 July 1815. GStA PK, III. HA I. no. 1461. See also Liverpool to Castlereagh, 21 July 1815, *WSD*, vol. 11, 47.

[81] Note from the Council, as annex 85 to the protocol of 18 August, addressed to Talleyrand, GStA PK, III. HA I. no. 1465.

why the principle of demilitarizing – 'the Dissolution of Bonaparte's Army', was the Allied Council's *first* priority. To this end, the French troops would first of all be forced to withdraw to south of the River Loire and then be decommissioned 'either by the power of the Allied Arms or by the King's authority . . . till it shall cease to exist as a military body'. The same fate awaited the National Guard, 'which consecrates their treason, perjury and hostile relations towards their own Sovereign and Europe'. In 1814, Alexander had not deactivated the guard, which subsequently had betrayed the Bourbon regime and joined Napoleon. Demilitarization was therefore the first condition for King Louis's government to create a stable base and construct a novel, royal and especially loyal army. This would furthermore benefit the rest of the continent, since it was the Allies' intention to see to it 'that Europe shall by some means or other be secured against the recurrence of a similar calamity'.[82]

Closely linked to this first principle was the need to de-Bonapartize the country. This *second* principle held in the first instance for Napoleon himself, who, on 13 July, was still 'at large'. But the remaining 'traitors' and Napoleon sympathizers also needed to be identified, arrested, tried and/or banned. At the same time, the Allies pledged to support the 'legitimate King Louis XVIII', 'to uphold and confirm his Royal authority, and to make it the instrument, if possible, of effectuating all their views in France. To dishonour or enfeeble that authority unnecessarily is in fact to weaken their own hands.' This *third* principle of stabilization was, however, quite ambivalently worded. On the one hand, the Allies pledged to support his authority, and suppress anything that would 'enfeeble' his rule. On the other hand, they confirmed that they would use the royal government as 'their instrument' to effectuate their plans: in short, an explicit form of potentially contentious 'indirect rule'. Stabilization also implied service to the people, the ministers asserted: 'It is also the duty of the Allied Powers to treat the nation with indulgence and conciliation, but to act towards them upon those principles of salutary precaution which their levity and invariable submissiveness to every successive usurpation enjoins.' Thus, stabilization would be enacted by supporting the king, providing benevolent guidance and even re-educating the French people, who had been caught up by the winds of change so often before.[83] The Allies' stated benevolence towards the French nation was nonetheless conditional and selective. They certainly did not reach out to the 'traitors and agitators in France who will inevitably organize a new Revolution'. With regard to that group, impunity was a sign of weakness and insincerity on the part of the new Bourbon government. That was the flip side of the stabilization coin: every trace of revolt and revolution had to be prosecuted and suppressed. Like the Bonapartists, the

[82] Talleyrand to the Allied Council, 11 July 1815, annex to the protocol of the first *séance*, 12 July 1815, GStA PK, III. HA I. no. 1464.
[83] Castlereagh, Memorandum.

revolutionary 'traitors' needed to know that they could not take their safety for granted. Here again, the seemingly clear-cut principles laid the groundwork for many headaches, since stabilizing and upholding the royal regime would most certainly come to clash with Allied interventions and interferences in societal and political disputes.

The *fourth* principle, the indemnifications and collective reparations, was equally double-edged. With the Allied Army of Occupation, that 'bond of peace', both peace and requisitions had to be enforced. Reparations, however, were certainly not viewed by the French citizens as beneficial to their domestic peace, but felt like Allied vindictiveness and superiority.

None of these four principles could be realized without the presence of the Allied forces. After all, the danger was 'that when the Allied Armies are removed from the Country, the System itself may fall to pieces, before it has by time been consolidated'. With the Memorandum of 13 July, the Allied Council therefore officially laid the foundation for the military occupation of France, not just during the negotiations for the Second Treaty of Paris, but also for the supervision and – if need be – enforcement of the treaty stipulations afterwards, for years to come. This was the first time that the prolonged presence of the Council for a period of multiple years was made explicit – the aim of which was to achieve these principles and, in so doing, to strengthen the 'Concert of Europe'. 'No time ought to be lost' in bringing about such a regime, and in convincing the French government that this was a necessary and beneficial step for the country and its people. Castlereagh did warn the Allies that it would be important to regulate the military and administrative practices of indirect rule well, to involve local administrators and allow them a degree of autonomy and to guarantee discipline and order in the occupied territories. In addition, the Allied troops would have to be well behaved and decent, and their officers aware of 'consistent regularity and sound method' in distributing and requisitioning what their soldiers stood in need of. In other words, the package instruction for these 'measures of salutary precaution' was clear enough: each Ally, and each commander, had to set a statutory example.[84]

The other Allies accepted and embraced the Memorandum straight away (turning it into binding law). But not without some extra additions. The Prussians wanted to see the payment of indemnities and reparations added as an explicit principle to the declaration, and not treated as an implicit or subordinate matter. Hardenberg formulated several arguments for compensating Prussia, in which he claimed more than 1,200 million francs for the joint German states. Prussia would wholeheartedly support the Bourbon regime, but only on the condition that that regime met its financial obligations. The

---

[84] Castlereagh, Memorandum, 13 July 1815, GStA PK, III. HA I. no. 1461. See also Houssaye, *1815. La seconde abdication*, 425–6.

question of the forts and fortifications along the border was, moreover, equally crucial for the Prussians, but Hardenberg agreed to discuss these later, in separate talks. The Austrians and the smaller states fully supported the points made by Hardenberg. Metternich furthermore urged the Council also to specifically underline the importance of fighting terror and revolution and making provisions for doing so. With the inclusion of Berlin and Vienna's call for reparations and Metternich's extra emphasis on forming an *haute police* force to counter terror, the Memorandum was confirmed and the Allied Council and its subcommittees could get down to work.[85]

The End of the Grande Armée

The first meetings of the Council, in July and August, were consequently devoted almost in their entirety to the most pressing principle – that of the demilitarization. Based on the Military Convention of 3 July, the imperial army had to withdraw to beyond the Loire. On 5 and 6 July, the troops streamed to the south, undisciplined and in complete disarray, and began to arrive there on 11 July. Despite the many who deserted, the main army still numbered some 70,000 men.[86] General Louis-Nicolas Davout, who was Napoleon's Marshal of the Empire, had indeed instructed his soldiers to put down their arms, since fighting the combined forces of the Allies, with Napoleon somewhere on the run, and Napoleon II in Vienna, would be a suicidal affair from the outset. Moreover, 'an army without a government ... is something of an inconceivable monstrosity. That would be a reminiscence of the banditry and the brigandage operated by du Guesclin' – referring to the fourteenth-century French guerilla wars.[87] But to simply submit himself to the king's new minister of war, Gouvion Saint-Cyr, was equally too risky. For what would happen to his soldiers, officers and generals? Could they keep their jobs, would they still be paid, or would they be fired or even taken prisoner? The limbo lasted a few days, after which Davout received extra guarantees and solemnly submitted himself to the king's authority:

> The armies of Europe have rushed into France to set the country ablaze; all hope to drive her out by force is lost. Only the government of Louis XVIII may bring the devastation and dismemberment of France to a halt. That is why the army should now rally behind him.[88]

---

[85] See for example Hardenberg, 'Memorandum', 22 July 1815, point 2; Humboldt, 'État des Négociations actuelles entre les Puissances Alliées et la France', 16–18 July 1815, GStA PK, III. HA I. no. 1461.

[86] Houssaye, *1815: La seconde abdication*, 403–6.

[87] Cited in Houssaye, *1815. La seconde abdication*, 407.

[88] Cited Ibid., 413.

In the end, Davout preferred to have a white lily rather than foreign banners blowing over France. The new king, however, could in no way guarantee Davout that he would work to support the integrity of Davout's army. With the Allies in the driver's seat, that question was really out of his hands.

Indeed, Alexander and Metternich had already expressed their preference for the permanent dissolution of the entire French army in 1814, as the only condition for a lasting and 'universal peace' in Europe.[89] On 12 July, after its first meeting, the Allied Council requested that Talleyrand formally disband the imperial army, and announce its 'reorganization'. Müffling's military government of Paris, supervised by Wellington as the chairman of the Military Committee, was to oversee the full demobilization of the French troops and their departure from the capital. Only a few British and Prussian elite regiments were allowed to remain in the city; the rest were dispatched to their zones of occupation. Some French garrisons, like those in Verdun, who had sworn loyalty to the king at a very early stage, requested to remain in the north as well. But Wellington had learned from Prince Frederick of Orange, his general over the army in the north, how the Allied forces were being pestered with blockades and all kinds of subversions by these allegedly loyal French regiments up north and would not hear of these demands at all.[90] All of the troops, whether royalist turncoats or staunch Bonapartists, were to transfer to south of the Loire. Cities could only be watched over by the city guard and they had to grant the Allies right of transit throughout the country.[91]

On 14 July, Davout handed the military command over to Marshal Jacques MacDonald, and submitted his resignation on 20 July. But not before once again imploring the Council that back salaries be paid and that further guidelines be established for the altogether disorientated and overwhelmed troops.[92] The Allied Council urged Talleyrand to appoint a new commander, one who was trustworthy and could better manage disbanding and then reorganizing the army. The Allies also ordained that special passports were necessary for any French soldier wanting to cross the border between occupied and non-occupied regions of the country. Metternich stipulated that such passports – understood more as a type of safe-conduct – could only be issued to trustworthy individuals of 'good character'. Thus, the Allied forces would be able to allow to move beyond the Loire only those who had an impeccable record. Only by way of an exception, when their home address was in occupied territory, and they could also demonstrate a perfect record, were persons allowed to cross over in the other direction. To manage these immense traffic

[89] Ibid., 417–18.
[90] Protocol of 16 July, report Wellington, GStA PK, III. HA I. no. 1464.
[91] Protocols of 1, 13, 14, 15 and 16 July 1815, GStA PK, III. HA I. no. 1464.
[92] Davout to Gouvion Saint-Cyr (minister of war), 21 July, annex to protocol of 20 July 1815, GStA PK, III. HA no. 1465.

controls, the Council instructed the Allied commanders, Müffling and the French government to set up a centre to administer all available information. Lists of vetted soldiers, their march routes and issued passports should be recorded. A passport document should include Allied signatures, remarks about the individual's character, intended destination and the time frame allowed for their passage to beyond the Loire. Only signatures issued by one of the four great powers would be valid; smaller states' signatures, or merely a French signature would fall through at the control posts. The Council also impressed on Talleyrand that only they decided on the issuing of passports and that they could withdraw the safe-conduct at their whim.[93]

On the Road with a Passport

Not just French or Allied soldiers required a passport while on the move. Civil travellers would not get far without such a document either; not just in France, but all over the continent, passports were the prerequisites for a safe journey. The more high-ranking signatures one collected, the more effective the safe conduct was – as a lady friend of Wellington's was about to experience.

For years, Frances Winckley, Lady Shelley (1787–1873), a British noble-woman, had wanted to take a trip through Europe. At the beginning of the nineteenth century that was no small task for a woman who held her reputation dear. Women venturing out alone was a phenomenon that – incidentally, just like the commercial production of tourist guides – would only come into vogue in the middle of that century, owing especially to the growing number and cultured popularity of spas.[94] Before then, 'respectable women' travelled only with a larger group, including servants. Ladies of title, including princesses and wives of diplomats, would travel, following their husbands so as to join them at friendly courts for special ceremonies or festivities, as did the aforementioned Louisa Adams, who made her way from St Petersburg to Paris in the winter of 1815.[95] But a 'Grand Tour', or other forms of tourism, usually

---

[93] Protocol and appendices, 29 July 1815, GStA PK, III. HA I. no. 1465.

[94] E. Hammer-Luza, 'Between Different Levels: The Journeys of Anna Plochl (1804–1885), Middle-Class Wife of Archduke John of Austria'; C. Vanja, 'Women Travel to Bad Ems: A Great Spa in the 18th and 19th Centuries'; M. Heidegger, 'Female Spa Guests in the 19th Century': papers presented at the 'European Social Science History Conference', 30 March–2 April 2016, Valencia. There were travel journals, and so-called *guides des voyageurs*, but it was only in the 1830s that John Murray (London) and Karl Baedeker (Koblenz) began to publish their commercial travel guides, filled with advertisements and systematic reviews of hotels, restaurants, cultural highlights and recommended routes. O'Brien, *Mrs. Adams in Winter*, 50.

[95] O'Brien, *Mrs. Adams in Winter*, 46. See, for an analysis of the 'travel writing' of British ladies, C. Barros and J. Smith, *Life-Writings by British Women 1660–1815. An Anthology* (Boston: Northeastern University Press, 2000), 31.

remained the prerogative of men. Women who travelled about were typically camp followers, women of loose morals or gang leaders.

Frances Winckley's marriage to Sir John Shelley in June 1807 was in that regard her ticket to travel. He literally allowed her to broaden her horizons. But the Napoleonic Wars had frustrated her dream. In March 1815, just when Lady Shelley and her husband were ready to depart for Europe, planning to leave their property and children in the hands of their loyal servants, the news reached them that Napoleon had escaped and had already arrived in Paris.[96] They had to wait another three months, but upon hearing about the outcome of the Battle of Waterloo,[97] they could leave for real. 'On the day that we heard that Paris had surrendered, we prepared to start; and, if possible, be the first to see, and to congratulate the hero' (indicating their friend Wellington).[98] In the early morning hours of 15 July they sailed for Calais, arriving some three hours later. The port town shone in the morning sun. The women with coloured petticoats, blue stockings and white clogs, and their 'decidedly pretty' children, made an impression on the British tour group. But as the coach drove further inland the consequences of the recent military campaigns could not help but be noticed. Bridges and fortifications were destroyed or in significant disrepair; farmlands looked neglected and shabby. 'I was struck by the scarcity of men and a multitude of squalid, and clamorous beggars, whose importunities at last drove me from the window.' White flags fluttered from the rooftops and the passengers were greeted cautiously with a 'vive les Anglais!' by French passers-by. Upon arriving in a city or town, the travellers had to hand over their passports to the local authorities. The signed safe-conducts that they had prepared in Britain had the envisaged effect: all Allied officers and French guards immediately accepted their presence, and often offered to escort them – given that their passports sported signatures from officials high up in the British government.

When they approached Saint-Denis on the outskirts of Paris, it was clear that the fighting had been intense. Trees were marked by gunshot, and here and there along the road were traces of bivouacs in the burned cornfields. Near Saint-Denis stood a battalion of heavy artillery; the place itself was swarming with British troops and other soldiers who were part of the Allied forces. Paris was in the hands of the British, or at least so it seemed to Lady Frances: 'As we passed slowly through the encumbered streets, every face seemed to be that of a friend; and we were met with answering smiles from our brave countrymen, who quickly recognized the English carriage.' The Shelleys registered at a hotel that during the first week of their stay changed its name four times: from 'Hôtel de Napoléon', to 'Bourbon', to 'Louis Dix-Huit' and finally to 'Hôtel de la Paix'.

[96] Edgcumbe (ed.), *The Diary of Frances Lady Shelley, 1787–1817*, 86.
[97] Ibid., 87.
[98] Ibid.

The initial highlight was of course seeing Wellington within an hour of settling in. 'In order to understand the delight which the Duke's courteous, and prompt visit caused me', Lady Shelley explained,

> it must be remembered that the hero of Waterloo was regarded by his countrymen with feelings of the deepest gratitude. His victories, crowned by the glory of Waterloo, had relieved Englishmen from a state of deep despondency; and had placed his reputation as a merciful conqueror on a plane with the heroes of chivalry in all ages.[99]

Shelley's travelogue provides a poignant vignette of the astounding compression and acceleration of events after Waterloo and conveys how effective the Allied Council's first interventions already were. The new European order depended on the presence of Allied troops – a presence not just in France, but on the roads towards the country and in the many staging posts and inns as well, as the Shelleys noticed to their delight.[100] This benevolent and protective presence of the Allied troops stood, in the eyes of Lady Shelley, in sharp contrast to the vandalism and disorder caused by the French Revolution. The Revolution had wrought destruction on churches and monuments, witnessed first-hand by the Shelleys in Dijon.[101] The Allied presence brought reconstruction and security. By the issuing of passports and implementation of mandatory inspections for those entering cities or crossing the borders, a degree of control took shape. That control was not all-pervasive, but it did create a perceived degree of predictability and security. That was true for safety on the roads, for the guaranteed presence of post-houses, post-riders and horse exchanges for carriages, as well as for safety in the woods and forests and along the waterways. One of the first orders given by the Allied governor general of Lorraine, David Alopeus, was for the maréchaussée to comb the forests and to protect against smugglers and robber gangs.[102] After their visit to Paris and Wellington, the Shelleys did not return to Britain straight away, but struck out on a Grand Tour of Europe, via Switzerland, Austria, the German lands and Italy, and then back again through France to their home country. They were not attacked, robbed or assaulted once during their entire trip; with the passports signed for them by Wellington, they would pass carefree through every control. A lady could once again travel safely, deep into Italy.

---

[99] Ibid., 88–95.
[100] Ibid., 192–3.
[101] Ibid., 215.
[102] Report of Alopeus, 15 May 1814, GStA PK, I. HA Rep. 92. Nl. Eichhorn, no. 22. See also H. Bald and R. Kuhn, *Die Spessarträuber. Legende und Wirklichkeit* (Würzburg: Königshausen & Neumann, 1991).

Surrender and Occupation

In some places, the Allied peace was, however, still wanting. In July and August 1815, while the Shelleys were already celebrating Allied victory in Paris, the last cities along the border still had to capitulate, sometimes only after fierce resistance and heavy Allied shelling. To this day, various French cities in the east and south of the country cherish their finely chiselled monuments praising the fact that their citizens did not surrender their bastions to the Allied forces, and thus prevented the seizure of arms stockpiles and food stocks. This type of memorial was usually put up only after the Allied departure in 1818.[103] Still, in July 1815, it was not yet clear how pervasive the Allied occupation would be, where it would be implemented and for how long the Allied forces would remain in France.

The occupation took shape step by step. It was the result of both practical considerations, informed by the necessity of petty daily problems, and more strategic calculations. Again, the different principles laid out in Castlereagh's memorandum kept interfering with each other. The Allied principle of stabilization and respect for the government of King Louis prompted the Allied Council to dictate a certain level of moderation to their generals and commanders.[104]

Wellington, who as supreme commander and chairman of the Military Committee oversaw the entire occupation, for example, prohibited the Allied armies and the military governors from confiscating any horse or livestock that smallholders needed to work the land. Farmers were to remain unhindered in their labours. Nesselrode and Pozzo di Borgo let the Russian governors and commanders know how much Tsar Alexander wanted them to follow through on the joint orders and decisions of the Council and Wellington. They had to be led by the *sentiments de justice* and not do anything that would exacerbate unstable or disorderly situations.[105] Both Wellington and Alexander introduced harsh disciplinary measures and penalties for soldiers or officers disobeying these orders.

Yet, their efficiency hinged on the assistance of French prefects, who had to submit to the authority of the governors in theory, but more often than not obstructed occupational instructions and, for example, turned a blind eye to fugitive or insubordinate soldiers or Bonapartist officers.[106] These prefects,

---

[103] Examples are to be found in the entry gate to the citadel of Briançon and in the marketplace of Antibes. There, the inscription reads: 'En août et septembre 1815 la place d'Antibes étant entourée de troupes étrangères les habitants quoique abandonnés a euxmêmes et sans le concours d'aucune garnison jurèrent de la défendre jusqu'à la dernière extremité. Leur patriotisme et leur courage sauvèrent cette ville de la honte d'une occupation.'

[104] Cited in protocol of 24 July, paragraph 2. GStA PK, III. HA I. no. 1465.

[105] Protocols of 22, 23, 24 July 1815, GStA PK, III. HA I. no. 1465.

[106] See for example the manifold complaints and protest letters of the prefects to the French minister of domestic affairs, such as: letter from a prefect to the Austrian governor and

moreover, were in charge of managing 'ordinary' police and judicial matters, since the Allied ministers had agreed to leave questions concerning religion, taxes and finances to the French authorities. In order to smoothen cooperation, each prefect was paired with an Allied commissioner (appointed by the Allied governor of the district), who was there to 'help' him. The Allied commanders in turn were from late July onwards instructed that they might no longer take or use cash from the economy, but had to submit their claims for supplies, support, clothing and the like centrally to the Allied administrative council, which would deal with them via the French commission for contributions and requisitions – an instruction that the Allied Council needed to repeat several times, since the governors and commanders did not always display the patience required to wait for the lukewarm French services and rather helped themselves.[107] This serve-yourself attitude caused a steady stream of complaints – predominantly from the German-occupied areas – and an incessant knocking by Talleyrand on the doors of the British embassy. The Allied Council heard out his anthology of grievances and complaints about Allied misconduct, but could not do much with this general 'information'. Talleyrand would have to provide names, times and places; vague objections about the behaviour of 'Prussian' or 'Bavarian soldiers' did not pass muster.[108]

These administrative doublures and interloping Allied and French interventions also prolonged the unrest on the roads. Deserters, veterans and soldiers discharged from the army roamed the area and caused a nuisance.[109] As per 1 August, every French officer and soldier without a permit for Paris was ordered to leave the capital. But they could only leave by displaying a passport. And even with a couple of days' respite until 5 August, Müffling's administration was still not able to process all requests in time. The Allied system of micromanagement had run aground. The Allied Council therefore appointed two additional French secretaries to assist Müffling in eliminating the passport backlog.[110] Meanwhile, Müffling had ordered the preventative incarceration of all free-roaming, passportless French soldiers, since they were in violation of the military convention of 3 July and could hence be taken as prisoners of war:[111] an intervention that was both unjust (since the soldiers could not help the passport backlog) and not very helpful, since it further increased tensions in the already heated atmosphere in the capital city.

French minister, 'Correspondance des Préfets avec le Ministère de l'Intérieure', CAdN, no. 8ACN/4.
[107] Protocols of 20, 21, 22, 23, 24, 25, 26 July 1815, GStA PK, III. HA I. no. 1465.
[108] Protocols and appendices of 16, 17, 18, 19 and 20 July 1815, GStA PK, III. HA I. no. 1464 and no. 1465.
[109] Cf. Guerrin, La France après Napoléon, 65.
[110] Protocols of 1 and 3 August 1815, GStA PK, III. HA I. no. 1465.
[111] Protocols of 5 August 1815, GStA PK, III. HA I. no. 1465.

That the occupation was necessary, both from the vantage point of security and with an eye on ensuring reparation payments, was something the Allied ministers had agreed upon. But its exact operation, term and character were still open for debate. The Prussian ministers, for example, contended that instead of a temporary occupation, parts of the occupied territories should be surrendered to Germany permanently, especially the strip of land bordering the German lands. Only the incorporation of this line of French fortresses alongside the French north-eastern frontier could give the Allied powers a substantial sense of security. Firm guarantees, both 'durables & réelles', against future French aggression were required.[112] That is why some Prussian representatives argued for harsher measures and a permanent partition of some of the French borderlands. Others, such as Hardenberg's advisor, General Karl Friedrich von dem Knesebeck, were more in favour of substantial financial guarantees: 'A nation so full off egoism and patriotism' would find it less difficult to pay its debts with money than with land.[113]

Metternich initially supported the Prussian desire to undermine French military prowess and occupy the country with an overwhelming use of force. He also supported decommissioning or at least downsizing a series of French garrisons along the north-eastern borders and in the Midi-Pyrénées. But after talks with Wellington, he concluded that Prussia's territorial demands had to be adjusted downwards, as did the financial ones. Not doing so would cause too much turmoil, and in time even lead to further destabilization.[114] The Russians concurred – Pozzo di Borgo and the young confidant of Alexander I, Count Ioannis Kapodistrias, generally agreed with Wellington's arguments; few objections or memoranda emerged from the Russian corner.

Hence, Wellington's voice proved decisive. On 11 August, he informed Castlereagh that the strategic dice regarding the occupation were cast. It was true that France was still very, and perhaps even too powerful, given its military power, territory and forward-looking line of defence. But he did not share Humboldt's assessment that the Allies had the right, on the basis of previous treaties (Humboldt invoked the General Alliance Treaty of 25 March 1815 and the Treaty of Paris of 1814) to significantly revise the territorial definition of France's borders. Neither did Wellington believe that the French nation had forfeited its right to preserve its territory because it had supported Napoleon. The opposite, he felt, was actually the case: 'It would be ridiculous to suppose that the Allies would have been in possession of Paris in a fortnight after one battle fought, if the French people in general had not been favourably disposed to the cause which the Allies were supposed to favour.' The goal was to stabilize

[112] Humboldt, 'État des Négociations actuelles entre les Puissances Alliées et la France', 16–18 July 1815, GStA PK, III. HA I. no. 1461, 61–2.
[113] Knesebeck, Memorandum, 4 August 1815, GStA PK, III. HA I. no. 1461, 65–6.
[114] Metternich, Memorandum, 6 August 1815, GStA PK, III. HA I. no. 1461, 75–81.

Louis XVIII's regime (one of the main Allied principles). If the king would not agree to ceding sections of the country to the Allies, all of France would put their internal divisions to the side and stand shoulder-to-shoulder behind the king; and France's neighbours would once again have to fix their gaze on Paris – 'there would be no genuine peace for the world; no nation could disarm; no Sovereign could turn his attention from the affairs of this country'. And even should the king agree, Wellington opined, Europe would then return to the misery of the year before, with a French army and populace that would be ready to revolt and to retake their lands at the drop of a hat.[115]

Although on the ground things remained messy, amongst the Allied ministers, at least, 'an appearance of moderation in all that has been written' dominated the discussions on France's future. Every minister agreed that the measures taken should serve the overall peace and stability of the regime. A temporary military occupation therefore emerged as being preferable to a major redefinition and realignment of France's northern and eastern provinces. As Wellington neatly summed it up:

> These measures will not only give us, during the period of occupation, all the military security which could be expected from the permanent cession, but if carried into execution in the spirit in which they are conceived, they are in themselves the bond of peace.

In other words, a military occupation for the next few years would not only provide more security arms-wise, it would also be the best way to press King Louis's government for reparation payments and at the same time uphold his regime in France. Moreover – and this was a remarkable strategic decision, flowing fully from Wellington's quill – the neighbouring countries could use that time to restore, reconstruct and expand their own lines of defence (the future Wellington Barrier, on which see Chapter 8). On the contrary, incorporation of the Rhenish provinces into German lands would only amount to 'immediate plunder' and would place a considerable burden on the post-war European peace and security – a very wise and forward-looking admonition.[116]

In so doing, the Allies, and particularly Wellington, dictated the strategic form of the occupation regime. They 'whispered', or better put, insisted that the French government would implement constitutional reforms. On the other hand, they proclaimed loudly how they respected the autonomy and sovereignty of the French state. That ambiguity – the French nation was helped up, but not allowed to stand alone – would spark new rounds of friction in the days and years to come.

For the time being, however, the Allied whispers had impact. On 12 August, the French government presented its plans for political reform and

---

[115] Wellington to Castlereagh, 11 August 1815, GStA PK, III. HA I. no. 1461, 82–7.
[116] Ibid., 86. See also Wellington to Castlereagh, 11 August 1815, in *WD*, vol. 8, 235–8.

reorganization of its military force to the Allied Council – a direct and tangible operationalization of the Allied Council's principles of demilitarization, de-Bonapartization and stabilization. The French plans were clearly informed by the fear of new rounds of terror. The source of the last spell of terror had been, according to the French memorandum, the notion of 'equality' that had nested itself so deep into French political culture and had enthralled the country for twenty-six years in a web of deceit. It had resulted in 'la domination de la multitude' and 'sa tyrannie'. This spirit of egalitarian despotism had subsequently been translated into extraterritorial aggression and 'l'esprit de conquête'. Revolutionary delusions of an 'imaginary world' had to be put down for ever – by means of a new, royal army, a hereditary Chamber of Peers and the provision that the Chamber of Deputies was to share legal prerogative with the king. The king was above the parties and the most important guarantee against renewed revolts and uprisings. In addition, a council of ministers was to serve as a 'measure of precaution' against an 'aberration of power' on the part of the king and the chambers. Restrictions on the freedom of the press were also formally abolished. The French memorandum, moreover, established a clear link between reforms in France and peace in Europe. French despotism had thrived where Europe was divided. Against a united Europe, the remnant of tyranny would not stand a chance.[117]

The Council was pleased with the memorandum; considering the upcoming elections for the Chamber of Deputies, the reforms as laid down in the memorandum were an important step towards stabilizing the French government. Although Prussian suspicions lingered on,[118] the other Council members agreed that the Allied powers had to make sure the French received strong guidance and 'help' in reconstructing their country and had to stick to the four Allied principles. Between July and October they therefore painstakingly negotiated the Second Treaty of Paris and the exact stipulations of the occupation – with the French, but even more amongst each other.

The Treaty of Paris

In 1814, France had been dealt with in a highly lenient fashion. The Peace Treaty of 30 May 1814 was set forth in a context of reconciliation. Tsar Alexander had personally advocated for a merciful and forgiving relationship with the defeated people of France. The Allied powers had not imposed war bounties or indemnities, nor was restitution required for many of the stolen artworks. But France did have to go into liquidation or 'settlements' with the

[117] Memorandum from the French government regarding the dissolution of Bonaparte's army, to the Allied Council. Annex to the protocols of 12 August 1815, GStA PK, III. HA I. no. 1465.
[118] Protocols of 15 and 18 August 1815, GStA PK, III. HA I. no. 1465.

Allied countries, primarily where private property was concerned. Private creditors had been invited to submit claims for arrears for delivered goods and services or for damage owing to the operations of war. Soldiers and civil servants could expect that arrears in salary, pensions and disability benefits would be met. Civil guarantees also fell under the liquidation, as well as the goods and possessions that municipalities and (charitable) organizations had to hand over for the benefit of the French 'sinking funds'.[119] On the other hand, countries whose territories were enlarged through the incorporation of formerly French soil had to settle all arrear debts attached to them as well.[120] Nothing came of all this, however, due to the endless training of the French negotiators and lax enforcement on the part of the Allies – and the subsequent return of Napoleon. The private claims and the French debt default were never paid or settled. During the Congress of Vienna debt payments and reparations were not discussed, and the Final Act of Vienna (signed on 9 June) also makes no mention of the liquidation of debts. That is why the peace of 1815 came at an even higher price.

After Waterloo, the European powers therefore agreed that this time, the Second Treaty of Paris seriously had to address the financial dimensions of peace and collective security.[121] During July and August, the terms and conditions of all forms of financial settlements and compensation were discussed continuously, preferably without Talleyrand. Only in rare instances was he invited to come by and explain a specific point. Agreements had to be hammered out regarding all kinds of compensation and disbursements: for the salary and maintenance of the troops, and the means of payment; regarding reparations and the financing needed to restore defensive emplacements along the border; and on following through on the settlement of private claims previously agreed to in 1814.[122] When, in late August, still no agreement had been reached between the sky-high demands of (most notably) the Prussian envoys and the other delegates, Tsar Alexander increased the pressure: the treaty should be concluded anytime now, since 'he cannot keep his army in France after the middle of September without exposing them to a march in winter'.[123]

Just in time, between 15 and 20 September 1815, the four powers finally reached a compromise between the extreme Prussian demands, Metternich's

---

[119] A financial institution meant to collect and set aside funds in order to pay off the debt from a bond or another public debt issue.

[120] H. Landheer, 'Afrekenen met het verleden: De vereffening van de achterstallige schulden van het Koninkrijk der Nederlanden in het begin van de negentiende eeuw', in H. Boels (ed.), *Overheidsfinanciën tijdens de Republiek en het Koninkrijk, 1600–1850* (Hilversum: Verloren, 2013), 217–19.

[121] Nicolson, *The Congress of Vienna.*

[122] See protocols from August and September 1815, GStA PK, III. HA I. no. 1465.

[123] Castlereagh, 'Observations', mid-August 1815, GStA PK, III. HA I. no. 1461, 108–9.

concerns about the French 'Jacobin spirit', and the more strategic and moderate position of Britain and Russia. France was to pay a war indemnity of 800 million francs and return most of the area it had conquered between 1790 and 1792. For seven years, the country would have to put up (with) an army of occupation, wholly at its own expense, and numbering 150,000 soldiers. That brought with it an additional 140 million francs to be disbursed per year for the Allied troops' clothing, equipment and salaries, based on the ratio, calculated per annum, of the number of men (and horses) who were officially stationed inside France. And the French were not only obliged to pay the debt for the great powers; the day before – on the 19th – the Allied Council had also invited the other partners of the 25 March alliance to submit their claims. Based on the number of troops that the smaller countries had contributed to the Seventh Coalition, they too could profit from the outcome of the peace treaty and participate in the occupation.[124]

The occupation of France was now confirmed by treaty as a project of 'European alliance', exercised both as a 'physical' and 'moral' pressure on France to comply.[125] The Treaty moreover confirmed that for the remainder of the occupation French troops had to stay outside the occupied area. They were demobilized and, pending the military reorganization of the royal French army, put on half salary. In addition, France had to set up a fund to pay for the (re)building of military fortifications along its northern and eastern borders, had to cede a few extra cities and areas to Germany and the Netherlands (but not Lille and Strasbourg, as the Dutch and Germans had asked), and plundered art treasures had to be returned. Furthermore, the articles regarding financial settlements found in the Peace Treaty of May 1814, which France had not acted on, would now also be enforced. The Second Treaty of Paris thus also included the Paris Convention of 30 May 1814.[126]

During the short two weeks between the Allies' submitting this compromise to the French king on 20 September and his accepting the same on 2 October, Talleyrand let it be known that he had had enough. This doyen of French diplomacy had with his skills and intrigues saved the day for the Bourbon regime in 1814 and at the Congress of Vienna. In 1814–15, France had kept several revolutionary conquests and its myriad of stolen artworks did not have to be returned. But now the expiration date had arrived. The Second Treaty of Paris gave short shrift to the status of France within the Concert of Europe: instead of being treated as a first-rank nation, it was reduced to a 'colony' of the other powers. When Talleyrand realized that there was not much left to save, he played his last card and tendered his resignation on 19 September, so as to

---

[124] Protocols of 19 and 20 September 1815, GStA PK, III. HA I. no. 1465.
[125] Castlereagh, 'Confidential Note', mid-August, GStA PK, III. HA I. no. 1461, 117–24.
[126] Allied Council, protocol of 19 September 1815, GStA PK, III. HA I. no. 1465; Castlereagh, 'Observations', mid-August 1815, GStA PK, III. HA I. no. 1461, 114.

shy away from any responsibility for the embarrassing treaty. The Prince of Benevento had in the meantime fallen into disgrace with both the king and the tsar, and clung to the last straw of disappearing from the stage now, in the vain hope of returning some time later in the future. He left the dubious honour of presenting the humiliation to the French population to his successor.

That was the Duke of Richelieu (Fig. 4.3), a relative of the historical Cardinal Richelieu, who was appointed as president of the Council of Ministers and foreign minister on 24 September. Under Napoleon he had fled and built a career in the service of Tsar Alexander as the governor of Odessa and the Crimea. He could count on the unreserved goodwill of the Russian envoys, Pozzo di Borgo, Razumovsky and Kapodistrias. As a relieved Council concluded: 'With mr. the Duke of Richelieu in charge of the negotiations, the spirit of reconciliation . . . has substantially contributed to a speeding up the process.'[127] As a result of this,

Figure 4.3   Armand du Plessis, Duke of Richelieu, prime minister of France. Portrait by Thomas Lawrence, 1818. (Royal Collection Trust / © Her Majesty Queen Elizabeth II 2019)

---

[127] Allied Council to Richelieu, annex to the protocol of 27 October 1815, GStA PK, III. HA I. no. 1469, 29.

Richelieu was able to reduce the length of the occupation from seven to five years and to lower the indemnity to 700 million francs.[128]

The Second Treaty of Paris defined the broad outline of the arrangement; financial and military details would be set forth in separate conventions.[129] Contrary to previous treaties, the execution of the stipulations was not left to France, but carried out and supervised by the Allied Council. For the next stage of the occupation, Wellington was again confirmed as commander-in-chief of the Allied Army and chair of the Military Committee.[130] The Council expanded its administrative empire with a new committee that had to execute the financial stipulations of the Paris Treaty, including the management of the reparations, the indemnities and the settlement of the arrear payments. A fund for subsidizing the reconstruction of the fortresses was also created, and put under Wellington's supervision.[131]

It is noteworthy that the four great powers now indeed formally invited the other partners in the Alliance Treaty of 25 March to submit compensatory claims for expenditures and damages incurred; but also that they gave the French government the opportunity to voice its take on defining the extent of these debts and the measures for repaying them. The Netherlands, for example, as a signatory to the General Alliance Treaty of 25 March 1815 and the Final Act of the Congress of Vienna of 9 June, and as a country supplying troops for the final campaign, counted as one the 'allies'. Consequently, King Willem I was invited to send representatives to participate in the military and financial committees.[132] It profited even more from the arrangements, since France had to cede the fortified cities of Philippeville, Mariembourg, Chimay and Bouillon to the Netherlands. From the above-mentioned fortification fund of 137.5 million francs, 60 million would be paid to the Netherlands.[133] Bavaria was a net receiver as well, since it was awarded the fortified city of Landau in the Palatinate. Countries like Spain and Portugal were also keen to join the others around the table, and requested as much. But because they had not yet signed the Final Act, they were not allowed to participate as of yet.

On Monday evening, 20 November 1815, the peace treaty and corresponding conventions were signed by all of the plenipotentiaries. That happened at the house of the Duke of Richelieu, who affixed his signature to the humiliating

---

[128] A. Zamoyski, *De ondergang van Napoleon en het Congres van Wenen* (Amsterdam: Balans, 2011), 488–94. For the English-language original, see Zamoyski, *Rites of Peace*.
[129] C. Dupuis, *Le ministère de Talleyrand en 1814*, vol. 2 (Paris: Plon-Nourrit, 1920), 333–404.
[130] Allied Council, protocol of 3 November 1815, TNA, FO 146/6.
[131] H. von Gagern, *Der zweite Pariser Frieden* (Leipzig: Brockhaus, 1845), 316–22.
[132] Ibid., 345.
[133] Allied Council, 2, 6, 7 and 8 October 1815, GStA PK III. HA I. no. 1469; Correspondence of Kraijenhoff and Wellington, December 1815, TNA, FO 92/15.

verdict with tears in his eyes.[134] In a special note to Richelieu, the Allies added
that the Treaty was intended to support France in its fight against revolutionary 'convulsions', and to guarantee the return of the 'general peace and order in
Europe'.[135] The Allied powers had delivered 'France and Europe for the second
time from the agitation caused by the late enterprise of Napoleon Bonaparte
and by the Revolutionary system reproduced in France'.[136] This Treaty was
their response to both the 'system of revolution' and the 'system of conquests' –
their two-part definition of terror – that France had imposed on Europe.[137]
They would therefore 'coordinate their measures in concert', in order 'to
prevent all that would endanger the domestic peace and security of France'.
This side letter was not a dry document, but transpired the high-pitched lyrics
of these first post-war months. In contrast with the 'reckless and passionate
opinions', the 'resentment', the 'alarmism', 'hatred and discord', the Allied
ministers presented their proposal in constructive emotives: 'calm spirits',
'heartfelt confidence' and a 'just balance' between the different parties would
prevail, if 'sagacity', 'persistence, moderation and resoluteness' were
pursued.[138]

Theirs was not only a matter of hope; they were there to guarantee the same.
After the signing ceremony, the four major powers signed another agreement –
but this time only amongst themselves – in which they confirmed their
cooperative commitment to work together as a Quadruple Alliance 'to guar-
anty Europe from the dangers by which she may still be menaced'. In order to
ensure stability and security, and to monitor the implementation of the peace
treaty and conventions, the four would continue to meet as the Allied Council.
They also agreed to organize larger international congresses on a regular
basis.[139] The new security order, and the preference for 'balance', peace and
order, was now anchored in an occupational guarantee and monitored by
a security council *avant la lettre*. Article VI expresses the Council's legal basis
as follows:

> To facilitate and to secure the execution of the present Treaty, and to
> consolidate the connections, which at the present moment so closely unite
> the 4 Sovereigns for the happiness of the World, the High Contracting

---

[134] The text of the treaty and conventions can be found in the *Buitengewone Nederlandsche
Staatscourant*, Monday 27 November 1815, no. 14; Gagern, *Der zweite Pariser Frieden*,
401–7.

[135] Note from the Allied Council to Richelieu, 20 November 1815, annex to the protocol of
the *séance* of 20 November, GStA PK, III. HA I. no. 1469.

[136] Foreign Office (ed.), *British and Foreign State Papers*, vol. 3, 281.

[137] Préambule to the Second Treaty of Paris, 20 November 1815, cited in Schulz, *Normen
und Praxis*, 60.

[138] Allied Council, note to Richelieu, 20 November 1815, GStA PK, III. HA I. no. 1469.

[139] *Buitengewone Nederlandsche Staatscourant*, no. 14, 27 November 1815; Foreign Office
(ed.), *British and Foreign State Papers*, vol. 3, 281.

Parties have agreed to renew their Meetings at fixed periods, either under the immediate auspices of the Sovereigns themselves, or by their respective Ministers, for the purpose of consulting upon their common interests, and for the consideration of the measures which at each of those periods shall be considered the most salutary, for the repose and prosperity of Nations, and for the maintenance of the Peace of Europe.[140]

The ministers subsequently handed Wellington a letter granting him as commander-in-chief of the Allied Occupation Army the full discretionary power to act as chair and *trait d'union* between the Council and the French king and government. Upon signing the Treaty, the sovereigns prepared their departure, leaving their ministers in Paris. The Allied Council, which was from now on often identified as the Ministerial Council or Conference, now consisted of ministers and special envoys: Charles Stuart, Baron Stuart de Rothesay (on behalf of Britain), Nikolaus Karl Baron von Vincent (for Austria), Karl Friedrich Count von der Goltz (for Prussia) and Carlo Andrea Count Pozzo di Borgo (for Russia). When he was not in the capital, their chair Wellington would receive a weekly report from the Council. He himself would also inform the European heads of state regarding developments in peace and security in France and Europe on a weekly basis.[141] In sum, the Iron Duke had moved from being a 'whisper behind the throne' in France to become the uncrowned governor of France, king of the Allied coalition, and with that, of practically all Europe. He was the one who was called 'sur le meilleur mode de réaliser le concert [de l'Europe]', and who had to see to 'non seulement la tranquillité intérieure de la France, mais le repos et la sureté générale de l'Europe' as a whole:[142] an almost too heavy burden to carry.

Inflicting a 'Cultural Waterloo'

It was high time the Council issued general guidelines for dealing with the French reparations and indemnities, since lower Allied officials and generals had already started to carry them out in their own fashion. Rather than restoring peace and tranquillity, Prussian, British and Dutch officers had already started to inflict 'a cultural Waterloo' by removing and retrieving looted artwork on their own account.[143]

---

[140] Foreign Office (ed.), British and Foreign State Papers, vol. 3, 279. See also E. Hertslet, *The Map of Europe by Treaty. Showing the Various Political and Territorial Changes which have Taken Place since the General Peace 1814* (London: Butterworths, 1875), 372–6.

[141] Allied Council, protocol of 20 November 1815; letter to Wellington, GStA PK, III. HA I. no. 1469, 97–9.

[142] Letter to Wellington, annex to protocol of 3 November, signed 20 November 1815, GStA PK, III. HA I. no. 1469, 52.

[143] Guerrin, *La France après Napoléon*, 92.

'Reconquering these objects, which are generally regarded as inalienable property of the people, greatly affects the spirits in Germany. In the previous Peace of Paris, they were among what was lost and forgotten; this time they are front and centre ... A nation may not be deprived of its history,' the strongly patriotist *Rheinischer Merkur* reminded the Prussian ministers.[144] Blücher and Hardenberg indeed felt that the German commissioners and envoys, Jakob Grimm and Alexander and Wilhelm von Humboldt, had been hoodwinked by their French art friends in 1814, and as a result, had not brought home any of the looted artworks.[145] This time, the Prussians got the smaller German principalities and the Dutch provinces who had also been severely duped to join them,[146] and after arriving in Paris, immediately set to work on this.[147]

Blücher and his sentries ordered the resistant Louvre director, Egyptologist Vivant Denon, to immediately return all artworks taken from Germany, lest he be arrested and deported to the Prussian prison in Fort Graudentz. The governor of the capital city, Müffling, underscored the order by appearing at the museum gates with a party of twenty-five soldiers in tow. Denon passionately defended his museum; thanks to Napoleon, the Louvre had become a 'universal gallery', an 'encyclopedia of art', for everyone there to visit and admire. Rather than rotting away in dungeons and dens in Dutch and German provinces, would not the artworks themselves shine much brighter in Paris? But in vain, for that same day a first series of paintings and busts was already on its way back to Germany.[148]

The other creditors, however – representatives from the Netherlands, the smaller German states and the Vatican – were less successful. The Netherlands were represented in Paris by Freiherr Hans Christoph Ernst von Gagern, who had just arrived from Vienna, where he had been part of the Dutch delegation.[149] Diligent and upstanding bureaucrat that he was, he followed the proper channels and submitted a request to the Allied Council in early August to assist him in retrieving the Dutch artworks from the French museums and collections. The council decided that, rather than dealing with every request upon submission, they would begin to compile a general catalogue of all stolen works of art.[150] Wellington and Castlereagh were somewhat at a loss; the French government and the Louvre director flatly refused to lend

[144] 'Die Zurücknahme der Kunst und wissenschaftlichen Werke', *Rheinischer Merkur*, 6 August 1815, 1.
[145] There was something to this accusation. See B. Savoy, *Patrimoine annexé. Les saisies de biens culturels pratiqués par la France en Allemagne autour de 1800*, vol. 1 (Paris: Éditions de la Maison des sciences de l'homme, 2003), 161–82.
[146] Savoy, *Patrimoine annexé*, 183–95.
[147] Houssaye, *1815. La seconde abdication*, 538–9.
[148] Ibid.
[149] (De) Graaf, 'Second-tier Diplomacy', 48–9; Gagern, *Der zweite Pariser Frieden*, 559.
[150] Protocol no. 36, 17 August 1815. Letter of Gagern and the deliberating board; note about the art committee, 4 September 1815, protocol no. 49, 14 September 1815, GStA PK, III. HA I. no. 1465.

assistance in dismantling the French museums. The British delegates were, moreover, afraid that continuing the art retrieval operation could very well trigger significant commotion in the already heated Paris climate of the late summer and autumn of 1815. They therefore also cautioned the Prussians to wait with further militant confiscations. But prime minister Liverpool and the Prince Regent (the future King George IV) were less patient with the French outrage and confirmed that the treaty stipulations of 1814 and the return of all artwork should indeed be upheld.[151]

The Vatican's papal envoy, the sculptor Canova, fell in with the Dutch and Prussian pleas. He had also been dispatched to Paris as *emballeur* ('packing agent'), rather than as ambassador, Talleyrand quipped. Canova's claim to all the artworks that were 'taken by Napoleon by force' equally fell on deaf ears with the French government. The French reasoned that the papal art treasures had been used to offset the war contributions that Napoleon had levied on the papal state. So, the more than a hundred paintings and other works of art confiscated from the Vatican had been one of the terms of surrender imposed by the French, and signed off on by Pope Pius VI, in the Treaty of Tolentino (February 1797). But according to Canova, who, like the Dutch envoy Hendrik Fagel, escalated his claims to the Allied Council, that Treaty had been 'unjust'. The French Revolution had 'subverted' all moral principles; whereas Pope Pius had done everything he could to help the French royalists – granting asylum to refugee priests, and taking in two of Louis's aunts – the French government now left the Vatican in the dark. Canova brought one last convincing argument to the table of the Allied ministers: the 'sacred right' of property. That right had been violated by the French Revolution and Napoleon, and for the new order to prosper, possessions needed to be returned to their rightful owners. The pope wanted his statues, manuscripts, paintings, medallions, cameos, stamps and seals back; not for the sake of these things themselves, but on behalf of and for the benefit of all civilized nations. Was not Rome the 'second Athens', where artists came from far and wide – also from France – for further training in the fine arts? It was therefore a matter of duty and decency to return what one had taken. With these equally passionate and eloquent appeals to the Allies' sense of justice and honour, Canova struck a nerve.[152]

The Allied ministers instituted a committee, and sealed its tasks in their draft Treaty of Paris, which spelled out the obligation to return all stolen works of art. The committee – consisting of Baron Wessenberg for Austria, Charles Stuart for Britain, Altenstein for Prussia and Baron d'Anstett for Russia – started its work halfway through September and found in favour of the claimants. The three Allied field marshals – Schwarzenberg, Wellington and Blücher – instructed Müffling and their own commanders to track down all the spoils of war taken by the French, to support the Dutch and German envoys and to aid Canova.[153]

From 17 September, things began to fall into place. Denon had to open the doors of the Louvre to the consul general of the Netherlands, Isaac Thuret. The Dutch commissioners began their work with Wellington's aide-de-camp, Colonel Fremantle, and his regiment. A Prussian regiment took care of the Grande Galerie. Initially, the Louvre's attendants claimed not to know where the stolen artworks were. Likewise, all the keys to the depots had allegedly gone missing. But with some military insistence, the Dutch and the British were able to amass a large cache of art by the end of October.[154] The inventories and exhibitions of Notre-Dame, the Musée de Dijon, the Bibliothèque de l'Arsenal and the Bibliothèque Royale were all combed as well – under strong protests, not only on the part of the conservators, but also of the Parisian population, which, according to Talleyrand, lamented the loss of these artefacts at least as much as it would the loss of *ancien territoire*.[155]

Müffling's most important objective, however – as instructed by Canova – was the Horses of St Mark's. That bronze four-span, probably dating from the second or third century before Christ, was brought to Venice during the Fourth Crusade and the sacking of Constantinople, and placed above the great central door of the basilica of St Mark's in Venice. After the fall of Venice in 1797, Napoleon took the horses to Paris and placed them on top of the Arc de Triomphe du Carrousel, by the entrance to the gardens of the Tuileries. Due to the weight and size of the horses and chariot – the four-span was well anchored in the stonework – Müffling asked Wellington to borrow an experienced company of sappers and miners that could help dismantle this sort of move-able real estate. Müffling informed the French head of the National Guard, General Dessoles, that he intended to remove the quadriga at night, in order not to shock King Louis XVIII, who would otherwise oversee the whole operation from his chambers. Undisturbed by Dessoles's pleas not to take them, Müffling gave the sappers the green light. The following morning,

---

[153] Letter of Schwarzenberg, Wellington and Blücher to Müffling, 20 September 1815. See Müffling, *The Memoirs*, 266–7, 277. Contrary to Freeman's suggestion, the return was not owing to Canova's fluency in English or his knowing a certain William (Bill) Hamilton, but to a decision of the Council that held for all stolen works of art, and not just those of the pope; cf. C. Freeman, *The Horses of St Mark's. A Story of Triumph in Byzantium, Paris and Venice* (London: Little, Brown, 2004), ch. 15: 'Antonio Canova and The Return of the Horses to Venice'.

[154] V. Herremans, 'Van oorlogsbuit tot kerncollectie: Hoe het KMSKA een Rubensstempel werd', in F. Judo and S. van de Perre (eds.), *Belg en Bataaf. De wording van het Verenigd Koninkrijk* (Antwerpen: Polis, 2015), 158–73, here: 165.

[155] Houssaye, *1815. La seconde abdication*, 540–1.

however, the four horses and chariot were still standing tall. The sappers had started in as night fell but were stopped in their tracks before midnight by a regiment of the king's *Garde du Corps*. The next evening, Müffling took another go, this time with two battalions of the National Guard in waiting. But this time they ran into a crowd of angry Parisians shouting and protesting outside the gates of the palace. Even for Müffling, deploying the National Guard against their own people was too bold a move. But the next morning he marched four battalions of Austrian troops and a cavalry division down and encircled the triumphal arch. The four Venetian horses and bronze chariot were hoisted away in broad daylight, under great protest of an even larger crowd than the night before. When the Austrian helpers tried also to pack up the winged Lion of Venice, the bronze sculpture fell and lost its wings, paws, tail and stone bible – causing even louder uproar and delight. For Dessoles, the story had a bad ending; he was mercilessly dismissed by an upset King Louis.[156]

King Louis could not face the falling apart of French glory. While the Allied commissioners rifled through the French museums and palaces, Louis squirrelled a favourite of his away in his bedroom. The painting in question – *Jupiter punissant les vices* – was a 5.6 by 3.3 m canvas of the Renaissance artist Paul Veronese (1556) that Napoleon had taken from the Doge's Palace in Venice in 1798. The painting depicted the god Jupiter (or Zeus), who with his hurled thunderbolts cleanses the heavens of crimes and vices (slander, excess, insurrection and corruption). It symbolized the power of the Venetian Council of Ten that protected the Venetian Republic against crime and threats. Not wanting to part with it and the other two ceiling side panels, Louis offered three paintings from his own collection in exchange. Thanks to the emperor of Austria, King Louis got his way.[157] And indeed, Veronese's *Jupiter* can still be seen in the Louvre. The other paintings from Venice, including Veronese's *Juno Bestowing her Gifts on Venice* and his *Old Man Wearing a Turban*, were all returned. King Louis did not need to feel to bereft; although the Prussian, Dutch and remaining German commissioners did their utmost, the Louvre director's bureaucratic obstruction tactics allowed him to keep a good number of artworks hidden. Probably only half of the more than a thousand first-rate works of art taken by Napoleon were returned to their original owners. Of the 506 stolen works from Italy, only 249 were sent back, 248 remained in France and 9 'disappeared'. Tintoretto's *Paradise* – taken from Verona – and Veronese's *Wedding at Cana* remained in the Louvre,[158] which was perhaps not for the worse, since although Venice received a good deal of its art back, the paintings were still rolled up in 1816 and randomly stored; there was insufficient expertise available to display them as beautifully as before. So too,

[156] Müffling, *The Memoirs*, 262–5.
[157] Edgcumbe (ed.), *The Diary of Frances Lady Shelley, 1787–1817*, 329–32.
[158] B. Oliver, *From Royal to National. The Louvre Museum and the Bibliothèque Nationale* (Lanham/New York: Lexington, 2007), 66–7.

shipments to Germany did not always arrive at the correct address; some got lost altogether, with manuscripts from Salzburg ending up in Bavaria, and pieces from Rome in Heidelberg.

But there was also reason for rejoicing. Lady Shelley, while on her Grand Tour in 1816, did find some artwork restored and exhibited in their original sites.[159] And also in the Netherlands gratitude for Allied support of the return of the looted treasures prevailed. Late in 1815, more than thirty works that had been taken as war booty in 1794 from Antwerp, including the famous altarpieces from the cathedral by Peter Paul Rubens, were returned. With church bells ringing, the entire city celebrated their return with festivities and fireworks. The Flemish artist Verellen documented the festive homecoming of the abducted objects of art and science.

His drawing from 1821 (Fig. 4.4), dedicated to Willem I, depicts a wagon with crated paintings entering Antwerp through the Emperor's Gate. The city,

ZEGEPRAAL der WAPENEN.   TRIOMPHE des ARMES.

Figure 4.4   Allegory of the return of the paintings of Rubens to Antwerp, 1815. The triumvirate, the heroes of Waterloo, sit on a cloud: the Prince of Orange, Blücher and Wellington. By A. G. van Prooijen, after J. J. Verellen, 1821. (Rijksmuseum, Amsterdam)

---

[159] Edgcumbe (ed.), *The Diary of Frances Lady Shelley, 1787–1817*, 329–32; Oliver, *From Royal to National*, 68.

personified as a young woman, conveys the good news to Lady Art herself, who was sadly pining away in her tent, while the three heroes of Waterloo – the Prince of Orange, Blücher and Wellington – look on approvingly from the clouds.[160] Ironically, through their abduction and exhibition in the Louvre, the pieces by Rubens, 'ce dieu de la peinture', truly became famous. Their return marked the beginning of the nineteenth century's celebration of Rubens as part of the Flemish identity.[161] A similar spectacle unfolded in Cologne, where the return of Rubens's painting *Die Kreuzigung Petri* coincided with the commemoration of the Battle of Nations on 18 October 1815. With a procession, a *Te Deum*, dances, open-air festivals and a sensational display of fireworks, the success of this 'holy mission' and the homecoming of the 'German' patrimony was celebrated.[162]

Wellington himself retained an impressive souvenir from this episode. In the Louvre, behind a curtain, his soldiers found a colossal more than 3 m high statue of the emperor, Napoleon, in the naked guise of the Roman god Mars the Peacemaker, carved in white, velvety marble by Canova himself between 1802 and 1806 (Fig. 4.5). The statue was so heroic and muscularly proportioned that the somewhat compact emperor had it immediately tucked away; he found it 'too athletic'. The British Prince Regent bought the image, had its 13 tons shipped to London, and then presented it to Wellington. Wellington placed his trophy in the vestibule of his Apsley House in London in 1817, and took immense pleasure in confronting visiting women with a 3 m tall nude Napoleon.[163]

The loss of the 'cultural Waterloo' lingered on; it took the Louvre quite some time to recover from the legally sanctified 'plunder'. The British satirist George Cruikshank, who despite his young age (twenty-three) enjoyed European notoriety, immortalized the French misgivings in a classic caricature (Fig. 4.6). Due to the rather liberal British policies on censorship, his images were printed there and disseminated throughout the continent.[164]

In November 1815 a caricature was published entitled 'The afterpiece to the tragedy of Waterloo – or Madame Françoise & her managers!!!', holding all elements of the Allied Council's activities up to ridicule. Madame Françoise is

[160] J. Verellen, *Zegepraal der wapenen of de plegtige terugkomst der ontvoerde voorwerpen van kunst en wetenschap / Triomphe des Armes ou le retour solemnel des objets des sciences et des beaux arts 1815*, 1821. Etching and engraving, Rijksmuseum, Amsterdam, via: www.rijksmuseum.nl/nl/collectie/RP-P-OB-87.343 (last viewed: 26 March 2019).
[161] Herremans, 'Van oorlogsbuit tot kerncollectie'.
[162] Guerrin, *La France après Napoleon*, 95.
[163] Explanation of the image in the vestibule, Apsley House, London; J. Bryant, 'How Canova and Wellington Honoured Napoleon',*Apollo*, 162 (2005), 38–40; S. Jenkins, 'Buying Bonaparte', *Apollo* 172 (2010), 50–5. See also Freeman, *The Horses of St. Mark's*, ch. 15.
[164] J. Gabriëls, 'Cutting the Cake: The Congress of Vienna in British, French and German Political Caricature', *European Review of History*, 24:1 (2017), 131–57.

Figure 4.5 *Napoleon as Mars the Peacemaker*. Statue by Antonio Canova in Apsley House, London. (Heritage Images)

on her back, with a heavy fetter attached to her wrist, while a kneeling Wellington hammers her chain to the ground and declares: '"We enter France as Friends" – well, I've crippled her Arms if that will do her any good.' Tsar Alexander, to the left, locks a padlock chaining her legs, while proclaiming: 'It is necessary that France should be great & powerfull in order to keep up the Ballance of Power for the security of Europe. But 'tis the great I who must preponderate in this Ballance.' The Dutch king Willem, depicted as a fat Dutchman, is cutting off a piece of her skirt, labelled 'The Netherlands'. Emperor Franz I assists the tsar with the chain and contentedly states: 'We come to restore France to her Ancient rights & Liberties.' The spiked knight in armour represents the Allied army, with its various national contingents (the feathers on his helmet). With his bayonet he force-feeds her tiny figures, the fat bottom of King Louis protruding from her mouth. Behind her, Blücher is trying to pinch her purse and necklace, while a bit further in the back Castlereagh declares: 'It delights me when I see a Country enjoy her Old established Privileges – My Own Country to wit.' In the

Figure 4.6 'France in the hands of the allies'. Anonymous cartoon, after George Cruikshank, 1815. (Rijksmuseum, Amsterdam)

background, the rectangular building of the Louvre stands upside down, while Allied soldiers in the foreground, right, are carrying away the artworks. An enormous billboard states:

> In consequence of the 'removal of the pictures & other things', The public are respectly inform'd That this Building will in future be used as a Bastille – artists are therefore invited to send in plans of alteration, improvement &c &c – NB The Holy Inquisition of Spain have kindly offered to supply the necessary instruments.

French citizens are staring at the spectacle in dismay. Thus, the picture quite correctly represented the dramatic scenes in Paris, in the autumn of 1815.[165]

An Imperial Concert

The Allied Council was set up to organize the practical matters of the occupation and to put together a peace treaty. But, as is often the case with

[165] G. Cruikshank, 'The afterpiece to the tragedy of Waterloo – or Madame Françoise & her managers!!!', 9 November 1815, British Museum/Rijksmuseum. Cf. also the description of the cartoon on the British Museum website: www.britishmuseum.org/research/collection_online/collection_object_details.aspx?assetId=173760001&objectId=1646426&partId=1 (last viewed: 26 March 2019).

international organizations, the council took on more and more tasks during
the negotiations. These came to include France's finances, its domestic administration, the question of the constitution and the defence of its borders. So too,
other European countries took the opportunity to put their own conflicts and
interests on the table. Their doing so made sense, given that negotiations
around the Treaty of Paris picked up where the Congress of Vienna had left
off, and took the next step in reorganizing the map of France. In that context,
Austria, for example, appealed to the other three powers for help in reclaiming
the areas it had lost to Bavaria in 1805. The inter-imperial Allied solidarity
functioned as intended, and the other ministers duly lent their support to
Metternich. Hardenberg and Humboldt, in turn, were able to arrange for
enlarging the area for Coburg, Oldenburg, Mecklenburg-Strelitz, Hessen-
Homburg and Pappenheim.[166]

The Council also solved the question of the Ionian Islands. The islands were
part of the Venetian Republic, incorporated by Napoleon and subsequently
reconquered, bit by bit, by the British forces. In Vienna, the powers had
announced that the islands would be brought under British rule, as
a protectorate. On 5 November, all Allied ministers voted, on behalf of their
courts, for the creation of the United States of the Ionian Islands and recognized the territory as a protectorate under British military rule. In return,
Castlereagh and Wellington promised their Allied colleagues that they would
enable and monitor the formation of a legal administration and the implementation of a constitution and a parliament. In addition, the other three great
powers would enjoy the same trade privileges as Britain.[167]

What was remarkable in these discussions was not just the way the Council
quite naturally considered itself an imperial concert, but also that the other
European powers hardly disputed the fact that the ministers of the four major
powers were entitled to call the shots. They were, as Metternich put it, 'les
premières Puissances de l'Europe'.[168] The acceptance of this international
stratification was perhaps smoothened out by the fact that the 'second-string'
powers (Pitt) were sometimes allowed to join them at the table, or have one of
them lobby for their cause. Gagern, for example, mentioned previously, was
very adept in that regard. Gagern, Elias Canneman and Fagel knew how to play
the Allied ministers, and by means of their British and Prussian advocates were
quite successful in cashing in (see Chapter 7). However, when smaller powers
locked horns with the 'greater' ones and tried to interfere with their strategy, all
indulgence was over. Attempts initiated by the smaller German states and the

---

[166] See GStA PK, III. HA I. no. 1485 and no. 1486. Negotiations dragged on until the end of
the nineteenth century. See no. 1487 and no. 1488.
[167] Protocol of 28 October 1815; Treaty of 5 November, GStA PK, III. HA I. no. 1469, 33.
[168] Metternich, note, as annex to the protocol of 3 November 1815, GStA PK, III. HA I. no.
1469, 50.

Netherlands to cream off more territory, especially fortified places, from France stranded. Prussia saw some merit in the requests, but Britain and Russia saw such territorial concessions as a recipe for future border conflicts. In the end, the smaller German and Dutch allies were no match for the Allied quartet that, despite various internal differences of opinion, kept its ranks tight.

That also proved to be the case when Spain and Portugal demanded a seat in the consortium. Around 20 August, the Council was informed that a Spanish army of some 80,000 soldiers was on its way and had already been sighted in the Pyrenees. The Spanish Bourbon king Ferdinand VII was on his way to lend 'assistance' to his cousin Louis, and wanted to deploy his troops in France as part of the Allied Occupation Force. This time Talleyrand and the Allied Council were in full agreement. Four powers were enough. Having Spanish troops stationed in the non-occupied portion of France, where the demobilized remnants of the Grande Armée were also quartered, given that things were already restless enough, could only add fat to the fire. The Allied Council pulled together and warned Spain off: Spain was too late and had to turn right around. In March the Allies had called on Madrid to join the alliance against Napoleon – the General Alliance Treaty of Vienna of 25 March. But Spain had remained mute. Now, with Bonaparte long defeated, Spain entered the scene to take part in the spoils of the occupation. Moreover, Spain had not discussed its troop movement with the powers at all – 'nullement concerté' – and in the Midi-Pyrénées the population was so sympathetic to the Bourbon regime that no assistance was needed at all. Madrid was told, 'in concert', to withdraw its troops at once. Aggrieved, the troops indeed turned and went.[169]

Requests from other powers, who had joined the coalition of 25 March, such as Hesse, Nassau, Kassel, Baden, Sweden, Denmark or the Netherlands, to accede to the Allied Council were equally turned down. But to alleviate that imperial rejection, they were invited to submit their ideas or desires in writing. The Allied ministers also promised to inform them on the proceedings of the peace talks.[170] However, one level down, there was some room for the lesser powers to participate in the decision-making process: they did have a voice, and even a seat, in the military and financial committees. Wellington saw to it that the first large amount that France paid out for salaries and upkeep (for the period 15 July–15 September), 50 million francs, was distributed to all those who had joined the alliance of 25 March and had actually delivered troops to the cause. The four powers claimed 10 million francs each, leaving the 10 million remaining to be divided among the other powers. Those who believed that they were entitled to a disbursement were invited to stop by 5

[169] Protocols of 24 August 1815; annex: 'Projet de dépêche pour Madrid', GStA PK, III. HA I. no. 1465.
[170] Protocol of 10 August 1815, GStA PK, III. HA I. no. 1465.

Place Vendôme, and submit their claims to Baron von Baldacci, the Austrian member of the Allied Administrative Committee (the *conseil administratif*).[171]

Smaller powers operating on their own were, however, censured forthwith. Acting 'in concert' did not allow for that. For example, the Council caught wind of the Kingdom of Sardinia trying to make bilateral agreements directly with the Tuileries regarding reparations. But doing so without Allied involvement was, according to Castlereagh, 'entièrement contraire' to the spirit of the treaties. The final result was indeed that Turin had to recall its envoy, count Ignazio Thaon di Revel, void the bilateral treaty that had been agreed upon with Louis and fall in line with the concert master.[172]

A seminal point of imperial discussion, broached by the British, regarded the abolition of slavery. Pushed by public petitioners, Wellington, on behalf of London, had put international condemnation of the slave trade to the negotiation table in Vienna. Both in the First Treaty of Paris and in Vienna, the restored Bourbon regime was forced to ban the trade in slaves. But during the first and now the second restoration, the mercantile marine had weighed in and immediately resumed the African trade. Fouché's family, for example, had made a fortune in the *noirs* trade and wished to continue doing so. But Castlereagh made it very clear to the Council that trading in slaves was from now on point-blank prohibited. After the first restoration, the Allies had granted Louis and the traders five years to make the transition. But that kind of window was now out of the question; public opinion in Britain would not tolerate that. Wellington was dispatched to persuade the unconvinced King Louis, via 'insinuations confidentielles', to counter the impression that the French government bluntly ignored the current liberal preferences and the stipulations of Vienna. Wellington did his job, and on 1 August King Louis issued a ban on the slave trade with immediate effect.[173]

The daily meetings of the big players of the moment were highly advantageous to the impact of this 'forum talk'. Without the interference of courtiers, formal pretensions, circumstances or other royal interjections, the ministers and diplomats could informally discuss and negotiate emerging issues as they saw fit – and even solve some of them before lunch (they always convened at eleven in the morning, with coffee and cocoa). In the coming years, the Allied Council would increasingly address issues that went beyond the French occupation, some of which had repercussions even as far away as South America.

---

[171] 6, 24, 31 August and 7 September 1815. See especially: 'Nombre de trouppes fixés dans les traités de participation & d'accession à l'alliance du 25 Mars, 1815', annex to protocol of 24 August; and the 'Tableau', as annex to the protocols of 7 September, GStA PK, III. HA I. no. 1465.

[172] Protocol of 21 September 1815, GStA PK, III. HA I. no. 1465.

[173] Protocols of 26 July and 1 August 1815, GStA PK, III. HA I. no. 1465.

Normalizing the Occupation

At the beginning of September at least 1,135,000 Allied soldiers (some estimates cite 1.2 million) were still in France. Austria, Prussia and Russia each provided some 300,000 troops. Britain had fewer deployed (128,000) but compensated for this with large military subsidies. Next to the great powers, Bavaria (60,000), Württemberg (20,000), Baden (16,000) and Piedmont (15,000) also contributed substantial contingents. Hessen-Darmstadt and Saxony each fielded 8,000 troops. Some Danish, and later Spanish and Swiss regiments were there as well. The Dutch and Belgian forces were included in Wellington's army. The Allied ministers asked Wellington to reduce the armies to 300,000 by late July, with 15,000 stationed in Paris and 150,000 in the surrounding area.[174] Once the peace treaty was officially approved in November, troops for the coming years could be reduced to 150,000 men, 30,000 for each of the four major powers, and 30,000 for the other Allies. Paris was cleared, and the troops were moved to the provinces in the north and east.[175]

Around December, all the troops had arrived where they needed to be, the last fortresses had surrendered and Allied commanders could set up their districts for the coming years. From June until December 1815, the Allied forces occupied two thirds of the French territories; from December 1815 onwards, that was to be gradually reduced to a smaller strip of land along the border (Map 4.2).

The Prussians initially occupied parts of Normandy, Maine, Anjou and Brittany, bordered by the Loire in the south and the English Channel in the north, the Seine in the east and north-east and the British sector in the north-west. The Russians had Île-de-France, Champagne and Lorraine (more specifically, the districts of Aisne, Marne, Meurthe, Meuse and Moselle, parts of the Ardennes, Aube and Seine-et-Marne). The British and the Dutch were in Picardy, Artois and French Flanders, bordered by the Prussian sector and the Seine, Oise and Sambre rivers. The Württembergers and Bavarians had Orléanais, Nivernais, Bourbonnais and part of Auvergne. Baden and Saxony had their troops stationed in Alsace, the Austrians in Burgundy, Franche-Comté, Dauphiné, Lyonnais, Provence and Languedoc. Sixty French departments were therefore in the hands of the Allies for the first stage of the occupation.[176] Broadly speaking, the British were in the far north, the Prussians just below in a strip from east to west, the Russians in the north-east and the Austrians along the eastern border, down to the Mediterranean. In addition, a narrow demilitarized buffer zone was designated between the

---

[174] Military Committee, 'Délibération du Comité militaire central des alliés', annex to the protocol of 17 July 1815, GStA PK, III. HA I. no. 1464.
[175] See Wacker, *Die alliierte Besetzung*, 143, 224–5.
[176] Houssaye, *1815. La seconde abdication*, 484.

Map 4.2   The Allied occupation according to the Treaty of Paris, December 1815–18. (Erik Goosmann © 2020, Mappa Mundi Cartography)

occupied and non-occupied regions, to keep the French and foreign troops separated from each other.[177]

The Council asked Wellington to stay in Paris for a few months and then, after that, to travel back and forth between the capital and the military headquarters that were to be set up in Cambrai in the north. When Wellington was gone, ensconced in his military headquarters or off inspecting the troops and fortifications along the border, Castlereagh – and after his departure for home

___

[177] See the map in Wacker, *Die alliierte Besetzung*, 142–6, 224–31.

in December 1815, the British ambassador Sir Charles Stuart – bore the torch in Paris and chaired the Allied Council.

Wellington very much enjoyed his new role. Although there was diplomatically speaking plenty to arrange, mediate and reconcile amongst the Allies and between the Allied commanders and their French 'hosts', he would come to revel in a number of more peaceful years. His wife, Kitty, with whom he had enjoyed a distant relationship, happy while separated, now came over. Friends who visited Wellington encountered a host who organized jolly evenings in the castle where he had set up shop, including a game that had folks racing in a goat cart through the hallways. But the field marshal also saw to his troops. To prevent the men from getting bored and roaming the area, he used his time during the occupation drilling his men and sent those who rode poorly off to attend riding classes. Wellington also made sure the commanders from the different zones of occupation cooperated closely. He arranged and executed joint exercises and devised manoeuvres with other commanders, after which they all happily decorated each other with medals and ribbons.[178]

The sovereigns, ministers and commanders highly enjoyed the exercises and the joint demonstration of splendour, pride and power – as opposed to the soldiers, who had to carry out the drill, they were seated in marquees, and served chilled wine and bites. Lady Shelley was invited to attend just such a parade with Wellington. Being as much a lover of horses as the duke, she gladly accepted:

> Of course, I was delighted! . . . I rode at the Duke's side. The Emperor of Russia spoke to me. A great honour indeed! . . . The Russian troops are very fine fellows. . . . The cavalry horses very large and handsome. Those of the artillery are small, but very beautiful. The crowd was not so great as at previous reviews. . . . How I love a Review.[179]

The reviews also provided an opportunity for the commanders and their generals to learn about each other's military customs and practices, and exchange new trends and tips. According to Lady Shelley, Tsar Alexander was much impressed by the

> manner in which our troops marched. He considered that they marched so much faster and freer than his own. The Russians had, up to that time, been accustomed to 'point their toes' and take very short steps in marching. In the six weeks that intervened between our review and the review at Vertus all this had changed. His troops now marched like ours. In consequence, the Russian review, which the Duke of Wellington expected to last nine hours under the old system, was over in about six hours and a half.[180]

---

[178] Cf. Veve, *The Duke of Wellington and the British Army of Occupation in France.*
[179] Edgcumbe (ed.), *The Diary of Frances Lady Shelley, 1787–1817*, 130–1. For other descriptions of such reviews, see 141–7, 151–9.
[180] Ibid., 158–9.

Conversely, the Duke of Wellington complimented the Prussian king a year later, asking Hardenberg in October 1816 to convey to the king that he was very impressed with how the Prussian troops had carried out their manoeuvres. Hardenberg and the king were, of course, 'infinement flatté[s]'.[181]

Lady Shelley and her companions, sitting under a shade-producing canopy, thoroughly enjoyed the spectacle. But for the soldiers it was, for many, a downer: 'Owing to the heat, one man dropped down in a fit just at the saluting-point, but otherwise all went off with *éclat*.'[182] The troops, given the wind and weather, mud and rain, and the long wait time in tight formation, generally hated these reviews:

> This sham fighting, without prize or glory,
> was to the poor soldiers not exciting,
> They droop'd, and fell as fast I can assure ye,
> as if they had been really fighting.[183]

'Une harmonie parfaite'?

The sovereigns and their entourage found it all rather exhilarating, the troops less so. But for the French the first months of the occupation were a trial. Not that most of them longed for Napoleon to return once again; they truly welcomed the end of the endless wars, but at the same time they heartily resented the humiliating defeat and the confrontational occupation. François Guizot, made Professor in Modern History at the Sorbonne in 1812 and secretary-general at the new Ministry of Justice in 1815, later described the ambivalent and conflicting emotions within the French society:

> In fact, a mutilated and exhausted nation. Side by side with this physical suffering, I also remarked a great moral perplexity, the uneasiness of opposing sentiments, an ardent longing for peace, a deadly hatred of foreign invaders, with alternating feelings, as regarded Napoleon, of anger and sympathy.[184]

Indeed, most French citizens bemoaned what they took to be an unjustly onerous occupation and how much it was costing them to billet all those soldiers; but most of them equally complied, albeit with great resentment.

The weight of the occupation was heavy, but differed in severity, depending on the area and the rank, status or gender of the populace, but also on the commander and situation. In the north, comparatively more troops were

---

[181] Correspondence between Hardenberg and Wellington, October–November 1816, GStA PK, III. HA I. no. 913.
[182] Edgcumbe (ed.), *The Diary of Frances Lady Shelley, 1787–1817*, 158–9.
[183] Cited in Veve, 'Wellington and the Army of Occupation in France', 103.
[184] F. Guizot, *Memoirs to Illustrate the History of my Time*, vol. 1 (London: Bentley, 1858), 25–6. Guizot, born in 1787, soon afterwards became prime minister of France in 1847.

deployed, and more battles had been waged: the costs of recovery, maintenance of troops and reparation soared much higher there.[185] From a social point of view, women and girls from the lower strata in society were far worse off in any case. French police reports repeatedly speak of rape and assault, the most telling and flagrant excesses of which the troops were guilty.[186] Raids of pillaging and looting forces were also very much the order of the day, especially during the first months of the occupation. The French population especially dreaded the Prussian soldiers, next to the Russian Cossacks, who were also terrifying to behold with their shaggy beards and colourful uniforms. For the Prussians, the occupation provided them in the first instance with the only way to replenish their depleted war treasury and to provide for the essentials that their troops sorely needed – while that was hardly the case for Britain and also less so for Russia. For Alexander and Wellington, moreover, the occupation was not an expression of revenge, but a strategic instrument, to enforce political change in France – this influenced the way they drilled their troops and held their generals to account.[187] Wellington had even laid this down in his order from 20 June 1815:

> As the army is about to enter the French territory, the troops of the nations which are at present under the command of Field Marshal the Duke of Wellington, are desired to recollect that their respective Sovereigns are the Allies of His Majesty the King of France, and that France ought, therefore to be treated as a friendly country.[188]

There were, of course, also excesses in the British and Russian sectors, but they were hardly tolerated. Both Wellington and Alexander explicitly and documentedly tried very hard to keep their troops in line. Wellington for example sent soldiers caught stealing or plundering straight home ignominiously – a heavy punishment, since it could imply a forfeit of their pension.[189] Wellington organized the army of occupation by district and left the commanders quite some leeway. He did, however, did make them commit to general standards of good conduct, meting out disciplinary measures and sanctions for trespasses. Commanders were to send up daily briefs on incidents or

---

[185] See L. Chène, L'occupation Russe dans le Département du Nord (1815–1818) (unpublished MA Thesis, University of Lille, France). Thanks to Catherine Dénys.

[186] C. Haynes, 'Face à l'occupation étrangère de 1815–1818: Les sorties de guerre des Alsaciens', Source(s), 4 (2014), 37–50, here: 44; Haynes, 'Making Peace: The Allied Occupation of France, 1815–1818', in Forrest, Hagemann and Rowe (eds.), War, 51–67.

[187] Wacker, Die alliierte Besetzung, 186–7.

[188] Proclamation, 20 June 1815, Nivelles, in J. Gurwood (ed.), Selections from the Dispatches and General Orders of Field Marshal the Duke of Wellington (London: John Murray, 1851), 865.

[189] Muir, Wellington. Waterloo and the Fortunes of Peace; Wellington to Talleyrand, 14 July 1816, in WD, vol. 12, 558–9; Wellington to Castlereagh, 14 July, Ibid.

complaints. Wellington, moreover, kept drilling his troops, making them march in lines, in echelons, or other strict formations, and practise attacks.[190]

The field marshal also applied that attitude of strict but just discipline to the French population. A Frenchwoman who threatened to take aim if British soldiers damaged her garden fence one more time was told that there would be a price to pay if she didn't quiet down – 'Let her know . . . that I will hang her.' But another Frenchwoman, who politely requested that he rescind the order to billet troops in her home because it was actually a boarding school for girls, could immediately count on Wellington's understanding. Trusting the cat to guard the cream was not an option; the soldiers had to leave the girls' guest house straight away.[191]

That did not stop the complaints from being lodged. The head of the Allied secret police, Justus Gruner (see Chapter 5), reported various 'Russian excesses'. An inhabitant of Angers had been put in a wooden cage; women jumped out of the windows to escape their occupiers. The French authorities, moreover, blamed the British soldiers, who, 'as soon as they have been drinking, start to cause mayhem. Usually they compel local musicians to play "God save the King" during public dances.'[192] The complaints indeed mostly regarded excesses that occurred in every zone, and that did abate somewhat in the course of 1815. In the French telling, however, the Prussian and other German troops were especially unpopular, particularly during the first months; Houssaye even talks about *La Terreur Prussienne*.[193] On 14 July, the French Ministry of the Interior published a whole list of serious offences allegedly committed by the Prussian troops: 'their excesses push whole communities to despair'.[194] Even King Friedrich Wilhelm III complained to the army leadership about the poorly organized and mangy German soldiers.[195] While Blücher and Gneisenau remained in France, the Prussian commanders kept continuing to collect cash amounts to compensate for the costs of the occupation – although the Allied Council had already prohibited this.[196] This malpractice only came to a halt after November.

It was not just the Prussians who lay violent hands on French citizens and their property. A whole gamut of complaints reached the Council: about Bavarian soldiers who cut down too many trees in the woods, hampered travel

[190] Ibid., 102–4.
[191] Letter of Mrs Huard de Merendol to Wellington, 28 August 1815; Mrs Sinon to Wellington, 29 August 1815, with his response scribbled in the margins. TNA, War Office (WO) 37/12.
[192] Report of Gruner, August, 11 September 1815, GStA PK, VI. HA Nl. Hardenberg 10a.
[193] See, for example, Houssaye, *1815. La seconde abdication*, 481–98.
[194] 'Bulletin de la Correspondance', 14 July 1815. Attachment to the protocol of 19 July, GStA PK, III. HA I. no. 1464.
[195] Wacker, *Die alliierte Besetzung*, 190–1.
[196] Protocols of 5, 6, 15 August 1815, GStA PK, III. HA I. no. 1465.

on the Briare Canal and interfered with the mail; about Russian abuses in Reims; or about the misconduct of Allied generals, such as the famous Austrian general Hieronymus Colloredo-Mansfeld, who had threatened a prefect and beat up a French official. A complaint was also lodged against the Prussian officer Leutner, in the department of Oise. He had put pressure on the local prefect to give him a list of the names of all the French citizens in the department who had voted for Napoleon's constitution.[197] Prussian commanders were feared for their stern demeanour; when a prefect failed to cooperate, it could happen that he was carted off to Germany and detained or held hostage for several months or even years. Wilhelm von Humboldt, a great Francophile, and a friend of Denon, lamented in a letter to his wife in August: 'Wir sind durchaus verhaßt, es heißt durchaus, daß wir lauter Exaktionen und Erpressungen machen.'[198]

The Council considered all the complaints, but usually responded very predictably. Most of the grievances were dismissed as being too vague and general. Talleyrand and the ultra-royalist Baron Vitrolles were told that they had to stop publishing comments about Allied excesses in the *Bulletin*, the explanation being that those kinds of objections were so 'vague' that they were not 'useful' and were sooner based on 'frivolous complaints' than on 'reality'. They would, moreover, fan resentment and mobilize unrest.[199] Lady Shelley, who accompanied the Duke of Wellington almost every day on his outings and visits to the opera, observed how he dealt with these complaints:

> Went into the Duke's sitting-room. He showed me about one dozen boxes, with portraits of various sovereigns, set with diamonds, which they had given to him. I took possession of one of his pens; and saw him receive, and answer several letters, by simply fixing a mark upon their margins. Others, containing the most absurd complaints, he threw away. One of these letters requested him to compensate the writer for mischief done to his property by the Prussians! The Duke told me that he receives similar letters daily.[200]

At the same time, she also witnessed misconduct first-hand:

> A Prussian division marched into Marle on the day previous to our arrival. Here, as everywhere, we heard nothing but complaints of their misconduct. Immediately on entering the town they published an order to the effect that every inhabitant who did not salute their soldiers whenever they passed them in the streets should be taken to the Hôtel de Ville and

---

[197] See the complaints and discussions attached to the protocols of 5, 7, 8, 10 and 20 August 1815, GStA PK, III. HA I. no. 1465.

[198] Wacker, *Die alliierte Besetzung*, 190–202.

[199] Protocol of 18 July 1815; letter of Allies to Talleyrand, 19 July 1815, GStA PK, III. HA I. no. 1464.

[200] Edgcumbe (ed.), *The Diary of Frances Lady Shelley, 1787–1817*, 127.

receive fifty *coups de bâton*! They also took by force everything that they
wanted in the town and its neighbourhood. If their search after brandy,
etc., proved unsuccessful, they vented their rage upon the inhabitants by
stripping them, and then throwing them, bound hand and foot, into the
fields or the woods. In one instance, when this was done to an infirm old
man of seventy, a formal complaint was lodged with the officer in command of the regiment. But instead of giving any redress, he ordered the
complainants to receive a flogging, and sent them away, promising to
repeat the punishment if they ever came back![201]

Only when the complaint contained names, numbers and concrete facts did the
Council refer the grievance on to the commander of the troops in question. But
then the complaint had to be accompanied by an official report with documented
evidence. In the case of Colloredo – a brave man, according to the ministers – his
commander (Schwarzenberg) was assigned the task of convincing him to back off
and to show more restraint. The Bavarians had to be reprimanded by
Schwarzenberg as well. Leutner, the Prussian listing Bonapartist citizens, was
also told that this kind of political intimidation was dangerous, and was a risk to
Allied order in itself. De-Bonapartization was a sensitive issue, preferably carried
out by the French government rather than by Allied commanders directly.[202]

The murder (*assassinat*) of five Prussian officers in the forest near Loret was,
naturally, also taken very seriously. The Council instructed Talleyrand to
immediately track down and prosecute the killers, who had probably fled to
Laon. When Talleyrand announced a few weeks later that according to the
prefect of Laon five officers had not been slain there at all, the Council was very
annoyed. The Prussians, as they had made very clear, were murdered elsewhere, but the culprits had fled to Laon. And so they commanded Talleyrand
to reopen the investigation and this time only come back with results.[203]

In practice, things began to stabilize somewhat during the autumn of 1815,
as people got used to the practices of the occupation. The ban on confiscating
cash and other goods, which the Council had issued on 24 July, was being
observed more consistently – which helped a lot. Most important, however,
was the Allied decision to place the troops in barracks outside towns and
villages, and stop billeting them.[204] Only high-placed officers were still quartered with French citizens, but only with prominent individuals, high in society
and with and nice manors and town palaces. All that is not to say that people's

---

[201] Ibid., 163.
[202] See the attachments to protocols of 5, 7, 8, 10 and 20 August 1815, GStA PK, III. HA I. no.
1465.
[203] Protocols of 5 and 22 August 1815, GStA PK, III. HA I. no. 1465.
[204] Wacker, *Die alliierte Besetzung*, 146–81. See also Chène, *L'occupation Russe dans le
Département du Nord*, 23–4. The shift from billeting to barracks was a rather slow
process. It was implemented fully only over the course of 1816, when a large proportion
of the Allied troops was repatriated (reducing them from 1.2 million to 150,000).

discontent dissipated. There were so many violent incidents, on both sides, that in some places the Allied Council was not wrong to speak of real French resistance. This was also behind the decision in November to keep direct contact between the Allied soldiers and French residents to a minimum.[205]

In the Military Convention of the Treaty of Paris, the Council had tried to circumscribe the hybrid administrative situation as best it could. In theory, the Allies fully acknowledged France's sovereignty when it came to legal issues, taxes and the levying of tolls: 'the Commanders of the Allied Troops shall throw no obstacle in the way of the measures to be taken'.[206] But in matters of security and public order, the Allies retained the right to intervene. In December 1815, for example, Wellington instructed the Allied commanders to review all police regulations before they were posted. So too, lines did sometimes blur when it came to settling legal disputes. In theory, Allied soldiers were prosecuted and punished by their own military police. But when it came to conflicts between citizens and the military, that was more difficult. France rejected the idea of mixed courts, with a combination of Allied and French officials. The principle of segregated case law was, however, a permanent source of conflict. The Allies and the French palpably accused each other of partiality when sentencing, or of letting litigation drag on when things were not going their way.[207] In practice, this meant that French judicial authorities structurally tried to prevent and hamper Allied interference via administrative obstruction and foot-dragging.

It is difficult to formulate a general assessment of France's attitude. Some of the positive reports about apparent camaraderie and joint celebrations were sooner meant as propaganda, or to temper the Allies' demeanour, than as accurate reflections of the general mood. For example, the French minister of justice, Marbois, ordered the local prefects to make sure that the relationships were excellent. He expected them to commit themselves to a 'parfaite harmonie'.[208] Sometimes, however, French residents did really speak highly of the troops. For example, they often had words of praise for the Russian officers, certainly after 1816, when Count Woronzow set his men back on the straight and narrow.[209] Baron Müffling furthermore received a lyrical letter of goodbye, composed by the prefect of the Seine department, Chabrol. Chabrol had been bestowed by Müffling with the Order of the Red Eagle and now paid back his dues in 'endless gratitude' to the general, praising his loyalty and integrity; they had almost become friends.[210]

---

[205] Wacker, *Die alliierte Besetzung*, 233–4.
[206] Article VI of the Military Convention, 20 November 1815, Foreign Office (ed.), *British and Foreign State Papers*, vol. 3, 280–1, 303.
[207] Wacker, *Die alliierte Besetzung*, 238–42.
[208] Ibid., 249.
[209] Ibid., 246–7.
[210] Chabrol to Müffling, 7 May 1816, GStA PK, VI. HA Familienarchiv und Nachlässe (Nl.) Müffling A7.

Because of these fluctuations over time and between areas, the occupation –
as a set of events and practices on the ground – should perhaps best be studied
and evaluated in a decentralized fashion.[211] For example, given their simila-
rities in language and tradition, the German-speaking troops in Alsace were
able to connect well with the population; various marriages were performed
between Allied officers and indigenous girls. In the provinces, members of the
upper class were quite pleased with the additional balls and festivities organized by the officers.[212] As said above, the lower classes – the farmers, workers
and their women – probably suffered the most by the Allied soldiers, with their
extravagant outings, hunting parties and sometimes still very rapacious
inclinations.

A Moderate Occupation

By the end of 1815, the Allied Council and its subcommittees had completed
their first major assignment – the Treaty of Paris had been composed and
adopted. The Allied infrastructure was also in place and had begun its work.
The Military Committee, the Joint Financial Committee, the Looted Art
Committee and the Administrative Committee were all running at full
steam. This resulted in a very well-thought-out, finely tuned and, given the
various courts and parliaments represented, rational form of conference sanctioned by diplomatic legitimacy, guaranteed and upheld by a military occupation force.[213] Moreover, internal disputes amongst the Allies had been solved,
compromise had been reached and the – especially Prussian – desire for
revenge had been tamed. What was special about this Allied Council was
that they, with their 'principles of salutary precaution', had set up
a European consortium that dedicated itself, like a security council *avant la
lettre*, to peace and security on the continent. They did so not only in close
consultation with each other, but also with the other countries of Europe –
albeit in a thoroughly imperialist manner. In this fashion, moreover, a new
reading of 'security' emerged: instead of pointing to 'Providence' (as Blücher
and Gneisenau still did), an 'Allied Machine' would take care of
the *ménagement* of mutual security in peacetime, indicating the collective
battle against both the 'system of revolution' and the 'system of despotism'.
After 1815, collective security was not preparing for war, but cooperating in
risk management on the continent.

This type of collective security, and the accompanying Allied concert that set
the tone in 1815, can moreover hardly be compared to the democratic way in
which international institutions such as NATO or the EU were designed after

---

[211] Which has been done by C. Haynes, *Our Friends the Enemies*.
[212] Haynes, 'Face à l'occupation étrangère', 37–50.
[213] See protocols from July and August, GStA PK, III. HA I. no. 1464.

1918 or 1945. The four major powers called the shots. France was humiliated and had to comply. The lesser powers had to be content when allowed to play the part of extras and to participate in subordinate committees. Obviously, this system of 'mutual security' was not the culmination of 'disinterestedness', as Castlereagh tried to present it. Britain consistently tried to keep its maritime and colonial interests out of the game in Vienna and Paris, and, as the preponderant power, could afford to do so. However, even Britain let itself be drawn into the web of mutual dependencies and deliberations, and found that it could not completely avoid having to discuss the Greek question, the slave trade or piracy issues with the other powers, thereby willingly curtailing its unilateral leeway in favour of multilateral gains on the continent. After 1815, compared with the Napoleonic rule prior to 1815, or with the situation of the *ancien régime*, considerable progress had been made. A security culture based on consultation and uniform agreements that were characterized by moderation and balance – at least on paper or in the words chosen – and constrained by self-imposed references to laws and justice, spread across the continent.

Signs of this new chapter in European history were evident already during the last half of 1815. Although some local Allied commanders – Prussian, Bavarian, but sometimes also Russian or Austrian – preferred to bind and sacrifice the French virgin on the altar of vengeance, Wellington and the other Allied ministers (including Prussian chancellor Hardenberg) wanted instead to teach her a few manners. It was not she, but her great seducer, Napoleon, who needed to be punished. And even that punishment ended up being quite civil. At the end of June, a few Prussian generals still demanded the exclusive right to execute Napoleon. A few weeks later, however, the entire Allied Council with few exceptions agreed to the British proposal to exile Napoleon to the South Atlantic island of St Helena. In the 'name of security', Napoleon would be accompanied by a British convoy to the island.[214] As a sign of communal solidarity, however, Napoleon's banishment was organized as a joint undertaking. To that end, each ally sent a delegate to join the supervisory contingent on St Helena. Even the French government was invited to join the multilateral security mission, 'cette mesure de sureté générale'.[215] And so it was that the emperor who on his own had tried to subdue 'this old Europe' – *ce vieil Europe* – was jointly tamed by that same Europe. Not with an iron fist, but with velvet gloves.

The double-headed monster of revolutionary terror and Napoleonic despotism was in chains. Demilitarization and restoration of the Bourbon regime had been achieved by means of a systematically applied military occupation. But

[214] Protocol of 28 July 1815, GStA PK, III. HA I. no. 1465.
[215] Protocols of 29 July and 3 August 1815, GStA PK, III. HA I. no. 1464.

the objectives of de-Bonapartization, stabilization and the completion of reparation payments had not been met yet. Whether the moderate Allied peace could tame France's 'eternal hatred' was still an open question. The spectre of 'armed Jacobinism' still hung in the air and kept emotions running high.

5

Fausses nouvelles and 'Blacklists'

The Allied Struggle against 'Armed Jacobinism'

Hortense on the Run

In the late summer of 1815, the French capital was still in turmoil. Rumours whirled like autumn leaves through the crowded streets. Louise Cochelet, a lady-in-waiting and confidante to Queen Hortense, sighed, 'Here I am in 1815, a time so magnificent and brilliant and so wretched, all at once. These days are confounding given the gravity of the events and the rapidity with which they are compounded in so short a time.'[1] One of the many victims of the post-Napoleonic turbulence was Louise's friend and employer, Hortense (Fig. 5.1). The daughter of Empress Joséphine de Beauharnais, she had married Napoleon's brother Louis, and had been Queen of the Netherlands between 1806 and 1810. But neither her husband nor her kingdom appealed to her, and she lived separated from them both in Paris from 1810 onwards. Hortense was one of the Bonapartists who remained true to the emperor to the bitter end. In 1814, Tsar Alexander took pity on her and her two young sons, Napoléon-Louis and Charles Louis Napoléon (known as Louis Napoléon, the future Emperor Napoleon III), and more or less protected her from the rage of the royalists. However, contrary to his advice, Hortense once again chose Napoleon's side during the Hundred Days. After that, the Russian emperor kept his distance, also in part because it was now the Prussians and the British who ruled the day in the capital.

On 17 July, the prefect of police, Decazes, informed Hortense that she had to leave the city. On behalf of the Allied Council, Governor Müffling let her know that she must be on her way within two hours. Accompanied by Count Edouard de Woyna, aide-de-camp to General Schwarzenberg, and a passport for Switzerland, signed by both French and Allied authorities, she left Paris at nine o'clock the same evening.[2] The very next day, she was waylaid by a group of unruly British soldiers, and shortly after almost arrested by French officers. Her

---

[1] Cochelet, *Mémoires*, 167.
[2] Cochelet, *Mémoires*, 185–93; Le prince Napoléon (ed.), *Mémoires de la Reine Hortense*, vol. 3 (Paris: Plon, 1927), 65–7.

205

Figure 5.1   Hortense de Beauharnais, queen of Holland. Portrait by A.-L. Girodet-Trioson, *c.*1805–9. (Rijksmuseum, Amsterdam)

Austrian escort saved her twice, and Hortense realized the gravity and absurdity of the situation: 'Enemies taking my part, Frenchmen acting as my foes. For the pleasure of persecuting me, they had placed themselves in a humiliating position, and allowed themselves to be reminded that they had been defeated.'[3] After arriving in Geneva, she was still harassed. Neither Hortense nor Napoleon's mother, who was initially expelled to Switzerland, was given permission to stay there. Where to go? Hortense did not want to return to the Netherlands: 'I ruled there once.' The French ambassador informed her that she had to wait for further orders from the Allied powers. Escorted, spied on and pursued by all sorts of agents and observers, in December 1815, after travelling via Aix-les-Bains and Bern, she finally arrived in the city of Konstanz in Baden. But here the *persécutions* continued as well: 'Espionage surrounds me on all sides and in every imaginable form.'[4] An official at the Baden court informed Hortense that international treaties did not allow the Baden government to grant a member of the Bonapartist family asylum, and that they could only settle in one of the four countries of the Quadruple Alliance.[5] Intensely cold winter weather had come in the meantime, but she and her children had to get on their way again.

---

[3] Le prince Napoléon (ed.), *Mémoires de la Reine Hortense*, vol. 3, 69.
[4] Ibid., 77–103, here: 109.
[5] Ibid., 77–103.

Hortense had become the target of the first Allied security measures, which will be discussed below. She belonged to that first category of Allied enemies: the Bonapartes and their immediate supporters. This was the one side of the terror threat. The other side, 'armed Jacobinism', was considered equally threatening and active in 1815. Against this double-faced threat, Bonapartism and 'armed Jacobinism', the Allied Council decided to take action. In addition to negotiating a peace treaty, seeing to the demilitarization, the execution of political reforms and the prompt payment of reparations, the four great powers applied themselves to the task of fighting the threat of terror. That included quieting the flood of rumours, singling out conspiracy plans in a timely fashion, and identifying and apprehending roaming enemies of the state. To that end, the Council devised a series of proactive measures, in line with the 'principles of salutary precaution' presented in the previous chapter.

Security through Management

As noted in Chapter 2, the Allied Council made use of the experience gained in 1814, especially with Stein's Central Administration – the organization that handled the communication, logistics and management of the conquered German and French territories on behalf of the Allies.[6] Some additional explications on the shaping of the Allied security policies are called for here. The measure and effect of the internal security policies of the Allies were very much dependent on the extent to which risks and threats could be managed centrally; and, of course, much had changed in that regard since the late eighteenth century. Stein's administration was part of the so-called 'territorial revolution' taking place between 1794 and 1815, when, under the influence of the Napoleonic Wars and reforms, the countries in Europe underwent a fundamental process of centralization and modernization. The rise of a class of local officials, legal professionalism and the development of all kinds of centralized government agencies had given a substantial boost to bureaucracies on the continent.[7] The Allies, too, made grateful use of the many barristers, solicitors and notables who assisted the commanders in the conquered areas. The Allied Council was likewise party to the ongoing trend of 'internal colonization projects', not only found in Prussia, Poland and the Caucasus region, but now also applied west of the Rhine. Stein's administration had initially assisted the Sixth Coalition and saw to a continuous supply of provisions and housing for the troops, the management of the liberated territories, maintaining the order there and preventing a glut of excesses towards the civilian population. But the second and no less important task was making

---

[6] Memorandum of Allied Council to Müffling, protocols of 12 July 1815, GStA PK, III. HA I. no. 1464.
[7] L. Raphael, *Recht und Ordnung. Herrschaft durch Verwaltung im 19. Jahrhundert* (Frankfurt: Fischer, 2000), 17, 21–40.

sure that the local authorities acquiesced to the Allied rule, as a form of so-called *Herrschaft durch Verwaltung* ('ruling by managing').[8]

These administrative efforts had been a short-term affair in 1814. But in 1815 the Allies' plan was to stay on until they were able 'to bring back the people of France to moral and peaceful habits', as Castlereagh wrote to the Allied ministers on 11 September 1815.[9] Now without Stein, the Allied Council, as quadripartite directorate, would monitor the implementation of Castlereagh's principles of salutary precaution.[10] The military commission and the financial committees were mentioned previously; but to manage security properly, more bureaucratic support was called for, namely, an Allied police-and-security agency, with a corresponding network of agents. Such an Allied police force was indeed set up straight away on 16 July, with the Prussian Justus Gruner (Fig. 5.2) at its head.[11]

Figure 5.2   Justus (von) Gruner, in charge of the Allied secret police, 1814. Artist unknown. (© bpk-Bildagentur)

---

[8] Cf. M. Rowe, *From Reich to State. The Rhineland in the Revolutionary Age, 1780–1830* (Cambridge: Cambridge University Press, 2003), 227–8.

[9] Note of Castlereagh to the Allied Ministers, 11 September 1815, *Journals of the House of Commons*, 71 (1816), 731.

[10] Castlereagh, Memorandum, 13 July 1815, GStA PK, III. HA I. no. 1461. See also Liverpool to Castlereagh, 21 July 1815, *WSD*, vol. 11, 47.

[11] Protocol of 13 July 1815, GStA PK, III. HA I. no. 1464. He was ennobled later, so here he is still called Justus Gruner; the 'von' came afterwards.

An Allied Security Service

During the first meetings of the Allied Council, which began on 12 July 1815 , the ministers discussed in detail how they could restore domestic peace and security in France and Paris. They insisted that the four courts had to act as a 'single authority'.[12] In order to have a sound sense of all the unrest, the Council decided on 13 July that, in addition to all military and financial oversight, there needed to be an official forum for police affairs. This agency would assist and supervise the French police, providing the Allies with information daily.[13] French officials would be put under Allied supervision regarding both 'major political issues' and the actions of the *haute police* (high police). In these two areas, the powers retained the right to 'decide by mutual agreement'.[14] Talleyrand was informed of this decision and asked to report on the status of domestic security as soon as possible.[15]

The Council believed that the threat could come from two corners: from the Bonapartists, but equally from the *Système révolutionaire*, which had put themselves on the throne in France prior to Napoleon.[16] Hardenberg tried to convince the other ministers that the former was the most pressing, since 'They [the Bonapartists] know about almost everything we discuss among ourselves. Everything this faction does is focused on countering the foreigner, and we believe that the government favours it.' And even if all these dangers could be neutralized, there was still the risk that 'new commotions' would break out, 'which could not but compromise the repose of Europe, bought with such effort and sacrifice'.[17]

That is why priority number one was to 'stabilize' France – on this, the Allies all agreed. The principle of stabilization manifested itself in restoring the Bourbons and occupying the country, but also in equipping and monitoring a central security service. The Prussians were particularly interested in the latter, but they immediately found Wellington equally supportive. Based on his time in India as well as his military campaigns, he had come to see the value of 'indirect rule' – inasmuch as it was based on and could count on a thorough intelligence and security network manned by local agents and directors. On 22 July, the Council, pushed by Hardenberg, officially approved setting up their own secret police, which would oversee Fouché's *haute police*, and have jurisdiction in Paris as well as throughout the rest of the occupied territories and incidentally also in other parts of France, when necessary.[18]

---

[12] Protocol of 12 July 1815, GStA PK, III. HA I. no. 1464.
[13] See reports by Gruner, 22 July–November 1815, GStA PK, VI. HA Nl. Gruner, no. 86; GStA PK, VI. HA Nl. Hardenberg 10a.
[14] Annex 6 to the protocol of 13 July 1815, GStA PK, III. HA I. no. 1464.
[15] Protocol of 14 July, comments of Pozzo di Borgo, GStA PK, III. HA I. no. 1464.
[16] Hardenberg, 'État des Négociations actuelles entre les Puissances Alliées & la France', 16–28 July 1815, GStA PK, III. HA I. no. 1461, 54.
[17] Hardenberg, Memorandum, 22 July 1815, GStA PK, III. HA I. no. 1461.
[18] See Hardenberg, Memorandum, 22 July 1815, point 1.b, GStA PK, III. HA I. no. 1461.

On Hardenberg's recommendation, the Allied Council appointed Justus Gruner as head of both the Allied secret police (*Verbündetenpolizei*) in France and the occupational police force in Paris, where he was to assist Müffling in overseeing the French capital. Gruner was an example of the modern, highly educated bureaucrat that, although not belonging to the nobility, increasingly came to the fore around the turn of the century. Born in 1777 as son of a simple lawyer, Gruner had studied law and political science at the universities in Halle and Göttingen, and then initially worked in Osnabrück. He came to be known as a careful and hard-working civil servant in the newly conquered Polish areas, especially in the province of Posen, where he worked for an organization that helped German settlers there. Gruner stood out for his ambition, wit and impatience; he could not tolerate indecision and incompetence. He was an avid writer, and published about criminal law, the prison system, and about public order and morality. He combined his fervency for modernizing bureaucracy with a passionate and even Romantic position on good manners and morals.[19]

Gruner steadily climbed the public service ladder, with positions in Posen, East Prussia and West Pomerania, and was appointed director of the police force in Berlin in 1809. Stein and Hardenberg were impressed by his unremitting commitment, patriotism and penchant for reform. Gruner made good on those impressions, proving his organizational talent in Berlin as well, where he centralized the police, extended their jurisdiction to Berlin's suburbs, reformed the fire department, brought order to the city's waste management services and devised all sorts of measures to combat corruption. Subsequently, he was appointed to the Secret Council of State and as chief of the 'higher police' in Prussia. But, when dissatisfied with the hesitancy of Prussia's King Friedrich Wilhelm III, whom he found to be far too afraid of turning against Napoleon, Gruner resigned in February 1812. Hardenberg and the king assured him straight away that under other circumstances he could return to Prussian service immediately.

In the meantime, he could turn to building an anti-Napoleonic spy network from Prague, on behalf of Tsar Alexander. But only a couple of months into the spying business, he was discovered and arrested by Metternich's police – Austria was, after all, still formally an ally of France. After Austria joined the Sixth Coalition in 1813, Gruner was released and immediately appointed as governor of the general government of the liberated duchy of Berg, which was

---

[19] J. Gruner, *Versuch über Strafen in vorzüglicher Rücksicht auf Todes- und Gefängnisstrafen* (Göttingen, 1799); *Actenmäßige Erzählung der Betrügereien eines angeblichen Wundermädchens* (Berlin, 1800); *Leidenschaft und Pflicht. Eine Sammlung moralischer Gemälde* (Berlin, 1800); *Versuch über die rechte und zweckmäßigste Einrichtung öffentlicher Sicherheitsinstitute und deren Verbesserung* (Frankfurt, 1802); *Meine Wallfahrt zur Ruhe und Hoffnung oder Schilderung des sittlichen und bürgerlichen Zustandes Westphalens am Ende des 18. Jahrhunderts* (Frankfurt, 1802).

now brought under Allied supervision. There, and in the reconquered French departments of the general government of the Middle Rhine (west bank), Gruner could further hone his organizational and bureaucratic talents. In 1815, thanks to his excellent contacts with Stein and Chancellor Hardenberg, Gruner was the Prussian dream candidate for the new Allied security service. Müffling, too, thought it was a great idea; he had got to know the young Justus when stationed at the Prussian garrison in Osnabrück, and found him to be a fellow patriot and reformer.[20] Gruner was indeed a close friend of Joseph Görres, the radical, Romantic patriot and publisher of the *Rheinische Merkur*. Thus, Gruner brought with him to Paris a remarkable combination of fervent dedication to modernizing bureaucracy and passionate patriotism. He arrived on 9 July, tasked by the Allies with establishing both an Allied General Directorate of Police (*Generaldirekzion der Policey*) as well as an Allied military police force (*Verbündetenpolizei*).[21]

Gruner and the 'Miracle' of Fouché

Gruner's service was responsible for assisting *and* keeping an eye on the French administration, for equitably distributing amongst the Allies the income from the occupied territories, and for ensuring the safety of the occupying forces. According to Gruner and Hardenberg, these efforts were also intended to make sure 'that the weakening of France was effected systematically and in an appropriate manner' – a somewhat wayward interpretation of the precautionary principles of de-Bonapartizing, stabilizing and de-revolutionizing. Clearly, the Prussian passion for revenge had not been completely tamed.[22] Around the end of July, Gruner informed all the relevant prefects and ministers of his new title, and announced that the Allies had put him 'in charge of the general police of the Allies, and particularly of the surveillance of safety measures for the troops in and around the garrison of Paris'.[23] He asked Fouché and Decazes politely but forcefully to provide him with daily briefs on all matters important to the Allies, especially regarding the safety and security of the troops. But, at the same time, he expressed his deep admiration for Fouché's talents and successes as head of the French police. He

---

[20] See K. Zeisler, 'Justus von Gruner: Eine biographische Skizze', in W. Breunig and U. Schaper (eds.), *Berlin in Geschichte und Gegenwart* (Berlin: Gebr. Mann Verlag, 1994), 81–105; J. Gruner, 'Gruner, Justus von', in *Allgemeine Deutsche Biographie*, vol. 10 (Leipzig: Duncker & Humblot, 1879), 42–8.

[21] The official order, signed by the four Allied powers, was issued on 8 August at Gruner's request. Letter from the Administrative Committee of the Allied Council to Gruner, 8 August 1815, GStA PK, VI. HA, Nl. Gruner, no. 86.

[22] Message from Gruner, 'Die Aufgabe ist', no date, probably late July 1815, GStA PK, VI. HA, Nl. Gruner, no. 86.

[23] Gruner to Fouché, no date, probably late July 1815, GStA PK, VI. HA, Nl. Gruner, no. 86.

described it as a great honour that he, as an Allied occupant, could now work with someone of the likes of Fouché[24] – even though the latter was a dyed-in-the-wool Bonapartist and, before that, a revolutionary. What impressed Gruner most, apparently, was Fouché's status as the architect of modern, centralized police and security services.

That said, Gruner was not an uncritical admirer of Fouché. In August, he outlined a detailed portrait of the French minister, explaining to the Allies what made Fouché so special. Fouché was 'not so much a secretive (*geheime*) person, as he was an important (*wichtige*) person . . . An equally great genius as Talleyrand, but he has not adapted to modern times.' Whereas Talleyrand played a 'subtle role, full of spirit', Fouché had begun as a 'crude revolutionary'. Thanks to Napoleon and his own 'orderly housekeeping', he had become a wealthy man. Fouché, in contrast to Talleyrand, had 'no burning desires or passions'. 'He governs cold-bloodedly, and in full possession of his wits. Talleyrand, on the contrary, loves the game, and on top of that, maintains women, needs to maintain his far too luxurious household and his inordinate ambition.' Fouché was at the top 'owing to fear'; Talleyrand, by contrast, 'has consistently invested himself in all affairs'.[25] Fouché, who had indeed started out as a revolutionary, had voted for Louis XVI's execution (and was thus a *régicide*), but fell into disrepute during the Reign of Terror (1793–4). After betraying some of his fellow supporters of the Jacobin Club and casting his lot in with Napoleon, he eventually found his niche: modernizing France's police force. By 1799 he had taken to leading the administrative agency in charge of 'the all-encompassing, grand machine of communal spirit and public opinion', leaving the 'torture' to others.[26] During the first and second restoration, Fouché had managed to retain his post as minister – a veritable 'miracle'. There was, continued Gruner, 'the most remarkable contrast' between Fouché's 'brutal and terrifying' measures at the time of the Revolution and his 'moderation', 'system of tolerance' and 'compliant, courtly tone' now. He could not hide his adoration for the manner in which Fouché had been able to manoeuvre himself into the role of a 'vital, indispensable and popular person', first in the eyes of the revolutionaries, then under Napoleon, subsequently under King Louis and now for the Allies.[27]

Unlike in East Prussia, the process of 'internal colonization' – tempering the hearts and rebellious spirits of the French – was less a case of pioneering and creating bureaucracies out of nothing. Paris had enough administrative

[24] See especially letter of Gruner to Fouché, 22 July and to Decazes, 3 August 1815, GStA PK, VI. HA, Nl. Gruner, no. 86; Gruner to Fouché, 3 August 1815, GStA PK, VI. HA, Nl. Hardenberg 10a.
[25] Message of Gruner, 'Ueber Fouché', 24 August 1815, GStA PK, VI. HA, Nl. Gruner, no. 32.
[26] Message of Gruner, 'Ueber Fouché. Fortsetzung', 26 August 1815, GStA PK, VI. HA, Nl. Gruner, no. 32.
[27] Message of Gruner, 'Ueber Fouché', 24 August 1815, GStA PK, VI. HA, Nl. Gruner, no. 32.

institutions in place. In fact, for Gruner, the Paris agencies, and the way in which Fouché had centralized the police, were his prime example. Fouché had done precisely what Gruner had attempted to emulate in Berlin and the eastern provinces of Prussia – to build a centrally led, modern, efficient police organization that included not only enforcement, prosecution and a penal system, but also assessed the 'general disposition' and public spirit. In doing so, both Fouché and Gruner combined tasks that today are found in separate agencies; his secret police encompassed a constabulary, intelligence, security and counter-intelligence services, all rolled into one.[28] In this highly complex and dense French network of competencies, Gruner wanted to try to get a foot on the ground. He would, however, find out that the Polish and Eastern Prussian territories were level terrain compared to the quagmire of French intrigues and interests that would ensnare his ambitions here.

'We Know the French!'

To fight terror effectively, 'counter-measures' were urgently needed; in particular, the strict enforcement of criminal law in the occupied provinces, preventative 'precautionary measures' in the rest of France, and an alert 'high and security police'.[29] In the jurisdiction of the 'high police', activities were indicated that nowadays would be situated within security and intelligence agencies, in particular domestic security operations and surveillance. Gruner discussed with Wellington how this type of security police should look and how it should be organized. It 'had, of course, to serve the government of the king of France', but was to be controlled by the Allies. 'A thousand difficulties, complications and diffusions' would arise without such a 'clear arrangement'. 'We know the French!' quipped a cynical Gruner, 'And whatever colour they wear, they are all against us.' As far as he was concerned, because 'the French people had not called him [King Louis] back', the Allies were in no way obliged to the French monarch. He agreed with Wellington that 'the Bourbons are for us the best option', but 'they have no right to make demands on us'. Gruner also thought that the Duke's assessment of French internal affairs was far too rosy; he was too 'confident about the present situation – which is certainly his right as a great hero, but to me does not seem well-founded'. Gruner believed that the threat of an insurgency was still far too great – 'a moment can devour us'. That is why oversight, control and a robust, unfettered police force were so important. Wellington thought so as well.[30]

---

[28] C. Fijnaut, *Opdat de macht een toevlucht zij? Een historische studie van het politieapparaat als een politieke instelling* (Arnhem: Gouda Quint, 1979), 489–616, 730–50.

[29] Message of Gruner, 12 July 1815, GStA PK, VI. HA Nl. Hardenberg 10a.

[30] Gruner, report of a conversation with Wellington, 24 July 1815, GStA PK, VI. HA Nl. Hardenberg 10a.

The means and funds for such a security force, however, were falling behind the commitments made. After the Council had made its decision (22 July) and Wellington and Hardenberg sent their letter of appointment (28 July informally, and in writing on 8 August), Gruner still had no budget to appoint his own personnel. It soon became apparent that Müffling saw Gruner primarily as his office manager and assistant, and did not plan on handing the maintenance of order and security over to him. The army leadership, too, was not prepared to place the 'war commissioners', who fell under the supervision of the Military Committee, at the disposal of Gruner in matters relating to public order and security. This irritated Gruner immensely because, in the meantime, the occupied territories and Paris were being run by 'commissioners who neither knew the language nor the culture of the country', by people who 'never would have led a directorate had we been in charge'. And while the Austrian and Russian managers still 'administrated their territories with dignity, Prussia had handed their departments over to civil servants who were not trusted to rule in their own country and only knew plunder as their governing principle'.[31] 'Order, discipline and the management of resources' were urgently needed in the occupied territories. 'This objective is a top priority; our security, honour and humanity demand it.' But Müffling did not budge an inch, and declared that the army leadership had 'not authorized' him to acknowledge Gruner's security service or military police as an autonomously operating unit. The fact that Gruner was rather vocal about the lack of discipline among Prussian troops, of course, did not make his relationship with Müffling and the generals any better.[32]

Metternich, too, threw sand in Gruner's gears, who complained to Hardenberg that the haughty Austrian minister had reproached him for abusing the Allied service as a vehicle for Prussian interests. Highly upset, the principled and quite incorruptible Gruner asked Hardenberg on 5 August to relieve him of the task of setting up a military police force, and to just assign him once again to a position in the Prussian provinces. 'I must have full command, or otherwise nothing; working on half authority will not do.'[33] But Hardenberg would have none of it and talked Gruner back to his post. From now on, Gruner needed to focus primarily on setting up an Allied secret police force, and could abandon attempts to create a military police as well. Hardenberg also encouraged the other ministers to express their support for Gruner's service, which they duly did. An official letter, with signatures of each of the Allies, worked wonders. On 10 August, Metternich even personally assured Gruner of his gratitude and praise – according to the Austrian

---

[31] Message of Gruner, 19 July 1815, GStA PK, VI. HA Nl. Hardenberg 10a.
[32] Message of Gruner, 24 July 1815, GStA PK, VI. HA Nl. Hardenberg 10a.
[33] Message of Gruner, 5 August 1815, GStA PK, VI. HA Nl. Hardenberg 10a.

minister, Gruner's police work was essential.[34] So much flattery was hard to resist, and Gruner decided to give it another go.

Intermittently, Gruner had indeed booked some successes with his efforts to launch a secret police force. Already on 16 July, before Gruner had officially reported to Fouché, his agents stood with Gruner on the doorstep 'and seem to want to create a kind of partnership'. But a few key figures from the 'royalist party' also came by and offered their services as well.[35] That is why Gruner first pencilled in for himself and for the Allies what the French political landscape looked like, and who he believed would be the best partners and collaborators for the Allied security service. According to Gruner, there were four parties: 'the Jacobins, the Bonapartists, the constitutional-monarchists and the royalists'. The 'triumph' of the last party was merely skin-deep; 'the first three are the stronger ones'. And the most troublesome – 'and easily possible' – would be an alliance of all three. In addition, the royalists were divided internally, the minority being moderates and the majority seemingly favourably inclined to the Count of Artois, Louis's ultra-conservative brother. The 'public mood' was quite frankly poor: 'terminate the Bourbons – hatred of the Prussians – contempt for Austria ... – veneration for Alexander – repressed anger with the English', and utter rage about the cost of the occupation.[36] Thus Gruner summarized the public climate in the French capital.

Gruner initially recommended that the Allied Council support the constitutional party. As he saw it, the combination of constitutionalism, legitimacy and royal authority would provide France with the most stability; he wanted nothing to do with zealotry, extremism or any other adventurous solutions. 'I have put Prussians on the road to winning over the whole of France's great constitutional party', he reported to Hardenberg. 'If we fail in this, the consequences will be incalculable.' In that endeavour, Gruner initially saw Fouché as a partner, the French minister being someone equally well versed in law, management and effective authority as Gruner himself.[37] Wellington had made a similar assessment; Fouché was the only one who knew the 'Jacobin party' and could also keep its members in line. Louis's position was still too vulnerable, especially in the east of the country, where the population's proclivity was profoundly anti-royalist. But also in the south, where the Ultras' preference was for Louis's arch-conservative brother. Even Paris was not stable. With his network of agents, spies and confidants, Fouché was therefore dearly needed.[38]

---

[34] Gruner to Hardenberg, 10 August 1815, report of a conversation with Metternich that same day, GStA PK, VI. HA Nl. Hardenberg 10a.

[35] Gruner to Hardenberg, 16 July, GStA PK, VI. HA Nl. Hardenberg 10a.

[36] Message of Gruner, 12 July 1815, GStA PK, VI. HA Nl. Hardenberg 10a.

[37] Gruner to Hardenberg, 8 August 1815, GStA PK, VI. HA Nl. Gruner, no. 86.

[38] Waresquiel, *Fouché*, 588–9.

Despite these considerations, having a fruitful collaboration with Fouché proved to be an illusion. It started with the fact that French officials did not take Gruner seriously at all. They would listen to him, answer him and sometimes share information with him, but only bits and pieces. To have an effective secret police force, however, Gruner really depended on the support of the ordinary police. 'The secret police cannot operate without the municipal police; its effort is in vain if it does not have access to the local police agencies', he complained. For the recruitment of spies, Gruner was equally left on his own. Although a successful recruitment process was totally 'dependent on their attitude and rightful spirit, operations would only be reliable when guided by this mentality'. One could 'buy' secret agents 'with gold or party spirit', but without intrinsic motivation and support from the French authorities, he would not be able to 'book reliable results'. Unfortunately, the French police did not feel at all inclined to compensate for that lack of good, motivated spies with extra help or information. 'The unmitigated disposition in France is against us; so, we ought not to count on them.'[39]

That is why Gruner had to make do with what he had, in particular the royalists, returning *émigrés* and some Germans living in France that had been offering their services to the Allies from the beginning. Today we would call them 'walk-ins' – people who on their own initiative volunteered as spies. Gruner's self-motivated recruits were driven by anger stemming from the appointment of Fouché and other Bonapartists. They hoped to find support for their cause with Gruner and his Allied police; otherwise 'things will turn out as they have before', opined a certain Marquis de Viennay ('one of the heads of the royalists'). According to the marquis, Gruner urgently needed help, because Fouché had already 'surrounded him' with spies.[40] The Swiss bookseller Louis Fauche-Borel, who had made a name for himself as the publisher of Louis XVIII's 1804 manifesto to the French people, and in Prussia had been a secret agent of Hardenberg, also stood on the doorstep in early August. As a royalist, and negotiator for the Bourbons, he came to warn Gruner of a 'terrible conspiracy' to 'assassinate' the kings of France and Prussia. According to Fauche-Borel, Michel Regnault de Saint-Jean d'Angély, minister of state under Napoleon, was personally involved (this could not be true, since Saint-Jean d'Angély, who would die in 1819, had already been exiled to the United States).[41] Another 'walk-in' was the author of French-nationalist and anti-British pamphlets, the knight Coffin de Rony, who, wanting to make things right again, offered Gruner a fully elaborated organizational chart for a secret police force, which, according to Gruner, was not bad at all. Coffin de

---

[39] Message of Gruner, 'Über die deutsche Polizei von Paris', undated, probably 5 August, GStA PK, VI. HA Nl. Hardenberg 10a.

[40] Message of Gruner, 19 July 1815, GStA PK, VI. HA Nl. Hardenberg 10a.

[41] Fauche-Borel to Gruner, 8 August 1815, GStA PK, VI. HA Nl. Hardenberg 10a.

Rony proposed, for example, recruiting ten female agents, in addition to the male spies that had to be recruited from within the armed forces, literary circles and the business community, since female agents may well be better equipped to work their way into well-known circles and salons.[42]

As a result of including these royalist and ultra-royalist agents, émigrés and penitents in his ranks, however, the ethos within Gruner's police force became fiercely anti-republican, anti-Bonapartist, anti-liberal and especially ultra-royalist. His original idea, to have the Allied service work with the more constitutional, moderate and liberal party, disappeared from sight. With his new ultra-royalist agents, there was no end to their denigrating Fouché and his Bonapartist retinue. With their bias and preoccupation with the 'Red Terror' scare, Gruner only realized around the middle of August that the Ultras were waging a veritable campaign of 'White Terror' in southern France.[43] This was the epitaph given to the anti-revolutionary wave of violence that responded to the 'Red Terror' of the Jacobins, and that had swept over France in bouts, starting in 1793. In 1814, 'White Terror' again started to wreak havoc. French Protestants and Bonapartists were systematically harassed and assaulted. The intelligence on this type of political violence, however, reached Gruner too late, and only haphazardly, possibly due in part to the fact that he did not have any Bonapartist spies in his network any more. Consequently, the Allied Council had a blind spot on the right, and lacked a true grasp of the excesses resulting from the White Terror.

For Metternich, the Allied Council's primary task was not just a prevention of another war and bloodletting. His greatest scare was the revolutionary character of those Napoleonic Wars. Not 'war', but political upheaval and revolt, leading to large-scale destruction or expropriation of private property, was Metternich's worst nightmare. His family had first-hand experience with this. His parents had to leave all their possessions on the Left Bank of the Rhine behind while fleeing from the advancing French armies in 1794. They had lost everything there.[44] Metternich therefore urged Gruner: 'It is finally time to name the evil that we are fighting: armed Jacobinism.'[45] To prevent any sort of revolutionary 'disruption' of society and expropriation of private ownership from ever occurring again, the evil of Jacobinism had to be eradicated root and branch.[46] And, as both Metternich and Hardenberg heartily agreed, that was precisely the purpose of Gruner's secret police.

[42] Message of Gruner, 19 July 1815, GStA PK, VI. HA Nl. Hardenberg 10a.
[43] See S. Clay, 'White Terror: Factions, Reactions and the Politics of Vengeance', in P. McPhee (ed.), A Companion to the French Revolution (Oxford: Oxford University Press, 2015), 359–78.
[44] Siemann, Metternich, 89–90, 166, 169–73.
[45] Metternich, Memorandum sent to Hardenberg, 6 August 1815, GStA PK, III. HA I. no. 1461, 75.
[46] Metternich, Memorandum, 6 August 1815, GStA PK, III. HA I. no. 1461, 78–80.

Fausses nouvelles: The Rumour Mill Starts Turning

From that moment on, Gruner was granted more leeway to collect information and map rumours and potential conspiracies. Intelligence is processed information, and that was exactly what Gruner went after. His budget, meanwhile, had already improved considerably. Initially, Gruner had to make an advance payment of 5,000 francs from his own capital in order to finance his modest staff. But he was soon able to come up with a better arrangement. With the assistance of Müffling, Gruner signed a contract with a certain Mr Bernard, owner of a Parisian *Spielbank* – a kind of state casino. In exchange for Allied protection, he paid the Prussians 2,000 francs a day. These payments allowed Bernard to improve his competitive advantage over the handful of other French casinos. In return, Müffling and Gruner could keep some of the payments as 'table money' for themselves (eventually netting a total of 8,500 francs each). The amount that remained amply funded Gruner's police force and related spy network.[47] During the very first weeks, Gruner had six employees, not counting the secret agents. By September he had more than twenty on the payroll.[48] Gruner also paid his spies well. La Coudraye was one of his top spies, receiving more than 1,000 francs per month. The others received between 50 and 400 francs – more than spies under the revolutionary regime or Napoleon had earned.[49]

His first big success was not long in coming. Gruner (and not Blücher, as is often claimed in the literature) was able to arrest the infamous French spy Charles Schulmeister just outside Paris. For years, he had been on the most-wanted list for missions he carried out as an agent of Napoleon. 'We have saved the honour of our police!' a jubilant Gruner wrote to Hardenberg. His force had bared its teeth. Schulmeister was transported under heavy escort to the Prussian fortress near Wesel (where he was again released in November, returning to a secluded life on his estate Boissy-Saint-Léger, south-east of Paris, until his death in 1853).[50]

---

[47] Müffling to Gruner, 13 August 1815. Contract with Bernard, with notes from Gruner, 20 August 1815, GStA PK, VI. HA Nl. Gruner, nr. 86. See also J. von Gruner Jr, 'Müffling und Gruner bei Beschaffung eines Fonds für die Polizeiverwaltung während der Occupation im J. 1815', *Deutsche Zeitschrift für Geschichtswissenschaft*, 11:1 (1894), 364–8.

[48] 'Nachweisung', 15 August–15 September 1815, GStA PK, VI. HA Nl. Gruner, no. 86. At the back of the folder a table of revenues and expenses is included.

[49] 'Nachweisung', 15 August–15 September 1815. 'Geheime agences'. See also the 'Nachweisung' of 15 September to 21 October, and the 'Nachweisung' of 1 November, GStA PK, VI. HA Nl. Gruner, no. 86. For more expenditures, see 15 September–21 October 1815, GStA PK, VI. HA Nl. Hardenberg 10a.

[50] Message of Gruner, 15 August 1815, GStA PK, VI. HA Nl. Hardenberg 10a. See also A. Douay and G. Hertault, *Schulmeister. Dans les coulisses de la Grande Armée* (Paris: Éditions de la Fondation Napoléon, 2002); L. Ferdinand Dieffenbach, *Karl Ludwig Schulmeister. Der Hauptspion, Parteigänger, Polizeipräfekt und Geheime Agent Napoleons I* (Leipzig: Webel, 1879), 74ff.

To gather, process and interpret information, Gruner developed his own specific and very modern routine. Following in the footsteps of Fouché's efforts to map *l'esprit public* for Napoleon, Gruner gave primary importance to creating a central registration of 'public rumours' (*Gerüchte*). What is more, he also gave special attention to checking and, when necessary, debunking *fausses nouvelles* (sometimes also referred to as *falsche Gerüchte*). Almost daily, he sent reports to Hardenberg in which he first wrote a paragraph about recent events and incidents, and then, much more extensively (often several pages' worth), gave an account of the 'rumours' that were circulating. And, as noted, incidentally debunked them as false. Through his agents, he kept track of what people in strategic places and in the cafes of Paris were whispering about and second-guessing. His top spy, a royalist *émigré*, the Marquis de La Coudraye, was a navy man who had served in various armies and had lived in Germany until 1814. Upon arriving in France, he was deeply shocked by the shadow of Bonapartism that still lingered in the country, and, in a pamphlet, called for a turnaround and return to the 'eternal truths' of Crown and Religion.[51] The arch-conservative marquis was particularly agitated by Fouché and Talleyrand's 'revolutionary' friends and manoeuvrings; but also by Wellington's alleged escapades and his frequenting houses of ill repute. Other agents kept an eye on alleged rivalries and on conflicts between Austrians and Prussians. A modern police force needed to have eyes and ears in place throughout the city, Gruner contended. At every key crossroads or cafe he made his agents gauge the public and political temperature of the day. Sometimes, 'Long live the emperor!' was the popular cry; on other days, 'Long live the young Napoleon!' was more *en vogue*. His agents, moreover, eagerly snapped up the countless political cartoons and diatribes against the king and his family – a stream that went on relentlessly.[52]

Gruner's battle against terror was mostly a shadow fight. His main targets were the many rumours and conspiracy theories that came in all sorts and sizes. Gruner recounted them regularly to Hardenberg in one continuous listing, in dozens of pages. His criteria for filtering them were the direct Allied security needs: he was triggered by remarks revealing (the lack of) Allied unity, comments on the (in)stability of the French Bourbon regime, or by expressions indicating a threat to public and political security. With respect to the latter, the rumours on coups and conspiracies – against Louis XVIII, or against Allied sovereigns and ministers – were obviously of the highest interest. Such rumours entailed stories about an imminent Bonapartist revolt, about the return of Napoleon I or II, about unrest and rebellion elsewhere in the

---

[51] 'De La Coudraye', in L. G. Michaud and F.-C. le chevalier de Loynes (eds.), *Biographie universelle, ancienne et moderne. KM-LAL* Supplement 69 (Paris: Michaud, 1841), 308. The person in question here is the oldest brother.

[52] Message of Gruner, 13 September 1815, GStA PK, VI. HA Nl. Hardenberg 10a.

country, or touched on the deep-seated great fear of 'brigands' (as they were known during the days of the Revolution).

The source of the rumour usually remained nameless, often introduced with a 'people say' or 'it is being told'. Sometimes the gossip was attributed to someone by name, but even then couched in an 'I've heard tell'. Hence, Gruner mostly wrote in the typical German subjunctive style that indicated a possibility and not a certainty. He reported, for example, that the French minister of war, Gouvion Saint-Cyr, had said that 'had we won over one of the Allied powers and been able to assemble 150,000 Frenchmen, we would be able to dislodge the Allies' – in the original German form, covered with all kinds of reservations. Or, another example: that a Mr von Wehrenberg was heard to have said that Austria could easily bide its time because they would probably have Napoleon II waiting in the wings.

Sometimes, with regard to highly sensitive questions or dramatic rumours, Gruner would spend some time commenting on the quality of the rumours, indicating whether he considered their substance plausible or not. In the above-mentioned case, for example, he believed that the rumour should not be considered fake news, but that the French minister Gouvion Saint-Cyr in fact stood in close contact with Russian representatives.[53] Regarding some other rumours, Gruner forthrightly indicated that they were nonsense. According to Gruner, the story making the rounds that an army of 200,000 Turks had taken Berlin proved again how 'gullible' Parisians were. Likewise, he found the rumour that the Austrian archduke Karl wanted to put the 'little Napoleon' on the throne 'silly' (15–18 August). But other rumours shocked him, not because of their fake nature or lack of substance, but because he considered them pernicious in their effects. They could severely undermine both the security of the Allied troops and the stability of the French government: for example, the malicious gossip about alleged disagreement among the Allies. Those rumours, he believed, could be traced back directly to Talleyrand – which did not do much good to the process of confidence-building with the French officials.[54]

The degree to which the information gathered by Gruner was true is difficult to determine. In 1815, with the memories of 'the Great Fear' – *La Grande Peur* – still present, and the direct experience of a dizzying series of revolutions and shock waves, France was still a hotbed for all kinds of 'fake news', rumours and stories.[55] Some of the rumours Gruner reported could be corroborated

---

[53] Message of Gruner, 'Euer Durchlaucht, Bemerke ich zu der einliegenden Anzeige ganz gefasst', no date, probably early August 1815, GStA PK, VI. HA Nl. Hardenberg 10a.

[54] Message of Gruner, 13 September 1815, GStA PK, VI. HA Nl. Hardenberg 10a.

[55] A good deal of research has focused on the function and interpretation of rumours, clamour and fake news: M. Bloch, *Réflexions d'un historien sur les fausses nouvelles de la guerre* (Paris: Allia, 1999 [1921]); F. Ploux, 'L'imaginaire social et politique de la rumeur dans la France du XIXe siècle (1815–1870)', *Revue historique*, 302:2 (April–June 2000),

and were based on empirically verifiable facts. The rumour that Tsar Alexander had helped Joseph Bonaparte flee the capital is a case in point, as were the many stories about French corps that refused to capitulate and kept fighting, or the suspicion that Hortense had helped a number of fugitives faithful to Napoleon (Duhamel) financially, by giving them some of her diamonds. Of greater importance, however, is that Gruner himself was not only, or even predominantly, interested in the veracity of the news. He was first and foremost concerned about what these rumours transmitted with respect to the prevailing mood in France – and whether that was, from an Allied perspective, favourable or not. Next to that, he also listed and analysed what the French population itself expressed to be its greatest hopes and fears. For example, reports that 'Maria Louise was on the way with the little Duke of Parma' (that is, Napoleon II) to claim the throne with help from the Austrians was one such 'hope' – for the anti-Bourbon camp, at least. Likewise, that Napoleon's generals (Exelmans, Vandamme) were preparing to continue the war against the Allies, acting independently as free corps, and that '30,000 conspirators' stood ready to liberate France. The numerous stories about Allied troops who carried out 'bloodbaths', or their plans to divide up parts of France – for example, that Alsace and Lorraine would go to Prussia – were among the nightmares the French feared most. The 'hate and bitterness' about the billeting of German soldiers was, of course, also very real, as were the fears and concerns about the future of France.[56]

For the effective management of internal order and security these 'rumour reports' were of key importance. With these overviews, the Allied ministers were able to gauge the political atmosphere in society. From the run of the rumours, the Allies, for example, could deduce that the fear (or hope) that the Bourbons would be deposed still prevailed in August. In September, however, all Paris was buzzing with concern about the upcoming Allied treaty, and in particular with worries over a possible dismemberment of France. Throughout, all kinds of tales about disagreement amongst the Allies were gleefully shared. In October, furthermore, popular rage framed after the Treaty was made public, mention of insurgency and plots surfaced, but in the end, resignation prevailed and the direct threat to Allied and public security abated. The most remarkable insight that can be drawn from Gruner's 'stream of public consciousness' is, however, the fact that the announcement of the Duke of Richelieu's appointment as prime minister proved to be a turning point. While Fouché and Talleyrand lasted in office, fodder for agitation on both sides continued to be produced. But after the news of the king's choice of

395–434; P. Triomphe, 'Des bruits qui courent aux mots qui tuent: Rumeurs et violences dans le Gard en 1815', *Revue d'Histoire du XIXe Siècle*, 36 (2008), 59–73.

[56] See messages from August, September and October 1815, GStA PK, VI. HA Nl. Hardenberg 10a.

Richelieu came through, a small wave of relief seemed to sweep over a highly anxious Paris and surrounding areas. Even Gruner's most alarmist agent, de La Coudraye, had to admit that Richelieu was widely known for his 'loyalty, liberal ideas and noble designs'. After that, public trust in the king's government seemed gradually to increase, and outright outrage over the Allied presence subsided a bit, partly because the worst nightmares (about the dismemberment of France) were now off the table, with the publication of the first draft of the Paris Treaty.[57]

Irrespective of whether the content of the circulating rumours could be proven or empirically verified or not (usually not), they were from an intelligence and security perspective in any case very real and substantial, to the extent that they could provoke unrest, rebellion or danger. Rumours could be a source of insecurity, certainly when they could possibly have adverse consequences for the Allies. For example, Gruner asked that Fouché take steps to vigorously counteract the 'malicious defamation' of the Prussian troops (who made up the bulk of the officers and soldiers in Paris) that he felt was being spread day in and day out in the French press. That some individuals in the Prussian army had misbehaved on occasion was certainly true, but that did not justify spreading 'slander and malice' against the Allied troops as a whole. That the people in the streets complained about the billeting of Prussians was understandable, but that official French newspapers should publish calumnies about 'a village near Versailles' that was torched by Prussian troops, or alleging that they perpetrated 'horrors' on a grand scale, was unacceptable. Prussia had sacrificed 33,000 of their sons to the liberation of France and deserved more admiration and respect than that. In addition, the rumours were detrimental to the security of the troops, and to peace and the public order in the country. They confused and upset people. So Gruner suggested that Fouché make an appointment as soon as possible to discuss together how this public defamation in the media could be brought to an end.[58] Little came of this specific plan (on 14 September), because the next day Fouché was sacked. It would take until November before the new royalist government, under the direction of Richelieu, would take action; but we hav not got that far yet. Other interventions on Gruner's part proved to be more effective.

A New St Bartholomew's Night

Another set of rumours that took on serious forms was the growing stream of stories about the persecution and slaughter of Protestants in departments in the south of France. In this case, Gruner's rumour-gathering network produced enough intelligence to give rise to action, at least eventually.

---

[57] Message of de La Coudraye, 8 October 1815, GStA PK, VI. HA Nl. Hardenberg 10a.
[58] Gruner to Fouché, 14 September 1815, GStA PK, VI. HA Nl. Gruner, no. 41.

During the summer of 1815, ultra-royalists in southern France launched
a literal manhunt for 'Bonapartist brigands', Jacobins and revolutionaries: in
short, for anyone whom they took to be an enemy of the Bourbon restoration.
Although the Allies, with their occupation force and administration, kept
a close eye on the dynamics of revolutionary or reactionary unrest in northern
and western France and in Paris, anarchy and a struggle for power did hold
sway for a few months in the south, where no Allied troops were deployed. The
Duke of Angoulême (the eldest son of the count of Artois, also known as
'Monsieur'), who ruled in those parts, tried with all his might to counteract the
directives and attempts at control coming from Paris, where his uncle, King
Louis, tried to direct the country towards a politics of reconciliation. As
a consequence, a wave of White Terror swept over the Midi, the Vendée,
Brittany and Maine. Some of those royalist groups wore green and white
epaulets and medals on their uniform – a combination of the colours of
Bourbon and Angoulême – and were called 'Verdets'. They went around
pillaging, kidnapping and killing. They had a large following especially around
Marseilles and Toulouse, where the conscription quotas had been very high
and economic life lay in ruins because of the continental blockade.[59] In these
areas, royalist gangs not only killed dozens of Napoleonic soldiers, but were
also able to create a veritable people's revolt.[60] In addition to the murder of
Guillaume Brune in Avignon on 2 August, General Ramel also fell at the hands
of the White Terror on 15 August. Armed gangs in the department of Gard in
the Languedoc region vented their anger against alleged 'nests' of Bonapartist
supporters. Protestant towns were heavily afflicted; dozens of Protestant
Christians lost their lives, were persecuted, ended up in prison or simply
chose to flee. Between July and October 1815, in Nîmes alone – the capital of
the department – 2,500 people were forced to leave their homes, including 400
employers, 1,500 employees and 600 day labourers and farmers. They left,
taking half a million francs as capital with them.[61] In and through this
pandemonium, however, some of the Ultras tried to raise society up and create
a revolt, intended to expel the foreign forces from the country.[62]

What the Ultras realized too late was that reports of open anarchy and
royalist violence were, on the contrary, the exact reason for the Allies (and
a reticent king) not to leave matters in the hands of the Ultras but intervene
even more forcefully. In late August, Gruner had amassed a pile of reports on

[59] D. Resnick, *The White Terror and the Political Reaction after Waterloo* (Cambridge, MA: Harvard University Press, 1966), 5–6. See also R. Blaufarb, *Bonapartists in the Borderlands. French Exiles and Refugees on the Gulf Coast, 1815–1835* (Tuscaloosa: University of Alabama Press, 2005), 3.
[60] C. H. Pouthas (ed.), *Charles de Rémusat. Mémoires de ma vie, 1797–1820*, vol. 1 (Paris: Perrin, 1958), 225–6.
[61] Vidal to the minister of justice, 19 August 1815, cited in Resnick, *The White Terror*, 55–6.
[62] Pouthas, *Charles de Rémusat*, vol. 1, 214–15. Also cited in Resnick, *The White Terror*, 39.

the 'atrocities' that occurred in the department of the Gard on his desk.[63] On 24 August, Gruner received a detailed memorandum from a Mr Martin, pastor of the église de Orange, who urged the authorities to intervene, since the Ultras were getting ready to unleash a new St Bartholomew's night in Nîmes ('une nouvelle Barthelemy'). Nominally, the Ultras were targeting Bonapartists, but in reality, their eye was on inciting a new religious war against Protestants, according to Martin. Protestant women were openly beaten with whips and iron-tipped batons.[64] More reports were passed on to Gruner, listing incident after incident.

Thus, the king and the French government, who had remained passive throughout, now decided to issue a formal protest in response to the reported events. On 25 August, Fouché ordered the Marquis d'Arbaud de Jouques, the prefect of the Gard (and close friend of Fouché), to put an end to these excesses. The events in Nîmes and the Midi 'filled the heart of the king with sadness', and caused 'astonishment and indignation' among the Allies. 'Justice' and 'moderation' needed to be restored; this 'most intolerable anarchy' must be stopped immediately. But Fouché remained very abstract in his description of those responsible and the guilty, and refused to call a spade a spade. He kept it at 'vengeance' and 'disorder', made no mention of Protestants and was careful not to specify who the perpetrators were, and who the victims. According to him, the violence was, in general terms, targeting the royal order, the constitution and 'the law'. And the perpetrators were not 'Catholics' or 'Ultras', but were simply referred to as 'the guilty ones', or in abstract terms as 'the anarchy'. What the prefect was supposed to do exactly remained unclear. Fouché expressed more worry about the appearance of anarchy than any sympathy with the victims. The last thing the king needed in negotiating with the Allied authorities, Fouché penned down angrily to the prefect, was a department in anarchy. But how the prefect was to restore order, and particularly, who was to be taken into custody, Fouché did not say.[65]

Consequently, this sort of decree from the capital understandably accomplished little. The prefect of the Gard did his best, but was not allotted more funds or forces. His dispirited attempts to condemn and prosecute these misdeeds only led to even greater outbursts of violence. The more and less organized gangs simply went on with their raids and lynchings. That is why the Allied Council, acting upon Gruner's reports, tasked the Austrian occupation forces, who were stationed nearby, with invading the Gard and restoring order. The Austrian forces, led by Lieutenant General Nugent, were to 'appease the

[63] See Gruner to Hardenberg, 'Gerüchte', 20 August 1815, GStA PK, VI. HA Nl. Hardenberg 10a.
[64] Martin, 'Mémoire', to Gruner, with attachment: 'Bulletin de ce qui s'est passé à Nîmes', 24 August 1815, GStA PK, VI. HA Nl. Gruner, no. 88.
[65] Fouché to the prefect of the Gard, 25 August 1815, copy in the Gruner archives, GStA PK, VI. HA Nl. Gruner, no. 88.

troubles and reassure the inhabitants'. But the insurgents on the right bank of the Rhône were not that easily waylaid. Therefore, 'given the new uprisings', another six battalions and eight squads followed suit. In the end, the Austrians succeeded in expelling a gang of fifty Ultras from the city.[66] But these Catholic troops were by no means the most ideal patrons for the French Protestants. When the group of ultra-royalists from Nîmes leaving the city came to fisticuffs with a group of Protestant farmers, the Ultras had no qualms about calling on the Austrians for help. They brought the confrontation to an end, killed some fifty to sixty Protestant farmers and put the blame for the skirmish on the Protestants. Protestant households were punished with having to provide extra quartering for Austrian troops.[67]

With dismay, Gruner observed the developments from Paris. He gave all his effort into putting the fight against White Terror higher on the Allied agenda; he even went over the heads of the Allied ministers to go straight to the sovereigns. First, he wrote a letter to his own king, Friedrich Wilhelm III, on 30 August, calling on him to rescue the Protestants: 'Your great ancestor [Friedrich the Great] has already once been the provider for our fellow believers who fled to France.' The current Prussian king was now in a position to do more than that – to be 'the saviour of those being persecuted in his own country'.[68] Then, on 31 August, he appealed to Castlereagh: the news in the French papers about the troubles was far too 'vague', which is why he had sent out his own agents and been able to get a clear picture of what was happening. In the Midi, targeted attacks and the assassination of Protestants – Gruner included examples – was the order of the day. The Allies needed to intervene; it was a sacred task, especially for the Prussians and the British. 'The trembling world is hoping for Allied sovereigns, whose wisdom and energy will prevent such a sinister event, and protect the best part of the French nation from its degenerate citizens.' It was, after all, the Protestants who fixed their 'plaintive eyes' on Britain and Prussia. 'I brought their complaints in the sacred name of faith to the throne of my sovereign', and now he hoped that Castlereagh would do the same. Both countries were 'the old protectors of the Protestant church'; therefore, they had to stand up for the religious freedom of 'our church in France'.[69]

---

[66] Report of Schwarzenberg to the Allied Council, 16 August 1815; Schwarzenberg, Memorandum, 27 August, attachment nr. 97, GStA PK III. HA I. no. 1465, 62ff., 109ff.
[67] Resnick, *The White Terror*, 56–7.
[68] Gruner to Friedrich Wilhelm III, 30 August 1815; copy to Hardenberg, 5 September 1815, GStA PK, VI. HA Nl. Hardenberg 10a.
[69] Gruner to Castlereagh, 31 August 1815, GStA PK, VI. HA Nl. Gruner, no. 88.

Some British Protestants, especially the so-called 'dissenters', in the meantime had also became concerned about the fate of their fellow believers, and, with an appeal to 'the liberties of Britain' and 'the most enlightened principles', called on their government to take action from Britain.[70] They also collected money for the Protestant refugees.[71] By then, Castlereagh and Wellington could not avoid addressing the issue any more. The Liverpool government instructed the British ambassador, Charles Stuart, to file a protest with the French court against the treatment of Protestants in the south.[72] Colonel Ross, who was sent from London to the Midi as an inspector on behalf of the British government, soon found that the royalists were circulating all sorts of conspiracy theories. They were spreading the myth that it was actually the Protestants, as disguised Bonapartists, who were the ones about to unleash a civil war, allegedly led by the Bonapartist general Gilly.[73]

Wellington brought the complaints to the king's attention again. The Allies' pressure on the French government to put an end to the intimidation and the partiality of the judges and magistrates was intensified.[74] It came, however, primarily from the Germans and the British; Metternich and the Russians did not comment on the matter in the Allied Council. It was not until 1 September, after a proclamation of Louis XVIII denouncing 'the excesses in the south', that this series of outbursts of uncontrolled violence and banditry under the royalist flag subsided. But the White Terror was not tamed yet; it was instead transformed into a legal form of reckoning with alleged Bonapartists.[75] The French government in Paris did prod the provinces' public prosecutor's offices to bring the White terrorists to trial, but even when it came to that, the judges and commissioners in the province found ways to make the jury release the suspects forthwith. What is more, on the flip side, so-called Protestant conspirators were arrested, convicted and publicly executed.[76] A proposal to investigate abuses in the Gard, put forward in the French parliament itself, was booed off the platform by most of the Ultras.[77] The French government, nonetheless, continued to bend over backwards to deny any suggestion that this conflict was a matter of religious persecution. Stuart wrote to Castlereagh:

---

[70] Circular of 28 November 1815, cited in Resnick, *The White Terror*, 60.

[71] Resnick, *The White Terror*, 60–2.

[72] See correspondence in TNA, FO 27/130, 27/119.

[73] Colonel Ross to Charles Stuart, 11 February 1816, TNA, FO, 27/130. See P. Lauze de Péret, *Causes et précis des troubles, crimes et désordres dans le département du Gard et dans d'autres lieux du Midi de la France* (Paris: Poulet, 1818).

[74] Wellington to Louis XVIII, 29 February 1816, *WSD*, vol. 11, 309–10.

[75] Resnick, *The White Terror*, 40.

[76] B. Fitzpatrick, *Catholic Royalism in the Department of the Gard, 1814–1852* (Cambridge: Cambridge University Press, 1983), 52.

[77] Resnick, *The White Terror*, 62.

the Court is very anxious on the subject, they take pains to make it believed that Religion has nothing to do with it, that it was merely a jealous effervescence on the part of the Royalists against the Jacobins of Nismes who happen to be all Protestants.[78]

According to the Englishman Colonel Ross, who had been sent there to take stock of the situation, many Protestants had by now lost any hope for a peaceful existence in the Gard. In January 1816, he reported:

> It is true that many of them believe that the king is personally sincere in his desire to protect them and to restore the Department to its former happy state of tranquillity; but they equally believe that his orders will always be evaded, that misrepresentations which they cannot contradict will reach the Royal Ear from priests and many of the catholic magistrates and that they are always labouring under the imputation of disloyalty, treachery and hatred of the Bourbons.[79]

But the French Protestants no longer had much confidence in the Allied forces, whose commander-in-chief, Wellington, had tried – quite unconvincingly – to assure British Protestants 'that the French king had done all he could'.[80] Hence, many chose to relocate, assisted by the Prussian government, which also saw emigration as the best solution.[81]

It would indeed take until 1819 before the most malicious Ultras in the judiciary and in public administration were replaced in part by more neutral guardians of law and order. In this case, the arm of the Allies did not reach out far enough to the victims in the south. Despite Gruner's appeals and Wellington's interventions, the underlying tensions and the ultra-royalist networks 'on the ground' in and around Nîmes were too firmly entrenched. To effectively fight the White Terror, the Allies would have had to take over the administration in the south, and that was wholly out of the question. Such an 'invasion' would have only further undermined the king's authority. Except for the Prussians, Allied ministers were, moreover, themselves somewhat sceptical regarding the complaints of the Protestants. The British Ambassador to France, Charles Stuart, was initially of a mind that there were indeed bona fide Jacobins and radicals hiding among the Protestants, 'and that both parties were guilty'. According to Wellington, always the stoic,

[78] Stuart to Castlereagh, 14 December 1815, TNA, FO 27/120.
[79] 'Extraits des rapports du Colonel Ross', January 1816, in D. Robert (ed.), *Textes et documents relatifs à l'histoire des églises reformées en France (période 1800–1830)* (Paris: Droz, 1962), 307–8.
[80] See letter of Wellington to the British Protestants, 28 November 1815, and the scorn that that earned him in Britain: E. Baines, *History of the Wars of the French Revolution*, vol. 2 (London: Longman, 1818), 524. See also 'Persecutions of the Protestants in France', 22 May 1816, in Hansard (ed.), *The Parliamentary Debates*, vol. 34, 739–71.
[81] Stuart to Castlereagh (regarding Prussian 'encouragement of emigration'), 14 December 1815, TNA, FO 27/120.

in this kind of transitional situation, with significant divisions within the country, violence was only 'normal'. Perhaps, as a law-abiding Brit, he did not really fathom the extent to which justice and law enforcement in the Midi were completely subject to the political whim of the Ultras.[82] Wellington, despite his outward laconic posture, did continue to insist on the matter with the king, going so far as to allude to a possible intervention on the part of the Allies.[83]

Nîmes was far away, the political situation too polarized and the king's authority weak – that was the limbo Protestants found themselves in for a few more years. Gruner must have found some consolation in the fact that his 'rumour machine' could contribute somewhat to convincing his Allied masters of the difference between real intelligence and 'exaggeration'. Richelieu, who became the new prime minister at the end of September, also understood that 'false news' and alarmist stories did not help, and that respect for the legitimacy of the king's authority had to be the first step towards restoring order and the rule of law. Hence, in early November, his government adopted a law that made the spreading of rumours and inciting action against legitimate authority punishable offences. Severe punishment lay in store for anyone who 'tended to alarm or undermine citizens' loyalty to the legitimate authority'.[84] For the Allied Council that was good enough for the time being. The ministers preferred not to intervene directly in the administration in the Midi. Thanks to Gruner's interference, however, the Protestants were granted exile in Prussia. His intelligence did also enhance their sensibility to the White Terror. In the end, Allied advocacy for stricter enforcement of the religious guarantees in the *Charte Constitutionelle* of constitutional impartiality and moderation did have some effect, but with a marked delay of a few years, and only indirectly.

The Blacklist of 24 July

Intelligence was equally inadmissible for the next stage in the fight against terror: executing judicial and administrative 'purification' of officials who were deemed to be corrupt and implicated in the years of terror. The question of such *épurations* as an instrument in the battle against terror was in 1815 as important as it was complex and contested. The Allied ministers carefully considered the matter. In contrast to the Allied occupation regime of 1945, there was no talk of externally enforced, systematic purges and processes in 1815. Large-scale, high-profile collective trials of war criminals, such as the Nuremberg Tribunals, were absent. Categorically dealing with all Bonapartists

---

[82] Correspondence, TNA, FO 27/119. See also A. Wemyss, 'L'Angleterre et la Terreur blanche de 1815 dans le Midi', *Annales du Midi*, 73:55 (1963), 287–310, here: 295–6.

[83] See Wellington to Louis XVIII, *WSD*, vol. 11, 309.

[84] Triomphe, 'Des bruits qui courent aux mots qui tuent', 59–73.

and opponents of the Bourbon rule by means of judicial and administrative purges was not a priority of the Allies. The Council formally wanted to leave that to the French government, for they were the ones responsible for internal order and justice. Behind the scenes, however, the ministers did share their advice. They felt that the principle of de-Bonapartization had to be applied by judicial means as well – but carefully and selectively. An across-the-board score-settling approach would only fan the flames of dissatisfaction, unrest and rebellion among an already defeated and humiliated people. And Louis XVIII stood in urgent need of more support and a broader base. Purifications had to take place to set examples, but in a highly constricted and temperate manner.

In fact, on 28 June, the king had declared that he would be a father to all the French, and that former Bonapartists did not have to fear for their lives. Likewise, the military Convention of Saint-Cloud, signed on 3 July 1815, marking the end of the hostilities, explicitly stated that no persecutions would take place, and that anyone who wanted to emigrate based on political convictions need not fear losing their property or possessions due to expro-priation or punishment. For many, that left the impression that a general amnesty had been announced. But that appearance was deceiving – because the Treaty only held for the Allies, vowing to restrain themselves during the ceasefire; what the king did after 8 July, once his authority had been re-established, was his business, as Marshal Ney would find out the hard way.

The royal *oubli* – pardon, amnesty or forgetting – did not hold for everyone.[85] Behind the scenes, the French government endured a good deal of pressure from vindictive emigrants and ultra-royalists. The Allied partners, too, differed in their openness to moderation and forgiving spirit, and inter-fered in the question. While the ink of the ceasefire treaty was still drying, British newspapers were filled with language provoking revenge. *The Times* even published a list of 'traitors' to prosecute. In July, Lord Liverpool, the prime minister, repeatedly told Castlereagh that, as far as he was concerned, Bonaparte and his 'accomplices' had to be punished, with those most guilty sentenced to death and the others exiled. 'To conclude, we wish that the King of France would hang or shoot Bonaparte as the best termination of the business', but if that was too 'impracticable', then he should be banished to St Helena.[86] That did not differ all that much from Blücher's vengeful desire to execute Napoleon point-blank. In the meantime, Tsar Alexander and Hardenberg let it be known that a 'general law' was called for, 'sanctioned by all of Europe', to remove Bonaparte and 'his family' from the lines of power

---

[85] Cf. Lok, *Windvanen*; Lok, '"Un oubli total du passé?" The Political and Social Construction of Silence in Restoration Europe (1813–1830)', *History & Memory*, 26:2 (2014), 40–75.

[86] Liverpool to Castlereagh, 21 July 1815, *WSD*, vol. 11, 45–7. See also Liverpool to Castlereagh, 30 June and 7 July, *WSD*, vol. 10, 630, 675.

forever – admittedly in a more decent way than that hoped for by the Prussian generals.[87] Castlereagh and Wellington therefore looked for a middle way, and hence advised the French king to swiftly set some examples. A rapid demonstration of resoluteness and strength by castigating a few key figures would enhance the king's weak position, and at the same time, the scope of the purges could remain limited.

Wellington, as the highest military commander, explained the connection between the need for purges on the one hand, and the 'tranquillity' in France and Europe on the other, as a logical implication of Castlereagh's 13 July 'principles of sound precaution'. As a first move, he also included a list of names:

> The Allied Sovereigns have asked three guarantees: for Napoleon, for the army, for future tranquillity. The first is taken, the second ordered to disband. To insure tranquillity, the Sovereigns have handed in a list of 200 persons to be banished France, some others only the capital. The Council has reduced this list to 80. Whether that will be satisfactory is not yet known. Alexander seems particularly anxious and impatient respecting this point. It is said that two of the Sovereigns have demanded the death of Napoleon, Francis his imprisonment for life.[88]

The minutes of the Allied Council of July report no further discussion in this regard. Nor can it be determined whether this list of eighty people overlaps with the list with which the French came. The Allied list probably included mostly Bonapartist generals and officers, as well as a few regicides.

Louis could see the logic of drafting a short list. He discussed the Allies' demands with Talleyrand and Fouché, and decided that Fouché should compile the list. Fouché, who was actually in favour of an overall amnesty, decided to swallow his objections for fear of the repercussions that might well come his way from the British and the Ultras – for he himself was a perfect fit for the category of 'Bonapartist suspects'. On 24 July, Fouché posted his list, which actually consisted of two lists: a list of nineteen Bonapartist generals who ought to be prosecuted, tried and probably executed, and a list of thirty-eight subordinates who had 'only' been put under police surveillance for the time being, awaiting their trial and possible expulsion from the country.[89] The list was drawn up based on two criteria: clearly contributing to efforts to violently overthrow royal authority, and level of public support for the return of Napoleon (and participating in his Hundred Days rule). Old regicides – members of the Convention who voted to send Louis XVI to the guillotine –

---

[87] Hardenberg, 'État des Négociations actuelles entre les Puissances Alliées & la France', 16–28 July 1815, GStA PK, III. HA I. no. 1461, 59.

[88] 'Private intelligence from Paris', 19 July 1815, *WSD*, vol. 11, 45; Pozzo di Borgo to Talleyrand, in Houssaye, *1815. La seconde abdication*, 425–6.

[89] Houssaye, *1815. La seconde abdication*, 426–9.

were among them, but also several who held a ministerial post during the Hundred Days. Of these, thirty-one were charged with supporting Napoleon's march on Paris, or for accepting a public function before 23 March 1815. The list included a series of high-ranking generals: Marshal Ney, generals de la Bédoyère, Drouet d'Erlon, Fressinet, Lamarque, Exelmans, Savary, Carnot, Count Lavalette and the Protestant general Gilly, who had fought the royalist volunteers in the south, but only joined ranks with Napoleon after 23 March.[90]

It could have been worse, but the criteria for being blacklisted were not very clear and were inconsistently applied. It seemed as though Fouché had rather randomly pulled some names out of his hat, including those of former comrades and colleagues. As a result, the list only generated more indignation. Many of the 'guilty' went scot-free, like Cambacérès, Cambon, Chartran, Talleyrand and, of course, Fouché himself. Many citizens wondered why Napoleon could while his time away on St Helena, while lesser figures were sentenced to death. According to the historian Houssaye, this fostered the impression that the list was primarily motivated by revenge, jealousy and political vendetta. But the Ultras, too, who found the list far too short, were also largely indignant. They had hoped that the purge and the prosecutions would affect a much larger group of Bonapartists.[91]

The unrest was aggravated by the fact that Fouché – as always – was playing two sides off against each other, and was actually leading the Allied 'security managers', in this case Gruner, around by the nose. Fouché understood the sense of issuing a blacklist. With those names in hand, the arbitrary and massive arrests in the south could be halted. By pointing to the official policy and purges and prosecutions, Fouché was able to put an end to the extraordinary powers of the special commissioners who had restored order in their own ultra-royalist fashion in the south after the Allied forces had invaded France.[92] At the same time, Fouché did his best to keep the list as short as possible. He appealed for understanding and forgiveness for the regicides of the Convention, as well as for those who had sided with Napoleon in March 1815 – in other words, before Louis XVIII fled across the Belgian border, to Ghent.

Fouché also played a far darker role, sowing confusion and ambivalence where possible. On 6 August, a glowing plea appeared in l'Indépendant for the release of General Charles de la Bédoyère. De la Bédoyère, one of Napoleon's most loyal generals, had briefly subjected himself to the king's authority after the first restoration and was subsequently sent out to arrest Napoleon when the news broke of his landing in southern France, only to side immediately with 'his' emperor once they met. After the Battle of Waterloo was lost (for which he

[90] Resnick, The White Terror, 68–70.
[91] Houssaye, 1815. La seconde abdication, 430–3.
[92] Waresquiel, Fouché, 605.

was partly responsible), de la Bédoyère fled to Switzerland. But when he returned to Paris on 2 August, with a passport for America and a letter of credit in hand from the banker Ouvrard, to say goodbye to his wife and son, he was arrested by Fouché's agents. He was to appear before a French military tribunal on 9 August, but *l'Indépendant* took up his cause straight away, arguing that the young 29-year-old general had lived almost his entire life under Napoleon, compared to only ten months under the French king. So, what else could he be but faithful to his emperor? To punish him for that now was not legitimate or morally correct.[93] Interestingly enough, Fouché was himself owner of this very first French newspaper, having founded it during the Hundred Days period. Antoine Jay, the former tutor of Fouché's sons, was in charge of *l'Indépendant* and fiercely held to enlightened, constitutional viewpoints. However, the article in question caused so much agitation and indignation among the royalists that Fouché was forced to ban the newspaper for the time being, and to set up a censorship committee.[94]

Interestingly, the equally zealous and passionate Gruner let himself be drawn in by Fouché's machinations and spoke out in defence of both Fouché and de la Bédoyère. *L'Indépendant* was very popular, with a circulation of 40,000 copies, and gave voice to the constitutionalists' cause – the party Gruner had favoured from the start. What was more, Fouché had promised the Allies a deal. 'People there [Fouché and his agents] trust me', Gruner explained to Hardenberg, 'and have promised me that once the newspaper is allowed to appear again, they will include all of the articles from us that I submit to the editors.' He saw this as a decidedly influential inside track: 'I cannot over-emphasize how crucial this advantage is!' Gruner asked Hardenberg to do everything within his power to have the Allied Council lobby for the newspaper's return and to bolster the cause of the French constitutionalists.[95] So, while Fouché at first blush seemed to cooperate with the royalists – by creating a blacklist and arranging for a censorship committee – behind the scenes he was using the Allies to mitigate those same measures. He could only do so because the Allied Council was driven by a variety of – often conflicting – principles, and staffed by ministers who translated them into different courses of action. Strategically, Wellington and Castlereagh favoured the blacklisting and banishment of a limited group of key figures – an initiative conceived to bolster and stabilize King Louis's rule. Gruner, however, worried more about public unrest occasioned by the list, and therefore, from the perspective of Allied security policies, advocated a more liberal press policy and granting

[93] *L'Indépendant*, 6 August 1815.
[94] See Waresquiel, *Fouché*, 605, 743 n. 14. See also J. Brisson and F. Ribeyre, *Les grands journaux de France* (Paris: Jouaust, 1862), 267–70.
[95] Gruner to Hardenberg, 8 August 1815, GStA PK, VI. HA Nl. Gruner, no. 86.

a pardon to de La Bédoyère. All of which Fouché – the master of deceiving and manipulating the media – understood through and through.

On 6 August, Gruner urgently petitioned the Allied Council to intervene immediately with Louis XVIII on behalf of de la Bédoyère. He did so not so much because he was against the death penalty per se, but because of the public unrest that an execution would elicit, and the adverse consequences that would accrue to the Allies. 'Many Frenchmen have approached me about this', he wrote worriedly, reporting in no uncertain terms: 'the king's decree of 24 July made a very poor impression; the majority of the French nation mistakenly believes that it was the Allies who provoked that list'. He received petitions and threatening letters daily from people complaining that his Allied police would have to live with de la Bédoyère's arrest on their conscience.[96] If Napoleon's youngest general was going to be executed, his blood would be on the Allies' hands: it would provide 'new fuel for the French hatred of foreigners, the fury of the factions would find new ammunition, and the cause of the Bourbons would suffer further'. Moreover, the 'ordinary, sensible person' would hardly understand why someone serving under Napoleon would be sentenced while the emperor himself was handled with so much respect. This was not about the 'fate of a single individual'; the case of de la Bédoyère had 'significant consequences for the entire French nation, and that also affects the interests of the major Allied powers'.[97]

Unlike Gruner, the Council did not let itself be carried away by Fouché and the suggestion of collective unrest. It could not, nor did it want to, follow Gruner's advice. In surrendering to the pressure and indeed granting pardon to de La Bédoyère, the king would undermine his authority further, instead of strengthening it with a display of vigour. Hence, the pleas of de la Bédoyère's mother and of his wife, who threw herself at the feet of King Louis XVIII, were to no avail.[98] Napoleon's loyal staff officer and general was executed on the plain of Grenelle on 19 August, after pointing to his own chest and issuing the order to fire, adding 'above all! do not miss'. With that, he became one of the two 'martyrs' who were sacrificed to confirm the decisiveness of the royalists and the principle of de-Bonapartization. However, probably thanks to Gruner, Fouché did book a small success: a few days later, his newspaper – now renamed – was allowed to appear again as usual.

---

[96] In his reports to Hardenberg, these protests against the execution of Ney and de la Bédoyère are indeed referred to time and again, as are the expletives directed at the Bourbons and the Allies. See 'Gerüchte', August–September 1815, GStA PK, VI. HA Nl. Hardenberg 10a.

[97] Memo of Gruner, intended for the Council, 6 August 1815, GStA PK, VI. HA Nl. Hardenberg 10a.

[98] Houssaye, *1815. La seconde abdication*, 508–11.

The Ney Affair

The other victim of this limited criminal campaign against high-ranking Bonapartists was Marshal Ney (Fig. 5.3). That the Allies had an influence on French security measures, and that they took their principle of de-Bonapartization seriously, was evident once again, but so was the fact that this influence could have unforeseen and detrimental consequences. Even more than with de la Bédoyère, the Ney case became an apotheosis of the public discussion about the royalist *oubli* – as well as of the indignation regarding the (as they thought) duplicitous Allied role in it. For years, the Allies, the French ministers and the king blamed each other for Ney's final conviction and execution. Here again Fouché subtly played a dual role in the affair. He was in fact the one who had to compile the definitive list, but he

Figure 5.3   Marshal Michel Ney. Portrait by J. S. Rouillard, 1815. (Musée de l'Histoire de France, Versailles/Heritage Images)

repeatedly tried to have others – the French parliament, the king or the Allies – be seen as shouldering that responsibility. Once the names were finally committed to paper, he personally saw to it that warnings were sent to each of the intended victims. Ney also received such a tip-off. But the Marshal was so deeply convinced of his own integrity and innocence that he refused to leave the country like a thief in the night. In fact, he was certain that a fair trial and subsequent acquittal awaited him.[99] The Ney case deserves a more elaborate explication, since the ambivalence and the unintended consequences of the Allied fight against terror were epitomized in this tragic affair.

Ney's life was replete with contradictions: he was modest but stiff-necked, temperamental and resolute, extremely loyal, but also very much a Romantic. His origins were ambiguous as well. He was born in 1769 – the same year that marked the birth of Napoleon, Wellington and Soult – in the fluctuating French–German border region of Saarland. Michel Ney was the son of a German family living in Saarlouis, where his father was a successful master barrel-cooper. He grew up bilingual, and impressed his parents as a good speaker and writer.[100] At the age of nineteen, he left his pursuit of a career in law, which his father had preferred, and enlisted in Metz with the French army. Under Napoleon, the barriers of the *ancien régime* fell away, and in 1799, after Ney and the Army of the Rhine conquered the heavily fortified city of Mannheim in an equally adventurous and inventive manner, Ney was made a general.[101] In 1802, Napoleon's wife Joséphine was instrumental in Ney's marrying one of her ladies-in-waiting, Aglaé Louise Auguié, whose mother, as lady-in-waiting of Marie-Antoinette, had committed suicide after her queen had succumbed to the guillotine. Aglaé and Michel had four sons, and to Napoleon's court their marriage was considered exemplary.[102] Ney fell out of favour when Wellington advanced up the Iberian Peninsula and he and the generals Marmont and Massena were not able to stop him. But he (with his III Corps) rehabilitated himself at the Battle of Borodino in 1812. After the devastating defeat at Leipzig and the capitulation of Paris in late March 1814, it was Marshal Ney who compelled Napoleon to abandon a march on Paris.[103] A month later, Louis XVIII offered him the same post as marshal, plus another title, Prince of Moscow, the Order of Saint-Louis and a seat in the Chamber of Peers.

Under the new Bourbon regime, Ney soon felt uncomfortable. He found the way in which the Count of Artois and his son, the Duke of Berry, compensated for their military ignorance with an extraordinary arrogance and presumption

---

[99] See H. Kurtz, *The Trial of Marshal Ney. His Last Years and Death* (New York: Knopf, 1957).
[100] R. Horricks, *Marshal Ney. The Romance and the Real* (London: Archway, 1988), 3.
[101] Horricks, *Marshal Ney*, 26–8.
[102] Ibid, 41–9.
[103] On 3 April, see Ibid., 167–9.

downright disgusting. He was even less patient with how Wellington was extolled by the French court.[104] But what did Ney in were the vicious insults of the *émigré* ladies returning with the Duchess of Angoulême, aimed at his beloved Aglaé. He hesitated one week after hearing the news of Napoleon's return, but on 14 March tipped his hat to his former master and joined the Eagle's camp – together they met their Waterloo in June. Ney did not flee the country after Waterloo, but decided on June 22 to explain in person to the Chamber of Peers that it was over, and that this time the Empire of Napoleon was truly done for. Given the military convention signed by France and the Allies on 3 July, Ney thought he would not be prosecuted. After all, in Article XII the Allies stated that they would not turn against France and the French, nor would they deprive French citizens of their possessions or liberties.

His wife, Aglaé, however, was more realistic, and tried to persuade him to leave town. He fled the city, under protest, on 6 July in the direction of Geneva, two days before the return of the Bourbons. When he heard in Lyons that Austrian forces had closed the border, he saw no reason to travel on and repaired instead to the mineral waters at Saint-Alban. On 25 July, he heard from his wife that his name was at the top of the king's blacklist. On Aglaé's urging, he moved on to a relative of hers at Château de Bessonies, but was discovered and arrested there on 3 August. The king, who would have preferred to see Ney disappear across the border, sighed upon hearing the news: 'Now he has done us more harm in getting himself arrested than he did on the day he betrayed us.'[105]

Initially, things did not look so bad for Ney. He was charged with high treason for deliberately helping to plan for Napoleon's return. But the military tribunal that was to try him consisted of fellow generals, and even the most hardened of royalists would not dare condemn to death the commander who had so famously defended France's honour and glory in Russia. But Ney's stubbornness did him in again. He was not just a soldier, he was a Peer of France, and demanded that he be tried in a normal, civil process at the highest level, by the Chamber of Peers itself. That was a huge mistake, because the majority of the new royalist parliamentarians wanted to see blood. So, Ney's lawyers introduced a surprising sleight of hand. The process began on 21 November, a day after the Treaty of Paris had gone into effect. And because under that treaty the city of Saarlouis had been assigned to Prussia, they argued that Ney could no longer be tried by a French court because he was now German. The room exploded. Finally, Ney himself took the bull by the horns: 'I am French', he roared through the hall with his heavy voice – and the room fell silent – 'And I will die as a Frenchman.'[106] The room burst into applause. Yet, the verdict was cast.

---

[104] Ibid, 181.
[105] Ibid., 251.
[106] Ibid., 266–7.

That November, Ney played his last card. Together with his wife and lawyers, he tried to place his fate in the hands of the Allies by appealing to the Saint-Cloud Convention of 3 July in which the Allies had promised the king that they would not prosecute anyone. On 13 November, he sent Wellington and the four central ministers of the Allied Council a letter in which, given his 'extremely critical situation', he made a final appeal to Europe's power brokers. They had helped liberate France, and had concluded a 'holy treaty', on which he now was counting. He could not imagine that the Allies would betray the trust that Article XII had inspired. He therefore urgently petitioned the Allied ministers and Wellington 'to mediate' on his behalf.[107] At Wellington's suggestion, the Council formulated a joint response that was disappointingly brief. Wellington explained to Ney that that treaty was a military agreement between Prussian and British Allied army commanders and the French army (Davout), and governed only the conditions of the military occupation of Paris. Article XII was therefore only intended to prevent excesses on the part of the occupiers during that first armistice: 'it was never intended and could not be intended to prevent either the existing French government under whose authority the French commander-in-chief must have acted, or any French government which should succeed to it, from acting in this respect, as it might seem fit'.[108]

A day later, however, Mrs Ney, Aglaé, paid Charles Stuart and Wellington a visit, personally delivering her husband's dossier. She threw all her charm and tears into the effort, appealing to Great Britain's rich history of law and justice. It simply could not be that Wellington and his government would bear the 'heavy weight of this judicial aberration'! She pointed once again to the Capitulation Treaty of 3 July, unable to believe that the Allies would so easily dismiss it as irrelevant. Wellington and his cohort were still the occupying power – 'no one may enter or leave the city without an Allied passport'. But the duke, on behalf of his own government and the Allied Council, stuck by the official standpoint: Ney's trial was now a matter for French justice.[109]

The Chambers of Peers, this time around, agreed with Wellington completely; they would determine what happened to Ney, and not the foreigners. On 7 December, the court reached its verdict. In the first round, thirteen deputies voted for deportation, one for death by the guillotine, and 142 for execution. In the second round, seventeen opted for deportation, five abstained and proposed to send a petition for clemency to the king and 137 voted for a military

[107] Letter of Ney to the Allied ministers and Wellington, discussion in the Council, 13 November 1815, 16 November 1815, GStA PK, III. HA I. no. 1469, 74–7.
[108] Letter of Wellington to Ney, appended to the protocol of 16 November, GStA PK, III. HA I. no. 1469, 77.
[109] See report and letters of 14, 15, 16 November, TNA, FO 92/15. See also House of Commons, *Papers Concerning the Case of Marshall Ney*, 14 February 1816 (London: House of Commons, 1816).

execution. Dressed in black knee-breeches and silk stockings, a white cravat and a dark blue overcoat, Ney approached the firing squad in the garden of the Tuileries at nine o'clock in the morning. (Louis XVIII was afraid that an execution on the Champs de Mars – as was usual – would end in spectacle and total chaos and had therefore designated the gardens along the Avenue de l'Observatoire as the site for the execution.) Ney had kissed Aglaé and his sons *adieu*, and written a final farewell letter. Wanting no blindfold, he gave the command himself: 'Soldiers, . . . I have fought a hundred battles for France, and not one against her. Soldiers, fire!' Eleven bullets hit Ney, including six in the chest and three in the head, and the last of the twelve lodged itself high in the wall behind him – a way of protesting the dishonourable execution.[110]

Ney was immediately lauded by the French populace and put in the pantheon of national heroes, which served neither the Bourbons nor the Allies well. Publicists straight away hounded the king for his lack of mercy, and blamed him for allowing the revenge of the Allies to cut down one of France's national heroes. They, in their turn, had accepted Ney's plight to help the Bourbon regime show that this time around it was serious about the restoration. But neither Louis nor Wellington was willing to take responsibility for Ney's execution. The verbal jousting around the moral responsibility for the verdict laid bare the ambiguity of the Allied occupation: was it there to undermine or uphold the sovereignty and autonomy of the French government? On 18 December, Richelieu officially complained to Charles Stuart about the tone of the news coverage in the British media, and about remarks made by 'foreigners' during the trial and in the Paris salons – that Ney's execution was owing to the intransigence and vindictiveness of the Ultras. The French government asked the British envoys to cooperate in the spirit of the November law against fake news, 'to suppress the circulation of opinions which are prejudiced'.[111]

Public opinion was indeed very much prejudiced against the king and his foreign ministers, the more so since Aglaé, Ney's wife, drew all the attention to her plight. The fate of this tragic widow, so young and attractive, mother of four small children, captured their imagination, and it was she who blamed the hero of Waterloo for mercilessly allowing her husband to be shot. Yet Ney had, in his final plea, also put his fate in the hands of the victorious Allies he so despised. Not the king, who refused to see Aglaé while he breakfasted on the morning of 8 December, not wanting to hear her plea for mercy; not Ney, with his honourable but futile efforts; nor the uncalled-for, hypocritical revenge of the Ultras – in the eyes of the French and the British, it was Wellington who quickly became the culprit and the murderer of Aglaé's tragic husband and hero. Years later, Wellington would complain about how people perceived him

---

[110] Horricks, *Marshal Ney*, 271.
[111] Richelieu to Stuart, 18 December 1815, TNA, FO 27/130.

in this regard, and he tried time and again to explain that Ney's execution had been part of the effort to restore security in France and Europe.[112] In the fight against terror, people died, but reputations perished as well.

An Allied Conspiracy: Tsar Alexander, Bergasse and Gruner

Gruner, Metternich and the British were not the only ones inventing ways and means of fighting terror, cleansing society and stabilizing the country. Tsar Alexander had not been idle either. He was working behind the scenes to launch a rather incredible plan for improving the public spirit of France and the security of Europe. At the end of August, a 'secret society' of French royalists, mesmerists and the tsar himself thought that the time was ripe to roll out their plan and involve the Prussians and the Allied security service in its implementation.

At that time, Fouché's posturing had become increasingly untenable. On 9 August, Gruner reported for the first time, 'Both parties find Fouché suspect.' The royalists thought he was supporting 'the interests of the Allies', the Bonapartists distrusted his duplicity, his 'jugglery'.[113] And Gruner himself also had started to seriously doubt the sincerity of Fouché's intentions, as well as the effectiveness of his police administration. He had been receiving a steady stream of reports from his agents that Fouché surrounded himself exclusively with 'die-hard Bonapartists', that he fired a spectrum of 'reliable' – royalist – civil servants and administrators, replacing them with 'scoundrels', and that he covered for all sorts of 'partisans du système anarchique'. Jean-Baptiste Boucheseiche was mentioned as an example, but also Lemontey de Lyon, who had been appointed by Fouché to head up his 'division de l'esprit public et de la police morale', but who in 1791 had mocked the king and also written pro-Napoleonic novels. That appointment had been a particularly treacherous move in the eyes of the royalists.[114]

Around 19–20 August, Gruner had had enough of Fouché. This breach of confidence was occasioned by two reports from Fouché to King Louis XVIII that circulated in Paris describing the 'deplorable situation of France' in the most apocalyptic terms. The miseries were attributed to the anarchy and rebellious-ness of the French themselves, but even more so to the indiscriminate pillaging on the part of the Allied troops, who did not keep order and lacked discipline. France was 'despoiled and plundered'; and Fouché summoned the king to put an end to it – without saying exactly how that was to be done, except by suggesting the possibility of an armed revolt against the Allies.[115] Fouché's

[112] Muir, *Wellington. Waterloo and the Fortunes of Peace*, 96–7.
[113] Report of Gruner, 9 August 1815, GStA PK, VI. HA Nl. Gruner, no. 86.
[114] Reports to Gruner, between 13 and 20 August, GStA PK, VI. HA Nl. Gruner, no. 86.
[115] See a copy of the report in GStA PK, VI. HA Nl. Gruner, no. 86, 13ff., also 37ff.

plea to the king (leaked to the public by Fouché himself) hit like a bomb. The Allies were furious. Stein fumed with anger at the accusations aimed at the Prussians, and the king was profoundly irritated with Fouché's manoeuvrings. Only Wellington stood up for the Duke of Otranto, and kept the king from firing him immediately.[116]

Gruner's spies reported that Fouché's accusations were the talk of the town, and were severely stoking the negative sentiment against the Allies. Gruner was deeply shocked. Initially, he could hardly believe that Fouché was actually the author of these alarmist lines, since 'the writer of the report could have fore-seen that disastrous outcome'. 'Convince me that the report did not come from you', he wrote Fouché on 31 August. And if Fouché had indeed written this, he was to retract it at once.[117] The minister of police arrogantly informed Gruner almost immediately, on 2 September, that there were indeed a few counterfeit copies in circulation, and that his words had come across and been taken more dramatically and negatively than he intended, but that the report was indeed from him, and that he was in no way inclined to retract it. While he did not doubt the noble intentions of the powers, he saw it to be his duty to inform his own sovereign of the miserable conduct of the Allied troops and to tell him what the mood was among the people. The Allies had helped end the 'tyranny that suppressed France', but the presence of their troops was now wreaking 'havoc', and 'civil discord' was worsening by the day. 'All Europe thought the sovereigns' entry into Paris would end the war', but now, 'what an abuse of force!'[118]

Whatever Fouché's intentions had been, they backfired, and he lost the last ounce of credit he had with Gruner. Gruner had now experienced first-hand what the Ultras and his own royalist agents were saying all along: that Fouché was stirring up unrest and inciting the French against each other and against the Allies with an eye to triggering another revolution. With these French ministers – Talleyrand and Fouché – cooperation was obviously impossible, inasmuch as Wellington had urged the other Allied officials to attempt it. With bitter feelings about his Allied machine that increasingly got stuck in the shifting sands of French bureaucracy, Gruner was looking for alternatives. Against that background, around late August, Gruner received a very special offer. One of Gruner's agents, a certain Chr. Deliége, a lawyer belonging to the reinstated order of king's counsels and to the court of cassation, a loyal royalist, invited Gruner to help set up an association to save the honour of France and the civilization of Europe from the 'scourge of our time' – Bonapartism and

---

[116] Houssaye, *1815: La seconde abdication*, 531–3.
[117] 'Gerüchte', 20 August 1815, GStA PK, VI. HA Nl. Hardenberg 10a; letter of Gruner to Fouché, 31 August 1815, GStA PK, VI. HA Nl. Gruner no. 86, 35, 42.
[118] Fouché to Gruner, 2 September 1815, GStA PK, VI. HA Nl. Gruner, no. 86, 36–7. See also GStA PK, VI. HA Nl. Hardenberg 10a.

revolutionary rebellion. In medical metaphors Deliége explained that Fouché and his cronies were consistently working not to 'heal', but simply to further enflame the 'hot fever that had pushed the French by the millions into the field of carnage'. According to Deliége, Alexander thought the same way; he had said to 'my illustrious friend [Nicolas] Bergasse': 'You are going to have to deal with a revolution after we leave.' In order to avert the threatening revolution of Bonapartists, Deliége now revealed a plan, designed by Tsar Alexander, and directed to the Prussians (Gneisenau, Hardenberg, Gruner, Humboldt – 'Les Héros de la Vertu'), to rescue the honour and security of France, and thus the fate of Europe as a whole.[119]

Gruner initially gave the correct, constitutionally sound response: we have just been released from that terrible Bonapartist yoke, and we do not need any new conspiracies. 'Sincere patriots should not look for secret measures or secret laws; only by re-establishing the eternal principles of virtue can you save your unhappy homeland.' In other words: please, abstain from any new plots. But Gruner was curious enough to let himself be persuaded to talk with Deliége's friend and comrade Nicolas Bergasse. By accepting Bergasse as his interlocutor, he entered an extremely remarkable ensemble. Bergasse enjoyed great fame in France as a prophet and apostle of radical mesmerism.[120]

Bergasse, a son of a wealthy merchant family, had come under the spell of the Austrian physician-charlatan Franz Mesmer before the French Revolution. This Austrian doctor taught that a single universal fluid surrounds and permeates all things, linking the cosmos, the earth, planets and people. Via 'animal magnetism', as opposed to mineral magnetism, human beings were thought to communicate with their environs and their fellows. According to Mesmer, when this communication was disturbed, by certain 'obstacles', dis-harmony arose and the system became unbalanced. Through 'crises', convul-sions and special seances, some people were able, as 'magnetizers', to remove the obstacles and restore the harmony. By carrying out certain cleansing moves, such as stroking parts of peoples' bodies, these 'magnetizers' were able to realign magnetic streams, poles, both in individual human beings and in larger groups and settings. Afflicted people would literally sweat out or vomit harmful substances. This 'scientific' theory and practice solicited so much acclamation and criticism that both the French and the British Royal Academies initiated a thorough assessment, in order to establish whether mesmerism could be accepted as science. This lifted mesmerism even further up in public and scientific attention. While Franz Mesmer primarily applied his theory to nature, developing a kind of medicinal health therapy with it, Bergasse and his associates also applied mesmerism to politics. Obstacles and disharmony were after all also inhibiting French politics. At the time of the

---

[119] Deliége to Gruner, 24 August 1815, GStA PK, VI. HA Nl. Gruner, no. 86, 29–33.
[120] Gruner to Deliége, 3 September 1815, GStA PK, VI. HA Nl. Gruner, no. 86, 47.

French Revolution, this brand of radical mesmerism had many followers, including Lafayette and Jacques-Pierre Brissot and Jean-Louis Carra. But Bergasse was the most fervent disciple, and with his financial means and organizational talent made it into a veritable cult.[121]

Around 1800, and still in 1815, it was by no means unusual to connect physical phenomena – such as electricity, magnetism and physical disorders – with each other in a kind of holistic theory. Science, superstition, religion and transcendent theories merged seamlessly. Scientists discovered only later in the nineteenth century that light does not flow through a fluid, that magnetism has to do with electrons and that the human body does not have 'poles'. But in 1815 everything could still be connected to everything, and gravity was just as much a God-given force as mesmerism seemed to be a 'scientifically' substantiated force to heal and purify man, animal and society.

Such theories immediately appealed to Tsar Alexander. After the second victory over Napoleon, and Alexander's return to Paris early in July 1815, his circle of friends and admirers had grown in proportion. Arriving on 10 July, he sought out a hotel at the Rue du Faubourg Saint-Honoré for his headquarters (close to the British headquarters), and invited his pious and by many considered almost fanatically religious friend Julie, the Baroness von Krüdener over with her daughter to stay in a city palace adjacent to his, at number 35. They received the Russian emperor almost daily, and succeeded in convincing him that his calling was not over yet. He was to be the redeemer of France and Europe: to liberate the French people from revolutionary convulsions; he was the 'second Abraham',[122] who needed to prepare France for a second Exodus out of their heathen ways, and save Europe as a whole. Alexander's salvific vision in Moscow and his victories had instilled in him a robust confidence in God, and in himself as God's apostle. With great aplomb, such as at the ecumenical mass on the Place de la Concorde in 1814, he had already demonstrated this confidence; yet now, in 1815, given his messianic perspective and his impatience with the ongoing meticulous and politically difficult negotiations in the Allied Council about compensation and reparations, Alexander wanted to do greater things, and save France from destruction – as quickly as possible. Wellington's diplomatic and organizational footsteps were far too small and too slow.

---

[121] See R. Darnton, *Mesmerism and the End of the Enlightenment in France* (Cambridge, MA: Harvard University Press, 1968). See also N. Bergasse, *Considérations sur le magnétisme animal, ou sur la théorie du monde et des êtres organisés, d'après les principes de M. Mesmer* (The Hague, 1784). See also A. Beeler, *Het dierlijk magnetismus beknopt in deszelfsverschijnselen en manieren van aanwending voorgesteld* (The Hague: Allart, 1814).

[122] See Krüdener's references in her diary, 11 July, as printed in F. Ley, *Alexandre 1er et sa Sainte-Alliance (1811–1825). Avec des documents inedits* (Paris: Fischbacher, 1975), 131.

The series of visits by Bergasse to the Baroness von Krüdener's salon, in which he came by to demonstrate his scientific talents by means of a sphere (a 'melon'), gave the tsar the inspiration he needed.[123] An association had to be set up, with himself as its shining middle point, inspired by the spark of the Eternal, and with the aim of spreading 'anti-revolutionary sentiments and virtues throughout Europe'.[124] In so doing, France, indeed all of Europe, could be purged of the Bonapartist convulsions, and the earth and the divine order be restored. The central mesmerizing role would of course be appropriated by the tsar himself, in an apotheosis of both his existing salvific beliefs and this new, semi-scientific creed of radical political mesmerism.

On 24 August, this group, consisting of Bergasse, Deliége, a number of royalist allies (including Chateaubriand) and Tsar Alexander's entourage, expressly sought rapprochement with Gruner and the Prussians. On 4 September, Gruner had a meeting with Bergasse, who told him that the tsar had great faith in Gruner, and wanted him to help the tsar further develop his 'religious insights'. According to Bergasse, the tsar was already busy arranging secret meetings in France with an eye to putting 'religion and virtue' back on the throne of Europe. The next day, Chateaubriand paid a somewhat overwhelmed Gruner a visit to underscore the same message again, but this time with a concrete political twist – not only the tsar, but King Louis too wanted to dismiss Talleyrand and Fouché as soon as possible because their 'depravity and falsity' hindered any recovery. Indeed, these two ministers were, in the mesmerist discourse, the main concrete obstacles to the restoration of social harmony. Their 'depravity and viciousness' were impeding every sort of recovery. But nothing was going to happen, in terms of healing, without the support and injunction of the Allies.[125] In other words, the royalists tried, together with the Russians, to use Gruner to undermine British resistance to the dismissal of Fouché, and to reconnect with Tsar Alexander's mesmerist ideas of purification and expiation.

Gruner was highly flattered and by now fully convinced of the plan, and about setting up such an alliance. He also found political merit in it for the Prussian cause. To Hardenberg he explained that although he had indeed at first set his hopes on Fouché and the constitutionals, it had now become clear to him that the Allies could best back the royalists. 'This is our chance to settle the lot of France … The new ministry will work with us in a way that Talleyrand's did not.' The door to cooperating with the Bourbons would finally open.[126] Three days later, he sent another reminder, with an additional

---

[123] See Krüdener's diary, printed in Ley, *Alexandre 1er et sa Sainte-Alliance*, 131–3.

[124] Gruner's retelling of the plans, 5 September 1815, GStA PK, VI. HA Nl. Hardenberg 10a.

[125] Accounts by Gruner and letter to Hardenberg, 5 September 1815, GStA PK, VI. HA Nl. Hardenberg 10a.

[126] Report of Gruner, 5 September 1815, GStA PK, VI. HA Nl. Hardenberg 10a.

argument to win Hardenberg over to the secret alliance. Talleyrand and Fouché not only had their eyes fixed on a revolution in France; they wanted to set all of Europe 'in flames' again. They were 'sworn enemies of Germany and Prussia. The one because of political interests, the other because of national concerns.' Gruner also frankly admitted now that he had let Fouché pull the wool over his eyes: 'Fouché shared very many pleasant insights with me; suggesting that he was truly convinced that Prussia was the most enlightened state.' But 'that is why he fears us!' 'France's general bitterness against Prussia is Fouché's work. He could work to dissolve that bitterness, but he chooses not to. Hardenberg knows better than anyone else what Talleyrand did to us in Vienna.' Russia would support the plans, probably Metternich too, but he was still somewhat indifferent. Only Britain's 'powerful ministers' (Castlereagh or Wellington) 'would object'. 'But they will not be able to oppose public opinion once the fall happens and is loudly acclaimed en bloc throughout Europe.'[127]

And then Gruner let his true colours shine through. There was only one solution imaginable: 'Power alone can bring this blow about.' He had allowed himself to be drawn into a full-fledged coup. The idea was to whisk Fouché and Talleyrand from their beds in the middle of the night, send them packing and confiscate their papers, under the pretext of having 'discovered a conspiracy against us' – a conspiracy that would have surfaced in 'the secret papers' that Gruner himself would draw up and plant. Gruner suggested to Hardenberg that he would himself conduct this investigation. The benefits of this plan were numerous: 'The gratitude of the French family, the glee of the army, the admiration of our people, a "lightening of the load" for Germany and all of Europe, the preservation of tranquillity in the future and the creation of an honourable peace.' And Prussia would be 'delivered' once and for all.[128]

The constant stream of rumours from his spies and the flattery of Bergasse and Chateaubriand had made Gruner's head spin. But he was not alone with his overheated sentiments. Indeed, the elections of 14 and 22 August for the French Chamber of Deputies, the many upheavals and disturbances in the country and the initial rumours surrounding the final outcomes of the Allies' deliberations had deflated morale and stoked emotions throughout Paris. It also did not help that Talleyrand and Fouché incessantly blamed the Allied Council for the deplorable 'moral state' of the country; those rising 'passions', that soured mood, were all owing to the presence of the Allied troops, which undermined the authority of the king, according to Talleyrand in one of his lengthy epistles to the Allied Council.[129] For the Council, and certainly for

[127] Ibid.
[128] Gruner to Hardenberg, 8 September 1815, GStA PK, VI. HA Nl. Hardenberg 10a.
[129] Talleyrand to the Allied Council, 19 August 1815, annex 89 to the protocols of 20 August, GStA PK, III. HA I. no. 1465, 82–3.

Gruner and his association, his claims were like adding fuel to the fire. They saw proof of an imminent revolt in his defiance.

Tsar Alexander's Redemptive Move

Against the backdrop of this hothouse of public and official resentments, and supported by an ensemble of admirers, spy masters and true believers, Tsar Alexander made his redemptive move. At four o'clock in the morning on 10 September the Allied forces engulfed the plains of Vertus, north-east of Paris. Tsar Alexander, flanked by the emperor of Austria and the king of Prussia, the Duke of Wellington and some other princes positioned themselves on top of the Mont Aimé, arising from the plains. Thousands of spectators were drawn from Paris to watch the spectacle of over 150,000 Russian soldiers spreading like crescents over fields, punctuated by the sound of 540 cannons. The next day transformed this military spectacle into an almost eschatological event. That day, in honour of Saint Alexander Nevski, Tsar Alexander staged an ecumenical mass. For the onlookers, the sight of the thousands of soldiers kneeling before seven altars, organized into seven squares, was unbelievably impressive. 'It was an imposing sight, to watch 150,000 men simultaneously throw themselves on their knees and celebrate mass', Julie Krüdener, the daughter of Alexander's pietist religious friend and prophetess remarked.[130]

Apart from this spectacular demonstration of Allied and Russian power and magnanimity towards the French people, a far more momentous event, but less visibly so, unwound behind the scenes: the preparation of a 'secret plan for the benefit of Europe' – originating from Tsar Alexander and his entourage. This plan, which became known as the Holy Alliance, has entered the history textbooks as a plan for the repression of reformist and liberal ideals, and a blueprint for a return to the *ancien régime* order.[131] In its first conceptions, however, Alexander's Holy Alliance was far less conservative, and far more revolutionary than it came to be understood to be, given the fact that it was the unique product of an amalgam of Christian pietism, semi-scientific enlightenment theories and a new political religion of reformism. The Holy Alliance did contain conservative ingredients, but the liberal and provocative elements stood out – within a few years, however, these were suppressed by political appropriations by other statesmen.

Two days after Alexander's demonstration of public healing at Vertus, Bergasse's 'secret association' came to Gruner again, this time bringing with them their general regulations and their ideas for new laws. According to

---

[130] Cf. S. Brown, 'Movements of Christian Awakening in Revolutionary Europe', in S. Brown and T. Tackett (eds.), *Enlightenment, Reawakening and Revolution, 1660–1815* (Cambridge: Cambridge University Press, 2006), 575.

[131] See especially Menger, *Die Heilige Allianz.*

Bergasse, Tsar Alexander had designed and initiated a 'great secret plan to unite all the peoples of the world – irrespective of their diversity – and finds the secret way the most suitable means to that end'. In other words, Alexander tried to work behind the back of the Allied Council – in particular behind the backs of Castlereagh and Wellington – and win over partners for his religious–political association. He already knew the French royalists were at his side, and hoped that the Prussians would join his camp as well. The tsar maintained that the time was now ripe.[132] On 14 September, his plans transpired in more detail. He had asked Bergasse to write a first draft for something that would enter history under the epitaph 'Holy Alliance'. Alexander personally edited and complemented the text, but the final result very much breathed the mesmeristic ideals of Bergasse *cum suis*.

All three elements were visible: Christian messianism, enlightened ideas about a fraternity of peoples and a mesmerizing approach. The declaration referred to the general bond of 'indissoluble fraternity' that connects all peoples and sovereigns, which was tarnished and infected, but now had to be healed by the 'influence' of a divine spirit. One may read Christian messianism in it, Orthodox and conservative-political obscurantism – the text was imbued with notions of providence, divine power, and 'the Holy Religion of the Divine Saviour'. But the roots and influences of a spiritual and political mesmerism also shone through: only the 'influence' of the 'Council of Princes' (of which Alexander, with his ensemble, considered himself the first and foremost magnetizer) would serve to 'consolidate the human institutions and remedy their imperfections'. Only thus, humankind, so 'agitated' by revolutionary passions, could be 'healed', could become united and inspired again. In short, in this combination of religious principles, Enlightenment ideas and new, allegedly scientific insights, the text had become an exalted brew.[133]

Even more telling are the concrete measures that accompanied the drafting of the Holy Alliance Treaty – measures that have been omitted in the historiography of a text that has always been portrayed as a merely spiritual and politically vacuous one. In fact, Tsar Alexander truly intended to deploy the Holy Alliance as a scientifically (via mesmerism) and religiously substantiated means to 'purify' and 'cleanse' France of its revolutionary and despotic obstipations, and help her embark on a new course of reform and moderation.[134]

---

[132] Report of Gruner to Hardenberg, 12 September 1815, GStA PK, VI. HA Nl. Hardenberg 10a.

[133] 'Treaty between Austria, Prussia, and Russia', Paris, 26 September 1815 (hereafter: the 'Holy Alliance'), in E. Hertslet (ed.), *The Map of Europe by Treaty*, vol. 1, 317–20.

[134] Cf. A. Tsygankov, *Russia and the West from Alexander to Putin. Honor in International Relations* (Cambridge: Cambridge University Press, 2012), 63–77; S. Ghervas, 'La Sainte-Alliance: Un pacte pacifique européen comme antidote à l'Empire', in S. Aprile et al. (eds.), *Europe de Papier. Projets Européens au XIXe siècle* (Lille: Septentrion, 2015), 47–64.

That he and his ensemble of fellow believers indeed saw the Holy Alliance as the beginning of a concrete reform project, albeit a highly ethereal one, was evidenced by the next steps that were taken towards 'cleaning up' French administration, right after the disclosure of the text. From a mesmeristic point of view, it was equally important to proclaim unity and to remove as quickly as possible all the obstacles that stood in the way of this fraternity. The way to do this was by triggering a 'crisis'. The obstacles were, of course, Fouché and Talleyrand, the evil twins responsible for the continuation of revolutionary Bonapartism and *ancien régime* Machiavellian politics. On 15 September, the support for deposing Fouché was broad enough; the Chamber now consisted of Ultras, who made it clear that the current ministry was no longer sustainable. The Prussian king and Russian tsar agreed entirely, and Wellington, on his own, could no longer keep Louis from saying yes as well. And so, Fouché was relieved of his post and sent to Dresden as an ambassador – admittedly, not in the manner suggested by Gruner, via a night-time arrest and the planting of evidence, but in broad daylight. Talleyrand took the initiative himself and on 19 September he submitted his resignation (in part, to avoid having to take the responsibility for the Treaty of Paris, of which he had received the first draft that day).[135]

On 22 September the Allies received a copy of Alexander's plan, and Metternich proceeded to try to tone down the text somewhat: the appeal to all 'states' was replaced by 'great powers', and the all-too-utopian references to the 'federation of states' were substituted by the less political and more vague imagery of the 'family'.[136] On 24 September, the tsar, the Prussian king, and the Austrian Emperor Franz signed the Treaty; the British Prince Regent signed the declaration on his personal account, but not on behalf of his country, as parliament would not ratify the Treaty.[137] Alexander had completed his divine mission, and four days later, on 28 September, the Russians left for home. Gruner, the royalists and their secret association had achieved their goal, and

[135] Letter to Talleyrand, 19 September, Allied Council, 19 September 1815, GStA PK, III. HA I. no. 1465; letter of Talleyrand to the Council, 20 September, annex 124, GStA PK, III. HA I. no. 1465, 177.

[136] For a comparison of the different versions of the Holy Alliance Treaty, see Ley, *Alexandre Ier et sa Sainte-Alliance*, 148–53. See also W. Näf, *Zur Geschichte der Heiligen Allianz* (Bern: Paul Haupt, 1928), 8–19.

[137] 'Letter of the Prince Regent to the Emperor of Russia, the Emperor of Austria and the King of Prussia', 6 October 1815, printed in Näf, *Zur Geschichte der Heiligen Allianz*, 41; J. Miller, *The History of Great Britain from the Death of George III to the Coronation of George IV* (London, Jones & Co, 1825), 378. Cf. also S. Ghervas, *Réinventer la tradition. Alexandre Stourdza et l'Europe de la Sainte-Alliance* (Paris: Honoré Champion, 2008); P. Menger, 'Die Heilige Allianz – "La Garantie Religieuse du nouveau système Européen"?', in W. Pyta (ed.), *Das europäische Mächtekonzert. Friedens- und Sicherheitspolitik vom Wiener Kongress 1815 bis zum Krimkrieg 1853* (Cologne: Böhlau, 2009), 209–36.

in Richelieu a notably virtuous, extremely loyal and upstanding first minister had been appointed to run the French government.[138]

The envisioned spirit of fraternity was not embraced as quickly as Alexander and his supporters had hoped, however.[139] 'Concern and fear' filled the air. 'Tension and ferment' still rose all around. 'The "anti-bourbon" party holds its breath for the present, the "royalist party", for the future', wrote Gruner.[140] On 20 September, the newspapers finally published the dreaded text of the Paris Convention. It was bad news for France, but less disastrous than feared. France would not be apportioned, but merely cut back to its 1790 borders. And one of the greatest sources of unrest was defused as well: the troops would be evacuated from the French capital immediately, and the humiliating billeting of Prussian soldiers in the parlours and hotels of the Parisians would be over.[141]

With the departure of the troops, the pervasive and demeaning presence of 26,000 Allied soldiers in the city came to an end, and the public order in the capital somewhat normalized. By the end of November, the Allies' control and military administration of the capital was therefore no longer necessary. The Prussians moved their headquarters to Caen. Totally unexpected for Gruner came the announcement that his security service was to be dismantled as well. With his manoeuvring and dabbling in French and Russian intrigues, he had lost considerable goodwill with Hardenberg and Wellington. He received his last salary as chief of the Allied police in January 1816 and was sent to Switzerland as a diplomat – not exactly a promotion.[142] He did succeed in convincing the Swiss cantons to accede to the Treaty of the Holy Alliance, but soon afterwards he died – a lonely and bitter man. The important role that he had imagined himself playing in the new Prussia was not to be. His top spy, the Marquis de La Coudraye, was – were that possible – even more disappointed. The conversations with 'my prince' Hardenberg, which he so had longed for, would never take place.[143] And he did not like living in France either. He pulled up stakes again and left for 'the north of Europe', and died in 1817.[144] Bergasse, however, was rewarded a couple of years later by French king Charles

[138] Report of de La Coudraye, 8 October 1815, GStA PK, VI. HA Nl. Hardenberg 10a.
[139] Reports of Gruner and de La Coudraye, 20, 22, 24, 28, 29 September, 6, 8, 11 October, GStA PK, VI. HA Nl. Hardenberg 10a.
[140] Report of Gruner, 20 October 1815, GStA PK, VI. HA Nl. Hardenberg 10a.
[141] That was the opinion of the Military Committee of the Allied Council. 'Délibération du Comité Militaire central des Alliés', annex sub 17 with the protocol of the sixth *séance*, 17 July 1815, GStA PK, III. HA I. no. 1464, 41.
[142] See 'Nachweisungen', in the back of the folder, GStA PK, VI. HA Nl. Gruner, no. 86.
[143] See de La Coudraye's repeated requests to Gruner, e.g. on 20 October, GStA PK, VI. HA Nl. Hardenberg 10a.
[144] 'De La Coudraye', in Michaud and de Loynes (eds.), *Biographie universelle*, vol. 69, 308.

X for his royalist loyalty, and was appointed to the Council of State, days before Charles was toppled in 1830.

The Holy Alliance and its Afterlife

Tsar Alexander's Holy Alliance did live on, and lingered on after his departure for Russia as a spectre, intimidating liberal reformers and irritating British diplomats alike. Since the Holy Alliance was not linked to a concrete administrative body or executive organization, such as the Allied Council (being the executive organization of the Quadruple Alliance and the Second Treaty of Paris), its effect was psychological rather than political. All traces and influences of the mesmerist discourse, moreover, soon retreated into oblivion when, around 1820, new insights on electromagnetism replaced the primitive notions on 'animal magnetism'. Moreover, not the mesmerist background, but Castlereagh's and Wellington's attempts to ridicule the tsar and his Orthodox beliefs – their political counterweight – survived as its legacy. 'It was not without difficulty that we went through the interview with becoming gravity', Castlereagh reported to his prime minister, Liverpool. 'The fact is, that the Emperor's mind is not completely sound'[145] – a citation that has made it into numerous textbooks ever since; as has the remark ascribed to Castlereagh on 28 September, when the British minister simply discarded the Treaty as 'this piece of sublime mysticism and nonsense'.[146] Metternich similarly is said to have quipped that, to him, the Treaty was nothing more than a 'laut tönendes nichts'. It was nothing more than 'the expression of the Emperor Alexander's mystical sentiments, and the application of these Christian principles to politics'.[147]

Yet it is too simple for historians nowadays to uncritically follow these early qualifications and to dismiss Alexander as a religiously derailed autocrat. First of all, Alexander was doing exactly what Castlereagh had suggested in the Allied Council, the body that was convened to discuss the future of France and design a security arrangement for Europe as a whole: thinking about the overall context of European peace – it is just that his doing so turned out to be much more religious and grandiose than the British had anticipated.[148] Secondly, it would be an uncritical reiteration of Alexander's competitors, and an overlooking of their agenda in discrediting the tsar's intentions. That the Holy

[145] Castlereagh to Liverpool, 28 September 1815, cited in Bew, *Castlereagh*, 410–11. Also in *WSD*, vol. 11, 176–7.
[146] Castlereagh to Liverpool, 28 September 1815, *WSD*, vol. 11, 175.
[147] G. de Bertier de Sauvigny, 'Sainte-Alliance et Alliance dans les conceptions de Metternich', *Revue Historique*, 223:2 (1960), 249–74, here: 251.
[148] Bew, *Castlereagh*, 410–11. See Alexander's invitation to the other Christian monarchs of Europe: 'Reskript Alexander I', 22 March/3 April 1816, in Ministerstvo inostrannykh del CCCP (ed.), *Vneshniaia politika Rossii*, vol. 1, 113–15.

Alliance was soon thereafter reduced to a conservative ploy was due to a combination of the British attempts to sideline the tsar, Metternich's astute political manoeuvring and Alexander's own preoccupation with domestic uprisings after returning home.

In Russia, the proclamation of Tsar Alexander's Holy Alliance did not meet with a warm reception at all, probably because of all the liberal, mesmerist, ecumenical and even Freemasonry-related symbols and wordings it contained. Tsar Alexander himself sent Krüdener into exile and forgot about his mesmerist friends. A few traces of the mesmerizing and revolutionary ideals expressed by Alexander in 1815 remained, as a residue: in 1818, Alexander still considered France as having been stricken by a 'vehement disease', as demonstrated by its suffering from so many revolutionary 'convulsions' that still taunted the patient.[149] In Aix-la-Chapelle, in October 1818, he therefore once again proposed a 'medicine' and remedy in the form of a general alliance and a moral guarantee.[150] At this time, however, his appeal to the other powers was waning, whereas Metternich's attempts to use Alexander's arguments for stepping up security monitoring and repression were far more successful.[151]

From 1815 onwards, together with Gentz, and with the knowledge of Wellington, Metternich consistently tried to rewrite and appropriate the Holy Alliance and turn it into a ploy for conserving the existing legal order, and legitimizing the military interventions necessary to uphold that order, as in Spain or Greece. His ambassador and former Allied Council colleague Vincent suggested to Wellington in January 1819 that it would be a good idea to use Tsar Alexander as a 'powerful antidote' to 'the principles which everywhere threaten the social order ... by occupying his mind and by interesting his heart in the sense of the Holy Alliance'. Because, 'the effect of an uneasy policy on his part is dampened and made to contribute to the preservation of the conservative principles of the general edifice'. Metternich insisted on this manipulative line when he wrote in 1821 to Alexander, 'the single principle with which the monarchs need to oppose this plan of universal destruction [as carried out by the revolutionary factions] is the conservation of all existing legal things' ('la conservation de toute chose légalement existante'). The only means of obtaining this aim

[149] As described by Castlereagh; see Castlereagh to Bathurst, 19 October 1818, TNA, FO 92/35, 138–47.
[150] Castlereagh to Bathurst, 3 October 1818, TNA, FO 92/35, 10–17.
[151] Via a letter from Nesselrode and Kapodistrias to Castlereagh and Wellington, 8 October 1818, WSD, vol. 12, 742–51. On 14 October, the ministers of all five courts deliberated on the matter collectively; see 'Projet de protocole', 14 October 1818, WSD, vol. 12, 770–3. See also the report and original memorandum, addressed to Metternich, 8 October 1818, Österreichisches Staatsarchiv, Haus-, Hof-, und Staatsarchiv, Vienna (AT-OeStA/HHStA), Staatskanzlei (StK), Kongressakten, Subfolder, Protokolle Aachen 1818, inv. no. 17, 33–56.

would be 'to not innovate at all'.[152] In reality, this meant that Metternich successfully deflected Alexander from bringing forward his ideas for a unity of peoples, of constitutional reforms and of invading the Balkans and reined him in, committing him safely and squarely to the existing order of things.

Two influential contemporaries did notice Metternich's rewriting of the Treaty's history and manipulation of Alexander's heritage – during his life, and then after his death in 1825. Benjamin Constant argued in *Le Courrier Français*, on 28 October 1822, that the original nature of the Holy Alliance had in the hands of Metternich and Austria been manipulated and turned into a ploy to destroy the 'independence of peoples in the name of the independence of the sovereigns'. Its original 'philantropical character and the pious direction', the design of Alexander, was now 'only a distant memory'.[153] And Goethe, in conversation with his friend Eckermann, on 3 January 1827 struck a similar chord, when he remarked that with the Holy Alliance, 'nothing greater and more benevolent for humankind had been invented'; but 'its greatness is too awkward for them; ... they cannot bear it'.[154] In sum, Metternich appropriated the Alliance in the years after its conception, used it to bind Alexander to his continental conservative policies and prevented him from unleashing all kinds of libertarian, reformist ideas on the continent.[155] Hence, in the public understanding and historical interpretation, the tsar's original ideas, and the Treaty itself, were conflated with this conservative instrumentalization by Metternich and Austria's security police in the years thereafter – quite a tragic outcome, since Metternich never really understood Alexander's true intentions and only saw the Treaty as a tactical instrument.[156]

Metternich's System of 'Uniform Measures'

With Gruner and Tsar Alexander outwitted, now Metternich was the one trying to work himself up as the patron of Allied security policies. He was the one who came up with the most drastic measures and – unlike Gruner and Alexander – actually succeeded in implementing them. For Metternich, in the summer and autumn of 1815, the greatest danger lay in the extent to which the lingering remnants of Bonapartism and revolutionary defiance could freely

---

[152] Cited in Ley, *Alexandre 1er et sa Sainte-Alliance*, 295–6.
[153] Benjamin Constant, *Le Courrier Français*, 28 October 1822, no. 92, in É. Harpaz (ed.), *Benjamin Constant. Récueil d'articles, 1820–1824* (Geneva: Droz, 1981), 202–5, here: 203.
[154] J. P. Eckermann, *Gespräche mit Goethe in den letzten Jahren seines Lebens, 1823–1832*, vol. 1 (Leipzig: Brockhaus, 1837), 277–8.
[155] See also H. Delfiner, 'Alexander I, The Holy Alliance and Clemens Metternich: A Reappraisal', *East European Quarterly*, 37:2 (2003), 127–50, here: 146.
[156] Bertier de Sauvigny makes this point as well; see 'Sainte-Alliance et Alliance dans les conceptions de Metternich', 256.

move among veterans, banished exiles and travelling publicists beyond the borders and throughout Europe, giving public voice to the spirit of rebellion. At his instigation, therefore, the Allied Council of Ministers had already decided on 14 August that 'uniform measures' would be taken to curb unrestricted travel and movement – not only in France, but also beyond its borders. Metternich first of all focused on the issuing of passports. Only passports issued by the Allied powers or, when issued by lesser powers or by France, endorsed and signed by the Allies would be recognized as valid. That was a far-reaching decision.

In 1815, 'passports' were very different from current, permanent and difficult-to-forge identity cards. They were documents that stipulated the reason for the journey, the designation of those travelling together, their names and titles and who it was that provided the letter of safe conduct. Such a passport was valid for a certain period and in a specified area, depending on the status and identity of the person who had issued and signed the letter. It also often indicated the intended route ('which runs from x via y to z') and destination. In 1815, passports from one of the four major Allied powers were the most reliable travel documents, allowing one to pass through most every checkpoint (Fig. 5.4). The higher up the authority behind the signature was, the more effective the travel document was in helping the traveller overcome borders and control posts. Passports issued by lesser powers, or by the French king, were therefore not enough to guarantee safety and freedom of movement. On 17 July, already, the Allied ministers had agreed that a standard form of passport had to be issued to regulate the travel of persons between the various occupied and unoccupied departments in France, and that that passport would be 'the only valid' means, 'to the exclusion of any other'.[157] The French government could also issue that passport, but the Allies reserved the right to 'ratify or not ratify' that passport at any time and to be able to declare it null and void at their behest.[158]

In this, Metternich knew the governor of Paris, Müffling, was on his side, hoping to manage the enormous influx of demobilized French soldiers more effectively with this measure. Only with a valid passport could a veteran, for example, cross the Loire and enter the unoccupied part of France, or, with the permission of the Allies, settle in one of the occupied territories. An officer could keep his arms, but an ordinary soldier had to hand over his arms when issued a passport. The same rule also applied to civil servants, parliamentarians, administrators and merchants who wanted to stay in the capital, or to cross the Loire. To handle all of that administratively, Müffling needed some extra staff, because the pile of requests and groups of waiting soldiers quickly got out of hand.[159]

---

[157] Protocol of 17 July 1815, GStA PK, III. HA I. no. 1464, 34. See also annex 18, 42.
[158] Protocol of 22 July 1815, GStA PK, III. HA I. no. 1464, 100.
[159] Protocol of 26 July; see also annex 42, GStA PK, III. HA I. no. 1464, 133 and annex 58, with the protocols of 3 August 1815, 176.

Figure 5.4   Passport of Justus von Gruner. (GStA PK, VI. HA, Nachlass Gruner, J. K., No. 27)

Besides regulating the flow of displaced persons, there was another import-ant argument for implementing uniform, Allied passports: designing a general Allied passport policy would support the principle of 'de-Bonapartizing' France and getting rid of revolutionary threats. Immediately during its first session on 12 July, the Allied Council had decided to give the boot to all of Napoleon's immediate family members, ministers, generals and close friends. On 25 July, the Council discussed the list drawn up on the

24th.[160] Metternich, in particular, insisted on a uniform decision; the Allied powers had to draw one line in dealing with the blacklisted persons. A general passport policy would create the instrument to monitor all people who passed border and control posts. For Metternich, the blacklisted persons were not just a danger for France, but for Europe as a whole. The first group on the list included not only those who had been arrested with Napoleon or had taken part in the French government prior to 23 March, but also those who had already fled France and settled elsewhere, believing that in doing so they could circumvent prosecution. Because persons beyond France's border should not be allowed to evade punishment, Metternich proposed to the Council (with success) that these individuals be arrested and then be given the choice of extradition to France or imprisonment in the country of arrest.[161]

The second group included those who had already been slated for deportation by the French. They were not allowed to settle wherever they wanted, but had to be well removed from the French border. They could, moreover, seek asylum only within one of the countries of the Quadruple Alliance. According to Metternich, only those countries had an adequate security infrastructure that was extensive enough to effectively supervise these exiles. The exiles were not allowed to settle in the Netherlands, Italy or Switzerland, for example, because these countries were not expected to have enough spies on hand to keep these security risks in check. Russia, Austria and Prussia were up to the task, so these were their only options. After conferring with the French government, it was decided that these measures equally held for the whole 'House of Bonaparte', in particular for Joseph and Jérôme, but also for Hortense and Napoleon's mother. Moreover, their free movement and the offer of asylum did not apply unconditionally – the persons in question had to abstain from involvement in 'political intrigues' at all times.[162]

The issuing of passports – including the indication of the provider, the addressee and the destination – was an equally crucial and innovative means of monitoring and enforcing 'the list'. This innovation was applied not only in France, but in the other European countries as well. Rather than being limited to one country, the Allies' 'precautionary measures' stretched as far as the threats reached.[163] The arm of the Allied Council was a long one; all the European courts received a copy of the list (some from Gruner directly), with the urgent request to comply with Metternich's guidelines straight away. They were, moreover, summoned to inform the Council immediately if anyone on that list was holed up in their area and if that person could be

---

[160] Protocol of 25 July 1815, GStA PK, III. HA I. no. 1464, 123.
[161] Memo of Metternich to the Allied Council, annex 93, protocol of 22 August 1815, GStA PK, III. HA I. no. 1465, 89. The Council's approval of Metternich's suggestion, protocol of 27 August, annex 96.
[162] Ibid. See also protocols of 7 and 14 August 1815, GStA PK, III. HA I. no. 1465, 22.
[163] Annex 87, 19 August 1815, GStA PK, III. HA I. no. 1465, 79.

extradited or put under surveillance. Almost all courts complied.[164] With this 'uniform measure', Metternich's policy could even be considered a forerunner to the current 'European Arrest Warrant' and the database on blacklisted individuals kept by Europol.

Hortense's Destiny

Hortense de Beauharnais, Napoleon's loyal stepdaughter, was one of the first affected by the new Allied security arrangements. On 26 and 29 August 1815, the Allied Council met to discuss her case. Her name was not on the list of persons to be banished per se, but as part of the network of Napoléonides she was nevertheless included under that category. The degree of culpability was determined individually. Hortense's case was a complex one and was brought up at several meetings. As a single mother (she lived separated from her husband, Louis Bonaparte), she did not seem capable of doing much harm. On the other hand, however, she had remained loyal to Napoleon to the bitter end, and was being associated, rightly or wrongly, with all kinds of Bonapartist intrigues. That is why the Allied Council politely, but bindingly, advised her to settle in one of the four countries of the Allies, purportedly also with an eye on her safety. If she really wanted to stay in Switzerland, that was acceptable, but only by way of an exception and as a temporary solution. She would have to be tailed closely, and be put under Allied 'protection'. In fact, she was placed under the legal guardianship and tutelage of the powers; her freedom was very limited and conditional. Something similar was the case for Napoleon's brothers: Jérôme could stay in Württemberg; Lucien was granted asylum in Rome, as was Louis. Murat and Joseph would eventually be granted asylum in Austria. Tsar Alexander did suggest that the entire family could always come and settle in his endless realm, but none of the Bonapartes felt much inclined to take up that offer.[165] Via the king of Württemberg, the Council consequently received an unsolicited contract of sorts, signed by Jérôme Bonaparte and a Württemberg minister himself. In this letter, Napoleon's youngest brother promised on his word of honour to abide by the stipulations of the Allied powers, and to receive no one into his home who was not in good standing. As a token of his good faith he even brought up, by way of example, the names of a few such shady characters in passing.[166]

---

[164] Hardenberg to Gruner, with the request to bring the circular and the list of 24 July to the attention of the courts in other countries, 18 October 1815, GStA PK, VI. HA, Nl. Gruner, no. 86.

[165] Protocols of the Allied Council, 19, 26, 27, 29, 31 August 1815, GStA PK, III. HA I. no. 1465.

[166] Contract, and letter from the Comte de Winzigerode to the Council, 21 September 1815, GStA PK, III. HA I. no. 1465, 188–9.

But Metternich was uneasy about it all, and continued to find ways to put the issue on the agenda – with the other ambassadors (Goltz, Nesselrode and Pozzo di Borgo) siding with his sensitivities. His greatest fear was a revival of the spirit of Napoleon, be it through his person, or via one of his loyal supporters. Hortense was herself not a direct threat to the Bourbons,[167] and kept a low profile, but her place was definitely the hub for a network of Bonapartists, with whom she corresponded, and who gathered around her in devising new plans. The cheering from faithful Bonapartists that accompanied her coach along the roads in France spoke volumes. As became clear later, that did not make Metternich altogether paranoid. Hortense maintained contact with Ney's widow, and did offer financial support to the family of Bonapartist generals, such as Duhamel, who was in prison. She also stayed in contact with Count de Lavalette, who ended up staying with Hortense's brother Eugène in Bavaria – after escaping a Paris prison the night before his execution with the help of his wife, who changed clothes and places with him (and was released within two months). A number of years later, both of Hortense's sons became involved with the Carbonari, who were fighting Austria's domination in northern Italy. Her son Napoléon-Louis, sick with the measles, died in 1831 while fleeing an offensive against the Carbonari in Romagna. Much later, in 1852, her other son, Charles Louis Napoléon, would become another Bonaparte on the throne, as Emperor Napoleon III. But even during those first post-Napoleonic months in 1815, the song 'Partant pour la Syrie' remained very popular: a notorious Napoleonic battle song, composed (c.1807) by Hortense for her stepfather, which later became the unofficial national anthem during Napoleon III's reign. According to Gruner, it was sung and whistled freely in the streets of Paris.[168]

That is why Metternich, at the end of 1815, personally invited Hortense to avail herself of some 'Austrian hospitality'. Yet, Hortense decided that she rather 'preferred an uneasy freedom [in Konstanz] to a protective prison [under Metternich's curatorship]'.[169] In the mountains of Switzerland, Hortense sought to escape the rumours and suspicions and to come to terms with her unrest. During a visit to the Benedictine monastery in the village of Einsiedeln, she received consolation from a priest and concluded that her own 'pride' and 'vanity' had been her greatest enemies. In gratitude, she gave the monastery a few of her remaining diamonds. In 1817, with what remained of her fortune, she bought a small chateau near Konstanz, Schloss Arenenberg, on the southern shore of Lower Lake Constance, just inside the border of the (to

---

[167] As the Council noted on 21 October. Annex to the protocol of 21 October 1815, GStA PK, III. HA I. no. 1469, 23.

[168] See reports of Gruner, July–August 1815, GStA PK, VI. HA Nl. Hardenberg 10a. See also Le prince Napoleon (ed.), *Mémoires de la Reine Hortense*.

[169] Le prince Napoléon, *Mémoires de la Reine Hortense*, vol. 3, 114.

her mind) more independent and hence safer Switzerland. After diverse wanderings – via Augsburg, Rome, Britain and France – she was finally allowed to move into her own place at Arenenberg in 1819. Her home became a meeting place for writers, philosophers and royalist and Bonapartist nobility. Given her musical and cultural interests, Chateaubriand was just as welcome as was her brother Eugène. But she was not able to enjoy her recouped rest for long. Napoléon Louis would die in 1831 (another son had died at a very young age), and in 1837, at the age of fifty-two, she herself succumbed to uterine cancer.[170]

Hortense was a pawn in the power games of the Allies' security arrangements. But she did not let them break her. Moreover, one unintended consequence of her exile was that she took the spirit of Bonapartism and patriotic resistance with her, instilled it in her children and, despite (or because of) Metternich's surveillance, managed to function as the hub of a network of liberal patriots and freedom fighters.

This chapter has discussed the increasing flow of security measures. The French found these measures so insufferable, that their introduction – the creation of an Allied security agency, the implementation of uniform passport procedures, plus censorship and banishment – only made matters worse. Hotbeds of radicalization arose around blacklisted persons, terrorists and exiles that would even start to threaten the commander of the Allied forces, Wellington. Striking the right balance between fighting terror and restoring harmony and order, moreover, pushed the discussion on the scope and essence of the Allied Council to the limits. How far did the Allied mandate stretch, and what was the nature of the 'Allied Machine' to be – should the ministers transform themselves into a European police directorate (as some advocated), or was that beyond the pale?

---

[170] Ibid., 131–65.

6

Fighting *terroristes* Together

Towards a 'European Police Directorate'?

Terroristes dangereux

It was Metternich who, on behalf of the Allies, took the lead and developed a system and repertoire of anti-revolutionary control that would continue to exist even after the occupation of France had ended. After the dissolution of Gruner's security service, the departure of Tsar Alexander and the conclusion of the Treaty of Paris, the Allied Council continued to concern itself with security in France and beyond. On 20 November 1815, the Council assured Richelieu that the Allies would respect the domestic administration of the French government and no longer perform policing duties, but that they would, however, see to it that they remained well informed about all major 'events', and that, as soon as they noted any 'revolutionary convulsions', Wellington was authorized to send in troops as he deemed necessary.[1]

In addition to attempting to keep the Bonapartist threat in check via the Allies' passport control policies, Metternich's next goal was to fight the 'dangerous terrorists' at work within and beyond France's borders. 'Terrorism' in 1815 was not the same as in the twentieth or twenty-first century. It did not point to violent attacks carried out by non-state groups or individuals motivated by political, ideological or religious beliefs, but to the Reign of Terror imposed by the French revolutionaries under Robespierre. This era nevertheless laid the groundwork for the modern understanding of the concept of terrorism, and the expansion thereof to include non-state terrorist perpetrators. The category of *terroristes* for Metternich, in 1815, did already point to a broader group of people and threats than merely those who had voted for the execution of Louis XVI, the *régicides*. For Metternich, and the other Allied ministers with him, this category comprised all individuals culpable of revolutionary outpourings, ranging along a scale from those organizing violent uprisings to those producing non-violent seditious writings. During this transitional period, right after the conclusion of a twenty-six-year spell of revolution and war, in the midst of instability and political uncertainties,

---

[1] Letter of Allied Council to Richelieu, 20 November 1815, GStA PK, III. HA I. no. 1469, 93.

Metternich's fear of terror was real. Terror was not only that phenomenon with which gods and princes instilled fear in their enemies, the righteous, salutary and majestic 'terror of God'; it had since Robespierre's Reign of Terror morphed into that devilish phenomenon, the 'terror of the people', the 'tyranny of the multitude': in short, into a 'term of abuse that could be used to discredit political adversaries' in 1815.[2]

Metternich's primary concern, then, was not the occurrence of riots and violence as such. During those first months, pugnacity was the order of the day. Gruner's reports sketched a picture of a city and a country in which people came to blows, were beaten up or egged on to violence and hate on a daily basis. For the Allied soldiers, wearing a uniform alone or at night was seriously discouraged by their superiors; one could easily end up in the Seine. Moreover, between wandering vagabonds, discharged soldiers, farmers and field hands frustrated by the deplorable weather conditions in 1815 and 1816, there were countless groups among the population who had reason enough to resort to violence. The post-1815 violence ran the whole gamut, from insults, windows pummelled by potatoes, raids on Allied soldiers, planned massacres (in the Gard), housewives protesting the price of bread, food riots and popular uprisings. Variations on civil disobedience were commonplace throughout Europe.[3]

Metternich's greatest grief, however – and the same was true for the Prussian and Russian envoys – was not owing to these relatively spontaneous outbursts of violence. These were merely symptoms of something deeper. He was far more apprehensive about the articulation of radical grievances: about the many publicists and revolutionary activists who distributed pamphlets throughout Europe and filled newspapers and magazines, spewing their bile about the crowned heads of Europe and their ministers. He was concerned about the freedom of expression and the printed word, about the speed with which the revolutionary spirit – both orally and in writing – spread through Europe. Little distinction was made at all between violent radicals and those who turned to the power of words; nor between Bonapartists, Jacobins and regicides, and sometimes moderate liberals were lumped together with these radicals as well. They were, after all, radicals; heirs of the French Revolution, adherents of the Terror, who embraced Thomas Paine's *The Rights of Man* as their foundational text. Most of them were republicans, especially in France, Italy and the Low Countries. They favoured a representative democracy, based on universal suffrage (and the elimination of class and censitary suffrage), and

[2] See Schechter, *A Genealogy of Terror in Eighteenth-Century France*, 204–5.
[3] J. Bohstedt, 'The Myth of the Feminine Food Riot. Women as Proto-Citizens in English Community Politics, 1790–1810', in H. Applewhite and D. Levy, *Women and Politics in the Age of Democratic Revolution* (Ann Arbor: University of Michigan Press, 1990), 21–60; R. Marjolin, 'Troubles provoqués en France par la disette de 1816–1817', *Revue d'histoire moderne*, 8: Nov.–Dec. (1933), 423–60.

passionately believed in the sovereignty and power of the people. They advocated the constitution of year two of the French Revolution and the Spanish constitution of 1812. They were the sharpest critics of the Vienna Convention, and of the way in which areas were confiscated and borders drawn over the heads of the people.[4] In the Rhineland, which was assigned to Prussia,[5] in Lombardy, which went to Austria,[6] in Belgium, which was annexed by Dutch King Willem I,[7] and in Poland, which was divvied up between Prussia and Russia, Metternich's alleged 'radicals' (real or supposed) coupled their resentment to a growing sense of nationalism as well. Radicalism was also primarily elitist and conspiratorial, and often lost itself in its own overly secretive plotting and scheming.[8] But radicalism became first and foremost a calling, a martyr's cause and a professional activity in reaction to the repression people had to endure from 1814 onwards. The 'professional radical' or revolutionary thus entered an unintended alliance with the new guard of professional policemen, deployed by the 'men of 1815' to fight 'terror'.

The problem in France was, moreover, according to the Allied ministers, that these radicals had made a pact with remnants of the army. Dangerous malcontents of demobilized, discharged and dismissed soldiers made for a separate category of disgruntled citizens – that, from Metternich's perspective, reinforced the already existing amalgam of radical rascals and played into the Allied fear of terror as the two-headed monster of revolutionary zeal and Bonapartist military aggression. In this case (as in others), Metternich's assessment was, however, exaggerated. Even though that cohort of veterans, soldiers and officers on half pay made up about 3.7 per cent of the French population, they were less of a risk for peace and order than Metternich thought.[9] The veterans were more often than not themselves the victims of violent outbursts; for example, in Marseilles, a large number of North African veterans from Napoleon's Egyptian army were murdered by the ultra-royalist population. On 2 August, the Bonapartist general Brune was attacked and shot down while briefly visiting Avignon to have his passport checked.[10] Moreover, these veteran groups certainly were not all cut from the same cloth. That they were

[4] J. Dinwiddy, 'English Radicals and the French Revolution, 1800–1850', in F. Furet and M. Ozouf (eds.), *The Transformation of Political Culture 1789–1848*, vol. 3, (Oxford: Pergamon Press, 1990), 447–66.
[5] J. Sperber, *Rhineland Radicals. The Democratic Movement and the Revolution of 1848–1849* (Princeton: Princeton University Press, 1991).
[6] F. Della Peruta, 'Le campagne lombarde nel Risorgimento', in F. Della Peruta (ed.), *Democrazia e socialismo nel Risorgimento* (Rome: Riuniti, 1965), 37–58.
[7] Cf. M. Robijns, *Radicalen in Nederland, 1840–1851* (Leiden: Universitaire Pers, 1967).
[8] Broers, *Europe after Napoleon*, 67–79.
[9] A. Spitzer, *Old Hatreds and Young Hopes. The French Carbonari against the Bourbon Restoration* (Cambridge, MA: Harvard University Press, 1971), 20–1; Cookson, 'Regimental Worlds', 23–42; Petiteau, 'Survivors of War', 50.
[10] Petiteau, 'Survivors of War', 48–9.

lurking on the edges of society, behind the scenes or in the bowels of the larger
cities, waiting for their chance to unseat the Bourbons again, was therefore
much more of a legend than a real threat.[11]

Yet, via the Council, Metternich unleashed a veritable hunt for radical plots and
collaborators. The twin brother of the Revolution was sedition, the fear of the fifth
column, the conspiratorial circle, which, having once beheaded a legitimate prince
with the consent of parliament, had no qualms about that happening a second or
third time. In 1815, in addition to the revolutionary and Napoleonic legacy of
a centralized police state, the European monarchs also inherited the spectre of
conspiracy. On the left and on the right that apparition was bandied about,
conjured up and used and abused for one's own political purposes.

In France, conspiratorial clubs with adventurous names, such as *Nain
Tricolore*, the *Lion Dormant*, the *Patriotes*, the *Amis de la Patrie*, and the
Épingle Noire, did indeed exist. They were consequently rolled up one after
the other and brought to trial, leading to long prison sentences and executions.
According to historians like Zamoyski, these kinds of clubs were not at all
dangerous, but were targeted by royalist police forces to make a political point,
to satisfy the premonitions of the conservative chamber and to expand the
police's own clout.[12] Yet, that inference does not give credit to the fact that the
fear of terror was very real, both within French bureaucratic circles and
amongst the Allies. Gruner's reports, moreover, proved that incidents and
alarmist rumours kept the country on alert. At the same time, the Allied secret
service was not expanded, but dissolved in 1816, and the new French minister
of police, Decazes, was far more moderate than the Ultras pressed him to be.
Both the French and the Allied ministers were wedged between two fires. On
the one hand, the Ultras pressed them for being too tolerant and even negligent
when it came to the alleged terrorist and radical practices and plots. On the
other, commanders like Wellington, and initially also Gruner, tried to work
with the Bonapartist officials in government. Decazes also was no dogmatist,
and attempted to pacify the loyal liberals. For him, excessively harsh policies
and measures would have an adverse effect, and would sooner incite the many
veterans, soldiers on half pay and radicals towards more hostility and actual
rebellion than placate them.[13]

However, with Gruner and Tsar Alexander sidelined and occupied with
their divine designs for salvation and security, Metternich took the initiative
into his own hands, and urged the Allied Council to hold to a tighter course
and address the 'Jacobin' threat more firmly – for, according to Metternich,

---

[11] Ibid., 55.

[12] Zamoyski, *Phantom Terror*.

[13] Spitzer, *Old Hatreds*, 24–5; J. Robert, *La Police sous MM. les Duc Decazes, Comte Anglès et
      Baron Mounier* (Paris, 1821); A. Ducoin, *Paul Didier. Histoire de la conspiration de 1816*
      (Paris: Dentu, 1844).

there was a direct connection between radical writings, alleged Bonapartist conspiracies and the security of Europe as a whole. Moreover, while Metternich was in search of alleged radical plotters, the radical publicists themselves found in him, and in the 'council of princes', a welcome target for taking stabs at.

On to a Police State

Metternich's imperial fears regarding the centrifugal forces of rebellion, succession and republicanism fit seamlessly with the vengeful, ultra-royalist tendencies of the Chamber of Deputies – or as Louis XVIII called it, the *Chambre Introuvable* ('Unobtainable Chamber'). In December 1815, a few hours after Ney's execution, Richelieu had tried to mitigate the social climate by introducing a more extensive amnesty law. In Richelieu's bill, everyone active during the Hundred Days would be pardoned, except for those on the king's list of 24 July, the Bonaparte family and those already charged. But Richelieu had failed to consult with the Ultras, who were able to turn Richelieu's conciliatory proposal around, after extending the list of those excluded from amnesty even further – mainly with the addition of regicides and still more of Napoleon's generals.[14] That was 'an unexpected turn', according to the British ambassador Stuart, who (quite rightly) saw the measure to be an alarming 'engine of violence'.[15]

Starting in October, the Chamber had already passed a series of laws that made it much easier to arrest and detain people without trial. On 23 October 1815, 56 deputies voted against and 294 in favour of legalizing what was in effect the right of arbitrary detention. Incitement, more broadly defined in a new law, was also made a criminal offence; anyone who threatened or insulted the life, authority or person of the king or his family, orally or in writing, was subject to prosecution.[16] Although Richelieu and his government tried to use 'moderation' and legitimacy, the ministerial guidelines for a restrained and limited purification of the administrative system were interpreted and applied much more broadly by the many vengeful and conservative provincial prefects.[17] Based on these new laws, legislative revisions and the creation of military courts, six to nine thousand of those accused were convicted between 1815 and 1818, often without a jury and without the possibility of appeal.[18] Under the pretext of 'public security', civil rights were suspended,

---

[14] Resnick, *The White Terror*, 71–7.
[15] Report of Stuart to Castlereagh, 14 December 1815, TNA, FO 27/120.
[16] Resnick, *The White Terror*, 78–80.
[17] Ibid., 11–12, 17.
[18] Resnick contests the usual number of 9,000, which circulated among those living at the time. He considers the number of 70,000 arrests, which arose later, as impossible, and suggests instead that there were approximately 6,000 convictions. See Ibid., 114–15.

suspects imprisoned without trial and 'seditious writings' forbidden. All regicides were banned eternally from France. This was still far fewer than in the
Red Terror, between 1793 and 1794, when some 17,000 suspects were sentenced to death.[19] But, for the Ultras, it was apparent that even with a *Charte*
and a constitutional regime, their White Terror could very well be institutionalized (once open massacres were avoided) and that, even more importantly,
the Allied ministers stood by and let it happen.[20]

This increase in repressive legislation and the political 'shift to the right' did
not only occur in France. Elsewhere in Europe, too, even in Britain, constitutional liberties were curtailed and protests were decisively suppressed. The
hard core of the state's authority, common to most every regime after 1815,
was what Marc Raeff referred to as a 'well-ordered police state'.[21] Whether
constitutional monarchies, the parliamentary British government or the
enlightened authoritarian regimes of Prussia, Russia and Austria, they all
embraced Napoleon's reforms in the areas of the police, criminal justice and
domestic oversight. According to Broers, this form of reformed centralized
administration was especially appreciated in Prussia and Austria, both in
principle and in practice.[22] But echoes of such centralized bureaucratic systems
can also be found in countries such as the Netherlands, Baden, Bavaria and
Italy. Even liberal Britain implemented its own form of centralized police
regulation. As Castlereagh – who had experienced Irish rebellion personally –
explained in parliament, the threat of terror was not only a French concern, for
the spirit of revolution, cached 'in the concentration of military Jacobinism',
spread through the whole of the continent.[23]

The question, therefore, was not whether there was a union of police states
in post-Napoleonic Europe, but the degree to which those police states differed
from each other; likewise, the extent to which they used that framework to
focus on the enemies of the new order – the revolutionaries, republicans,
Bonapartists or also the moderate liberals – and how many liberties they
were willing to relinquish or curtail. The Allied Council in Paris was in any
case the central forum in which the pivotal, imperialist players discussed their
security preferences and polities. After the implementation of the uniform
passport and the Bonapartist exiles, in 1816 Metternich succeeded in putting
the radical publicists, writers and editors at the top of the Allied agenda.

---

[19] Ibid., 95–7.
[20] Ibid., 120.
[21] M. Raeff, *The Well-Ordered Police State. Social and Institutional Change through Law in
the Germanies and Russia, 1600–1800* (New Haven: Yale University Press, 1983).
[22] Broers, *Europe after Napoleon*, 22–3. See also Sperber, *Revolutionary Europe*, 325–48;
D. Laven and L. Riall (eds.), *Napoleon's Legacy. Problems of Government in Restoration
Europe* (Oxford: Berg, 2000).
[23] Castlereagh, 'Address upon the Treaties with Foreign Powers', 19 February 1816, in
Hansard (ed.), *The Parliamentary Debates*, vol. 33, 692–3.

The Brussels Hotbed

In the more conservative, enlightened-absolutist countries, the police state was hardly ever tempered by constitutional restrictions that sought to protect civil liberties. In countries where a liberal government was in power, or where a liberal opposition could make itself heard in parliament, these restrictions were less easily sidestepped. In Britain, the Netherlands, some German principalities such as Baden, but also in France there was talk of a very vocal culture of opposition and debate. From October 1815 onwards, however, the margin of latitude in France gradually decreased.[24] In anticipation of the amnesty law, which was announced on 7 January 1816, a steady stream of radicals – those banished or earmarked for prosecution, or simply departing of their own accord – left for the Netherlands, and for French-speaking Brussels in particular. Officially banished or not, they hoped to escape the long arm of the Ultras, and to be able to build a new life for themselves. The Dutch historian Colenbrander has noted how their move replicated the flight of Dutch patriots in 1787, who sought their refuge in France.[25] In that relatively safe haven, they sought each other out around newspapers and in salons, and continued their work even more vigorously.

The Netherlands as such was not known as a hotbed of radicalism and rebellion. Admittedly, a culture of resistance and protest had developed under the rule of Napoleon's brother Louis and during the period of incorporation into France, such that Napoleon would note in response to an uprising in Amsterdam in 1810 that '[t]he people are never right to start a revolt'.[26] But because the majority of the protests stemmed from dissatisfaction with the French occupation and the continental blockade, things had become much calmer after Willem I's return.[27] Yet, in the Netherlands, just as elsewhere in Europe,[28] (violent) protest during the Napoleonic turmoil had become a tried and tested stock-in-trade, a political repertoire that did not promptly dissipate after 1813.[29] And unlike Louis Napoleon or his brother, both of whom stood ready to suppress with brute force those who revolted, Willem I (Fig. 6.1) was not inclined to forfeit the goodwill in the Netherlands and the new Belgian provinces, or to infringe his

---

[24] Broers, *Europe after Napoleon*, 39–40.

[25] H. Colenbrander, 'Willem I en de mogendheden, 1815–1824', *De Gids*, 95 (1931), 370–407, here: 375.

[26] J. Joor, '"A Very Rebellious Disposition": Dutch Experience and Popular Protest under the Napoleonic Regime (1806–1813)', in Forrest, Hagemann and Rendall (eds.), *Soldiers*, 186–9.

[27] Joor, 'A Very Rebellious Disposition', 191.

[28] See S. Woolf, *Napoleon's Integration of Europe* (London/New York: Routledge, 1991); Broers, *Europe under Napoleon*; M. Rowe (ed.), *Collaboration and Resistance in Napoleonic Europe. State-Formation in an Age of Upheaval, 1800–1815* (Basingstoke: Palgrave Macmillan, 2003).

[29] Joor, 'A Very Rebellious Disposition', 193–7.

Figure 6.1   Willem I, Sovereign Prince of the Netherlands 1813–15, king of the Netherlands 1815–40. Portrait by Joseph Paelinck, 1819. (Rijksmuseum, Amsterdam)

own constitution, the ink of which was barely dry. Brussels therefore quickly became a hub of liberal and Catholic dissatisfaction with Willem I's centralizing ambitions, and likewise a magnet for French exiles. Radical writers, bookshops and publishing houses found a welcome base in the Burgundian city of Brussels. Pamphlets, diatribes, caricatures and articles soon appeared, aimed primarily at the Bourbons and the restoration regime. But the Allied sovereigns also got an earful.[30]

The Allies initially had no idea as to the clouds of opposition that were beginning to gather – owing in part to their own security measures and

[30]   See W. Lemmens, '"Une terre hospitalière et libre"? Franse migranten tussen restauratie en revolutie in het Brussel van Willem I, 1815–1830', *De Negentiende Eeuw*, 36:4 (2012), 263–84; Lemmens, 'Het ontluikend liberalisme: Franse migranten, hun netwerken en journalistieke activiteiten in de Zuidelijke Nederlanden, 1815–1830', *Revue Belge de philologie et d'histoire*, 89: 3/4 (2011), 1165–91.

France's repressive legislation – just across the border. But it did not take long before they started to see the smoke curling, emitted by the fires of radical opposition. In October 1815, the French diplomat Caraman lodged a first formal complaint with the Dutch government regarding the presence of Fouché in Belgium, who had not set off for Dresden straight away, but hung around in Brussels. He was not alone; 'enemies of state' such as the Bonapartist Count Réal and the regicides Merlin de Douai and Garnier de Saintes had also made themselves a new living in exile there. De Saintes had immediately set to publishing an opposition periodical, *Le Surveillant*. More veteran regicides followed suit, such as Cambacérès, the painter David, and Sieyès, and many other convention members, such as Prieur, Ramel, Letourneur, Cochon, Cambon, Pommereul and Alquier. The generals Lobau, Vandamme, Davout and Cunéo d'Ornano also took refuge there. Napoleon's former general Exelmans even strode through the Brussels salons proclaiming that Ney would be avenged.[31]

The regicides were not the threat that loomed the largest. Richelieu himself admitted that most of them were far too old to be up to new malice. But others, young Frenchmen, former soldiers or journalists who had to flee France, continued their forays from the Netherlands' southern provinces. A certain Jean-Baptiste Teste had settled in Liège and published from there the anti-Russian and anti-Austrian political magazine *Le Mercure*. Teste was a lawyer from Provence, who had briefly been the director of police in Lyons under Napoleon. After Napoleon's defeat, he turned to the Allies to help him find employment. For example, he had offered Justus Gruner his services as a liaison between the Allied ministers and a British group that claimed, on behalf of Castlereagh, to be able to put the Duke of Orleans – Louis Philippe II – on the throne. Gruner, who initially felt for this kind of constitutional-liberal initiative, became intrigued with Teste. But at the end of October, Teste had to leave the country at short notice, with the French police hot on his heels. Filled with 'bitterness' for the British and the French, as well as for being forced to leave a 'beloved young lady' behind, with Gruner's help he fled France in a Prussian uniform, accompanied by Fallenstein, a Prussian lieutenant.[32] Hence, provided with an Allied passport (a consequence of Metternich's uniform rule), Teste was able to continue his opposition to the authoritarian regimes of Europe from Belgium. It seemed as though the Allied (and French) fight against terror was now generating its own hotbed of radicalization.

---

[31] Colenbrander, 'Willem I en de mogendheden', 377.
[32] Reports of Gruner, 18, 20, 23 October 1815, GStA PK, VI. HA Nl. Hardenberg 10a.

Another List

In the Allied fight against terror, the exiles in Belgium and the role of the Netherlands became one of the hottest issues in Allied talks, and the subject of the first major dispute among the ministers.[33]

On 25 February 1816, the Council discussed at length the Belgian exiles and various ways in which to silence them. According to Metternich, the inflammatory writings and flares of revolution spread from Brussels throughout Europe. The Austrian minister was quite incensed that his 'uniform measures' had not been implemented consistently by the French and Dutch police. That these regicides and Bonapartists had been banished was fine; that was what the lists of 24 July 1815 and January 1816 were meant to accomplish. But the Allied Council, as instigated by Metternich, had also made it known that the exiles were only to be allowed to settle in one of the four countries of the Quadruple Alliance, where they could be placed under proper supervision. The Netherlands was too close, and Willem's government was too liberal and too weak to keep these exiles under control. The Council therefore decided to ask Richelieu for a list of names of all the French refugees in Belgium: who was involved, who had issued them a passport, and what was to happen to them now? The Prussian envoy, in addition, requested that an overview of all the exiles from France (including those staying in other countries) be compiled, so that he could see if some had defected to any of the smaller German states.[34]

Subsequently, Robbert Fagel, the Dutch envoy to Paris, and Nagell, the Netherlands' minister of foreign affairs, were summoned. The Austrian envoy in The Hague, Franz Baron Binder von Krieglstein, impressed on the Dutch government that its task as a European stronghold was not only to build physical forts and barriers, but that the tide of revolutionary words and writings also had to be stemmed. It was, after all, 'the noble calling conferred upon it by the European alliance to be one of the main barriers countering the spirit of revolution'. That is why introducing stricter regulations for the press and the expulsion of French refugees was a 'measure to maintain both security and order in Europe'.[35] But King Willem and Falck, his general secretary and advisor, would only yield marginally. 'I have had Réal [one of the blacklisted radicals] set sail for America', the king replied. And Pommereul (another one) was to leave the country as soon as he was healthy. For the rest, since most of the refugees had a valid French passport with them, and next to none were even on the list of 24 July, nothing could be done. Likewise, the regicides that were banished in January 1816 had arrived wholly legally in the Netherlands before

---

[33] See especially (Van) Sas, *Onze natuurlijkste bondgenoot*, 125–62.

[34] Discussion of Allied Council, plus exchange of letters with Richelieu, 25 February 1816, TNA, FO 146/6, 24ff.

[35] Colenbrander (ed.), *Gedenkstukken*, vol. 8.1, 216, 470. See also (Van) Sas, *Onze natuurlijkste bondgenoot*, 129.

that time. According to the tenacious monarch, out to defend his country's young national autonomy and constitutional rule against the pressures of the Allied Council, given that laws cannot work retroactively, there was no legal ground for extradition.[36] For Binder, representing the absolutist rule of Austria, this reasoning was absurd and, once again, proof of 'the fundamental inferiority of revolutionary creations such as constitutions'.[37]

In April 1816, a compromise seemed to have been found. The French envoy, La Tour du Pin, acknowledged 'the [Dutch] king's rigid, but scrupulous, observance of constitutional principles', and realized that France had to provide more legal evidence to substantiate its case.[38] Richelieu promised to draw up a list that indicated which refugees were actually dangerous. The passports of these would be rescinded, which would allow the Dutch government to treat them as exiles without a passport and deport them by 15 May 1816. Wellington, who had been asked by the Council to settle matters between The Hague and Paris, found it a sufficient step. The duke had had a visit from the young wife of Lobau (one of nineteen generals on the list of 24 July), who had charmed him into believing that her husband was decidedly harmless. Moreover, not being nearly the alarmist that Metternich was, the down-to-earth Wellington tried to set the minds of the Paris Conference at rest; after all, the Dutch king did have a point. Most of the exiles were 'old and infirm', and the king was already transferring them to the northern provinces, beyond the Rhine and away from France and the salons of Brussels. Wellington was also keenly aware of how thorny Willem's position was. The Dutch monarch had to deal with a strong constitution and a parliament that did not shy away from critique. In both the north and south, there was little empathy for the ultra-royalist French Chamber and the laws it enacted. Why would Willem want to defy his own parliament, and then 'submit himself to the dictates of the folly of the French Chamber of Deputies'? Wellington reminded the Allied Council that none of them had been very pleased with the wretched amnesty law of January:

> I believe there are none of us who did not feel that the Chamber of Deputies not only adopted a measure upon that occasion which every view of the internal policy of France ought to have induced them to refrain from, but that by adopting it they dragged the King and his ministers through the dirt.[39]

[36] Colenbrander, 'Willem I en de mogendheden', 377–9.
[37] (Van) Sas, *Onze natuurlijkste bondgenoot*, 131.
[38] Cited in Colenbrander (ed.), *Gedenkstukken*, vol. 8.1, 214. See also (Van) Sas, *Onze natuurlijkste bondgenoot*, 131.
[39] Wellington to Stuart, 9 May 1816, cited in Colenbrander, 'Willem I en de mogendheden', 378–9. The entire letter is in the protocols of the Allied Council of 12 May 1816, TNA, FO 146/6.

In addition, Stuart had let it be known that one of the radical newspapers in question, *Le Nain Tricolore*, was not being printed and distributed in Brussels at all, but in France itself.[40] In brief, decision makers had become a bit more patient with Willem, and their pressure on the Dutch government was tempered slightly.

The Allied Council accepted Wellington's advice for the time being, expecting that their priorities would not be provoked again anytime soon.[41] But these developments brought Castlereagh little solace, and Metternich even less. A coup by soldiers in Grenoble had just been thwarted, and the Council had also been informed, via 'the latest telegraphic news', that the uprisings in Dauphiné had been quashed, but the king had to send 4,000 men to Lyons and 3,000 to Grenoble to get the rioting under control.[42] In May, the Council discussed a plot against the French king by the alleged 'Patriots of 1816'. Sixty plotters had been arrested, and some of those had active contacts with refugees in the Netherlands.[43] In the meantime, invective pamphlets had started to flow again. Jean-Baptiste Teste's *Mercure* and Garnier de Saintes's *Surveillant* were merged into *Le Mercure Surveillant*, published in Liège. Guyet and Cauchois-Lemaire's *Nain Jaune* was printed in Brussels, and Lallemand's *Vrai Libéral* appeared in Ghent. The Dutch government was not in much of a hurry to take action against these journals or to deport these refugees. For Metternich, however, an all-too-familiar picture emerged: all these people, and the incidents surrounding them, were one of a kind and evidenced an increasingly active and organized 'armed Jacobinism'.[44]

Richelieu fuelled the concerns further. In mid-May, the ministers received an extensive list of names of 'conventional regicides', who, according to French records, had received a passport and had left for the Netherlands.[45] He explained to the Council in minute detail why these people were a risk to the security of France and Europe, and why they had to leave the Netherlands. Names were presented in an eleven-page table that included their geographical departments of origin and 'intelligence' detailing the specific risks associated with each individual in question.

Surprisingly, these risks were not expressed in the detailing of their politically disruptive activities. Neither was there any mention of someone's concrete criminal record. What was listed was the individual's emotional state, in

---

[40] Discussion of Allied Council, 3 March 1816, TNA, FO 146/6.
[41] Letter of Allied Council to Wellington, 12 May 1816, TNA, FO 146/6.
[42] Protocol of Allied Council, 15 May 1816, TNA, FO 146/6.
[43] Discussion of Allied Council, 5, 8, 12 May 1815, TNA, FO 146/6.
[44] In April, King Willem I had announced that Cambacérès and Sieyès could stay, owing to old age and illness. But Exelmans, Vandamme, Davoust, Dumonceau and Lavelli, among others, were still in the Netherlands. Discussion of Allied Council, 3, 7, 28 April, 1 May 1816, TNA, FO 146/6.
[45] Letter of Richelieu to the Allied Council, 19 May 1816, TNA, FO 146/6, 179.

combination with that person's financial means – these two dimensions taken together qualified someone as a greater or lesser danger for society. For example, it was noted that Alquier had the 'means' to finance 'plots abroad'. Beffroy, on the other hand, had 'no budget whatsoever'. The entry for André Dumont, from the department of the Somme, included an explicit warning: he was 'one of the most dangerous terrorists, a dangerous man', and still 'only' fifty-one years old. The epithet 'angry demagogue' suffices for many of those listed. Garnier de Saintes, who published *Le Surveillant*, was also considered dangerous. Apparently, someone's long-term influence also mattered. For example, Gleizal was also categorized as 'very dangerous', primarily because his epistles could light a fire under people in his department, the Ardèche. This table certainly did not entail sufficient judicial proof or concrete evidence to start an extradition request. Neither was it merely a listing of vengeful grievances. The table was a central, national and even international instrument to redraw boundaries of threat and insecurity. The logics of evidence were risk-oriented: not someone's concrete criminal record or criminal behaviour, but their potential danger for posing a political threat in the near future was the decisive criterion here. Not even the individual's alleged intention was the most significant point; financial means, good health, age (not being too old) and established contacts were sufficient causes. Remarkably enough, temperament was decisive as well. The table detailed whether an individual had an 'exalted', 'ardent revolutionary', 'furious republican', 'bloodthirsty' or 'violent' temperament – all epitaphs intended to disqualify someone on emotional grounds. Interestingly enough, the logic of the list also dictated when suspects were not considered an immediate risk to society. A small number of regicides were absolved from being a direct threat based on their alleged emotional state: 'Mathieu', from Oise, was 'moderate', and had voted against 'the terrorists' in 1795.[46] The counterpoint to extremism and intensity was composure and 'moderation'. With these risk assessments, neatly transcribed and categorized, the fear of 'the spirit of 1789' resurfaced again – only to be tamed by 'the spirit of 1815': that of calm, tranquillity and balance. Dangerous were the unruly and passionate souls, who with their energy and resources could stir up and

---

[46] 'Notice sur les Conventionnels Régicides qui ont pris des Passeports pour le Royaume des Paysbas'. Appended to protocol of 19 May 1816, TNA, FO 146/6. Names: Alquier, Beffroy, Begard [Beaugeard], Bonet fils [Bonnet], Bouillerot, Boussion, Cambacérès, Cambon, Carpentier, Cavaignac, Choudieu [Charlier?], Cochon, Cordier, David, Debry, Dulaure, Dumont, Duval, Eschassériaux, François, Garnier de Saintes, Gamon, Gay de Vernon, Gleizal, Goupilleau, Granet, Guyot [Florent-Guiot], Hounier [?], Ingrand, Jouenne [Jouenne-Longchamp], Lahosdinière [La Bossière?], Lalloy, Lefiot, Lejeune, Lesage-Senault, Le Tourneur (×2) [?], Maigrit, Mailhe, Mallarmé, Marragon, Massieu, Matthieu, Méaulle, Merlin de Douai, Mioche [?], Nion, Paganel, Piorry, Pocholle, Pottier [?], Prieur, Ramel, Ribui [Ribérau?], Robert, Rouband, Roux, Savornin, Sieyès, Thabaud de Bois-La-Reine, Vadier.

support revolution and terror again. The elderly, impoverished and moderate or meek spirits were considered less risky.

The list did little to abate the confusion among the Allied ministers concerning the right course of action. The Austrians were in favour of tougher measures, and could not care less about the constitutional and legal concerns of the Dutch. Castlereagh was increasingly fed up with the Dutch and their scruples. Richelieu supported this harsh approach, but felt that each of the Allied countries had to act separately, since his apprehensions about the Paris Conference, developing more and more in the direction of a European directorate, had mounted. Then again, Wellington and the British envoy in The Hague, Clancarty, were more sympathetic to the position of the Dutch government. However dangerous, most of the people on this list nonetheless had a valid and legal passport for the Netherlands, which they had received from the French authorities themselves. The Prussian minister Goltz, coming from an impeccable bureaucratic background, also let his colleagues in Paris know that this blunder was France's, and not a Dutch one. Willem I had the right and the paragraphs on his side.[47]

Once again, it was up to Wellington to solve the impasse. He advised Richelieu to collect more evidence during the summer, and especially concrete judicial proof, to further substantiate the charge of 'calumny'. At the same time, he enjoined the Dutch monarch to subject the persons on the list to stricter control, to prepare for their deportation nonetheless, and to adopt stricter press laws straight away. He reinforced this admonition with an ominous warning: given such an 'abuse' directed to the address of the French king – the Belgian pamphlets being the case in point – it was not illogical that the French court would see in it 'grounds for war'.[48]

Allied 'Help' for the Netherlands

During the summer, Richelieu, and the Austrian representatives especially, jacked up the pressure within the Allied Conference. Richelieu produced a list of people who had been granted a passport to Austria, to determine whether any had secretly fled to the Netherlands – which proved not to be the case. The French government also officially rescinded all passports issued to regicides.[49] But that was not enough for Austria. In the meantime, Emperor Franz had personally read a copy of Le Nain Jaune and, according to the Austrian envoy Baron von Vincent, had been outraged. He found the satirizing of European

[47] Communiqué from the Prussian court to the Council, discussed during its meeting of 19 June 1816, TNA, FO 146/6, 284ff.

[48] Protocols of Allied Council, 9 June 1816, TNA, FO 146/6.

[49] Letter of Richelieu to the Council, 24 June, with 'Notice sur les régicides exclus de France par l'Art 7 de la Loi du 12 Janvier. Et sur les individués compris dans l'ordonnance du 23 Juillet qui ont reçu des Passeports pour l'Autriche', TNA, FO 146/6.

monarchs 'scandalous'; what kind of constitution was it that would keep one from acting against such publishers? That is why Metternich had drawn up a plan of action and submitted it, via Vincent, to the Paris Conference on 24 August.

The first and simplest step towards doing something about this was to ensure that the troublemakers did not land up in France's neighbouring countries. Each of the European courts was once again called upon to monitor this matter more closely. Likewise, a 'curtain' had to be erected between the Netherlands and France, via the implementation of border controls on traffic and the dissemination of writings, so that these sorts of insults and attacks would no longer assail the French court. Secondly, the Council had to be more active in countering 'this strange tolerance' in the Netherlands, because it was clearly losing its grip as a stronghold against agitation and revolution. The Dutch government was apparently too 'weak' and too hamstrung by its own constitution and parliament. Since it was determined to hold on to 'the most devastating interpretation' of 'citizens' rights', it was the duty of the other courts to 'help' the Dutch monarch. The way in which the Netherlands gave shape to the 'constitutional principles' was simply incompatible with 'the repose of Europe'.[50]

The young Dutch monarchy now found itself at the sharp end. Emperor Franz, with the support of the Russian tsar, his envoy, and now also the Prussian diplomats – both the Russians and the Prussians now also no longer wished to tolerate the steady stream of insults lobbed at the European monarchs from Belgium – seemed intent on using the Council as a European police force against the Netherlands.[51] If the Netherlands was not able to fulfil its function as 'bulwark', then it was no longer the 'lapdog of the powers' – and its very right to exist, or at least the autonomy of the new state, was up for discussion.

Once again, France and Britain defended the Netherlands' right to self-determination – not because they wanted to protect Willem, or were such great advocates of constitutional freedoms, but because they wanted to avert another dynamic: the Council was not to behave like a European intervention force that interfered with the internal affairs of other states based on its own authority and of its own accord. Wellington wearily saw how the foreign ministers in Paris were on the way 'to erect themselves into a Power'.[52] And Richelieu, too, who saw the need for measures, was not in favour of collective action on the

---

[50] 'Déclaration', from the Viennese court to the Council, annex 50 to the protocol of 24 August 1816, TNA, FO 146/14.

[51] See for example Nesselrode to Alexander I, reporting on Pozzo di Borgo's *dépêches* from the Allied Council, 17/29 August 1816, in Ministerstvo inostrannykh del CCCP (ed.), *Vneshniaia politika Rossii*, vol. 1, 241.

[52] Colenbrander (ed.), *Gedenkstukken*, vol. 8.1, 38; (Van) Sas, *Onze natuurlijkste bondgenoot*, 131 n. 60.

part of the Council itself. A standing Allied institution that intervened in the internal affairs of other countries, as 'a kind of dictatorship', was not an attractive prospect for the French government either.[53] So, Wellington trumped Metternich by, four days later, submitting a 'Memorandum regarding the libels published in the Low Countries' of his own. In this note, he admitted that things were going from bad to worse, as not only refugees and exiles but also more and more young journalists and other agitators had begun to associate with the oppositional salons and publications. Their 'rogue writings' sparked 'rebellion', 'perverting public opinion'. The Dutch king was proving to be an ungrateful monarch; after all, the kingdom had been the fruit of the Allies' efforts.[54]

With these condemning words, Wellington joined the chorus of irritated Allied ministers. He proposed a package of measures that was, however, different from the Austrian plan and did not provide for a military intervention. First, not the Conference, but the four courts separately would present their protests (démarches) to the Dutch government. Second, all four courts would merge the lists of July 1815, January 1816 and Richelieu's list of May 1816, and consider that new inventory in its entirety as the list of those 'to be banished' – with the list being dispatched throughout Europe. Third, the Dutch government had to prosecute and punish (punir) everyone who misused the freedom of the press and went against the spirit of friendship (amitié) with the other European states. And finally, all other French refugees who were not on a list would be deported immediately if they were associates (associés) of persons on the July or January lists. The Conference found these stipulations acceptable, and Wellington's plan was adopted.[55]

On 8 September, in The Hague, La Tour du Pin's high-pitched complaint – about the cowardice of the Dutch government towards 'anarchy, unrest and disorder' caused by 'revolutionaries' and 'assassins' – arrived on the doorstep of the minister of foreign affairs, Van Nagell. He did not understand why the Dutch government did not intervene, since not only the king of France, but every king, yes, the société Européenne as a whole was under attack from the sordid Belgian press.[56] Within the Paris Council, Richelieu (as ex officio member) and Wellington also spoke with force about the failing Dutch government. But, at the same time, the British diplomats in The Hague, Clancarty and Chad, acted as buffer. Fencing with a threatening intervention by the Conference (and Austria), they presented themselves as helpful allies,

---

[53] (Van) Sas, *Onze natuurlijkste bondgenoot*, 132, 134; G. de Bertier de Sauvigny, *Metternich et la France après le Congrès de Vienne*, vol. 1 (Paris: Presses Continentales, 1968), 115; Colenbrander (ed.), *Gedenkstukken*, vol. 8.1, 225.

[54] Memorandum, 29 August 1816, attachment of Wellington to the protocol of 29 August 1816, TNA, FO 146/14.

[55] Ibid.

[56] La Tour du Pin to Van Nagell, 8 September 1816, NL-HaNA, 2.05.01, inv. no. 22.

making suggestions to the king and his ministers for a more effective approach on their part. Van Nagell could find some understanding for the Allies' ideas. As he explained in a report to the king, he fully agreed with the protests from Paris regarding 'the shameful abuse of the freedom of the press' and the condemnation of 'an evil that threatens the general tranquillity of Europe'. He also opined that the government had to put an end to the 'incendiary tracts and diatribes against the monarchs and peoples of Europe', to those 'wretched Jacobin pamphlets' coming from that 'horde of mere scribblers who find their reason for being in sending the most heinous libels into the world'. It was especially annoying that

> these diatribes are written by foreigners who, as a token of their acknowl-
> edgement of the hospitality that they enjoy under the mild blessings of
> your Majesty in these provinces, spare no effort ... to instigate insurrec-
> tion in the neighbouring realms and to make this kingdom look like the
> source of all the venom disturbing Europe.

According to the lawyer Van Nagell, also citing the 'immortal Burke', the king had to step in. It was certainly not contrary to 'the general law of nations' when a state took action against 'foreigners' within its borders who were busy 'giving rise to civil wars'.[57]

At the end of September, the Lower House adopted, by a large majority (64 to 4), a law proposed by the government that made offending foreign sovereigns and governments a criminal act.[58] At the same time, that was to be enough; a separate 'Alien Bill' that would see unwanted foreigners deported without due process – which is what Binder wanted – was a bridge too far. The Allied ministers had to distance themselves from 'the pretension ... of governing Europe', according to Nagell. 'The tone and line of their proceedings are calculated to disgust and irritate all the minor governments.'[59]

Calamity Avoided?

With the new law in place, minister of justice Van Maanen could finally charge and fine the editor of *Le Mercure Surveillant*, Garnier de Saintes – the law made provision for a penalty of 500 florins. However, it was hard to corner the effervescent opposition figures in Brussels. They quickly set up an emergency fund, a *caisse de sustentation*, from which they could pay the fines. The wealthy

---

[57] Report from Van Nagell to the king, 11 September 1816, NL-HaNA, 2.05.01, inv. no. 28. See also W. Sautyn Kluit, 'Dagbladvervolgingen in België', *Bijdragen voor Vaderlandsche Geschiedenis en Oudheidkunde*, 3:6 (1892), 318–19.

[58] (Van) Sas, *Onze natuurlijkste bondgenoot*, 133–4; Tweede Kamer (ed.), *Handelingen*, 20 September 1816, 264–9; annexes, 1028–30.

[59] (Van) Sas, *Onze natuurlijkste bondgenoot*, 135; Colenbrander (ed.), *Gedenkstukken*, vol. 8.1, 43–4.

regicides, journalists and even the French Duke of Orleans and the British Duke of Kent (who lived on the continent) contributed.[60] The Dutch 500-florin fine, therefore, had hardly any effect – except for demonstrating that Richelieu, with his logic in estimating risks based on financial resources, did have a point. Garnier paid his with a chuckle, and within two months was back to publishing. The other magazines also sharpened their pens. At the beginning of 1817, *Le Libéral*, which regarded itself as the torchbearer of the *opposition européenne* against the restoration regimes, focused its cross hairs on the French envoy La Tour du Pin.[61]

The Dutch government did not seem to realize what the outcome of their legally sound but politically lax attitude would be; for the envoys of Austria, Prussia and Russia were already discussing together the possibility of establishing an administrative division between the north and the south, i.e. of installing that 'curtain' between the Netherlands and France themselves.[62] In February 1817, Metternich congratulated Wellington on the decisive action of the British government against the 1816 Spa Fields riots in Islington and the introduction of repressive legislation.[63] But he warned the duke in the same letter: 'the kingdom of the Netherlands is today one of the centres, and perhaps the most active centre of disorder of every kind'. How else was it possible that the British Lord Kinnaird's call for a 'universal republic' and the abolition of hereditary monarchy met hardly any opposition in Brussels? After having written a friendly but firm warning to King Willem I, Tsar Alexander circulated a memorandum in March 1817 in which he called on the Allied ministers to take firmer action against the French political refugees, 'the representatives, the organs of the revolutionary spirit which hovers over Europe and perhaps over the two hemispheres of the globe'.[64] Metternich agreed with the tsar completely: only the Allied ministers were in a position to put a stop to this; for example, by having the Duke of Wellington inform the Dutch government of the possibility of a military intervention.[65]

[60] (Van) Sas, *Onze natuurlijkste bondgenoot*, 153.
[61] Ibid., 139; Sautyn Kluit, 'Dagbladvervolgingen in België', 324. See also Clancarty's letter to Wellington, 5 April 1817, NL-HaNA, 2.05.01, inv. no. 770.
[62] (Van) Sas, *Onze natuurlijkste bondgenoot*, 138–9. See, for example, Metternich's letter to his ambassador, Lebzeltern, in St Petersburg, 26 March 1817. Intercepted copy in NL-HaNA, 2.05.01, inv. no. 770.
[63] Metternich to Wellington, 17 February 1817, *WSD*, vol. 11, 632.
[64] Letter of Alexander I to Willem I, 27 September/9 October 1816, in Ministerstvo inostrannykh del CCCP (ed.), *Vneshniaia politika Rossii*, vol. 1, 255–6; N. Mikhailovich (ed.), *Doniesienia avstriiskovgo poslannika pri russkom dvore Lebzelterna za 1816–1828 gody* (St Petersburg, 1913), 34; A. Polovtsoff, *Le Duc de Richelieu. Correspondance et Documents, 1766–1823*, vol. 1, 222, 475, 546.
[65] Metternich to Lebzeltern (the Austrian envoy in St Petersburg), 26 March 1817, NL-HaNA, 2.05.01, inv. no. 770.

On 11 April 1817, the Paris Conference met to discuss the 'domestic tranquillity' of France and Europe. In doing so, all the ministers agreed that the Belgian threat did not stand alone; revolutionary fires were smouldering throughout Europe; the French refugees were spreading unrest and 'revolutionary behaviour' everywhere. 'Perturbations' were also occurring in Germany, Poland and Italy, directed at 'overthrowing the established and legally recognized treaty system'.[66] In other words, the Allied edifice, with its foundation of treaties that had taken so much blood, sweat and tears (of the ministers themselves) to negotiate, was crumbling at the corners. Each court, therefore, had to be summoned to curb that danger, which was increasing by the day, at once. At the same time, the British ministers once again had to play a double game. They agreed with Metternich's threat assessment, and made that well known. His suggestion of a joint military intervention, however, went directly against their grain. They therefore managed to convince the Allied Council to ask the respective constitutive courts to intervene in The Hague. The envoys of Berlin, St Petersburg and Vienna would indeed each emphatically urge the Dutch government to take action against and improve surveillance of the French exiles in Belgium.[67] And this was all the British ministers were prepared to do for The Hague. Castlereagh's patience with the Dutch was pretty much spent. He related to Clancarty in The Hague that he could no longer support the existence of an independent Dutch kingdom if it remained 'a nest of traitors and libellers'.[68]

Finally realizing the seriousness of the situation, thanks in large part to Clancarty, the British envoy in The Hague, the Dutch authorities saw to it that the *émigrés* Guyet, Cauchois-Lemaire, Lallemand and Brissot were escorted across the border by the end of May. The king personally tried to reassure the tsar, 'my brother', by announcing that he had now expelled everyone concerned and would no longer make any exceptions. If the 'High Allies' wanted to consolidate 'more and more the bases of the political and social order', then he could not be against it.[69] Van Nagell also announced new legislative proposals for October to keep a tighter lid on the press.[70] Wellington, who had gone to see how things were in Brussels – that 'nest of foreign

---

[66] See also Tsar Alexander's instructions, via Nesselrode, to Lieven (London), Stackelberg (Vienna) and Alopeus (Berlin), 5/17 April 1817, in Ministerstvo inostrannykh del CCCP (ed.), *Vneshniaia politika Rossii*, vol. 1, 507–8.

[67] Protocol of 11 April 1817 and Metternich's report, 17 May 1817, TNA, FO 146/15. See also Hardenberg's letter to Lebzeltern, 12 April 1817. Intercepted copy in NL-HaNA, 2.05.01, inv. no. 770.

[68] Castlereagh to Clancarty, 16 May 1817, cited in (Van) Sas, *Onze natuurlijkste bondgenoot*, 145.

[69] Tsar Alexander's letter to Willem I, 12 May; and Willem I to the tsar, 27 June 1817, NL-HaNA, 2.05.01, inv. no. 770.

[70] (Van) Sas, *Onze natuurlijkste bondgenoot*, 143–4.

libellers'[71] – was able to report satisfactorily to the Conference on 2 June that only the Count de Lobau and Mr Arnault were still in Brussels, that the Netherlands was now only allowing French people with valid passports to enter the country, and that every individual whose passport was rescinded by Paris would be deported from the country immediately. The government would also be taking temporary measures against journalists, albeit based on concrete evidence of bad behaviour. A generic 'Alien Bill' was too much to ask; Dutch criminal law did have provisions against crimes committed against persons, and these also held for foreigners. But crimes 'against the state', or against the 'security of the state' were unknown in that country – and required amendments to the constitution.[72] At that point Wellington found himself in the position of having to teach the Allied ministers a brief lesson on Dutch public administration. He explained to the Council that passing through a 'fundamental piece of legislation' in a system with two parliamentary chambers was a highly intricate and difficult business, especially if it concerned something – the comprehensive censorship of the press or the deportation of all foreigners – that touched on constitutional cornerstones.[73]

The ministers grudgingly accepted that explanation. The Austrian ministers even subscribed to the statement – quite far-reaching for the Allied Council – that all security measures had to be in accordance with the 'rights of the people'.[74] But that was theory. In practice, apart from Lobau, all regicides would be required to have left the Netherlands by August 1817. That same edict was sent as a circular (dated 14 July 1817) to all other small states. The question of rebellious refugees also concerned other countries, for example Italy. With so many Bonapartes living there, the Italian states were likewise considered a liability. The ministers thought that it would probably be better if Lucien Bonaparte were to move to Austria or Prussia. (Vincent proposed directing Lucien to Prussia, because there were so many French exiles in Austria, making it 'more difficult' to maintain the proper level of surveillance.)[75] Although the Dutch King Willem I personally approached the Paris Conference to argue for an exception, the generals Hullin and Lamarque, and the well-known lawyer Merlin, in spite of their advanced age

[71] Wellington to Clancarty, 3 December 1817, in Colenbrander (ed.), *Gedenkstukken*, vol. 8.1, 76.
[72] Report of the ministers of justice (Van Maanen) and foreign affairs (Van Nagell), secretary of state (A. R. Falck) and vice president of the Council of State (J. H. Mollerus) to the king. This report was a record of their deliberations, and contained a proposal to send to Clancarty and Wellington, 21 April 1817, NL-HaNA, 2.05.01, inv. no. 301.
[73] Protocol of 2 June 1817, TNA, FO 146/22.
[74] Protocol of 11 April 1817, TNA, FO 146/15.
[75] Protocol of 28 (or 30) June 1817 and protocols of 10, 19 July 1817, 6 August 1817, TNA, FO 146/22.

and weak constitution, also had to move to one of the countries of the
Quadruple Alliance.[76] In close consultation with the British envoy Clancarty,
and with the advice of Castlereagh and Wellington, the Dutch government
again set itself to redrafting the press law. On 10 November, the French envoy,
La Tour du Pin, returned to The Hague, to resume his diplomatic post. The
disaster seemed to have been averted for the time being.[77]

The stubborn resistance of the Dutch to the involvement of the Allied
Council did not go unnoticed. Other minor states were far more compliant.
Offers to help with the extradition came in immediately from Baden, the
Hanseatic cities and Parma.[78] The Court of Naples approached the Allied
ministers of its own accord. There, in the Kingdom of the Two Sicilies, the
government was worried about the Bonaparte family that was living in Rome.
In view of the impending elections for a new pope, and the ongoing corre-
spondence of Lucien in Rome with Joseph in the United States (where he had
fled at the end of August 1815), the risk of sedition and conspiracy was real. In
September 1817, the ambassador from Naples therefore asked the Allied
Council to extend Metternich's measure to include members of the
Bonaparte clan. Why should they be allowed to continue living in Rome?
That was too great a risk for the 'common security' in Italy. The Council
agreed, but contended that France had a say in the matter as well, and asked
Richelieu for advice.[79] A response was not forthcoming in the months that
followed; it took until 1821 for France to follow up. By then Napoleon was
dead, and the Bonapartist threat had passed. Minister Pasquier found 'no
objection' any more to issuing Lucien's son Charles a passport for
Philadelphia, where this Bonaparte offspring made a career as an
ornithologist.[80]

Ultra-royalist repression had begun to run its course already before the
death of Napoleon, so that many exiles and refugees were able to return to
France between 1818 and 1820.[81] The Allied pressure on the Netherlands,
therefore, also subsided. Between September 1817 and 1821, the Allied
Conference no longer put the refugee question on its agenda either. The
Belgian story did have a follow-up, however. Metternich's fear of the spreading
revolutionary flames seemed to come true in 1818, with Brussels as the seat of

---

[76] Protocol, with letter Willem I, of 27 August 1817, TNA, FO 146/15.
[77] (Van) Sas, *Onze natuurlijkste bondgenoot*, 151–5.
[78] Letter of Baden to the Council, 8 September 1817, attachment to the protocol of
13 September, TNA, FO 146/22; letter of Parma, attachment to the protocol of
30 August 1817, TNA, FO 146/22.
[79] Protocol of 13 September 1817; letter of Naples' ambassador to the Council,
12 September 1817; the Council's response to Richelieu, TNA, FO 146/22, 304ff.
[80] Discussion and protocol of September 1821, Paris ambassador's conference, TNA, FO
146/41.
[81] Colenbrander, 'Willem I en de mogendheden', 379–80.

the fire. Owing in part to strict French laws and the pressure of the Allies, many radicals had fled France and ended up in the Netherlands. The Dutch king correctly maintained that the old regicides had kept a low profile. But among the young radicals and the journalists – whom Wellington and Willem I had claimed fell under the rules on the freedom of the press, or were doing no one any harm – a bona fide conspiracy was brewing that would end in a terrorist attack – or so it seemed.

Assassins and 'Diabolical Plots'

Around 1815, real assailants, those who were actually motivated to kill for political reasons, were not (yet) labelled as terrorists, but as assassins, and their acts as 'attacks' (*attentats*). Conversely, the label 'terrorists' could be tagged to anyone relating to the revolutionary Reign of Terror in the 1790s, but increasingly also to individuals spreading revolutionary ideas – as was Metternich's habit. Real politically motivated attacks were rare, but Gruner's reports do indeed refer in a few places to concrete 'assassination' attempts. In August 1815, a plot to kill the Prussian King Friedrich Wilhelm III was unmasked as a provocation.[82] In his letter to the prefect of the Gard, Fouché decries the perpetrators of the White Terror attacks and describes 'assassins' as people who kill 'without the king's command'.[83] On 15 February 1817, Friedrich Wilhelm III congratulated 'my brother' George, the Prince Regent of Britain, on the foiled *assassinat* against his person after he had opened the parliamentary year.[84] In other words, there was a growing awareness and wariness in Europe of a dangerous phenomenon, that of the 'assassin' – someone who carried out politically motivated attacks. In public and political perception, these attacks were also increasingly tied to non-violent revolutionary, seditious or even 'terrorist' writings and expressions. Zamoyski describes how the 'phantom of terror' dominated public debates in Europe, although he underestimates the extent to which this scare in these first post-war years was very real, and not (yet) instrumentalized for budget purposes or expanding executive competences. In Britain, too, prompted by the fear of revolutionary rebellion – suspecting 'the existence of an extensive plan of insurrection' – a law was passed in March 1817 that suspended the *habeas corpus* provision and allowed for more repressive and preventative measures.[85] All sorts of resistance and rebellion, from food riots to the resistance of weavers

---

[82] Decazes to Hardenberg, 11 August 1815, GStA PK, III. HA I. no. 903.

[83] Fouché to the prefect, 26 August 1815, GStA PK, VI. HA Nl. Gruner, no. 41.

[84] Friedrich Wilhelm III to Prince Regent George of the United Kingdom, 15 February 1817; and George's response to Friedrich Wilhelm, 17 May 1817, GStA PK, III. HA I. no. 8884.

[85] Zamoyski, *Phantom Terror*, 149–51. The quote is from Home Secretary Sidmouth, from a speech to parliament on 24 February 1817.

in Manchester and London, were raked together and considered attempts at revolution and 'sedition'.[86]

Literature also contributed to the dissemination of the scare, or, conversely, to the glorification of terror and rebellion. In 1816 the British poet Percy Bysshe Shelley was working on a novel, *The Assassins* – which, however, remained incomplete at his death in 1822. The manuscript was set up as an unadulterated tribute to the righteousness, purity and dedication of the assassin community, which Shelley placed in a rather indefinite period around the time of the Roman occupation of Israel. Shelley glorified the passionate rebel, adding – in line with Schiller's Karl Moor and Goethe's Faust – a romantically dangerous (and violent) hero to the pantheon of European literature. Sir Walter Scott's *Marmion* also fit into that trend, as a novel whose main character is a heroic crook who shakes off the yoke of the law and other conventions. In a similar vein, Byron created works like *Childe Harold's Pilgrimage*, *The Giaour*, *The Corsair* and *Manfred*, whose main characters were all 'moody outcasts with the mark of Cain upon them, mad, bad and dangerous to know'.[87] The 'romantic poet-rebel' was an ideal that, in the period after the Napoleonic Wars and the restoration, appealed to the imagination of radical and liberal thinkers, of publicists and of a readership that appreciated uncanny plots of the Gothic genre. In 1820, the French writer Charles Nodier linked this genre of the violent rebel to the social, political and economic shock that the new era after the Revolution had brought: 'Romantic poetry springs from our agony and our despair. This is not a fault in our art, but a necessary consequence of the advances made in our progressive society.'[88]

Although not all of these writers were equally political or progressive, Shelley, Byron and Hazlitt were among the sharpest critics of Allied politics.[89] Following the introduction of the laws mentioned above in 1817 – and the Seditious Meetings Act of that same year – Shelley, Peacock, Hunt and Hazlitt immediately opted for the radical opposition.[90] In the spring of 1817, William Hazlitt, the most productive journalist of *The Examiner*, published an extensive history of the French monarchy, from the founder Hugh Capet to the current Louis XVIII, in which he presented the Bourbon family as a mafia-like clan of robber barons.[91] Against that background, therefore, to eliminate a tyrant was the only noble course of action. Even if – or particularly because – it involved the 'hero of Waterloo'.

---

[86] Hilton, *A Mad, Bad and Dangerous People?*
[87] M. Butler, *Romantics, Rebels & Reactionaries. English Literature and its Background 1760–1830* (Oxford/New York: Oxford University Press, 1981), 2–3, 118–37.
[88] Cited in Butler, *Romantics*, 3.
[89] Ibid., 94–7.
[90] Ibid., 127, 138–9.
[91] Ibid., 149.

A Duke under Fire

From the beginning of his time in France, the 'manager of Europe' had to watch out for his own safety. From his first stay in Paris onwards, the Duke of Wellington had come under fire from disgruntled and humiliated Frenchmen. In the autumn of 1815, his house was defaced and posters affixed to it, on which he was accused of colluding with the Jacobins.[92] In the theatre, a tragedy, *Adélaïde du Guesclin*, was being staged in which the drama of the French–Breton freedom fighter Bertrand du Guesclin and his beloved Adélaïde was re-enacted. References to foreign, notably British rulers were numerous. Wellington personally was portrayed as 'the tyrant of Cambray' – referring to his military headquarters in the garrison of Cambrai.[93] The satire went hand in glove with real attacks. In June 1816, in the month marking the first anniversary of the Battle of Waterloo, Wellington almost died in a case of attempted arson. Gunpowder and ball cartridges had been hidden inside one of the lower windows on the street side of his house. When they were detonated, the iron security bars on the window were blown off, shattered to smithereens, and the window frame was soon in flames. Fortunately, one of the duke's footmen quickly noticed the fire and made sure that it spread no further. The minister of police himself, Decazes, came by in the morning, but quickly concluded that the culprit was past finding out.[94] Wellington tried to reassure his friend, Frances Lady Shelley, by pointing out that he could have easily escaped the arson attack, had it been any worse, by fleeing through the large windows opening into the garden.[95]

But in February 1818, during carnival, the threat took on more serious forms. Around midnight, on the night of 10/11 February, Wellington returned from his evening at the opera. Suddenly, just before the carriage turned into the gates of his residence on the Champs-Elysées, the Hôtel de Charost, a man emerged and fired a shot at close range. The man had a moustache, wore a large round hat and was well dressed. Before Wellington's sentries could seize him, he disappeared into the night. The bullet had not touched the carriage, but if the shooter had had a 'firmer hand and cooler head', the field marshal would have been done for, as Wellington wrote to the British minister of war Bathurst a day later.[96] The attack has been written about often, usually only in an anecdotal and trivializing manner. According to Zamoyski, it was an 'absurd incident'. Wellington's biographer Rory Muir also sees the attack more as

---

[92] Reports of Gruner, September–October 1815, GStA PK, VI. HA Nl. Hardenberg 10a.

[93] Edgcumbe (ed.), *The Diary of Frances Lady Shelley, 1787–1817*, 200.

[94] Ibid., 202–3. Shelley refers to 'de Cage', an English phonetic rendering of the French name of Éli Decazes, the French minister of the interior and police.

[95] Ibid., 203.

[96] *The Edinburgh Annual Register for 1819*, vol. 12 (Edinburgh: Archibald Constable, 1823), 306–7; Wellington to Bathurst, 12 February 1818, *WSD*, vol. 12, 271–3.

a symptom of the turbulent mood in the French capital than as a serious matter. Siemann, Metternich's biographer, attaches more significance to it, seeing it as a serious attempt by Bonapartists to set the tone for a regime change.[97] Indeed, the various accounts diverge, and changed over time. For this study, however, the attack is of crucial importance – it shows both the effectiveness and the collapse of the European attempts at a collective form of security management.[98]

A Lone Assassin or a Conspiracy?

Was it the work of one reckless carnival partygoer, or was the man with the hat and moustache a sign of the international revolutionary conspiracy that Metternich and Alexander had warned of? Wellington himself dismissed it as an unimportant trifle ('bagatelle'), that had probably been the work of a drunken good-for-nothing. Publicly, Richelieu and Decazes were more than happy to accept that explanation. Decazes had used a similar relativizing, minimalizing strategy in 1815, when a conspiracy against the Prussian king was discovered. The French government, after all, was not at all interested in this kind of negative publicity. Priority number one for them was to convince the Allies that everything was peaceful and quiet in France, and that the occupation could easily be ended sooner rather than later. That is why Richelieu quickly sent the French ambassador, the Marquis de Bonnay, to Berlin, to assure the German government that nothing was amiss. While they were frantically looking into the possibility of an international conspiracy back at home, the marquis dutifully informed his colleague in Berlin, the Count de Lottum, that the 'event with the Duke of Wellington' was in no way 'a formal intent to assassinate' him, but simply 'a criminal act' with the probable goal of causing 'unrest'.[99]

But, behind the scenes, none of those involved took the matter lightly, and de Bonnay's attempt at trivializing the matter did not match the French police's assessment of a veritable revolutionary plot. Wellington wrote up his will a few days later.[100] He realized all too well how the foiled attack

---

[97] A. Roberts, *Napoleon and Wellington. The Battle of Waterloo and the Great Commanders Who Fought It* (New York: Simon and Schuster, 2001), 234; Siemann, *Metternich*, 641, 647, 660; Zamoyski, *Phantom Terror*, 16, 171, 566–7; Muir, *Wellington. Waterloo and the Fortunes of Peace*, 110–11.

[98] With thanks to Yannick Balk; see Y. Balk, The Diabolical Conspiracy. An Inquiry into the Plotting, Rumouring and the Rise of a European Security Culture after the Assassination Attempt on the Duke of Wellington in 1818 (unpublished MA thesis, Utrecht University, 2017).

[99] Richelieu to de Bonnay, 23 February 1818 and letter of de Bonnay to the Comte de Lottum, 23 February 1818, GStA PK, III. HA I. no. 8886.

[100] On 17 February. See W. Stirling-Maxwell, *Napoleon's Bequest to Cantillon. A Fragment of International History* (London: Longwood, 1858), 7–8.

underscored the vulnerability of his position in France. Castlereagh was also very concerned: 'this diabolical plot . . . has augmented all our anxieties'. The British Prince Regent also wrote to express the 'sentiments of horror and indignation with which I am impressed by the infamy and baseness of the foul attempt'.[101] Upon further reflection, on 21 February, the British Cabinet decided to withdraw Wellington from all negotiations with France, and to have him return home.[102] But the duke was not so inclined; doing so would be a sign of weakness for the entire Allied presence. And it would only stir up more unrest: 'the spirit against the Allies . . . would become everyday more exaggerated, while all respect would be lost for the only person who has the power to keep it within bounds'. Hastily quitting Paris would 'give the most fatal shake to everything that is going forward'. In addition, he added, while the attack was bad enough, it was not the start of an overall uprising, nor did it seem 'that the conspirators had more in view than to create confusion [or] putting out of the way a person whom they imagined their enemy'.[103]

Louis XVIII immediately sent Richelieu and Decazes to congratulate the duke personally on safely escaping this attack. They in turn set everything they could in motion to track down the perpetrators. At about half past nine that morning the police were informed of the attack, and by eleven o'clock commissioners were at the duke's residence interrogating him and his servants and taking down the accounts of those who had witnessed the crime. Wellington was able to inform Bathurst the following day, 12 February, that 'the government, the police, and indeed every individual here, are doing everything in their power to discover the criminal'.[104]

That was certainly true. It is no exaggeration to say that all of Paris's agents were sent out to follow up on the handful of clues and potential avenues of exploration. Thousands of pages of witness and police reports were recorded in the months of February and March.[105] Richelieu, Decazes and Jules Anglès, the Paris prefect of police, were on top of things. All arms dealers, all men who had come home after one o'clock in the morning, or had left the city in the early morning hours, as well as all soldiers (both French and foreign) who had arrived at their boarding house after one o'clock, were screened. But to the great despair and shame of Richelieu, the police came up empty-handed. 'The way forward for the police is necessarily vague and uncertain', Anglès wrote to

---

[101] Castlereagh to Wellington, 15 February 1818, *WSD*, vol. 12, 291; Prince Regent to Wellington, 14 February 1818, *WSD*, vol. 12, 285.
[102] Bathurst to Wellington, 20–1 February 1818, *WSD*, vol. 12, 324–6.
[103] Wellington to Bathurst, 25 February, 8 March, *WSD*, vol. 12, 333–5, 380–1.
[104] Wellington to Bathurst, 12 February 1818, *WSD*, vol. 12, 271–3.
[105] See the folder 'enquête concernant la tentative d'assassinat sur Lord Wellington, février–mars 1818', in the French National Archives, Paris (ANF), F7.6673. See also the files of the prefecture of the Paris police, 'attentat contre le duc de Wellington', in Archives de la Préfecture de Police, Paris (APP), 342.

Decazes.[106] The description of the suspect was too general; he had disappeared too quickly into the fog for anyone to see which direction he took; and the weapon they recovered lacked any tell-tale features. So too, a possible bullet, lodged in the wall of a house down the road, would have had to follow an impossible trajectory – coming from under the carriage – to land where it did, so that by the end of February Richelieu was beginning to wonder if the musket had even been loaded, or whether it merely fired a blank cartridge,[107] causing Wellington to comment to Bathurst with great indignation: 'As if … the conversations in all the coffee-houses and salons of Paris did not prove the existence of the plot and the night of the 10th the execution of the scheme in every part excepting the death of the victim.'[108]

Wild Rumours and Censorship

The flood of rumours was an aggravating circumstance; police efforts could hardly keep up with the rumour mill. Via semaphore (optical telegraph; Fig. 6.2), the British troops in Calais announced on 14 February that they stood ready to advance on the capital. Elsewhere, flags were flying at half mast because some had been given false news of Wellington's death.[109] In the days that followed, Decazes's informants carefully recorded the extent of the alarm. In Saint-Dénis, 'the attempted murder of General Wellington … plunged the minds of all into consternation'. And while 'everyone was chattering away about what had happened to the Duke of Wellington, wise people were seriously aggrieved by the event'. 'Each one had their own version of the event'; 'commoners' saw it as a 'blow to the English', but the 'reasonable people', by contrast, interpreted the attack as a 'case of personal revenge'. Or deeper yet, as a 'deed by those who wanted to sow unrest in the minds of the people'. It did not take long before the feeling in the salons was that the attack was 'the result of a political manoeuvre'.[110]

Such a surge in conspiracy theories was not on the French government's wish list. With an appeal to the censorship already in place, and the existing ban on alarmism and spreading slander, journalists were prohibited from writing further on this matter.[111] The authorities in the Netherlands were

[106] Anglès to Decazes, 16 February 1818, ANF, F7.6675.
[107] Richelieu to de Bonnay, 23 February 1818, GStA PK, III. HA I. no. 8886. See also Court of Assizes of the Seine, 'Acte d'Accusation contre Marie André Cantillon et Louis Joseph Stanislas Marinet', 23 February 1819, ANF, F7.6675.
[108] Wellington to Bathurst, 16 February 1818, *WSD*, vol. 12, 292–3.
[109] Semaphore notice from Calais, 14 February, and semaphore notice from the post, 14 February 1818, in the police dossier on Wellington, ANF, F7.6673.
[110] Rumour reports from the police of 12, 13, 16 February 1818, 'Extraits des rapports commissaires de police de Paris 1818', ANF, F7.3839.
[111] On 12 February, *Le Moniteur* still discussed the matter, but the following week all reporting had stopped. Stirling, *Napoleon's Bequest*, 28.

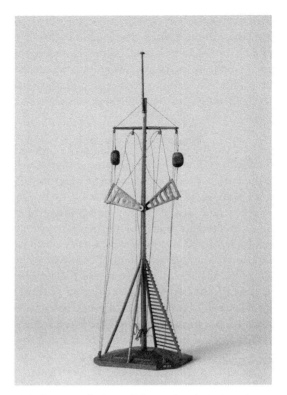

Figure 6.2 Model of an optical telegraph (semaphore). Artist unknown, *c.*1798–1800. (Rijksmuseum, Amsterdam)

deeply disturbed as well, and stressed the importance of secrecy, arguing that no one would benefit from the publication of details related to the investigation and the possible involvement of the refugees in Brussels.[112] But the suspicions kept circulating, not least through (foreign) newspapers in Britain, Austria and the Netherlands. The headlines in *The Times* of 16 February read: 'We are sorry to have to announce to our readers an attempt made at Paris, on Wednesday last, upon the life of the Duke of Wellington.'[113] Some newspapers believed that the Ultras were behind the plot, because they did not want the Allied forces to leave, lest the royalist government be replaced by the liberal opposition. Others thought, as did most French officials, that the British themselves had had a hand in it.[114] The majority of details, however, were to be gleaned

[112] See letters of Thiennes, Van Maanen, February–March 1818, NL-HaNA (State Secretariat of the Cabinet, 1813–1840), 2.02.01, inv. no. 6534.
[113] 'Private correspondence', *The Times*, 16 February 1818, 2.
[114] See e.g. *The Times*, 17 February 1818; the *Morning Chronicle*, 25 March 1818; *The Courier*, 24 March 1818; *The Observer*, 30 March 1818. See also Stirling-Maxwell,

from the Austrian newspapers, in large part because Metternich was of the opinion that the 'disposition toward assassination' shared by the armed Jacobins in France and Belgium should be denounced openly. The world needed to know that the spirit of the Revolution was still running wild: a warning that Metternich announced via a number of articles in the *Oesterreichischer Beobachter* (Austria's official newspaper).[115]

Brussels Once Again

In the end, it was Wellington who, quite unintentionally, tossed the French an anchor to free itself from that pool of terrorist suspicions. The duke had received an anonymous letter in Cambrai as early as 15 January 1818, in which he was warned of a possible attack on his life. And on 30 January, Lord Kinnaird – not the best friend of the British government and her diplomats – had also informed Wellington, by a letter which reached him via his chief of staff George Murray, of a group of conspirators in Brussels who were planning an attack. Wellington showed that second letter to Anglès, when the French police commissioners came to his place on 11 February, right after the attack. As Richelieu and Decazes started to realize in the following days, the letter was a godsend and a breakthrough for the French, because they could now tighten up their forensic investigation and turn it in a specific direction: the suspect could well have come from the circle of French refugees, officers on half pay and Belgian radicals. That meant that the police had to focus primarily on traffic to and from Brussels, and to keep an eye on all couriers and coach traffic. It also meant that the source of the threat shifted from Paris to Brussels, and specifically to the people who had been a thorn in the side of the French government for months already. According to Anglès, the letter from Kinnaird led to the type of threat 'which the government could not disregard' any more, namely the French 'refugees in Belgium'. Decazes could concentrate his investigation on that group 'with less uncertainty'. Research in that direction – across the border – was politically more desirable, forensically more straightforward and publicity-wise more effective than having to admit to conspiracies in France itself.[116]

As Anglès put it, this was about the 'centres in Brussels and London', and not the liberal societies in Paris. The 'revolutionaries who have relationships throughout Europe' were in London and Brussels. For them, Wellington was the:

Napoleon's Bequest, 27. For reporting by Dutch newspapers, see *Journal de la province de Limbourg, Leydse Courant, Arnhemsche Courant, Opregte Haarlemsche Courant, Nederlandsche Staatscourant*, 16–26 February 1818.
[115] See *Oesterreichischer Beobachter*, 24, 26 February, 1, 13, 16 March, 1 May, 11 July 1818, 13, 21, 22 May 1819.
[116] Anglès to Decazes, 16 February 1818, ANF, F7.6673.

defender of the authorities, the enemy of the prevalent ideas of the ultra-liberals and the destroyer of the last revolutionary army. He was the man whose assassination would shake the whole of Europe to its core, which would produce all kinds of disorders, that would subsequently allow the destructive, anti-monarchic forces to profit in their attempt to overturn the existing social order.

It was plainly inconceivable, according to Anglès, that 'the origin of the plot be in France', given the fact that there were no more supporters of that ultra-liberal movement in France who could commit such a crime. With Kinnaird's letter in hand, the world made sense again.[117]

Decazes immediately called for all their communications with Belgium to be transmitted by semaphore as soon as was possible. He also straight away found a zealous accomplice in the person of La Tour du Pin. La Tour du Pin's father had lost his life to the guillotine during the Reign of Terror in 1793, and his wife had been a lady-in-waiting to Queen Marie Antoinette. In 1815, this anti-revolutionary and conservative ambassador had voted in favour of the death penalty for Marshal Ney. He had been forced to move to the Netherlands, presumably because of his short-lived flirtation with the Bonapartist regime, and personally found himself in a heart-breaking state: his daughter Cécile had died of tuberculosis in March 1817, his son Humbert had died in a duel that he, his father, had himself encouraged and his wife was grief-stricken.[118] Decazes did not need to spend any more time on convincing La Tour du Pin of his suspicions. The latter immediately gave vent to all his frustrations towards the Dutch government. He could not comprehend why the Dutch Lower House, the king and the ministers did not take firmer action against the revolutionary enclave in Brussels and kept delaying the promised press legislation. On 3 February, a week before the attack on Wellington, Van Maanen, the minister of justice, had submitted the long-promised bill to the Lower House, with an eye to addressing issues related to the radical agitation of the French refugees. The 500-florin law was expanded considerably. Along with slighting foreign sovereigns, insulting their envoys was now also punishable. Moreover, not only the authorship of a rabble-rousing piece, but also printing or publishing the same were now also libel. The penalty was increased, and the public prosecutor could take action himself and did not have to wait for a ruling or the lodging of a complaint. Domestic press offences, however, were not covered by the law. (The British suggestions to abolish the entire free press, to impose fines of 50,000 florins, or to have all newspapers appear in Dutch only, which would keep French-speakers from publishing, did not pass muster.) But, after escalated debate, the Lower House rejected Van Maanen's

[117] Anglès to Decazes, 15 February 1818, ANF, F7.6673.
[118] See the memoirs of La Tour du Pin's wife, the Marquise de La Tour du Pin, *Journal d'une femme de cinquante ans, 1778–1815*, vol. 1 (Paris: Chapelot, 1913), v–xxxii.

compromise bill with 39 votes to 36. The disaffected had won the battle for an open forum for public opinion.[119] The liberal members of the Lower House did not consider the radical salons in Brussels to be a major threat. In fact, when the now exiled journalists Guyet and Cauchois-Lemaire sent a petition from Germany to the States General, asking the Lower House to recognize the unconstitutionality of their exile and deportation and to prosecute the ministers who had banished them, they found thirty-seven delegates on their side (fifty were opposed).[120]

The attack on Wellington was after this affront a gift from heaven for La Tour du Pin. Finally, he could vent his grievances and be heard by Decazes. He was more than happy to supply suspicions and the names of a variety of liberal and allegedly radical individuals to the French police. Decazes made good use of these hunches. According to him, it was precisely this 'parti de bonaparte', these 'writers, correspondents, outlaws and refugees' who, together with the liberal representatives in the Netherlands and Belgium, drummed up sentiment against the French government. As he saw it, the attack was intended to sour the life of the French king even more. In a postscript, Decazes and Richelieu therefore promised La Tour du Pin all the funds he needed to launch investigations in the Netherlands.[121] Kinnaird had already mentioned the (infamous) names of Brice, Marinet (alias Nicol(l)e, the name he bore in the Low Countries), Guyet and Cauchois-Lemaire. The Dutch minister of police, Thiennes, and the attorney general in Brussels, Vanderfosse, received the information by semaphore, with the request to interrogate these people (with more names to follow on a daily basis) and thus support the French investigation. La Tour du Pin, always eager to suggest additional suspects, stood ready to assist them with advice and action.[122]

Lord Kinnaird's network was the first to be interrogated.[123] His informant, the one who had tipped him off about the conspiracy, was a certain Louis Joseph Stanislas Marinet (Fig. 6.3), a lawyer who had served as auditor of the Council of State during the Hundred Days regime, had been sentenced to

---

[119] (Van) Sas, *Onze natuurlijkste bondgenoot*, 155–9.

[120] See the Cabinet deliberations of 3 December 1817, NL-HaNA, 2.02.01, inv. no. 6051, as well as the 287-page printed petition: L. Cauchois-Lemaire and I. Guyet, *Appel à l'opinion publique et aux états-généraux du royaume des Pays-Bas, en faveur des proscrits français, contre leurs proscripteurs* (The Hague: Wallez, 1817); Tweede Kamer (ed.), *Handelingen*, 1817–1818, 263–4, Appendix XV. See also (Van) Sas, *Onze natuurlijkste bondgenoot*, 156–7.

[121] Decazes to La Tour du Pin, 13 February 1818, ANF, F7.6673.

[122] Dispatches to Thiennes and Vanderfosse, 13 February 1818, ANF, F7.6675. See also the correspondence of Van Maanen and Vanderfosse to the king, February–March 1818, NL-HaNA, 2.02.01, inv. no. 6534.

[123] The Dutch minister of justice, Van Maanen, issued an extensive report on this matter in April 1818; see Van Maanen, 'Onderzoek in Belgien omtrent den aanslag op het leven van den Hertog van Wellington', 19 April 1818, NL-HaNA, 2.05.01, inv. no. 767.

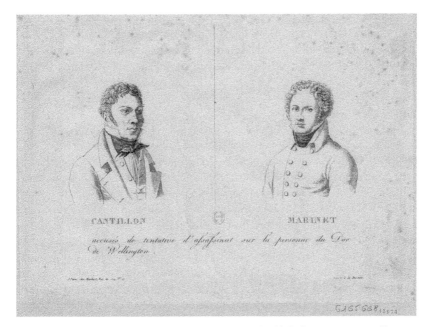

Figure 6.3   Cantillon and Marinet, the suspects in the (failed) attempt on Wellington in February 1818. Print from 1819. (Bibliothèque nationale de France)

death by the Assize Court in Dijon and had then fled to Belgium. There he had befriended Guyet, Cauchois-Lemaire and Brice, and had also come to know Cantillon. After consulting the French police and Wellington, Kinnaird himself came to Paris on 21 February – with his friend Marinet – assuming that Wellington had promised him safe passage for his acquaintance. Wellington and the French saw that differently. Marinet gave such contradictory and muddled testimonies and acted so secretively and suspiciously that he found himself arrested and in prison by 26 February, where he remained for months in solitary confinement, pending further investigation and his trial. Marie André Nicholas Cantillon (Fig. 6.3), Marinet's alleged accomplice, also had no clear alibi – a jealous mistress, Julie Frémont, would not vouch for his whereabouts. A former jeweller, the 36-year-old Cantillon had served in Napoleon's Grande Armée, as well as with the regiment of Chasseurs à Cheval of the Imperial Guard. He had been convicted of 'deeds of cruelty towards the enemy' as well as violent behaviour against his superiors, but was pardoned 'for his extraordinary bravery' by Napoleon himself.[124] In 1813, angry and embittered, he had quit the army on half pension, returning to the ranks during the Hundred Days. In the meantime, he worked as a servant in

---

[124]   Stirling-Maxwell, *Napoleon's Bequest*, 27.

Brussels and Paris, for Brice, his former major, and Marinet. But the net did not immediately fall on all these men – Cantillon, for example, was not found until the end of March. Some seventy other witnesses were interrogated, including, in particular, the wives of Guyet and Cauchois-Lemaire, as they were initially considered linchpins in the conspiracy.[125]

The Collusion of Two Women

By 1 March, the authorities on both sides of the border were certain of this: they were dealing with a conspiracy – indeed, a 'plot ... woven together by their wives, in concert with Lord Kinnaird, Nicole and Croquembourg'. Felicité Guyet (36) and Judith Cauchois-Lemaire (only 21) were the pivotal figures in this web of intrigues and had to be arrested immediately for questioning. Together, these women hosted a salon in Brussels where they accommodated numerous refugees, correspondents and other radical Bonapartists. Given such provocatively independent behaviour, they played into the hands of both the heavily Catholic La Tour du Pin and the conservative Thiennes. Moreover, they still resented the petition their husbands had made to the Lower House – that Thiennes and friends be prosecuted. Without their husbands and without a fixed source of income, these two women also led a risky and precarious existence. Kinnaird, who was suspected of having an affair with Felicité Guyet, paid for their lodging with a *rente*. Spies of Thiennes had moreover overheard Felicité telling friends in Antwerp all sorts of details about the attack on Wellington, and reported on her familiarity with the French expatriate François Stévenotte, a journalist for *Le Vrai Libéral*.[126] In Antwerp, she stayed for a time with the Stappaerts family, which was known for receiving all kinds of 'malcontents'.[127] From the perspective of the French and Dutch police, a veritable conspiracy had indeed been brewing: one that could directly be related to the attack on Wellington.

The Dutch attorneys and their ministers were not quite comfortable over all the unrest. 'I do not think His Highness the Prince of Waterloo will be very fond of this once he learns about it all', Vanderfosse nervously wrote to Van Maanen.[128] That fear was confirmed; Wellington was 'not amused'. He wrote to the British ambassador in The Hague, Clancarty:

---

[125] Correspondence of Thiennes, Vanderfosse, Decazes, February–March 1818, ANF, F7.6673.

[126] Thiennes to Decazes, 1 March 1818, ANF, F7.6673; Vanderfosse to Van Maanen, 30 April 1818, NL-HaNA, 2.02.01, inv. no. 6534.

[127] Gouvernement d'Anvers to Thiennes, 10 March 1818, ANF, F7.6673. See also R. Merecy, 'De Antwerpsche pers onder het "Vereenigd Koninkrijk"', *De Gulden Passer*, 23 (1945), 81–95.

[128] Vanderfosse to Van Maanen, with a copy also sent to King Willem I, 1 March 1818, NL-HaNA, 2.02.01 inv. no. 6534.

a plot has been formed in the Netherlands by these very people to assassinate me; not, I presume, because they did not like my face, or my manners, or the colour of my coat, but because I was the General of the Allies, and the main support of the system of tranquillity and order which it is wished to establish in the world.[129]

Indeed, in Antwerp, but also in Brussels and Liège, all sorts of satirical poems were being circulated about the attack and the alleged arrogance of the duke – who had become the target of all anti-Allied resentment. One example from the police files went as follows:

> Ajuster mal est un defaut.
> Il l'a manqué mais voici comme[nt].
> L'imbecile a tiré trop haut.
> Il le prenait [Wellington] pour un grand homme.[130]

Thiennes, the minister of state in change of supervising the police and security in the southern Netherlands, presented a detailed account of the suspicions surrounding Kinnaird and the refugees in Brussels to King Willem I. According to Thiennes, despite all their denials, the conspiracy was the joint effort of Cauchois-Lemaire and Guyet, as authors of the pamphlet to the Lower House, and their wives – the *femmes des Nains* (the women of the periodical *Le Nain Jaune*) – who orchestrated their evil plans 'in concert' with Kinnaird and Marinet.[131] It could not be otherwise. The salon of Guyet and Cauchois-Lemaire was the hotbed of the conspiracy – a plot that could have all kinds of objectives: simply to get rid of Wellington, or perhaps only to scare him off, so that he returned to Britain. Van Maanen even contended that the whole ploy may have been invented just to manipulate Wellington into believing that Kinnaird had helped save his life, so that he would allow the families of Guyet and Cauchois-Lemaire to return to France. (The latter interpretation would also become the conclusion of the Dutch criminal investigation.) Whatever the case, the target of the plot was the Allied presence in Paris; that was certain.[132]

'Telegraphic bulletins', crossing the border back and forth, were used to keep the authorities up to date on their travels and conversations. The prefect in Lille wrote that there was 'no doubt' that these two women were directly involved in the scheming – 'these facts are certain'. Some reports spoke of an affair between Kinnaird and Felicité Guyet/Judith Cauchois-Lemaire, or between Marinet and Felicité Guyet. From the sum of these reports, denials,

---

[129] Wellington to Clancarty, 24 March 1818, *WSD*, vol. 12, 433–5; Vane (ed.), *Correspondence*, vol. 11, 419–20.

[130] Poem, sent by Thiennes to Willem I, 2 March 1818, NL-HaNA, 2.02.01, inv. no. 6534. Paraphrased: 'The inability to aim is a flaw. / He's missed him, and here's how. / The fool aimed too high. / He took him for a great man.'

[131] Thiennes to Willem I, 2 March 1818, NL-HaNA, 2.02.01, inv. no. 6534.

[132] See Van Maanen's account to Willem I, 5 September 1818, NL-HaNA, 2.02.01, inv. no. 6534, especially the final pages of the file.

confirmations and contradictions, Thiennes drew a clear conclusion: 'these last clues, these intimate and shameful connections, do they not confirm the thought that Lord Kinnaird, Marinet and Guyet have come to play a malicious comedy?'[133] Felicité Guyet was arrested in Antwerp and interrogated. Judith Cauchois-Lemaire left for France on 11 February to deal with personal affairs, wanting to sell her home there to replenish her dwindling funds. Upon arrival in Paris, she was arrested as well, and put away in the infamous Madelonnettes prison in Paris for a series of interrogations.

Guyet, tears flowing, was able to convince the Belgian police of her innocence. She admitted to talking with her friends about the attack, but explained that what she knew came from the newspaper, assuring them that she had never been involved in dishonourable things. She was only trying to keep her head above water by writing books together with Judith, and if her fate remained so tragic, they would both return to their families in France.[134] However, a loyal friend she was not; rather than standing up for Judith, Felicité informed the Belgian magistrates investigating her case that 'it may well be that Cauchois-Lemaire and his wife are involved to some extent in the case in question, but that she herself and her husband are "beings too pure to employ means of this nature"'.[135]

The 21-year-old Judith had a far harder time in the Parisian prison. She was in prison for several weeks and was interrogated for days on end about the smallest and innermost details. From the reports, she seems to have carried herself in a very controlled and business-like manner, her answers kept as short as possible (unlike the lengthy, tearful responses of her friend). The friends with whom she had been staying – the owners and employees of the Foulon bookshop – sent an extensive petition on 6 March to Decazes, the minister of police, in which they argued for her immediate release. Judith had a 'moral character of high quality', her 'innocence' was 'unquestionable', she was an 'unhappy' young woman, 'known by all her friends for the amiability of her character, for the purity of her soul', and she was in no way a danger.[136] In the end, it was perhaps that plea – which still pointed to 'the weakness of her sex' – that was decisive for her. Two such innocent, tragic women could not be tied to a pistol and an attack. Cauchois was released in early April, and the focus shifted again to the men, Marinet and Cantillon.[137]

---

[133] Thiennes to Willem I, 6 March 1818, NL-HaNA, 2.02.01, inv. no. 6534.

[134] Interrogation of Guyet in Brussels, 30, 31 March 1818, ANF, F7.6673.

[135] See Van Maanen's report to Willem I, 5 September 1818; in particular, the note in the appendix, 26 March 1818, NL-HaNA, 2.02.01, inv. no. 6534.

[136] Interrogation of Cauchois-Lemaire, 4, 16, 31 March 1818; interrogation of Guyet, Antwerp, Brussels, 30 and 31 March 1818; letter of Foulon 'et employés' to Decazes, 6 March 1818, ANF, F7.6673.

[137] See also the correspondence, late March–April, of Van Maanen, Vanderfosse, Thiennes to Willem I, in particular, the 'Rapport au Roi, par le Ministre d'État Comte de Thiennes',

Machinating Men, after All

The phantom of a Bonapartist conspiracy by French exiles who spun their intrigues from Brussels – even though they were not women – was too good to let go. The French government, in cooperation with the Dutch authorities, could present Wellington with the ideal conspiracy: it was French exiles, congregating in liberal Brussels, who had wanted to reward Wellington with a bullet for all his efforts and constitutional empathy. Unfortunately, apart from rumours, presumption and reciprocal imputations, no solid evidence could be brought to bear on the case. In early March, Thiennes complained to King Willem I that he had never been able to confirm that police measures in Antwerp – where Guyet was staying – were ever implemented 'with secrecy and success'.[138] And Vanderfosse wrote to Van Maanen, with a sigh, that 'the threads of the weft ... became so numerous and complicated' that he simply did not have a chance to investigate all those different lines, and slowly got lost in the maze of details.[139]

At the end of April, the Dutch and French authorities nevertheless agreed that Cantillon had pulled the trigger, that Marinet was the 'author' of the plan, and that Kinnaird was the 1,400-franc paymaster behind the scenes.[140] Based on some letters, Marinet could, moreover, be associated with Joseph Bonaparte, who had fled to the United States.[141] In short, instead of hard evidence, the police deployed the epistemological logic of relying on the fact that the three men were surrounded by a cloud of half-retired soldiers, correspondents and Bonapartist exiles (the extent of which was indeed abundantly estimated) – and therefore must somehow be responsible for the agitation and the attack. Had not Marinet asserted that Lord Kinnaird 'had long been meditating a plan, of which the world would soon be talking'? Enough witnesses, meanwhile, claimed that Marinet himself was also deeply involved in the plotting. He had told his friends in Brussels, regarding Cantillon, that he was 'an instrument to be used, and then broken'.[142] According to Wellington and the Dutch minister of justice, there was 'no doubt' that at least Marinet was part of the group that had hatched this plot. There was 'ample evidence to convict' Cantillon and Marinet in a guilt-by-association case. But only if the French authorities wanted that – because,

31 March 1818, as well as the report of Van Maanen to Willem I, 5 September 1818, NL-HaNA, 2.02.01, inv. no. 6534.

[138] Thiennes to Willem I, 6 March 1818, NL-HaNA, 2.02.01, inv. no. 6534.

[139] Vanderfosse to Van Maanen, 20 March 1818, NL-HaNa, 2.01.01, inv. no. 6534.

[140] Letter from the public prosecutor, Van de Casteele, to Van Maanen, 26 April 1818, NL-HaNA, 2.02.01, inv. no. 6534.

[141] Ms Elisa sent Joseph Bonaparte a letter warmly recommending Marinet to him. See Vanderfosse to Van Maanen, 30 April 1818, NL-HaNa, 2.02.01, inv. no. 6534.

[142] See Van Maanen's correspondence with Vanderfosse, April 1818, NL-HaNA, 2.02.01, inv. no. 6534. See also Stirling-Maxwell, *Napoleon's Bequest*, 32–4.

while there was evidence of a conspiracy (the network, the plans, the contacts and the financial transactions), 'they have no positive proof to produce in a court of justice' yet regarding their presence at the scene of the crime.[143]

Despite, or precisely because of the lack of positive proof, the conspiracy took on even more improbable forms. In order to exonerate themselves, or simply to stir the pot, Kinnaird and Marinet suggested that they were not the ones, but that a much higher-ranking person – a 'great personage' – was behind the attack. By getting rid of Wellington, this person would have wanted to become the supreme commander of the Allied forces himself. They were hinting at Tsar Alexander, or the Prince of Orange (the oldest son of Willem I, and later King Willem II).[144] This former adjutant and general in Wellington's army had very much distanced himself from his father. He avoided The Hague and, hurt and embittered, surrounded himself in Brussels with 'people whose sole purpose is agitation and disorder'.[145] There were even reports of friends and adjutants of the crown prince who were involved in 'orgies' and 'treachery' with suspects in the conspiracy.[146]

Metternich had long been concerned about a plot to put the Duke of Orléans or 'a prince from the House of Orange' on the throne.[147] The attack on Wellington could well be a first step in that direction. The French police rose to that bait. The intrigue and rumours escalated so much that Tsar Alexander, the brother-in-law of Crown Prince Willem (who was married to Anna Pavlovna, the tsar's youngest sister), let it be known from Moscow that he strongly condemned the prince's rebellious behaviour and poor choice of friends. The rumours were so persistent because they were based on a couple of facts. The Prince of Orange had indeed surrounded himself with a coterie of aggrieved and like-minded people and, as it turned out, got himself black-mailed because of his homosexual escapades.[148] He was friends with the Bonapartist veterans Brice and Croquembourg (who were being questioned as suspects at the time) in Brussels, having met them in the Masonic lodge 'L'Espérance', and in the salon 'La Vieille Garde'. Wellington, too, knew of Willem's friendship with notorious Jacobins; he was 'intimately connected with them' and 'they considered him as their head, and wished to place him on

---

[143] Wellington to Clancarty, 17, 21 July 1818, *WSD*, vol. 12, 601–2, 621–2; Clancarty to Castlereagh, 4 August 1818, Vane (ed.), *Correspondence*, vol. 11, 467–8.

[144] Memorandum of the Dutch examining magistrate, 4 August 1818, *WSD*, vol. 12, 646–50; see also 330, 383, 481.

[145] Robbert Fagel to the Princess-Mother, 20 December 1817, Colenbrander (ed.), *Gedenkstukken*, vol. 8.2, 167.

[146] Vanderfosse to Van Maanen, 20 March 1818, NL-HaNA, 2.02.01, inv. no. 6534.

[147] Metternich to Lebzeltern, 26 March 1817, intercepted copy, NL-HaNA, 2.05.01, inv. no. 770.

[148] Cf. J. van Zanten, *Koning Willem II, 1792–1849* (Amsterdam: Boom, 2013), 259–63.

the throne of France'.[149] But Willem had not been involved in a direct attack on the life of his former superior, and so he saw the need to assure Wellington of his devotion. He wrote, in an emotional letter, that he sincerely hoped that the duke would not believe the rumours that he, the crown prince, would have been party to 'such a dirty business'.[150] The duke accepted the clarification, and assured the prince that he 'would as soon suspect my own son as I could your Royal Highness', but warned the prince that his poor judgement had been a debit to the entire situation. The prince should never have let himself get involved with those 'conspirators' in the first place, those advocates of the 'revolutionary party in every kingdom of Europe'.[151]

Along with the Prince of Orange, Wellington was of the opinion that the rumours regarding some 'high-level involvement' in the conspiracy were a 'complete fabrication', conjured up by certain French persons, and intended to sow division among the Allies.[152] The idea that the French were now actively conspiring against the Allied occupiers gained ground, however, and fuelled mounting concerns in London about the French occupation. In late March 1818, the British government sent a memorandum to all the Allies about the 'system of security' in France. According to Castlereagh, the conspiracy and, in particular, its treatment by the French authorities and the reaction of the French people made it clear that public opinion had now turned against the Allied presence. The French government was too weak or too unwilling to curb the unrest, or was even, via the Ultras, itself in part responsible for that anti-Allied sentiment. Castlereagh was not particularly impressed with the French argument that it was primarily owing to the Belgian exiles. 'Though principally traced in evidence to French exiles in the Low Countries, [the plot] appears to have been connected with the effort of a certain party within France to produce a state of confusion by which they hoped to profit.' The attack on Wellington was thus a 'serious ground for additional uneasiness', because it was 'impossible to regard it as an insulated outrage confined to two or three desperate and profligate assassins, who conspired against his Grace's personal safety'. It was, in short, 'a plot of wider extent', which demonstrated that 'the peace and security of Europe' had now seriously been compromised by the 'political confusion' in France. For the British, these unintended consequences of their fight against terror were the writing on the wall: it may well be time to leave. Whether the other ministers drew a similar conclusion, and under what conditions the occupation could be terminated early, had to be discussed further by the ministers,

---

[149] Wellington to Bathurst, 8 March 1818, *WSD*, vol. 12, 382–3.
[150] Prince of Orange to Wellington, 15 April 1818, *WSD*, vol. 12, 471.
[151] Wellington to the Prince of Orange, 18 April 1818, *WSD*, vol. 12, 480–1.
[152] Clancarty to Castlereagh, 11 August 1818, Vane (ed.), *Correspondence*, vol. 11, 468–70; Wellington to Bathurst, 23 February 1818, *WSD*, vol. 12, 330–1.

come October, when they would meet in Aix-la-Chapelle. Serious financial negotiations would be pivotal to such a premature exit at the very least (see Chapter 7).[153]

The End of the Story

It took a while for the story to play itself out, because the suspects – who remained in detention – were only brought to justice in May 1819. For Wellington and the Allied Council, the whole affair was one big disappointment, if not a deception. The French police proved incapable of bringing the most notorious post-war attack to date to clarity. But the failure of the Council's pressure and of Wellington's mediation in this matter had also become clear. The Council was unable to neutralize the moral panic that the attack elicited; instead, with their alarmist circulars, they had aggravated the situation further. The torches of radicalism burning in Belgium were not snuffed out, but fanned into flaming flares by the expulsion of so many Bonapartists and liberals from France – who subsequently flocked to Brussels to continue their conspiracies even more furtively from there. The man who, as Prince of Waterloo, had constantly worked for the well-being and security of the Netherlands had become the victim of a Belgian conspiracy – or so it seemed. For Wellington, the attack was indeed proof of the fact that his time in Paris was coming to an end. The paradox of the Allied occupation in France could not have manifested itself more clearly: as commander-in-chief, Wellington was the guardian of the new system of collective security. But his very presence became a magnet for Bonapartist intrigues and conspiracies. When, after a few months, the occupation was terminated, Wellington wiped the dust from his cape and never looked back on this ignominious story.

That was probably a good attitude to adopt, because, in May 1819, the trial against Marinet and Cantillon took an unexpected turn. The trial took place in Paris from 10 to 14 May, in the Assize Court of the Seine. Seventy witnesses were summoned, including Wellington (who did not come). Marinet and Cantillon were accused of having organized a conspiracy with the intent of killing the Duke of Wellington.[154] Their lawyers defended them by pointing out the suggestive, insinuating nature of the indictment and the lack of concrete evidence.[155] In his closing argument, the prosecutor stated that

---

[153] Castlereagh to Cathcart, 27 March 1818 and Bathurst to Wellington, 31 March 1818, *WSD*, vol. 12, 446–9, with the appended memorandum of 27 March, signed by Castlereagh.

[154] Court of Assizes of the Seine, 'Acte d'accusation contre Marie André Nicolas Cantillon et Louis Joseph Stanislas Marinet', ANF, F7.6675.

[155] See e.g. M. Claveau, 'Memorial on behalf of Cantillon, accused of having fired a pistol-shot at the carriage of the Duke of Wellington', ANF, F7.6675. See also *The Times*, 21 November 1818.

there had been a conspiracy and a shooter, but that the gun, the bullet – concrete evidence – had never been found. It was also very unlikely that it had been a French perpetrator – because 'Frenchmen never try to assassinate people', and France was not a 'hotbed of revolutions', or 'a den of assassins'. With the day of being liberated from the Allied yoke fast approaching, it was inconceivable and completely illogical back in February 1818 that a Frenchman would have committed such a 'useless crime'. It could only have been 'a conspiracy abroad', of which Marinet and Cantillon had become the victim. Given that the *Agememnonat* (an unfriendly reference to Agamemnon, commander-in-chief of the Greeks and king of Mycenae) of Wellington had come to an end, it no longer made sense to burden French citizens with this matter. The jury therefore acquitted Marinet and Cantillon of all charges. The two – by now – public heroes received congratulations from the judge and the public prosecutor; Marinet was furthermore granted a safe-conduct to return to Belgium and a passport for Dijon.[156] With this acquittal, the French justice system shook off the last of Allied patronage. Insecurity and disorder – these were the foreigners. The French knew where their national interest lay. When they left the courthouse, Marinet and Cantillon were 'warmly greeted by the multitude'.[157] Napoleon also posthumously contributed to the party by leaving 10,000 francs to Cantillon in his will, signed April 1821. According to the quite unsportsmanlike emperor, Cantillon had as much right to 'assassinate' Wellington as that 'oligarch' had to send him, Napoleon, to St Helena. No evidence exists, however, of any direct involvement of Napoleon in, or inside information on his part about this conspiracy.

The whole affair had been a stain on the white lily banner of France. That is why Decazes and Richelieu had been so happy pointing fingers across the border, to Belgium. After the Allied departure, every public and political necessity to come to a conviction had evaporated. The other suspects in the conspiracy were also free to go. The ladies Guyet and Cauchois-Lemaire returned to Paris in 1819, with their husbands. There, Louis Augustin François Cauchois-Lemaire in particular made a name for himself as a fervent opponent of Louis XVIII and Charles X, and after 1830, during the July Monarchy, finally found a permanent job and honourable position as the director of the royal archives. The steadfastness and independence of his wife, Judith, were also not fractured by her stay in the women's prison; she made her name as a writer of textbooks, led a kindergarten and was later appointed an inspector of education.[158] La Tour du Pin's career eventually went in the

---

[156] Stirling-Maxwell, *Napoleon's Bequest*, 48–53.
[157] 'French Papers', *The Times*, 20 May 1819, 2.
[158] H. Chisholm, 'Cauchois-Lemaire, Louis François Auguste',*Encyclopaedia Britannica*, vol. 11 (Cambridge: Cambridge University Press, 1911); L. Clark, *The Rise of Professional Women in France. Gender and Public Administration since 1830* (Cambridge: Cambridge University Press, 2001), 30, 36.

opposite direction. He was promoted in 1820 and left for the Court of Sardinia in Turin as ambassador. The July Monarchy, however, became his Waterloo. He supported the Duchess of Berry (the widow of the Duke of Berry – Charles X's youngest son – who was a former advocate for the White Terror, and had been assassinated by an anti-royal Bonapartist in 1820) in her attempt to take over power, disappeared behind bars and eventually died in exile at Lausanne in 1837.

Towards a 'European Police Directorate'?

In 1817, the Allied Council underwent its most severe crisis. The issues related to the French refugees brought the identity of the Council itself into question. Should the Council now transform what were, up to then, separate projects related to security and surveillance (passports, lists, influencing the fate of exiles, identified Bonapartists and radicals) into one centrally regulated 'European Council', a 'European Police Directorate'? Or did that go too far? And what would the alternative 'intermediate' positions be?

When it came to peace and security in Europe, none of the four ministers doubted that the primary European powers had a larger say than did the secondary powers. They also saw no reason not to interfere in the domestic affairs of other European countries. Wellington himself wrote to the Council that he was continuously working at 'persuading' the Dutch king regarding the French refugees in Brussels.[159] The Austrian, Russian and Prussian ministers and ambassadors in particular took quite a number of steps in the direction of an Allied security council. The Prussians had attempted to establish a centralized system of security management, administered meticulously by their own civil servants (Stein and Gruner). That attempt had become stuck as early as 1816 in the French swamp of plots and schemes and of politicians committed to playing two hands at the same time. But it had equally met a wall of resistance amongst their own army headquarters, where the generals had not been inclined to hand policing matters over to civil servants and their bureaucracies. The Russian approach, in turn, had been too megalomaniacal and too esoteric at the same time, although it had produced a treaty, the Holy Alliance, that especially in later years and in the eyes of the liberal opposition was taken very seriously in its potential for repressive consequences. The one able to advance the Council the furthest along the road towards a 'European Police' was Metternich. In 1816 and in the summer of 1817, with the support of the Russian and Prussian ministers, Metternich almost succeeded in turning the Council into a forum for collective intervention in the southern provinces of the Netherlands.

---

[159] Letter of Wellington, 9 May 1816, enclosure to the protocols of the Allied Council, 12 May 1816, TNA, FO 146/6.

The Allied ministers developed, via the Allied Council, a whole series of general principles and security measures. The spectre of an unfettered 'armed Jacobinism' that spread freely via the spoken word, writings and general mobility throughout Europe forged a bond between the power brokers in Europe. Their epistemological logics of security converged in a general threat assessment that lumped together everything on the spectrum from liberal writings via libels to seditious pamphlets, unrest and incitement to terror. This shared threat assessment was only further fed by real-life insurrections and attacks in their own home countries, such as the German student fraternities' protests at the Wartburg Castle in 1817, the British uprisings and foiled attacks in those same years, or uprisings of the Carbonari in Italy and revolts in Spain. Even in Britain, on 16 August 1819, the government resorted to bloody counter-insurgent tactics to suppress the peaceful demonstrations on St Peter's Field in Manchester, an infamous intervention that satirically came to be known as the Peterloo Massacre, and adopted new repressive laws.[160]

Up until late 1818, the Allied Council was the communal forum for discussing and designing the joint fight against terror – directed more against Red rather than against White Terror. The Council came close to not just translating their jointly forged security culture into circular letters and declarations but also undertaking collective military and police interventions. That this did not happen was mostly owing to British uneasiness. Castlereagh warned Stuart in the summer of 1817: 'The Allied Ministers at Paris must be kept within the bounds of their original institution and not be suffered to present themselves as an European Council for the management of the affairs of the world.'[161] Neither was Castlereagh much enchanted by 'Metternich's inordinate taste for Spies and Police'.[162] Indeed, by the beginning of 1818, Metternich's momentum was waning. The fires in Belgium were extinguished, and, as Castlereagh wrote to Clancarty, 'we must have no more circular letters from our Ministers at Paris, which cannot fail to disgust the Powers to whom they are addressed, and, in fact, to diminish our means of managing by negotiation what the common interests require'. Uni- or bilateral interventions were sufficient; London did not want to be chained to the other powers and be hauled into unpredictable continental or military adventures.[163] The British people were not at all ready for an autonomous European council that would begin to develop its own continental dynamics. 'It may be too much to assert that no

---

[160] Muir, *Wellington. Waterloo and the Fortunes of Peace*, 141–6; Zamoyski, *Phantom Terror*, 179–89, 258–61.

[161] Castlereagh to Stuart, 22 July 1817, in C. Webster, *The Foreign Policy of Castlereagh, 1815–1822. Britain and the European Alliance*, vol. 2 (London: G. Bells and Sons, 1931–47), 71.

[162] Cited in Bew, *Castlereagh*, 430.

[163] Castlereagh to Clancarty, 7 August 1817, Colenbrander (ed.), *Gedenkstukken*, vol. 8.1, 70; Muir, *Wellington. Waterloo and the Fortunes of Peace*, 110.

case could occur in Europe to render an authoritative remonstrance on the part of the Great Powers conjointly to any particular Court expedient', Castlereagh wrote, 'but such a mode of acting ought not to be of habitual occurrence, and especially ought not to proceed from the ministers in conference at Paris, as if it were done in the execution of their acknowledged functions'.[164] British national interests and thinking in terms of spheres of influence could not be combined with a supranational 'European Security Council'. In this way, Castlereagh effectively put an end to the 'function creep' of the Allied Conference in Paris.

Metternich's idea of a *centre de surveillance* did not get off the ground[165] – in any case, not as an international, European project with the British included. For France, the Netherlands and other 'secondary' powers, such as Spain, Portugal and Sardinia, this was a great relief. With reference to either their constitution, their parliament or simply their national pride, they each rejected any notion of an 'Allied government', as well as its intervening in their national security policies. The Dutch minister of foreign affairs, Van Nagell, who had (unsuccessfully) tried to resign a couple of times over precisely this foreign interference, was convinced that the Allied Conference of Ministers had too often crossed the line and, as already stated above, hence 'irritated all minor governments'.[166]

The coalition of authoritarian-absolutist states did, however, continue the fight against terror – albeit not as a joint enterprise of an Allied Conference any more, but as bilateral or unilateral endeavours. Austria and Prussia opened their *Zentralbeobachtungszentrale* (Central Intelligence Agency) in Mainz and, after the murder of the conservative playwright August von Kotzebue in 1819, agreed on a joint registration and security service.[167] In France, the deadly attack on the Duke of Berry in 1820 set a spate of new security measures in motion.[168] Decazes, the moderate and modern minister of police, was given his marching orders. For Tsar Alexander also started to tilt towards more repression. While he still hung on to his belief that a charter for France and a constitution for Poland were not only important but also necessary, he was not willing to grant either country full autonomy. He considered both national autonomy and civil liberties in the context of smaller states to be luxuries, and

---

[164] Castlereagh to Stuart, 22 August 1817, in Webster, *The Foreign Policy of Castlereagh*, vol. 2, 72. See also (Van) Sas, *Onze natuurlijkste bondgenoot*, 149–50, who found this quotation.
[165] See also Bertier de Sauvigny, *Metternich et la France*, vol. 1, 116–17; (Van) Sas, *Onze natuurlijkste bondgenoot*, 149.
[166] Colenbrander (ed.), *Gedenkstukken*, vol. 8.1, 43–4.
[167] J. van Zanten, '"Met verscheidene dolkstoten afgemaakt": Moraal en politiek in de berichten over de moord op August von Kotzebue', *De Negentiende Eeuw*, 27:1 (2003), 39–49.
[168] Zamoyski, *Phantom Terror*, 232–7, 246–8, 262–3, 271–7.

fully conditional on the provision of great powers' security considerations. In Aix-la-Chapelle, a few months after the attack on Wellington, he would even put a plan on the table that would provide an operational and executive basis for his Holy Alliance, and a continuation of the Allied Council on an even larger scale: a European Intervention Force. For Metternich, the new areas of the Habsburg Empire, in particular the Italian provinces, were a playing ground for his ideas on security and surveillance.[169] Via indirect 'advice' or direct surveillance centres, such as in Milan, he tried to bring the unruly radicals as well as the reactionary and extremist Ultras under control.

In 1818, the fight against terror in France was only partially successful. The principles of stabilization of the Bourbon regime, of de-Bonapartization and demilitarization had been implemented. The Allied Council had also put serious effort into designing, monitoring and enforcing uniform security measures in their fight against terror. The first Allied security service had been created, circular letters and uniform passports had been drafted and issued, policies on deportation and expulsion had been enforced. The Allied occupiers had, however, discovered that implementing 'indirect rule' in a country that was among the most highly developed in Europe – in terms of governance and state structure – was like trying to wade through deep mud. Increasing resistance among the populace and the duplicity of French administrators raised doubts among the Allies about whether or not the occupation contributed to security in France (and Europe). The unrest caused by the Allied measures, culminating in the attack on Wellington, moreover, induced the ministers to question the unintended consequences of their security policies. The Allied occupation was intended to 'colonize the evil passions', but instead seemed to fuel further polarization and radicalization in France and beyond. As a secondary effect of the strict disciplinary actions against the alleged Bonapartist and radicals – in particular the expulsions – the revolutionary extremism had spread and festered beyond the borders, into precisely the vulnerable neighbouring states of France, such as Belgium. In addition to this, the costs of the occupation and the ongoing humiliation of the reparation measures placed a very heavy burden on all attempts to restore political and social peace.

---

[169] Broers, *Europe after Napoleon*, 111.

7

The Price of Security

The Price of Peace

If there was anything that the people of Neufchâtel disliked, it was taxes. In the eighteenth century, this idyllic Swiss mountain village had become a principality under Prussian rule and was awash in the wealth that its Protestant patricians had earned from the slave trade. In 1806, Napoleon forced Friedrich Wilhelm III to cede sovereignty over it in exchange for Hanover, but in 1814 the population immediately rebelled against the French governor and re-embraced Prussian rule. They did so under one condition: that they would not have to pay taxes. When it seemed for a while in 1814 and 1815 that the Allies were going to levy a tax on the principality, the wealthy citizens swiftly sprang into action. The amount of the voluntary contributions they amassed in short order was so significant that they were able to convince the Allied commanders to change their minds. They were happy to pay the price for peace, but preferably to Prussia rather than to France, and then only on a voluntary basis and not because of a compulsory levy. Lady Shelley, who visited the city in July 1816, was as lyrical about the beauty of the surroundings as about the inventiveness and independence of the inhabitants:

> The *bourgeoisie* here has so great a dread of taxation in any form, that when it became necessary to raise a trifling sum for the Allies by taxation, the people at once raised the money required by voluntary contributions ... The extra money is now being spent on the improvement of the town by lengthening the quays.[1]

Neufchâtel was, regrettably, an exception – it could slip out from under the Allied yoke quite easily. Most of the towns and cities in Napoleonic France were not as fortunate. Their inhabitants had had a tough time of it during the Napoleonic Wars and as far as taxes were concerned that was not about to

---

[1] Edgcumbe (ed.), *The Diary of Frances Lady Shelley, 1787-1817*, 220-1. See also J. Courvoisier, *Le maréchal Berthier et sa principauté de Neuchâtel (1806-1814)* (Neuchâtel: Société d'histoire et d'archéologie, 1959).

change straight away after 1815. Both war and peace came at a high price. In times of war, the reserves in the war chests and the daily allowance rates for soldiers were decisive for the course of battle. The Sixth and Seventh Coalitions counted on Russian and Prussian bayonets, Austrian horses, but most of all on British pounds sterling. Months after the Battle of Waterloo, the coalition's commander, the Duke of Wellington, was still negotiating with all the small and medium-sized countries that had sent troops to France on the assumption that the British would be subsidizing their efforts.[2]

Britain, however, was not about to bear the cost of peace – and the occupation – alone. The other states also agreed that the high debts and damages occasioned by France's military campaigns, conquests and occupation had to be settled. By July 1815, the Allied Council wholeheartedly agreed on one principle: peace and security may come at a price, but those costs must be paid not by the occupiers, but by the occupied nation. The new agreements on the price of peace confirmed and extended earlier treaties: the Treaty of Chaumont (1 March 1814), the Vienna General Alliance Treaty (25 March 1815), and the Final Act of the Congress of Vienna (9 June 1815). But most of all, the reparations demanded were an expression of that fourth 'precautionary principle' that the Allied Council had formulated, and laid down in the Second Treaty of Paris (20 November 1815): the enforcement of the payment of compensatory damages (*dédommagements*) as a condition for the termination of the Allied occupation.[3]

In the previous chapters, the demilitarization, the stabilization and the fight against Bonapartist and revolutionary terror have been discussed. The principle of indemnities was for the Allied ministers equally if not more important for the pacification of France, and Europe for that matter. At the same time, this principle, not unlike the other three, was a paradoxical instrument. On the one hand, this financial prod was intended to keep the new regime of Louis XVIII in line and to ensure and pay for the occupation and security costs. But at the same time, these imposed payments caused further unrest and rebellion; not to mention the fact that France's financial reserves were all but depleted. The function of these payments was, moreover, ambiguous. They were indeed reparations, but also helped pay down overdue debts and help cover the cost of maintaining the occupying troops. These *dédommagements* were, therefore, a combination of institutional and fiduciary compensation, an instrument of law and justice, but they also served as an anchor point for the French. Meeting these payments allowed France the opportunity to show that it could earn back its place in the Concert of Europe. At the same time, the country had to come to realize that it could not afford to return to the ways of Bonapartist defiance

---

[2] See correspondence of Wellington, May–December 1815, TNA, FO 92/15.
[3] The objectives are listed in the protocol of the Allied Council of Ministers, 20 November 1815, GStA PK, III. HA I. no. 1469.

or revolutionary unrest. Peace in France in 1815 had come at a high cost for the Allies. That is why the peace had to be high-priced for France as well. What was special was that not only the four great powers used their 'victory rights' to fleece France, but other European powers were also invited to file debt and damage claims. These discussions took place around the tables of the Financial Committee of the Allied Council, composed of appointed Allied Liquidators. Before long, bankers and high-level financiers were also invited to the negotiating table. They were needed to ensure that the ruling class would become a stakeholder in French security.

Little attention has been given to the complex package of French reparations and the role of the Allied Council in these arrangements. Literature regarding this period focuses primarily on the Congress of Vienna, with some research given to the Paris Convention, but little or none to the financial settlement.[4] A number of recent publications dealing with the loans extended to France do discuss the financial–economic dimensions of these loans, but do not – or only briefly – touch on the political negotiations surrounding their settlement.[5] The role of smaller countries, such as the Netherlands, in regard to the compensation settlement in the Second Treaty of Paris has also not been investigated before.[6] In particular, the place of these financial security payments in the broader security system that the Allied Council tried to set up has remained a closed book. With

---

[4] Mark Jarrett touches on it briefly. Jarrett, *The Congress of Vienna and its Legacy*, 172, 180. Some of the older literature mentions the financial paragraphs, albeit briefly: Dupuis, *Le ministère de Talleyrand en 1814*, vol. 1, 358–68; Kissinger, *A World Restored*; T. Chapman, *The Congress of Vienna. Origins, Processes and Results* (Oxford: Routledge, 1998), 54; Landheer, 'Afrekenen met het verleden', especially 206–8, 217–22; Veve, *The Duke of Wellington and the British Army of Occupation in France*, 12–17.

[5] J. Greenfield, 'Financing a New Order: The Payment of Reparations by Restoration France, 1817–1818', *French History*, 30:3 (2016), 376–400; E. White, 'Making the French Pay: The Costs and Consequences of the Napoleonic Reparations', *European Review of Economic History*, 5:3 (2001), 337–65; K. Oosterlinck, L. Ureche-Rangau and J.-M. Vaslin, 'Baring, Wellington and the Resurrection of French Public Finances Following Waterloo', *The Journal of Economic History*, 74:4 (2014), 1072–102; A. Nicolle, 'The Problem of Reparations after the Hundred Days', *The Journal of Modern History*, 25:4 (1953), 343–54; D. Platt, *Foreign Finance in Continental Europe and the United States, 1815–1870. Quantities, Origins, Functions and Distribution* (London: Allen & Unwin, 1984); P. Ziegler, *The Sixth Great Power. Barings, 1762–1929* (London: Knopf, 1988); N. Ferguson, *The World's Banker. The History of the House of Rothschild* (London: Weidenfeld & Nicolson, 1998). See also G. Sluga, '"Who Hold the Balance of the World?" Bankers at the Congress of Vienna, and in International History', *The American Historical Review*, 122:5 (2017), 1403–30; Sluga, 'Economic Insecurity, "Securities" and a European Security Culture after the Napoleonic Wars', in De Graaf, De Haan and Vick (eds.), *Securing Europe after Napoleon*, 288–305.

[6] Paragraphs on the overdue debt are based in part on a previously published article by B. de Graaf and M. van Leeuwen-Canneman, 'De prijs van de vrede: De Nederlandse inbreng in het Europees Concert, 1815–1818', *BMGN*, 133:1 (2018), 21–51.

new archive materials available, the story of the intended and unintended consequences of that financial security policy can now be investigated. What was the price of peace, and did these financial investments actually facilitate a safer situation in France and for Europe? Fighting terror and securing peace in Europe proved to be a capitalist venture; it was paid for with money from high-powered financiers, and also served to further the security of that internationally interwoven ruling class.

Reparations in the Era of the 'Balance of Power'

In 1815, the place and purpose of compensation and reparations as a logical part of a *sortie de guerre* were not codified.[7] They could finance an occupational force, but also be used as retribution and compensation for damages suffered. Today, reparations are described as 'compensation for an injury or wrong, esp. for wartime damages or breach of an international obligation'.[8] This can apply to all kinds of financial compensation for injustices committed against individuals or groups (war crimes, slavery, colonialism, genocide, etc.). In a more classical sense, reparations primarily concern payments between states. As codified in 1907, the victorious state could request compensation after a war for the damages incurred.[9] In 1815, none of those regulations were in place yet. The victor determined what the economic relationship with the conquered nation would look like. For the Greeks and Romans, that happened via organized vandalism, plunder and imposed tributes. Until well into the eighteenth century, these types of war contributions and systematic plundering were a standard component of warfare, and more particularly, of a *sortie de guerre*. That is how Louis XIV financed a quarter of his war chest. During the Seven Years War, Prussia also fell prey to Austrian, French, Russian and British raids.[10]

Napoleon was readily inclined to impose ruthless levies. As often as was possible, he milked the countries he conquered and occupied. Robbery, looting, imposed indemnities and the mandatory billeting of his troops were all standard means to have the countries he conquered cover the costs of his

---

[7] With thanks to Daan den Braven; see D. den Braven, A Just Contribution. On the Reparations Imposed on Post-Napoleonic France (unpublished MA thesis, Utrecht University, 2017).

[8] S. Wolfe, *The Politics of Reparations and Apologies* (New York: Springer, 2014), 23.

[9] 'Convention (IV) respecting the Laws and Customs of War on Land and its annex', The Hague, 18 October 1907, *The Avalon Project*, via http://avalon.law.yale.edu/20th_century/hague04.asp (last viewed: 30 April 2019).

[10] J. Lynn, 'Looting/Plunder/Booty', in R. Cowley and G. Parker (eds.), *The Reader's Companion to Military History* (New York: Houghton Mifflin, 1996), 271; A. Gillespie, *History of the Laws of War*, vol. 2: *The Customs and Laws of War with Regards to Civilians in Times of Conflict* (Oxford: Bloomsbury, 2011), 241–2.

expeditions and invasions.[11] Starting in 1803, Spain had to cough up 6 million francs a month to maintain its neutrality. Austria and Prussia were required to pay contributions of 350 and 515 million francs respectively.[12] Even after the battles were over, Napoleon continued to press the vanquished states for more. In 1803, he forced the Batavian Republic (the newly minted Dutch republic) to fully provide for a French and a Batavian expeditionary and occupation army.[13] In the 1805 Treaty of Pressburg, Napoleon not only stripped Austria of one sixth of its territory and 3 million of its inhabitants, offering only Salzburg as a minor compensation, he also imposed an additional contribution on her and demanded that Austria bear the costs of his occupation army as well.[14] The Treaty of Tilsit of 1808 was even more ruthless. Napoleon confiscated about half of Prussia's pre-war territories, had his French troops occupy the Prussian forts and forced Prussia to join the Continental System (against the British Empire). He also imposed a war contribution of 140 million francs on Prussia, and ordered the Prussian state treasury to pay for the maintenance of the imperial garrisons.[15] In this way, between 1802 and 1814, Napoleon diverted the payment of 41 per cent of the funds necessary for waging his wars to the occupied territories.[16]

Given this background, the attitude of the Prussian army command, hiding behind 'the will of Providence' to freely dip into the French coffers, is understandable. At the same time, the contours of the Allied Ministerial Conference's moderation stand out more clearly. The agreed-upon occupation of France was in service to European security and not intended to line the pockets of the victors or to exploit the vanquished – Napoleon had shown how disastrous that was. The ministerial arrangements constituted a radical decision and evidenced the new paradigm that characterized international politics and warfare at the beginning of the nineteenth century.[17] The rejuvenated balance-of-power paradigm, as we saw in Chapter 3, tied power to justice, reasonableness and moderation. Organized plunder no longer fitted those parameters, any more than the unilateral imposition of reparations. States that had joined together in the war effort would also share any post-war

[11] Kennedy, *The Rise and Fall of the Great Powers*, 133–5; P. Dwyer, *Napoleon and Europe* (New York: Routledge, 2014), 10–11.
[12] Esdaile, *Napoleon's Wars*, 459.
[13] Already in 1795, the Batavian Republic had committed to pay a 'liberation contribution' (indemnity) of 100 million guilders. See T. Pfeil, *'Tot redding van het vaderland'. Het primaat van de Nederlandse overheidsfinanciën in de Bataafs-Franse tijd, 1795–1810* (Amsterdam: Amsterdam University Press, 1998), 126–30, 331–45.
[14] Schroeder, *The Transformation of European Politics*, 284; M. Leggiere, *Napoleon and the Struggle for Germany* (Cambridge: Cambridge University Press, 2015), 27; Gillespie, *A History of the Laws of War*, vol. 2, 248.
[15] Leggiere, *Napoleon and the Struggle for Germany*, 25–8.
[16] P. Branda, 'La guerre a-t-elle payé la guerre?', in T. Lentz (ed.), *Napoléon et l'Europe. Regards sur une politique* (Paris: Fayard, 2005), 270–1.
[17] Schroeder, *The Transformation of European Politics*, 6–7.

revenues in a reasonable manner. That was already apparent from Wellington's disapproving response to Blücher's attempt to impose a war contribution on the Parisians (to benefit the Prussian war chest) of 100 million francs. 'In regard to the contribution laid on the city of Paris', as Wellington instructed Blücher on 9 July 1815, 'it appears to me that the Allies will contend that one party to a general alliance ought not to derive all the benefit resulting from the operations of the armies'.[18]

If this paradigm shift was evident anywhere, it was in the discussions about financial reparations. Blücher did not get the 100-million-franc indemnity he hoped for, at least not straight away and not in his inimitable blunt fashion. The Prussian troops would have to wait patiently together with the other armies for a fair distribution of the contributions that all of France, and not just Paris, would be paying. The ministers would decide 'in conference' on the amount of those contributions, and even grant French officials an executive and mitigating role in that process.[19] The imposed sanctions also had to be subjected to a moderate reading of the 'balance of power'.

The French Have to Pay – But How?

Already on 19 July, the Allied Council of Ministers decreed that, effective immediately, commanders and generals would not be allowed to submit requisitions or collect their 'booty' on their own.[20] Claiming otherwise, Talleyrand continued to bombard the Council for weeks with lists and evidence to the contrary. According to him, a Prussian commander, for example, pocketing 2,329 francs, had emptied the departmental coffers of Eure, and in the district of Vernins a quarter of the workhorses had been stolen, worth 600,000 francs.[21] According to a frustrated Talleyrand, the Allies had already collected approximately 57 million in unorganized contributions by the end of July, 33.5 million of which had been siphoned off by the Prussians alone – a claim that Prussia's General Gneisenau strongly denied. According to his own calculations, his commanders had 'picked up' only 1.3 million.[22] Be that as it may, as of 22 July (at least on paper), these sorts of requisitions were disallowed. Collecting contributions (via taxes and other sources of income) was left to officials of the French government, who would disburse them centrally and directly to the Allies at set intervals. It was only when the French government failed to do so that the commanders were allowed to

[18] Wellington to Blücher, 9 July 1815, in *WD*, vol. 12, 552–4.
[19] 'Aucun des Cabinets ne voudra et ne pourra conséquemment sous sa propre & seule responsabilité agir isolément.' See annex 6 to the protocol of 13 July 1815, GStA PK, III. HA I. no. 1464.
[20] Annex 25, protocol of 19 July 1815, GStA PK, III. HA I. no. 1464.
[21] Annex 29, protocol of 20 July 1815, GStA PK, III. HA I. no. 1464.
[22] Protocol of 22 July 1815, GStA PK, III. HA I. no. 1464.

take what was due them for the maintenance of their troops – a provision that of course did not exclude future conflicts.[23]

Although the final format and scale of the desired reparations was still in the making, this would be the principle implemented for the months of July and August. The Allied Council demanded 50 million francs for the maintenance of the troops, the first half of which had to be paid by 25 August. According to Castlereagh, this was a fair and reasonable compromise between what the French treasury and citizenry could handle, and what the Allies needed.[24] But he had failed to factor Talleyrand into the equation, who let it be known that he was not in a position to meet that first instalment:

> He states that since the civil and financial administration has not been fully and unreservedly handed back to him, it was not in his powers to procure the funds for the payment of the first 25 million for which the date of payment is August 25.[25]

Talleyrand indeed flipped the Allies' financial mandate into an attempted form of blackmail and suggested that the French would show the money once the occupation was rescinded and France had its autonomy back.

Before Prussia's anger could explode in France's face, the French minister of finance, Baron Louis, came up with a proposal that was as elegant as it was modern: the French government could not pay from what was not in the treasury, nor from what they could not expect as eventual income. But it could pay the amount in instalments, assuming that it could procure a loan; because, 'with the help of this loan, we cannot help but look confidently towards the future'. The French and the Allies were in the same boat, and no one would benefit from a prolonged feud over finances. The Allies would set a fixed amount for maintenance per soldier per day and the French would issue the required treasury notes. The value of these vouchers depended on the reliability and regularity of the daily disbursements and the stability of the state and its institutions. It was, therefore, in the interest of the Allies to respect that arrangement *and* those French institutions. Relieved, and for want of better alternatives, the Allied Ministerial Conference agreed to this plan on 7 September.[26]

---

[23] Protocols of 1 and 4 August 1815, GStA PK, III. HA I. no. 1464.
[24] Castlereagh's memorandum, annex 65, protocol of 5 August; protocol of 6 August 1815, GStA PK, III. HA I. no. 1464.
[25] Protocol of 27 August 1815, GStA PK, III. HA I. no. 1464.
[26] Annex 95, protocol of 27 August 1815; protocol of 7 September 1815, GStA PK, III. HA I. no. 1465.

Twelve Hundred Million

Fifty million in vouchers was only the beginning. Blücher and Gneisenau, with the other Prussian generals following suit, felt that more French bloodletting was called for. Their bid for Napoleon's execution and Blücher's fervent desire to destroy the Pont d'Iéna in Paris had already failed to materialize, just like the 100 million he demanded in compensatory damages. With some clamour Blücher therefore pressured Hardenberg not to give in to the accommodating attitude of the British and the Russians this time.[27] Hardenberg was not planning on doing anything of the sort, because 'in 1814 the Prussians had graciously relinquished their claims. It was enough to be duped once [by the French], and that that will not happen again.'[28] Unlike Blücher and Gneisenau, however, Hardenberg was not a brawler, but a bureaucrat. He wanted to calculate the costs fairly, and agreed with Wellington and Metternich that ascertaining the debt and indemnities should not be carried out as an act of blind revenge. 'We are going to stop with this kind of arbitrary measures, disarray, depredations, imposed contributions and requisitions', Hardenberg told the army command.[29] As a respectable bureaucrat and diplomat, Hardenberg realized that the new order should be predictable and reasonable. That is why, in preparation for the first discussions within the Allied Council, Hardenberg compiled numerous lists and notes in which he meticulously calculated the damage that Napoleon had inflicted on the Prussian monarchy. He was able to show that the Prussian claims were 'fair' compared to those of the other countries.

In July, Hardenberg came up with a tally of 350 million francs for the damage suffered by Prussia. That amount was calculated by adding the 90 million in war contributions imposed by Napoleon (80 million paid by the German provinces following the 1808 Treaty of Tilsit, 10 million of which was paid on behalf of the city of Königsberg) to the 10 million, plus 120 million and still another 130 million in requisitions demanded by the French after 1808. That amount did not even include the cost of maintaining and billeting the troops and their daily provisions.[30] Extrapolating to include the claims of the other Allies, Hardenberg arrived at an amount of 1,200 million in damages that the Allies reckoned for the French. That amount was excessively high – it far exceeded the gross domestic product of France – and did not even include the cost of maintaining the Allied occupation forces in France.[31]

Metternich was not on board with that amount. The Allies were in France to lay a solid foundation for a French restoration that would provide peace and

[27] Cf. Petonke, *Der Konflikt*, 1–54.
[28] Hardenberg, *Mémoire*, 22 July 1815, 27, GStA PK, III. HA I. no. 1461.
[29] Hardenberg, memorandum, 22 July 1815, point 1, GStA PK, III. HA I. no. 1461.
[30] Sum of the balance, July 1815. Probably compiled by Hardenberg. GStA PK, III. HA I. no. 1461.
[31] Hardenberg, *Mémoire*, 22 July 1815, 27, GStA PK, III. HA I. no. 1461.

security throughout Europe. Just as he disapproved of Blücher's pillaging, he also rejected Hardenberg's financial 'war of conquest'. Predatory and 'counter-predatory pillaging' was no guarantee for security. This made sense for Metternich, since for him, the greatest threat to security was a new reversal in property and ownership.[32] The Allied ministers, therefore, had to urgently 'curb the subversive principles that undermine the social order and on which Bonaparte had based his usurpation'.[33] For Prussian commanders and ministers to demand major territorial revisions and exorbitant indemnities would only feed the spectre of terror. The extent of the reparations had to be such that it did not provoke an unnecessary amount of instability in France. Metternich was therefore looking for a system of compensation that was 'based on the spirit of the treaties, on the actual situation in France, and on the need to keep the calm on the continent'. That system had to provide both 'guarantees that France could give to the powers' and 'guarantees that France would receive from the powers': in other words, a 'balance of payments' that would not jeopardize the security of the ruling classes either in France or in Europe.[34] According to Gentz, Metternich sought 'a middle way between these two extremes', referring to the moderate position of the British and Russians on the one hand, and the aggressive Prussian position on the other.[35]

Money or Land?

Having come this far, Metternich, supported by the British, made an interesting move: he brought fortifications into the discussion. Two reasons brought him to conclude that the potential for French insurgence should not only be kept in line with financial assurances, but could also be addressed by removing the French line of defence along its borders. First of all, based on the Austrian and German experience of France's ruthless occupational presence under Napoleon, he feared that an Allied occupation might sooner undermine the sense of peace within France than promote it.[36] Secondly, as mentioned above, he felt that the Allies had to take their own system of treaties and moderate security initiatives seriously. This meant that the Allies had to 'help' France transition from an offensive to a defensive security policy. Crucial to this transition was the line of forts along France's northern and eastern border, which, positioned as they were so close to the neighbouring countries'

[32] Metternich, memorandum, 6 August 1815, GStA PK, III. HA I. no. 1461, 70, 75.
[33] Ibid., 75.
[34] Ibid.
[35] Gentz to Caradja, 'Friedenspräludien', late August 1815, in R. Metternich-Winneburg (ed.), *Oesterreichs Teilnahme an den Befreiungskriegen* (Vienna: Gerold's Sohn, 1887), 707.
[36] Metternich, memorandum, 6 August 1815, GStA PK, III. HA I. no. 1461, 75. See also (Den) Braven, A Just Contribution.

territorial borders, could never serve as an exclusively defensive presence. Given the balance-of-power framework, it was logical, according to Metternich, that this French system of fortifications should be modified – especially because all the forts in the Low Countries and Germany were destroyed or in a state of disrepair. It would take far too long and be too expensive to wait until those countries could restore their forts. So, in anticipation of the reconstruction of the forts in these neighbouring countries, France could begin to help pay for new forts, or possibly also dismantle their own forts or transfer them to the Allies.[37] On the remaining reparations that needed to be paid after the damages were paid for with fortresses, the Austrian position was ambivalent: the Austrian ministers did expect some payment of indemnities, but Metternich did not say how much exactly, nor how much of these indemnities was payable either in francs or in forts, or in a combination of these.

Tsar Alexander was happy to pick up the gauntlet. Entirely in line with the generosity he showed in 1814 and his mesmerist–messianic inclinations, he did not even mention money. He was thinking politically. As Castlereagh and Liverpool rightly surmised, Russia was remote, and it was to the tsar's advantage not to humiliate France too much, so as to be able to use France as a counterweight to Austria on the continent.[38] Russia categorically rejected Prussia's demands. Pozzo di Borgo, the Russian ambassador, along with Nesselrode, felt that Prussia's claims would only generate a 'toxic aura', and that the 'inevitable problems that would arise in implementing them would become a source of discontent'.[39] Alexander also realized that, expressing himself in the mesmerist discourse he still adhered to in these months, 'in the present convulsed state of France, no government . . . can in itself afford to the Allies and to Europe that security which they are entitled to expect'. That is why a Russian memorandum suggested that the occupation should not exceed five to seven years, and that the French reparations should be enough to pay for a new line of defence for the protection of the neighbouring countries and for the Allies' occupation of the French fortresses until that new line was complete[40] – the reason being that 'within just limits the Allies are entitled to the fruits of conquest, and therefore to such permanent acquisitions as they might deem necessary for their own security'.[41]

[37] Metternich, memorandum, 77, 80.
[38] Castlereagh to Liverpool, 24 July 1815, WSD, vol. 11, 122; Liverpool to Castlereagh, 28 July 1815, Vane (ed.), Correspondence, vol. 10, 445. See also J. Hartley, Alexander I (London: Longman, 1994), 142.
[39] Pozzo di Borgo to Nesselrode, 5 and 17 October 1815, in Pozzo di Borgo (ed.), Correspondance, 227. See also Alopeus to Nesselrode, 16 (28) December 1815, in Ministerstvo inostrannykh del CCCP (ed.), Vneshniaia politika Rossii, vol. 1, 52–3.
[40] Enclosure ('an official memorandum in consequence of the Russian paper'), included in Liverpool's letter to Castlereagh, 3 August 1815, WSD, vol. 11, 86–9.
[41] Ibid., 87.

This combination of financial demands (albeit restrained ones) and territorial claims was well received within the governmental offices in London.
Friedrich Gentz, Metternich's assistant, knew that the majority of the British
population was in favour of imposing hefty reparations, both in land and in
capital. Public outrage in Britain was tamed only because of Wellington's
shining reputation on the home front.[42] In August 1815, Liverpool, the
British prime minister, impressed upon Castlereagh that the British must not
be given the runaround, and that their government had 'a right to expect a fair
indemnity for our losses'. Liverpool believed that this could also be met by
France ceding territory, but that 'if the French government are unwilling to pay
that indemnity by sacrifices of territory, we must require it of them in such
means as may render the territories of our Allies secure against future
aggression'.[43] Agreeing with London, Spain and the Netherlands also saw the
sense of considering certain border areas and fortified cities; after all, these had
been Napoleon's front line of defence and the springboard for his attacks. With
this, a consensus had been achieved that the reparations could indeed be paid
both in francs and in fortresses – but there remained an open debate as to how
extensive the amount of the payments had to be.[44]

Indemnities – But for What?

In August, the problem had still not been resolved, and unrest was on the rise
in France. As noted earlier, Wellington's chief of intelligence, Gruner, reported
that all kinds of wild rumours were circulating among the people of Paris about
France being parcelled up. The Council of Ministers had to publish their
decisions quickly in order to neutralize the *fausses nouvelles*, the 'fake news'
avant la lettre. But in order to determine the price tag for the reparations, the
extent of the damages had to be defined first. As Lord Bathurst, the British
minister of war, summarized it: 'The Allies have an unquestionable right to be
indemnified by France. But for what?' Lacking today's conventions regarding
'crimes against humanity', or other international law provisions, the Allied
Council tried to figure out the correct formula for calculating France's war
debt. The guiding principle for that formula was the idea of a 'balanced peace'
and a general security for Europe. According to Bathurst, there was only one
clear answer to the question regarding the nature of the damage. The reparations were intended as compensation 'for the expense they [the Allies] have
incurred by the violation of the Treaty of Paris' – encompassing all costs
incurred by the military campaigns of the Seventh Coalition, calculating

[42] Gentz to Karadja, 5 September 1815, in Prokesch-Osten (ed.), *Dépêches inédites*, 172–5.
[43] Liverpool to Castlereagh, 11 August 1815, *WSD*, vol. 11, 114.
[44] See Jarrett, *The Congress of Vienna and its Legacy*, 171.

from the return of Napoleon onwards.[45] Liverpool, too, believed that the Allies were 'fully entitled ... to indemnity and security' on the basis of France's 'violation of the most sacred treaties'.[46] That sounded more dramatic than it was, because Bathurst's reference to the Paris Treaty implied that France did not have to answer for the costs incurred by the Allies during the campaign prior to 1814.

Yet, because such a general declaration of guilt, laid on the doorstep of the entire country, was inconsistent with the Allies' offer regarding 'mutual security' in its General Alliance Treaty of 25 March 1815, this was still not the solution. In Article VIII, the Allies had clearly distinguished between Napoleon and his followers on the one hand, against whom the war efforts were directed, and the French people and the king, who were seen as allies. Gentz also noted this discrepancy; the Treaty of 25 March promised Allied support for France against Napoleon. The ministers could not now suddenly claim compensation from the same people. Wellington agreed – not all of France embraced Napoleon's resurgence after 20 March.[47] There was also a minority in parliament that agreed with that line of reasoning. Demanding too much would not be fair, and would prove to be counterproductive. According to parliamentarian Francis Horner, 'It was the first time he had heard that to subject any people to a large pecuniary contribution was a good mode of producing their tranquillity.' That would never work in England; why did Castlereagh think that it would work in France?[48] His comments hit the nail on the head, correctly describing the paradox of the peace: the price that had to be paid would more likely undermine the peace within France than reinforce it.

So, a compromise had to be found between Prussia's demand for total debt repayment (the 1,200 million), which went too far back in history, the overly vague parameters of the moderate reparations that Metternich and Alexander were broaching, the 'will of the people' in Europe who thought it just fine that France should 'bleed', and the practical approach of the British ministers to combine the one (security) with the other (compensation) in a meaningful fashion. That is why Bathurst's suggestion that the starting point for the indemnifications should be the violation of the Paris treaties kept coming up in the discussions. His position also provided for a reduction of France's

[45] Bathurst to Castlereagh, 25 August 1815, Vane (ed.), *Correspondence*, vol. 10, 500–2.

[46] Liverpool to Castlereagh, 15 July 1815, *WSD*, vol. 11, 33.

[47] See Gentz to Karadja, 19 July 1815, Metternich-Winneburg (ed.), *Oesterreichs Teilnahme an den Befreiungskriegen*, 675. See also 'Traité de la quadruple alliance conclu à Vienne le 25 mars 1815', in A. de Clercq (ed.), *Recueil des traités de la France, 1803–1815*, vol. 2 (Paris: Amyot, 1864), 474–6; Wellington to Castlereagh, 11 August 1815, *WD*, vol. 12, 596.

[48] See discussion in parliament regarding the 'Address upon the Treaties with Foreign Powers', 19 February 1816, in Hansard (ed.), *The Parliamentary Debates*, vol. 32, 773–4.

territory to the borders of 1790 and no further. Castlereagh could fully agree with that. He could only imagine that ceding territory within those borders would be extremely difficult for the French king to accept. Lands conquered by Napoleon were one thing, but the land that his predecessor, Louis XVI, had ruled was sacred. A Bourbon could not let that realm be circumcised. Moreover, that kind of territorial chastening would contribute little to the security of Europe. Finally, it was likewise questionable which countries would be allowed to benefit from that eventual change of hands. With an eye to the balance of power, that would create all sorts of new problems.[49]

By the end of September, after weeks of negotiations, reconciliation between the British and Russian push for a 'moderate' peace and Prussia's preference for retaliation and Austria's inclination to demand more territorial reductions still eluded them. What was worse, another financial claim was put on the table that had to be dealt with first.

Outstanding Debt

There was one very clear category of payments about which the Allied Conference wholeheartedly agreed – the so-called arrears payments.[50] These payments affected every country in Europe and exceeded all other financial security instruments in terms of size. Even though their significance and consequences were immense, they have not been addressed as such elsewhere before.[51] It will be worth our while to give more extensive attention to them. The case can be made that France's liquidation of outstanding debts, with the corresponding lengthy political negotiations, was the first successful project of a common European, capitalist security culture.

When we bear in mind that the greatest fear of the European security community in 1815–16 was the *Umwertung aller Werte* – the revaluation of all values – and in particular that of property value, then it becomes clear that security also had an economic and financial core. In line with Rafe Blaufarb's analysis of how the French Revolution created a new framework for private property-holding, we could argue that the question of handling the outstanding debt demonstrates the emergence of these new power alignments between national governments and private property owners.[52] Napoleonic expropriations were not reversed; *émigrés* and the clergy could for the most part forget

---

[49] Castlereagh, 'Address upon the Treaties with Foreign Powers', 19 February 1816, in Hansard (ed.), *The Parliamentary Debates*, vol. 32, 695–6. See also Castlereagh to Liverpool, 24 July 1815, 'Précis of correspondence on settlement with France', *WSD*, vol. 11, 122.

[50] See also (De) Graaf and Van Leeuwen-Canneman, 'De prijs van de vrede', 21–51.

[51] See the literature references at the beginning of this chapter.

[52] Cf. R. Blaufarb, *The Great Demarcation. The French Revolution and the Invention of Modern Property* (Oxford: Oxford University Press, 2016).

about the *domaines nationaux* – their expropriated land and possessions, which had now passed into the hands of the state. At the same time, the outstanding debt of the French state to private creditors soon became a core priority for the Allied powers. According to the Allied ministers, propelled by the overwhelming lobby of private creditors at home, this was a moral obligation that had to be dealt with justly. It was also a systemic principle upon which consolidation and stabilization of the post-war economy rested. After all, an economy could only flourish when the payment of debts was assured. Already in 1814, almost one third of the articles of the First Treaty of Paris (30 May) had to do with settling these financial matters.[53] They dealt in the first place with private property: private creditors could submit claims for overdue payments for goods and services they provided, or for damage caused by warfare. Soldiers and civil servants could anticipate past-due salaries, pensions and disability benefits. The guarantees issued by civil servants also fell under these settlements, as did the possessions that municipalities and (charitable) organizations had to relinquish for the benefit of the French amortization coffers. (These kinds of debt settlements worked in both directions, however. Then, countries whose territory had been or was to be enlarged with former French areas had to settle the arrear debts that rested on these lands with France as well.)[54]

Little came of these provisions in 1814, in part because Napoleon's return undermined most of the arrangements, but also because of the obstructive policies of the French commissioners appointed to implement them. In July 1815, the Allied Council immediately informed the Allies that everyone in Europe could submit their claims to France as long as that was done before 1 March 1817 – and that this time the correct settlement would be monitored and enforced. For the Allies, Europe's security was equated with the security of the ruling class. For French contemporaries and later historians, the financial arrangements were an affront. According to the historian André Nicolle, this provision 'was destined to encourage all sorts of grossly exaggerated claims for reparation'.[55] And indeed, a first harvest would result in a pile of claims totalling more than 1.5 billion francs.

The Dutch Claims

In order to get a sense of how this process of claims and redress worked, and to emphasize how much this affected all the countries of Europe, we will consider how the Dutch lobby in France worked the ropes. The issue of private claims

---

[53] See 'Traité de paix signé à Paris le 30 mai 1814 entre la France, l'Autriche, la Russie, la Grande-Bretagne et la Prusse', in Clercq (ed.), *Recueil des traités*, vol. 2, 421.

[54] Landheer, 'Afrekenen met het verleden', 217–19.

[55] Nicolle, 'The Problem of Reparations after the Hundred Days', 343.

was particularly pressing for the Netherlands, because it – with private claims from the (combined) northern and southern parts of the newly established kingdom – was France's greatest creditor. One consequence of the Allies' 'concert diplomacy' was that the great powers supported the medium-sized ones, as the United Kingdom did the Netherlands, in soliciting and submitting claims to the extent that they were judged legitimate and fit into the framework of the presumed principles and peace treaties. The Netherlands was thus a country that, like no other, reaped the benefits of this moderated peace. When the details of the Paris Peace Treaty reached the Netherlands, King Willem I appointed Elias Canneman as 'Commissioner-General, in charge of the liquidation that must take place between this State and His Most Christian Majesty [the French king] as a result of the peace treaty'.[56]

Canneman seemed to be a suitable candidate for the negotiations in Paris. He was a mathematical wizard, a master of precision and, owing to years of experience at the Ministry of Finance – between 1798 and 1811 he had risen to be its secretary general – well versed in public finances. He also knew how the French worked, and how shrewd France's officials could be. During the last two years of the French annexation, he had been the director of direct taxation in the department of Bouches-de-la-Meuse – an area near the mouth of the Meuse River in the Netherlands. In November 1813, he joined the provisional government, which prepared the way for the return of the Sovereign Prince Willem to the Netherlands. After the restoration of independence, he was the minister of finance for a few months, and thereafter was appointed a member of the Council of State. In the meantime, he had also become the chairman of the 'commission for the settlement of domestic public debts engaged and contracted for Our arrival to rule the United Netherlands'.[57] So, it was logical that he left for Paris, where he represented the Dutch financial interests from December 1814 until the beginning of March 1815.[58]

But, despite his seasoned disposition, things did not go so well for him in Paris. The French commissioners made it clear to Canneman that nothing would be paid to Dutch individuals if the Netherlands did not first pay its debt to France. The French counterclaim had to do with the 'Belgian debt' – debts related to former Belgian territories that had gone to the Netherlands and were

[56] Sovereign Decree (SB) of 20 July 1814, no. 28.28, NL-HaNA (General Secretary of State (ASS)), 2.02.01, inv. no. 31.
[57] M. van Leeuwen-Canneman (ed.), *Een vriendschap in het teken van 's Lands financiën. Briefwisseling tussen Elias Canneman en Isaac Jan Alexander Gogel, 1799–1813* (The Hague: Instituut voor Nederlandse Geschiedenis, 2009), xli–xlix. See also A. Alsche, 'Levensberigt van Elias Canneman', *Jaarboek van de Maatschappij der Nederlandse Letterkunde* (1862), 47–69.
[58] Canneman's assignment to go to Paris, with corresponding instructions, SB, 3 December 1814, no. 26, NL-HaNA, 2.02.01, inv. no. 59.

registered in France's general ledger.[59] A claim for interest owed to the Netherlands that Canneman submitted for the year 1813 was rejected out of hand. With no further progress in sight, Canneman sought support from the commissioners of Prussia, Austria and the Hanseatic cities, with whom he quickly aligned himself. The French commissioners, however, did not give an inch.[60] Frustrated, the Allied commissions wrote home with the request to inform the Congress of Vienna. On 1 March 1815, Napoleon landed in the south of France.[61] The Hundred Days were about to begin; and with that, the negotiations ended.

In Vienna, where the Allies had begun to redraw the map of Europe in September 1814, the topic of the debts had yet to be broached. The settlement of private claims was also not addressed in the Final Act of the Vienna Congress. After Waterloo, however, it was clear to the great powers that the second Paris convention would also have to address the financial dimensions of the collective security and peace to which they were committed. The Netherlands was not a member of the Allied Council. However, as a signatory to the General Alliance Treaty of 25 March 1815 and the Final Act of Vienna of 9 June, and as a supplier of troops for the last campaign, the Netherlands was regarded as 'allied' and was invited to be a full member of the Allies' financial and military committee. Countries such as Spain and Portugal were as well, but had not yet signed the Final Act of Vienna – which was a condition for cherry-picking from the French grove. The plenipotentiary for the Netherlands, Gagern (Fig. 7.1), who was already in Paris to search for stolen Dutch artworks, heard from his German contacts that the Netherlands was eligible for a share of the first 50 million francs for the remuneration and maintenance of the Allied troops. The four great powers each received 10 million francs; smaller countries that had supplied a substantial share of the troops at Waterloo, such as the Netherlands, were allowed to divvy up the remaining 10 million amongst themselves.[62]

---

[59] Debts registered in the general ledger were perpetual and inalienable. Canneman could not negotiate the 'Belgian debt' because his mandate was limited to the area that the Sovereign Prince then governed. H. Colenbrander, *Vestiging van het Koninkrijk* (Amsterdam: Meulenhoff, 1927), 186–7; J. Koch, *Koning Willem I, 1772–1843* (Amsterdam: Boom, 2013), 268–73; W. Uitterhoeve, *'Een innige vereeniging'. Naar één koninkrijk van Nederland en België in 1815* (Nijmegen: Vantilt, 2015), 97.

[60] Canneman to the Sovereign Prince (Willem), 13 January, 25 January and 16 February 1815, NL-HaNA, 2.02.01, inv. no. 84; Canneman to Willem, 2 March 1815, 2.02.01, inv. no. 147; 'Note communiquée à M.M. les commissaires des Hautes Puissances Alliés pour la liquidation avec la France, par le Commissaire de S. A. R. le Prince Souverain des Provinces Unies des Pays-Bas', 22 January 1815, NL-HaNA (Collection Canneman), 2.21.005.30, inv. no. 36. In addition to Willem I, Canneman also let the Dutch envoy in Vienna, Gerrit Carel van Spaen van Voorstonden, know what was happening. See Canneman to Van Spaen, 18 February 1815, NL-HaNA, 2.21.005.30, inv. no. 36.

[61] SB, 2 March 1815, no. 147, NL-HaNA, 2.02.01, inv. no. 84.

[62] Protocol no. 41, of 24 August 1815; see also protocol of 6 August 1815, GStA PK, III. HA I. no. 1465.

Figure 7.1 Hans von Gagern, envoy for the Netherlands at the Congress of Vienna. Artist unknown, *c.*1815. (National Archive, The Hague)

The most important financial demand of the Netherlands remained the private debt claims. Gagern and Canneman (who came back to Paris to support his colleague with financial calculations) together started an intense lobby for support with the other allies.[63] The committee had not yet started its deliberations, but Gagern, Canneman and Robbert Fagel, the Dutch ambassador, set out straight away to win the British to their cause, ambassador Stuart and Castlereagh in particular.[64] They in turn tried to cool the heels of their Dutch colleagues: inviting smaller powers around the table was one thing, but these should not create a pertinent imbalance of payments. It was, after all, not just about the Netherlands. The British were concerned that the invitation to the Allies would lead to millions of claims on top of the already agreed-upon 700 million francs in reparations. That would push France over the brink of bankruptcy and endanger the stability of the country. France had already indicated at the end of

---

[63] Royal Decree (KB) of 22 September 1815, NL-HaNA, 2.21.005.30, inv. no. 28; Gagern, *Der zweite Pariser Frieden*, 244–5. Gagern had received a memorandum regarding the general state of affairs from the Dutch minister of finance, Charles Six, which he forwarded to Stuart. Memorandum (in both Dutch and French) in NL-HaNA, 2.05.01, inv. no. 15, 688; Tweede Kamer (ed.), *Handelingen*, special session, 21–9 September 1815, 36.

[64] Gagern, *Der zweite Pariser Frieden*, 257.

August that it could not even come up with the first down payment of 50 million.[65] That was why the British proposed alternative solutions: France could be forgiven part of its debt to individuals, pay later or arrange for a lump-sum payment per country. Canneman and Gagern preferred the latter option.[66]

Help from Prussia

Meanwhile, Gagern and Canneman also solicited support from Karl Sigmund Baron vom Stein zum Altenstein,[67] a forceful Prussian statesman who was in Paris to see to the restitution and return of stolen art to his country. Altenstein had been named as a candidate for the Financial Committee on behalf of Prussia and was prepared to promote the interests of 'the unfortunate creditors' from the Low Countries in the committee.[68] But Altenstein also tempered their expectations, pointing out the dangers of financial collapse to his Dutch colleagues. Even less support was expected from the Russian envoy on the Finance Committee, Jean d'Anstett.[69] The Russian court repeated the tsar's gracious position of 1814, when he refused to impose large reparations on France. In the end, the Financial Committee did not go with the excessive demands of the Germans and the Dutch, but accepted the proposal of the Russian envoy d'Anstett, which included a variety of loopholes, such that France could elude most of the payments.[70]

The Russian proposal went to the Allied Council, with a memorandum from Canneman as an appendix, where it was examined further by Wilhelm von

[65] Allied Council, protocol no. 30, of 11 August 1815, GStA PK, III. HA I. no. 1465.

[66] Reports of Canneman to the king, 28 September 1815, NL-HaNA, 2.02.01, inv. no. 144, 4 October 1815, no. 32; Report of Canneman to the king, 1 October 1815, NL-HaNA, 2.02.01, inv. no. 145, 6 October 1815, no. 32.

[67] Referred to below as 'Altenstein', as is standard in the literature.

[68] Gagern, *Der zweite Pariser Frieden*, 244–5; Allied Council, protocol no. 53, of 21 September 1815, GStA PK, III. HA I. no. 1465.

[69] Reports of Canneman to the king, 1 and 3 October 1815, NL-HaNA, 2.02.01, inv. no. 145; Canneman, report of 6 October 1815, no. 32; 'Articles projettés par le ministre de la Russie, M. de Anstetten, communiqué au Comité le 2 octobre 1815', NL-HaNA, 2.21.005.30, no. 36.

[70] Amendments from members not represented came from Hamburg, Hanover and the Netherlands; see 'Memorandum sur les articles du Traité de Paris qui n'ont pas été exécutées de la part du gouvernement français et sur les moyens d'en assurer mieux l'exécution dans la prochaine transaction avec ce gouvernement', signed by the members of the Finance Committee in NL-HaNA, 2.21.005.30, inv. no. 36. See further report of Canneman to the king no. 11, 12 November 1815, NL-HaNA, 2.02.01, inv no. 158, 12. See also Gagern, *Der zweite Pariser Frieden*, 313–15; report of Canneman to the king no. 32, 3 October 1815, NL-HaNA, 2.02.01, inv. no. 145, 6 October 1815, no. 32; 'Projet et article additionel'; NL-HaNA, 2.02.01, 158, 12 November 1815, no. 11; 'Note confidentielle pour S. E. Mr l'Ambassadeur de la Grande Bretagne à Paris, remise par le Commissaire général de S. M. le Roi des Pays-Bas pour la liquidation avec la France', NL-HaNA, 2.02.01, inv. no. 145, 6 October 1815, no. 32.

Humboldt, the Prussian plenipotentiary for negotiations with France.[71]
Humboldt's 'preparatory investigation and report' noted that France had failed
to fulfil its obligations in ten of the thirty-three articles of the Peace Treaty of
30 May 1814,[72] and that that treaty had lacked sufficient rigour. With that in
mind, the Russian proposal had to be honed and tightened up.[73] Subsequently,
a new report was handed over to the recently installed French prime minister
Richelieu. In the meantime, the obstructive French commissioners had been
replaced and the new ones seemed more accommodating and reasonable than
their predecessors. On 29 October they made a counter-offer: once the foreign
claims were deemed to be legitimate, France would acknowledge them as
a bona fide debt and register them in its 'Great Book of the Public Debt'. The
disbursement would not take place in cash, but with debt securities (*rentes*)
issued by the French government, which gave the holder a right to 5 per cent
interest per annum. This arrangement allowed France to spread the settlement
of its debt over a longer period – thus also committing its creditors to the
necessity of upholding the arrangement and the stability of the overall economic situation. It was an important step forward. Canneman, however,
remained on his guard, because he suspected that the French were speculating
against a future depreciation of the franc.[74]

At the beginning of November, agreement had been reached on the articles
of the anticipated peace treaty and on two of the three conventions. The
Netherlands fared well. France had to transfer the fortified towns of
Philippeville, Mariembourg, Chimay and Bouillon to the Netherlands. Some
of the barrier forts on the French side would be dismantled. A fund of
137.5 million francs was set aside for the construction of forts along the
French border, of which 60 million would be paid to the Netherlands for the
Boulevard de l'Europe – or, as it would later be called, the 'Wellington
Barrier'.[75]

Liquidating the private claims turned out to be the toughest nut to crack.
The Dutch and Germans (Prussia, Hanover and the Hanseatic cities) acted
together and reached a number of important concessions: a payment of
75 per cent would be guaranteed when paying off securities, dispositions and

[71] Dupuis, *Le ministère de Talleyrand*, vol. 2, 358–68; report of Canneman to the king,
      10 October 1815, NL-HaNA, 2.02.01, inv. no. 158, 12 November 1815, no. 11.
[72] It concerned Articles XIX–XXVI and XXX–XXXI.
[73] 'Rapport sur le travail de la Commission nommée pour assurer l'exécution des articles de
      la Paix de Paris du 30 Mai 1814 auxquels il n'y a pas été satisfait jusqu'ici par la France', as
      well as a piece without a title, prefaced in Canneman's handwriting with the words 'travail
      de M. de Humboldt', NL-HaNA, 2.21.005.30, inv. no. 36.
[74] Report of Canneman to the king and 'projet écrit par la main du conseiller d'État Dudon,
      reçu de M. Thuret, dimanche 29 octobre 1815', NL-HaNA, 2.02.01, inv. no. 158; report of
      Canneman to the king, 19 October 1815, NL-HaNA, 2.02.01, inv. no. 158.
[75] Allied Council, protocols of 2, 6, 7 and 8 October 1815, GStA PK, III. HA I. no. 1469;
      correspondence of Kraijenhoff and Wellington, December 1815, TNA, FO 92/15.

consignments; 60 per cent would apply to other claims. If the exchange rate of
the debt instruments fell below this percentage, the French government would
adjust the difference.[76] Every two months a docket would be drawn up, of
verified and confirmed liquidations. These would all be inscribed in France's
Great Book of the Public Debt, at par. France would set up a guarantee fund to
the tune of 3.5 million francs, from which the payment of claims would take
place.[77] If these funds were not sufficient, they would be 'replenished' when
needed. Calculations regarding debts owed to France by the Allies for former
French areas were also capped.[78] In spite of French opposition to a *force
majeure* of Allied liquidation commissioners, a 'European Commission of
Liquidators' was assembled to supervise the proceedings and to consult
directly with the French commissioners of liquidation. Participating countries
were also allowed to appoint arbitrating 'umpires', who would move to Paris,
and constitute an authority of appeal.[79]

Things began to stagnate, however, in the final stage of the negotiations. The
Dutch stubbornly held on to the demand that France pay the overdue interest
on government debt owed to the Netherlands for 1813, appealing to Article XX
of the Paris Peace Treaty of 1814. Canneman figured that this amount (some
20 million francs) by and large cancelled out the Belgian debt (estimated at
24 million francs that the Dutch owed the French[80]) – an argument with which
Humboldt agreed. But in the light of the other articles and provisions, and the
commitments that France had made, the British in particular did not want to
try the *esprit de conciliation* of Richelieu and the French government any
further. They noted that the limit of French financial security and flexibility
had been reached and that the issue of the outstanding debt from 1813 owed to
the Dutch could not be resolved in short order. On the advice of Castlereagh,
who was highly skilled in the art of 'settling by postponing', the case was
referred to an international arbitration committee (that had yet to be
formed).[81] The particular interests of a 'secondary power' were sacrificed to
the greater good of completing the peace negotiations amongst the principal
powers. Disappointed, Canneman returned home.[82]

---

[76] Royal Decree (KB) of 6 November 1815, no. 68, NL-HaNA, 2.02.01, inv. no. 153; report of
Canneman to the king, 10 November 1815 and protocol of Allied and French
Commissioners of 6 November 1815, NL-HaNA, 2.21.005.30, inv. no. 36.

[77] One French franc in 1815 was worth about 0.05 British pounds.

[78] Convention on private claims upon France, as annex to Second Peace of Paris Treaty,
20 November 1815, Articles XX–XXIII, Clercq (ed.), *Recueil des traités*, vol. 2, 651–3.

[79] Ibid., Article V.

[80] Concept-report of Canneman to the king, 9 November 1815, NL-HaNA, 2.21.005.30, inv.
no. 36.

[81] Letter (copy) of 11 November 1815, NL-HaNA, 2.21.005.30, inv. no. 36. See also Allied
Council, protocol of 11 and 18 November 1815, GStA PK, III. HA I. no. 1469.

[82] See Article VIII in the financial convention annexed to the Second Treaty of Paris,
20 November 1815. See further concept-reports of Canneman to the king, 11, 12, 13

What Can France Pay?

In the meantime, the Allied Ministerial Conference also had greater clarity about the cost of the reparations. As early as the end of August, Castlereagh had indicated that this amount would not be less than 600 million francs, to which needed to be added 2 francs per soldier per day for the upkeep of the troops.[83] With an occupational force of 100,000 – which is what Castlereagh expected in August, but which would become 150,000 by 1816 – this would amount to 6 million francs per month, or 72 million per year. Castlereagh believed that this was not too much for France to bear: 'the pressure is likely to be as heavy in a pecuniary shape as the country can be expected quietly to submit to' – a heavy burden, but still doable, he reasoned.[84]

The country was financially healthy, according to Castlereagh, 'for as soon as they had created armies they turned them loose to prey on mankind'. Because Napoleon had been able to finance most of France's campaigns with monies from foreign countries, Castlereagh believed that 'France was in a state of greater financial affluence than any other country in Europe', and that the 'contributions demanded could be met by the revenues of that country'. He suggested that it was a 'very inconsiderable payment' that would not be an 'extraordinary calamity' for France, if compared to all the expenses that the late war had thrown upon Britain.[85] A memorandum from October 1815 records how he made his calculations. He suggested that if France were to impose a 25 per cent increase in taxation for five years, the government could raise 750 million francs in revenue (instead of the expected 600 million) per annum. And supposing that its public expenditures in peacetime amounted to about 500 million per year, then they would have some 250 million available per year (or, over five years, some 1,250 million) to apply to the charge of war. If the Allies were to demand 800 million in reparations and 800 million for the cost of the occupation (which came to less than that in the end), the total claim would be 1,600 million francs, and, given the five-year balance from above, would leave France to finance the remaining 350 million to bridge the deficit on the debt to the Allies. According to Castlereagh, 'this is really nothing as an operation of finance'. Or, the French government could also simply sell its national forests, which alone were worth 300 million francs.[86]

---

and 15 November 1815, NL-HaNA, 2.21.005.30, inv. no. 36; Gagern, *Der zweite Pariser Frieden*, 373–4, 393–4.

[83]   Castlereagh to Liverpool, 'Précis', 17 August 1815, *WSD*, vol. 11, 127–8.

[84]   Ibid.

[85]   Hansard (ed.), *The Parliamentary Debates*, vol. 32, 694–9.

[86]   'Memorandum from Lord Castlereagh on the Means of Increasing the French Revenue', *WSD*, vol. 11, 192.

Yet, Castlereagh got it wrong. The contributions required of France came in lower than he had projected, but the expenses were higher. The problem was that France, unlike Britain, had not yet developed a sound economic understanding of the national debt. In Britain, given the process of checks and balances and its modern means of accounting, openness was the order of the day when it came to the budget and the national debt. Parliament, society at large and the Bank of England worked together and took joint responsibility for managing the public debt.[87] This was not the case in France; as a British magazine observed in 1858: 'France was not at that time initiated into the mysteries of public credit.'[88]

Although economic growth picked up somewhat in 1815, the Napoleonic regime had borrowed heavily and the treasury was virtually empty. The French government tried to collect the revenue set for that year via additional assessments and taxes. Prior to the signing of the Second Treaty of Paris, France had already committed to pay 180 million francs towards the costs of the occupation forces. To that end, the government implemented a compulsory loan to the state of 100 million, targeting wealthier French citizens, and only in those regions of the country that could bear it, that is, those not having to endure the occupation or those that had not suffered severely because of the war. The French finance minister, Baron Louis, had thrown his persuasive powers behind this move: 'I am relying entirely on the patriotism of the most important business leaders, proprietors and capitalists', and he hoped that they would commit themselves to 'the enlightenment of their compatriots who have been ruined by these recent events'.[89] That appeal to the solidarity of the well-to-do yielded 92.7 million francs, which enabled the government to cover a large part of the intended amount of 180 million. A popular way to collect extra funds, however, it was not. And the shortages continued to increase. Revenue (615.3 million) and expenses (618.6 million) would have been in balance in 1815 had it not been for the 180 million to cover the additional costs of the occupation forces. So, with the 92.7 million added to the treasury, there was still a budget shortfall of 90 million. Even with an additional new loan of 35.8 million, France still ended the year 54.8 million in the red.[90]

[87] See N. Ferguson, *The Cash Nexus. Money and Power in the Modern World, 1700–2000* (New York: Penguin, 2001), 111–16.

[88] C. Dickens, et al. (eds.), *Bentley's Miscellany*, vol. 43 (London: Bentley, 1858), 249.

[89] ' La contribution extraordinaire à lever comme réquisition de guerre', 20 August 1815, *Correspondance de M. le Préfet du Département de la Seine-Inférieure*, vol. 21 (1811–1818) (Arouen: Periaux, 1815), 69–73. See also 'Copie d'une Lettre adressée aux Préfets par S. Exc. Le Ministre des finances', 18 August 1815, Ibid., 79.

[90] White, 'Making the French Pay', 339, 342–3 (with footnotes).

The Price is Set: The Main Provisions

In September, there was still a world of difference between the Prussian claim of 1,200 million francs and the British sum of 600 million. Meanwhile, it was clear that all parties were in favour of a disbursement of part of these reparations (probably about 200 million) into a fund for the financing of fortifications.[91] However, everyone had to make concessions. The Prussians lowered their demands, from 1,200 to 800 million francs, in exchange for the French transfer of Saarlouis to Prussia.[92] The territory of Savoy went to the Kingdom of Sardinia, and some fortifications in northern France were added to the Kingdom of the Netherlands. The 20 September figure of 800 million was then further lowered to 700, as noted above.[93] The complaint of Louis XVIII to the tsar, that the Allies' demands combined 'ruin with dishonour', had made an impression.[94] Richelieu also succeeded in reducing the duration of the occupation to five years.[95]

On Monday evening, 20 November 1815, at the home of Richelieu, the Second Treaty of Paris and its conventions were signed by all the plenipotentiaries. The convention on not executing some of the articles of the First Treaty of Paris of 30 May 1814 had twenty-six articles and was based on Article IX of the main treaty.[96] The price was set. France had to pay a war contribution of 700 million francs and had to relinquish the greater part of the areas captured between 1790 and 1792. It would have to pay an additional 150 million francs per year for the clothing, equipment and pay for the occupational forces – 150,000 Allied troops – for five years. France would also have to set up a fund to finance the construction of (foreign) military fortifications along its northern and eastern borders. Looted art treasures had to be returned. And, of great importance for the other Allied countries: France also had to take up the private claims upon France that had been mentioned in the Peace Treaty of 30 May 1814, but had never been evaluated and acted on. Moreover, the articles of that treaty relating to financial settlements, which France had not

---

[91] Gentz to Caradja, 5 September 1815, Metternich-Winneburg (ed.), *Oesterreichs Teilnahme an den Befreiungskriegen*, 717–19.

[92] See the discussions of the 'Conférence militaire', 16 September 1815, GStA PK, III. HA I. no. 1465; Hardenberg to the Prince Regent, 18 September 1815, *WSD*, vol. 11, 162–3.

[93] Letter of thanks from Richelieu to the Russian tsar, 5, 17 October 1815, in Polovtsoff (ed.), *Le Duc de Richelieu*, 451.

[94] Louis XVIII to the Russian tsar Alexander, 11/23 September 1815, Pozzo di Borgo (ed.), *Correspondance*, vol. 1, 209–10.

[95] Wellington to Richelieu, *WSD*, vol. 12, 652–3.

[96] The text of the treaty and its conventions is available in various sources. See, for example, Foreign Office (ed.), *British and Foreign State Papers, 1815–1816*, vol. 3 (London: Ridgway, 1838), 273–358. See also Allied Council, protocol, sent to Richelieu, 20 November 1815, GStA PK, III. HA I. no. 1469; Gagern, *Der zweite Pariser Frieden*, 401–7.

implemented, would be clarified and defined more specifically. The starting point when negotiating the 1815 treaty was that the 1814 treaty would remain in full force and form the basis for the new 1815 Peace Treaty.[97]

The Second Treaty of Paris laid out in broad terms how the 700 million would be distributed, which had been quite a puzzle to create (and for historians to unpick). First of all – according to the protocol – one quarter of that amount would be spent on the construction and maintenance of fortifications.[98] Since the fortified city of Saarlouis was also included in this programme, another 50 million francs (the estimated net worth of the city) was added to the 700 million for reparations, so that eventually one quarter of the 750 million (or 187.5 million) was allocated for the fortification project. Of the remaining 562.5 million, Spain, Portugal, Denmark and Switzerland were allowed to have and distribute 12.5 million among themselves, and 50 million was awarded as 'prize money' to the armies that had helped win the final battle: that is, 25 million each to Prussia and Britain, which honoured in part Blücher's demand and Hardenberg's claim, albeit that the 100 million requested was reduced to 25 million francs. The remaining 500 million was divided equally by five. The four 'great powers', Prussia, Austria, Russia and Britain, each received a share, and the remaining 100 million was divided among the other Allied troops, the 'acceding powers' who had also signed the General Alliance Treaty of 25 March 1815.[99]

In surveying the distribution of the funds, it is clear that the most substantial part of the 700 million – the amount of 562.5 million – served as compensation, and was thus an amount that looked back in time. The fortification fund of 137.5 million plus Saarlouis, on the other hand, was an investment in the future, since these funds were devoted to European security through the enhancement or (re)construction of fortifications. On that score, the general notion of 'indemnities' was somewhat misplaced. The sum of 700 million was less reactive and vindictive than it could have been (1,200 million), and can sooner be taken as a moderate and even constructive resolution. Its distribution was also an interesting compromise, because, although not everyone got the same amount, each country did eventually make concessions. The four great powers received 100 million each. In addition, Prussia received another 20 million for improving their own fortifications, 25 million as 'prize money', plus Saarlouis. The German Confederation also received another 25 million for border fortifications in Mainz and along the upper Rhine, which also benefited Prussia. The United Kingdom received a total of 125 million, Austria

---

[97] Allied Council, protocol of 19 September 1815, GStA PK, III. HA I. no. 1465.

[98] 'Protocole de la conférence de Paris, du 6 novembre 1815, sur la répartition des 700 payables par la France aux Puissances Alliées', Clercq (ed.), *Recueil des traités*, vol. 2, 637–42.

[99] Ibid. See also the protocol of 7 and 8 October 1815, where this was all discussed, GStA PK, III. HA I. no. 1469.

Table 7.1 *French payments: treaty provisions*

Provisions	Amounts in millions of francs
War damage compensation for the Hundred Days period	700 (of which 137.5 goes to the construction of fortifications)
Liquidation of private claims	3.5 for *rentes* (capitalized 70) for the continental Allies (with the possibility of being supplemented)
	3.5 for *rentes* (capitalized 70) for Great Britain
Occupation costs 1815	180
Occupation costs 1816–20	450–750
Total	**Unknown, expected: 1,470–1,770**

113.8 million and Russia 100 million. Then followed the Netherlands, which received a substantial amount (60 million) for fortifications along its southern border, plus another, smaller amount, to be estimated, for its participation in the general alliance.[100]

The treaty's financial and military details were set out in separate conventions.[101] The Allied Council was there to see to it that these agreements were honoured.[102] All told, it was a significant financial operation: 700 million in reparations, an additional 180 million for costs related to the occupation in the first year, another 140 million per year for maintaining the Allied forces, plus 3.5 million in annuities from the guarantee fund (Table 7.1).[103]

How to Redeem the Debts?

The big question was then how France would be able to disburse these amounts to the Allies when its treasury was pretty much empty. Richelieu had to use all his talents, and even have the king appear in the Chamber of Deputies of the French parliament, to persuade the delegates to approve the budgets – perhaps his most astonishing and impressive achievement over the

---

[100] Ibid.
[101] Dupuis, *Le ministère de Talleyrand*, vol. 2, 333–404.
[102] Allied Council, protocol of 3 November 1815, TNA, FO 146/6.
[103] These amounts differ slightly from what Nicolle and White have calculated. A. Nicolle, *Comment la France a payé après Waterloo* (Paris: E. de Boccard, 1929), 186–9; White, 'Making the French Pay', 340–1.

whole of his career. Talleyrand had been on the mark: politicians, publicists and the people took the Second Treaty of Paris to be a disgrace. The king who had entered the capital thanks to the efforts of the Allies was now handing the French treasury over to foreigners. France had a bitter pill to swallow. That was made possible by taking the bitterness in smaller portions.

Over a period of five years, France was to pay the 700 million in fifteen instalments of about 46.7 million francs each. That amount was to be paid in 'bearer notes' on a daily basis in equal portions from the first to the last day of the month. So as not to unsettle the financial markets, no more than 50 million francs in these payment notes were allowed into circulation at any one time. No interest would have to be paid on the 700 million in reparations, but 5 per cent interest would accrue if the disbursement of these notes was delayed. To guarantee these payments, a credit of 7 million in interest was inscribed in France's Great Book of the Public Debt as a counterpart to a capital of 140 million. This fund was intended to cover shortfalls in the debt payment. The first major payments were scheduled for 31 March 1816, four months after the treaty was signed.[104]

The Allied Council would supervise these transactions (payments, loans, calculations) with the help of the Finance Committee, which had to sort out the terms and guarantees for the compensation payments. The French had to set up and manage a fund for the construction of the fortresses, as well as for the maintenance of the troops. In addition, the Finance Committee had to attend to the interpretation and execution of the liquidation articles of the First Treaty of Paris of 30 May 1814.[105] All Allied committees also had a discussion partner on the French side. This would help to ensure that the financial security was organized and regulated – and that the wayward and autonomous practices of the occupation forces in the provinces assigned to them would also come to an end.[106]

Here too, as was noted in Chapters 4 and 5, security was a matter of management, committees, lists (of names, debts and financial compensations) and compromises that the Allies agreed upon with each other and with the French. This form of security management was – just like Gruner's security forces and Metternich's uniform measures – another innovation: instead of plunder and predatory behaviour on the one hand, and Napoleon's unilaterally imposed war contributions on the other, the costs of peace and security were dealt with and negotiated from the perspective of European solidarity. Everyone was involved as a stakeholder in France's and Europe's financial

---

[104] See White, 'Making the French Pay', 339–40; 'Convention conclue à Paris, le 20 Novembre 1815 en conformité de l'article IV du traité principal du même jour, et relative au payement de l'indemnité pécuniaire à fournir par la France aux Puissances Alliées', Clercq (ed.), Recueil des traités, vol. 2, 651–3.

[105] Gagern, Der zweite Pariser Frieden, 316–22. See also Gagern, Mein Antheil an der Politik, vol, 5, 316–22.

[106] Hardenberg, Mémoire, 22 July 1815, GStA PK, III. HA I. no. 1469.

security and stability. Room was even made in those negotiations for the smaller allies as well as the defeated party (via the French commissioners) – even though the French tried to fill their role as negotiating partner in their own unique way. With the reign of Louis XVIII, the tax inspectors, prefects and local administrators had also returned. As happened in the top ranks among the police, the Allied ministers ruled the roost, but the French administrators made all the day-to-day decisions.

The French administrators and ministers were certainly not only bent on opposition or obstruction. They were very well aware of the fact that, by signing the Second Treaty of Paris and fulfilling its provisions, the government of Louis XVIII was able to recoup its independence. And although prime minister Richelieu was dejected by the humiliating treaty, he was convinced that making these payments was the only way to pull France out of its misery. He explained to parliament that this outrageous treaty was as unique as the fate of the unfortunate French people themselves. So, even in France's humiliation and in the size of the imposed reparations, there was still a measure of grandeur. It is probably here that Richelieu displayed his greatest skill and finesse as prime minister. In the light of the great confusion, agitation and sense of injustice – as recorded by Gruner – it is a miracle that the French parliament, full of Ultras, agreed to comply with this financial yoke. Richelieu's persuasiveness and integrity and, of course, the support of the king were decisive. The French, who had lived in uncertainty through November, and had been sent in every which direction by Talleyrand and Fouché, finally – in general terms – knew what they were facing.[107] And at least the worst was averted: the country was not to be parcelled, ripped apart indefinitely, but only occupied temporarily, until the debts were redeemed.

The Second Treaty of Paris put an 'essentially European system' in place,[108] resting on three pillars: a military one, a political one and a financial one. Under extreme pressure, the Chamber of Deputies, dominated by ultra-royalist representatives, adopted a law on 23 December 1815 to secure the necessary funding for the war indemnity and the guarantee fund.[109] Unlike after the First World War, when the German debts were not paid and were finally written off, France accepted the financial burden and met her obligations within the set period. But that did not happen without a struggle. The reparations and the cost of maintaining the troops was less of a problem than the payment of overdue debts, which the French found to be very unjust and

---

[107] 'Discours prononcé par le Duc de Richelieu le 25 Novembre 1815, en donnant communication a la Chambre des Députés, des Traités et Conventions du 20 Novembre', Clercq (ed.), *Recueil des traités*, vol. 2, 684–90.

[108] Allied Council, protocol of 21 November 1815, GStA PK, III. HA I. no. 1469.

[109] ' De Loi relative à la création des rentes nécessaires pour l'exécution du traité du 20 novembre 1815', of 23 December 1815, in J. Duvergier (ed.), *Collection complète des lois, décrets, ordonnances, réglements*, vol. 20 (Paris: A. Guyot, 1837), 203.

exaggerated. Because the amount of those debts had not yet been determined in the treaty itself – the claims for damages and the receipts still had to be submitted by the creditors – the negotiations stalled several times.

The Devil is in the Details, and he's a French Commissioner

Metternich, Castlereagh, Humboldt and Gneisenau left for home at the end of November 1815, handing the baton off to their ministers and the British ambassador (Stuart). As noted earlier, they had also invited envoys and ambassadors from the other, lesser powers to take part in the financial deliberations.

As in 1814, each country delegated a commissioner to represent the interests of private creditors in his country. Representatives from six countries met for the first time in February 1816, but their numbers grew and by February 1818 there were twenty-one delegates around the table, representing thirty-nine countries or (combinations of) regions.[110] Each of the Allied partners also delegated one or more judges to an *Assemblée Générale*. If a claim was rejected by the French liquidators, appeal could be made to the Assembly. The case was then handed over to three judges, chosen by lot, for assessment. Their judgement was binding.

Management of the guarantee fund – created by French law in December 1815 – was entrusted to two French and two Allied commissioners.[111] From December 1815 on, the Allied commissioners met every Wednesday – and more often in the week if there was good reason – in the British embassy (the same place where the Allied Council met), now rebaptized as the 'House of the Commission of the Four Allied Powers'. The chests holding the annuities payments from the guarantee fund were also kept here.[112] Spain and Portugal, co-signatories to the First Treaty of Paris of 1814, were only allowed to join the Committee of Allied Liquidators after they signed the Treaty of Vienna, in November 1816 and February 1818 respectively. Sweden's interests were represented by the Netherlands.[113] British representatives only joined the Committee in February 1818, presumably as observers. The British had their own guarantee fund, containing a collateral of 3.5 million francs for them alone – as had been agreed upon in a separate convention of the Second Treaty of Paris.

---

[110] See the protocols of the meetings of the Committee of Allied Liquidators, added as annexes to the reports of Canneman to the king, NL-HaNA, 2.02.01, inv. no. 6365–7.

[111] These commissioners (*commissaires-dépositeurs*) were not members of the Finance Committee.

[112] Report of Canneman to the king, 2 March 1816, NL-HaNA, 2.02.01, inv. no. 6365.

[113] This is evident from the description in the index to the resolutions, 1816, NL-HaNA, 2.02.01, inv. no. 5066. The pieces themselves are missing from the series, 4 March 1816, no. 143, NL-HaNA, 2.02.01, inv. no. 202.

The counterpart of the Allied Committee was the French Commission of Liquidators, consisting of five people under the chairmanship of Jean François Dudon, a member of the state council. Dudon, who came from a family of attorneys in Bordeaux, was an overzealous and staunch monarchist. He had nonetheless rendered service to Napoleon's cause with the exploitation of Spain and Portugal. After 1814, Talleyrand had charged him with travelling to Orléans to recover the imperial treasures of Marie-Louise.[114] He and his colleagues delivered formidable resistance to these foreign claims. For example, in October 1816, Dudon refused to handle claims if the proofs of payment, which ran into the tens of metres of receipts and bills, were not accompanied by a proof of order or dispatch. Without an original proof of an agreed-upon transaction, the liquidators would not even consider paying on a claim.[115] In these sorts of disputes, when the Allied liquidators were unable to reach a bilateral agreement with the French liquidators, they looked to the Allied Council for support, which in turn turned to Richelieu with the deadlock and tried to work things out at the highest level. On the receipt issue, Wellington and Richelieu agreed that submitting some 'general rules of evidence' would be sufficient support for claims submitted; after all, it made sense that many purchase orders and proofs of payment had not made it through the turbulent years of the war.[116]

It soon became apparent that the French commissioners respected the great powers, but tried to do what they could to torpedo the claims of the smaller countries, such as the Netherlands. In February 1816, Canneman returned to Paris and, with some degree of wariness, resumed his position as commissioner general. This time the interests of creditors from the Southern Netherlands were also entrusted to him. These were considerable, because this part of the kingdom was invaded by France as early as 1794, and had been burdened by the French yoke for a long time. The Dutch rented office space in Paris for their liquidation tasks, and hired staff members to verify and register the claims and to write up and transcribe reports and letters. It was an enormous challenge to meet all the requirements of the financial commission. In 1817, the staff included twenty-two people, some Dutch (from both north and south), some French.[117] All claims had to be submitted to the French government before 1 March 1817. That is why, in early 1816, the Dutch king had placards posted throughout the southern Netherlands summoning citizens to submit their claims for compensation to the government.[118] The appeal

---

[114] G. Sarrut and B. Saint-Edme (eds.), *Biographie des Hommes du Jour*, vol. 2 (Paris: H. Krabe, 1836), 82–4.

[115] Protocol of 11 October 1816, TNA, FO 146/3.

[116] Ibid.

[117] See the reports in NL-HaNA, 2.21.005.30, inv. no. 46.

[118] There were dozens of claims from Oudenaarde, a city of around 4,000 inhabitants (*intra muros*). See, for example, the receipts and bills submitted to the city, intended for debt

led to a huge influx of claims, all of which had to be investigated – and many of which turned out to be inadmissible. It soon became clear that, compared to all the other allied countries, the Netherlands had submitted the largest number of claims. That being so, the Netherlands had a strong position within the circle of liquidators from medium-sized countries. On the other hand, the Dutch envoys had a tough row to hoe with the French commissioners.

Given the above, the Netherlands encountered a major setback in pursuing the annuities it thought it had coming. As stipulated in the convention of 1815, an ad hoc arbitration committee of seven diplomats was assembled to address the matter in June and October 1816. On 16 October, with a 4 to 3 vote, the Dutch pretensions were rejected.[119] And that was not all. In April 1816, the French commissioners also presented Canneman with a bill regarding what the Dutch owed when it came to Belgium. This related to interest due, registered in the French Book of the Public Debt, and amounted to 2,263,605 francs annually. France demanded twenty times that as capital – 45,272,100 francs. Canneman spent sleepless nights filtering out the errors and deceptive moves in their calculations. In November 1816, he filed an official protest with the Allied Council against the French demand, which came with little or no documented support; all the while, they still expected the same of the Dutch. The issue dragged on for months – demonstrating how much international diplomacy could be drained by such seemingly minor details as receipts.[120]

French commissioners continued to remain obstructive regarding the claims of secondary or third-rank powers. Not only the Netherlands, but a whole series of smaller allied countries complained in memos of protest to the Allied Ministerial Conference about the unfair and dilatory behaviour of the French partners, and with good reason.[121] The system of paying with vouchers led to a fatal fall in the market, and a trade in receivables was on the rise. Canneman reported in early 1816 about an attempt at corruption on

---

claims in Paris: City Archive Oudenaarde (SAO), Hollands Bestuur (HB) VIII D.b., SAO, 463.103A; 'Aanplakbrieven namens het Hollands Bestuur', January–February 1816, SAO, 583, 79Bis.

[119] All the relevant documents are printed in Recueil de pièces officielles, relatives au procès concernant la dette d'Hollande, entre le Gouvernement français et celui des Pays-Bas, qui a été jugé par des arbitres, le 16 octobre 1816 (Paris, 1817), a copy of which can be found in NL-HaNA, 2.02.01, inv. no. 6366.

[120] Dudon to Canneman, 18 April 1816, appended to Canneman's report to the king, 23 April 1816, NL-HaNA, 2.02.01, inv. no. 6365; copy of the letter to the four ambassadors, 14 November 1816, appended to Canneman's report to the king, 15 November 1816, NL-HaNA, 2.02.01, inv. no. 6366; appended to his reports to the king, 8 February, 24 June and November 1817. A specification of the counter pretensions, appended to Canneman's report to the king, 10 March 1817, NL-HaNA, 2.02.01, inv. no. 6366.

[121] Protocol of 12 September 1816, TNA, FO 146/14.

the part of the French. Commissioner Dudon and an accomplice had tried to persuade the Dutch consul-general in Paris, Isaac Thuret, and him to take part in a fraudulent scheme to buy pretensions. Outraged, he told the Dutch general secretary, Anton Reinhard Falck, that 'everything here is corrupt, and everyone complicit'.[122] French obstruction, however, was not only based on a lack of will and corruption, but also on financial straits – France's finances were no longer what they had been.

1816: An *annus horribilis*

In the spring of 1816, the fragile relationship between payments and French stability was seriously disrupted. What Russia's Pozzo di Borgo and the British parliamentarian Horner had warned would happen, did. The French treasury could no longer meet the Allied payments, and the two-headed monster of a financial impasse and a political crisis lay in wait. As a result of the eruption of the volcano Tambora on the Indonesian island of Sumbawa in April 1815, violent storms pummelled Europe, beginning in early 1816. France was hit particularly hard. Snow fell until June, and crop failure was common. Grain prices soared and the state started to capsize financially.[123] Attempts by the French government to sell the national domains and forests, as suggested by Wellington and Castlereagh, came to nothing because of the opposition of the French Chamber. The ultra-royalist Chamber thwarted the Allies, but also the king and Richelieu, refusing to approve budgets, and reverted repeatedly to incendiary rhetoric. When the payments for maintaining and paying the troops did not materialize in January and February 1816, Wellington was instructed by the Allied Council to let King Louis XVIII and his brother, 'Monsieur' (who later became Charles X), know in no uncertain terms where things stood: 'Crisis was imminent.' The situation deteriorated by the day. If the king did not get his brother and the Chamber back on course, he, Wellington, would not shy away from calling the Allied Army to arms again.[124]

That seemed to help. In April, the Chamber approved budgets and payments. The liquidations were again set in motion. Indirect taxes were increased, and the government just managed to disburse the two payments of 47 million francs due on 31 March and 31 July respectively, as mandated.[125] But then things went awry again. Angry Bonapartists conspired against the king, and riots broke out in

---

[122] Report of Canneman to the king, 31 May 1816; letter of Canneman to Falck, 29 May 1816, NL-HaNA, 2.02.01, inv. no. 6365.

[123] P. Mallez, *La Restauration des finances françaises après 1814* (Paris: Dalloz, 1927); G. de Bertier de Sauvigny, *La Restauration* (Paris: Flammarion, 1955).

[124] Allied Council, protocols of 28 February 1816, 6 March 1816, TNA, FO 146/6.

[125] The 46.7 million figure was one fifteenth of the war indemnity due to be paid on 31 March and 31 July. These were the first two payments. See Article II of the financial convention to the Second Treaty of Paris, 20 November 1815.

various places.[126] The French liquidation commissioners, too, dug in their heels. They snubbed their Allied partners, engaged in delaying tactics and provided faulty calculations of reimbursements and annuities.[127]

All this resistance could be traced back, in part, to the magnitude of these payments. With the 180 million France had to pay for the first year, paired with 150 million for the second year of the occupation, the shoe began to pinch quite severely. Salaries were reduced and money for public affairs was decreased; even the king returned 10 million of his 25-million-franc allowance. The price of tobacco and other luxury goods rose – which in itself generated a tax revenue of 742.7 million francs (an increase of 140 million). Yet this was still not enough. The disappointing harvests also made the increase in taxes more palpable – which forced the government to expend more to help subsidize the price of bread.[128]

Mitigating the Need

After the summer of 1816, the guarantee fund was bottoming out. In October, Richelieu requested that the costs be lightened, preferably by reducing the Allied Occupation Army.[129] So, in late December 1816, Russia and Austria proposed to the Allied Council that some of the troops be sent home.[130] That would at least help alleviate the costs of maintenance. Wellington, however, found that to be an ill-conceived plan. Those troops were needed to keep the occupied territory under control and to take action should revolution break out again. Based on Gruner's reports and those of his own agents, neither the terror of the right nor that of the left had abated. It was even questionable whether the many incidents did not signal a new trend of increased resistance. France therefore first had to *earn* a reduction in Allied troops. Richelieu had dissolved the Chamber of Deputies in September 1816 and, in effect, sent the Ultras packing. Wellington maintained that if Richelieu's move led to a better and above all quieter political situation, a reduction of 30,000 troops could be discussed in April.[131] He first wanted to see what the French budget for the next year looked like. Wellington's reasoning was the exact inverse of Richelieu's: 'Whereas the French

---

[126] Allied Council, protocols of 5, 8, 29 May 1816, TNA, FO 146/6.

[127] Complaints submitted by the Allied Council, 11 October 1816, TNA, FO 146/13. See also the Allied Council protocol and the protest letters of the Allied Liquidators, 12 September 1816; protocol of 30 September 1816, TNA, FO 146/14.

[128] Cf. C. Oppenheimer, 'Climatic, Environmental and Human Consequences of the Largest Known Historic Eruption: Tambora Volcano (Indonesia) 1815', *Progress in Physical Geography*, 27:2 (2003), 251; White, 'Making the French Pay', 344.

[129] Richelieu to Wellington, 7 September 1816, *WSD*, vol. 11, 486–7; Wellington to the Allied Council, 16 October 1816, TNA, FO 146/15.

[130] Protocol of 28 December 1816, TNA, FO 146/13.

[131] Protocol of 2 December 1816, TNA, FO 146/15.

government looked upon the reduction of the army of occupation as
a necessary prelude to its financial arrangements, the British cabinet regarded
such arrangements as preliminary to any reduction of the army.'[132] That was
a setback for Richelieu. Frustrated, he wrote to Kapodistrias: 'By pulling on the
rope, it will eventually break. The revolutionary spirit will reappear in France
and bring misfortune to all of Europe.'[133] The French government was indeed
unable to pay the third instalment of 47 million francs for November. On
7 December 1816, Richelieu had to announce that he could not deliver on the
daily vouchers – which also meant, as agreed, that France would have to pay an
extra 5 per cent interest on the postponed payment.[134]

Wellington was a strict commander, who first and foremost cared for the
safety of his troops. At the same time, he was enough of a politician to
understand that Richelieu needed a way out. So, after consulting with the
king and Richelieu, Wellington initiated negotiations with the British banking
house Baring Brothers and the Dutch (Barings-related) Hope & Company.[135]
These bankers had already provided France with a small loan of some
70 million francs in April 1816. That loan had been sold to Dutch investors
(among others). Wellington announced that he would explore the conditions
for a much larger loan. In the meantime, France would be granted a deferment
of indemnity payments for the next two periods.[136] Richelieu heartily supported this plan; in fact, French bankers had already been putting out feelers
themselves. Via the bankers Lafitte and Hottinguer, as well as through
Napoleon's former financial advisor, the crafty Gabriel-Julien Ouvrard, the
French government had itself already tried to contact the banking houses of
Baring and Hope.[137]

Wellington's plan did not come to him from out of the blue, but was in fact
built on a previous contact with Ouvrard. The 47-year-old Ouvrard, son of
a paper-mill owner, started speculating in the paper trade at the age of nineteen,
and thereafter had earned a fortune through overseas trade in products from the
Americas and military contracts with France, Spain and Italy. Starting with
France's Iberian campaign, he began to specialize in the buying and selling of
public debt. According to Nicolle, he was 'truly the apostle of loans'.[138] Ouvrard
first got to know Wellington when he was the British ambassador in Paris for

---

[132] Nicolle, 'The Problem of Reparations after the Hundred Days', 345; Jarrett, *The Congress
of Vienna and its Legacy*, 179.

[133] Richelieu to Kapodistrias, 15 October 1816, Polovtsoff (ed.), *Le Duc de Richelieu*, 490.

[134] White, 'Making the French Pay', 344.

[135] The Baring Brothers banking house was sometimes referred to as 'Barings' (the House of
Barings), sometimes as 'Baring & Hope'. The family name was 'Baring'.

[136] Protocol of 2 December 1816, TNA, FO 146/15.

[137] Greenfield, 'Financing a New Order', 385.

[138] 'Ouvrard', in J. Tulard (ed.), *Dictionnaire Napoléon* (Paris: Fayard, 1987), 1279–80;
Nicolle, *Comment la France a payé après Waterloo*, 25.

a brief time, in 1814. Since then, the cunning trader had tried to convince both Alexander Baring and Pierre César Labouchère (Hope's partner), and Wellington and Richelieu, of the mutual benefit of a large loan for France. That had already led to that first small loan in 1816.[139] At the end of 1816, Ouvrard again put out feelers in that direction, for the situation had become so acute for the French government that 'its means for liquidating claims decreases inversely with the increase of its debt'. In 1816, he visited Wellington in Brussels. On 8 January 1817, he wrote Wellington a long letter in which he appealed to his good contacts with Baring and Hope, suggesting to the duke a solution to the problem at hand, one that also involved the 'security of the Allies'. Ouvrard outlined a plan for a large loan to be provided by Baring and Hope and for which the Allies would act as guarantor (and then, of course, also an indication of the commission that he would want to expect).[140]

A day later, Wellington, always up for pragmatic and creative solutions, took the idea for discussion to the Allied Ministerial Conference. On 9 January 1817, the ministers met to discuss the plan, and unanimously believed that a loan of this type could be the solution. This loan would finally become a real *sécurité*, both for France and for Europe. With this loan, France would be able both to meet its annual obligation of 140 million francs for the maintenance of the Allied forces, and to start settling what it held in arrears.[141] As a sign of goodwill, Richelieu announced on 22 January 1817 that he had dismissed four of the five French liquidation commissioners (including Dudon) for malpractice and had appointed four new ones. The guarantee fund, which was completely depleted, was supplemented by 5.5 million francs. Likewise, the French king also committed himself to making sure that the payments were processed in a prompt fashion.[142] The paradox of paying versus stabilizing seemed to have become slightly less paradoxical. As Pozzo di Borgo wrote to Count Lieven: 'By encouraging this loan, the British government has done the world a great service.' The tsar was also pleased that the political and financial security remained guaranteed.[143]

---

[139] Ziegler, *The Sixth Great Power*, 78–9. See also: Greenfield, 'Financing a New Order', 379–80.

[140] Ouvrard to Wellington, 8 January 1817, City Archives, Amsterdam (SAA), Archive of Banker's and Family Affairs Sillem, no. 675/52. See also Greenfield, 'Financing a New Order', 389, who found the letter from Ouvrard in the archives of the French Ministry of Foreign Affairs.

[141] Allied Council, protocol and attachments, 9 January 1817, TNA, FO 146/15; Oosterlinck, Ureche-Rangau and Vaslin, 'Baring, Wellington and the Resurrection of French Public Finances', 1083.

[142] Protocol of 22 January 1817, TNA, FO 146/15.

[143] Pozzo di Borgo to Lieven, 3/7 January 1817, Pozzo di Borgo (ed.), *Correspondance*, vol. 2, 7.

The First Large Loan

The banking houses of Baring and Hope were already working closely with the British government, and had also provided the first small loan to France.[144] To ask Barings for a large loan, therefore, seemed to be the next logical step. But that is not to say that such a loan was necessarily attractive to Barings. France might well be one of the richest countries in Europe, but there was a world of difference between the wealth of French individuals and the credit rating of their government. There were plenty of wealthy citizens, but they were wary about investing in the national debt of a country that had been so unstable for years. They were only willing to do so if they had confidence in their government.[145] And so, in the summer of 1817, the government was caught in a vicious circle of instability and insolvency. To be recognized as a stable state, France had to pay the Allies. To do so, France found itself forced to take out loans, because not enough money was coming in through taxes.[146] To lend such immense amounts, investors and debtors demanded a stable and creditworthy political situation. France could hardly escape this vicious circle on its own. It had been able to borrow 70 million in 1816, but the market was not amenable to a vastly larger loan. As the French banker Jacques Lafitte had told the Russian ambassador Pozzo di Borgo, there was simply not one single extra écu to borrow in Europe.[147] Likewise, the French statesman Étienne-Denis Pasquier,[148] who among other things was responsible for the foreign debt commission in 1816, sighed rhetorically: 'Is our country in a situation that inspires confidence?' Against the background of all these storms, political and meteorological, France was scraping the bottom of the barrel: 'Is it any wonder that, against the background of a future that promises so little peace of mind, the capitalists hesitate to commit themselves?'[149] Not surprisingly, at the beginning of 1816, Alexander Baring had informed Richelieu that it was inconceivable, given the instability of the French governments, which were all prepared, at the drop of a hat, to commit political suicide and risk defaulting on France's foreign debt, that he should extend a large loan to the country now. French politics

---

[144] See Baring to Richelieu, 7 October 1817, appended to protocol of 8 October 1817, TNA, FO 146/22. See also Oosterlinck, Ureche-Rangau and Vaslin, 'Baring, Wellington and the Resurrection of French Public Finances', 1081–3.

[145] See Ziegler, *The Sixth Great Power*, 78.

[146] Greenfield, 'Financing a New Order', 382–3.

[147] White, 'Making the French Pay', 344–5.

[148] In 1815 and 1817–18 he was the minister of justice of France.

[149] É.-D. Pasquier, *Histoire de mon temps. Mémoires du chancelier Pasquier*, vol. 4 (Paris: Plon, 1893–5), 147.

was its own worst enemy, and the predominant source of France's credit-unworthiness.[150] Castlereagh shared that sense.[151]

France's deplorable credit rating was not only due to the policy of the current French government. France was structurally lagging behind countries like Britain and the Netherlands when it came to the reform of its financial institutions.[152] Unlike those two countries, France had been unable, over the course of the eighteenth century, to repay its public loans and to meet the interest payments, which rose ever higher; the country had to default five times over.[153] Britain had introduced a double-entry bookkeeping system already in the seventeenth century, to combat financial fraud and corruption, and it had set up a central bank to prevent inflation. A representative political system also ensured that governmental budgets were transparent and had to be submitted to parliament, and in this way also gave the lobby of bankers and creditors access to the decision-making process. In 1786, the then prime minister and chancellor of the exchequer (minister of finance), William Pitt the Younger, had set up a 'sinking fund' to set aside budget surpluses for debt repayment. In that way, Britain – like the Italian states – built up a reliable reputation. This, in turn, had led to low interest rates on the public debt and a correspondingly low tax burden. The story of the Netherlands was slightly more complicated. From the seventeenth century onwards, because of the intensity of its trade-based economy and low interest rates, the country had amassed a large capital surplus, making investing in government debt attractive. In the second half of the eighteenth century, however, the national debt increased. The associated interest burden rose, leading to an increase in capital flight. Centralizing the collection of taxes and introducing a sinking fund in 1799 did help reduce the debt, but at the end of the French occupation, the Netherlands still struggled with a huge national debt. The merger of the north and south, however, brought some relief because Belgium had virtually no debt.[154] Although this unequal state of affairs would also increase political tensions between the north

---

[150] See Ferguson, *The Cash Nexus*, 146; White, 'Making the French Pay', 344; L. de Viel-Castel, *Histoire de la Restauration*, vol. 5 (Paris: Michel Lévy frères, 1862), 318–19.

[151] Ziegler, *The Sixth Great Power*, 79.

[152] See K. Dyson, *States, Debts and Power. 'Saints' and 'Sinners' in European History and Integration* (Oxford: Oxford University Press, 2014), 101; M. Bordo and E. White, 'A Tale of Two Currencies: British and French Finance during the Napoleonic Wars', *Journal of Economic History*, 51:2 (1991), 303–4.

[153] Dyson, *States*, 141, 143, 179.

[154] Cf. Pfeil, 'Tot redding van het vaderland'; Van Leeuwen-Canneman (ed.), *Een vriendschap in het teken van 's Lands financiën*, appendix 4, 649. See also H. Riemens, *Het Amortisatiesyndicaat. Een studie over de staatsfinanciën onder Willem I* (Amsterdam: Paris, 1935), 20–7. See also E. Buyst, 'De onmogelijke integratie: Economische ontwikkelingen in Nederland en België', in I. de Haan, P. den Hoed and H. te Velde (eds.), *Een Nieuwe Staat. Het begin van het koninkrijk der Nederlanden* (Amsterdam: Bert Bakker, 2013), 189, 196.

and the south in the longer run, in 1815, thanks to financial reforms and stable political institutions, it was relatively easy and attractive for both the British and Dutch governments to borrow money.

France, on the other hand, still struggled with a very poor credit rating, and hyperinflation, high taxes and the failure to repay debts during the Napoleonic regime had not improved things. Implementing an amortization fund (1799) and creating the Banque de France (1800) had not changed things substantially. The national debt remained a state secret, the parliament had little or no control over it and no one knew how monies were being spent. On top of that came the high cost of the Hundred Days period, which had undermined the last remnants of France's creditworthiness.[155]

Confidence in France's solvency started to improve only in 1817, due in large part to Richelieu's efforts and the political reforms carried out under Allied pressure. The Ultras were gone, and a more moderate parliament had taken office. The Allied Council indicated that if this parliament were to take the constitution, the *Charte*, more to heart and pay the reparations more faithfully, it would be possible to talk about an earlier or partial reduction of the occupation. If France were to show its good side, the Allied Conference stood ready to help the government look for a solution to making its payments.[156]

In the meantime, everyone was waiting on the others. European high finance was reluctant to invest in France's national debt. French banks, before engaging in the risk themselves, were waiting for foreign participation. The French government, in turn, was less than confident about the ability of its own French banks to mobilize the necessary funds, and the Allies, at least formally, did want to stand behind such a loan. Castlereagh warned Baring of what he should expect:

> No guarantee of any description on the part of Gt Britain, but no obstacle to your dealing with France on her own credit, and upon your own account. In short, you must judge and act upon the terms and the securities, the French Govt has to propose, as you think best for your own private interests.[157]

In the light of the above, it was Wellington who cut the knot a few weeks later. A reduction of the debt was possible, but only if the French government was willing to work with a banking house that was sufficiently sound financially. The Allied Occupation Army would then function as an informal form of guarantee.

---

[155] See Bordo and White, 'A Tale', 307–15; Ferguson, *The Cash Nexus*, 180; Dyson, *States*, 103.

[156] Protocol of 9 December 1816, TNA, FO 146/15.

[157] Castlereagh to Baring, 23 December 1816, SAA, Hope & Co, no. 735/1936.

Barings' Financial Securities

From Wellington's perspective, Baring and Hope were indeed the most suitable for realizing this plan. They were a British–Dutch consortium of two banking houses that were related through family ties and had also serviced the British government well during the period of the Napoleonic Wars and the war with America.[158] Even more important was the fact that Barings was the richest banking house in Europe – the Allied Ministerial Conference agreed unanimously on this. The French king informed them, via Richelieu, that Barings appealed to him as well. The capital reserves and the status of Baring and Hope (represented by Labouchère) were urgently needed, because the amount called for was immense: the indemnities, the maintenance of the troops and the overdue debt had to be settled.

On 9 January 1817, Wellington secured the support of three of the four Allied ministers (from Austria, Russia and Britain) plus Richelieu for engaging Baring and Hope. Prussia refused that support and was outraged that Baring and Hope were the only parties in the picture and German banks had not been consulted. In London, on 17 January, Castlereagh, prime minister Liverpool and chancellor of the exchequer Vansittart tried to further warm Baring to the plan – who shortly thereafter left for Paris to further consider the matter – but he was not yet willing to commit.[159] Wellington, who was in Paris, chimed in as well, writing to Castlereagh on 27 January:

> I have been hard at work on the finances here. As you stated, Baring was very unwilling to act upon Ouvrard's romances . . . and I should have been myself so much involved in it, that I thought it best to go into the whole question of the French Budget, and to see whether we could not bring the wants to such a sum as that Baring could undertake to supply them without the aid which he expected to derive from being the agent of the Allies.

In other words, Wellington had to try to persuade Baring to proceed, without directly guaranteeing him that he was acting on the Allies' behalf. Baring was only interested if he could make such a huge loan without any obligations to a third party, so that he could be certain of deriving sufficiently high earnings for himself – a high-risk, high-gain game, in short. At the same time, the Allies wanted to be assured that they would receive their money within a reasonable time frame. In consultation with Wellington, Richelieu, Corvetto (France's new minister of finance) and Baring, it seemed that a loan of 315 million would, in the end, be sufficient. That amount would be split

---

[158] Ziegler, *The Sixth Great Power*, 43–77.
[159] Castlereagh to Wellington, 17 January 1817, *WSD*, vol. 11, 601–2.

across three tranches: one of 100 million in February, another of 100 million in April and a last one of 115 million in July 1817.[160]

On 10 February 1817, the contract for the first loan was signed. Each month, Baring and Hope would deliver part of the 100 million francs in the form of bills of exchange or promissory notes to the bearer. These could be redeemed three months after being issued. In exchange, the bankers put 9,090,909 *rentes* (in fact, a kind of bond) on the market. The purchase price of those *rentes* by Barings from the French ministry was 55 francs each. Barings was then able to sell the *rentes* on the market for 57.75 francs.[161] Baring and Hope then signed a separate contract with the French trading houses Baguenault, Greffulhe, Hottinguer and Perregaux Lafitte. As subcontractors, these French bankers would buy one quarter of the *rentes*.[162] They would then together sell the *rentes* on the capital market. Both the Allied ministers and their French colleagues rightly assumed that putting these up for tender would be well received by public opinion and the stock markets.[163]

Baring and Hope remained the ultimate risk bearers.[164] Alexander Baring (Fig. 7.2), however, had a fine nose for business and knew that he could count on the statesmanship of Wellington. Although Wellington had not issued a formal declaration of assurance, he did, of course, provide a substantial military security deposit with his Allied Occupation Army. The first loan was indeed such a success that in April the second loan of another 100 million could be put on the market. This time, 8,620,689 *rentes* were bought at 58 francs each.[165] The announcement of the first loan of 1817 by Baring and Hope had given France's credit rating internationally a significant shot in the arm. France's attractiveness for foreign and domestic investors increased dramatically. That was reflected in the price of the *rentes*, which rose from 57.75 to 61 francs between 8 and 11 January 1817.[166] Wellington and Baring's venture had paid off.

Against this background of the upward trend of French interest rates, the third envisaged loan of 115.2 million francs was taken out in July 1817. This time the French government saw to it that French houses could also participate. To that end, a consortium of seven banking houses was set up, consisting

[160] Wellington to Castlereagh, 27 January 1817, *WSD*, vol. 11, 609–10. See also Ziegler, *The Sixth Great Power*, 80.
[161] Calculation: 100,000,000 x 5 = 500,000,000. The exchange rate is 55. That 500,000,000 divided by 55 = 9,090,909. See the contract of 10 February 1817, between Corvetto and the banking houses Baring and Hope, SAA, Hope & Co, no. 735/1940.
[162] Platt, *Foreign Finance*, 9.
[163] See protocol of 9 January 1817, TNA, FO 146/15; memorandum of Richelieu, 10 February 1817, TNA, FO 146/15; Ziegler, *The Sixth Great Power*, 79–81.
[164] Letter of Corvetto, 13 February, SAA, Hope & Co, no. 735/1940.
[165] Letter, 11 March 1817, SAA, Hope & Co, no. 735/1940.
[166] Oosterlinck, Ureche-Rangau and Vaslin, 'Baring, Wellington and the Resurrection of French Public Finances', 1091, 1096–7.

Figure 7.2   Alexander Baring. Portrait by Thomas Lawrence, c.1815. (The Baring Archive, London)

of Baguenault, Barings, Delessert, Greffulhe, Hope (represented by Labouchère), Hottinguer and Perregaux Lafitte. The French houses together participated for one half of the *rentes*, and Baring and Hope for the other half. Each financial transaction had to be accepted by at least five of the seven signatories.[167] According to the contract, between September and December 1817, the bankers would pay 19,200,000 francs per month to the French treasury, and 12,800,000 francs per month between January and March 1818: in total, 115.2 million francs. On the other hand, from 1 March 1817 on, the bankers had access to a capital of 9 million *rentes* at the rate of 64 francs each, as the price had increased further.[168]

The loans were offered through the stock exchanges in London, Amsterdam and Paris. The French banks arranged for one quarter of the sales for the first and second loans, and one half of them for the third loan. A large part of the

[167] 'Traité' of their 'société commerciale', 24 July 1817, SAA, Hope & Co, no. 735/1940.

[168] See Convention between Corvetto and Barings, Hope and Perregaux Lafitte. Similar conventions were made with the other French banks, 22 July 1817. The banking consortium was established on 24 July by treaty, SAA, Hope & Co, no. 735/1940.

stock ended up in the hands of French investors. However, besides the 'major houses' mentioned above, it was a European company of elite bankers and high financiers that 'bought' French security in this way. Those buying *rentes* included: Reid Irving, Sillem, Sartoris, Haldimand, Ouvrard himself, Liebert & Wiesen, Parish, Rothschild, Welles & Williams, Oppermann/Mandrot, Oppenheim, Scherer & Finguerlin and a number of wealthy individuals.[169] Of the first series of *rentes* (the 9,090,909), 4,533,650 went to Paris, 2,429,750 to London and 1,100,000 to Amsterdam. The rest remained in the hands of the bankers themselves.[170] In September 1818, the demand in France was so high that the *rentes* of the third loan were by and large bought by French investors and banks.[171] Eventually, German bankers and investors also got involved, like Stieglitz, who opened up the Hamburg market.[172]

Things were going so well that Alexander Baring began to worry. 'Too much stock has been emitted, and credit thereby overstretched', he wrote worriedly to Wellington. 'Our sales move very heavily, or rather for a long time we have sold nothing, and I should calculate that there must be still in our hands or in those of other speculators, at least 80 million unliquidated.'[173] Indeed, a great burden of responsibility was resting on Barings' shoulders. 'The fact is', Wellington wrote with some worry to Liverpool,

> that Baring having the French finances in his hands, and French loans being in fashion in England, has to a certain degree the command of the money market of the world. He feels his power, and it is not a very easy task to succeed in counteracting him.[174]

Even the Rothschilds, who would far exceed Barings in their power and influence over the financial world after 1818, complained in 1817 about the overpowering influence of their competitor. 'He is quite a crook, this Baring', Salomon Rothschild reported to his brother Nathan from Paris:

> We must certainly watch our step . . . The Baring lot is and was well versed in the way of using influence, as we are. There is not a single man of importance among the authorities here who would not work with Baring hand-in-glove. Baring and the French minister of finance are sharing the profit.[175]

---

[169] See lists of the sale of the 'stocks' for the loans of 1817, SAA, Hope & Co, no. 735/1938.

[170] See lists of 'sales', 5 April 1817, SAA, Hope & Co, no. 735/218; Greenfield, 'Financing a New Order', 391.

[171] Ibid., 391.

[172] See the balance of May 1818, SAA, Hope & Co, no. 735/1939.

[173] Baring to Wellington, 4 December 1817, *WSD*, vol. 12, 171–4; Ziegler, *The Sixth Great Power*, 81.

[174] Wellington to Liverpool, 4 February 1818, *WSD*, vol. 12, 247–9.

[175] Cited by Ziegler, *The Sixth Great Power*, 82; Greenfield, 'Financing a New Order', 393.

Keeping the Mountain of Debt Contained

The loans helped France through the spring and summer of 1817. Because France had met the payment of two instalments, Wellington fulfilled his promise on 1 April 1817. Each occupying power withdrew one fifth of its troops, meaning that 30,000 troops could be repatriated.[176] But, as the Allied Council informed Richelieu on 2 April, France had to continue paying the agreed-upon amounts for the fortifications. Richelieu also had to urge Luigi Emanuele Corvetto, his minister of finance, to transfer 200 million francs for the interest on the arrears due the Allied creditors, and to do so quickly, as the 'unhappy creditors' had been waiting for such a long time.[177] However, these arrears were still the biggest stumbling block. The mountain of submitted claims was by now exceeding their worst expectations.

As a result, after a few weeks, the recently supplemented guarantee fund for private liquidations was again empty, and would remain so. The liquidation activities came to a standstill, and after October 1817 no more notes of remittance were drawn up.[178] Only a quarter of the total number of debt claims had been liquidated. In September, after the Council and Committee of Liquidators had debated the entire summer with Richelieu and the French commissioners about the details and conditions of the payouts, the prime minister came out with an unambiguous announcement. He made it clear that there would be no new guarantee fund, that he would not reconvene parliament for that purpose and that a new law was not in the works. In a long memorandum dated 10 September, Richelieu invoked the 'law of necessity': the French people were exhausted and could no longer pay for that extra fund. Allied creditors were asking too much. When the First Treaty of Paris of 30 May 1814 was signed, Richelieu argued, no one had foreseen that such a mountain of debt claims would materialize. France was 'deeply disappointed'. The original 3.5-million-franc interest fund would have to be increased 'not twofold, not fourfold, but tenfold' in order to be able to pay all those private debt claims, which by now were already higher than half of the entire French national debt. That is why Richelieu wanted to talk again about the conditions for admissible claims. The valid claims would not be paid in the

---

[176] Wellington to Charles Stuart, 'Memorandum of a note on the reduction of the army of occupation', 9 January 1817, *WSD*, vol. 11, 589–94.

[177] Allied Council, protocol plus attachments, 2 April 1817, TNA, FO 145/15. Articles XVII and XVIII of the convention stipulated that, starting on 22 March 1816, France's debt to creditors, 'either in principal, or arrears of interest', had to be paid in cash.

[178] Nine notes of remittance were drawn up for the Kingdom of the Netherlands, six of which were paid in full or in part. See report to the king, 22 October 1817, with attachments, NL-HaNA, 2.02.01, inv. no. 6366.

meantime, but would be considered as debt claims against the French government.[179]

So, what now? The Allied ministers and their commissioners were decidedly fed up with the unending squabbles with the French commissioners. Under no circumstances were the ministers willing to withdraw the occupying forces if the Paris Convention had not been fulfilled beforehand. Creditors who had already been paid might well be satisfied, but most of the others could pretty much forget about what was owed them – an estimated 1,310 million all told.[180] The Dutch – Canneman, Robbert Fagel and his brother Hendrik, the Dutch ambassador to the British court, who was visiting his brother – put pressure on Wellington, arguing that to fail to honour these claims would be unjust, a violation of public law and the promises France had made.[181] Wellington was not insensitive to this argument. Canneman also warned him about sympathizing too much with France, which, 'although the richest nation in Europe, used poverty to win time and will soon resume its old role and projects of encroachment'.[182] In the meantime, Canneman had also spoken with Baring and heard that Baring was able to finance a loan for 12 million *rentes* that would allow France to finally settle the liquidation of the private claims.[183]

So, once again, there was only one possible solution: more loans. At the end of October 1817, rumours began to circulate about a new loan. The initial steps were taken in December.[184] The negotiations on the loans coincided with attempts on the part of the Allied ministers and commissioners to reduce the claims in arrears to a somewhat acceptable level. Again, Wellington was the one who was in a position to negotiate a compromise between debtor and

---

[179] The Allied Liquidators to the Allied Council, 16 September 1817; protocol of 20 September 1817, TNA, FO 146/22.

[180] This amount is mentioned a number of times. See also the memorandum annexed to the protocols of 31 January 1818, no. 199, TNA, FO 146/23. But this estimated amount of 1,300 million francs was higher than the actual claims submitted (1,200 million); see Table 7.2. This difference can presumably be explained by the ineptitude of the French commissioners, about which Canneman complained to the king in his reports. Another explanation could be that the French inflated the debt as high as possible for tactical reasons.

[181] Hendrik Fagel began a journey through France on 4 July 1817, with Paris as his point of departure. See NL-HaNA, 1.10.29 (Fagel Collection), inv. no. 199. Presumably, this conversation with his brother Robbert, Wellington and Canneman took place before his departure.

[182] Report to the king, 28 August 1817, NL-HaNA, 2.02.01, inv. no. 6366. Canneman's assumptions about the financial strength of the French were based on the success of the third loan from Baring and Hope, half of which was subscribed to by French investors (in contrast to the first two loans, which mainly sold in London and Amsterdam). See Platt, *Foreign Finance*, 9; Ziegler, *The Sixth Great Power*, 81.

[183] Report of Canneman to the king, 12 October 1817, NL-HaNA, 2.02.01, inv. no. 6366.

[184] Message about a new loan, 9 December 1817, SAA, Hope & Co, no. 735/1940.

Table 7.2 *Overview of the claims filed, liquidated and paid, of amounts granted to participants in the Convention of 25 April 1818 and corresponding* rentes *granted to Allies on the continent*[a]

Country / combined (parts of) countries[b]	Total of claims submitted,1816–18	Claims liquidated and paid	Amount granted to participate in the agreement of 25 April 1818	*Rentes* granted
Anhalt-Bernburg	446,194	* (no data)	350,000	17,500
Anhalt-Dessau	379,719	6,211	373,507	18,500
Austria	189,383,506	2,612,642	25,000,000	1,250,000
Baden	1,444,886	117,006	650,000	32,500
Bavaria	78,023,766	1,244,060	10,000,000	500,000
Bremen	3,769,376	689,923	1,000,000	50,000
Denmark	46,599,611	2,734,077	7,000,000	350,000
Frankfurt	3,861,038	15,818	700,000	35,000
Hamburg	81,927,374	6,948,850	20,000,000	1,000,000
Bank of Hamburg	10,000,000	10,000,000	*	*
Hanover	40,607,700	7,677,422	10,000,000	500,000
The Electorate of Hessen	643,047	85,118	507,099	25,000
The Electorate of Hessen and Saxe-Weimar	17,512	*		14,000	7,000
The Electorate of Hessen and Saxe-Weimar	7,099	*	*	7,000
The Electorate of Hessen, Bavaria and Saxe-Weimar	856,066	*	*	40,000

Table 7.2 (Cont.)

Country / combined (parts of) countries	Total of claims submitted,1816–18	Claims liquidated and paid	Amount granted to participate in the agreement of 25 April 1818	Rentes granted
The Electorate of Hessen, Prussia, Hanover and Brunswick	260,015	*	*	8,000
Hessen-Darmstadt and Bavaria	556,937	*	200,000	8,000
Hessen-Darmstadt, Prussia and Bavaria	2,745,877	*	800,000	40,000
Ionian Islands & Isle de France (Mauritius)	19,995,311	*	3,000,000	150,000
Lübeck	5,718,958	881,269	2,000,000	100,000
Mecklenburg-Schwerin	1,625,969	125,420	500,000	25,000
Duchy of Nassau	1,459,242	*	127,000	6,000
Netherlands	219,404,504	28,672,959	33,000,000	1,650,000
Duchy of Parma	4,716,102	888,383	1,000,000	50,000
Pontifical States	29,728,487	1,299,074	5,000,000	250,000
Portugal	32,024,531	*	818,736	40,900
Prussia	135,054,118	19,269,923	52,003,289	2,600,000

Table 7.2 *(Cont.)*

Country / combined (parts of) countries	Total of claims submitted,1816–18	Claims liquidated and paid	Amount granted to participate in the agree-ment of 25 April 1818	*Rentes* granted
Sardinia	85,805,594	7,944,460	25,000,000	1,250,000
Saxe-Meiningen	45,255	*	20,694	1,000
Kingdom of Saxony	15,654,580	632,559	4,500,000	225,000
Saxony and Prussia	5,624,845	567,092	2,200,000	110,000
Spain	215,014,775	3,497,185	17,000,000	850,000
Switzerland	28,115,021	426,831	5,000,000	250,000
Tuscany	10,315,615	4,594,620	4,500,000	225,000
Württemberg	702,030	1,903	400,000	20,000
Grand Duchy of Hesse	10,628,217	1,207,843	8,000,000	348,150 (together with Oldenburg)
Mecklenburg-Strelitz	35,098	*		1,750
Oldenburg	11,529,060	181,754		
Reuss	115,107	5,651		3,250
Saxe-Gotha	1,320,351	8,161		30,000
Saxe-Weimar	536,341	10,520		9,250
Schwarzburg	255,748	5,738		7,500
Total[c]	**1,296,954,562**	**102,352,499**	**230,664,325**	**12,040,000**

[a] See 'Résultat de la liquidation en exécution de la Convention du 20 novembre 1815', HL-HaNA, 2.21.005.30, 36, and the Convention of 25 April 1818, Article X. This Table was also printed in (De) Graaf and Van Leeuwen-Canneman, 'De prijs van de vrede', 49. With thanks to Mieke van Leeuwen-Canneman.

[b] This table has been copied from the tables used by Wellington and the financial liquidators themselves. They sometimes listed groups of counties/duchies twice,

depending on how they were realigned during the Congress of Vienna. That process of realignment and territorial rearrangement caused some to be mentioned more than once.

^{c} These totals, like the other figures, have been copied straight from the files, which contain copies made from the numbers Wellington used, and they do not reflect the actual totals of the numbers listed above. Perhaps the copiers made mistakes, or perhaps Wellington computed the numbers in haste. However, the differences are not substantial. For the calculation of the *rentes* it did not matter whether the total of the claims amounted to 230,664,325 francs or 236,927,066 francs. In Article I of the Convention of 25 April 1818 it is stipulated that a sum of 240,800,000 should be inscribed in the French Great Book of Public Debt. The numbers in this table should therefore be read as a working plan for Wellington, and as indicative of the final stipulations.

creditor, between the French and the Allies. Canneman offered to help him by starting to divide the outstanding debts into various categories.[185] He also advised Wellington to make sure that France did not play any one of the Allies off against the others.[186] Wellington took Canneman's plan with him, but first had to receive his official instructions. He left for London at the end of October 1817 to confer with Castlereagh and to take a break for his health.[187] In Wellington's absence, the unrest among the Allied Liquidators grew. Canneman expressed his concern to King Willem I about private meetings between Austria and Prussia, which would lead to separate negotiations with France, without involving the other Allied countries. The Allied Council tried to speed up the process by designing a complex model that would incorporate the claims and especially include the interests of the great powers. From London, Wellington also urged the Prussian ambassador Goltz to take the countries and commissioners of the smaller powers into account. Indeed, Canneman found the tone of the foursome 'unbecoming' and was relieved when Wellington returned to Paris at the end of January 1818.[188]

[185] For example, security deposits, back pay and pensions were not negotiable or open to reduction.
[186] Reports of Canneman to the king, 26 October 1817, NL-HaNA, 2.02.01, inv. no. 6366; copies of letters from Canneman to Wellington, 22 October and 26 November 1817, NL-HaNA, 2.21.005.30, inv. no. 37.
[187] Allied Council, protocol of 19 November 1817, TNA, FO 146/22.
[188] Report of Canneman to the king, 1 February 1818; copy of the letter of 19 January 1818 in Canneman's report to the king, 6 February 1818, NL-HaNA, 2.02.01, inv. no. 6367. See also the protest memorandum from the Allied Liquidators to the Council, annex to the protocol of 4 December 1817, TNA, FO 146/23.

By now, the tsar had proposed, via Pozzo di Borgo, that Wellington should – again – make some decisions. Tsar Alexander acknowledged that private creditors were entitled to redress under the conventions of 20 November 1815. At the same time, the claims were much higher than expected. And they did not even include the Russian and Polish creditors; their claims would come 'later', the tsar temporized. Wellington would have to find a middle position between these two extremes, based on a 'strictly impartial basis', and 'reconcile' France with its creditors.[189] The Council agreed; the ball was in Wellington's court.[190]

The Convention of 25 April 1818

Wellington resumed his duties on 2 February 1818 and made it clear to the Allied Council that he would factor in all the interests, including those of the smaller countries. He was probably also the only one who could fill the role of mediator. He dared to act independently of the wishes of the British government, he had the ear of the French king and the deep (or grudging) respect of all the other ministers and diplomats. The task at hand was not an easy one. He had to bridge the gap between what the French could (or wanted to) pay and what the Allies were demanding. In point of fact, Wellington followed Canneman's advice. He would first ask each commissioner for an overview of their legitimate claims, and then initiate a discussion with each of them separately and with France, all of which would remain secret from the others. Based on what he came to learn in this way, he would determine the final sum.[191]

Each commissioner submitted his list to Wellington. The list from the Netherlands was the most complicated, because the issue of the Belgian debt made comparisons difficult.[192] Although Canneman had demonstrated the inadequacy of the French calculations, and had hoped that an agreement regarding the Belgian debt would lead to a result 'with no extra cost', the conversation ended with a difference of more than 22 million francs in France's favour.[193] 'What will the Field Marshal do now? On what do they base this insolence?', Canneman complained

---

[189] Russian memorandum, 'Mémoire. Affaires Liquidations', November/December 1817, annex to the protocol of 4 December 1817, TNA, FO 146/23.

[190] See Prussia's consent, protocol of 14 January 1818 and Austria's, 24 January 1818, TNA, FO 146/23.

[191] Protocol of 2 February 1818, TNA, FO 146/23.

[192] Report of Canneman to the king, with attachments, 18 February 1818, NL-HaNA, 2.02.01, inv. no. 6367, no. 81.

[193] See French reclamations, including calculations and other annexes: 'Reclamation contre les Pays-Bas', 1817–1819, CAdN, no. 8ACN/294. France filed reclamations to other countries, such as Denmark, as well, CAdN, no. 8ACN/258.

to the Dutch king. Yet, he need not have worried; Wellington proved to be a reasonable advocate of the Dutch cause. The Netherlands was allocated 55 million, from which 22 million was deducted for the Belgian debt, leaving a final amount of 33 million francs. Both parties accepted the final verdict.[194]

After agreements were reached with each country, only one question remained. The financial convention of the Second Treaty of Paris stipulated that starting on 22 March 1816 France had to pay the interest on its current and future debts in cash. Reckoned up retroactively, that would amount to some 30 million francs. France refused, but Wellington found the requirement to be just, in part because the Allies had already made so many concessions. In this decisive phase of the negotiations, however, the four ambassadors left him a bit in the lurch. When the liquidation commissioners were informed as to where things stood,

> I [Canneman, in his report to King Willem I] found the Prince [of Waterloo] quite timid, but also embittered against the Duke of Richelieu. France can thank the Russian ambassador and the cowardly weakness of his three colleagues that the case has been abandoned and the interests of the creditors left to languish in an unheard-of manner.[195]

Wellington distanced himself from the proceedings, and was unwilling to take up the task of mediation after this. After endless and increasingly emotional negotiations, the French and Allied commissioners finally reached an agreement on 23 April. They brought the results to Richelieu. Wellington, who was now properly fed up with the deal, had gone hunting. Somewhat embarrassed with their own actions, the Allied commissioners made sure that his role was honoured and praised in the preamble of the agreement. At half past three in the morning, the final act was signed.[196]

For the first time, it became clear to everyone involved how large the amount and everyone's share of it was. The lump sum that France made available for settling the outstanding private claims from the Allied countries (minus Britain[197]) was 12 million francs in *rentes* against a capital of 241 million

---

[194] Report of Canneman to the king, 28 March 1818, with the final sum; the final settlement of the Belgian debt is in Canneman's report to the king, 11 May 1818, NL-HaNA, 2.02.01, inv. no. 6367.

[195] Report of Canneman to the king, 25 April 1818, NL-HaNA, 2.02.01, inv. no. 6367.

[196] Ibid.; Duvergier (ed.), *Collection complète*, vol. 21, 496–500; Dutch text in *Nederlandsche Staatscourant*, 30 June 1818, no. 51.

[197] In a separate convention, 3 million francs (capitalized 60 million francs) were also granted to Britain: Duvergier (ed.), *Collection complète*, 500–1.

Table 7.3 *Payments: Expected and final*

Treaty provisions	Reparations in millions of francs	Final payments (in cash)
Compensation for war damage during the Hundred Days period	700	685.8
Liquidation of private claims	3.5 *rentes* (= capitalized 70, continental Allies) 3.5 *rentes* (= capitalized 70, Great Britain)	3.5 + 5.5 + 12.04 *rentes* (capitalized 180 + 240.8, continental Allies) 3.5 + 3 *rentes* (capitalized 70 +60, Great Britain)
Occupation costs for 1815	180	180
Occupation costs 1816–20	450–750	453
Total	**Unknown, expected: 1,470–1,770**	**1,869.6**

francs. The Dutch share in this was set at 1.65 million in *rentes*. It could have been almost double that, if the Belgian debt had not been calculated into the final amount. Nevertheless, after Prussia, which had been awarded 2 million, the Netherlands took second place among the thirty-nine candidates who participated in the arranged settlement.

Thanks in part to the authority of Wellington, who during the process increasingly took on the role of impartial and supranational arbiter, the Allies succeeded in having France pay the price of peace. Of the more than a billion in private claims submitted, France paid the substantial amount of more than 550 million francs (see Table 7.3).

To enable them to make these payments, Baring and Hope negotiated a loan with the French government on 30 May 1818 for the unprecedented amount of 321,068,000 francs. Twenty-four million *rentes* were duly entered in the Great Book of the Public Debt at a purchase price of 67 francs each. In addition to the *rentes* set by Baring and Hope, the French government would also issue 14.6 million *rentes* directly to the public at the price of 66.5 francs each.

The loans were explicitly made with the goal of achieving the 'total liberation' of France from the 'foreign powers', as well as the 'complete evacuation' of foreign troops from its borders.[198] Unlike with the third loan of 1817, Baring and Hope did not include the French banks in their arrangements with the government – much to the consternation of the bankers Thuret, Lafitte and Perier, who had already been busy preparing a loan themselves (which, incidentally, was not going to include Baring and Hope).[199] When it was announced that the French government had negotiated a loan with the British, the French financiers poured out their wrath on Corvetto and Richelieu. After some political haggling, they finally got a small share. Lafitte could lend 20 million, and the Rothschilds had to settle for a consolation prize of 10 million.

With the signing of the 25 April convention, the securing of the May 1818 loan and the successful completion of its first round of payments, France had met one of the main objectives of the Second Treaty of Paris of 20 November 1815, namely, the redress of and payment on its debt. The Allied Council was more ambivalent about the settling of the political unrest, taming the domestic 'spirit' and achieving 'tranquillity'. The attack on Wellington and the ongoing disorder proved that the revolutionary passions had not yet subsided. The paradox of the occupation and the payment of reparations was no less abrasive: the Allies were in France to stabilize the country and to restore security, but their presence and strict demands were at least in part responsible for the ongoing discontent. Until the end of 1817, the Allied Council had made a firm hand its priority. Now that France had pulled through the most important test and shouldered the financial 'penalty', it was time for it to be compensated.[200] The Allied Council decided that terminating the occupation early – after three years instead of five – was a possibility. In May, the ministers announced that they would convene a congress that autumn, during which, among other things, the end of the occupation would be discussed. In doing so, they implemented Article V of the Second Treaty of Paris.[201]

Canneman stayed in Paris for another year to collect and take care of the documentation and receipts of the outstanding claims. After that, his colleague de Peñeranda took over the work – a process that would continue through to

---

[198] Agreement between Baring & Hope and Richelieu and Corvetto, 30 May 1818, ING London, Baring Archives, HACA inventory no. 204229. See also Greenfield, 'Financing a New Order', 393.

[199] Ibid., 394–7.

[200] Extensive discussion of the state of affairs in France, Allied Council, protocol of 21 April 1818, TNA, FO 146/29.

[201] Allied Council, protocol of 4 May 1818, TNA, FO 126/29.

1843.[202] With the efforts of Canneman, Gagern and Fagel, the Netherlands had succeeded in playing a substantial role in the negotiations surrounding post-war European peace and security. The Netherlands was one of the largest net recipients of the Treaty of Paris, in absolute terms, and entirely so in a relative sense. The Dutch example proved that, while an imperial concert was in place after the Congress of Vienna, the envoys from smaller countries could indeed increase their room to manoeuvre when they wisely joined in with one or more of the larger powers – as the Netherlands did with the British and the Prussians. Canneman was also an example of a new professional class of non-noble bureaucrats, financial experts and security managers who began to dominate national and international policymaking after 1815. Not only the aristocratic envoys with their titles, but deft financial and pragmatic men like Canneman and Baring, with their detailed memoranda, thorough calculations and well-timed suggestions, were clearly able to influence the negotiations.

Security through Financial Interdependence

The security of 1815 was a capitalist one. No one had yet heard of 'retributive justice'. Trials for 'crimes against humanity' and the international enforcement of human rights were simply not part of the picture. And yet, the peace of 1815 was not merely a case of *Siegerjustiz* – victor's justice. Vengeance or retaliation did not characterize the collective security policy. Nor was it about just turning back the clock. That is why 'restoration' does not cover the breadth of this highly transformative post-war order. Stolen property and confiscated territories often did not revert to their pre-revolutionary owners. Significant components of the arrears were never settled. The collective security order after 1815 did, however, at least symbolically restore the rights of private landowners and citizens' savings by elevating reparations and compensatory damages to a central principle. The security was anti-revolutionary in the sense that it was intended to prevent future expropriations and upheavals by administratively sealing the notion of 'mine and thine'.

By 1818, the contours of a new system of international relations were visible: one that was much more collective and regulated, but at the same time more imperialist and capitalist in nature than was previously the case in the feudal situation of the *ancien régime*. The phenomenon of sovereigns and their governments finding their way to capital markets in Amsterdam and London had already emerged in the seventeenth and

---

[202] Landheer, 'Afrekenen met het verleden', 208–10, 220–2. See also Landheer, 'Arm Vlissingen: Hulpverlening en schadevergoeding', in V. Enthoven (ed.), *Een haven te ver. De Britse expeditie naar de Schelde van 1809* (Nijmegen: Vantilt, 2009), 257–77.

eighteenth centuries.[203] However, after 1815, this practice of transnational loans developed into a pivotal component of the international system of collective security. Finance became an important counterweight in maintaining the balance of power. Via Wellington, the Allied Council helped facilitate a risky loan for France from Baring and Hope, after which the *rentes* were subsequently sold in London, Amsterdam, Paris and later also in Hamburg. In this way, European investors, citizens, bankers, the French government and the Allied courts together formed a financial circuit that was embedded in a collective European political system, allowing money to flow freely, pumping it into the economy and ensuring that the peace was also sealed economically.

This was not just a matter of course. After the First World War, the Allied forces were not able to get Germany to pay all that it owed; consensus among the Allies was completely lacking, and the German debtor proved to be a more difficult sparring partner than the French government had been in 1815.[204] Also, it was not a foregone conclusion that France could or would pay the price of security, or that the Allies could agree on the nature and extent of the reparations. In 1815, matters were held hostage by Prussian vindictiveness; repression and exploitation were on the top of their list. In addition, tax revenues were far from sufficient to pay for the maintenance of the occupying forces and reparations, which led to French speculators as well as local Allied commanders taking matters into their own hands. But nonetheless, three years later, security had become a matter of mutual financial dependence, of orderly compromises and consistent criteria.

The tipping point for France's creditworthiness – the most crucial aspect of the financial security situation – happened in January 1817, when the Allied Council of Ministers, again via Wellington, used its collective persuasiveness and military influence to get the bankers and the French government on the same page. When Baring was found willing to put his reputation and financial means on the line, thanks in large part to Wellington's covert and never formally issued guarantee of the Allied occupation forces, France's international credit rating rose significantly, as did the mutual financial interdependence of the French and European

---

[203] See J. Riley, *International Government Finance and the Amsterdam Capital Market 1740–1815* (Cambridge: Marten, 1980); M. Buist, *At spes non fracta. Hope & Co, 1750–1815. Merchant Bankers and Diplomats at Work* (The Hague: Kluwer, 1974); Ziegler, *Sixth Great Power,* 43–99.

[204] Oosterlinck, Ureche-Rangau and Vaslin also make this argument, in 'Baring, Wellington, and the Resurrection of French Public Finances', 1083.

partners. The Allies were not the only ones to benefit from France's payments for reparations; France itself very much did as well. In the summer of 1817, after the first two loans were successfully secured, also thanks to Richelieu's clever and conciliatory mediation, five French banks were invited to form a consortium of equal partners with Baring and Hope.[205] This capitalist safety net was so robust because the Allied ministers had linked Europe's security both to financial interests and to demands for political reforms and stabilization within France. As the powerful banker Nathan Rothschild put it in a letter to the Prussian government:

> the late investments by British subjects in the French Funds have proceeded upon the general belief that in consequence of the representative system now established in that Country, the sanction of the Chamber to the national debt incurred by the Government affords a guarantee to the Public Creditor which could not be found in a Contract with any Sovereign uncontrolled in the exercise of the executive powers.[206]

In other words, the financial obligations that had been so humiliating had nonetheless led to political reforms in France and an intertwining of financial interests in Europe. That capitalist–security nexus was in fact also collective. The property rights of smaller countries and private individuals were just as well respected as the demands of the great powers. Bankers from Britain, the Netherlands, France and finally also the German lands benefited from the loans. Further beneficiaries included wealthy European citizens who bought the *rentes*, and who in so doing helped finance France's security. The amounts involved were huge. Barings booked an astronomical profit of 720,000 pounds: according to a Barings associate, 'the most profitable undertaking in which any mercantile House ever engaged'. By 1818, the power of the big four was now shared by two more: 'There are six great powers in Europe', Richelieu is said to have quipped: 'Britain, France, Prussia, Austria, Russia and the Baring Brothers'.[207]

The price of French and European security was paid, and rested on the capitalist foundation of financial 'securities'. The 'men of 1815' did something remarkable: they made the payment of reparations and arrear debts into the cornerstone of the treaty work underpinning and securing the new peace order. Thus, they sealed a transformation towards a new system of

[205] Pasquier, *Histoire de mon temps*, 150–2; Nicolle, *Comment la France a payé après Waterloo*, 348–9.
[206] Letter, December 1817, cited in Ferguson, *The Cash Nexus*, 288.
[207] Unfortunately, this aphorism cannot be documented beyond doubt. But according to Ziegler, it was nonetheless true. Both cited by: Ziegler, *Sixth Great Power*, 85.

financial and capitalist power alignments, summarized in the formula 'indemnity for the past and security for the future'.[208] But before this edifice could be declared complete, a final congress was called for. Arrangements had to be made for the troops returning home, and new safeguards – in the form of fortifications along the border – had to be put in place before the Allies could really organize their final departure.

---

[208] J. Meeks, *France, Britain and the Struggle for the Western Mediterranean* (Cham 2017), 13 and 113.

8

Fortress Europe

Constructing the 'Wellington Barrier'

Important Dignitaries in Oudenaarde

For centuries, fortifications and fortresses were the most visible sign of security in a country. Ramparts and fortified walls marked out the city limits and provided protection to its inhabitants. But they also forced them to bear the costs and consequences of border protection and national defence, such as sieges and artillery bombardment in times of war. Fortifications were built as strategic reinforcements, erecting a barrier against possible invaders along the border of one's territory. Walls and earthworks were also constructed along access routes and by storage depots. Border fortifications could consist of one or more lines of defence. One such important line – referred to as 'barriers' after the seventeenth century – was the Scheldt River, which flows from northern France through Belgium to the North Sea.[1]

From early on, castles and ramparts had been built along this river. The town of Oudenaarde was founded in the twelfth century at an extremely strategic spot along the Scheldt, some 30 km south of Ghent. It was the site of the only bridge across the Scheldt between Tournai and Ghent, and was on the primary supply road to Ghent. Oudenaarde was also the traditional invasion route from France northwards. By shutting the sluices of the Scheldt, the entire valley could be inundated.[2] A cycle of sieges, deterioration and reconstruction of the fortifications followed over the years. Nobles and common folk, Calvinists and Catholics, Spaniards and the French all waged war around

---

[1] See R. Gils, *De versterkingen van de Wellingtonbarrière in Oost-Vlaanderen. De vesting Dendermonde, de Gentse citadel en de vesting Oudenaarde* (Gent: Dienst Monumentenzorg, 2005); P. Borremans, *Het Kezelfort van de vesting Oudenaarde* (Erpe: Krijger, 2006). One often thinks of Antwerp in discussing the Scheldt, and the Eastern and Western Scheldt. But the Scheldt estuary has many tributaries, such as the Lys (Leie), which flows into the Scheldt in Ghent, or the Dender, which joins the Scheldt in Dendermonde, flowing eastwards from there. These were important defensive positions.

[2] Gils, *De versterkingen*, 67–8. See also 'Report on the Re-Establishment of the Fortresses of the Netherlands, by the Committee of British Engineers', November 1815, in H. Jones (ed.), *Reports Relating to the Re-Establishment of the Fortresses in the Netherlands from 1814 to 1830* (London: Spottiswoode, 1861), 11–39, here: 27–30.

358 FORTRESS EUROPE: CONSTRUCTING THE 'WELLINGTON BARRIER'

the Scheldt fortress. In 1668 the fortress came into the hands of Louis XIV, who charged his brilliant military strategist and designer of fortifications Vauban with turning it into a bastioned border town. He constructed a maze of narrow passageways and counter-mine tunnels around and under the fortress and perfected the bastions on the heights on both sides of the river. In 1713, a number of dramatic sieges later, the Spanish Netherlands (roughly comprising present-day Belgium and Luxembourg) were ceded to Austria. In 1715, a so-called Barrier Treaty was signed, in which Austria gave the Dutch Republic the right to establish garrisons in the barrier fortresses. This was to prevent France from returning to 'its politics of dynastic imperialism'. The Scheldt remained closed and Dutch garrisons occupied the fortified frontier towns of Veurne, Ypres, Namur and Oudenaarde. As part of the Treaty of Utrecht, Oudenaarde's ramparts were a visible sign of the European system of a balance of power expressed in stone and border fortifications.[3] That system lasted less than half a century. After the Treaty of Aix-la-Chapelle in 1748, Maria Theresa informed the United Provinces that she no longer wanted to pay for the occupation costs of barrier garrisons and fortresses. Vauban's bastioned fortifications slowly fell into disrepair and were demolished in 1782 by order of Emperor Joseph II of Austria. The barrier cities were allowed to sell the land to local inhabitants on the condition that they dismantle the forts. It was only after the French Revolution, and after Napoleon had come to power, that Menin, Ypres, Ostend, Nieuwpoort and Antwerp were restored to a state such that they were able to defend these strategic gateways to the continent for Britain. By 1803, there was little left of the other barrier fortifications.[4]

Old times returned in 1814. Between 1814 and 1815, Oudenaarde was subjected to the constant advances and withdrawals of French, Dutch, British and German troops. Between February and June 1815 alone, 180,000 soldiers streamed through the town, which almost collapsed under the burden of the occupation, billeting and need for sufficient fodder. But Oudenaarde was to be restored to its former splendour; that was the plan. At the end of March 1814, the Allies decided that the old barrier fortifications needed to be repaired again. The Kingdom of the Netherlands, which had yet to be formally established, was to line its border with France with a wall of fortified cities (fortresses). Reconstruction began as early as the summer of 1814. On 20 April 1815, the Duke of Wellington even came by to inspect the progress being made. He ordered that Oudenaarde should become part of the new

---

[3] J. Pirenne, *Geschiedenis van Europa*, vol. 2 (Brussels: Renaissance du Livre, 1960), 182.

[4] Borremans, *Het Kezelfort*, 7–17. For Ypres, see R. Opsommer, *Ieper en de Frans-Belgische grens (17ᵉ–18ᵉ eeuw). 300 jaar vredesverdragen van Utrecht en Rastatt* (Ypres: City Archives, 2013).

fortification plan, which was later named in his honour – the Wellington Barrier.[5] Another important visitor would follow suit.

Willem I had already declared himself king on 16 March 1815. Oudenaarde replaced France's tricolour with the House of Orange's orange-white-blue Prince's Flag, and heralded the new monarch in with a solemn *Te Deum* and tolling bells.[6] Two years later, on 7 July 1817, the king came by again for an unannounced lightning visit. And a few years after that, a grand visit was planned to celebrate the completion of the Kezelfort (Fig. 8.1), a landmark of the Wellington Barrier.[7] On 27 June 1823, all the inhabitants were standing on the slopes of the Kezelberg. They had set up a beautifully decorated tent, with

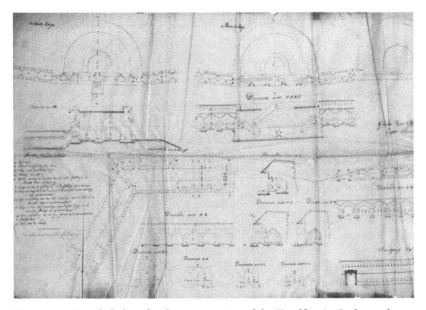

Figure 8.1   Detailed plans for the construction of the Kezelfort in Oudenaarde, *c.*1830. (City Archive Oudenaarde, Vandermeersch family trust)

[5] Borremans, *Het Kezelfort*, 17–22.
[6] M. de Smet (ed.), *Het dagboek van Bartolomeus de Rantere. Beschrijving van al het merkweerdigste dat er voorgevallen is in de stad en casselrije van Audenaerde zedert het jaer zeventhien hondert zevenentachentig tot het jaer achthien hondert vijfentwintig* (Oudenaarde: Sanderus, 1973), 193.
[7] 'Onthaal van den Koning', meeting of the government's council, 21 June and 1 July 1823, SAO, Modern Archive, Deliberations of the city council, 3 January 1820–24 September 1825.

wine to honour the special occasion. Together with Colonel Hennequin from Ghent, the head of the third Directorate of Fortifications, the king studied the building plans with approval. He also took a look at the passageways and fortified chambers – casemates – which had been dug into the hillside and were secured with skilful geometric masonry. But then things went awry. De Rantere, the chronicler of Oudenaarde, wrote: 'A few minutes after the king had emerged from one casemate, a good amount of dirt caved in on the front side of that very casemate, much to the great surprise of the spectators.' The (mini) landslide caused a good deal of hilarity among the onlookers, but Willem was not amused: 'The king was offered a skilfully carved stone with his name and the date on it to install in a prepared opening in the tower's wall. But he chose not to do so.'[8] To this day, during carnival, the citizens of Oudenaarde search for that royal stone, which disappeared in the commotion of the landslide and has never surfaced again.

King Willem I, despite his displeasure, nonetheless remained gracious, distributing 150 guilders to the barge-pullers when he left and treating the workers to twelve casks of beer with bread and cheese. Things did not go so well, however, for Colonel Hennequin, nor with the fortifications. But for the time being, during those first years after 1815, the pursuit of a new European balance of power and efforts to curb the menace of France expressed themselves in visible forms of security: fortified ramparts, citadels and fortifications along the Dutch–French border, via the Rhine and Germany and all the way to Italy and the Mediterranean coast. These fortifications became the safeguard and collateral of Allied solidarity on the one hand, and evidence of France's adaptation to the new system of order and security on the other. The Wellington Barrier was the visible symbol of the new balance of power, the artefact of the Allies' cooperation and their conquest of France. Power and authority cannot endure without visible and tangible images, as Hobbes already knew.[9] The Allied power had to be visible, even in the future, once the gigantic Allied Army of Occupation had left France.

The forts were the foundation and final element of the new Allied order, which had to take over the role of the European occupation army after 1820. Before that could happen, and the framework of imperialist, capitalist security could be equipped with a coat of armour, the financing for these forts, their construction and the relationship between the fortifications and the occupation forces had to be arranged and confirmed. Between 1815 and 1818, the military safeguards for their system were grounded in the presence of the troops, but Wellington and the Allied Council now had to anchor these guarantees in a different way – with a balance of deterrence in the form of forts and barriers, including, eventually, an army of observation and

---

[8] (De) Smet (ed.), *Het dagboek van Bartolomeus de Rantere*, 240–2.
[9] See Stollberg-Rilinger, 'State and Political History in a Culturalist Perspective', 47.

garrisoned troops. That transition from occupation forces to a system of forts and garrisons was beginning to take shape. Bricks (forts), earth (defensive ramparts) and paper (treaties and financial bonds) had to hold up the imperialist peace and security in concert. The episode in Oudenaarde suggests that not everything thus constructed was equally solid. Moreover, the artefacts of collective security did not always live up to the repute of Allied power.

In this chapter the construction process will be mapped out, understood here as the translation of the balance-of-power concept of 1815 into a balance of deterrence via fortresses. With the project of the fortifications ongoing and the reparation payments being made, two years earlier than planned, Britain, Austria, Prussia and Russia decided on withdrawing the occupying forces from France. At the Congress of Aix-la-Chapelle in September 1818 the evacuation of France for 30 November that same year was announced. Whether constructing a 'Wellington Barrier' would indeed provide a sustainable substitute for the Army of Occupation was another question.

The Forts and the European Balance of Power

For the British ministers it was clear that the 'Allied Machine', as Castlereagh and Wellington liked to call the Allied Council, was intended to restore peace and security on the continent and to anchor the European balance of power with various sanctions and practices. Given the machine metaphor, and the four driving principles associated with it – to demilitarize, de-Bonapartize, stabilize and indemnify – building a reinforced barrier around France was the next logical step. The line of forts, fortresses and fortified cities would serve the European balance of power, as British prime minister Pitt had anticipated in 1805. The future barrier would fulfil a threefold function: it would act as a deterrent against renewed French aggression, as a buffer between Prussia and the North Sea and, demonstrating the special relationship between the Netherlands and Great Britain, serve as a sign of Britain's advanced defence system and active sphere of influence on the continent.[10] The latter function was primarily intended for Russia, which had, via control over Poland, expanded very far to the west in 1815. Moreover, the fortresses would enable the government to avoid obligations towards authoritarian and absolutist states that would not sit well with audiences at home. Britain's troops could be sent home, and France could be left to itself. From 1814 on, the British government therefore strongly supported and even supervised the construction of the forts. In 1815, Wellington, as commander-in-chief of the Allied Occupation Army and informal chairman of the Allied Council, made it clear that their construction was priority number one. A third of the costs were paid with British pounds, and the remainder with Dutch guilders and French

---

[10] See (Van) Sas, *Onze natuurlijkste bondgenoot.*

francs. It was thanks (or due) to him that the European balance of power between 1815 and 1818 would manifest itself primarily in bricks and mortar. Later British ministers and generals attached much less value to this initiative. The Russians and Austrians were also much less concerned about a balance of power that hinged on stone. Only the Prussians and King Willem I were as enthusiastic as Wellington about 'all that masonry', as Willem's son Frederik would later derogatorily put it.

The Prussian interest in the fortresses was, however, quite differently delineated; for the generals, the forts were part of their passionately patriotic plans to protect the German lands against future French agression. As early as July 1815, Chancellor Hardenberg, his envoy Wilhelm von Humboldt and military advisor Lieutenant-General Karl Friedrich von dem Knesebeck had made it clear to the other ministers that it was all about restraining the French people's 'hatred' of Prussia. This had to happen through concrete measures, such as the appropriation of large areas along the border. It was, after all, 'Divine Providence' that had put the French territories into Prussian hands. The Prussian ministers and generals submitted several memoranda in which they proposed such a new territorial arrangement, along with the legitimations for these plans. According to Hardenberg, France's peace could not simply be left up to its new government; nor could the neighbouring countries of the Netherlands and Germany protect their borders on their own. The Netherlands was still 'very vulnerable, and would be the most at risk' if a French army were to move outwards from their northern fortifications. Had it not been for Waterloo, Napoleon would once again have been standing at the mouth of the Scheldt and the Rhine. The Allies, therefore, had both 'the power' and 'the right' to take possession of the forts on the French side of the border in order to redress the balance of power.[11] This intended territorial reduction was 'not at all led by the spirit of conquest'. The Prussian emotional vocabulary was saturated with notions of legality, law and a justified desire for security. The fortified cities from the North Sea to the Mediterranean that Napoleon had used as a springboard for his invasions of his neighbours, the *points offensifs*, had to change hands or be dismantled. 'Our contemporaries and offspring will condemn us and sharply accuse us, and with reason, if we fail to address a matter of such great importance.' Hardenberg believed that not only the Prussians, but the other German countries, the Netherlands, Austria, Switzerland and the king of Sardinia shared that desire. Russia was strong enough, and sufficiently far away, to worry less about border defences, he granted. Yet Russia and Britain also benefited from peace and security on the continent. The soft forces of 'sound management and generosity', of rules and concessions, were therefore not enough any more. Not after 1815. 'Let us exercise moderation, but not shy away from taking what is necessary for our

---

[11] Hardenberg, Memorandum, 22 July 1815, GStA PK, III. HA I. no. 1461.

security, and to which we have every right – granted to us by eternal and acknowledged principles.' Stopgap measures (*palliatifs*) were no longer sufficient; the Allies had the right to use force to defuse France's ability to attack once and for all.[12]

The solution was obvious, according to General Knesebeck, Hardenberg's strategically well-versed advisor. The Alsace should be divided between Prussia and Austria, Prussia should be given the French fortresses along the Mosel and the Saar. Savoy should be governed by the king of Sardinia, and Switzerland should get part of Franche-Comté. As noted previously, the Prussians were in favour of cutting away large swathes of French territory. For clarity's sake Knesebeck had drawn a blue line on a map of France to indicate the width of those swathes. A stretch on the north and east side that included Lille, Mézières, Montmédy, Metz, Strasbourg, Colmar and, further to the south, Châtillon and Barraux would be cut off from France. This would create a 'good line of defence' and the most crucial French forts would be in the hands of neighbouring countries. When coupled with occupation forces in the heart of France for the first years, this would certainly ensure peace.[13] 'Today, we can still do this', opined Knesebeck (who, here too, echoed Blücher's firm conviction). 'The hand of providence has demonstrably granted us this opportunity. If we let this chance pass, rivers of blood will flow later to attain the same goal, and the groaning of the hapless ones will call us to account!'[14]

Metternich – though in less dramatic terms – agreed to a certain extent with the Prussian ministers and generals. For the Austrian chancellor, however, the 'balance of power' metaphor had less to do with borders and fortifications than with the domestic politics of the European sovereignties. It was, for him, also a metaphor for the right and prudent balance between the various ranks and classes within society, a balance of orders.[15] That is why the Austrian chancellor, like his Prussian colleagues, was deeply concerned about the revolutionary and Jacobin tendencies of those French people who did not want to follow the path of gradualism and moderation, but repeatedly threatened to embrace radical change and conflict: a penchant that also threatened order and peace in the immense Austrian Empire. The 'offensive disposition' of France, with its spirit of rebellion, could possibly spread to Austria. From that perspective, the fortresses therefore were not only a military line of defence, but could also serve as a defence against France's revolutionary spirit. They were the rock-solid concretization of the rather abstract 'balance of power' metaphor. France

---

[12] Hardenberg, Memorandum, 4 August 1815, GStA PK, III. HA I. no. 1461.
[13] Hardenberg, Memorandum, 22 July 1815, GStA PK, III. HA I. no. 1461; Knesebeck, Memorandum, 4 August 1815, GStA PK, III. HA I. no. 1461, 65–6. See also Humboldt, 'Mémoire entièrement confidentiel', 4 August 1815, GStA PK, III. HA I. no. 1461, 51.
[14] Knesebeck, Memorandum, 4 August 1815, GStA PK, III. HA I. no. 1461, 68. See also the clean version, 69–73.
[15] Siemann, *Metternich*, 392, 410, 436, 638–41.

might well have a national defence line and a standing army, but the forts and arms depots in Alsace, Lorraine, Franche-Comté and Midi-Pyrénées had to be down-sized or demolished. The forts in Germany and the Netherlands (Ehrenbreitstein, Philippebourg, Ingolstadt and several others) should be completely destroyed. It was, after all, Metternich argued, about finding an 'equilibrium in their military attitude'. France's neighbours had to be able to assume that they no longer ran the risk of France attacking them – which had been a real and constant danger since the time of Louis XIV. And yet that risk was still present, given 'the egoism and total lack of public spirit that characterizes the French nation'.[16]

The only party that was less concerned about the military threat still emanating from France was Tsar Alexander. His minister was the only one who did not issue a separate memorandum on France's borders and their fortifications. The tsar, given his messianic (and mesmeristic) tendencies, was still more interested in reconciliation with France and a spirit of moderation than in mundane financial compensation or military guarantees. Moreover, amongst the Russian diplomats, the Prussian spirit of patriotism and vindictiveness, as fanned by radical patriotic journals, was considered dangerous and insulting towards the sovereigns of Europe.[17] As described in Chapters 4 and 7, the tsar therefore supported Wellington's view that territorial vengeance in this case would make matters worse, and that a sensible line of defence had to be drawn up, manned by Dutch and German troops. As to the specifics of defining that boundary, the tsar was rather indifferent. Most importantly, a large-scale reduction of France's territory had to be avoided. Like Wellington, Tsar Alexander was worried that such an enormous intervention would only lead to more instability and heighten the risk of revenge.[18] In the end, taking into account all positions, the Allied Council in Paris did not agree to Prussia's push for substantial territorial changes, but did take the Prussian and Austrian concerns seriously enough to announce an upgrading of the fortifications along the French border.

Boulevard de l'Europe

The first visible signs of the Allies' security order, apart from the occupation army, were the forts, whether dismantled or newly revamped. On her journey across the continent, Lady Shelley came past the fortifications in Ulm, which had been destroyed after the Austrian general Mack had surrendered to Napoleon in 1805, and where gardens had been laid out on top of artillery batteries and along the former ramparts. She witnessed how new

---

[16] Metternich, Memorandum, 6 August 1815. Sent to Hardenberg. GStA PK, III. HA I. no. 1461, 77–8.

[17] Alopeus to Nesselrode, 16 (28) December 1815, in Ministerstvo inostrannykh del CCCP (ed.), *Vneshniaia politika Rossii*, vol. 1, 52–3. The *Rheinische Merkur* and the *Wächter* are mentioned explicitly.

[18] See, among other sources, the protocol of 22 July 1815, GStA PK, III. HA I. no. 1464.

fortresses were being built in the soft, green Belgian landscape, and visited the fortified towns of Vauban, along the Franco-Swiss border, such as Besançon and Auxonne on the banks of the Saône. The inhabitants of these towns had for months resisted the transfer of their forts to the Austrian Allied troops. She noted that '[Auxonne] is a *ville de guerre* into which the Allies did not enter. Its inhabitants are very proud of this, for it saved them from much discomfort.' She could understand the residents: 'Although it is said that the Austrians always behaved very well on these occasions, yet the quartering of troops is a dreadful infliction at all times.'[19] In other words, the forts not only brought security, but could also be a huge source of unrest and insecurity for both the Allies and the French, for both the generals and the local residents.

In July 1815 it became immediately evident how relevant the control of the forts and fortifications in the French border region was – and to what extent these fortresses could become focal points of rebellion and national pride (on the French side) and indignation and frustration (on the Allied side). Despite Napoleon's capitulation, many fortified towns in the north and east of France refused to surrender to the Allies. On 16 July, the Allied Council discussed this problem. The Duke of Wellington had to inform the council that the oldest son of Willem I (the Prince of Orange), who was a general in Wellington's army and commander of the troops in the north of France, was encountering all sorts of blockades and felt very frustrated about these acts of sabotage. He reported that several cities in northern France had indeed hoisted the white banner of the Bourbons, but that the French garrisons stationed there refused to obey the Allied demand that they close up shop and leave. The agreement was that French troops were to remove themselves to south of the Loire, where Napoleon's Grande Armée would be disbanded and then be reorganized again under the royal banner. But pockets of resistance remained north of the Loire, particularly in places where the French troops could count on the patriotism of inhabitants along the border.[20] French garrison troops from fortresses near Mézières and Longwy attacked the Allied Prussian troops time and again. Deaths and injuries resulted from these skirmishes. According to the Allied commanders, the French soldiers there were not to be trusted. Switching out the tricolour for the white flag was merely cosmetics.[21]

In addition, the garrisons in the fortified towns would not let the Allied troops pass through those towns, which meant that supply and transit routes for the (until January 1816) circa 1 million Allied troops were obstructed or blocked. The Military Committee, chaired by Wellington,[22] therefore quickly issued clearer

[19] Edgcumbe (ed.), *The Diary of Frances Lady Shelley, 1787–1817*, 215–16, 276, here: 215.
[20] See Wacker, *Die alliierte Besetzung*, 143.
[21] Report of Frederik of Orange and Wellington. Discussion led by Wellington in the Allied Council, 18 August 1815, GStA PK, III. HA I. no. 1465.
[22] The other committee members were the Allied generals Schwarzenberg, Gneisenau, Wolkonsky, Radetzky and Wrede.

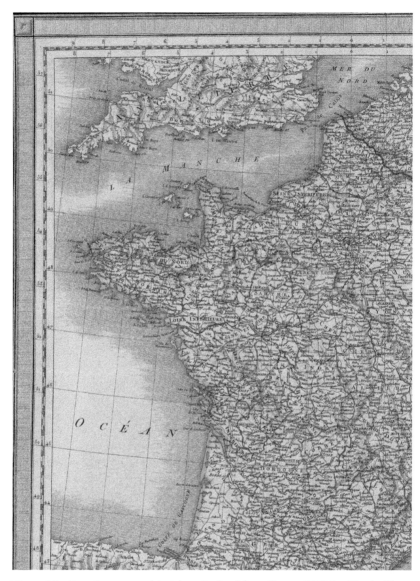

Figure 8.2   Prussian proposal to take extra land from France, 1815 (outlined with a bold line). (GStA PK, III. HA, MdA, I. no. 1461)

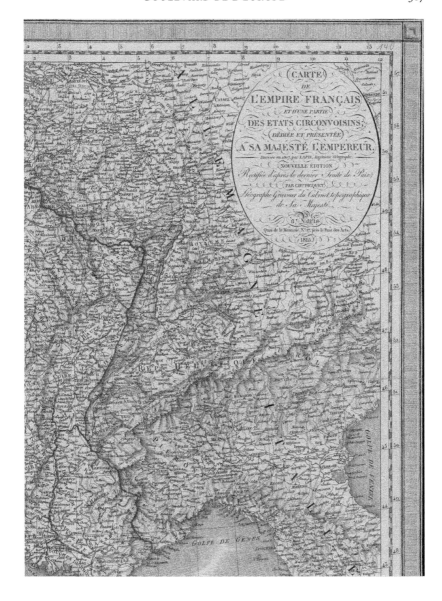

orders: the French troops had to leave the occupied part of France, and do so immediately. The fortresses had to be vacated, pending further negotiations about France's borders and the eradication of the forts or their allocation either to France or to neighbouring countries.[23] That evacuation would take a few more months. Cities such as Vitry, Metz, Thionville and Verdun complied with the summons in July and August. At the end of July, skirmishes were still common around Auxonne and Mézières. The population and troops in and around the citadel of Briançon kept up their resistance through the beginning of 1816.[24]

For both sides, the Allies and the French, the forts were a visible and volatile symbol, a matter of prestige. The French saw the fortified ramparts along their border as an expression of sovereignty. For the Allies, the surrender of the forts was proof of France's submission to their authority. That is why the Allied ministers, during their negotiations on the Second Treaty of Paris in September 1815, were in complete agreement on this point. Most of the fortifications on France's side of its northern and eastern border indeed had to be demolished – or transferred to neighbouring countries. The military line of occupied France would run along the forts of Condé, Valenciennes, Bouchain, Cambrai, Le Quesnoy Maubeuge, Landrecy, Avesnes, Rocroy, Givet, Mézières, Sedan, Montmédy, Thionville, Longy, Bitsch and Fort-Louis. Their agreeing upon the return to the territorial borders as they were in 1790 meant that the Landau, Saarlouis, Philippeville, Mariembourg and Versoix fortresses would be transferred to the Allies (that is, to the Netherlands and Prussia). For the French this was a painful territorial reduction, although the appropriated areas came nowhere close to the wide swathe that Prussia had wanted to see excised from France (Fig. 8.2).

Sardinia and Switzerland each also received some territory. In addition, 187.5 million francs in reparations would be reserved for the construction of fortifications on the Dutch and German side of the border. Because Saarlouis eventually went to Prussia (as previously noted), 50 million was deducted from that fortress fund, leaving 137.5 million francs.[25] Of that amount, 60 million was earmarked for fortifications in the Netherlands. The other 77.5 million francs were distributed among fortifications in the Bas-Rhin, Haut-Rhin and Piedmont regions. Spain, too, would in due course, after signing the Treaty of Vienna, receive a few million francs for (re)constructing fortifications along its border.[26]

---

[23] Protocols of 16 and 17 July 1815, GStA PK, III. HA I. no. 1464.

[24] See mention of this on 29 July, 2 August 1815, GStA PK, III. HA I. no. 1464. Also the protocols of 16, 17, 18 August 1815, GStA PK, III. HA I. no. 1465.

[25] Decision of 19 September 1815, GStA PK, III. HA I. no. 1465. See also the protocol of 2 October 1815, GStA PK, III. HA I. no. 1469.

[26] Protocol of 7 and 8 October 1815, GStA PK, III. HA I. no. 1469. Territorial additions to the Netherlands, Switzerland and Sardinia were adopted on 6 November and added to the Treaty of Paris. Protocol of 6 November 1815, GStA PK, III. HA I. no. 1469.

The significance that Wellington attached to the matter of fortifications stood out throughout the occupation period. As the commander-in-chief of the occupation army and chairman of the Military Committee, he would manage the fortress fund. In practice that meant that requests would be discussed by the Allied Council, but that the final approval and allocation of funds would run via Wellington. In other words, the process of building a visible and tangible European system of defence was in the hands of the Prince of Waterloo, which only helped to increase his power and influence even more. His overriding influence also expressed itself in the Allies' strategic planning and in the symbolism of the 'bulwark of Europe' that would be set up along a line from the North Sea to Mainz – a presence that in Belgium was soon christened the 'Wellington Barrier' (Map 8.1).[27]

The idea behind this military barrier was by no means devised by Wellington. Even though he gave it a new twist, he was building on the earlier plans of others. Britain had long embraced the importance of a ring of fortifications around France. During the reign of Louis XIV, France's neighbours had already invested in extra fortifications along the border with an eye to limiting the expansionist leanings of French politics. The Pitt Memorandum of 1805 went back to the Peace of Utrecht's Barrier Treaty of 1713, and confirmed the role of the Netherlands as *Boulevard de l'Europe*.[28] In addition to the Rhine States of the German Confederation, Switzerland, Piedmont–Sardinia and Spain, the Kingdom of the Netherlands was crucial for the restoration of the European balance of power. These medium-sized countries were in themselves too small to pose a threat to France, and too large to be easily trampled underfoot in an initial attack. But taken together they formed a belt around France. They could also be quickly supplied by Britain, Prussia and Austria, and served as a buffer for the great powers against the possibility of renewed French aggression. As an independent state just across the English Channel, the Netherlands clearly fell within Britain's sphere of influence; it was a bridgehead for British troops, a buffer between Prussia and the North Sea and a stronghold against France. Although the Netherlands would never be able to completely withstand a strong French offensive, it could weather an attack long enough to give British or Prussian troops an opportunity to regroup, to advance or to retreat or relocate.[29]

---

[27] See Wellington, Memorandum, 22 July 1816, TNA, FO 92/31, 77–80; Fagel to Wellington, 18 October 1816, TNA, FO 92/31, 93–7.

[28] For the early history of the barrier, see R. Geikie and I. Montgomery, *The Dutch Barrier, 1705–1719* (London: Cambridge University Press, 1930).

[29] (Van) Sas, *Onze natuurlijkste bondgenoot, 41, 55*. See also Gils, *De versterkingen van de Wellingtonbarrière, 8–9*. And, of course, G. J. Renier, *Great Britain and the Establishment of the Kingdom of the Netherlands, 1813–1815. A Study in British Foreign Policy* (London: Allen & Unwin, 1930). See also C. Nelson, 'The Duke of Wellington and the Barrier Fortresses after Waterloo', *Army Historical Research*, 42 (1964), 36–43.

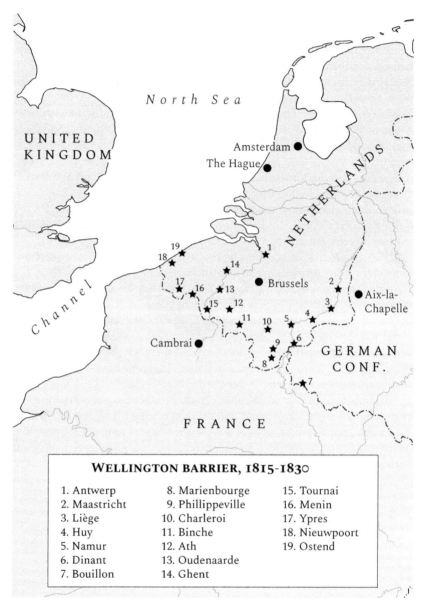

WELLINGTON BARRIER, 1815-1830

1. Antwerp
2. Maastricht
3. Liège
4. Huy
5. Namur
6. Dinant
7. Bouillon
8. Marienbourge
9. Phillippeville
10. Charleroi
11. Binche
12. Ath
13. Oudenaarde
14. Ghent
15. Tournai
16. Menin
17. Ypres
18. Nieuwpoort
19. Ostend

Map 8.1 Map of the Wellington Barrier, 1815–30. (Erik Goosmann © 2020, Mappa Mundi Cartography)

The question was how exactly this bulwark should be constructed, and how the abstract idea of a balance of power could best be translated into actual lines of defence and specific territorial changes between France, Prussia and the Netherlands. From a military perspective, investing in fortifications was already a fairly old-fashioned method at the start of the Napoleonic Wars. In the eighteenth century, so many more roads had been built that in times of war nowhere near all of them could be closed off effectively with barriers or fortresses. Armies were also much larger, so that a commander could easily put a fortress under siege with some of their troops, while the rest of the main army could make its way around it. Improved artillery trains, the greater agility of armies and more convenient ways of supplying provisions allowed army corps to manoeuvre with greater ease and speed. Napoleon had already shown how quickly large armies could move out, simply leaving fortresses to stand where they were, and force the enemy to engage them on a battlefield of his choosing.[30]

Likewise, as became apparent on the fields of Waterloo in 1815, artillery had become too powerful to still fight battles in open country in this way. That did not mean that the role of fortresses was altogether passé, but operationally speaking, it was far easier simply to ignore them. In other words, the eighteenth-century tactics of sieges and battles belonged to the past rather than to the future of warfare. Wellington was himself the first to admit that from the military-technical point of view building fortresses was somewhat outdated. On 22 September 1814, in a memorandum to Bathurst, Wellington did not shy away from sharing his hesitations about investing in new fortresses: 'The operations of the revolutionary war have tended in some degree to put strong places out of fashion.' The recent campaigns against Napoleon had also shown 'that strong places are but little useful, and at all events are not worth the expense which they cost'.[31] Why then did the Allied Council bother so much with the role of forts and fortresses after 1815?[32]

An 'Essentially European System'

First of all, there was specific cause in July 1815 to give extensive attention to the fortresses in and just outside France, namely, the persisting French insubordination, and the widespread use of these fortifications as a base for a kind of insurgency against the occupation forces. Likewise, with an eye to logistics and open supply lines for the occupation army, control of the access roads leading

---

[30] See Uitterhoeve, *Cornelis Kraijenhoff*, 289–90; J. Kaufmann and H. Kaufmann, *Forts and Fortifications of Europe, 1815–1945*, vol. 1: *The Central States* (Barnsley: Pen and Sword, 2014), 5–6. See also vol 2: *The Neutral States*, 81–2.

[31] Wellington to Bathurst, 'Memorandum on the Frontier of the Defence of the Netherlands', 22 September 1814, in *WD*, vol. 12, 125–9, here: 126.

[32] Gils, *De versterkingen van de Wellingtonbarrière*, 8–9.

into and out of France, and hence of the fortifications along the border, was also crucial for the Allies. But there were more reasons – of a strategic and security-policy nature – to maintain and even to rebuild these facilities.

There was, according to Wellington, simply still no other way to defend a country at that moment, although he admitted having seriously considered other options. Given the situation in 1815, he concluded that 'the country must be fortified upon the old principle'. The small effort required to restore the existing fortifications would, in any case, slow the French down significantly should they decide to invade Belgium and the Netherlands again. Improving those sites would increase the likelihood of a protracted and more gruelling confrontation for the enemy, and was hence still a useful and even necessary investment.[33] From a military-operational point of view, these investments were furthermore worth the effort when these fortresses were constructed in places that were important for the effective use of the field army. When situated more spread out, in the back country, they provided a safe operating base for the troops in the field, as well as a safe haven to which they could withdraw should they have to recuperate from defeat elsewhere (e.g. the ring of forts – the National Redoubt – built around Antwerp in later years).[34]

There was, however, an even more important reason to invest in those fortifications and the southern border areas of the Netherlands. In 1815, those forts actually had much more of a political-strategic significance, with an eye to France as well as to a common Allied security policy. They constituted both a military and a political bulwark. First of all, the occupation of France assured the payment of reparations and of outstanding debt. The occupation was temporary; the fortifications were not. France, therefore, was financially obliged to invest in its own military dismantling, and in the construction of defensive works that were directed against possible new French aggression. In addition, building the fortifications was a communal project of the Allies, also intended to deflect Prussian vengeance and lust for territorial compensations, and to redirect anti-French resentments into the construction of future-oriented defence projects. It was, along with Gruner's security service, Metternich's passports and the occupation army itself, the most tangible and, so it was thought, sustainable way of binding the Quadruple Alliance together. It was a pledge in stone of their reciprocal security obligations, and a visible manifestation of the Allied concert. On 21 November 1815, one day after the signing of the Second Treaty of Paris, the ministers agreed that they would indeed jointly maintain this 'essentially European system'. The great powers would jointly supervise the 'defensive line of countries bordering France'. More specifically, this 'concert' would be performed by Britain in collaboration with the Netherlands, by Austria and Prussia in collaboration

[33] Wellington to Bathurst, 'Memorandum', 22 September 1814, *WD*, vol. 12, 127–9.
[34] Gils, *De versterkingen van de Wellingtonbarrière*, 9.

with the smaller German states and Austria in cooperation with Sardinia. Each government would keep the others informed as to the progress being made with their fortifications. Other military measures and the spending on the forts would be arranged by the Allied Council and managed by Wellington.[35]

Practically speaking, this meant that the countries bordering France, and the Netherlands and Prussia in particular, could request funds to finance the construction of their fortifications. The Council appointed special commissioners who would issue the vouchers for paying for the fortifications and see to it that these funds were actually used for the intended purpose.[36] According to the protocols of the Allied Council, the Dutch requests were always granted. In May 1816, however, Sardinia experienced a slap on the wrist because it had asked for too much money. The king of Sardinia had been promised 10 million francs, but he now threatened to exceed that amount. The claims from the small German states did comply with what had been agreed upon, and were also honoured. The funds were closely monitored and protected in Paris.[37] In March 1816, Prussia tried to get the till for the forts moved to Frankfurt, because, at that time, the largest building projects were taking place there. Austria, too, thought that the funds belonged to the country in which the building projects were to take place. But the other ministers foiled that argument, pointing out that Spain, Sardinia and the Netherlands had projects as well. The fund was a pool of resources held in common by the 'princes of the coalition'; its management remained in Paris, under Wellington's control.[38]

Herein lay the significance of the fortress barrier: taking on the construction of such an immense line of defence along the French border as a joint project of the Allied Council decreased the risk of the alliance's disintegrating, of individual countries making separate treaties with France or of carrying out any self-willed aggression. The fortress fund and Wellington's supervision were an effective guarantee of the Allies' solidarity when it came to security policies. Their pledge to finance and build these fortifications bound them together. Remarkably, historians have failed to appreciate the very symbolic role of these fortifications and how this project contributed to security policies at the time. Most are satisfied to note in passing that these forts were rather useless from a military point of view. But their true meaning lay in the strategic and long-term significance of such a *systema* of mutual obligation and deterrence against future enemies.

That said, the fortresses were not completely useless militarily. Even if they could not withstand the accumulated strength of artillery bombardments, and

---

[35] Agreements of 21 November 1815, GStA PK, III. HA I. no. 1469.
[36] Protocol of 24 November 1816, TNA, FO 146/15.
[37] See, for example, the protocol of 26 May 1816 in which the additional claim from Sardinia is discussed and rejected, TNA, FO 146/15.
[38] Protocol of 10 March, 2 June 1816, TNA, FO 146/6.

large armies could easily pass them by, the fortifications along the projected Wellington Barrier ensured the Allied forces of open lines of communication between the North Sea and the Alps. Tactically, the forts could serve as fallback bases and arms depots. Strategically, they were a guarantee of Britain's obligations to assist on the continent when necessary. At the time, the same logic applied to the British garrisons stationed on the Ionian Islands (off the west coast of Greece), which was an indication that the 'United States of the Ionian Islands' had been placed, per treaty, under the protection of Britain.[39] The fortifications were thus tangible evidence and an operational pivot point in the system of military and strategic deterrence, the practical and concrete implementation of the hitherto still very thin paper of the new treaties on the European balance of power.

Lapdog and Net Recipient

Secondary powers were given a major role in implementing the fortifications project. That was especially true for the Netherlands. Back in Vienna, Metternich had informed King Willem I's envoy, Gagern, that he saw 'Holland' as the 'lapdog of the great powers'.[40] Though meant to humiliate, that pat on the head worked to the Netherlands' advantage, through independence, the establishment of a monarchy and territorial expansion. The Netherlands also became the largest net recipient of monies from the fortress fund – even though this handout would come to hang like a millstone around the neck of Willem I.

The Dutch king was certainly not opposed to the British and Allied plans. As early as 1813, the Sovereign Prince (he was not yet king then) had pleaded with the British to let the Netherlands take on its former role as the 'boulevard' defending the 'independence and tranquillity of Europe', and to that end to extend the territory of the new state. During secret talks in London, recorded in the London protocol of 20 June 1814, the British had agreed to the establishment of the United Kingdom of the Netherlands, consisting of the northern Netherlands and Belgium (the former Austrian Netherlands). In the same period, Willem asked his advisors to figure out what the southern frontier in Belgium should look like. As noted above, Wellington drew up a detailed memorandum on the topic in September 1814.[41] The Anglo-Dutch consensus emerged from the agreements they reached regarding the reinforcement and expansion of the fortresses and garrisons along a number of lines of defence

---

[39] See negotiations regarding the Ionian Islands, and the decision that Britain would serve as their *Puissance Protectrice*. Annex, 31 October, GStA PK, III. HA I. no. 1469.

[40] Gagern, *Mein Antheil and der Politik*, vol. 2: 118–19.

[41] Uitterhoeve, *Cornelis Kraijenhoff*, 291.

from Nieuwpoort on the North Sea to Mainz on the east side of France and Belgium.[42]

This was also urgently needed, because the Austrian Habsburgs had not rebuilt the fortresses that had been almost completely demolished at the end of the War of the Austrian Succession by Louis XV. In 1782, Emperor Joseph II had relinquished all the fortresses, except for those in Luxembourg and the citadels of Antwerp and Ghent, selling them to the cities' inhabitants. Even during the period of annexation in France, the fortifications were not rebuilt. Only Antwerp, Ypres, Menin, Nieuwpoort, Ostend and the citadels of Tournai, Ghent and Luxembourg remained somewhat intact. When Wellington, as British ambassador to Louis XVIII, went to check on the fortresses that were once again part of the Netherlands in June 1814, after the First Treaty of Paris, he had to conclude that the line of defence was so weak that Belgium would immediately fall into the hands of the aggressor after one lost battle. There was not a single fortress secure enough to serve as a safe operating base for the troops in the field, let alone the thought that the derelict ruins could hold back the enemy in any way. However, he did inform Willem I and his own government that the old locations had not been chosen so badly and that reconstruction of the fortifications along the former barrier would save time and money.[43]

Napoleon's return in early March 1815 accelerated the decision-making. Willem I proclaimed himself king of the United Netherlands on 16 March. On 17 March, in one of his first decrees as the new king over the whole of the Low Countries, he ordered his engineers and commanders to ready the line of defence. Around 20 March, 10,000 people were already at work in the fortified towns and cities.[44] Although Willem hoped that he could prove his independence and sovereignty by working on these fortifications, it turned out that doing so only sucked him deeper into the Allied system. Wellington's engineers were responsible for the construction of fortifications, and likewise for providing the resources, manpower and building plans. For the manning of the forts, Willem not only had to tolerate the presence of Prussian generals and their troops, but also – dragging his feet – to feed and sustain them as well. When the British troops (financed by their own treasury) arrived in Belgium, Willem I tried to send the Germans back across the border. That, however, was not an option. Troop movements were no longer the prerogative of individual generals and commanders, according to Müffling, 'but become a matter of the Allies jointly'. At the urging of Wellington, who wanted to keep both the

---

[42] Willem Frederik of Oranje-Nassau to Castlereagh, 27 April 1813, Colenbrander (ed.), *Gedenkstukken*, vol. 6.2, 1876–8. See also (Van) Sas, *Onze natuurlijkste bondgenoot*, 41, 55; Gils, *De versterkingen van de Wellingtonbarrière*, 10.

[43] Gils, *De versterkingen van de Wellingtonbarrière*, 12.

[44] Borremans, *Het Kezelfort*, 20.

Prussian and British armies near Brussels, Willem had to accept that the Prussian troops would be staying on for some time at the expense of the Netherlands.[45]

The same sort of thing threatened to repeat itself at the end of 1815, because the Netherlands had too few deployable troops to man the new fortifications and still have enough remaining to dispatch as an expeditionary force. Waterloo had, moreover, demonstrated how quickly and without much of an obstacle French forces could (almost) push right through to Brussels. At the same time, expenditures for the fortifications were a disproportionate drain on the government's budget. With the Congress of Vienna and the Second Treaty of Paris, all the fortifications along France's northern border were officially apportioned to the Netherlands, plus those in Philippeville, Mariembourg and part of the district of Bouillon. As compensation for the loss of the patrimonial lands of Nassau, Luxembourg was assigned to Willem I in a personal capacity. Luxembourg was part of the German Confederation and, as a result, its fortress housed a Prussian garrison, while the civil administration was under Willem I. Executing the (re) construction of all these older and newer fortifications, as well as seeing to it that they were manned, was the responsibility of the Netherlands. The Second Treaty of Paris, which included special provisions for a fortress fund, helped to resolve the matter. As noted above, 60 million francs went to the Netherlands, and Britain contributed an additional 2 million pounds sterling as compensation for the Cape Colony and possessions on the north coast of South America,[46] which the Dutch had officially ceded to Britain in the Anglo-Dutch Treaty of 1814. During the Napoleonic occupation of the Netherlands, the British had taken possession of these colonies. The Netherlands agreed to invest 2 million pounds of its own in the barrier. Wellington managed the funds, and all the expenditures and budgets were to be controlled and approved by him. The construction would be carried out by Dutch and British engineers together, with Prussia advising when it came to Luxembourg (and funded in part by the French).[47] The fortification projects were at the time, then, clearly not a manifestation of Dutch independence, but sooner a confirmation of its role as lapdog – or better put, as a watchdog for the Allies.

Building the Wellington Barrier

Willem was thus forced to go along with Wellington's plans and to contribute to the barrier from the Netherlands' own funds as well. The entire endeavour would end up costing 70 million guilders.[48] Thus, more than half of the Dutch

---

[45] Müffling (ed.), *The Memoirs*, 219–20.
[46] The possessions were Demerara, Essequibo and Berbice.
[47] Gils, *De versterkingen van de Wellingtonbarrière*, 13–16.
[48] Uitterhoeve, *Cornelis Kraijenhoff*, 292–3.

Figure 8.3 Lieutenant General Cornelis Kraijenhoff. Portrait by H. J. Slothouwer, 1838. (Rijksmuseum, Amsterdam)

defence budget went into the project. Dutch engineers carried out the plans drawn up by the Dutch inspector general Cornelis Kraijenhoff (Fig. 8.3). Kraijenhoff was a kind of jack of all trades and celebrated hydraulic engineer among his contemporaries. With degrees in law, philosophy and medicine, he had made a name for himself during the Batavian and French period as a physicist. He was an authority on electricity and lightning, had reorganized the Department of Water Management and begun his life's work: mapping the Netherlands in detail using a system of triangulation. His sons also served under Napoleon and worked as far away as Moscow. However, after Napoleon's defeat at Leipzig in the Battle of the Nations, Kraijenhoff chose the side of the Allies. Willem I appointed him inspector general of all fortifications on 12 March 1814 and bestowed on him the title of baron. He proceeded to display unbridled energy, mediated between Willem I and Tsar Alexander and conferred with Wellington regarding progress on the fortifications. Kraijenhoff reported directly to Willem and maintained close contact with the monarch. They corresponded and consulted together several times a year. Wellington also frequently joined the two of them and their entourage on their (bi)annual multi-week-long inspection tours of the fortifications.

Kraijenhoff began his activities in August 1815, and by October he presented his first sketches to Willem I, who loved the blueprints. In November 1815, Wellington also received an extensive report from his military engineers on the state of the fortifications in Flanders.[49] According to the British ambassador Clancarty, Kraijenhoff, who was enjoying this new, prominent position and his proximity to the heroes of Waterloo, carried himself as 'a second Vauban'. On 19 and 20 December, Wellington and Kraijenhoff devoted two days to discussions related to the construction of the first fortifications.[50]

Wellington and Kraijenhoff agreed straight away on the first line of defence. It should run via Antwerp, Ostend, Ypres, Menin, Tournai, Ath, Charleroi and Namur to Maastricht. According to Kraijenhoff, the costs would amount to 42 million guilders – 'just close your eyes and pay the price'. Binche, Mariembourg, Philippeville, Dinant, Bouillon and Arlon were added to this line of defence. Arlon and Binche were in the end never fortified, and Wellington's wish to reinforce Courtrai did not come to fruition either, owing to the overly high costs. Regarding the second line, however, an extended difference of opinion arose between the British and the Dutch that could be traced back to diverging strategic intentions for the bulwark of Europe. Wellington wanted a second line of defence close to the west coast, from Dendermonde via Ghent, Ostend, Oudenaarde and – with an eye to defending Brussels – via Halle to Mont-Saint-Jean, near Waterloo. But Kraijenhoff and the Dutch were afraid that, should defeat (in a hypothetical war) appear imminent, the British could too easily leave the area quickly by embarking at Ostend. And so they proposed a different second line: via Oudenaarde, Dendermonde and Antwerp to Maastricht, with a road and a fortress near Hasselt. Kraijenhoff also found that Brussels was insufficiently covered by fortifications at Halle and Waterloo. On paper, Wellington prevailed. Ghent, Oudenaarde and Dendermonde would be reinforced, but Kraijenhoff managed to postpone the planned construction of fortifications at Halle and Mont-Saint-Jean. In the end, nothing came of reinforced fortifications around the fields of Waterloo. To appease Wellington's wishes somewhat, but to spare the Dutch treasury, only a few field fortifications – actually earthworks – were introduced. The defence of the Rupel-Dyle-Demer valleys, between Maastricht and Antwerp, was also put on the back burner, and the Fortifications Service did not even start on the fort at Oosterlo. After the occupation troops left France, Wellington returned to London, where he joined the Liverpool cabinet as Master General of the Ordnance – one of the highest military positions – in December 1818. As a result, he could not involve himself nearly as much with the fortifications. But he never completely lost

---

[49] Inspector general of fortification, 'State of the Fortresses in Flanders, November 1815'. Prepared by Captain Wedekind, on behalf of Wellington, TNA, WO 55, no. 1553/9.
[50] Uitterhoeve, *Cornelis Kraijenhoff*, 296.

interest either. In 1821, he again conducted an inspection tour, and continued to correspond with Kraijenhoff for a number of years.[51]

And so it happened that between 1815 and 1824 a defensive barrier took shape, consisting of twenty-one fortresses, including the one manned by Germans in Luxembourg. The fortifications could be interpreted as two lines parallel to the French border, one near it, one some distance deeper into the country, but they could also be seen as two lines at a right angle to the French border, and parallel to the North Sea coast. The right-angled line was the British way of picturing the strategic depth of the defence system, the parallel line, the Dutch take on it. From a Dutch perspective, the first line was along the French border and ran from Nieuwpoort on the coast via Ypres, Menin, Tournai, Oudenaarde, Ath, Mons, Charleroi and Namur to Dinant (with Philippeville and Mariembourg as forward posts). In this way, all the major access roads to the Netherlands could be blocked (with Bouillon as an outpost of the Luxembourg fortress). The second line, behind it, ran along the Ghent–Ostend canal and further along the Scheldt and the Rupel-Dyle-Demer valleys in the direction of Maastricht. The citadels of Ghent and Dendermonde were part of this line. A third line, even further north, was located along the southern edge of the northern Dutch territory, running from Zeeschelde via Bergen op Zoom, Breda and 's-Hertogenbosch to Venlo. From a British perspective, however, the fortifications were pictured as lying along two operational lines that needed to be defended – the Meuse and Scheldt rivers, which were at right-angles to the border with France. Troops and goods could then easily be supplied via these rivers (since there were at the time no railroads yet).[52]

The Fortification System as an Elitist Project

In effect, the great powers imposed their own strategic and political objectives on the smaller powers. They could enforce these provisions because they possessed the funds and the military superiority and acted together. There were clear differences in how they dealt with top-, middle- and lower-level states. That was evident from the distinction the Allied Council made in processing a request submitted by Metternich on behalf of Austria on the one hand, and a similar request from Gagern, the envoy for the Netherlands and Nassau, on the other. Austria had lost territory to Bavaria during the 'unfortunate campaigns' of 1805 and 1809, and now appealed to the Council to get those areas back again with an eye to reinforcing its borders (in exchange for a much smaller area on the left bank of the Rhine). The Allied ministers immediately expressed their support for Metternich, who certainly did not act

[51] Gils, *De versterkingen van de Wellingtonbarrière*, 14–18; Uitterhoeve, *Cornelis Kraijenhoff*, 296–314.
[52] Gils, *De versterkingen van de Wellingtonbarrière*, 18–19.

as an honest broker in these negotiations, but as a diehard advocate of the Austrian emperor. Gagern, by contrast, who had requested the same arbitration in a Duchy of Nassau case (namely, lands of the duchy that had already been added to the fortress grounds in Mainz), got nowhere with his petition.[53]

The Allied Council determined where the boundary lines would run and who got what, and when, from the fortress fund. The ministers did this with centrally established instructions to the supervisory directors who issued the vouchers for paying for the fortifications. First, it was the Netherlands, the Haut-Rhin and Mainz's turn, because of the strategic importance and efforts of those countries for the coalition. Then came Spain and Sardinia. Portugal was also allowed to join in May 1816, under the auspices of Britain. The United Kingdom of Portugal, Brazil and the Algarves (as it was officially known between 1815 and 1822) lay – as did the Netherlands – within the British sphere of influence. London maintained a 'special relationship' with both kingdoms.[54] After Austria had transferred the Rhine District to Bavaria in 1816, the Allied Council also agreed, early in June 1816, to an amount of 5 million francs for the construction of forts on this left bank of the Rhine.[55]

Some protested this imperialist arrogance. Spain, for example, initially refused to accept the dictates of the Allied ministers or to sign the Vienna Convention. Wellington and the ministers, however, did not beat around the bush: if Spain did not first abolish the slave trade and affix its signature to the Final Act of the Vienna Congress, it would not be granted access to the fortress fund or be allowed to join the committee of Allied liquidators.[56] The Spanish envoy Labrador sharply protested this authoritarian attitude: Spain was as much an 'equal power' as the other four. The Spanish court found the 'innovation' of the Allied ministers in acting as a foursome simply off-putting. Spain wanted to negotiate with France on its own and act on the basis of its own sovereignty. But there was no chance that Labrador would even get his foot in the door, because Richelieu knew all too well that Wellington had the last word in the matter. After a multitude of memoranda and angry letters had been sent back and forth, Spain finally accepted the inevitable. When Labrador showed them the evidence of Spain's having signed the convention, which they had demanded, he still had to stand in line at the Allied cashier's window to receive what they would give Spain from the fortress

---

[53] Protocol of 3, 17, 18 November 1815, GStA PK, III. HA I. no. 1469. See also S. Laux, '"Errors of statesmanship" en 1815? Le Congrès de Vienne et les régions allemandes', *Austriaca*, 84 (2017), 157–76.
[54] Protocol of 22 May 1816, TNA, FO 146/6.
[55] Protocol of 2 June 1816, TNA, FO 146/6.
[56] Protocol of 21 August 1816, TNA, FO 146/14. See also the request to Labrador to provide evidence that Spain had truly joined the treaty, protocol of 20 March 1816, TNA, FO 146/6.

fund (which was not much),[57] all the while knowing that the Allied commissioners would scrupulously check, as was the Council's prerogative, to see whether Spain really used the money for work on its fortifications.[58]

In another case, it was Wellington himself who left the execution of the Allied defence plan to a middle-level country when he transferred the daily management, planning and execution of the Wellington Barrier entirely to Kraijenhoff at the end of 1815. He had won Wellington's confidence already at their first meeting, not that long before – impressed as he very much was with the hydraulic engineering expertise and military knowledge of this Dutch 'grand technician'. Wellington abandoned his initial plan to put the (re)construction projects under the practical supervision of British engineers, and turned to Kraijenhoff to take care of their execution on behalf of Willem I.[59] Apparently, smaller powers within the elitist Allied security culture could gain influence, provided that their contribution was in line with that of the Allied Council. In this case, it was Kraijenhoff's useful knowledge and expertise that Wellington was pleased to take advantage of.

Protection – But at What Price?

The fortifications were meant to defend the new European order. This grounding for Europe's balance of power, however, was built without the involvement, or better put, at the expense of the inhabitants of the border region. Little or no consideration was given to their wishes, possessions, fears and worries. The Allied security culture not infrequently led to more uncertainty and stress for the citizens in those regions.

The inhabitants of Oudenaarde had experienced this first-hand already in 1813–15, when they were constantly the victims of troops moving back and forth through their town. They had to hand over carts, horses and supplies, and endure the billeting of French, British, Dutch and German armies. Wellington himself had visited the place on 20 April 1815 to inspect their fortress, and in early June, just prior to the Battle of Waterloo, had explained to the people that he was commander-in-chief of the Allied troops. In his statement, he called on the local administrators of Oudenaarde and its residents to report or detain deserting soldiers: an order that was softened with the promise of a reward of 23 Belgian francs per deserter.[60]

When the construction of the Wellington Barrier in the southern Netherlands actually began in late 1815, the local population experienced the move as a veritable invasion. Work on the fortifications was carried out by

[57] See protocols of 24, 27, 31 March 1816, TNA, FO 146/6.
[58] See protocols of 7 and 10 April 1816, TNA, FO 146/6.
[59] Borremans, *Het Kezelfort*, 23–7; Uitterhoeve, *Cornelis Kraijenhoff*, 293–6.
[60] See Wellington, 'Proclamation', beginning of June 1815, SAO, no. 584; 583.

local contractors, but they were at the beck and call of the Fortifications Service, and under the supervision of inspector general Kraijenhoff. His department had six directorates, including Ghent, Antwerp and Namur, each with a colonel director at its head. All sorts of officers, engineers, overseers, but also military guards – field wardens, one might say – caretakers and other personnel were stationed at each of the fortresses. Most of them came from elsewhere. Among the 128 Dutch officers/engineers in 1830, only six were Belgian. The few (French-speaking) Belgian soldiers and engineers who were allowed to join in complained that they first had to learn Dutch.[61]

But there was more to it than that. In early 1816, the provincial governors began announcing expropriations on a large scale. Prior to Napoleon, cities saw to the maintenance of their own fortifications. The monarch, of course, could involve himself in their form and design, but in peacetime the city magistrate could decide for himself what he did with them. He could break them down, rent them, or let townsfolk plant little gardens on the ramparts. After the French Revolution, a law in 1791 transferred the ownership of all city fortifications to the state and they were put under the control of the army. Walks on the ramparts became a thing of the past; the commanders determined when the gates would open and close and it was they who chose the contractors. To keep the outer sweep of the ramparts free of obstacles, inhabitants were no longer allowed to build within 585 m of the glacis.[62] From the Napoleonic period onward, the fortifications, which the townsfolk and city councils found to be useful or handy in the eighteenth century, therefore became more and more of a burden to the inhabitants, who no longer had anything to say about them. Instead of a symbol of security and protection, the fortresses and fortifications became a source of unrest and uncertainty – in part because of the unpredictable expropriations and the costs related to the same.[63]

Willem I simply adopted the Napoleonic regulations. In 1816, by royal decree, he declared the plots for the fortresses being built to be state property. The lists of those whose farmlands and houses would be appropriated were announced 'with the roll of drums'.[64] The residents then had eight days to have their property appraised. A special committee saw to their redress and compensation, but because that turned out to be minimal, the number of appeals to be processed increased exponentially. One could hardly speak of an 'amicable settlement'. The construction projects did lead to jobs and employment for many, but workers could just as easily be let go when the weather changed for the worse. Their lives were uncertain from one day to the next, and their labour

---

[61] Gils, *De versterkingen van de Wellingtonbarrière*, 20–1.
[62] That is: the long, slightly sloping bank around the outer edge of the fortress.
[63] Gils, *De versterkingen van de Wellingtonbarrière*, 38–40.
[64] See, for example, the announced 'roll of the drum', published in the newspaper: 'Vestingwerken der stad Oudenaarde', *Feuille d'Annonces*, Oudenaarde, 9 October 1825.

thankless. Those who had to hoist the clay bricks up the Kezelberg to build the casemates had an especially hard time of it. Some lost fingers to frostbite, others were buried in rubble thanks to sudden landslides. Oudenaarde's chronicler, De Rantere, refers to all kinds of accidents. He also attributes the high number of suicides during these years to work on the forts; workers would be fired on the spot if the pace slowed or the weather was not cooperating.[65]

As a consequence of these hardships and uncertainties, the residents took stock of the new situation and started to find ways to engage in more or less open resistance or obstruction. For example, the curate of Oudenaarde's Saint Walburga Church and the city council, citing various prohibitions and regulations, were able to delay the construction of a Protestant church for years. That church was meant to provide the soldiers from the garrison and the officers and engineers from the north the opportunity to hold their own Protestant worship services. In the meantime, they had made do with a shabby hall in town. Likewise, when a funeral service for a Protestant was held in the hospital chapel, family members were not allowed into the chapel. Only after persistent objections did the governor of East Flanders relent. But he made it very clear that during such services 'the outer door shall not be opened, and that the access of the families of the deceased shall transpire discreetly'. Oudenaarde's city council, in responding to their submission to the Dutch authorities, with their imperialist forts, clearly dealt with the Protestant soldiers as second-class citizens. In early 1829, King Willem I had to intervene personally to see to it that funeral services for the military were dealt with equitably. That same year, the Protestant church was finally built – admittedly in the form of an elongated townhouse, and with no steeple.[66]

The new Dutch subjects also tried to put one over on the 'Hollanders' in other ways. Local contractors were especially skilled in this. The Dutch board had decided to keep the prices low by soliciting bids. Potential contractors could then submit their offers at a price higher or lower than that set by the engineers for moved earth per cubic metre, masonry work, the delivery of stone and bricks and the like. By offering a lower price, but in the end also delivering a much lower quality of stone or masonry work than agreed upon, contractors could make a killing.[67] Sometimes the military engineering office also made a deal with the contractor on the spot, allowing them, with a blind eye and their bribe in hand, to make do with shoddy brickwork.[68] In addition

---

[65] Borremans, *Het Kezelfort*, 29–36; (De) Smet, *Het dagboek van Bartolomeus De Rantere*, vol. 1, 149–231.

[66] Letter of the *Burgerhospital* to the mayor of Oudenaarde, 14 June 1826; the governor of East Flanders' response, 3 October 1828; ordinance of Willem I, 7 April 1829, SAO, HB XVII.A. MOA SN 567.1. See also E. Vandermeersch-Lantmeeters, *Uit de geschiedenis van het Geslacht Vandermeersch te Oudenaarde* (Sanderus: Oudenaarde, 1973), 74–5.

[67] Various official reports against contractors, SAO, HB no. 583.

[68] See also Uitterhoeve, *Cornelis Kraijenhoff*, 337–9, 345–50.

to the incident in Oudenaarde during Willem I's visit in 1823, landslides and collapsing embankments also occurred in Ath and Charleroi. The greatest scandal occurred in Ypres in 1824. After the gunpowder magazine collapsed there, an investigative committee discovered ample evidence of corruption. The local supervisor, engineer Lieutenant Colonel Lobry, was sentenced to twenty years in prison; Captain Pasteur, also an engineer, was given one year, and his lieutenant six months. The director of the Third Fortification Directorate, Major General Hennequin, who had been with Willem I during his visit in 1823, committed suicide in prison. This affair had another unpleasant consequence, because Kraijenhoff, Willem's inspector general, was also accused of untoward management and oversight. His function was discontinued and he was put on non-active duty in 1826. Even after he was formally rehabilitated and acquitted four years later, his old lustre never returned; he had more or less lost the king's favour.[69]

The rumours about malpractice and troubles on the southern frontier were so persistent that even Wellington began to worry. He sent his colonel John T. Jones to inspect matters in the Netherlands. On behalf of the British co-financiers, he had been monitoring the construction projects for years and knew everyone. According to Jones, two things were going on, but the alarmism, he felt, was unwarranted. Owing to the 'great haste' and the pressure put on completing these fortifications, some construction errors had indeed been made here and there. But they were not so serious as to compromise the military value of the fortresses. His sense was that what had really happened was that the 'jealous ire of the Belgians' had blown up the limited number of mistakes that had happened into a national affair. Kraijenhoff was also, indirectly, responsible for this, because, as Jones reported, 'by a very impolitic and unnational arrangement, scarcely any but native-born Dutch officers were employed on the new frontier'.[70] Support for the construction of the fortifications was minimal, and among Belgians many saw it as a hobby horse of Willem I.[71]

Whether the fortifications project was popular at all in the Netherlands, aside from with Willem and Kraijenhoff, is an open question. The variety in the forms and types of obstruction certainly increased their cost. And it was an expense sorely underestimated by Wellington and Willem in the first place. When the fund was dissolved in 1854, the total cost of the barrier proved to have risen to 88.56 million guilders. After deducting Britain's (one-time) contribution of 2 million pounds and the French contribution of 60 million

[69] Gils, *De versterkingen van de Wellingtonbarrière*, 22–3; Uitterhoeve, *Cornelis Kraijenhoff*, 350–63.

[70] See Jones, *Reports Relating to the Re-Establishment*, xv–xvi. See also Jones to Wellington, 28 September 1828, Ibid., 282–3.

[71] Uitterhoeve, *Cornelis Kraijenhoff*, 345–57.

francs, the 35.19 million guilders remaining was paid by the Dutch treasury.[72] The Oudenaarde fortress cost 3.4 million guilders, and the expenses for Dendermonde and Ghent were 3 and 3.3 million guilders respectively. Those costs had to be borne by the population. European security had come at a high price – something that Wellington realized as well. After his inspection tour in the summer of 1817, he likewise acknowledged to Castlereagh: 'I am a little afraid of the expense to the King, as the work is going on in really the best style.'[73] These costs were indeed too high, certainly for the inhabitants of Belgium, who, through all kinds of levies, had to bear the brunt of the additional costs. The majority were not at all excited about unifying with the northern part of the Netherlands or about the formation of a buffer state. However, the Allied security brokers at the time did not pay them much heed. Kraijenhoff was the first one to pay the price. But Willem I (and the Allies), too, suffered the consequences when the Belgians revolted in 1830.[74]

Irrespective of the costs, the fortifications were crucial for Wellington. What should be underlined here is that, in his assessment of the situation in France and the question of withdrawing the Allies' occupational forces in 1818, Wellington used the progress made in the construction of these fortifications as a yardstick. And if the Prince of Waterloo threw his importance behind the project, no other Allied minister was seriously willing to object to that call.

The First Troop Reduction

The construction of the forts and the completion of the first defence structures were well underway in the spring of 1816. In some places, such as Charleroi, the works were already almost done. According to British planning, most of the fortifications would be completed between 1818 and 1820.[75] With those in place, the need for occupational forces would also decrease somewhat. That is exactly what Wellington had intended: the fortifications and the joint military defence of the frontier by Prussia, the Netherlands and the German states would eventually take over as the guarantee of peace. As described in the previous chapters, the issue of troop reductions first appeared on the negotiating table of the Allied Council in the late summer of 1816. After the *Chambre*

---

[72] Gils, *De versterkingen van de Wellingtonbarrière*, 24.
[73] Wellington to Castlereagh, 7 August 1817, *WSD*, vol. 12, 23.
[74] Nelson, 'The Duke of Wellington and the Barrier Fortresses after Waterloo', 36–43.
[75] Including Nieuwpoort, Ypres, Menin, Oudenaarde, Ath, Dendermonde, Binch, Charleroi, Namur, Huy and Liège, which were well along and on schedule. See C. Kraijenhoff (ed.), *Levensbijzonderheden van den Luitenant-Generaal Baron C. R. T. Krayenhoff door hem zelfden in schrift gesteld, en op zijn verlangen in het licht gegeven door H. W. Tydeman* (Nijmegen: Vieweg, 1844), 150; see also 'Memo of the time computed for completing the Fortresses proposed in the Netherlands, with the yearly prospects in each', April 1816, on behalf of Wellington, TNA, FO 92/31.

Introuvable, the French reactionary parliament, had been dissolved, Wellington also felt that the time was ripe to follow through on this possibility, in part because he had received a number of encouraging reports from the Netherlands at the end of 1816 on the progress being made with the fortifications building project.[76] On behalf of the tsar, who equally wanted to demonstrate his generosity and saw France as a future ally, Pozzo di Borgo strongly urged Wellington in this direction as well.[77]

As for the political objectives, things were a bit more complicated. The occupation was also meant as a safeguard against a revival of revolutionary tendencies. Although the 'revolutionary spirit' was not altogether 'extinct' in May and June 1815, the fervour of the Revolution had been quenched. Things were more difficult when it came to the spirit of rebellion, short of open revolutions and revolts. The occupation was intended as a means to curb rebellion, but had itself given rise to a growing discontent. The French people had initially understood or at least grumblingly accepted the measures taken, but that had changed over time. As Wellington honestly assessed the situation:

> The measure of the occupation of a part of France by the Allied foreign force is no longer considered necessary for the interests of France herself, but is represented as a disgraceful condition imposed by the conquerors on the conquered, unjustifiable in its objects, and the expense of which is as intolerable as the measure is disgraceful to the French people.

Security was not only a matter of troops and fortresses, but as much a case of stable and calm sentiments, as Wellington knew too well. That is why reduction was not only a reward for the steps taken by the French king and parliament; it was also necessary with an eye to politically pacifying and alleviating the burden of the French people.[78]

Wellington, nonetheless, saw a major disadvantage in bringing the proposed 30,000 men home. His occupation army had to man seventeen spots along the entire border from Calais to Basel, each of which required hefty garrisons. Neither the loan (see Chapter 7) nor the troop reduction of twenty or thirty thousand had the 'effect of again reconciling the people of France to the occupation and to the conduct of the Allies'. The 'system of occupation, however still necessary for all the objects for which it had first been adopted, might no longer be one of peace'. In other words, Wellington was faced with a dilemma. Troop reductions were necessary, given the increased unrest and

---

[76] See reports from the Netherlands, May–December 1816, TNA, FO 92/31.

[77] See Pozzo di Borgo to Wellington, 10 September 1816, TNA, FO 92/31, 115–20. See also Pozzo di Borgo to Lieven, 29 November/11 December 1816, in Ministerstvo inostrannykh del CCCP (ed.), *Vneshniaia politika Rossii*, vol. 1, 306–8.

[78] Memorandum from Wellington to the Allied Council, discussed on 10 February 1817, TNA, FO 146/15. A version of this memorandum is reprinted as Wellington to Stuart, 9 January 1817, *WSD*, vol. 11, 589–94, here: 591.

the need to alleviate the people's burden. But, with an eye to the safety of the troops, they were also dangerous – with 30,000 fewer soldiers, Wellington could not keep his forts, and that 'might be attended with dangerous consequences'.[79]

Some of the forts on the French side of the border would have to be evacuated, lest the Allied occupation forces that remained be compromised. To compensate for this eviction, Wellington turned to Richelieu, asking him and the king to intensify their attempts to promote a spirit of 'moderation' among the people, including and especially towards the Allied soldiers – to which Richelieu dutifully complied.[80] He also saw the planned arrangement of France's meeting with the banking houses of Baring and Hope, mediated by himself and the Council, as a form of compensation. The occupation had, after all, served as a pledge guaranteeing France's reparations obligations. Fewer troops meant that France's willingness to pay had to be covered by extra assurances. In addition, Wellington set his hopes on an accelerated investment in the construction of forts on the other side of the border, with the fortress fund being transferred to Barings, so that the disbursement of the 'vouchers' was guaranteed.[81] He envisioned replacing the military security of an occupation army with a completed system of fortified deterrence. That system would thus entertain two functions: next to its physical, military impact, it had to exert a combined psychological, emotional effect: to scare off possible rebellious inclinations in France, and to instil in the Allied partners a sense of common security and solidarity.

The Prince of Waterloo's reputation was at stake if he did not keep a bead on the progress of that fortification system with his own eyes. He made his second major inspection tour from 28 July to 6 August 1817, and was pleased with what he saw. As he wrote to Castlereagh, 'A great deal of work has been done; it is remarkably well performed, and does the highest credit to the engineers of the Netherlands ... The King of the Netherlands will certainly have some of the finest fortresses in Europe.'[82] A December 1817 report from his right-hand man on the fortifications, Colonel John T. Jones, was somewhat more critical. According to Jones, 'the progress of the work has been retarded by difficulties ... particularly with respect to obtaining possession of the ground and forming contracts for the supply of the materials'. In other words, the obstruction antics of the residents along the Belgian frontier were not without consequences. However, 'notwithstanding this, nearly all the places have

[79] Ibid. See also Veve, *The Duke of Wellington and the British Army of Occupation in France*, 109–23.
[80] See the protocol of the Allied Council and Richelieu's letter to them, in which he expressed his gratitude for the reduction, and conveyed Louis XVIII's praise of the 'moderation' of the Allies, 19 February 1817, TNA, FO 146/15.
[81] Wellington to Castlereagh, 13 January 1817, *WSD*, vol. 11, 597–8.
[82] Wellington to Castlereagh, 7 August 1817, *WSD*, vol. 12, 23.

advanced agreeably to the expectations formed ... No doubt can therefore be entertained that everything essential to the defence of each fortress (except Mons) will be completed in 1820.'[83] That was good enough for Wellington. At the beginning of 1818, he assured General Müffling, who apprehensively inquired on behalf of the Prussian government as to where things stood, that the construction projects were 'well-advanced' and that he was 'very satisfied'.[84] On 19 August 1818, on the eve of the Congress of Aix-la-Chapelle, Wellington expressed his relief and gratitude for the progress made to Willem I. He was very pleased, both with 'the amount of work done, but also with the way it's been finished off so far'. Even a mishap – a small collapse in Charleroi – could not shake his pleased disposition. That 'misfortune' had been a 'minor accident' about which the builders could not have done anything. Briefly put, the military preparations for the troops' withdrawal was very much on track.[85] That was a good thing, because the political pressures within France had increased significantly, and several Allied ministers also thought that the occupation had lasted long enough.

An Imperialist *tête-à-tête*: Preparing to Withdraw from France

On 11 February 1818, Wellington's assessment of the unstable state of affairs in France was confirmed. The masked man who fired at him was not trying to rid France of the private person Arthur Wellesley; his barrel was aimed at the commander of the occupation forces. Wellington realized that all too well, as he admitted in his letters to Bathurst and Castlereagh – though not publicly. That attack was for him the last straw. His time in France, and that of the occupying forces, was over. The 'system of occupation' was 'no longer one of peace'. Wellington had come to the point where he could be content with leaving: the loans with Baring and Hope and the French bankers had been arranged, the final negotiations regarding the French arrears were almost complete – and the fortifications were coming along as planned. It was time to bring the occupation to an end and to dismantle the Allied Machine in France.

On 21 April 1818, the Allied Council discussed preparations for the next *réunion des souverains et cabinets alliés* that was due to take place in the autumn. That 'reunion' was meant to confirm the end of the occupation, to which all the ministers had by now agreed. The pressing question for now, however, was what the nature of that meeting would be. A congress,

---

[83] John T. Jones, 'Inspection Report', Cambrai, 8 December 1817, in Jones, *Reports Relating to the Re-Establishment*, 165–9, here: 169.

[84] Report of Müffling to Hardenberg, 'Unterredung mit dem Herzog Wellington zur Befestigung der Grenzen gegen Frankreich', February 1818, GStA PK, VI. HA Nl. Hardenberg 10a, 10–13.

[85] Wellington to Willem I, 19 August 1818, *WSD*, vol. 12, 652.

a conference, a mere consultation? Who would be invited to attend? Metternich took the lead and emphatically underscored the selective nature of the European security system. More than was the case in Vienna, the upcoming meeting should be, as Metternich put it, 'explicitly reserved for the four Allied sovereigns alone'. It should, of course, be about whether 'the moral and political situation of France' justified evacuating the Allied troops. A second, equally important issue concerned the form and character of the European treaty system itself. Should the 'spirit' and texts of the treaties be revised and renewed, or not? According to Metternich, the planned meeting in Aix-la-Chapelle (Aachen) was in accord with Article VI of the Quadruple Alliance Treaty of 20 November 1815, which established the regular gathering of the great powers as a mechanism for maintaining Europe's peace and security. These meetings were not, however, intended to be large congresses every time, where everything was on the table and had to be renegotiated all and sundry. That would only be 'dangerous'. Stuart added that the British government saw it that way as well. Even though the other 'princes of Europe' had now joined the Treaty of 25 March 1815, the Final Act of Vienna and the Second Treaty of Paris, and had also put their troops at risk in the peace efforts, the Quadruple Alliance remained a collaboration 'explicitly reserved for the principal contracting parties'. From the outset, Metternich spoke negatively about other countries joining the Quadruple Alliance. Such an 'extra-special right' for one country would only provoke jealousy and discontent at the other courts. In other words, France, Spain or Portugal should not count on being admitted.[86]

Pozzo di Borgo, on behalf of the Russian court, tried to oppose this imperialistic 'political excommunication' of Spain and France and argued for the admission of 'secondary powers', but the views of Castlereagh and Metternich prevailed.[87] The meeting in Aix would not be a special congress as was Vienna, in which all the Allies could participate, but a mere meeting under Article V of the Second Treaty of Paris (a 'deliberation', as the article has it), which provided for a consultation regarding the end of the occupation of France – something reserved for the four great powers only.[88] Prussia and Russia agreed to this as well; it would not be an open assembly, but a closed 'reunion', or a 'conference'.[89]

---

[86] Memorandum of Metternich, discussion in the Allied Council, protocol of 21 April 1818, TNA, FO 146/29.

[87] See for example the Russian attempts to influence the invitation policy to Aix-la-Chapelle: Golowkin (Vienna) to Kapodistrias, 4/16 April 1818, Lieven (London) to Kapodistrias, 6/18 May 1818, in Ministerstvo inostrannykh del CCCP (ed.), *Vneshniaia politika Rossii*, vol. 2, 297–301, 364–6.

[88] Jarrett, *The Congress of Vienna and its Legacy*, 180–1.

[89] Protocol of 4 May 1818, TNA, FO 146/29. See also, for instance, Castlereagh to Cathcart, 27 March 1818, *WSD*, vol. 12, 445–6.

Consequently, On 28 April, the Council sent a letter around to the other courts of Europe to inform them of the upcoming conference, indicating that it would not be a congress like Vienna, but only a conversation between the four great powers of the Quadruple Alliance. The ministers and envoys hence consistently referred to the meeting as a 'reunion' or 'conference', and not as a congress.[90] France was invited to the table only for specific points on the agenda, and not as a full participant. Ministers and ambassadors from the other courts were allowed to be present as observers, but not as participants with equal rights. Even more than in Vienna, Aix was an imperialist, great power get-together.[91] As Metternich had already explained to the Russian ambassador in Vienna, Count Golowkin, 'the European system [the four great powers of the Quadruple Alliance] is the kingpin of the political world', and the 'inferior powers' had better stop complaining. This assessment of inter-Allied superiority could only sit well with Golowkin: 'I don't have to tell you', he conceded to Kapodistrias, the foreign minister of the tsar, 'that it warms the Russian heart to hear someone wanting to give to Caesar what is Caesar's'.[92]

On 25 May 1818, the agenda was sent around to all the ministers and envoys of the Allied courts for their information. As Metternich had already proposed, the Aix-la-Chapelle conference would first of all be about 'the internal state' of France and the final conditions for terminating the occupation. There would be a few other issues on the table, but the meeting was emphatically not a congress.[93] The Austrian chancellor also repeated the same thing to the Ottomans, who had apprehensively inquired into the matter. The Reis Efendi – the sultan's chancellor and minister of foreign affairs – was told that the ministers and princes of the Quadruple Alliance would not be discussing Ottoman matters and that the French issue was the only item on the agenda. That (quite rightly) did not completely allay the anxiety of the Ottomans, however.[94] France, of course, would be present. When asked, Richelieu let the Allied Council know that the king's 'state of health' did not allow him to travel to Aix-la-Chapelle himself. Instead, Richelieu, as prime minister and minister of foreign affairs, would represent his country and the monarch.[95] Apart from Spain and Portugal, the other European countries

[90] Within a year, however, publicists spoke of a 'congress'. See C. Meyer, *Aachen der Monarchen-Kongress im Jahr 1818* (Aix-la-Chapelle: Weiss, 1819).

[91] Circular of 28 April 1818, TNA, FO 146/29.

[92] Golowkin to Kapodistrias, 15/27 March 1818, in Ministerstvo inostrannykh del CCCP (ed.), *Vneshniaia politika Rossii*, vol. 2, 265–7, here: 266. See also Golowkin to Kapodistrias, 2/14 May 1818, Ibid., 354–7.

[93] Protocol of 25 May 1818, TNA, FO 146/29.

[94] Stürmer to Metternich, 10, 25 July, 10 October, 25 December 1818, AT-OeStA/HHStA, StAbt, Türkei VI, 8, Berichte, 1818–1820.

[95] Protocol of 20 and 30 June 1818, TNA, FO 146/29.

seemed to accept the decree of the four courts of the Quadruple Alliance without protest. With that, the Conference of Aix-la-Chapelle was officially in the hands of the Allied imperial consortium.

'Measure of Precaution'

The meeting in Aix-la-Chapelle was a somewhat superfluous conference, because what had triggered it was in fact already resolved when the talks commenced in September. The most important decisions regarding the occupation of France and the security system that befitted the situation in Europe had been prearranged by the ministers in Paris during the spring and summer of 1818, and not by the sovereigns and their entourage. The decision to convene the Aix-la-Chapelle conference in 1818, three years after the Second Treaty of Paris instead of the originally agreed-upon five years, was in fact the most important step, made in April, after the final payment agreements had been arranged. A half-hearted attempt by the ultra-royalists to gum up the gears of Richelieu's government could not undo that decision. A camarilla led by the overly reactionary Baron Vitrolles had tried to give credence to the suggestion that a revolution was imminent. To frustrate Richelieu's efforts and to increase his own powerbase, he asked the Allied Council to postpone the end of the occupation and the evacuation of the troops. But no one took his plea seriously.[96] Briefly put, the meeting in Aix had more of a performative function, rather than indicating that much real work still had to be done. The conference was to demonstrate the solidarity of the Allies, to display their grip on European peace and security and to draw France back as an equal onto the stage of international relations.

Final conditions, however, were negotiated at Aix. These fell into two categories: the financial payments that France still owed, and the required military guarantee needed to compensate for the departure of the Allied troops. The financial negotiations were discussed in Chapter 7. Here we will focus on the military question and the related issue of fortifications. This issue was hotly debated from April to August, and opinions on the possible military risk that France posed differed widely.

British decision makers took the initiative and tried to cast the deliberations primarily in terms of the now notoriously elusive image of the 'European balance of power'. In this case, they conceived the metaphor above all as a container concept for setting up a system of deterrence. France was first and foremost a potential military threat to the continental balance of power

---

[96] See Pozzo's reference to this 'conspiracy': Pozzo di Borgo to Lieven, 29 July; Nesselrode to Pozzo di Borgo, 2 August 1818. All to be found in Pozzo di Borgo (ed.), *Correspondance*, 567–9. See also Veve, *The Duke of Wellington and the British Army of Occupation in France*, 148–50.

and therefore also had to be dissuaded with physical, military resources from giving in to its potentially aggressive tendencies. The forts were therefore a crucial part of this discussion. In a September 1818 memorandum, Castlereagh wondered about what the 'measure of precaution' should be when the occupational forces were withdrawn. In doing so, he was elaborating on Wellington's memorandum of January 1817.[97] To support the Allied security system, Castlereagh thought, one might think first of deploying an 'army of observation' along the borders with France. The problem with that tactic was that the states bordering France were not particularly excited about having to pay for those extra troops. The British parliament was also not about to approve additional funds for such a continental army; as a world power, Britain also had other irons in the fire that needed tending. Moreover, it was debatable whether such an observation force would serve the cause of security or just prod the 'military spirit' within France into action. The French army was at the time rather small – some seventy to eighty thousand men. The French had altogether no desire, let alone money, for new military adventures. But because such an army on its doorstep might well rekindle France's aspirations, that idea was set aside.[98]

Another solution was much more obvious: to involve the German Confederation in the European defence system. The Confederation was able to mobilize 300,000 soldiers, plus a reserve of 150,000. The question was whether that force was also sufficient to defend the Low Countries, which were, after all, central to the European defence system. The Dutch and German defence lines did not automatically mesh well with each other. The Duchy of Luxembourg was part of the Confederation (which meant that Willem I, as Grand Duke of Luxembourg, was represented in the Confederation), but the Netherlands as such was not. Could the Netherlands, then, be linked to the German line of defence in another way? For example, with an augmented security treaty of the Quadruple Alliance with Willem I? That was not a good idea either. If the four Allies signed a separate treaty with the Netherlands, this would have negative repercussions in the other countries. The new treaty 'would be appearing to weaken their duty of protecting other points of the line of defence against France, the immediate effect of which would be to excite jealousy in those states whose interests were thus apparently placed in the second line'.[99] It was also not really necessary, because the four powers of the Quadruple Alliance had already obliged themselves to intervene if the Netherlands were attacked.

---

[97] Castlereagh, 'First Memorandum on the approaching conference of Aix-La-Chapelle Foreign Office', 14 September 1818, TNA, FO 92/34.

[98] Castlereagh, 'First Memorandum', 19–23.

[99] Ibid., 24.

A third option was a general request to all the other states to join a kind of military assistance treaty that would commit them to their own 'proportion of force'. But that, too, went too far, as Castlereagh observed:

> But as the effect of such an acception, not made, as it was at Vienna, upon a specified and known danger, such as the return of Bonaparte from Elba, but upon an unforeseen Case, would be prematurely to embarrass the Councils of the Quadruple Alliance ... It was thought more prudent not to have recourse to a measure of this nature till the occasion should arise when a principle of common danger might facilitate such a combination.

In other words, such an expansive new treaty, or the inclusion of other countries in the alliance, would create a new dynamic, and might possibly even act as a blank cheque for countries that wanted to use the alliance for their own purposes.

There was still a final option. As a new power flanking the Netherlands, Prussia was the most 'important security' for the Low Countries. Prussia and the Netherlands shared a common interest in defending the border. That common interest simply needed to be arranged better and more explicitly than was presently the case. Why not set up a 'separate defensive system on their part', which Britain and Russia could then join? But Austria would then probably feel excluded again, which meant that this option would not result in 'great security'. In short, any separate, new alliances would only undermine the existing system and the corresponding 'general alliance' of the four powers.[100] Hence, the only possible option was that the Netherlands would have to work together with Prussia, within the existing framework of treaties, in a more structured format, in the practical implementation of the fortifications project and in jointly manning the garrisons. Castlereagh was in fact repeating Wellington's position in 1815. During the meetings in Aix, concrete agreements would have to be made to make the visible translation of the European balance of power – the *Boulevard de l'Europe* – also truly effective.

The New European Security System

Another security policy issue emerged in connection with the fortifications: the treaty-based obligatory dimension of the security system, and its repercussions for international law. Were the existing treaties still up to their task, or did they have to be tweaked somewhat or revised, given the developments in international relations after 1815? This quickly gave rise to a new conceptual conundrum regarding the discursive linchpin of the European security system: the notion of the balance of power. Was it a balance of power against France, or a European balance of power in which France could play a part? Did the

---

[100] Ibid., 24–8.

metaphor 'balance of power' even allow for a balance formed of linked-together states without a hostile state to act as 'counterweight'? According to the Allied Council in Paris, talk of a balance of power implied by definition that there was such a 'counterweight'. At the same time, the departure of the Allied troops from France confirmed the return of France to the circle of top-level Allied powers. The question, more specifically, was what to do with the Quadruple Alliance. The November 1815 treaty was an alliance against France. Could France now join this treaty, or was it a contradiction in terms for a country to join an alliance whose ground for existence was specifically intended as a defence against that same country?

Prussia and Austria proposed simply renaming the alliance a Quintuple Alliance. That would be the best and fastest way to incorporate France into the balance of power.[101] Things were somewhat more complicated for the British. In August, Castlereagh laid out the contradictions and options in a lengthy memorandum, in which he weighed both the concrete, political implications and the possible psychological effects.

In terms of treaty law, Allied cooperation was based on the Treaty of Alliance (the Quadruple Alliance) of November 1815. That treaty was itself based on the Treaty of Chaumont and the Final Act of the Congress of Vienna. The General Alliance Treaty of 25 March 1815 (against Napoleon) was no longer valid because it had been incorporated into the Treaty of Paris and the Quadruple Alliance. The *casus foederis* of the latter treaty – the obligation of all members to assist in the event of one treaty partner being attacked – included a commitment of 60,000 extra troops per country, in addition to the existing Allied army. After the occupation, this commitment of 60,000 soldiers per state, plus more when necessary, simply continued. The Treaty of Chaumont had been drawn up to hold for twenty years, and so still applied. Together, this system of treaties had three aims, as Castlereagh wrote to Stuart and Wellington: maintaining European peace, excluding Napoleon Bonaparte and his family from any administrative or political function and fighting terror and revolution in Europe. That third goal – preventing and combating the 'revolutionary spirit which had convulsed France, and endangered Europe' – was the most difficult. It was, after all, 'difficult to distinguish' revolution from 'other more ordinary cases of local disturbances'. This could not be unambiguously and generically defined in a treaty, but had to be left to the discretion of the 'contracting parties' on a case-by-case basis.[102]

Opening this treaty to renegotiation in Aix-la-Chapelle could lead to all sorts of unforeseen and undesirable consequences, to new insecurities, and, at the least, to 'serious differences of opinion'. It was also an open question whether the British parliament would ratify the treaty again. The stipulation

---

[101] Vincent to Wellington, including memorandum, 22 August 1818, *WSD*, vol. 12, 653–4.
[102] Memorandum, August/September 1818, TNA, FO 92/34, 30–2.

about excluding the Bonapartes was as such no longer necessary, and in 1818 would never have been included. If other states wanted to strike that passage from the treaty, that could eventually be discussed and voted on, but beyond that, the Treaty of Alliance should not be subject to renegotiation. A final point was the question of France's joining the alliance. Just like Metternich, Castlereagh had his reservations about that. The treaty was, after all, 'founded upon the principle of an exclusive surveillance of this state'. It would be very strange if the French king were to become party to a treaty that placed his own state under the guardianship of the Allies. At the same time, France could not expect that 'Europe should at once desist from the precautionary system against the power from which the revolutionary danger had flowed'.

Castlereagh's solution was, therefore, a pragmatic one. The treaty would not be dissolved, nor would France sign on to the treaty in its entirety. If it could not be otherwise, the French king would be invited to sign on to Article VI and, per protocol, become a contracting party to that part of the treaty. Article VI stipulated that the Allied powers would cooperate in a 'deliberative system for the purpose of consulting at fixed periods and upon common interests, and for the consideration of such measures as may be deemed most salutary for repose and prosperity of nations and for the maintenance of the peace of Europe'. The French king could thus join Article VI and, in doing so, be included in the deliberative system. That was better than 'having so great a power as France in a state of separation to create for herself some counterpoise to this alliance'. The European balance of power, then, had to encompass the entire continent and close the door to any attempt by one country to tip the scale or to form a counterweight against other states.[103]

These considerations laid the foundation for the negotiations in Aix-la-Chapelle, and were also decisive for the position taken by Prussia and Austria. Castlereagh's nuanced and cautious views on a partial entry for France lined up with Metternich's concerns about eventual domestic revolutionary stirrings. In this way, the notion of 'concert' – collective consultation and cooperation – could be reconciled with those of 'deterrence and balance of power'. The Austrian envoy Gentz saw things similarly – the latent spirit of revolt could only be tamed with a security policy defined by deterrent measures. The Austrian ministers believed that a balance of power in international relations would prevent any imbalances in domestic politics. With that as a bridge, the British and the Austrians found common ground. Prussia, too – which had from the start felt that a European balance of power needed a military cordon of fortifications along France's borders – agreed with Castlereagh's solution.

---

[103] Memorandum, August/September 1818, TNA, FO 92/34, 32–40.

Pozzo's 'Temple of Concord'

Having arrived at this point, Pozzo di Borgo – Russia's minister – launched his assault to change the Allied course of action substantially, towards both France and the rest of the world. Coming from a competing Corsican clan, Pozzo had turned to Bonaparte's nemesis, Tsar Alexander. Since 1812, he had been active as a diplomat at the Russian court to do what he could to restore the Bourbons, albeit the moderate branch of that house. He was not at all inclined towards Louis XVIII's brother and the clique of Ultras. On the other hand, he did have an excellent relationship with Richelieu. Via Pozzo, Richelieu kept the tsar well informed about all that was going on in France, and, in return, Pozzo was increasingly Richelieu's direct ally within the Allied Council. Pozzo had a good working relationship with Wellington, but it was clear to the other ministers that the Russian minister was a direct extension of France's foreign policy.[104]

It was therefore not surprising that in March and April Pozzo pleaded with his Russian master, in increasingly longer and fiercer memoranda, for the complete withdrawal of troops from France and a halt to further financial charges and other 'indignities'. From his perspective, Providence had shown that France was thriving under the current dynasty and had embraced order and peace. Now that France had arranged for its final financial obligations with the April 1818 convention, there was every reason for the Allies to turn to their side of the deal: complete political disengagement (*liquidation politique*) from France. That meant not only that all their troops would be sent home, but also that France would have to be invited to join the Quadruple Alliance as a full member. Or better yet, that a new alliance would replace the former one. France would then be able to join this new alliance in a celebratory fashion. Now that the Bourbon monarchy had been restored, Pozzo opined, France could no longer be regarded as the 'counterweight'. The argument of its being a balance of power against France was therefore no longer valid,[105] and framing things in these terms was inappropriate. It would be better to proceed from the concept of a federation or general alliance. A true 'temple of concord' was called for that included all the states of Europe[106] – with Alexander undoubtedly as high priest, as far as Pozzo was concerned. With the help of such a new, broad alliance, Tsar Alexander could also offer a counterweight to Britain's dominance on the continent. With France and hopefully Spain

---

[104] See Lieven to Kapodistrias, 13/25 May 1818, in Ministerstvo inostrannykh del CCCP (ed.), *Vneshniaia politika Rossii*, vol. 2, 373.

[105] Appendix to Pozzo di Borgo's memorandum of 25 April 1818, Pozzo (ed.), *Correspondance*, 484–500, here: 496, 498; see also Pozzo to Nesselrode, 5 August 1818, Ibid., 583.

[106] Pozzo to Nesselrode, 27 August 1818, Pozzo (ed.), *Correspondance*, 587.

and Portugal as part of the picture, the British–Austrian axis could be weakened.[107]

Pozzo's passion in defending the French cause as well as his criticism of the British–Austrian interpretation of the 'balance of power' concept was recognized in St Petersburg but not fully appreciated. Kapodistrias and Nesselrode, respectively Alexander's secretary of state and minister of foreign affairs, urged their overzealous minister in Paris not to irritate the other Allied ministers.[108] Alexander spoke less about a balance of power and in 1818 still preferred the metaphor of the European 'concert'. In fact, he saw himself as one of its conductors. He did not want that concert to be kept out of tune by an overly one-sided partiality towards France. In St Petersburg, Pozzo was considered to be France's shadow minister of foreign affairs. Hence, the tsar could also not appreciate the bitter accusations Pozzo aimed at Metternich and the Prussians. Although Pozzo could not help underscoring Wellington's 'upright' character, he was very critical of Castlereagh – which occasioned a reprimand from Kapodistrias and Alexander. Moreover, convinced as he was that the spectre of revolution was by no means vanquished, Alexander felt that Pozzo was far too optimistic about France's future. The Bourbon dynasty should certainly be invited to join the European Concert as a full member. There would, of course, have to be a clause or emergency plan built into the European system to 'help' the Bourbons should any new slip-ups or 'revolutionary upheavals' arise, because, according to the tsar (cited by Kapodistrias to Pozzo), 'the French will always remain the same'.[109]

In addition, the other Allies clearly needed each other. Alexander was not convinced that the fortifications were a sufficient precaution against the potential terror of the French. 'A little line of fortresses' is how Kapodistrias condescendingly referred to the Allied Council's plan to offset the evacuation of France with the Wellington Barrier. For the tsar, that line was a mere 'bagatelle', and completely inadequate to contain the dangers of revolution. More was needed: not a balance, but a serious 'moral guarantee', a reinvigoration of a 'general alliance'. What Kapodistrias and the tsar meant

[107] Pozzo to Kapodistrias, 24 March 1818, including memorandum; Pozzo to Nesselrode, Lieven, 24 March 1818, Pozzo (ed.), *Correspondance*, 403–14. For *liquidation politique*, see 410. See also Pozzo to Kapodistrias, 27 April 1818, Ibid., 442–5.
[108] Nesselrode to Pozzo, 17 June; Kapodistrias to Pozzo, 18 June, Pozzo (ed.), *Correspondance*, 537–40; Kapodistrias to Pozzo, with quotes from Tsar Alexander, 10 July 1818, Ibid., 553–61.
[109] Kapodistrias to Pozzo, 27 March 1818, Pozzo (ed.), *Correspondance*, 422–7; Pozzo to Kapodistrias, 27 April 1818, Ibid., 433–41. Regarding Wellington, see Pozzo to Kapodistrias, 29 May, Ibid., 519; citing Alexander in Kapodistrias's letter to Pozzo, 10 July, Ibid., 555. See also Gowkin to Nesselrode, 25 July/6 August 1818, in Ministerstvo inostrannykh del CCCP (ed.), *Vneshniaia politika Rossii*, vol. 2, 478–9.

by that initially remained vague.[110] Pozzo, too, was in the dark. The tsar's plan would not be revealed until 14 October, during the conference itself.

The Janus Face of the Aix-la-Chapelle Conference

The Conference of Aix-la-Chapelle, as contemporaries called it, had two faces. It was intended to look ahead, but focused primarily on the most recent threat. The shadow cast by the recent past of revolution and terror hung palpably over the negotiations among the sovereigns and their entourage. The conference was nonetheless a truly innovative platform of deliberation. It was a textbook example of modern, effective diplomacy – even more than the Congress of Vienna – in which ministers and their envoys had already deliberatively mapped out the areas of heightened tension and were able to resolve the final ambiguities during a large international session. Even though there were many sovereigns in attendance, there was much less partying going on than in Vienna. So as not to demand too much from the citizens of Aix-la-Chapelle, and to devote their time to actual negotiations and deliberations, the crowned heads were seldom out and about in Aix. For the most part they remained behind closed doors. As a result, forty-seven sessions took place between 30 September and 22 November, resulting in an extensive number of protocols and agreements. However modern and professional this form of 'summitry' was, the conference remained an instrument in the fight against the ghosts of the past. What no one had seen coming was that, halfway through, the conference was hijacked by Tsar Alexander and his ministers, who were still trying to force their European colleagues into an anti-revolutionary alliance.

It all started out very friendlily. 'I have never seen a prettier little Congress', Metternich wrote to his wife in early October.[111] It was warm reunion for the diplomats and envoys who had met in 1814 and 1815 in the wake of the last campaigns against Napoleon and had got to know each other at the whist tables in Vienna and possibly also in the British embassy in Paris. In the run-up to Aix-la-Chapelle, a number of the main figures had agreed to travel together. Kapodistrias had already spoken to Metternich and Hardenberg in Carlsbad, where these two, en route to Aix, were attending a session of the German Bundestag. They were both of the opinion that this congress was the culmination of the efforts of the Quadruple Alliance and the Allied Council in Paris to permanently curb the terror in France.

---

[110] Kapodistrias to Pozzo, 19 April 1818, Pozzo (ed.), *Correspondance*, 428–31. See also the memorandum 'Sur l'entrevue d'Aix-la-Chapelle', composed by the Russian Foreign Ministry, 24 June 1818, in Ministerstvo inostrannykh del CCCP (ed.), *Vneshniaia politika Rossii*, vol. 2, 409–23, in particular 417–19.

[111] In R. Metternich (ed.), *Memoirs of Prince Metternich, 1773–1835*, vol. 3 (New York: Scribner's Sons, 1880-2), 144. See also Jarrett, *The Congress of Vienna and its Legacy*, 204.

All the sovereigns and their entourage had arrived in Aix-la-Chapelle by the end of September. Franz I, the emperor of Austria, had Metternich, Gentz and the ambassadors Lebzeltern and Zichy with him. Friedrich Wilhelm III, the king of Prussia, had his 17-year-old son Carl, plus Hardenberg, Humboldt, Prince Wittgenstein and Count Bernstorff in his retinue. France was represented by Richelieu, Caraman, Rayvenal and Mounier, Britain by Castlereagh, his half-brother Lord Stewart and Wellington. The tsar had brought along Kapodistrias, Nesselrode and Count Lieven; and very much to the chagrin of Castlereagh and Metternich, who would have preferred that he had not come, Pozzo di Borgo arrived in Aix-la-Chapelle in early October. Likewise, a whole series of lesser princes, ministers and diplomats were also quartered in the city. Compared to the triumphant summit in Paris and Vienna three years earlier, the mood was more businesslike and sober. Moreover, only the diplomats and ministers of the four powers plus those of France were invited to join in the meetings. In addition to the presence of a few well-known activists, such as the social reformer Robert Owen, the abolitionist Thomas Clarkson and Lewis Way, the advocate for the emancipation of the Jews, what was also noteworthy was that an entire cadre of influential bankers and financiers showed up as well. The security sought for was very much contingent on a solid financial foundation, embodied by Alexander Baring, Hope's Pierre César Labouchère, two brothers from the Rothschild family and David Parish.[112]

The new era was embodied by a young woman, Wilhelmine Reichard, who did something both spectacular and very symbolic on 13 October. While the ministers were still in the middle of discussing the future of the Quadruple Alliance, dignitaries gathered in the park on the outskirts of the city. There, Reichard climbed into a gas balloon, which she had constructed herself. Earlier flights had not been without mishaps. In 1811, she had lost consciousness due to the altitude (25,600 ft), had crash-landed in a forest and, badly injured, had barely survived the fall. Now, everyone held their breath while she stepped into the basket, waved and ascended. It was a beautiful autumn day, and, from the blue sky above, Wilhelmine dropped flowers on those gathered – along with pamphlets with a poem on them in which she lauded the desire for peace that had blossomed in Europe since time immemorial, and had, via Charlemagne, also manifested itself in the current gathering of monarchs and emperors.[113] (A competing attempt by the French woman Élisa Garnerin (Fig. 8.4) failed miserably. Wellington, who was standing at the front of the group that witnessed the event, caught Élisa just as she fell from the balloon, which flew away unmanned and was eventually found back in Stuttgart. Though suffering

[112] Jarrett, *The Congress of Vienna and its Legacy*, 182.
[113] Meyer, *Aachen*, 38–41; E. Probst, *Königinnen der Lüfte in Deutschland. Biografien berühmter Fliegerinnen, Ballonfahrerinnen, Luftschifferinnen und Fallschirmspringerinnen* (Munich: Grin, 2010), 95–9.

Figure 8.4 'Pour la Féte Du Roy! Par Élisa Garnerin', print of the balloon ride during the celebration of the Allied victory over Napoleon, under the supervision of the Prussian King Friedrich Wilhelm III, 1815. Artist unknown, 1815. (© Smithsonian National Air & Space Museum)

some minor injuries, she went on to fly her balloons many times more, throughout Europe.)[114]

The future peace and security of Europe could be sealed most appropriately in Aix-la-Chapelle, the city where Charlemagne's tomb lies. That future was one of princes, ministers and citizens together. If anything in Aix pointed to the dawning age, it was the active involvement of a large group of citizens and notables in the programme of the conference. They were not allowed to participate in the negotiations, but factory owners, inventors, creators of chemical processes to add pigments to porcelain, producers of sewing needles and experts in mine-building were given plenty of room to share their craftsmanship, expertise and discoveries with the dignitaries. Tsar Alexander particularly enjoyed the German manufacturing industries, slipping out incognito

---

[114] 'Neueste Nachrichten aus Aachen', *Oesterreichischer Beobachter*, 23 October 1818, 1545–6; P. Caron and C. Gével, 'Mademoiselle Élisa Garnerin, aéronaute', *Revue politique et littéraire, Revue bleue* (1912), 434–9.

to explore the area, visit a few churches and admire the machines in the nearby textile factories.[115]

The dignitaries were not as optimistic and candid with respect to the future as were Wilhelmine and the industrious citizens of Aix-la-Chapelle. While the British and French, seeing Aix as a technical conference, worked primarily on the latest financial arrangements, the continental powers were deeply concerned about the tangible risk of future revolutions – in Europe and far beyond.

'No Publicity'

The time taken for excursions could not hide the fact that the Aix-la-Chapelle Conference had a different character from the spectacle that the Congress of Vienna afforded all visitors, from top to bottom, three years earlier. The conference was much shorter – the tsar wanted to have his troops and entourage on their way back to Russia before winter set in – and the meetings and discussions were also less visible. The Allied Council had already made the most important decisions in Paris. As a correspondent (possibly Gentz himself) explained to the *Oesterreichischer Beobachter*, the Austrian house magazine in the hands of Metternich and Gentz: 'If you want to hear secrets from me about the negotiations taking place here, you've got it all wrong. This is not a congress, and ministers are not plenipotentiaries. It is the sovereigns and their cabinets who have come together for deliberations.' The essentials had already been decided beforehand, and those preparations were secret: 'Ministerial conferences are not suited for openness and publicity. These ministerial discussions take place every day, sometimes even twice a day, in the morning and in the evening.' The negotiations went so smoothly that after a few days the convention on evacuating the troops could be concluded and Wellington gave the order for his commanders of the occupation army to begin to pull up stakes and head for home. 'The diplomats unanimously agree that things are proceeding here smoothly, quickly and better than was expected ... They will be finished before the world even realizes that they have already begun.'[116] That is why it was a good deal quieter in the city by early November. 'Most of the foreigners who came here out of curiosity, or to entertain themselves, have already left', wrote the *Oesterreichischer Beobachter* around 4 November. 'They did not find what they were looking for. There were no grand feasts, drinking sprees or parties.' Castlereagh, Metternich, Nesselrode and the Princess of Thurn and Taxis were the only ones to entertain

---

[115] Meyer, *Aachen*, 24–37, 42–3. See also 'Zusammenkunft der Monarchen in Aachen', *Oesterreichischer Beobachter*, 15 October 1818, 1503.

[116] 'Weitere Nachrichten aus Aachen bis zum 19. October', *Oesterreichischer Beobachter*, 29 October 1818, 1578.

guests at home. The three monarchs (Alexander, Friedrich Wilhelm III and Franz I) rarely appeared in public, and 'were primarily hard at work'.[117]

The citizens and guests in the city did, of course, see and experience something of the concord among the delegations. On a radiantly sunny 19 October, a grand memorial festival took place commemorating the victory of the Battle of Leipzig five years earlier. It included a simulated medieval religious altar spectacle on the fields outside the city, a lunch for the diplomats, officers and crowned heads and, in the evening, a light show for all the citizens of Aix-la-Chapelle and other interested parties. Standing under the clear sky and visible to everyone, King Friedrich Wilhelm III of Prussia, Emperor Franz of Austria and Tsar Alexander, hand in hand, let the 'Hallelujah' and the 'Amen' of the choirboys fill the evening air.[118]

What was tangibly visible and poignantly present to mind were not the discussions of the day, but the historical places and memorable moments that connected the sovereigns present there to one another – primarily the battles of Leipzig and, of course, of Waterloo. The British Prince Regent had sent Thomas Lawrence, his court painter, along with the British delegation, to Aix-la-Chapelle to continue the work that he had begun in 1814: painting life-size portraits of all 'the heroes of Waterloo'. In Aix, Lawrence was able to immortalize Metternich, Wellington himself and Tsar Alexander. (Blücher's portrait was finished, but Lawrence had to go to Vienna to finalize Schwarzenberg's painting.) Wellington sat with regal allure on his horse Copenhagen; Alexander, somewhat plumper than in 1815, stood with his legs spread wide; and Metternich gazed with mysterious contrivance from the frame.[119]

The actual significance of Aix-la-Chapelle thus lay not on the battlefields, which were soon declared epic events of the past, but in the final negotiations among the specialists: the financiers, bankers and military engineers. Another way in which the Aix conference became tangible was in the relocation and evacuation of the troops, in the ongoing construction of the Wellington Barrier and, of course, in the stock-market prices, which dropped frightfully low for a while during the conference.

The Last Loan

The first days in Aix-la-Chapelle were devoted to negotiations between the seats of power, the ministers and their diplomats, but also with the bankers and

---

[117] 'Neueste Nachrichten aus Aachen vom 4. November', *Oesterreichischer Beobachter*, 12 November 1818, 1647.

[118] 'Weitere Nachrichten aus Aachen bis zum 19. October', *Oesterreichischer Beobachter*, 29 October 1818, 1577.

[119] See 'Ausländische Nachrichten. Grossbrittannien', *Oesterreichischer Beobachter*, 18 October 1818, 1519. The portraits can now be admired in the Waterloo Chamber at Windsor Castle.

financiers. France's final financial obligations, which were still sizeable, were on the agenda. Louis XVIII, however, had given his prime minister clear instructions: 'M. de Richelieu, make every kind of sacrifice in order to obtain the evacuation of the territory. It is the first condition of our independence.'[120] Indeed, already on 1 October, during the third official session, the Allied ministers signed an agreement that provided for the evacuation of the occupation forces. Tsar Alexander gave his former assistant the benefit of the doubt when Richelieu assured him on 30 September that the French government sat firmly in the saddle. The Prussians were especially 'hard pressed for money', and also agreed with the evacuation.[121] With that agreement, the goal of the conference, as formulated in Article V of the Treaty of Paris, was achieved.[122] Castlereagh's earlier proposal, to leave the Quadruple Alliance between the four Allies intact and to invite France to sign on to Article VI of the treaty, was also adopted – much to the chagrin of Richelieu, Pozzo and Kapodistrias, who had advocated a broader coalition with France and Spain.[123]

The financial settlement relating to the evacuation of the troops and the settlement of the final payments was complicated, however, and would eventually come with a coda. As Castlereagh put it in a memorandum in August/September 1818, the 'pecuniary demands' of the Allies were the most important condition that France had to meet in order to obtain an early end to the military occupation of the country.[124] According to him, the amount involved was 280 million francs, as part of the reparations still owing for the years 1819 and 1820, plus what France had to pay to meet the terms of the past year. As was the case in 1817, France was simply not in a position to pay that amount directly from the treasury, and would have to secure another loan with Baring. That loan, he explained, would then be covered by individuals, so that the money was safely invested. Such a 'precautionary principle' gave the Allies 'every security which the joint credit of the French Government and of the contractors can give to it'. The French government could only refuse the credit if it went bankrupt, and the 'private contractors' were in it for their own benefit. No one, therefore, would profit from undermining the 'public credit' of the state. There was, at most, the risk that enforcing payments from the 'rentes held by the contractors' could have a detrimental effect on the money in Great Britain, 'this side of the water'. Castlereagh did have foresight in that regard. But for the time being, it seemed that the occupation forces' leaving would not immediately lead to payment insecurity.

---

[120] Cited in Veve, *The Duke of Wellington and the British Army of Occupation in France*, 155.
[121] Ibid., 155–6.
[122] See 'Protocole' of 1 and 2 October 1818, AT-OeStA/HHStA, StK, Kongressakten, inv. no. 17, Subfolder 'Protokolle', Aachen 1818, 5–7.
[123] See Jarrett, *The Congress of Vienna and its Legacy*, 184.
[124] Memorandum, August/September 1818, TNA, FO 92/34.

Conversations about the final payments could build on the earlier work of the Allied Council in Paris. With Wellington as chairman of the Military Committee and commander-in-chief of the occupation forces, it had already worked out and written up how the occupation could be ended and which financial transactions still needed to transpire. At eight o'clock in the evening of 9 October, the Council's document was signed by the five states at Metternich's accommodations in Aix-la-Chapelle.[125] This convention, made available to the public, manifestly showed how much completing the European peace and security system was based on the financial guarantees of European bankers.[126] In Article IV of the Convention, the sum that France still owed the Allies, stemming from the Treaty of Paris on 20 November 1815, was calculated at 265 million francs. That amount was based on the six terms of the indemnification that had not yet been paid (6 × 46,666,666 = 279,999,996), less the 15 million francs for the interest that the Allies did not have coming because the payment was to be made two years earlier than originally planned (in 1818, instead of in 1820). In addition, it was agreed that 165 million would be provided in bank drafts (*traites*) by Baring and Hope in nine monthly instalments, starting on 6 January 1819, after the Allied troops had left France. To finance this amount, France secured a loan with these two banking houses, which issued *rentes* to the tune of 6,615,944 francs for this purpose. Four Allied depository auditors would oversee the payments.[127] By organizing payments in this way, there seemed to be enough supervisory mechanisms in place, and the risk was spread between private investors, the bankers and the French treasury.

Yet this Allied payment mechanism did not run as smoothly as in 1817. Before the ink was even dry on the contract with Baring, Castlereagh voiced his concerns. The promised payment of 100 million francs was based on 'the double security of the contractors and the French government'. But was the loan of 165 million not based too heavily on the 'personal security' of Barings Bank alone? 'Suppose French *Rentes* to fall, and these houses to be ruined', Castlereagh wrote to Wellington with a worried tone.[128] His disquiet was justified, because that is exactly what happened at the end of October – *rentes*

---

[125] 'Zusammenkunft der Monarchen in Aachen', *Oesterreichischer Beobachter*, 17 October 1818, 1514; see also the French newspaper, *Le Moniteur*, 6 October 1818.

[126] See the Convention of 9 October 1818, Articles IV–VIII. See also 'protocole' of 9 October 1818, plus annexes, AT-OeStA/HHStA, StK, Kongressakten, inv. no. 17, Subfolder 'Protokolle', Aachen 1818, 30–2.

[127] These were Adrian Nicolas Joseph Baron Barbier for Austria, the Briton James Drummond, the Prussian Joseph Piautaz and for Russia Adolph André Baron de Mérian Falkach. Drummond and Barbier had also been involved with the Allied Council's Finance Committee.

[128] Castlereagh to Wellington, 10 October; Baring to Wellington, 11 October 1818, *WSD*, vol. 12, 761–3.

prices fell. Bond holders were probably concerned that the Allied Occupation Army's departure would lead to new instability in France and a devaluation of their *rentes*. Which is why they flooded the market with selling orders, making it impossible for the Baring–Hope consortium to sell the *rentes* for the old price.[129] Moreover, the Banque de France had counted on too high an increase in prices and had sold *rentes* at too great a discount. France's ability to meet its payment obligation was being threatened, because interest was to be paid every year on all those *rentes*. Unlike in 1817, the market panicked for a while in the light of falling prices. More and more British investors threw their holdings into the market, causing the price to drop from 76 to 71 francs. The stock exchanges collapsed and the bankers talked about not being able to meet their obligations to provide France with hard cash, which in turn would have consequences for France's payment to the Allies. The financial adventure almost ended in a catastrophe. Because this financial arrangement was too big to fail for everyone involved, the Allied ministers reconvened to renegotiate matters during the final weeks of the Conference of Aix-la-Chapelle.[130] Metternich, Nesselrode and Hardenberg had all invested personally in the loan.[131]

In mid-November the ministers adjusted the 9 October convention to allow France to postpone paying what it owed.[132] The 6,615,944 francs in *rentes* that France had granted to Austria, Britain, Prussia and Russia (as a counterpart to the agreed-upon 165 million) was entered into the General Ledger on 5 October 1818 and would remain ('frozen', that is, uncirculated) in the hands of the Allied plenipotentiaries until 5 June 1820, after which they were payable within nine months, through to 1 March 1821. In doing so, the Allies granted the banks and the French government a delay of eighteen months. The *Oesterreichischer Beobachter* was relieved to report that this measure would probably put an end to the selfish behaviour of financially adventurous speculators.[133] The postponement was officially ratified in a convention on 2 February 1819.[134] That agreement was drawn up and signed in Paris by the four ambassadors (who in effect took up their discussions again as the Allied

[129] Oosterlinck, Ureche-Rangau and Vaslin, 'Baring, Wellington and the Resurrection of French Public Finances', 1084–5.

[130] Baring to Wellington, 30 October 1818, *WSD*, vol. 12, 789–94; see also White, 'Making the French Pay', 347; Greenfield, 'Financing a New Order', 399.

[131] See Oosterlinck, Ureche-Rangau and Vaslin, 'Baring, Wellington, and the Resurrection of French Public Finances', 1084–5.

[132] Wellington to Baring, 4 November 1818, *WSD*, vol. 12, 816–17. See also protocol of 19 November 1818, Aachen; protocol and addenda, 15 November 1818, AT-OeStA /HHStA, StK, Kongressakten, inv. no. 17, Subfolder 'Protokolle', Aachen 1818, 183, 192–4.

[133] 'Frankreich', *Oesterreichischer Beobachter*, 12 November 1818, 1649–50.

[134] Convention of 2 February 1819, *Journal des Débats*, 21 February 1819.

Council) and by the Marquis Desolles on behalf of France. (On 29 December 1818, Richelieu had been replaced by a new government in France under the leadership of foreign minister Jean Joseph Marquis Desolles. Baron Louis had once again become the minister of finance, as he had been under Napoleon.)[135] The Allies were thus able to retain the certainty of being paid, and the bankers had more time to sell their current *rentes* on the market at a good price. It would take a few years, but in the end France was able fulfil all its obligations. That was an immense achievement, but one that the French government could not have honoured without the help of European investors. They were in turn convinced that investing in the French debt was a safe venture. Of course, the loans from Baring and Hope, the pressure from the Allies and the willingness that France showed to introduce constitutional reforms were also crucial to this endeavour. Financial, economic and political security completed the circle.[136]

To visibly demonstrate their satisfaction with France's accomplishment, the ministers looked for an opportunity to celebrate this financial feat as the foundation of the new security order. On 9 November, Louis Antoine, Duke of Angoulême, made a personal appearance in Aix-la-Chapelle. Visibly to all, and with loud jubilation, he was received by the representatives of the great powers, also for a splendid dinner in their midst, as an equal, and as a representative of the French crown. Even though the Quadruple Alliance continued to exist, and France was not a full member of that alliance, the window dressing of France's glory had in any case been restored. The reproach and the humiliation of it all were shed. The duke actually did not feel very comfortable in that position of being favoured in grace. He stayed in the city for only twenty-four hours and then quickly took his leave.[137] The conference, however, was not over yet.

Yet Another Guarantee?

The business side of the security order was arranged for, but another burning interest that moved the Allied Machine needed addressing – the desire for political and social security. Here, the emotional vocabulary still diverged widely. Tsar Alexander was afraid that the anti-revolutionary consensus of 1815 might well be disintegrating. That is why, in the months preceding the conference, he had worked with Kapodistrias (but without Pozzo di Borgo) on a grand plan to protect the safety of the current thrones and sovereigns from

---

[135] Baron Louis had been minister under Napoleon, and from 1 April 1814 to 10 March 1815, and again from 9 July to 26 September 1815, under Louis XVIII.

[136] Oosterlinck, Ureche-Rangau and Vaslin, 'Baring, Wellington, and the Resurrection of French Public Finances', 1085, 1097–9.

[137] 'Preussen', *Oesterreichischer Beobachter*, 20 November 1818, 1689.

the spirit of terror – in short, a renewed attempt to put the Holy Alliance into practice and give it institutional and military clout.[138] The plan provided for a 'common league, guaranteeing to each other the existing order of things, in Thrones as well as in Territories'.[139] It was officially intended to suppress new revolutionary threats, exemplified in the reforms and patriotic uprisings among citizens and students throughout Europe, and to obligate each other as military allies to provide mutual military assistance. Unofficially, the tsar tried to counterbalance the, in his eyes, Austrian–British dominance within the Allied Council.

When Alexander and Castlereagh met for the first time on 27 September, Alexander got right to the point. Unlike Pozzo di Borgo, the tsar was first of all highly concerned about the situation in France. According to him, nine tenths of the French people were 'either corrupted by bad principles or violent party sentiments, and the remainder had little experience or ability in conducting a government, especially one of a constitutional description'. Unlike Castlereagh or Metternich, who – using the terms of power politics – spoke of balance and precaution, Alexander's infatuation with mesmerism, which had captivated his mind in late 1815, remained robustly manifest. According to the tsar, the French patient was still critically ill, and subject to a 'violent malady' that could lead to all sorts of convulsions. Given those circumstances, the tsar was an avid proponent of maintaining the Quadruple Alliance. He was not interested in expanding his own territory, but solely lobbied for the implementation of a 'moral guarantee', a medicine to cure France of its moral decay and deadly disease.[140]

On 8 October, Alexander presented his plan to the other ministers, who met to discuss the matter on 14 October.[141] The Quadruple Alliance was a start, but a broader 'general alliance' was called for, to which all the signatories of the Final Act of the Congress of Vienna could be admitted. This alliance should confirm the current 'state of possessions' and guarantee the 'inviolability of territories as well as their legitimate representatives, or, in other terms, the principle of legitimacy'. Europe's current peace and security had come to it by the hand of Providence and had to be protected against the 'evil' of political and moral 'egoism'. This proposal, therefore, was not to replace the Holy

[138] See the Russian Foreign Ministry's memorandum of 24 June 1818, in Ministerstvo inostrannykh del CCCP (ed.), *Vneshniaia politika Rossii*, vol. 2, 409–23.
[139] Castlereagh's description, Castlereagh to Bathurst, 19 October 1818, TNA, FO 92/35, 138–47.
[140] Castlereagh to Bathurst, 3 October 1818, TNA, FO 92/35, 10–17.
[141] Via a letter from Nesselrode and Kapodistrias to Castlereagh and Wellington, 8 October 1818, *WSD*, vol. 12, 742–51. On 14 October, the ministers of all five powers met to discuss the matter. 'Projet de protocole', 14 October 1818, *WSD*, vol. 12, 770–3. See also the accompanying letter and the original memorandum addressed to Metternich, 8 October 1818, AT-OeStA/HHStA, StK, inv. no. 17, 33–56.

Alliance, but to give it a more solid political and concrete footing. Alexander wanted to link the alliance to a new military treaty that included a guarantee clause that defined the criteria for a *casus foederis*. Bulwark Europe needed more than just fortifications; it also had to have an automatic intervention clause to activate it militarily as the need arose. The tsar was not asking this just for himself, but 'in the interest of the entire universe'.[142]

Interestingly enough, Alexander, in making this proposal, was not the reactionary that others later made him out to be. His fear of terror also had a legal and legitimate component. For him, the danger consisted of a twofold threat: 'the return of revolutions, and the presumption that might makes right'. In other words, the tsar was indeed concerned about the possibility of a revolution, but he was equally engaged in maintaining the restored balance of power and the international resolve against new, one-sided aggression. In the latter case, he was rearticulating his earlier commitment to legal reforms. From 1814 on, he had made a strong case for a constitution on the home front, and international treaties and alliances in international relations. Now, in 1818, he went one step further and drew another innovative idea from his sleeve: a military-strategic one. The only adequate answer to the double threat of terror was, according to the Russian court, a *fédération armée*, set up by the parties of the Second Treaty of Paris. Such a military federation would be internationally and legally sanctioned (by the treaties of Chaumont, Vienna and Paris, on the basis of the 'law of the nations'), and militarily powerful enough to thereby also become a 'moral' barrier against new revolutions and seizures of power. The Quadruple Alliance would establish this federation on the basis of the agreements on 'mutual security' as laid down in the Treaty of Chaumont.[143] All the signatories of the treaties of Vienna and Paris could then join this alliance. The tsar clearly saw this proposal as part of the four great powers' legacy to Europe. He was convinced that by having the sovereigns take on obligations for mutual solidarity now, such an alliance would explicitly take an advance on 'the future', in order to stabilize European peace for the long term against 'the evil genius of revolutions or conquests'.[144]

Metternich and Gentz could thus follow Alexander's desire for a 'moral guarantee'.[145] Such a guarantee, after all, could also be brought to bear on any future Prussian and Russian attempts at territorial extension or possible

---

[142] Jarrett, *The Congress of Vienna and its Legacy*, 186; see also the Russian Foreign Ministry's memorandum of 24 June 1818, in Ministerstvo inostrannykh del CCCP (ed.), *Vneshniaia politika Rossii*, vol. 2, 409–23.

[143] See 'Projet de Protocole', 14 October 1818, *WSD*, vol. 12, 772.

[144] Nesselrode and Kapodistrias to Wellington and Castlereagh, including 'Mémoire confidentiel du cabinet de Russie', 8 October 1818, *WSD*, vol. 12, 742–51, here 743 and 748.

[145] Annex to protocol of 19 October, 'Principes unités', 19 October 1818, AT-OeStA /HHStA, StK, Kongressakten, inv. no. 17, Subfolder 'Protokolle', Aachen 1818, 61–3, here: 61b.

(military-Jacobin) seizures of power. The Austrians were also not complete strangers to Alexander's mesmeristic semantics (they had come to know the tsar and his exaltations over the last four years). For them, the tsar's contribution was important enough; it gave the metaphor of the 'balance of power' the moral content it clearly needed. Gentz even reiterated Alexander's style and spoke in medical idioms about the sick patient, describing how 'all European countries, without exception, are tormented by a burning fever, the companion or forerunner of the most violent convulsions which the civilised world has seen since the fall of the Roman Empire'.[146] The Austrian and British ministers' question, however, was whether Alexander's medicine of iron and armour offered the solution. They felt that such an *Alliance Solidarité* went too far and was also superfluous. The Quadruple Alliance had meanwhile proved itself; 'the destruction of that system would be a dreadful calamity'. A new alliance, which would irrevocably give Russia, France, Spain and Italy more power, would upset the existing balance of power. As Gentz explained to Metternich, such an alliance 'would have certainly provoked a counter combination between Austria, Prussia, and England'. Alexander's idea, to have the Quadruple Alliance exist alongside his new general alliance,[147] would also be too confusing for 'the powers of the second and third rank', or lead to all sorts of misunderstandings and double agendas – if, say, a (small) power was not able to safeguard its interests through one alliance, it could simply appeal to the other group or, even worse, play the two alliances off against each other. When it came to domestic troubles, Alexander's call for a 'moral' guarantee was just too confusing, and even too threatening – any uprising could in theory be perceived as an open invitation to Moscow to come and 'help' the sitting government. For Metternich and Gentz, the Quadruple Alliance already had such an explicit domestic task in 'preserving the old order of society, or at least to moderate and soften the changes which are indispensable'.[148]

Prussia had similar misgivings regarding Tsar Alexander's imaginings. A year earlier, on 18 October 1817, a student-organized combined festival commemorating the Battle of Leipzig (1813) and the 300th anniversary of the Reformation turned into patriotic protests and the call for democratic reforms. Now, a year later, as the monarchs prepared for their memorial service in Aix-la-Chapelle, the students assembled again. As they saw it, the Congress of Vienna had not gone far

---

[146] Gentz, 'Denkschrift. Die Ergebnisse des Aachener Congresses', to Metternich, November 1818, in Metternich (ed.), *Memoirs*, vol. 3, 190–6, here: 193. See also 'Remarques de M. de Gentz', 14 October 1818, AT-OeStA/HHStA, StK, Kongressakten, Aachen 1818, inv. no. 17, 67–9.

[147] See 'Mémoire confidentiel', 8 October, *WSD*, vol. 12, 748.

[148] Metternich, 'Aperçu sommaire de la situation au 1er Novembre 1818'; Gentz, 'Denkschrift. Die Ergebnisse des Aachener Congresses', to Metternich, November 1818, *Aus Metternichs Nachgelassenen Papieren*, vol. 1.2, 161–70; in translation: *Memoirs*, vol. 3, 191, 192 and 194.

enough, deliberately leaving off opportunities to make Europe not only more peaceful, but also more modern and democratic. In Jena, they founded the *Allgemeine Deutsche Burschenschaft* – a league of university students – to call for the unification of Germany and political reforms. Their efforts, however, were in vain. The governments of Prussia and other German states responded to this national-liberal movement with repressive measures and laws. Would the intervention clause that Alexander was proposing lead to other European countries interfering in German affairs? With this kind of thing in mind, Hardenberg and his security advisors focused mainly on manning the fortifications as a military and territorial guarantee. They were not inclined to wait for a political-moral alliance under Alexander's purview, or to follow the tsar in his liberal ideas on constitutions and federations. Instead, Metternich and the Prussian ministers were already working on something similar, but on their own initiative, within the remit of the German Confederation. A year later, in September 1819, they issued the Decrees of Carlsbad, thereby introducing a series of reactionary restrictions under Metternich's leadership, subscribed to by principal states of the German Confederation, banning university student leagues, among other things. The restrictions were to be enforced via the establishment of a central intelligence centre – the *Mainzer Zentraluntersuchungskommission*. With these provisions, Metternich and Wittgenstein would create their own security policy stronghold for the German Confederation – they therefore felt no need in late 1818 to play along with the tsar's equally far-flung and unpredictable ideas.[149]

For the British, things were even more clear-cut. A new alliance, general or not, was simply out of the question, and a non-negotiated intervention arrangement even more so.[150] The British parliament would never accept an obligation to intervene based on domestic developments or changes in a state's structure or political order. With great difficulty Castlereagh succeeded in helping the tsar to understand that the British situation was different from Russia's when it came to the parliamentary approval and support that such a clause would require. At the same time, Castlereagh was willing to go along with the tsar's preference for a greater degree of mutual commitment. 'We were all agreed upon the substance [of mutual solidarity]. And it was only a question of management.' The 'solid guarantee' that the tsar was looking for did not come in the form a treaty. That was also not necessary, because, according to Castlereagh, such a guarantee was already implied in the existing treaties of Chaumont, Paris and Vienna.[151] In the treaty of the Quadruple Alliance, they had all agreed that the powers would each contribute 60,000 troops in the event of war; and in Articles VII and VIII of the Treaty of Chaumont they had also stipulated that they would help each other when one of

---

[149] See, for example, the description of the meeting in Jena: 'Teutschland', *Oesterreichischer Beobachter*, 31 October 1818, 1587–8. See also Siemann, *Metternich*, 662–701.

[150] Liverpool to Castlereagh, 13 November 1818, *WSD*, vol. 12, 830–1.

[151] Jarrett, *The Congress of Vienna and its Legacy*, 184–94.

the powers was attacked.[152] In the final declaration of 15 November, the wording of the British and the Austrians prevailed: their security idiom was less vengeful than the Prussian, less exalted and alarmist than the Russian and far more carefully and pragmatically formulated. The Aix-la-Chapelle declaration did not refer to moral guarantees and curing convulsions, but was about the sealing of European peace and order based on existing treaties and the established form of joint consultation based on Article VI of the Quadruple Alliance.[153] On 4 November, the ministers had sent Richelieu an official memorandum inviting France to participate in future 'deliberations consecrated to the maintenance of peace'.[154]

The closing declaration of Aix-la-Chapelle, then, enigmatically referred to very divergent expectations about those future consultations. The metaphor of Europe's 'balance of power' left room for conflicting interpretations. The Russians had realized that all other cabinets were 'frightened by the mere idea of a general alliance' and that plans for constructing any type of new treaty organization had to be abandoned.[155] Yet, according to Tsar Alexander, an informal gentleman's agreement on military solidarity had been reached between the Allies, to assist each other when thrones or borders were being threatened. Even without a treaty, the 'grand alliance' had gained more support, and the *réunion* should thus be qualified as a 'success' and a confirmation of the 'most intimate union between the Allied powers'.[156]

The takeaway for Metternich and Gentz was a mutual moral responsibility to prevent or combat abrupt revolutionary turmoil. Gentz also did not take the 'balance of power' metaphor to imply a rigid fixation on the status quo. The Austrian documents clearly leave room for gradual change. By contrast, the British maintained that a gentleman's agreement on intervention had not been made at all. The Quadruple Alliance was allowed to take action only in the event of war and was not to interfere in political reforms and internal affairs. Bathurst had also urged his minister Castlereagh to keep the 'deliberative system' modest. Doing so would avoid arousing jealousy among the other powers. If France showed that she could ensure domestic peace and order, then all those conferences were no longer necessary. Article VI should not be abolished, but the

---

[152] Wellington, 'Memorandum upon the force to be employed by the Quadruple Alliance in case of a war', 5 November 1818, *WSD*, vol. 12, 817–19.

[153] Jarrett, *The Congress of Vienna and its Legacy*, 194. Final Declaration, Aix-la-Chapelle. Protocol no. 33 and 34, of 15 November 1818, AT-OeStA/HHStA, StK, Kongressakten, inv. no. 17, 157–71.

[154] Veve, *The Duke of Wellington and the British Army of Occupation in France*, 157.

[155] Kapodistrias to Alexander, 'Marche de la négociation', 20 October/1 November 1818, in Ministerstvo inostrannykh del CCCP (ed.), *Vneshniaia politika Rossii*, vol. 2, 531–3.

[156] Memorandum 'du ministère de Russie après les conferences d'Aix-la-Chapelle', 19/31 December 1818, in Ministerstvo inostrannykh del CCCP (ed.), *Vneshniaia politika Rossii*, vol. 2, 611–19, here: 611.

mechanism also did not have to be used so intensively as in the previous years. Bathurst's suggestion was that they set a date for one new conference; that would satisfy France, but would also make it clear that possible further actions would be the outcome of a deliberative decision and not mere automatism.[157]

The Allied ministers' very different readings and interpretations of the Aix-la-Chapelle Declaration would have serious consequences after 1818. In the years after Aix, some ministers would appeal to the final declaration to legitimize their intervention in the event of domestic unrest and revolution and to request assistance from their colleagues. However, Aix's final declaration was, in the eyes of liberal and radical movements, also a substantial document – in a negative sense. They took it to be – as was earlier the case for the Holy Alliance – a veritable declaration of war on the principles of freedom and national unification, even although that had not been the underlying rationale at the time at all. The Ottoman Porte was not comfortable with it either. Given the British and Russian movements near its borders, it kept asking for all kinds of assurances and explanations.[158]

The Declaration of Aix-la-Chapelle was, therefore, not just window dressing. It was not perceived to be such, and its military consequences proved that assessment to be accurate. It did institutionalize a European congress system, including procedures for convening European states. In fact, it was perhaps the most concrete and practical translation of the vague and ambiguous metaphor of the European 'balance of power': first of all, in inviting France to sign on to Article VI of the Quadruple Alliance, but perhaps even more so in the concrete agreements regarding the fortifications and the troops that would occupy them. Although the Russian plan for a 'League of Thrones and Territories', as well as a Prussian-inspired lighter version, which included a declaration of assurance regarding existing boundaries, did not pass muster, a secret, but nonetheless substantial protocol was added to the conference's declaration of 15 November. That protocol was drafted by the Duke of Wellington as commander of the occupation forces. It stipulated that within two months of an eventual *casus foederis*, troops from each of the four Allied powers in Europe would be called up and move out together as an Allied coalition. These troops would assemble at the fortifications of the Wellington Barrier and, further south, at the fortresses in Germany. This secret protocol, then, not only provided for a deterrent presence, but did so in terms of specific physical locations and the allocation of troops.[159]

---

[157] Bathurst to Castlereagh, 20 October 1818, TNA, FO 92/34.
[158] Stürmer to Metternich, 25 December 1818, HHStA, StAbt, Türkei VI, 8, Berichte, 1818–1820.
[159] Wellington, 'Memorandum', 5 November 1818; definitive version, 'Reserved protocol – Quadruple Alliance' and 'Protocole Militaire', 15 November 1818, WSD, vol. 12, 817–19, 835–7. See also the protocol and appendices, 15 November 1818, AT-OeStA/HHStA, StK, Kongressakten, inv. no. 17, Subfolder 'Protokolle', Aachen 1818, 157–72.

In connection with this secret protocol, it was proposed that an Allied observation force be permanently stationed in the Netherlands to man the forts of the Wellington Barrier and as visible proof of the fact that the Allies did not only deliberate together, but also stood ready collectively to take action as a military force[160] – not as a convention-based obligation to intervene, but simply as a visible sign of their intended deterrence potential. That permanent observation force was not constituted straight away, and when it was, it took on a different form. However, all the powers did ratify the provision that a joint Allied army could be mobilized in the event of war and could ready itself via the forts.[161] In linking the Aix-la-Chapelle declaration to the construction of the fortifications and the Wellington Barrier, a formal treaty-enforced balance of deterrence was created to which all the great powers had also committed themselves.

On Farewell Tour

On 16 October 1818, those gathered in Aix-la-Chapelle ratified the treaty on the evacuation of troops from France. Wellington officiated over that signing and was able to formally announce the conclusion of the occupation of France.[162] He left immediately thereafter for Valenciennes in northern France to preside as commander-in-chief of the Allied Occupation Army over one final grand review of the European troops. That, too, was a popular way in which to demonstrate and celebrate Europe's military strength and unity. The role-play involved depicted a battle between Europe's army and 'the enemy' – consisting of a joint cohort of British troops and Russian Cossacks. On 22 and 23 October, under Wellington's direction, British, Saxon, Hanoverian and Russian troops stole the show, while Tsar Alexander and the king of Prussia and their entourage looked on. Veterans of Waterloo, including the Dutch crown prince, a number of German princes and General Müffling were also in attendance.[163]

Alexander then went on to inspect Wellington's British cohorts, after which the group rode on to the fortress of Sedan. The farewell tour had to be completed with decorum and in style. Wellington had personally arranged for about sixty horses to be kept at the ready at each resting place between Aix-la-Chapelle and Valenciennes. He had also received serious rumours from the Netherlands that after the review of the troops an attempt

---

[160] 'Project of the Formation of an European Army under the Command of the Duke of Wellington', November 1818, WSD, vol. 12, 809–11.

[161] Jarrett, The Congress of Vienna and its Legacy, 194–7.

[162] Bathurst to Castlereagh, 16 October 1818, TNA, FO 92/34.

[163] Wellington to Murray, 6 October 1818; Wellington to Woronzow, 6 October 1818; to Campbell; to Murray, 7 October 1818; to Baron Constant, 13 October, WSD, vol. 12, 734–8, 765.

would made on the tsar's life while he was to make a detour via Brussels. To play it safe, Wellington advised Van Nagell, the Dutch minister of foreign affairs, to station as many cavalry and gendarmes as possible along the route from Liège to Brussels, but not to take too many further measures. He felt that overly attending to such precautions always implies 'a certain degree of ridicule', and would not please the emperor.[164] Everything went well. The affair was substantial enough, but the alleged French and Belgian conspirators were arrested in time, the weather was beautiful and the inspection proceeded without a hitch.[165] On the return journey from Valenciennes and Sedan to Aix-la-Chapelle, the dignitaries made another detour to meet with King Louis XVIII. This important visit was over by the beginning of November, and they were back in Aix for the final negotiations.

On 5 November, Tsar Alexander I expressed his thanks to Wellington by naming him Marshal of Russia; Emperor Franz I handed him the baton of Field Marshal of Austria (and an infantry regiment in Erbach); and King Friedrich Wilhelm III granted him the same honour for Prussia.[166] The talks about the South American colonies took a bit longer than expected, but by the end of November the conference was concluded. Three weeks earlier, the Allied troops had begun evacuating the territories they had occupied, exiting France according to agreed-upon lines of march, and dismantling their arms depots and camps as they left. Wellington had promised the French government that his troops would be gone by 30 November. Part of the Russian, Prussian and German armies headed east via the Netherlands. Another column crossed the Rhine near Mannheim. The Austrian troops had already passed the Rhine on 1 November, and had evacuated France entirely by 11 November. British troops, including their supplies, food, wood and ammunition, sailed home via Calais. The tsar left on 16 November, via the Netherlands. Because of the threat of plots against his life, he was accompanied by a military escort, which, as mentioned, had been given strict instructions not to let itself be noticed by the tsar.[167]

The fortresses in northern France were handed over to French commissioners and commanders in the presence of Wellington on 18 and

---

[164] Wellington to Van Nagell, 9 November 1818, *WSD*, vol. 12, 821–2.

[165] Wellington to Van Nagell, 12 November 1818, *WSD*, vol. 12, 829–30; Van Nagell, 'Details of Plot to Seize the Emperor of Russia', 17 November 1818, *WSD*, vol. 12, 840–4. See also for more details on this quite forgotten conspiracy: N.N., *Arrêts de la cour d'assises du Brabant Méridional, précédés de l'acte d'accusation et du plaidoyer, prononcé par M. le Substitut du Procureur-Général, dans l'affaire du complot contre la personne de S. M. l'Empereur de toutes les Russies* (Brussels, 1819), 5, in NL-HaNA, 2.05.44, inv. no. 8.

[166] Wellington to Bathurst, 5 November 1818; Franz I (Austrian emperor) to Wellington, 15 November; Friedrich Wilhelm III to Wellington, 16 November, *WSD*, vol. 12, 819, 839.

[167] Wellington to General Tripp, 15 November 1818, *WSD*, vol. 12, 832.

19 November. With barely disguised impatience, the French were at that very moment recruiting young men to man the fortresses and fortifications that Allies had just vacated with their 'own' French armed forces. France had paid the price of peace, and could not wait to demonstrate its newly acquired freedom and autonomy in the previously occupied territories.[168] The peasants in and around Cambrai were also extremely relieved that the British troops would no longer be stomping through their fields and crops while revelling in their favourite pastime (after confiscating the local wine) – hunting.[169] The head of the French civil administration there, the prefect du Nord, had taken ill and could not personally wave Wellington off. He nevertheless sent a letter with his equally honest and expansive praises. He thanked Wellington for the 'appropriate discipline ... to which we owe the good harmony that has been maintained between the troops and the inhabitants'. It was not always easy to maintain that harmony, but thanks to 'the excellent conduct of the British troops, and the zeal with which the officers and generals have constantly supported the views of Your Grace, [they were able] to lighten as much as possible the burden of the occupation'. Wellington kindly thanked him for this somewhat awkward compliment, noting that he was sorry if his efforts had not always had the intended effect.[170]

Wellington himself took leave of his troops in his own characteristic way. On 7 October, he had already given his aide-de-camp Murray the order to beginning planning the routes for the evacuation. With *ordre du jour* number 21, dated the end of October, he thanked all the commanders, liaison officers and military personnel for the three years that they had served under him. On 10 November he repeated his thanks to his own British soldiers. Had it not been for the 'conciliatory conduct' of the generals, commanders and officers, and for the discipline of their subordinates, the occupation would not have been as successful as it was. With deep feelings of 'regret', *le Feld Maréchal* took leave of his troops, and promised that he would keep a 'keen interest' in their well-being and further career. It was a promise that he held himself to in the future. Many soldiers who later turned to him in their times of – usually financial – need could count on his responding.[171]

On 27 November Wellington received a letter of deep appreciation from Bathurst, on behalf of the Prince Regent; Castlereagh received his letter of congratulations from them on 4 December. He had anticipated a favourable conclusion, Bathurst wrote, but he was very happy that it had now indeed

[168] Note of Wellington to Murray, 7 October 1818, *WSD*, vol. 12, 739.

[169] See, for example, correspondence, 4 December 1817, TNA, WO 55, inv. no. 1540.

[170] Letter of Préfet du Nord to Wellington, 25 October 1818; Wellington's response, 6 November 1818, *WSD*, vol. 12, 784, 819–20.

[171] 'Ordre du Jour', no. 21. Prepared by Murray for Wellington; 'General Order', 10 November 1818, *WSD*, vol. 12, 794–6, 826. See also Veve, *The Duke of Wellington and the British Army of Occupation in France*, 158–62.

materialized. Others also wanted 'harmony', but the favourable outcome was nonetheless due to the 'ingenuous' performance of Castlereagh and Wellington.[172]

On 5 December 1818, the Allied Council in Paris, composed of Charles Stuart, Karl Friedrich von der Goltz, Karl von Vincent and Carlo Andrea Pozzo di Borgo, also solemnly celebrated its last session. The dignitaries and ministers present in Aix-la-Chapelle (Metternich, Castlereagh, Hardenberg, Bernstorff, Nesselrode and Kapodistrias) had already dissolved the Allied Council in a letter dated 22 November. 'The Protocol of the Ministerial Conferences in Paris is considered closed' – and with that, the ministers shut the door behind them. Protocol 307 was the last binding document of the Allied Council. This did not mean, however, that the ministers would no longer be seeing each other. While the Council, 'as regarding matters relating to the military occupation of French territory, and to executing the peace treaty of 20 November 1815', was formally disbanded, the envoys continued on as ambassadors, in an 'ambassadorial conference'.[173]

They did indeed keep meeting regularly as representatives of the *Cinq Courts Médiatrices*, the Five Mediating Courts, but now also with a representative of the French court. In the context of ordinary ambassadors' conferences, these representatives of the five powers would from now on further mediate, for example, the question of the Spanish and Portuguese colonies in South America. The ministers in Aix-la-Chapelle had also left room for this. The Allies retained the right to hold new conferences 'in view of other matters of general interest' or 'as circumstances required', as they had previously announced in the letter of 22 November dissolving the Allied Council. In doing so, they were implicitly acknowledging a number of unresolved disputes concerning indemnities and liquidations between other allied countries that had requested the Council to act as mediators in this regard. However, the group – which was now referred to as an 'ambassadors' conference' or as 'mediators of the five powers' – lacked two crucial means of power: an Allied occupation army and a charismatic leader. The Prince of Waterloo – *l'homme de l'Europe* – had repeatedly been the decisive factor in crucial or deadlocked discussions. Yet Wellington had now returned to London, where he joined the cabinet of Lord Liverpool in December 1818. The deliberations, therefore, took on a different character; the status of both the members and the conference had been degraded somewhat.

[172] Letter of Bathurst, 13 November, 4 December 1818, TNA, FO 92/34; Bathurst to Wellington, 27 November 1818, *WSD*, vol. 12, 851–2.
[173] Letter of Metternich et al. to the Allied Council in Paris, 22 November 1818, (annex to protocol 307); protocol no. 307, 5 December 1818, TNA, FO 146/30, 310–13.

Müffling's New Assignment

Although the driving force behind the Allied Machine, the Allied Council, had been relieved of its duty, the engine kept running for a while. Müffling, Wellington's former adjutant and governor of Paris, received new orders in 1818. These flowed from the secret agreements that the four powers had reached in Aix-la-Chapelle in a separate protocol regarding the fortifications.[174] This commission was as surprising to Müffling as it was welcome – at first, that is.

Just like Kraijenhoff, Müffling, after completing his duties as governor of Paris, had concentrated on more military-technical activities, in particular, starting in 1816, on mapping the area around the Rhine and the line between Dunkirk (northern France) and Seeberg (Switzerland) using triangular measurements.[175] As was the case with Kraijenhoff in the Netherlands (whom he knew well), Müffling was part of a new caste of officers who had not been appointed based on their name or family history, but who stood out given a combination of professionalism, openness to new scientific insights and the transnational exchange of these ideas. Müffling gave lectures in Paris, had been the assistant of Professor Zach at the Seeberg Observatory in Gotha (Germany) and maintained correspondence with a variety of colleagues throughout Europe. Kraijenhoff's learning came from Dutch mathematicians and physicists and French cartographers and geodesists. He himself also wrote works on cartography and hydraulics.[176] In 1819, invited by the Prussian government as one of the *grands techniciens* of Europe, he travelled to Cologne and Koblenz to view the fortifications and fortresses there of the German Confederation.[177] Both Wellington and Willem I valued the knowledge and skills of these kinds of officers highly, and gave them broad responsibilities and power – as long as the steps they took did not interfere with the *raison d'état*.

Müffling's new assignment placed him at the crossroads of military and political as well as national and Allied interests. It had to do with manning and maintaining the fortifications of the Wellington Barrier, which by then were fairly well completed. Alexander's 'solidarity alliance', with accompanying intervention obligation, had been rejected, but the ministers in Aix-la-Chapelle had come up with a different security measure. As noted, they had agreed in a separate protocol that, in the event of a threat of war, they would use the ring of fortresses and fortifications around France to congregate and mobilize their troops. The question that remained was how to man them

---

[174] 'Protocole Militaire', 15 November 1818, signed by Metternich, Castlereagh, Hardenberg, Nesselrode, Wellington, Bernstorff and Kapodistrias, *WSD*, vol. 12, 836–7.
[175] Müffling, *The Memoirs*, 278–80.
[176] Ibid.; Uitterhoeve, *Cornelis Kraijenhoff*, 381–93.
[177] Ibid., 336–7.

from day to day. The Netherlands certainly did not have enough of their own armed forces to do so. The secret protocol had, however, set out what would happen should a concrete reason for them to band together arise. Once the *casus foederis* was triggered, within two months, the British corps would gather near Brussels, the Prussians near Cologne, the Austrians near Stuttgart and the Russians, a month later, near Mainz. The British would disembark at Ostend and Antwerp, and then operate from Ostend, Nieuwpoort and Ypres, while also manning the fortifications on the Scheldt. The troops from Prussia and the German Confederation would occupy the citadels of Dinant, Namur, Huy and Liège and the fortresses of Charleroi, Mariembourg and Philippeville. In this way, the Prussian, British and Dutch lines of operation could be connected to each other into a joint allied force. The Dutch king had agreed somewhat grouchily to this in mid-November.[178] As Castlereagh had already laid out in his memorandum of August 1818, it was mainly about facilitating a good sense of cooperation between Prussia and the Netherlands, which together would have to endure the first blows of an eventual new French aggression.

In Aix-la-Chapelle, Wellington and Hardenberg, the Prussian chancellor, gave Müffling the task of further fleshing out the Prussian–Dutch military partnership on behalf of the Quadruple Alliance. This not only involved preparations for joint action in the event of a possible war or attack, but also organizing an effective balance for deterrence in peacetime. The Allied Council had already discussed this before. On 7 November 1815, a 'just and equitable arrangement' had been devised to connect the 'defensive system' of the German Confederation with the Dutch line of defence. For example, the king of the Netherlands had to grant Prussia the right to garrison troops in Luxembourg, as well as the right to appoint the governor and commander of that place. The sovereignty and the civilian administration naturally remained in the hands of Willem I. A similar arrangement held also for Sardinia and Switzerland (which, for the rest, had to remain neutral).[179] But all that was not nearly enough. Metternich, Hardenberg and Wellington were convinced that a joint force in the Dutch and German Rhenish provinces had to be at the ready in peacetime, such that, in the event of a crisis or war, could hold the line until British reinforcements arrived. There was even talk of a 'European Army under the Command of the Duke of Wellington', to which France would also supply a cohort of 10,000 soldiers. That rumour – that the Allies would leave a 'cordon of troops' along the French border – had also made the rounds earlier in July 1818 in the Netherlands, and had made the French envoy, La Tour du Pin, rather nervous.[180] The anonymous correspondent of the

---

[178] Van Nagell to Wellington, 19 November 1818, AT-OeSt/HHStA, StK, Kongressakten, inv. no. 18, Aachen 1818. See also Gils, *De versterkingen van de Wellingtonbarrière*, 19.
[179] Protocol with annex, 7 November 1815, GStA PK, III. HA I. no. 1469.
[180] Clancarty to Castlereagh, 21 July 1818, Vane (ed.), *Correspondence*, vol. 2, 463–5.

Oesterreichischer Beobachter (probably Gentz) tried to reassure its readers in October: the establishment of such an observation force was highly unlikely.[181]

Yet that was precisely what the ministers in Aix-la-Chapelle were still discussing in October and November. There was indeed a plan to have Prussian, Russian and British troops man fortifications within the Netherlands during peacetime as a deterrent.[182] That idea was quickly downsized to an observation force that consisted mainly of Dutch and Prussian troops that would be spearheaded not by Wellington, but by Dutch and Prussian generals. Müffling was charged with the overall command of the Prussian contingents of that proposed international observation force. With this charge, he was also given the mandate to convince the king of the Netherlands that this assistance was necessary and to persuade him to allow his fortresses to be manned in part by Prussian – and, in instances of impending doom, also British – troops.[183]

Thus instructed, Müffling left the Aix-la-Chapelle conference for Brussels straight away – only to find out how small powers' sentiments could frustrate great powers' schemes. Tsar Alexander, the Russian dowager empress, her daughter Anna Pavlovna and the latter's husband, the Prince of Orange (the later king Willem II), had already arrived in Brussels. King Willem I and the Dutch court had settled in the southern Dutch capital to spend the winter months in Brussels. Müffling found an easy access to the king and was given a few hours to explain his plans. When Willem realized what the intention was, he quickly showed Müffling the door. He was not at all interested in even more tutelage and meddling by the Allied ministers. He had come to Brussels for the express purpose of presenting himself to the factious population of the southern Netherlands as an independent sovereign of his new kingdom. He could not and would not again allow himself to be seen as a marionette of the Allies. That he had to accept Prussia's right to appoint the military commander in his Grand Duchy of Luxembourg, and for their troops to be garrisoned there, was bad enough.[184] That that fortress was not a sign of Willem's sovereignty, but proof of his dependence and status as a secondary power, stung. The Dutch king, who kept a close eye on the purse strings, had also not forgotten that the war coffers of Blücher's troops were anything but full – as had been those of the British – and that Prussia's assistance had cost the Dutch treasury dearly, especially in 1815. He was relieved that the Allied Council had been disbanded, and that Paris was no longer imposing its will on the second- and third-ranked

---

[181] 'Weitere Nachrichten aus Aachen bis zum 19. October', *Oesterreichischer Beobachter*, 29 October 1818, 1578.
[182] 'Project of the Formation of an European Army under the Command of the Duke of Wellington', November 1818; Metternich to Wellington, 17 November 1818, *WSD*, vol. 12, 809–11, 840. See also Colenbrander, 'Willem I en de mogendheden', 397–8.
[183] Müffling, *The Memoirs*, 287–8; Wacker, *Die alliierte Besetzung*, 220–3.
[184] See the letter recording this annoyance, the memorandum of Müffling to Wellington, 15 and 17 December 1818, plus a few more notes, *WSD*, vol. 12, 868–74.

powers. With the passing of the pressure of the Allied ministers in Paris, King Willem was in no way compelled or inclined to accept Müffling's proposals.

Prussia's attempt to have the Netherlands contribute to the cost of restoring forts in Luxembourg, which were in a deplorable state – another point on Müffling's agenda – also did not pan out. A somewhat frustrated appeal to Wellington for help in this regard yielded little. The Duke not only altogether agreed with Willem I, but also did not want to impose his say-so on a sovereign. Monies from the French fortress fund were intended for the construction of forts in the Netherlands, and not to be dispersed to Prussia or the German Confederation.[185]

Either way, after Metternich and Wellington had left Brussels, Müffling could no longer turn to them to advocate for or mediate his agenda. Given the shared lack of tact between Willem I and the Prussian general, Müffling's mission was doomed to failure. He stayed in Brussels for another five months, but after a diverse series of terse and fruitless conversations with the Dutch king, he had had enough. He left for Berlin, where Hardenberg asked him to reorganize the Prussian general staff. With the diminishing threat of France and the absence of an active Allied Council of ministers that pulled the strings, nothing came of an international observation force.[186] The fear of French terror had diminished so much in 1818 that Willem I got away with his refusal to cooperate with Prussia. The Allies had to settle for the renewal of the Quadruple Alliance, the secret military protocol of Aix-la-Chapelle and the promised Dutch compliance with a Prussian–British occupation of the forts should war arise. However, work on the forts did continue in earnest for the next few years – a tangible manifestation, on Dutch soil, of the Allies' focus on deterrence and balance.[187]

What Remained

In the 1820s, widow Albertijn from Oudenaarde wrote long letters to the mayor, to the aldermen and to the governor of Flanders. She demanded restitution for the costs she had incurred for billeting eighty British soldiers who were passing through Belgium. She had seen the placards that the Dutch king had had posted, which urged the residents to submit their declarations, which the Dutch government would then recover from the French treasury.[188] She had, however, yet to see a penny for her expenses. What did European

---

[185] Müffling, The Memoirs, 278–90. See also Wellington's letter to Metternich, 22 December 1818, WSD, vol. 12, 874–7.
[186] Müffling, The Memoirs, 289–90.
[187] Wacker, Die alliierte Besetzung, 223.
[188] See, for example, the notice to submit debt claims for the governor of Flanders, De Coninck, 'Avis aux Créanciers qui ont réclamé sous le régime français la liquidation de rentes d'origine Belge', 5 November 1816, SAO, Old Archives, HB no. 583, no. 54.

security mean for her, a poor widow, while the generals and sovereigns celebrated war and peace on the backs of their subjects? But the city council of Oudenaarde had no sympathy for her appeals. It maintained that she had submitted her claim too late. She should have, at the time, simply passed that bill on to her local officers. The city could not begin to reimburse its citizens for feeding and housing Allied troops.[189]

The assurance of the thrones did not automatically imply financial securities for the royal subjects and citizens. That was only the case when the creditors accurately complied with the Allies' requirements, were able to submit detailed proof of payment for the right costs and to fill in the correct claim form – or when they hired (expensive) lawyers to arrange these liquidations for them.[190] By doing so, the Flemish trader Antheunis succeeded in getting his claim accepted. With the help of a business representative and using the correct forms, his claims were paid. In this case, the city of Oudenaarde, via the Dutch commissioners, was able to recover 1,600 francs from the French treasury for butter and charcoal delivered to the French troops. In contrast to the poor widow Albertijn, the tradesman Antheunis knew how to walk the right capitalist route.[191]

What remained of the European security order after 1815 – besides the unpaid bills and lingering declarations for ordinary citizens on the continent?[192] Was the Allied security culture also of benefit to them? Were the efforts to restrict terror in France and abroad with a common security order in any way apparent to them? According to the *Oesterreichischer Beobachter*, 'the entire edifice of civil society' had been rescued by Europe's monarchs. The British *Courier* was much more critical, and had hoped that the ministers in Aix-la-Chapelle would summon de Cortes back to Spain, arrange for the emancipation of Irish Catholics and unite Poland with Prussia. Nothing came of these sorts of 'radical operations' for the time being.[193]

The importance of European cooperation was manifest symbolically in stone and masonry from 1815 on. The new and refurbished fortifications were the most visible result and artefact of that enduring European struggle

---

[189] 'Weduwe Albertijn. Advies op eene rekwest', City Council Oudenaarde, 6 March 1826, SAO, Modern Archives, no. 4666. See also correspondence, SAO, no. 4665. City Council, 24 September 1825–3 January 1828.

[190] See the offerings and services of the law firm Rooman Frères, letter to the mayor of Oudenaarde, 9 April 1816. The lawyer offered the city's mayor to initiate the reimbursement process. See also other successful claims in the same folder, October 1816, SAO, HB VIII.D.b., no. 463/173b. See a sample claim form with explanation, C. Jubelt, 'Avis concernant les réclamations', 2 February 1816, SAO, HB 46, no. 583/73bis.

[191] Correspondence about Antheunis' claim, 1815–1821, SAO, HB VIII.D.b., no. 463/173b. For more debt claims and allocations, see SOA, HB VIII. no. 463/165b.

[192] For more information about languishing damage claims, see Landheer, 'Afrekenen met het Verleden', 206–8, 217–22.

[193] *Oesterreichischer Beobachter*, 19 September 1818, 1373–5.

against terror. They were meant to represent power and protection, explicitly professing the European spirit of order and peace in which they were grounded. Willem I, for example, had the white marble stele removed that Vauban had built into the beautiful facade of the (old) Menin Gate in the city walls around Ypres. The inscription 'Louis XIV' had been engraved in gold letters. Willem turned the stone around and had a new text engraved on the back side and put in place in 1822. That inscription reads (in English translation):

> After Europe found peace and Napoleon had been defeated, Willem I provided the city of Ypres – previously scantily fortified and then surrounded with stronger ramparts by Louis XIV – with new fortifications, after having removed the older ones. Citizens, recently returned under a government that grants you prosperity, feel safe; a magnanimous king, astute through consultation, valiant in his courage, unrelenting in his labour, dedicates himself wholeheartedly to your security. *Anno* 1820.[194]

The role of the Allied Council was here briefly reduced to 'consultation', and a single reference to 'Europe'. The sovereignty and heroic role of the Dutch king came first. In the citadel in Ghent, the role of the Wellington Barrier was emphasized and underlined. In the monumental entrance gate was chiselled *Nemo me impune lacesset*, and *Anno XI post proelium ad Waterloo extructa* – 'erected in the eleventh year after the Battle of Waterloo'.[195]

Whether the people of Belgium actually 'felt safe' with those fortresses, as the inscription on the Menin Gate proclaimed, was open for debate. Yet the memory of war and terror did not fade away immediately. The emotional vocabulary of the Allied Council echoed through in the manifold poems and inscriptions on Europe's peace, order and security. The sloping hills of Waterloo remained a permanent destination and even pilgrimage site for rulers, princes, diplomats and their contemporaries. After the Aix-la-Chapelle Conference, most participants travelled on to Brussels, where the court of King Willem I, and his son, Crown Prince Willem, with his wife, Anna Pavlovna, the sister of the tsar, ceremoniously received them. On 26 November, Wellington took Metternich on a walk down memory lane, to Waterloo. The company left for the fields of Waterloo in three carriages, recalling, according to a local newspaper, the 'immortal drama of the value of the Allied armies and the genius of the great captain who commanded

---

[194] Commemorative stone from the old Menin Gate, which was torn down after Belgium became independent; only the stele remains, and can still be seen from the Rijselpoort (or Lille Gate). Latin text (*sic*): *Pacata Europa subverso Napoleonte Gulielmus I Urbem Iprensem olim vale munieam a Ludovico XIV. Validioribus propugnculis cirxlmdatam novis denvo suppressis allies niumittonibus restituit civs felici imperio neiper restitu sicupupi estote. Rex magnanimous consilio sagm animo fortis labore indefessus. Incolumitati vestræ toto iectore incumbit. Anno MDCCCXX.*

[195] Gils, *De versterkingen van de Wellingtonbarrière*, 65.

them'.[196] Now, three years later, the 'ingenious' commander and his equally brilliant political companion were clearly moved by the historical importance of that tangible symbol of the Allies' unity and solidarity.

However, the presence of the fortifications inspired others to express wholly different sentiments of more or less boisterous and visible resistance. A few kilometres south of Waterloo, on the other side of the border, in the country where the terror began, the disgrace of the defeat and occupation was brushed over as quickly as possible and transformed into a national protest. In the fortified towns along the eastern and southern borders of France, where the Austrians had been stationed, the departure of the Allied troops in 1818 was marked with monuments that celebrated the heroic deeds of the courageous French population. A large plaque in the citadel of Briançon in south-eastern France commemorates the resistance displayed by the population and the garrison to the Allied siege. The inhabitants there had been able to defend the fortress against the Austrian troops until the end of November 1815, making it the only fortress that had never been evacuated by the French nor occupied by the Allies. In the market square of Antibes (Côte d'Azur), a column was erected immediately after the departure of the Allied troops (so, when the coast was clear) with the inscription (translated):

> In August and September 1815, the inhabitants of Antibes, though surrounded by foreign troops and without the assistance of a garrison, swore to defend this place with whatever it took. Their patriotism and courage saved this city from the shame of an occupation. (Fig. 8.5)

The monuments lamented the shame of the occupation and praised the continuity of the unbroken courage and resolute fortitude of the French people. They openly and brazenly expressed how the years of 1815–18 had been an aberration. From 1818 on, these forts would symbolize French autonomy, suppressing all memories of the 'European system of defence' that had been in place there as well.

Europe's bulwark was also undermined outside France. The enormous investment in the many fortification projects of the 1820s also led to the corrupt activities of a few dodgy commanders and shady local contractors. In several places the walls of the fortifications were not made entirely of bricks, but partly filled with sand, which led to instances of collapse and sinking surface structures. By the end of the 1820s, most of the reinforcements had been rebuilt, but less than two years later, in 1830, the Belgians revolted against the – in their eyes – harsh and unjust rule of Willem I that systematically favoured Protestants and the north. After a few military battles and years of

---

[196] Metternich to Dorothée Lieven, with newspaper clipping attached, 27 November 1818, J. Hanoteau (ed.), *Lettres du prince Metternich à la comtesse de Lieven, 1818–1819* (Paris: Plon-Nourrit, 1909), 26.

Figure 8.5 The monument in Antibes, France, in memory of its protection from the Allied occupation, erected in May 1818 (when the end of the occupation elsewhere in France came into view). (Photo by the author)

negotiations, the Belgians, with the support of the Allies, managed to force the separation of the Southern Netherlands and to establish their own kingdom. With that, the Dutch buffer state, the 'Boulevard of Europe', was split in two. The Wellington Barrier came to lie in Belgium, but the citizens there were more concerned with industrialization and modernization than with defence measures against France. In 1839, the first thing the new Belgian king Leopold decided was to dismantle the fortifications along the barrier. The old Menin Gate in Ypres, for example, gave way to city expansion; at 3 m, the passageway was too narrow and the recurrent cause of traffic jams.[197] From a military point of view, the fortresses were also a cause for concern. Maintaining them was too expensive, and the Belgian army was too small to occupy and defend them on their own. The London Ministerial Conference had furthermore stipulated that Belgium was to remain neutral at all times. Preventative occupation forces coming from Prussia and Britain – in accordance with an agreement that Willem I had painstakingly negotiated in 1818 in order to avoid maintaining a permanent army of observation – were, therefore, no longer an option.

The foremost line of the defensive barrier – Ypres, Menin, Ath, Philippeville and Mariembourg – was the first to go. The expensive, skilfully constructed fortifications with their complex ravelins and strongholds were, for the most part, all demolished. The first railway lines finished the job. Only the National Redoubt around Antwerp remained.[198] It functioned as a defensive post, a redoubt, to which the army could retreat and regroup, awaiting support from the great powers that stood behind Belgium's independence. After that, the second ring of fortifications was also demolished: Ostend, Nieuwpoort, Oudenaarde, Mons, Charleroi, Dinant and Huy. After 1870, the citadels of Ghent and Dendermonde had to make way for progress: for a city park, and later, in 1912, for the Festival Palace that was built on the grounds of the Ghent citadel on the occasion of the World Fair the next year.[199]

Only a few fortresses along the Meuse remained of the Wellington Barrier, and a commemorative plaque or two. Images of the Dutch coat of arms were replaced by Belgium's.[200] In 1914, the ramparts of a number of fortresses, including Dendermonde, were actually used as a defence. Thereafter, the Germans undid them once and for all. After the First World War, what remained of the fortifications was demolished – there was hardly a bastion or bulwark still intact.[201] What did remain were the underground networks of passageways, about which all kinds of rumours and legends continued to

---

[197] The Ypres fortresses were demolished around 1850; the gate was also dismantled, and a passageway 13 m wide was put in its place. The commemorative stone was placed on the Lille Gate.

[198] See H. Stück and A. Grelon, 'Die Ingenieure des Corps des Ponts et Chaussées: Von der Eroberung des nationalen Raumes zur Raumordnung', in Stück and Grelon (eds.), *Ingenieure in Frankreich, 1747–1990* (Frankfurt: Campus, 1994).

[199] Gils, *De versterkingen van de Wellingtonbarrière*, 43, 59, 65. The Redoubt was completed in 1859.

[200] Ibid., 24–6, 65.

[201] Ibid., 51.

circulate. (For example, some underground tunnels would extend far beyond the fortress and end up in a nunnery.) Most of what remains of the fortifications is no longer visible to the naked eye, nor do they enjoy legal protection. The Kezelfort in Oudenaarde, the only fort that remained intact, is owned by a private family and (partly because of its location as a nesting place for bats) is not open to the public.[202]

---

[202] Ibid., 76–8.

9

Beyond Europe

From Four to Five

The accolades and expressions of gratitude directed towards Wellington in 1818, the praise of sovereigns extended to their ministers and, in turn, their thanks to their ambassadors in Paris marked the last days of the Allied Council. The 'Allied Machine' had done what needed doing: the bulwark of Europe had been erected. Grounded on the bedrock of solid financial arrangements and a transnational capital market, it was bolstered by a network of forts and fortifications that was supported by an explicit hierarchy of states, ranked officials and persons of repute, and maintained via a series of anti-revolutionary measures.

Nonetheless, the forum for ongoing discussions remained decidedly intact. In addition to their discussions regarding France, the Allied Machine was given another assignment starting in 1817. After 1818, however, it was no longer in the capacity of the Allied Council of the Quadruple Alliance, but as a new body, consisting of the same representatives as before, but now also including France (with France's minister of foreign affairs as full member). The 'Five Mediating Courts' represented the five great powers of Europe and convened as an ambassadorial conference. From 1817 on, the protocols of the Allied Council and this Council of Five ran together, the reason being that as French payments started to come in via the loans, and as the construction of the fortresses progressed, the Allied Council saw reason to take on new tasks. The fight against terror on the continent was under control, but throughout Europe there was still plenty that needed to be mediated and nailed down. In 1817, the Spanish–Portuguese conflict in South America ended up on the Council's agenda.

The reason for expanding the security talks in Paris was the formal request that the Court of Madrid submitted in January 1817, initially via Russia, to the Allied Council and France for mediation in a dispute with Portugal.[1] The disagreement had to do with the chaotic situation in the colonies in South

---

[1] See Nesselrode to the Russian ambassador in Madrid, Tatischeff, report dated 15/ 27 May 1817, in Ministerstvo inostrannykh del CCCP (ed.), *Vneshniaia politika Rossii*, vol. 1, 553–6.

America, and was a bristly security issue that the Allied ministers and the Spanish and Portuguese envoys were finding difficult to resolve. We turn to this matter here because it seemed as if the Allied Council, in the guise of this Council of Five, might morph into a directorate that would even get involved with security issues overseas. It is a telling example of the extent and limitations of the nascent Allied security community.

Thus, while the Allied security order in Europe was declared 'completed' for the time being, the debate was now opened as to how far the great powers could project their trans-imperialist cooperation beyond the borders of fortified Europe. Would the European powers be able to export the fight against terror to the 'second', southern hemisphere, to Latin America, where all sorts of uprisings and independence movements were raging? An emotional vocabulary of terror, threat and moderation was again mobilized to put these threats on the agenda and to legitimate possible interventions. Before this chapter is out, we will have sized up how far the Eurocentrist security culture reached, and where the Allied Council's limits lay.

A Gaucho in World Politics

In the eyes of his Roman Catholic parents, José Artigas was already a handful at a young age. He came from a wealthy Spanish immigrant family in Montevideo, and his parents enrolled him a Franciscan convent school, from which he fled when he was twelve. Once he had moved to the countryside and distanced himself from his parents, he became involved in cattle smuggling. As a gaucho, he combined his adventurous tendencies with a passionate aversion to the outdated, monarchist, Spanish colonial regime. The ideas of the Enlightenment and Napoleon's victories had also made the leanings of many in South America ripe for revolution, sparking the Spanish-American wars of independence between patriots and royalists. In 1810, Buenos Aires deposed the Spanish viceroy, Cisneros, replacing him with the self-appointed *Primera Junta* (First Assembly) to govern Argentina. Madrid moved its colonial court to Montevideo in an attempt to hold the crumbling colonial empire together. However, there, in the area of the Rio de la Plata, Artigas was already working to trigger a popular uprising on behalf of Buenos Aires. A year later, in the Banda Oriental, he proclaimed himself *Primer Jefe de los Orientales* ('First Leader of the Orientals') and declared the area around the Rio de la Plata the Provincia Oriental ('Oriental Province' – today, in large part, the country of Uruguay), independent from Spain. He advocated for federation, freedom of religion and civil rights protections. Other South American provinces joined Artigas and his 1,500 Indios militias. They announced a review of foreign relations and called for economic revolt, including the confiscation of the haciendas.

After Artigas had explained these plans for a 'League of Free Peoples' in Concepción in 1815, Portugal had had enough. The Portuguese marched on the Provincia Oriental and occupied the region. They were already nearby, since the Portuguese court had moved to Brazil after Napoleon's invasion and occupation of the Iberian Peninsula, and had governed the United Kingdom of Portugal, Brazil and the Algarves from Rio de Janeiro since 1808. The spirit of revolution and republican principles reverberating from North America threatened to flood all of South America – which is why the Portuguese intervened. From 1816 on, they were engaged in constant skirmishes with Artigas's rebels, the Artiguists. They made no effort to leave the strategic area around Montevideo, even when Spain repeatedly insisted that they could better do without their 'neighbourly help'.[2]

In 1817, Spain approached the Allied ministers in Paris with the request that they intervene in the dispute with the Kingdom of Portugal. In the meantime, Rio de Janeiro had practically annexed the Banda Oriental, even though that area was formally still part of the Spanish colonies' domain in South America. Madrid could not accept that the spirit of independence was ranging abroad and that the political landscape had irrevocably changed. The Spanish king, Ferdinand VII, who had been restored to the throne with the help of Wellington and the Allies, hoped that they might also help him regain control of his colonies.[3]

The Allied Council was still busy in 1817 with issues relating to the reduction of troops in France and financial negotiations. But these discussions were moving right along and nearing completion, so that a number of ministers found that the Allied Machine was in a position to turn to the southern hemisphere and deal with the Spanish request. Terror did not only need to be stemmed in France and Europe; rebellion and a revolutionary spirit in the New World seemed also to be a problem that the ministers could tackle together. The only question was whether the Allied sense of solidarity in Europe was sufficiently well established to project the new security order beyond Europe's borders. Did the Parisian ministers dare to call the gauchos active in world politics to task? And, even more to the point, was there any chance of making these rebels listen to the voice from Europe at all?

'A European Mediation'

Prior to its formal request to the Allied Council, Spain had sought – and received – the support of Russia and Prussia. Nesselrode, the Russian minister, on behalf of Spain, asked his Allied colleagues in Paris to act 'in concert' and to

---

[2] J. Street, *Artigas and the Emancipation of Uruguay* (Cambridge: Cambridge University Press, 1971 [1959]); T. Reeder, '"Sovereign Lords" and "Dependent Administrators". Artigan Privateers, Atlantic Borderwaters, and State Building in the Early Nineteenth Century', *Journal of American History* 103:2 (2016), 323–46.

[3] See E. Resnick, 'A Family Imbroglio: Brazil's Invasion of the Banda Oriental in 1816 and Repercussions on the Iberian Peninsula', *Revista de História*, 51:101 (1975), 179–205.

find a way to reverse the invasion, which was in effect a violation of Spain's sovereignty. Nesselrode felt that with Europe's mediation the Portuguese king could possibly be brought to embrace an *esprit de conciliation*. The Prussian minister, Goltz, seconded the proposal. According to the Berlin court, the Allied ministers had to do everything they could to protect the rights of Spain. The Russian and Prussian ministers were also convinced that France should be involved in this important task as well. Stuart and Wellington were more hesitant, waiting on instructions from their government first. Moreover, there was also a problem with the 'delayed communication link ... owing to the vast distances'. As a result, the Allied ministers would be at a constant disadvantage, and could arrive at wrong conclusions based on 'fateful misinformation'.[4] Their misgivings did not sway the others. They understood very well that London preferred to keep the option of recognizing the independence of South American colonies open with an eye to their commercial connections there and their sensitive relationship with Washington. That is why Goltz suggested that they, in any case, ask the Spanish, but also their own contacts across the Atlantic, for more 'intelligence', and to put pressure on Portugal. In order to prevent the continental powers from conducting the mediation without Britain's involvement, Castlereagh finally gave Stuart the green light. At the end of February 1817, the Allied Council officially accepted the Spanish request for mediation.[5]

These talks about the colonies in South America overlapped in part with the deliberations of the London Ministerial Conference, where the European powers, since 1816, had been negotiating the abolition of the slave trade and a possible defensive alliance against the state-supported piracy of some Barbary States in North Africa. The British government linked the issue of the joint fight against piracy with the abolition of slavery, but Spain and Portugal had resisted that last point in particular. Castlereagh saw a clear analogy with the activities of the Allied Council in Paris. Why should a multinational Allied fleet not be sent into open waters to war against the corsairs? One commander-in-chief would be in charge of that fleet – as was the case in France. 'There seems to be no reason why the machine should not work as well as the army of occupation has done in France', opined Castlereagh optimistically.[6] That optimism was in this case just as unfounded as it was misleading, because, in addition to Spain and Portugal, France did not think that a new mandate from the four great powers was a good idea either – especially pushed as it was by Britain. Castlereagh was therefore unable to get the Allied Machine into gear. The proposal for an Allied maritime alliance

---

[4] Protocol of 19 January 1817, TNA, FO 146/15.
[5] Protocol of 14, 26 February 1817, TNA, FO 146/15.
[6] Castlereagh to Cathcart, 7 May 1817, Centre des archives diplomatique de La Courneuve (CADLC), 8CP/609. See also (De) Lange, Menacing Tides, chapter 3.

would once again be on the table in Aix-la-Chapelle, only to be stranded again on the protests of second- and third-level powers.[7]

Despite these setbacks, the ambassadorial conference, or Council of Five, from 1817 onward (and overlapping with the Allied Council for about a year) continued their debates on the colonies in South America even further than did the London Conference, both geographically and strategically. The logic behind their consultation was simple. When it became clear at the end of 1816 that a reduction of troops in France would be the prelude to the payment and departure of the occupying forces, and that achieving the Allies' objectives regarding the security of France (and Europe) was clearly on the horizon, more space was created for new ambitions. As early as 1815, topics had surfaced within the Allied Council that touched on security issues on the periphery of Europe and far beyond. In Paris, too, sovereigns and their emissaries had occasionally discussed the slave trade and piracy. The Council had addressed the issue of the Ionian Islands and resolved various other cases requiring mediation between major and minor powers in and around the borders of Europe.[8] It stood to reason that, as peace and security seemed to be under control in the heart of Europe, this system of order and peace would also be exported to the periphery and beyond.

Compared to its unwillingness in London, it was remarkable (though not inconceivable) that Madrid had now turned to the Allied Council. Earlier, Don Pedro Gómez Labrador, the Spanish ambassador to Paris, had been one of the sharpest critics of the Council. The fact that the four powers were keen to present themselves as the managers of Europe, and elevated themselves as a directorate above the other states and kingdoms, had repeatedly occasioned protest in Spain. But Spain was now in serious trouble. It sorely needed money from the fortress fund and was too weak in South America to be able to act independently against Portugal. That is why, at the end of 1816, Madrid began to take a somewhat more indulgent attitude towards the Council (and, in doing so, to gain direct access to funding for their fortresses). In approaching St Petersburg, London and Berlin at the same time, as well as the ministers in Paris, Madrid was also trying to play the Allies off against each other (rather to the vexation of Madrid's first advocate, the tsar, who reminded Spain to stick to the principle of Allied unity)[9]. What did not work in London – support for Spain's imperial power in South America – might pass muster in Paris. The

[7] See Vick, 'Power, Humanitarianism and the Global Liberal Order'. See also (De) Lange, Menacing Tides.

[8] See, for example, protocol of 28 October 1815; Treaty of 5 November, GStA PK, III HA I. no. 1469, 33.

[9] See for example Kapodistrias to the Russian ambassador in Madrid, Tatischeff, 19 April/ 1 May 1818, in Ministerstvo inostrannykh del CCCP (ed.), Vneshniaia politika Rossii, vol. 2, 330–2.

Spanish ambassador in Paris peppered the ministers with heavy reports and bulging side letters explaining how wrong Portugal was.

Portugal had signed an armistice with the Buenos Aires rebels and thus de facto recognized the independence of Argentina.[10] Given the region's strategically important location along the borders of its own kingdom, Brazil – also not wanting to jeopardize the unstable peace with the regime in Buenos Aires – did not want Rio de Janeiro to vacate the area along the Rio de la Plata. Portugal's argument was that it was in a better position than was Spain, with its vast holdings on the continent and far-removed government in Europe, to keep the Artiguists in check.[11] According to Spain, however, the ongoing 'aggression' of the Brazilian court, as demonstrated by the occupation of its territory, was 'disastrous'. This violation of Spanish sovereignty would not only have 'negative consequences' for Spain, but 'adversely affect both hemispheres'. Given this argument, the Allied Council granted Spain's request. The ministers praised Madrid's 'spirit of moderation' and 'wisdom' for choosing negotiation first rather than starting a new war.[12] After months of memos and meetings back and forth with the loutish Labrador and the beloved Portuguese ambassador Palmela – always separately, never together – the Five Mediating Courts got Portugal to at least formally accept Spain's right of ownership of the occupied territory, and to document that in writing.[13]

Palmela's Master Stroke

Pedro de Sousa Holstein, first Duke of Faial and Palmela, was as a cosmopolitan and savvy diplomat not easily categorized. He immediately appropriated Labrador's argument – the connection between peace and order in South America on the one hand, and in Europe on the other hand – to justify the continuation of the Portuguese occupation of the Banda Oriental. According to Portugal, the invasion and subsequent occupation was a much-needed initiative in response to the terror of the South American rebels. Just like the Allied occupation of France, the Portuguese occupation of the Banda Oriental was a 'counterrevolutionary measure'. It was the only way to protect the South American kingdoms against the advances of the Artiguist revolutionaries and their 'Republicks'.[14]

---

[10] The Congress of Tucumán in 1816 declared the United Provinces of South America independent of Spain. That territory included Argentina, Uruguay and parts of Bolivia.

[11] Note of Labrador to the Allied Council; deliberations and annex. Protocol of 16 March 1817, TNA, FO 146/15.

[12] Allied Council, protocol of 16 March 1817, TNA, FO 146/15.

[13] See, for example, Hardenberg's instructions to Goltz on behalf of the Allied Council, November 1817, AT-OeStA/HHStA, StAbt, Spain, Diplomatic Correspondence, no. 149.

[14] Allied Council, protocol of 18, 21 June 1817, TNA, FO 146/22.

With his rhetorical mastery, Palmela succeeded in getting at least two or even three members of the Allied Council on his side. Now that the Allies had succeeded in taming the *esprit révolutionnaire*, it was high time to engage with the bane of revolution in the rest of the world. Terror had to be curbed not only in Europe, but 'worldwide'. And especially in the New World, because the uprisings in 'the Americas' were a veritable 'attack on the morality of the nations and the security of the thrones of kings'. When thrones were wobbling in South America, it would not be long before they were again shaking at their core in Europe. In 1814 and 1815, had it not been the 'overarching goal' of the European 'confederation' to combat this 'anarchy' and defeat the 'enemies of the sovereigns and their peoples'?[15]

The discussion of the legality of the invasion on the one hand, and Portugal's right, given the extraordinary circumstances, to protect South American kingdoms against rebellion and terror with a 'pre-emptive' invasion on the other, dragged on for several months after July 1817. Given Spain's stubbornness, Palmela tried to break through the rather fruitless dialogue by arguing that Portugal had at least stepped forward. In March 1818, while the final negotiations on French arrears were still pending, and after the attack on Wellington, Palmela launched a new proposal. On behalf of his king, he requested that the Five Mediating Courts embed the dispute with Spain in a much larger plan for the 'pacification' of South America as a whole. 'The greatest interest of Spain, Portugal and the whole of Europe' dictated a joint effort to put an end to 'revolutionary agitation in America' once and for all. That plan was 'conformable to the spirit of the age'. Peace in Europe was near completion; now it was about 'the relations between the two worlds'. If the 'spirit of demagoguery' in the Americas was not undone, it would 'sooner or later' pop up in Europe.[16]

Palmela's coup hit like a bombshell. Wellington, who was there when Palmela explained his proposal to the ambassadors with great enthusiasm and drama, was very impressed. He had never seen the otherwise very calculating and cool Russian envoy Pozzo di Borgo so 'disturbed'. The Austrian and Prussian ambassadors were also moved by Palmela's dystopian panoramic views. Even Spain's ambassador Núñez (who was invited, along with Richelieu, to the Court of Five's session on 22 April 1818) admitted that Madrid was certainly in favour of a European commitment to the 'great work of peacekeeping in America', based on the 'principles laid down in the Congress of Vienna'.[17]

[15] Protocol of 20 July 1817, TNA, FO 146/22.
[16] Memorandum of Palmela to the Allied Council, discussion and annexes, 21 March 1818, TNA, FO 146/23.
[17] Memorandum of Núñez, protocol of the Allied Council/*Cinq Courts Médiatrices*, 22 April 1818, TNA, FO 146/29.

France and Russia especially saw this as an opportunity. Richelieu, before the Allies had departed France, was able to elevate his own country and his role to the level of the other Allies; all the while, Tsar Alexander and the Russian envoys were becoming both irritated over Spain's policy of obstruction and increasingly worried about the spirit of revolution within Russia and beyond.[18]

A New Mission for *l'homme de l'Europe*?

On 23 March 1818, Wellington was offered a very special assignment. The courts of France and Russia asked the commander-in-chief of the Allied occupation to extend his field of responsibility to include South America. Could he not accept the role of 'mediator' between Spain, Portugal and the colonies now that the French occupation was nearing its end? If he was to achieve the same brilliant result that he had facilitated in France, he would, of course, have to move from Paris to the Iberian capital in order to shepherd a similar project of mediation and occupation. Wellington, who had not anticipated this career move, could not help but take the offer seriously. In consultation with Castlereagh, he discussed the chances and actual possibilities of setting up such a peacekeeping, counter-revolutionary programme in South America.[19]

What he could imagine possible was to send an Allied expeditionary force to Montevideo: not a Spanish or Portuguese contingent force, but military forces under the command of a 'third power'. He had even thought about which country could possibly take this on, and came up with the Netherlands. But Castlereagh, who had not heard Palmela's dramatic exposé, was more detached. Watching the Spanish–Portuguese squabbling from a distance, he gave short shrift to that plan. Wellington was actually himself somewhat sceptical about the feasibility of the proposal. As Wellington explained to the ministers of the Five Mediating Courts, the first question was which European power could be prodded to take up such a thankless and costly military mission. Would the king of the Netherlands be willing to lend his name and army for such an adventure? Secondly, he could not see himself operating from Madrid. Although his younger brother Henry was ambassador there, without an extensive network or his own occupational forces there, he would not be able to function in as effective a manner as he had done in Paris. Even more problematic was the fact that he would have to mediate from Madrid a conflict involving revolutionaries who obviously had no accredited envoys in Madrid. So, how could he even initiate such a conversation, and with whom?

---

[18] Letters of Wellington to Castlereagh, 23, 26, 30 March 1818, TNA, FO 92/33. Letter of Kapodistrias to Tatischeff, 19 April/1 May 1818, in Ministerstvo inostrannykh del CCCP (ed.), *Vneshniaia politika Rossii*, vol. 2, 330–2.

[19] Letters of Wellington to Castlereagh, 23, 26, 30 March 1818, TNA, FO 92/33.

He saved the most devastating judgement for last, and only Castlereagh heard the negative wording. He explained to the Allied ministers that the conflict between Portugal, Spain and the Artiguist revolutionaries was a 'bye-battle'. It was a fait accompli. The times were geared towards reform and change, not absolutist revanchism. The colonial kingdoms in South America were doomed to failure. The liberator of the Iberian Peninsula (and Marquis of Douro) wrote bitterly that, since the end of the Napoleonic War, Spain had been 'too jealous' to take any advice from him and that for a Spaniard the word 'liberty' was not part of the political vocabulary – even although the term 'liberal' derived from the Spanish faction of the *liberales*, in the Cortes of 1812.[20] He was convinced that the Court of Madrid would not tolerate serious interference in its affairs from him or from any other European power. However honourable the Russian–French request was, he had to inform the ministers that he would not be able to get the Allied Machine to work in South America or in Madrid, let alone bring those efforts to a good end.[21]

The trans-imperialistic security culture had its limits. Those limits were obviously dictated not only by the practical impossibility of such a proposed mission, but also by Britain's imperial and unilateral interests. In the light of the expected recognition of the South American republics and revolutionaries by Washington, it was important that Great Britain's monopoly on trade relations, including with Brazil, not be jeopardized. Supporting Spain and Portugal would easily forestall relations with the new republics, and hence with new markets and raw-material suppliers. (Incidentally, the Netherlands followed the same course.) The second hemisphere was therefore left to its own devices; the trans-imperial security culture applied to the continent and the periphery, but did not reach across the ocean. That was also due to Spain itself. Madrid had, of course, first asked the Allies to mediate in the situation, but when it became clear that the great powers did not immediately deploy their gunboats to defend the Spanish interests against the insurgents and the brazen Portuguese, they paid that mediation little heed. In August 1818, the British ambassador to Madrid, Henry Wellesley, told Castlereagh that Pizarro, the Spanish foreign minister, turning a deaf ear to the Allied Council, was intentionally operating on his own. Instead of settling the matter via Paris, he tried to play the Allies off against each other via the

---

[20] See also the conversation that Wellington had with Pozzo di Borgo, Castlereagh and Baron von Vincent about Spanish conservativism, in the presence of Lady Shelley, Edgcumbe (ed.), *The Diary of Frances Lady Shelley, 1818–1873*, 199–200.
[21] Lengthy letters and memoranda, August 1818; 19 November 1818, TNA, FO 92/33; Castlereagh to Stuart, protocol of the Allied Council, 14 August 1816, TNA, FO 146/13. See also Labrador's complaint to the Allied Council, protocol of 22 December 1816, TNA, FO 146/15.

436   BEYOND EUROPE

courts of Russia, France and Berlin, still in the hope of securing the desired military support.[22]

The Concert Won't Play in South America

In Aix-la-Chapelle, in October 1818, the issue of the Banda Oriental was discussed extensively. Castlereagh himself, on the 23rd, brought the question of the Spanish colonies in South America to the attention of the conference. There was now also a direct link with the other issue of an Allied maritime alliance against piracy. Artigas's rebels were utterly unimpressed by the Paris talks and the Spanish–Portuguese anti-revolutionary threats. He had taken it a step further and issued letters of marque and reprisal, which authorized privateers or corsairs – often Americans who operated out of Baltimore – to attack and capture Spanish and Portuguese vessels on behalf of the rebels, sometimes as far away as the coast of Europe and North Africa.[23] Palmela tried to convince the powers in Aix-la-Chapelle that the rebels at sea and on land were two heads of the same monster. 'Soon', Palmela warned the ministers, 'there would not be any safety at sea for whatever flag' – the same argument that he had already used to support the potentially endlessly expanding danger of revolution and rebellion in South America for Europe. In this case, he even proposed that they also hold Washington to account, and discuss joint measures against the United States.[24]

Although Richelieu aligned himself with Palmela,[25] the Iberian diplomats chose to act in their own interest and to hold stubbornly to their mutual conflict. In the meantime, Portugal and Spain had already raised so many roadblocks and demands that the possibility of a such a 'concerted' approach and of European mediation soon deteriorated. By this time, Wellington was so 'very irritated with Spain', according to Pozzo, that he had become 'ill-tempered'. Although Russia had made a strong case for the Spanish cause, even Nesselrode complained from Warinas, on his way to Aix-la-Chapelle, that the Spanish court imagined that they still lived in the days of Philip II.[26]

[22] Henry Wellesley to Castlereagh, 22 August 1818, WSD, vol. 12, 652–3. See also the cautious but warning letter of Tatischeff to Pizarro, 1/13 May 1818, in Ministerstvo inostrannykh del CCCP (ed.), Vneshniaia politika Rossii, vol. 2, 351–3.

[23] See D. Head, 'A Different Kind of Maritime Predation: South American Privateering from Baltimore, 1816–1820', International Journal of Naval History, 7:2 (2008), 1–38; G. Brown, Latin American Rebels and the United States, 1806–1822 (Jefferson, NC: McFarland, 2015), 76–8. Thanks to Erik de Lange.

[24] Palmela, protocol no. 30, annex A, Aachen Conference, 11 November 1818, TNA, FO 139/42, 82–92. See also Palmela to Metternich, 8 October 1818, AT-OeStA/HHStA, StAbt, Spain, Diplomatic Conference, no. 148.

[25] Protocol no. 31, annex A, Aachen Conference, 13 November 1818, TNA, FO 139/42, 99–110.

[26] Pozzo to Lieven, 31 August 1818; Pozzo to Nesselrode, 27 August, Pozzo (ed.), Correspondance, 592–7; Nesselrode to Pozzo, 3 September, Warinas, Ibid., 597. See also

Spain demanded compensation from Portugal for income lost during the occupation. Portugal, on the other hand, requested compensation for its troops, which had protected the Spanish territory from the rebels. Portugal also felt that the borders had to be drawn differently.[27]

After several long sessions in Aix-la-Chapelle,[28] the Five Mediating Courts offered (again) to mediate in the situation. However, they made it clear to Madrid's court that this support consisted only of mediation between Spain and the rebels – with an eye to developing a general peace plan for South America that would also include legal concessions to the insurgents. There could not be military assistance alongside any form of counter-insurgency. A military expedition would put too much of a burden on both trade and the unstable relationship with the United States. Richelieu wanted to do more, and in mid-November, together with Spain, produced a memorandum inviting Wellington, as *l'homme de l'Europe*, to set up a new ministerial conference in Madrid. The United States would also be invited to join the 'general system of Europe', so as to prevent 'sentiments of rivalry and hatred' from driving the 'Old World' and the 'New World' apart.[29] Austria, Russia and Prussia had in the meantime realized that Wellington was in no way inclined to this approach, and that without Britain's naval power the courts of Europe could do little in South America.[30] Even Tsar Alexander now conceded and person-ally explained to the Spanish king that any military intervention was 'inad-missible in the eyes of the other powers because it would be de facto impratical'.[31] Moreover, they were all of the opinion that, if Spain and Portugal did not want to accept the conditions of the Allies,[32] no further support could be given. The ministers of the Five Courts in Paris continued

the Russian memorandum for Alexander, 13/25 October and 20 October/1 November 1818, in Ministerstvo inostrannykh del CCCP (ed.), *Vneshniaia politika Rossii*, vol. 2, 522–4, 525–8.

[27] Protocol of the Allied Council/*Cinq Courts Médiatrices*, 10, 11, 13, 21 July 1818, TNA, FO 146/29.

[28] The conference even lasted a few days longer. Metternich complained to his friend Dorothée Lieven and to Emperor Franz I. Metternich to Franz, 17 November 1818; Metternich to Dorothée Lieven, 17 November 1818, in Hanoteau (ed.), *Lettres du prince Metternich*, 14.

[29] 'Note of the French and Spanish Plenipotentiaries on the Question of Spanish South American Possessions', *WSD*, vol. 12, 805–9.

[30] See Wellington's answer to the French and Russian ministers, 24 November 1818, *WSD*, vol. 12, 846–51.

[31] Letter of Alexander I to Ferdinand VII, 10/22 December 1818, Vienna, in Ministerstvo inostrannykh del CCCP (ed.), *Vneshniaia politika Rossii*, vol. 2, 596–7.

[32] The conditions that Castlereagh formulated were: (1) a treaty abolishing the slave trade, (2) a general amnesty for all insurgents, (3) that South American subjects must have the same rights as the subjects in Spain, (4) that South America must be able to share in the benefits of free trade and (5) that mediation and support would not have a military character. Jarrett, *The Congress of Vienna and its Legacy*, 198.

their discussions for a number of years after the Aix-la-Chapelle Conference as
to the exact form of mediation that they could then offer, and the conditions
that Spain and Portugal would then have to meet.[33] But the Concert would not
play in South America.

Deeply disappointed in the European powers (and in Wellington), Spain
tried a year later on its own initiative to ship troops to South America to quell
the rebels there. Already during the Aix-la-Chapelle Conference there were
rumours that Spain was busy preparing, with the help of Russia, an expedition
that would leave from Cádiz, the principal home port of the Spanish Navy.[34]
However, the troops near Cádiz who were meant to suppress the revolution in
the colonies, and were awaiting transport to South America, themselves
became a source of rebellion. Colonel Rafael del Riego was given the command
of the Asturian Battalion. After arriving in Cádiz, he, with other liberal officers,
started a mutiny in January 1820, demanding a return to the constitution of
1812 and the restoration of a constitutional monarchy, which the king did
agree to in March.

At Spain's request, and through the mediation of Núñez, a European ally did
get involved in 1823, but not to fight the revolutionaries in South America. In
a one-sided military intervention, France invaded Spain. At the Congress of
Verona in December 1822, the Quintuple Alliance countries felt that Spain's
growing republicanism was threatening the balance in Europe and, much to
the chagrin of Wellington and the British, chose France to see to the restoration of the absolute monarchy. Under the military high command of the Duke
of Angoulême, the 'Hundred Thousand Sons of Saint Louis' overthrew the
rebels and put the Bourbon dynasty back in the saddle.[35] The Spanish court
had long ago lost its authority over the colonies. In the same year (1823), the
United States' Monroe Doctrine ensured that no European power would dare
reassert that authority. Until 1825, the ministers of the Five Mediating Courts
continued to discuss the status of the former Spanish colonies and their
relations with Europe, but just as in 1817–18, the 'restored' King Ferdinand
VII of Spain paid their advice no heed. He kept fighting his own 'bye-battles',
supported by his at least equally reactionary Bourbon cousin Charles X, who
succeeded Louis XVIII after his death on 16 September 1824.[36]

Colonel Riego was found guilty of treason and hanged by order of the king
on 7 November 1823. His fellow freedom fighter Artigas fared better. He had
been expelled from Uruguay in 1820 by the Portuguese under the command of

---

[33] Jarrett, *The Congress of Vienna and its Legacy*, 197–201. See also 'Médiation entre
l'Espagne et le Portugal', signed by Metternich, Richelieu, Castlereagh, Wellington,
Bernstorff, Nesselrode, Kapodistrias, 22 November 1818, AT-OeStA/HHStA, StK,
Kongressakten, Aachen 1818, inv. no. 17, 128–9.
[34] Palmela to Wellington, 8 October 1818, *WSD*, vol. 12, 740.
[35] A more accurate count would be about 60,000.
[36] Jarrett, *The Congress of Vienna and its Legacy*, 342–3.

General Carlos Frederico Lecor (a former comrade-in-arms of Wellington during the Iberian campaign), and fled to Paraguay. He was allowed to stay there, as long as he stayed out of politics. He died in 1850 at the age of eighty-six, reportedly in the saddle, a gaucho to the end. He was buried in the pantheon of South American folk heroes.[37] The Duke of Palmela drew the longest straw; he came to embrace a more liberal way of thinking, became the minister of foreign affairs in Brazil and the prime minister of Portugal three times between 1834 and 1846.

A More Modest Bulwark

The transition and expansion of the European security culture to the non-European world was aborted. The European powers were too divided, and the New World was not much interested in European interference either.

This did not mean that, after the departure of the occupying forces and the end of the Allied Council, the trend towards deliberation and consultation regarding security issues had run its course. The five major powers continued to assume a leading role in addressing the loose ends of the European security order. As mentioned, the ambassadorial conference of the Five Mediating Courts remained active until 1825. All kinds of other issues requiring mediation also continued to arise. For example, the ambassadors in Paris lent Switzerland their support when that republic sought mediation between Austria and the Vatican to set up a Swiss diocese for the parishes that had been ceded to Switzerland by Sardinia in 1815. That bishopric would eventually come, thanks in part to Allied support.[38] The ambassadors also put pressure on Bernadotte, king of Sweden, to fulfil his promise to compensate Denmark for the loss of Norway, which Denmark had ceded to Sweden.[39] A dispute between Willem I and the French Duke of Rohan about the financial settlement of the transfer of the Duchy of Bouillon to the Netherlands was also addressed by the Council of Ambassadors. In other words, thanks to the efforts of the five great powers, the wheels of the Allied Machine quietly continued to turn, albeit at a different pace and in a different gear. However, intensified military action based on solidarity clauses or extraterritorial expeditions were not part of the picture. The experimental, multinational phase of the first years was over.

Battling the Barbary pirates along the periphery of Europe was still discussed as a joint project – and sometimes carried out – although the momentum had ebbed there too. In Aix-la-Chapelle, Tsar Alexander had proposed establishing

[37] In 2011 a Spanish movie was made about Artigas, *Artigas – La Redota*, and in 2006, an animated film for children, *El pequeño héroe*.
[38] Protocol of the Allied Council, Paris, 13 May 1818, TNA, FO 146/29.
[39] Jarrett, *The Congress of Vienna and its Legacy*, 203.

a common European federation and 'maritime league', and linking up the common struggle of the Christian nations against piracy and the slave trade into a new international anti-slavery organization with an agency in North Africa. That sounded all well and good, but the discussions of the London Conference had already made it clear that none of the powers, not even Russia, was in fact prepared to transfer sovereignty over part of its own fleet to an Allied commander-in-chief. When the British abolitionist Thomas Clarkson lobbied the ministers and presented them with a plan to equip such a maritime alliance with real strength by linking it to a reciprocal 'right to search' arrangement, the tsar did not think that that was a good idea. Neither Prussia, Austria nor Russia wanted to commit to a provision that would give other powers the right to access and inspect their ships. France was not keen on a new Allied naval occupation force either.[40] What finally happened in Aix-la-Chapelle was that the possibility of setting up such an Allied fleet or multinational expedition in the future was explicitly discussed. The idea remained an open question. Moreover, the ministers had agreed in Protocol 39 that they would jointly confront those in power in North Africa and Constantinople regarding their involvement in piracy and privateering. They would then be in a position to link the threat of a European expedition to those discussions. An Allied multinational navy or sea federation did not materialize, but that possibility was consciously kept on the table, and after 1818 was also articulated in joint statements and memoranda to a very wary and anxious Ottoman Porte.[41]

That mutual imperialist support and solidarity remained present for the time being. In Verona in 1822, for example, the ministers discussed in detail Austria's occupation of Piedmont. The Allied imperialist system was based on very practical ways of doing things and mechanisms of consultation, of ministerial conferences and protocols, of meetings and the reciprocal exchange of information, although the hierarchy was clear at all times. According to Castlereagh, it was about the 'habitual confidential and free intercourse between the Ministers of the Great Powers as a body ... embracing in confidential and united discussions all the great points in which they were severally interested'.[42] The five great powers were open to proposing and disposing. Although they adjusted their shared ambitions after 1818, and kept the European edifice a bit more modest, their attitude led the other European countries to home in on their own latitude and independence, and they developed an entire repertoire of reactions, from refutation via tactical

---

[40] See letter of Clarkson to Wellington, *WSD*, vol. 12, 760–1; also J. Oldfield, *Transatlantic Abolitionism in the Age of Revolution. An International History of Anti-Slavery, c.1787--1820* (Cambridge: Cambridge University Press, 2013), 215–17.
[41] 'Protocol no. 39', Aix-la-Chapelle, 20 November 1818, TNA, FO 139/43, 219–20. See (De) Lange, *Menacing Tides*, chapter 3. Liston to Castlereagh, 27 July 1819; also the memorandum to the Porte, July 1819, TNA, FO 78/92, 195–208.
[42] Cited in Jarrett, *The Congress of Vienna and its Legacy*, 205.

accommodations to obstruction and protest. The non-European world, which was not in any way considered an equal partner, developed even more radical techniques of protest and resistance.[43]

With or Without Washington

The imperialist leanings of the four (plus one) major powers did mean that the European ministers missed the opportunity to invite the United States into the concert as an equal partner. John Quincy Adams, formerly the US ambassador in St Petersburg and London, had negotiated the Treaty of Ghent – the peace treaty after the British–American War of 1812 – on behalf of the United States in 1814. After returning to Washington with his wife Louisa, who had reported so vividly on her gruelling journey from St Petersburg to Paris, he had become secretary of state in 1817 (and he would move on to become president of the United States in 1825). After having made several unsuccessful attempts to glean information from Castlereagh, he informed the British envoy in Washington, Charles Bagot, in June 1818 that he was very disappointed by the reticence he had experienced at the European courts on the question of the Spanish colonies in South America. Earlier on, he had noticed as a diplomat in Europe 'how very small a space my person or my station occupy in the notice of these persons' (here referring to Wellington and Castlereagh).[44] None of these ministers had shared anything at all with him on the Spanish question, but, as he told Bagot, he had in the meantime obtained some information himself. Adams had a copy of a memorandum from Russia in his possession in which the Russian court proposed to the Allied ministers that they should seek to mediate in the Spanish question and perhaps also to send Wellington out on their behalf. Adams, however, would have liked to have heard personally from Castlereagh or the other European ministers as to what their plans were regarding the issue of the Spanish-American colonies. A 'rational interference of foreign powers in that quarrel' would be inconceivable, he opined. It was the 'earnest wish' of the United States to 'freely communicate' and be 'in concert' with 'the European principal Powers' about the future of South America.[45] Should Washington recognize the United Provinces of the Rio de la Plata or not? And in exchange for which concessions and provisions? The powers needed to answer that

---

[43] For the resistance of the North African warlords against European dictates, see (De) Lange, *Menacing Tides*.

[44] See for example John Quincy Adams' diary entries from July 1816, D. Waldstreicher (ed.), *The Diaries of John Quincy Adams, 1779–1821* (New York: Penguin, 2017), 392, 395.

[45] Bagot to Castlereagh, 29 June 1818, Vane (ed.) *Correspondence*, vol. 2, 458–9; citations in Waldstreicher, *The Diaries of John Quincy Adams, 1779–1821*, 444, 501.

question quickly, because, Adams expected, it would soon be too late, and the South American provinces would then simply be able to force that recognition.[46]

Washington very much wanted to join the system of European powers. Adams explained later, in one of his diary entries from 1820, that the United States had always pursued a policy that was 'best adapted to harmonize with those of Europe'. Europe, however, had 'never considered the United States as belonging to her system'. On the contrary,

> the European Alliance, consisting of the five principal powers had since the overthrow of the French revolutionary domination regulated the Affairs of all Europe; without ever calling the United States to their consultations. It was best for both parties, that they should continue to do so – for if the United States should become a member of the body, they would even now be a power entitled to great influence, and in a very few years must become a first rate power in the League.[47]

Yet, already in 1818, the American envoys were self-confident enough to tell Castlereagh that if the Europeans were not to make space for Washington, 'the time was fast approaching when the American Government could no longer avoid taking some positive line'.[48]

Despite that disguised threat, Britain did not accept the offer. In November 1818, Russia and France broached the possibility of inviting Washington to discussions on the South American colonies at a later date. Pressured by Castlereagh, however, the ambassadorial conference decided to continue their efforts only through to 1825, and to keep Washington at bay. Those discussions proved to be fairly fruitless. In the meantime, Adams, who was not at all impressed by the (in his eyes) outdated European courts, had taken some steps of his own. By the autumn of 1818, he had gathered enough information to conclude that there would be no European armed intervention or military expedition to South America, because of the simple fact that Britain did not want that. London followed a course of delay, so as finally to present the recognition of the South American states as a fait accompli.[49] Yet, in order to prevent London or St Petersburg from changing their course, Adams formulated a firm position in 1823. That was the famous Monroe Doctrine of 1823 (of which not President Monroe, but he himself was the *spiritus rector*), declaring on behalf of the United States that the door was closed to every form of European interference in South America. The Europeans had missed the

---

[46] S. Bemis, 'Early Diplomatic Missions from Buenos Aires to the United States, 1811–1824', *American Antiquarian Society*, 49:1 (1940), 11–101, here: 68–72, 97–101.

[47] Waldstreicher (ed.), *The Diaries of John Quincy Adams, 1779–1821*, 568–9.

[48] Bagot to Castlereagh, 29 June 1818, Vane (ed.) *Correspondence*, vol. 2, 458–9.

[49] Bemis, 'Early Diplomatic Missions', 71–2.

boat. In fact, their involvement had come to be seen by Washington as a threat to the United States' own sphere of influence.

All kinds of bilateral agreements would still be discussed and concluded, but this early nineteenth-century plan to pull the United States into the European 'system' in 1818 ran aground because of European self-interest and Iberian stubbornness. The European imperialist security community was too divided when it came to non-European issues to act with one voice, and too 'jealous' to give up its self-interest for the interests of Europe in general.

Meanwhile, in Europe, the political and cultural climate was undergoing swift changes in the 1820s, thereby stealthily eroding the security architecture of the *Boulevard de l'Europe*. From 1830 onwards, France was no longer considered an enemy or aggressor. The bulwark of Europe, as a network of fortifications, was losing its function. As those visible manifestations of collective security deteriorated, the reputation of Allied solidarity also crumbled. At the same time, the instruments and artefacts that were supposed to curb or restrain the terror had reawakened or spawned new protests to the plan. A novel, nationalist and radical rhetoric trumped the fading emotional vocabulary of Allied concord, 'balance', 'moderation' and collective security. In the eyes of the courts of Spain and Portugal, of the Belgian population, of German students, of liberals and radicals spread across the continent and in South America, the four great powers had erected a far too exclusive and imperialist security system. At best, these 'objects' of the European security inventions shrugged their shoulders and took little notice of the Allies' dictates. In the worst cases, imperial Allied hubris inspired new waves of rebellion and radical counter-violence.

10

Conclusion

'We Must Have Another Paris Dinner'

Early 1819, while in London, Lady Shelley ran into Wellington. The duke still had a special place in her heart, even though he no longer had the 'air of Waterloo' about him. Wellington also looked back nostalgically to their time in France. 'We must have another Paris dinner', he sighed. He was thinking less of Lady Shelley's company than of the short and unique period after Waterloo, when he was honoured as Marshal by all the great Allied powers and had the security of Europe in his hands. After returning to London in December 1818, Wellington had become caught up in conservative intrigues. His fame remained great, but when he was confronted with opposition in his own country as prime minister, from 1828 onwards, he reacted much less sovereignly and moderately than he had done while overseeing Allied matters in France. To Lady Shelley, he confessed his aversion to the current agitations and demonstrations for parliamentary reform: 'After all – despotism for despotism – it is better in the hands of one than in the hands of the mob!' Upon his return to Britain, his increasingly conservative and at times reactionary demeanour got the better of him and often did not sit well with the press – perhaps these headwinds coloured his time in France as Allied Commander with a rosy afterglow (Fig. 10.1).[1]

The period after Waterloo had indeed been unique. Napoleon had been forcibly defeated, but the new security order was not based on bayonets alone. The sovereigns, ministers and most generals realized in 1815 that terror could not simply be combated with terror. A new system had to be put in place that was supported by law and reason. This book has told that forgotten history as a story of generals, kings and statesmen, such as Wellington, Metternich, Tsar Alexander and Richelieu. But it was also the story of their officials, diplomats and experts, who had to translate that delicate balance between might and right, between restoring and transforming, into the troubled practices of the

---

[1] Edgcumbe (ed.), *The Diary of Frances Lady Shelley, 1818–1873*, 10, 29, 256–7; Muir, *Wellington. Waterloo and the Fortunes of Peace*, 472–4.

Figure 10.1   Wellington musing at Waterloo. Painting by B. R. Haydon, 1839. (©
National Portrait Gallery, London)

everyday. Bankers, directors and citizens, both in France and just across the
border – all of them wondered more or less about their place within this new
order, and whether it would accommodate or suffocate them.

The peace of 1815 took shape as a security community designed by the
leading sovereigns. Contrary to how they are often portrayed, these monarchs
and their ministers were not merely the narrow-minded representatives of
restoration and repression. They rather saw themselves, most of the time quite
accurately, as moderate and 'balanced'. In their preference for collective action
and deliberation in the international arena, but also for resolute bureaucratic
centralization on the homefront, they were decidedly modern. These 'modern'
tendencies towards centralization and administrative control also structured
and shaped their definition of that object of their concerted security policies,
'terror'. Characterizing this fight against terror as effective and legitimate
would be a gross exaggeration. Yet it can and should be, at the end of this
story, evaluated as a unique process of combining *moral dedication* and
innovative forms of cooperation with *imperialist optimism* – to say the least.

The first dimension, the moral dedication, expressed itself in a strongly
emotional framing of the new security order. An overwhelming sense of (often

religiously inspired) calling, of being responsible for the restoration of the European order, pervades not only the prepared public declarations, but also the various internal memoranda and preserved correspondence of the participants. Whether it was Providence or good morals, the sovereigns and their ministers were convinced of a general, European, Christian-ecumenical obligation to jointly counter the double-headed threat of despots and revolutionaries – those enemies of their newly established balanced order – even beyond Europe's borders. That was clearly evident from the common vernacular they developed. Notions such as 'revenge', 'conquest', 'usurpation' or 'revolution' were used to frame a specific policy of strategy as outside the accepted order. Instead, the envoys and ministers of Europe appealed to decency, morality, and order to advance their measures. Moderation, 'concert', solidarity (amongst the ruling elites) and deliberation were the magic words with which the new peace was secured and emerging conflicts quieted. The crowning moment of this joint struggle for order and security in the immediate post-war period took place in Aix-la-Chapelle, where the plenipotentiaries declared in superlatives their 'mutual good will that today unites the states into one European family'.[2] In doing so, of course, it was important to at least be *seen* as moderate; wanting to *be* so per se was often a different story. The efforts of Portugal and Spain to get the Allied Council to send a seasoned military naval force to South America under the flag of 'harmony, peace and order' testified to the hypocrisy with which the new emotional vocabulary was also applied to the international scene.

Secondly, this new security culture was based on a (professed) shared preference for innovative forms of cooperation in the fight against terror. The occupation of France by a joint Allied force as well as the novelty of financing reparations through international loans and collective European bonds (on the French treasury) was at the time nothing short of revolutionary. Something of this scope would not happen again until after the First World War. The form and make-up of the Allied Council made it possible to meet regularly and effectively without all the fuss of court culture and dynastic pomp and circumstance. A small committee of several ministers and ambassadors under Wellington's leadership turned the British embassy in Paris into the headquarters of the new European order.

This hybrid combination of traditional symbolism and innovation also became visible and tangible for the general public to behold and endure. Poems, paintings and large-scale military parades and public worship services celebrated the Allies' solidarity and sense of harmony, which was in turn sealed with mutual royal accolades and decorations. An Allied commission for stolen art recovered looted artworks and returned them to their rightful owners,

---

[2] Protocol and attachments, 15 November 1818, AT-OeStA/HHStA, StK, Kongressakten, inv. no. 17, Subfolder 'Protokolle', Aachen 1818, 157–72, here: 170b.

accompanied by great public spectacles. Spies and uniform passports helped guarantee safety on the roadways; bonds and other securities began to influence the financial markets and the investment climate. Blacklists of terror suspects kept local and national police forces hopping in France and throughout Europe. Thanks to Prussian bureaucratic innovators, such as Stein and Gruner, a bona fide bureaucracy and security apparatus were set up to support the occupation and maintain order, including a department for detecting *fausses nouvelles* and rumours.

Above all these activities and deliberations, the European Concert resounded with the imperialist-optimist tone of the major powers. This third dimension of this European security culture clearly shone through in the conviction of the four victors over Napoleon that it was their duty to colonize the rebellious hearts and minds in France and beyond, to reform the continent and to tame the terror. This conviction was also expressed in joint attempts to export this imperialist security to the periphery of Europe – Greece, the Mediterranean, North Africa – and defend the continent against Barbary corsairs and other unrest. This modern, post-war imperialism started in France, but was just as expansive and moralistic towards the rest of Europe and beyond. Pressured by Britain, with access to the Allies' fortress fund as a reward, second-level powers such as Spain and the Netherlands were persuaded, for example, to agree by treaty to abolish the slave trade.[3]

Taken together, these three dimensions of the post-war security culture between 1815 and 1818 laid the foundation for the nineteenth-century system of European collective security – which should here rather be understood as an ongoing *process* of integration, expansion and imperialist cooperation than as a ready-made edifice or institution. In the first decades after 1815, the absence of major conflicts between the European powers on colonial issues is particularly evident. And even though rivalries increased after that, the cooperative spirit in Europe continued to permeate and even propel the ongoing colonial and imperialist relationships with the non-European world throughout the century.[4]

---

[3] Cf. Treaty of Great Britain with the Netherlands, 4 May 1818; with Portugal, 28 July 1817; with Spain, 23 September 1817, AT-OeStA/HHStA, StK, Kongressakten, inv. no. 18, Aachen 1818.

[4] Cf. M. Borutta and S. Gekas, 'A Colonial Sea: The Mediterranean, 1798–1956', *European Review of History*, 19:1 (2012), 1–13; D. Todd, 'A French Imperial Meridian, 1814–1870', *Past & Present*, 210 (2011), 155–86, here: 161; S. Legêne and M. Eickhoff, 'Postwar Europe and the Colonial Past in Photographs', in A. Rigney and C. de Cesari (eds.), *Transnational Memory. Circulation, Articulation, Scales* (Berlin: De Gruyter, 2014), 287–311, here: 293. Legêne, Eickhoff and Todd make this point as well. In this sense, the period 1815–18 was much more than just a phase of 'technical cooperation', as suggested by Louise Richardson, 'The Concert of Europe', 57.

The Principle of Great Power Harmony

In 1814, the Russian diplomat Razumovsky expounded on the secret of European harmony: it consisted in the joint domination of the new European order by the four great powers. They could protect the social and political order of Europe from terror and despotism in the future only if they together formed a strong and united front.[5] Tsar Alexander was very clear about that. The primary goal for Alexander was to 'liberate Europe from the yoke that oppressed it; and to establish a political system based on law and on a firmly anchored balance of power'.[6] This political 'system of the balance of power' had to be protected by 'the first-ranked powers, who then had to protect it against any form of hegemony'.[7] It is true that the first Treaty of Paris (30 May 1814) stated in Article I that: 'The high contracting parties shall devote their best attention to maintain, not only between themselves, but, inasmuch as depends upon them, between all the states of Europe, that harmony and good understanding which are so necessary for their tranquility.' But it was understood that the four great Allied powers would take the lead in drafting the treaties of peace and signing them. The Final Act of Vienna was recorded by eight powers, including France, Portugal, Spain and Sweden. But the Second Treaty of Paris (20 November 1815) and the occupation of France were carried out by the Allied Council, in which only the four Allied powers were represented. They considered it their imperial task, as the four 'great powers', to put the European security machine together and to tend to it.[8]

That imperial alliance established a new explicit hierarchy in the European system. That hierarchy formed the basis for the expansion of imperial tendencies in two directions: externally and internally. The Allied Council extended its competencies to the European periphery and the non-European world, and at the same time began to get more involved with the design of domestic security on its own continent. The principle of security was the guiding principle for both domains. Security, that effervescent and insatiable principle of governance, was never bound by national borders or a country's autonomy, and surfaced in policies and strategies well before 1815. Yet, after 1815, it was interpreted by the great powers in more deliberation and more proactive and political concertation; moreover, it was no longer only understood as a military

---

[5] Nesselrode to Austria, England, Prussia, 31 December 1814, in Klüber, *Acten des Wiener Congresses in den Jahren 1814 und 1815*, vol. 7 (1815–18), 69ff.

[6] Russian memorandum to Castlereagh, 11 November 1814, in L. Chodźko (ed.), *Le Congrès de Vienne et les traités de 1815*, vol. 3 (Paris: Amyot, 1864), 452ff.

[7] Russian reply to Castlereagh's circular of 12 January 1815, 19 January 1815, in Chodźko (ed.), *Le Congrès de Vienne*, vol. 2, 799; Osiander, *The States System of Europe*, 225–6, citation on 229.

[8] The full texts of the various treaties and appendices can be found in Hertslet, *The Map of Europe by Treaty*, vol. 1. For example: the First Treaty of Paris, 30 May 1814, 2–28. For the Second Treaty of Paris, 20 November 1815, see Ibid., 342–411.

concept or discussed within a military or warlike setting. As of 1815, security became a matter of explicit national and international governance. Security became a matter of safeguarding one's colonial possessions, of protecting against terror on the periphery of Europe or in the New World – through concerted action. In Europe, the imperial security mandate that the Allied Council had given itself legitimized the increased intervention of the great powers in existing social and political institutions in order to shield them against alleged new revolutionary developments.

In fact, the Allied Council almost propped itself up as a 'European world government' (as Castlereagh warily and disapprovingly recorded). In addition to the ministers and diplomats of the great powers, financial experts, police corps and bankers were also increasingly part of the picture. Bankers, investors and security experts were needed to safeguard the interests of the great powers. This explains why the culture of treaties and fortified cities with which Europe had protected itself since 1713 was suddenly supplemented in 1815 with a whole series of new measures and practices. The new 'Wellington Barrier' was just as much a demonstration of this as was Gruner's intelligence agency, which was to collect information on conspiracies generated in France. After the French Revolution, the ambition of the victors was, therefore, at least as megalomaniac as that of Napoleon. Security in Europe meant that terror between states within Europe, but also far beyond, was to be tamed and prevented, but also that revolutionary outbursts on the domestic front, in the public square and in people's homes and hearts had to be tracked and chal- lenged. The populace – more or less informed and tacit – supported these measures for the time being. After 1815, a generation of new liberal thinkers relinquished the old eighteenth-century critiques of imperial expansion as formulated by Edmund Burke, Jeremy Bentham or Benjamin Constant. Philosophers like James and John Stuart Mill found that England's victory over Napoleon and the abolition of slavery were proof of the superiority of British civilization, and that that civilization could therefore safely be imposed through imperial expansion into 'inferior' or less developed countries. In France, Alexis de Tocqueville followed a similar line of reasoning, with the other great and secondary powers following suit.[9]

Indeed, the victory over revolutionary terror and Napoleonic despotism gave the four great powers the right to see themselves as superior, moderate and enlightened. They furthermore propagated that 'civilization' by dissemi- nating 'security' throughout Europe and beyond its borders – via the spread of their emotional vocabulary and by means of a series of concrete measures.

[9] J. Pitts, *A Turn to Empire. The Rise of Imperial Liberalism in Britain and France* (Princeton: Princeton University Press, 2005), 15–27.

CONCLUSION

Security as a Two-Edged Sword

The European security community used the fight against terror as a two-edged sword. The ministers and ambassadors in the Allied Council worked in relatively cooperative solidarity amongst themselves, but were all the more outwardly imperialistic and domineering towards their enemies for that. In other words, the collective security that the Council advocated was Janus-faced. The Allied ministers hid behind the law and constitutions, but were quick to use more modern police methods when they perceived a threat. The year 1815 did not represent a return to the despotism or absolutism of the *ancien régime*, but it also did not see the restoration of the 'liberty, equality and fraternity' of 1789. *La Loi et le Roi* – the law and the king – determined what terror was and how it had to be fought.[10] The Allied Council put a palette of real and imagined enemies on the European agenda: assassins, Jacobins, Ultras and liberals. Revolution, terror and 'passion' were the ghosts that haunted peace and order in society; 'jealousy' and 'egoism' were the enemy of harmony in international relations. The Council's primary focus was also clear: to restore property relations and create a stable investment climate, such that the post-war reconstruction could be tackled and colonial ambitions advanced.

That fight was effective because at critical moments the Allied Council facilitated the sway of one-man leadership for Wellington, allowing him to act as a crisis manager. With monies drawn from the British colonies and a supply of troops from Russia, an immense occupation army was mobilized, whose maintenance was then financed by France. Owing to the Napoleonic Wars, a large internal market had also emerged. And thanks to Napoleon's 'inner empire' (Michael Broers), the opponents of Bonapartism found each other as allies. Wellington had in the past mastered the art of broadening colonial power by co-opting subordinate chiefs and representatives of the local population (in India for example); Gruner had done so in Prussia and Richelieu in Crimea. They could now put that into practice in France and elsewhere in Europe. The Allied ministers' confidence in their own security management was given an additional boost by moral and 'Eurocentric Enlightenment thinking', by the remnants of Bonapartist centralization and by a Christian revival that triumphed after 1815 and benefited from its symbolic confirmation in the Holy Alliance (and the spread of all kinds of bible and missionary associations).[11]

---

[10] J.-C. Martin, *Contre-Révolution, Révolution et Nation en France 1789-1799* (Paris: Seuil, 1998).

[11] See, for example, Vick, 'Power, Humanitarianism and the Global Liberal Order', 13–14. For the spread of bible and missionary associations, see A. Kloes, *German Awakening. Protestant Renewal after the Enlightenment, 1815-1848* (Oxford: Oxford University Press), 94, 155–85.

Whether that new security culture was a sustainable one is more difficult to assess. In the context of their own professed aims, they succeeded, at least partially. These security managers and 'balancers' of 1815 sought to protect the future from the terrors of the past. In 1818, Tsar Alexander was still predominantly worried about Napoleon. Pozzo di Borgo forced the other Allied ministers in Aix-la-Chapelle to declare that they would not listen to the plethora of opposing voices – French or not – calling for a more liberal approach or even the release of the ailing emperor. Pozzo also impressed on his colleagues that Napoleon's relatives had to remain under supervision and in their assigned countries.[12] After 1818, however, the Bonapartes were no longer the most important security risk. (Napoleon himself died in 1821.) Nor was the resurrection of France as an aggressor going to put the guardians of Europe's security to the test in the coming years. Therefore, in this sense, the security managers were effective. Yet, in their zeal and dedication to anti-revolutionary measures, they unleashed another spectre: with their methods they fanned the flame of the desire for freedom nestled in the bosom of their own states and stoked the flare-up of national reform movements. In fact, the rulers of the absolutist-governed countries, those who had worked the hardest to set up central security services, intelligence bureaus, databases and black-lists, became the greatest threat to their subjects.

The collective fight against terror in these first immediate post-war years carved out the contours of nineteenth-century Europe in a more lasting and institutional form than has been assessed so far. These contours were pointed: hierarchical, asymmetrical, imperial. Many benefited, but many others were excluded. The collective definition of terror – as an overarching threat to estate-based, imperialist and anti-revolutionary interests – remained intact. Thus armed discursively, the Allied Council did not hesitate to halt the first attempts at democratization and modernization and to ramp up non-European colonial submission. Post-war European committees colonized the Rhine – the lifeblood of Europe – and opened the deltas of the Scheldt for free trade. European ships jointly undertook the fight against Barbary pirates and incorporated the Mediterranean into that system of security. At the same time, a veritably unprecedented transformation took place in the heart of Europe itself. The four great powers colonized the continent and transformed it into a region of industrious activity, peace and security that was based on a complex system of ranking social groups. Based on a hierarchy of profit-making and exploitation, this security framework can, therefore, not be broken down into an intra- and extra-European culture. Processes of 'othering' – excluding certain groups that were seen as a risk or threat – and of a unifying standardization on the continent and beyond were in line with each other. According to

---

[12] Pozzo di Borgo, 'Mémoire sur Napoleon', Aken, AT-OeStA/HHStA, StK, Kongressakten, inv. no. 18, Subfolder 'Protokolle', Aachen 1818, map fasc. 32, 34–47b.

Christopher Bayly, the facial features of father state were now much more clearly visible, and the government's actions much more evident, and more 'rational', than they had been in the eighteenth century.[13] These administrative interventions were expressed both in trade and in the enforcement of open markets via state-owned companies, both in the administrators' own countries and between the European countries themselves. That is why these European attempts to expand their realm of security and free trade irrevocably created enemies: in the bosom of their own states and societies, on the side of the oppressed, among the marginalized supporters of the *ancien régime*, but also in the New World, both in South America and the United States. As the geo-political and ideological ambitions increased, resistance grew.

This being the case, the fight against terror and enforced security were always subject to conditions, and connected to the tacit consent of the citizens and subjugated foreign nationals. As in the colonies, the central security policy and the superiority of the ruling government's police and military forces were invariably challenged by the endemic and regularly kindled resistance from the local population.[14] This was evident from the obstruction that the French populace and local administrators initiated against the Allied occupiers, or from the criticism of the publicists and radical pundits regarding the new European order, and certainly from the assassination attempts targeted at Wellington and Tsar Alexander in France and at the notables of the restoration elsewhere in Europe. Attacks on the Allied occupation forces in France con-tinued until they left in 1818, sometimes in the form of bouts of open violence and assault, sometimes more surreptitiously in conspiracies or corrupt prac-tices, such as during the construction of the Wellington Barrier, or as exem-plified in the *émigrés* averting exile and censorship in Belgium.[15]

The peace and order achieved was less stable than the signatories of the Quadruple Alliance had hoped for, not only with regard to social and political relationships domestically, but on the international front. Imperialist security, by definition, exhibits expansive and totalitarian tendencies, with the result that the great powers of Europe at times came to stand against each other. As memories of Napoleonic domination faded, the ties that bound Europe together loosened. During the nineteenth century, imperialist interests began to collide more and more, especially when nationalistically driven power brokers and demagogues began to define and determine international politics in a totally different, non-concerted vernacular.

---

[13] Bayly, *Birth of the Modern World*, 139.

[14] See, for example, A. Burton, *The Trouble with Empire. Challenges to Modern British Imperialism* (New York/Oxford: Oxford University Press, 2015).

[15] For more information on this episode, see Y. Balk, Threats to Tranquillity. Perceiving and Countering Security Threats in Britain and the Netherlands, 1815–1820 (unpublished MA thesis, Utrecht University, 2019).

What Remained?

Between 1815 and 1818, the 'Allied Machine' was running strong on all four cylinders, and all four of its principles had been implemented: demilitarization, de-Bonapartization, stabilization and the payment of reparations. (1) Napoleon's Grande Armée was dissolved. (2) The Bonapartes were banished and placed under supervision, and the Bonapartist generals were fired, convicted or purged. (3) The regime of Louis XVIII was stabilized and the spirit of revolutionary terror had been constrained, not only with an iron fist and the help of intelligence agencies, but also by obliging France to forever retain its 'constitutional shape', as was once again recorded in Aix-la-Chapelle.[16] (4) The price of peace as set by the Allies was, moreover, indeed paid by France. The bulwark of Europe was not only built on the bayonets of the occupation army; that was the case for only a few years. Rather, it was visibly sealed, and came together in a more sustainable manner – drawn on the paper of treaties, bonds and passports and built with the bricks of the Wellington Barrier. That process went so smoothly that second-level powers, who had initially been very critical and hostile towards the Allied consortium, were soon very eager to get on board (partly because doing so gave them access to financial support for building their fortifications and to compensation for past-due debts). In October 1818, the Allied Council was about to use their newly constructed European bulwark as a springboard to the New World, with an eye to restoring the imperial order there as well. But here, the Allied Machine faltered. The driving force behind the Allied Council, Britain, chose instead, when it came to the non-European world overseas, to go it alone and follow its own imperialist self-interests. Wellington was also – quite reasonably – not convinced that getting involved in fighting colonial rebellions and terror in the southern hemisphere would garner much success.

The generation of colonizers after 1815 was nimble and agile. They were open to reforms and innovations in the areas of management, high finances and governance. However, this generation bade farewell to international politics in the 1820s, causing the system of collective security to show fractures. Richelieu, whose resignation in December 1818 'all Europe should and does regret' (*dixit* Dorothea Lieven),[17] returned briefly in 1821, but died of a stroke in 1822. Castlereagh, that mastermind of balancing British and European great power interests, committed suicide in 1822, driven to this by an alleged psychological or medical condition.[18] Tsar Alexander died unexpectedly of

---

[16] 'Apperçus sommaires', 1 November 1818, included with the protocol of 9 October 1818, AT-OeStA, StK, Kongressakten, inv. no. 17, Subfolder 'Protokolle', 105.

[17] Dorothea Lieven to Alexander, 3/15 January 1819, in Robinson (ed.), *Letters of Dorothea*, 38.

[18] Castlereagh's biographer, John Bew, cannot say with certainty what drove him to suicide. It was perhaps a fit of madness caused by a venereal disease, perhaps depression or a total collapse resulting from the great political pressure with which he had to deal.

typhus in 1825. Spy master Gruner also did not live long after being promoted away to Switzerland. Managers-in-chief Metternich and Wellington remained in the saddle for a long time, but their political stardom soon faded.[19] When he was prime minister, Wellington's conservative government became entangled in the refusal to implement new parliamentary reforms. In France, Louis XVIII was consumed by gangrene and his brother, 'Monsieur', who came to power as Charles X in 1824, exacerbated the polarization and brought the House of Bourbon to its ruin. In 1830, the Bourbons had to clear the field for good.[20] The satellite state of the Netherlands was split in half, with Belgium becoming independent and neutral, so that the Wellington Barrier lost its value in one fell swoop.[21]

As the generation of sovereigns and ministers of 1815, with their matured rapport, was replaced by nationalistic power brokers and demagogues, these became more dependent on public opinion and political parties on the home front and they let solidarity with the European Concert fall by the wayside. What is more, popular support was from the 1820s and 1830s onwards increasingly bought off by launching offshore colonial projects, in India or North Africa, where the French, having endured their own foreign occupation, tried to occupy Algeria in turn. Rather than tapping into the great power idiom of 'balance', (alleged) 'disinterestedness' and 'moderation', domestically driven campaigns for national greatness were a catalyst for the disintegration of the Vienna system in the second half of the nineteenth century.[22] Wellington, who lived until 1853 and even ended up in a black-and-white photograph, in his old age made quite a fuss about these developments. He found the populists' catering to public sentiment through the press, and their blind eye to the need of collective security, both extremely distasteful and definitely harmful.[23]

The Legacy of the Allied Occupation

The joint Allied occupation of France, which set the precedent for all sorts of ministerial and ambassadorial conferences in the decades to come, was itself a novelty and remained in the collective memory. In the years that followed,

[19] Wellington's role in the 'Peterloo Massacre' in 1819 was controversial. The Manchester magistrates decided to suppress a meeting of 60,000 peaceful, picnicking demonstrators, resulting in eleven deaths. They nonetheless received a thank-you letter from the Prince Regent. As a member of the Cabinet, Wellington fully agreed with that. He, and the other ministers with him, had to endure the anger and indignation of many liberals and radical critics regarding the matter. Muir, *Wellington. Waterloo and the Fortunes of Peace*, 139–45.
[20] See Ibid., 383–400, 472–4.
[21] Belgium did not have an adequate army to man the forts.
[22] Osiander, *The States System of Europe*, 251.
[23] Ibid., 549.

the European powers would turn to such joint treaty-sanctioned military or armed security occupations and interventions more frequently: for example, in Syria (1860–1), Macedonia (1898) and China (1900).[24] We could therefore argue that the most impactful legacy of the Allied Council was twofold: it introduced both a joint allied military occupation and the method of convening ambassadorial/ministerial conferences to the repertoire of international relations.

Interestingly enough, France was the first to embrace the method of military occupation. While the (disgrace of the) military occupation of the Allies was usually tucked away and seldom mentioned (or if mentioned, reduced to a footnote) in the official French history books covering this period, the idea of this kind of great-power-sanctioned occupation was kept afloat in French politics and served as an example for France's own interventions. In 1829, the ultra-royalist and equally reactionary and megalomaniacal French minister of foreign affairs and prime minister Jules de Polignac distributed a plan to occupy Algeria. In doing so, France could take the lead in 'freeing Europe from the threefold scourge' of piracy, Christian slavery and the financial extortion of European ships and commercial convoys by Barbary sovereigns – and en passant underscore the place of France among the leading powers of Europe.[25] Polignac suggested to the French king, Charles X, that he would organize an international conference and invite the other great powers to think about a joint occupation of Algeria and about dividing up the Ottoman provinces amongst themselves. Polignac also sketched out a first move in this direction. His plan included a complete rearrangement of Vienna's Europe: the Kingdom of the Netherlands would be transplanted to Constantinople, which, together with Greece, would come under the authority of the House of Orange. In this way, the heart of the Ottoman Empire would once again be firmly in Christian (albeit Protestant) hands. The European parts of the Ottoman Empire would revert to Russia, and the Balkans to Austria. The Kingdom of the Netherlands in Europe would be dissolved, with the Dutch territory divided between France and Prussia, and the Dutch colonies going to Britain. France would thus gain 3.8 million Dutch citizens and, even more importantly, all the fortifications making up the Wellington Barrier. In a second plan, Polignac then laid out a design for a joint occupation of Algeria by the Allied powers, either as a temporary arrangement or a more definite one, supported by indigenous local princes and administrators – as an almost exact copy of the Allied occupation of France.[26]

[24] Cf. M. Schulz, 'Cultures of Peace and Security from the Vienna Congress to the Twenty-First Century', in De Graaf, De Haan and Vick (eds.), Securing Europe after Napoleon, 21–39.
[25] Letter of Polignac to Rayneval, the French ambassador in Vienna, 20 April 1830, CADLC, 11CP/412, fp. 148–51. With thanks to Erik de Lange.
[26] Cf. C.-A. Julien, Histoire de l'Algérie contemporaine, vol. 1: La conquête et les débuts de la colonisation (1827–1871) (Paris: Presses Universitaires de France, 1979), 59–60; A. Pingaud, 'Le projet Polignac (1829)', Revue d'histoire diplomatique, 14 (1900), 402–10.

With that, Polignac showed that he had taken the lessons of the Allied Council and the occupation of France to heart. Even the extremely reactionary and ultra-royalist Polignac knew by now that unilateral military or security operations in post-war times (after 1815) were not a good idea. The French desire for war would have more effect if it was embedded in European congress politics and could be implemented with the support of the other Allies. Although the plan of the Duke of Polignac sounded almost too outrageous to be true, it was nevertheless seriously discussed in Paris, Vienna and St Petersburg. But Polignac and Charles X never got around to executing such ambitious foreign projects. In July 1830, the French population rebelled against their autocratic leadership and its repressive domestic laws, and put an end to the Bourbon monarchy for good – with the king ending up in Britain and Polignac in jail.[27]

The idea of the French intervening and occupying the Ottoman provinces was, however, not entirely off the table. In June 1830, France had invaded Algeria, initially intending a temporary occupation 'in the name of Europe', in order to protect and defend the 'Christian civilizations' along the Mediterranean littoral. Yet, ultimately, France would leave its troops there for the next 130 years. Under Napoleon III, France would, moreover, play a crucial role in the occupation of Lebanon and during the European intervention in the Syrian civil war in 1860 – again under the pretext of protecting the Christians in the Ottoman Empire. The repertoire of Allied military interventions and (temporary) occupations was further transformed into the mandate system of the League of Nations after the First World War. In this way, the Allied military occupation of France can also be seen as having been an example for later colonial interventions.[28]

Expansive Security

The second pillar of the Allied Council's legacy was the method of proclaiming a ministerial or ambassadorial conference to discuss a specific, oftentimes highly complex and galling international issue over a longer period of time.

The meetings and conferences of 1814–18 laid the foundation for a new form of European collective politics. More congresses took place than ever before. Conferences between ministers or ambassadors were from 1815 onwards the tried and true means not always of resolving conflicts and security threats, but at least of bringing them out into the open and allowing them to become topics for possible mediation, instead of considering them as *casus*

---

[27] Cf. A. Stern, 'Der grosse Plan des Herzogs von Polignac vom Jahre 1829', *Historische Vierteljahresschrift*, 3 (1900), 49–77, here: 67–9.

[28] Cf. O. Ozavci, *Dangerous Gifts. Imperialism, Security and Civil Wars in the Levant, 1798–1864* (Oxford: Oxford University Press, forthcoming).

foederis. Between 1642 and 1814 only a handful of European congresses took place. With the Congress of Vienna and the Allied Council of 1815, a century began in which the number of congresses and ministerial conferences – including the appropriation of new, uniform measures and practices that resulted from them – increased exponentially. A ministerial conference was convened every few years: to discuss South America (1826), Greece (1827), the Belgian Question (1830), the return of the pope to Rome (1849), the Danish monarchy (1850); but also on thematic issues such as sanitation concerns and quarantines (1851), sugar tariffs (1863), telegraph cables (1863), the postal unions (1863) and many other international affairs.[29] These kinds of conferences gave the European countries a huge head start in terms of technical, economic, financial and military issues compared to the rest of the world. During the First World War, this form of transnational cooperation at a professional level continued to exist: for example, in the joint European membership in the Mixed Courts of Egypt and in the Central Commission for the Rhine and the Danube.[30] And another allied Conference of Ambassadors continued its deliberations after 1918 throughout the 1920s until 1931, when it was integrated into the League of Nations.[31]

The actual 'winners' and gatekeepers of this security revolution of 1815 were not necessarily the ministers, sovereigns or princes of that era, but their bureaucrats, deputies, officers, diplomats, experts, managers, bankers and lawyers. It was this professional caste of administrators that made the above-mentioned conferences and committees work that came out on top in the decades that followed. They reformed taxation policies, continued the standardization of identification and registration practices, drew up protocols, and built up transnational expertise regarding free maritime and Rhine River navigation. Thanks to their circulation of expertise and knowledge, the joint European powers managed to force the Ottoman Empire to its knees in the Greek wars for independence.[32] They were the ones who mapped the newly

[29] P. Macalister-Smith and J. Schwietzke, *Diplomatic Conferences and Congresses. A Bibliographical Compendium of State Practice, 1642 to 1919* (Graz: Neugebauer Verlag, 2017); Richardson, 'The Concert of Europe', 78–9.

[30] See, for example, M. Hoyle, *Mixed Courts of Egypt* (London: Graham & Trotman, 1991); J. Schenk, 'The Central Commission for Navigation of the Rhine: A First Step towards European Economic Security?', in De Graaf, De Haan and Vick (eds.), *Securing Europe after Napoleon*, 75–94; H. Klemann, 'The Central Commission for the Navigation on the Rhine, 1815–1914: Nineteenth-Century European Integration', ECHR working paper: ECHR-2013-1.

[31] Cf. G. Pink, *The Conference of Ambassadors (Paris 1920–1931). Its History, the Theoretical Aspect of its Work, and its Place in International Organization* (Geneva: Geneva Research Centre, 1942); J. Heideking, *Areopag der Diplomaten. Die Pariser Botschafterkonferenz der alliierten Hauptmächte und die Probleme der europäischen Politik, 1920–1931* (Husum: Mathiesen Verlag, 1979).

[32] See Bayly, *The Birth of the Modern World*, 140–4.

acquired or occupied territories and implemented a new, colonial or imperialist administration, not just in the second half of the nineteenth century, but already in 1815. 'Grand technicians', like Kraijenhoff and Müffling, met, sat together for long periods of time, exchanged views and came up with new metrics and all sorts of innovations for hydraulic engineering and military use. Security professionals, such as Gruner, staffed the new intelligence centres in Mainz, Vienna and Milan, and bankers, such as Baring, came up with new forms of transnational lending.

Against that backdrop of internationalization and circulation of new ideas and modes of cooperation, we therefore need to respond to the question raised in the Introduction with a cautious, but positive reply. Napoleon was in the wrong, Europe did not witness a withered reduction to insignificance, but would on many fronts experience a period of growth and expansion. Yet, on one point, Napoleon had the better of his victors: the United States would indeed at the end of the nineteenth century 'grow rich by our follies'. By excluding the United States (against its will) from the Concert of Europe and dawdling in realizing the 'inevitable emancipation of the colonies', Europe would in time fall behind.[33] In the years after 1815, however, not many paid heed to an exiled emperor. Notwithstanding these imperial admonitions, this book has outlined how the immediate post-war years, so often glossed over in the trendsetting historical surveys, were not the calm after the Napoleonic storm. In the fight against terror, the great powers planted the seed of a new, modern system of European collective security – including the irrevocably linked imperialist surveillance of one's own population, and increased territorial expansion at the expense of the non-European world. Both strategies would cost the European powers dearly in the longer run of the nineteenth century.

---

[33] Las Cases (ed.), *Memorial de Sainte Hélène*, vol. 1, 327.

BIBLIOGRAPHY

Archives

Austria

Österreichisches Staatsarchiv, Haus-, Hof- und Staatsarchiv, Vienna (AT-OeStA/HHStA)

Staatskanzlei (StK) (1500–1860), Kongressakten, Subfolder, Protokolle Aachen 1818
StAbt, Türkei VI, 8, Berichte 1818–1820
StAbt, Spanien, Diplomatische Korrespondenz

Belgium

City Archive, Oudenaarde (*Stadsarchief Oudenaarde*, SAO)

Hollands Bestuur (HB) VIII, no. 463, 567, 583, 584
Modern Archief (MA), *Beraadslagingen Gemeenteraad*, no. 4665, 4666
Oud Archief (OA), *Versterkingen*, no. 1344

Britain

Baring Archives, ING London

No. 204228, French Reparation Loans: 1817 Loan
No. 204229, French Reparation Loans: 1818 Loan

The National Archives, Kew, London (TNA)

Foreign Office (FO) 27, Foreign Office, Political and Other Departments, General Correspondence before 1906, France, 1781–1905
FO 78, Ottoman Empire
FO 92, Foreign Office, General Correspondence before 1906, Continent Conferences, 1814–1822
FO 139, Continent Conferences, Delegation Archives, 1813–1822

FO 146, Foreign Office and Foreign and Commonwealth Office: Embassy and
   Consulates, France: General Correspondence, 1814–1971
War Office (WO) 55, Ordnance Office and War Office: Miscellaneous Entry Books
   and Papers, 1568–1923
WO 37, War Office, Scovell, Sir George (1774–1861), Knight General, c.1801–1860

University College Library, London (UCL)

Bentham Manuscripts, unpublished notes, box 32, 61, 100

Czech Republic

Státní ústřední archiv, Prague (SUA)

Acta Clementina, Correspondance politique Autriche. Cart 49, vol. 5

France

Archives nationales de France, Paris (ANF)

F7.3839, Extraits des rapports commissaires de police de Paris 1818
F7.6673, Enquête concernant la tentative d'assassinat sur Lord Wellington, février–
   mars 1818
F7.6675, Acte d'Accusation contre Marie André Cantillon et Louis Joseph Stanislas
   Marinet

Archives de la Préfecture de Police, Paris (APP)

No. 342, attentat contre le duc de Wellington

Centre des archives diplomatique de La Courneuve, Paris (CADLC)

No. 8CP/609, Angleterre, Correspondance politique, 1817
No. 11CP/412, Autriche, Correspondance politique, jan.–sep. 1830

Archives du ministère des Affaires étrangères (AMAE)

Vol. 646, Mémoires et Documents, France – Fonds 'Bourbon'

Centre des Archives diplomatiques de Nantes (CAdN):

No. 8ACN/1, 'Commission des Requisitions, Procès Verbaux et correspondances,
   1815'
No. 8ACN/6, 'Correspondance de l'administration des douanes avec la
   Commission Royale des Réquisitions, novembre 1815 – mars 1816'
No. 8ACN/7[8], Commission des Requisitions, Procès Verbaux et correspon-
   dances, 1815'

No. 8ACN/4, Map 'Invasion de 1815'. 'Correspondence des Préfets avec le Ministère de l'Intèrieure, 1815'

No. 8ACN/294, 'Reclamations contre les Pays-Bas'

No. 8ACN/258, Reclamations', 1816–1818

Germany

Geheimes Staatsarchiv Preussischer Kulturbesitz, Berlin (GStA PK)

I. HA Rep. 92, Nachlass (Nl.) Eichhorn, no. 22

III. HA. Ministerium der auswärtigen Angelegenheiten, I

No. 862, Besetzung v Frankreich und den noch nicht vertheilten deutschen Territorien. Rückmarsch der verbündeten Heere. März–Juni 1814

No. 891, Vorübergehende Verwaltung Belgiens durch die alliierte Mächte, April 1814–Oktober 1816

No. 903, Polizeiverwaltung von Paris und der angebliche Plan eines Anschlags auf König Friedrich Wilhelm III

No. 913, Revuen und Manöver der preussischen und anderen alliierten Truppen, 1816

No. 1238, Administration von Belgien nach der Besetzung durch die alliierten Truppen, Februar–Augustus 1814

No. 1461/2/3, Militärische und politische Verhandlungen der Alliierten mit Frankreich. Korrespondenzen und Denkschriften, Juli–November 1815

No. 1464/5, Konferenzprotokolle der Minister der alliierten Mächte, Juli–Dezember 1815

No. 1469, Procès verbaux des Conférences à Paris, du 2. Octobre jusqu'au 22. Nov 1815

No. 1485, 1486, 1487, 1488, Zuweisung von Gebieten an Coburg etc. auf Grund der Wiener und Pariser Kongressverhandlungen, Juni 1815–Dez. 1883

No. 8884, Attentat Brit. Parlament, 1817

No. 8886, Mord-Versuch auf Wellington 1818

IV. HA Rep. 15 A Preussische Armee, no. 64

VI. HA, Nachlass Gneisenau, no. 452, 479

VI. HA, Nachlass Gruner, J. K., no. 27, 32, 41, 86, 88

VI. HA, Nachlass Hardenberg

VI. HA, Nachlass Müffling, A7

No. 10a, Berichte des Justus von Gruner aus Paris

No. 38, Schriftwechsel Gneisenau

No. K55, Schriftwechsel Müffling

Hessisches Staatsarchiv Darmstadt (HStD)

O11 B32, Familienarchiv Freiherren von Gagern

The Netherlands

Nationaal Archief, The Hague (NL-HaNA)

No. 1.10.29, Collectie Fagel
No. 2.02.01, Algemene Staatssecretarie (ASS)
No. 2.05.01, Ministerie van Buitenlandse Zaken 1813–1870
No. 2.05.44, Gezantschap Groot-Brittannië, standplaats London
No. 2.05.46, Gezantschap Spanje
No. 2.21.005.30, Collectie Canneman

Stadsarchief Amsterdam (SAA)

No. 675, Archief van Bankiers- en Familiezaken Sillem
No. 735, Archief van de Firma Hope & Co. met verwante archiefformers

Turkey

Başbakanlık Osmanlı Arşivleri, Istanbul (BOA)

Topkapı Sarayı Müzesi Arşivi Belgeler (TS.MA.e), 243/16/1
Hattı Hümayun (HAT.), 286/17183
HAT. 953/40926
HAT. 960/41184 U
HAT. 961/41197 M

Published Primary Sources

Anderson, F. M., *The Constitutions and Other Select Documents Illustrative of the History of France, 1789–1901* (Minneapolis: H. W. Wilson, 1904).
Anglesey, Marquess of (ed.), *The Capel Letters. Being the Correspondence of Lady Caroline Capel and her Daughters with the Dowager Countess of Uxbridge from Brussels and Switzerland 1814–1817* (London: Jonathan Cape, 1955).
Audiffret-Pasquier, E. d' (ed.), *Mémoires du Chancelier Pasquier. Révolution – Consulat – Empire, 1812–1814*, 2 vols. (Paris: Plon, 1893–4).
Austen, J., *Mansfield Park* (New York: Penguin, 2003 [1814]).
Baines, E., *History of the Wars of the French Revolution*, vol. 2 (London: Longman, 1818).
Beeler, A., *Het dierlijk magnetismus beknopt in deszelfsverschijnselen en manieren van aanwending voorgesteld* (The Hague: Allart, 1814).
Bergasse, N., *Considérations sur le magnétisme animal, ou sur la théorie du monde et des êtres organisés, d'après les principes de M. Mesmer* (The Hague, 1784).
Beugnot, A. (ed.), *Mémoires du Comte Beugnot, Ancién Ministre (1783–1815)* (Paris: Dentu, 1868).
Brockhaus, F. (ed.), *Conversations-Lexicon*, vol. 4 (Leipzig/Altenburg: Brockhaus, 1815).

Broglie, Comte de (ed.), *Charles-Maurice de Talleyrand-Périgord. Mémoires du prince de Talleyrand, 1809–1815*, 3 vols. (Paris: Calmann-Lévy, 1891–92).

Burns, J., and H. Hart (eds.), *The Collected Works of Jeremy Bentham* (Oxford: Oxford University Press, 1996).

Cauchois-Lemaire, L., and I. Guyet, *Appel à l'opinion publique et aux états-généraux du royaume des Pays-Bas, en faveur des proscrits français, contre leurs proscripteurs* (The Hague: Wallez, 1817).

Chateaubriand, F.-R., *Mémoires d'outre-tombe*, 12 vols. (Paris: Brodard & Taupin, 1973 [1849]).

Chodźko, J. L. [pseud. Comte d'Angeberg] (ed.), *Le Congrès de Vienne et les traités de 1815*, 4 vols. (Paris: Amyot, 1863–4).

Clare, I. (ed.), *Library of Universal History. Containing a Record of the Human Race from the Earliest Historical Period to the Present Time Embracing a General Survey of the Progress of Mankind in National and Social Life, Civil Government, Religion, Literature, Science and Art*, vol. 7 (New York: Peale & Hill, 1897).

Clausewitz, C. von, *On Wellington. A Critique of Waterloo* (trans. and ed. P. Hofschroër, Norman: University of Oklahoma Press, 2010).

Clercq, A. de (ed.), *Recueil des traités de la France, 1803–1815*, vol. 2 (Paris: Amyot, 1864).

Cochelet, L. (ed), *Mémoires sur la Reine Hortense et la Famille Impériale* (Paris: Ollendorf, 1907).

Colenbrander, H. (ed.), *Gedenkstukken der algemeene geschiedenis van Nederland van 1795 tot 1840*, 10 vols. (The Hague: Martinus Nijhoff, 1912).

Conway, S. (ed.), *The Collected Works of Jeremy Bentham. The Correspondence of Jeremy Bentham*, vol. 8 (Oxford: Oxford University Press, 1988).

Delavigne, C., *Trois Messéniennes* (Paris: Ladvocat, 1822).

Dickens, C., et al. (eds.), *Bentley's Miscellany*, vol. 43 (London: Bentley, 1858).

Ducoin, A., *Paul Didier. Histoire de la conspiration de 1816* (Paris: Dentu, 1844).

Dulaure, J., *Histoire civile, physique et morale de Paris*, vol. 9 (Paris: Baudouin Frères, 1825).

Duvergier, J. (ed.), *Collection complète des lois, décrets, ordonnances, réglements*, vol. 20 (Paris: A. Guyot, 1837).

Eckermann, J., *Gespräche mit Goethe in den letzten Jahren seines Lebens, 1823–1832*, vol. 1 (Leipzig: Brockhaus, 1837).

Edgcumbe, R. (ed.), *The Diary of Frances Lady Shelley, 1787–1817* (New York: Scribner's, 1912).

Edgcumbe, R. (ed.), *The Diary of Frances Lady Shelley, 1818–1873* (New York: Scribner's, 1913).

Edinburgh Annual Register for 1819, vol. 12 (Edinburgh: Archibald Constable, 1823).

Encycloaedia Britannica, vol. 4 (Edinburgh: Black, 1842).

Flitner, A., and K. Giel (eds.), *Wilhelm von Humboldt. Werke in fünf Bänden*, vol. 4 (Darmstadt, 1969).

Foreign Office (ed.), *British and Foreign State Papers, 1812–1816*, 3 vols. (London: Ridgway, 1838–42).

Freksa, F., *A Peace Congress of Intrigue (Vienna, 1815). A Vivid, Intimate Account of the Congress of Vienna Composed of the Personal Memoirs of its Important Participants* (New York: Century, 1919).

Gagern, H. von (ed.), *Das Leben des Generals Friedrich von Gagern*, vol. 1 (Leipzig/ Heidelberg: C. F. Winter, 1856).

Gagern, H. von, *Mein Antheil an der Politik*, vol. 1: *Unter Napoleons Herrschaft* (Stuttgart/Tübingen: Cotta, 1823).

Gagern, H. von, *Mein Antheil an der Politik*, vol. 2: *Nach Napoleons Fall. Der Congress zu Wien* (Stuttgart/Tübingen: Cotta, 1826).

Gagern, H. von, *Mein Antheil an der Politik*, vol. 3: *Der Bundestag* (Stuttgart and Tübingen: Cotta, 1830).

Gagern, H. von, *Der zweite Pariser Frieden* (Leipzig: Brockhaus, 1845).

Galignani, A., and W. Galignani, *Galignani's New Paris Guide for 1880* (Paris: Galignani Library, 1880 [1827]).

Galland, A., *Du Retour des Bourbons en France et du gouvernement paternel de Louis XVIII* (Paris, 1815).

Gentz, F. von, *Fragments upon the Balance of Power in Europe* (trans. London: Baldwin, 1806).

Gentz, F. von, 'Über de Pradt's Gemälde von Europa nach dem Kongress von Aachen', *Wiener Jahrbüchern der Literatur*, 5 (1819), 279–318.

Gifford, C., *History of the Wars Occasioned by the French Revolution, from the Commencement of Hostilities in 1792, to the End of 1816. Embracing a Complete History of the Revolution*, vol. 2 (London: Lewis, 1817).

Giraud, P. (ed.), *Campagne de Paris, en 1814, précédée d'un coup-d'oeil sur celle de 1813* (Paris: Chez les Marchands de Nouveautés, 1814).

Gladstone, W. (ed.) *Political Speeches in Scotland, November–December 1879* (Edinburgh: Elliott, 1880).

Gruner, J., *Actenmäßige Erzählung der Betrügereien eines angeblichen Wundermädchens* (Berlin, 1800).

Gruner, J., *Leidenschaft und Pflicht. Eine Sammlung moralischer Gemälde* (Berlin, 1800).

Gruner, J., *Meine Wallfahrt zur Ruhe und Hoffnung oder Schilderung des sittlichen und bürgerlichen Zustandes Westphalens am Ende des 18. Jahrhunderts* (Frankfurt, 1802).

Gruner, J., *Versuch über die rechte und zweckmäßigste Einrichtung öffentlicher Sicherheitsinstitute und deren Verbesserung* (Frankfurt, 1802).

Gruner, J., *Versuch über Strafen in vorzüglicher Rücksicht auf Todes- und Gefängnisstrafen* (Göttingen, 1799).

Gruner, J. Jr, 'Müffling und Gruner bei Beschaffung eines Fonds für die Polizeiverwaltung während der Occupation im J. 1815', *Deutsche Zeitschrift für Geschichtswissenschaft*, 11:1 (1894), 364–8.

Guizot, F., *Memoirs to Illustrate the History of my Time*, vol. 1 (trans. London: Bentley, 1858).

Gurwood, J. (ed.), *The Dispatches of Field Marshal the Duke of Wellington, K. G. during his Various Campaigns in India, Denmark, Portugal, Spain, the Low Countries and France* [abbreviated as *WD*], 13 vols. (London: John Murray, 1834–9).

Gurwood, J. (ed.), *Selections from the Dispatches and General Orders of Field Marshal the Duke of Wellington* (London: John Murray, 1851).

Hanoteau, J. (ed.), *Lettres du prince Metternich à la comtesse de Lieven, 1818–1819* (Paris: Plon-Nourrit, 1909).

Hansard, T. (ed.), *The Parliamentary Debates from the Year 1803 to the Present Time*, vol. 31 (London: Hansard, 1815).

Harpaz, E. (ed.), *Benjamin Constant. Récueil d'articles, 1820–1824* (Geneva: Droz, 1981).

Hertslet, E. (ed.), *The Map of Europe by Treaty. Showing the Various Political and Territorial Changes which have Taken Place since the General Peace 1814* (London: Butterworths, 1875).

Hobbes, T., *Leviathan* (London/New York: Routledge, 2008 [1651]).

House of Commons, *Papers Concerning the Case of Marshall Ney*, 14 February 1816 (London: House of Commons, 1816).

Jones, H. (ed.), *Reports Relating to the Re-Establishment of the Fortresses in the Netherlands from 1814 to 1830* (London: Spottiswoode, 1861).

Journals of the House of Commons (1547–).

Justi, J. von, *Natur und Wesen der Staaten als die Quelle aller Regierungswissenschaften und Gesetze* (Aalen: Scientia, 1969 [1771]).

Kant, I., 'Idee zu einer allgemeinen Geschichte in weltbürgerlicher Absicht', in *Kants Werke, Akademie-Ausgabe*, vol. 8 (Berlin: Georg Reimer, 1912 [1784]).

Klinkowström, C. von (ed.), *Aus der alten Registratur der Staatskanzlei. Briefe politischen Inhalts von und an Friedrich von Gentz aus den Jahren 1799–1827* (Vienna: Wilhelm Braumüller, 1870).

Klüber, J. (ed.), *Acten des Wiener Congresses in den Jahren 1814 und 1815*, 9 vols. (Erlangen: Palm & Enke, 1815–35).

Kraijenhoff, C. (ed.), *Levensbijzonderheden van den Luitenant-Generaal Baron C. R. T. Krayenhoff door hem zelfden in schrift gesteld, en op zijn verlangen in het licht gegeven door H. W. Tydeman* (Nijmegen: Vieweg, 1844).

Las Cases, Emmanuel, comte de (ed.), *Memoirs of the Life, Exile, and Conversations of the Emperor Napoleon*, vol. 3 (London: Colburn, 1836).

Las Cases, Emmanuel, comte de (ed.), *Memorial de Sainte Hélène. Journal of the Private Life and Conversations of the Emperor Napoleon at Saint Helena*, vol. 4 (London: Colburn, 1823).

La Tour du Pin, Marquise de (ed.), *Journal d'une femme de cinquante ans, 1778–1815*, vol. 1 (Paris: Chapelot, 1913).

Lauze de Péret, P., *Causes et précis des troubles, crimes et désordres dans le département du Gard et dans d'autres lieux du Midi de la France* (Paris: Poulet, 1818).

Leeuwen-Canneman, M. (ed.), *Een vriendschap in het teken van 's Lands financiën. Briefwisseling tussen Elias Canneman en Isaac Jan Alexander Gogel, 1799–1813* (The Hague: Instituut voor Nederlandse Geschiedenis, 2009).

Lockhart, J., *Memoirs of the Life of Sir Walter Scott*, vol. 3 (Edinburgh, 1837).

Martens, G. de (ed.), *Nouveau recueil de traités des puissances et états de l'Europe. Depuis 1808 jusqu'à présent*, vol. 3 (Göttingen: Dieterich, 1818).

Maurin, M., *À la gloire de l'auguste famille des Bourbons, épître à Louis XVIII, roi de France et de Navarre suivie de Ode sur la misère* (Dijon: Carion, 1814).

Maxwell, W., G. Wright and Alexander (eds.), *Leben und Feldzüge des Herzogs von Wellington. Mit Benutzung der übrigen neuesten englischen Quellen deutsch bearbeitet von F. Bauer*, vol. 6 (Quedlingburg/Leipzig: Basse, 1844).

Metternich, R. (ed.), *Memoirs of Prince Metternich, 1773–1835*, 3 vols. (New York: Scribner's Sons, 1880–2).

Metternich-Winneburg, R. (ed.), *Oesterreichs Teilnahme an den Befreiungskriegen* (Vienna: Gerold's Sohn, 1887).

Meyer, C., *Aachen der Monarchen-Kongress im Jahr 1818* (Aix-la-Chapelle: Weiss, 1819).

Michaud, L., and F.-C.. le chevalier de Loynes (eds.), *Biographie universelle, ancienne et moderne. KM-LAL* Supplement 69 (Paris: Michaud, 1841).

Mikhailofsky-Danilefsky, A., *History of the Campaign in France in the Year 1814* (London: Smith, Elder and Co., 1839).

Mikhailofsky-Danilefsky [Mikhailovsky-Danilevsky], A., *Memuary. Memoirs on the Campaign of 1813* (St Petersburg: RNB, 2001 [1834]).

Mikhailovich, N. (ed.), *Doniesienia avstriiskovgo poslannika pri russkom dvore Lebzelterna za 1816–1828 gody* (St Petersburg, 1913).

Miller, J., *The History of Great Britain from the Death of George III to the Coronation of George IV* (London: Jones & Co, 1825).

Ministerstvo inostrannykh del CCCP (ed.), *Vneshniaia politika Rossii XIX i nachala XX veka: dokumenty Rossiiskogo Ministerstva inostrannykh del, 1815–1830*, 2 vols. (Moscow: Izdatelstvo politicheskoy literatury, 1974–6).

Moens, P., *Bij het intrekken van Napoleon Buonaparte in Parijs* (Utrecht: Zimmerman, 1815).

Morris, T., *Recollections of Military Service in 1813, 1814, and 1815, through Germany, Holland and France* (London: Madden, 1845).

Müffling, C. von (ed.), *The Memoirs of Baron von Müffling. A Prussian Officer in the Napoleonic Wars* (London: Greenhill, 1997).

N.N., *Arrêts de la cour d'assises du Brabant Méridional, précédés de l'acte d'accusation et du plaidoyer, prononcé par M. le Substitut du Procureur-Général, dans l'affaire du complot contre la personne de S. M. l'Empereur de toutes les Russies* (Brussels, 1819).

N.N., *Collection des Discours du Trône*, 2nd ed. (Paris: Boucher, 1826).

N.N., *Correspondance de M. le Préfet du Département de la Seine-Inférieure*, vol. 21 (1811–18) (Rouen: Periaux, 1815).

N.N., *Recueil de pièces officielles, relatives au procès concernant la dette d'Hollande, entre le Gouvernement français et celui des Pays-Bas, qui a été jugé par des arbitres, le 16 octobre 1816* (Paris: Gratlot, 1817).

Napoléon, Le prince (ed.), *Mémoires de la Reine Hortense publiés par le prince Napoléon. Avec notes de Jean Hanoteau*, 3 vols. (Paris: Plon, 1927).

Palm, J. van der, *Geschied- en redekunstig gedenkschrift van Nederlands herstelling in den jare 1813* (Amsterdam, 1816).

Pange, V. de (ed.), *Madame de Staël et le duc de Wellington. Correspondance inédite 1815–1817* (Paris: Gallimard, 1967).

Paşa, A. C., *Tārīh-i Cevdet*, vol. 10 (Istanbul, 1858).

Pasquier, E.-D., *Histoire de mon temps. Mémoires du chancelier Pasquier*, 4 vols. (Paris: Plon, 1893–5).

Polovtsoff, A. (ed.), *Le Duc de Richelieu. Correspondance et Documents, 1766–1822* (St Petersburg: Société impériale d'Histoire de Russie, 1887).

Pouthas, C. H. (ed.), *Charles de Rémusat. Mémoires de ma vie, 1797–1820*, vol. 1 (Paris: Perrin, 1958).

Pozzo di Borgo, C. (ed.), *Correspondance diplomatique du comte Pozzo di Borgo, ambassadeur de Russie en France, et du comte de Nesselrode (1814–1818)*, 2 vols. (Paris: Calmann Lévy, 1890).

Prokesch-Osten, A. (ed.), *Dépêches inédites du Chevalier de Gentz aux Hospodars de Valachie pour servir à l'histoire de la politique européenne (1813 à 1828)*, 2 vols. (Paris: Plon, 1876).

Pushkin, A., 'Bova' (1814), cited in L. Melnikova, 'Orthodox Russia against "Godless" France. The Russian Church and the "Holy War" of 1812', in J. Hartley, P. Keenan and D. Lieven (eds.), *Russia and the Napoleonic Wars* (Basingstoke: Palgrave Macmillan, 2015), 179–95.

Reimarus, J., *Klagen der Völker des Continents von Europa die Handelssperre betreffend. Ihren Fürsten dargestellt* (Hamburg, 1809).

Robert, D. (ed.), *Textes et documents relatifs à l'histoire des églises reformées en France (période 1800–1830)* (Paris: Droz, 1962).

Robert, J., *La Police sous MM. les Duc Decazes, Comte Anglès et Baron Mounier* (Paris, 1821).

Robinson, L. (ed.), *Letters of Dorothea, Princess Lieven, during her Residence in London, 1812–1834* (London/New York: Longmans, Green and co., 1902).

Sarrut, G., and B. Saint-Edme (eds.), *Biographie des Hommes du Jour*, vol. 2 (Paris: H. Krabe, 1836).

Schlesier, G. (ed.), *Schriften von Friedrich Gentz. Ein Denkmal* (Mannheim: Hoff, 1838).

Scott, J., *Journal of a Tour to Waterloo and Paris, in Company with Walter Scott in 1815* (London: Saunders, 1842).

Scott, W., *Paul's Letters to his Kinsfolk* (Edinburgh: Ballantyne, 1816).

Scott, W., *Waverley; or, 'Tis Sixty Years Since* (London: Penguin, 2011 [1814]).

Smet, M. de (ed.), *Het dagboek van Bartolomeus de Rantere. beschrijving van al het merkweerdigste dat er voorgevallen is in de stad en casselrije van Audenaerde zedert het jaer zeventhien hondert zevenentachentig tot het jaer achthien hondert vijfentwintig* (Oudenaarde: Sanderus, 1973).

Stanhope, P., *Notes of Conversations with the Duke of Wellington, 1831–1851* (New York: Longmans, 1888).

Tweede Kamer der Staten-Generaal (ed.), *Handelingen Tweede Kamer* (The Hague: Tweede Kamer der Staten-Generaal, 1814–1995).

Vane, C. (ed.), *Correspondence, Despatches, and Other Papers of Viscount Castlereagh*, 12 vols. (London: Shoberl, 1848–52).

Waldstreicher, D. (ed.), *The Diaries of John Quincy Adams, 1779–1821*, 2 vols. (New York: Penguin, 2017).

Weigall, R. (ed.), *The Letters of Lady Burghersh (afterwards Countess of Westmorland). From Germany and France during the Campaign of 1813–14* (London: John Murray, 1893).

Wellesley, A. (ed.), *Supplementary Despatches and Memoranda of Field Marshal Arthur Wellesley, 1st Duke of Wellington* [abbreviated as *WSD*], 15 vols. (London: John Murray, 1858–72).

Wilkinson, W., *An Account of the Principalities of Wallachia and Moldavia with Various Political Observations Relating to Them* (London: Longman, 1820).

Williams, H., *Letters on the Events Which Have Passed in France since the Restoration in 1815* (London: Baldwin, 1819).

Secondary Literature

Aalders, A., *Met gevelde lans en losse teugel. Kozakken in Nederland, 1813–1814* (Bedum: Egbert Forsten, 2002).

Aaslestad, K., 'War without Battles: Civilian Experiences of Economic Warfare during the Napoleonic Era in Hamburg', in A. Forrest, K. Hagemann and J. Rendall (eds.) *Soldiers, Citizens and Civilians: Experiences and Perceptions of the Revolutionary and Napoleonic Wars, 1790–1820* (Basingstoke: Palgrave Macmillan, 2009), 118–36.

Abel, W., *Landwirtschaftspolitik* (Wiesbaden: Springer Fachmedien, 1950).

Adanır, F., 'Turkey's Entry into the Concert of Europe', *European Review*, 13:3 (2005), 395–417.

Ahmed, S., *The Cultural Politics of Emotion* (Edinburgh: Edinburgh University Press, 2004).

Alsche, A., 'Levensberigt van Elias Canneman', *Jaarboek van de Maatschappij der Nederlandse Letterkunde* (1862), 47–69.

Anderson, B., *Imagined Communities. Reflections on the Origin and Spread of Nations* (revised ed., London/New York: Verso, 2006 [1983]).

Anderson, M., 'Eighteenth-Century Theories of Balance of Power', in R. Hatton and M. Anderson (eds.), *Studies in Diplomatic History. Essays in Memory of David Bayne Horn* (London: Archon Books, 1970).

André, R., *L'Occupation de la France par les Alliées en 1815 (Juillet–Novembre)* (Paris: Boccard, 1924).

Armitage, D., *Foundations of Modern International Thought* (Cambridge, MA: Harvard University Press, 2004).

Armitage, D., 'Globalizing Jeremy Bentham', *History of Political Thought*, 32:1 (2011), 63–82.

Artz, F., 'The Electoral System in France during the Bourbon Restoration, 1815–30', *The Journal of Modern History*, 1:2 (1929), 205–18.

Bald, H., and R. Kuhn, *Die Spessarträuber. Legende und Wirklichkeit* (Würzburg: Königshausen & Neumann, 1991).

Balk, Y., The Diabolical Conspiracy. An Inquiry into the Plotting, Rumouring and the Rise of a European Security Culture after the Assassination Attempt on the Duke of Wellington in 1818 (Unpublished MA thesis, Utrecht University, 2017).

Balk, Y., Threats to Tranquillity. Perceiving and Countering Security Threats in Britain and the Netherlands, 1815–1820 (Unpublished MA thesis, Utrecht University, 2019).

Barbero, A., *The Battle. A New History of Waterloo* (London: Atlantic Books, 2013).

Barros, C., and J. Smith, *Life-Writings by British Women 1660–1815. An Anthology* (Boston: Northeastern University Press, 2000).

Barth, V., and R. Cvetkovski, 'Introduction. Encounters of Empires. Methodological Approaches', in V. Barth and R. Cvetkovski (eds.), *Imperial Cooperation and Transfer, 1870–1930. Empires and Encounters* (London: Bloomsbury, 2015), 3–34.

Barton, G., *Informal Empire and the Rise of One World Culture* (Basingstoke: Palgrave Macmillan, 2014).

Bayly, C., *The Birth of the Modern World 1780–1914. Global Connections and Comparisons* (Oxford: Blackwell, 2004).

Béguin, M., 'Les Prussiens à Evreux en 1815', *Revue Catholique de Normandie*, 31 (1922), 122–7.

Bell, D., *The First Total War: Napoleon's Europe and the Birth of Warfare as We Know It* (London: Bloomsbury, 2007).

Bemis, S., 'Early Diplomatic Missions from Buenos Aires to the United States, 1811–1824', *American Antiquarian Society*, 49:1 (1940), 11–101.

Bensaude-Vincent, B., 'The Balance. Between Chemistry and Politics', *The Eighteenth Century*, 33:3 (1992), 217–37.

Benz, W., *Potsdam 1945. Besatzungsherrschaft und Neuaufbau im Vier-Zonen-Deutschland* (Munich: DTV, 2012).

Bertier de Sauvigny, G. de, *The Bourbon Restoration* (Philadelphia: University of Pennsylvania Press, 1966).

Bertier de Sauvigny, G. de, *Metternich et la France après le Congrès de Vienne*, vol. 1 (Paris: Presses Continentales, 1968).

Bertier de Sauvigny, G. de, *La Restauration* (Paris: Flammarion, 1955).

Bertier de Sauvigny, G. de, 'Sainte-Alliance et Alliance dans les conceptions de Metternich', *Revue Historique*, 223:2 (1960), 249–74.

Bew, J., *Castlereagh. A Life* (Oxford: Oxford University Press, 2012).

Bezotosnyi, V., 'Factions and In-Fighting among Russian Generals in the 1812 Era', in J. Hartley, P. Keenan and D. Lieven (eds.), *Russia and the Napoleonic Wars* (Basingstoke: Palgrave Macmillan, 2015), 106–18.

Blaufarb, R., *Bonapartists in the Borderlands. French Exiles and Refugees on the Gulf Coast, 1815–1835* (Tuscaloosa: University of Alabama Press, 2005).

Blaufarb, R., *The Great Demarcation. The French Revolution and the Invention of Modern Property* (Oxford: Oxford University Press, 2016).

Blichner, L., and A. Molander, 'Mapping Juridification', *European Law Journal*, 14:1 (2008), 36–54.

Bloch, M., *Réflexions d'un historien sur les fausses nouvelles de la guerre* (Paris: Allia, 1999 [1921]).

Blomeyer-Bartenstein, H., 'Conferences of Ambassadors', in Y. Zhou (ed.), *Encyclopedia of Public International Law* (Amsterdam: Elsevier, 1984), 48–9.

Bohls, E., *Women Travel Writers and the Language of Aesthetics, 1716–1818* (Cambridge: Cambridge University Press, 1995).

Bohstedt, J., 'The Myth of the Feminine Food Riot. Women as Proto-Citizens in English Community Politics, 1790–1810', in H. Applewhite and D. Levy, *Women and Politics in the Age of Democratic Revolution* (Ann Arbor: University of Michigan Press, 1990), 21–60.

Boogman, J., *Nederland en de Duitse Bond 1815–1851*, 2 vols. (Groningen/Jakarta: J. B. Wolders, 1955).

Bordo, M., and E. White, 'A Tale of Two Currencies. British and French Finance during the Napoleonic Wars', *Journal of Economic History*, 51:2 (1991).

Borremans, P., *Het Kezelfort van de vesting Oudenaarde* (Erpe: Krijger, 2006).

Borutta, M., and S. Gekas, 'A Colonial Sea. The Mediterranean, 1798–1956', *European Review of History*, 19:1 (2012), 1–13.

Boudon, J., *Napoléon expliqué à mes enfants* (Paris: Seuil, 2009).

Branda, P., 'La guerre a-t-elle payé la guerre?', in T. Lentz (ed.), *Napoléon et l'Europe. Regards sur une politique* (Paris: Fayard, 2005).

Braven, D. den, A Just Contribution. On the Reparations Imposed on Post-Napoleonic France (Unpublished MA thesis, Utrecht University, 2017).

Bray, R., *Armies of Pestilence. The Impact of Diseases on History* (Cambridge: James Clarke, 2004).

Brisson, J., and F. Ribeyre, *Les grands journaux de France* (Paris: Jouaust, 1862).

Broers, M., *Europe after Napoleon. Revolution, Reaction and Romanticism, 1814–1848* (Manchester/New York: Manchester University Press, 1996).

Broers, M., *Europe under Napoleon 1799–1815* (London: Arnold, 1996).

Broers, M., *The Napoleonic Empire in Italy, 1796–1814. Cultural Imperialism in a European Context?* (Basingstoke: Palgrave Macmillan, 2005).

Brown, G., *Latin American Rebels and the United States, 1806–1822* (Jefferson, NC: McFarland, 2015).

Brown, S., 'Movements of Christian Awakening in Revolutionary Europe', in S. Brown and T. Tackett (eds.), *Enlightenment, Reawakening and Revolution, 1660–1815* (Cambridge: Cambridge University Press, 2006).

Bruin, R. de, 'Regenten en revolutionairen (1747–1851)', in R. de Bruin et al. (eds.), *'Een paradijs vol weelde'. Geschiedenis van de stad Utrecht* (Utrecht: Matrijs, 2000), 315–73.

Brunn, G., *Europe and the French Imperium, 1799–1814* (New York: Harper, 1938).
Bryant, J., 'How Canova and Wellington honoured Napoleon', *Apollo*, 162 (2005), 38–40.
Buist, M., *At spes non fracta. Hope & Co, 1750–1815. Merchant Bankers and Diplomats at Work* (The Hague: Kluwer, 1974).
Bullen, R., 'France and Europe 1815–1848. The Problems of Defeat and Recovery', in A. Sked (ed.), *Europe's Balance of Power, 1815–1848* (London: Macmillan, 1979).
Burbank, J., and F. Cooper, *Empires in World History. Power and the Politics of Difference* (Princeton: Princeton University Press, 2010).
Burton, A., *The Trouble with Empire. Challenges to Modern British Imperialism* (New York/Oxford: Oxford University Press, 2015).
Butler, M., *Romantics, Rebels and Reactionaries. English Literature and its Background 1760–1830* (Oxford/New York: Oxford University Press, 1981).
Buyst, E., 'De onmogelijke integratie. Economische ontwikkelingen in Nederland en België', in I. de Haan, P. den Hoed and H. te Velde (eds.), *Een Nieuwe Staat. Het begin van het koninkrijk der Nederlanden* (Amsterdam: Bert Bakker, 2013).
Buzan, B., O. Waever and J. de Wilde, *Security. A New Framework for Analysis* (Boulder, CO: Lynne Riener, 1998).
Cardosa, J. (ed.), *Paying for the Liberal State. The Rise of Public Finance in 19th Century Europe* (Cambridge: Cambridge University Press, 2010).
Carl, H., 'Religion and the Experience of War: A Comparative Approach to Belgium, the Netherlands and the Rhineland', in A. Forrest, K. Hagemann and J. Rendall (eds.), *Soldiers, Citizens and Civilians: Experiences and Perceptions of the Revolutionary and Napoleonic Wars, 1790–1820* (Basingstoke: Palgrave Macmillan, 2009), 222–42.
Carpenter, S., *Aesthetics of Fraudulence in Nineteenth-Century France. Frauds, Hoaxes, and Counterfeits* (Aldershot: Ashgate, 2009).
Cernovodeanu, P., and N. Edroiu (eds.), *Istoria românilor* ['History of the Romanians'], vol. 6: *Românii în epoca clasică și epoca luminilor* ['The Romanians in the Classical Age and during the Enlightenment'] (Bucharest: Editura Enciclopedică, 2002).
Chapman, T., *The Congress of Vienna. Origins, Processes and Results* (Oxford: Routledge, 1998).
Chasteen, J., *Americanos. Latin America's Struggle for Independence* (Oxford: Oxford University Press, 2008).
Chène, L., *L'occupation Russe dans le Département du Nord (1815–1818)* (Unpublished MA Thesis, University of Lille, 2008).
Chisholm, H., 'Cauchois-Lemaire, Louis François Auguste', *Encyclopaedia Britannica*, vol. 11 (Cambridge: Cambridge University Press, 1911).
Clark, L., *The Rise of Professional Women in France. Gender and Public Administration since 1830* (Cambridge: Cambridge University Press, 2001).

Clay, S., 'White Terror. Factions, Reactions and the Politics of Vengeance', in P. McPhee (ed.), *A Companion to the French Revolution* (Oxford: Oxford University Press, 2015), 359–78.

Cohrs, P., *The Unfinished Peace after World War I. America, Britain and the Stabilisation of Europe, 1919–1932* (Cambridge: Cambridge University Press, 2008).

Colenbrander, H., *Vestiging van het Koninkrijk (1813–1815)* (Amsterdam: Meulenhoff, 1927).

Colenbrander, H., *Willem I. Koning der Nederlanden*, 2 vols. (Amsterdam: Meulenhoff, 1931–5).

Colenbrander, H., 'Willem I en de mogendheden, 1815–1824', *De Gids*, 95 (1931), 370–407.

Conze, E., 'Abschied von Staat und Politik? Überlegungen zur Geschichte der internationalen Politik', in U. Lappenküper and G. Müller (eds.), *Geschichte der internationalen Beziehungen. Erneuerung und Erweiterung einer historischen Disziplin* (Cologne: Böhlau, 2004), 14–43.

Conze, E., *Geschichte der Sicherheit. Entwicklung – Themen – Perspektiven* (Göttingen: Vandenhoeck & Ruprecht, 2017).

Conze, E., '"Securitization": Gegenwartsdiagnose oder historische Analyseansatz?', *Geschichte und Gesellschaft*, 38 (2012), 453–67.

Conze, W., 'Sicherheit, Schutz', in W. Conze et al. (eds.), *Geschichtliche Grundbegriffe*, vol. 5 (Stuttgart: Klett-Cotta, 1984), 831–62.

Cookson, J., 'Regimental Worlds: Interpreting the Experience of British Soldiers during the Napoleonic Wars', in A. Forrest, K. Hagemann and J. Rendall (eds.), *Soldiers, Citizens and Civilians: Experiences and Perceptions of the Revolutionary and Napoleonic Wars, 1790–1820* (Basingstoke: Palgrave Macmillan, 2009), 23–42.

Cooper, F., *Colonialism in Question. Theory, Knowledge, History* (Los Angeles: University of California Press, 2005).

Costeloe, M., *Response to Revolution. Imperial Spain and the Spanish American Revolutions, 1810–1840* (Cambridge: Cambridge University Press, 1986).

Courvoisier, J., *Le maréchal Berthier et sa principauté de Neuchâtel (1806–1814)* (Neuchâtel: Société d'histoire et d'archéologie, 1959).

Craig, G., *Politics of the Prussian Army, 1640–1945* (Oxford: Clarendon Press, 1955).

Craiutu, A., *Le Centre introuvable. La pensée politique des doctrinaires sous la Restauration* (Paris: Plon, 2006).

Craiutu, A., *A Virtue for Courageous Minds. Moderation in French Political Thought, 1748–1830* (Princeton/Oxford: Princeton University Press, 2012).

Crepon, T., *Leberecht von Blücher. Leben und Kämpfe. Biografie* (Berlin: Neues Leben, 1988).

Crowder, M., 'Indirect Rule: French and British Style', *Africa. Journal of the International African Institute*, 34:3 (1964), 197–205.

D'Arcy Wood, G., *Tambora. The Eruption that Changed the World* (Princeton: Princeton University Press, 2014).

Darnton, R., *Mesmerism and the End of the Enlightenment in France* (Cambridge, MA: Harvard University Press, 1968).

Davidson, D., C. Haynes and J. Heuer, 'Ending War: Revisiting the Aftermath of the Napoleonic Wars', *Journal of Military History*, 80 (2016), 11–30.

Delfiner, H., 'Alexander I, The Holy Alliance and Clemens Metternich: A Reappraisal', *East European Quarterly*, 37:2 (2003), 127–50.

Della Peruta, F., 'Le campagne lombarde nel Risorgimento', in F. Della Peruta (ed.), *Democrazia e socialismo nel Risorgimento* (Rome: Riuniti, 1965), 37–58.

Démier, F., *La France sous la Restauration (1814–1830)* (Paris: Gallimard, 2012).

Dieffenbach, L., *Karl Ludwig Schulmeister. Der Hauptspion, Parteigänger, Polizeipräfekt und Geheime Agent Napoleons I* (Leipzig: Webel, 1879).

Dinwiddy, J., 'English Radicals and the French Revolution, 1800–1850', in F. Furet and M. Ozouf (eds.), *The Transformation of Political Culture 1789–1848*, vol. 3 (Oxford: Pergamon Press, 1990), 447–66.

Douay, A., and G. Hertault, *Schulmeister. Dans les coulisses de la Grande Armée* (Paris: Éditions de la Fondation Napoléon, 2002).

Duchhardt, H., *Gleichgewicht der Kräfte, Convenance, Europäisches Konzert. Friedenskongresse und Friedensschlüsse vom Zeitalter Ludwigs XIV. bis zum Wiener Kongreß* (Darmstadt: Wissenschaftliche Buchgesellschaft, 1976).

Dülffer, J., M. Kröger and H. Wippich (eds.), *Vermiedene Kriege. Deeskalation von Konflikten der Grossmächte zwischen Krimkrieg und Erstem Weltkrieg (1856–1914)* (Munich: Oldenbourg, 1997).

Dupuis, C., *Le ministère de Talleyrand en 1814*, 2 vols. (Paris: Plon-Nourrit, 1919–20).

Dutacq, F., 'L'occupation autrichienne à Lyon en 1815', *Revue des Études Napoléoniennes*, 43 (1936), 270–91.

Dwyer, P., *Napoleon and Europe* (New York: Routledge, 2014).

Dyson, K., *States, Debts and Power. 'Saints' and 'Sinners' in European History and Integration* (Oxford: Oxford University Press, 2014).

Erlichman, C., and C. Knowles, 'Introduction: Reframing Occupation as a System of Rule', in C. Erlichman and C. Knowles (eds.), *Transforming Occupation in the Western Zones of Germany: Politics, Everyday Life and Social Interactions, 1945–55* (London: Bloomsbury, 2018), 3–24.

Esdaile, C., *Napoleon's Wars. An International History, 1803–1815* (London: Allen Lane, 2007).

Eustace, K., '"Questa scabrosa missione". Canova in Paris and London in 1815', in K. Eustace (ed.), *Canova Ideal Heads* (Oxford: Ashmolean Museum, 1997), 9–38.

Eustace, N., et al., 'AHR Conversation: The Historical Study of Emotions', *American Historical Review*, 117:5 (2012), 1487–531.

Evans, R., *The Pursuit of Power. Europe, 1815–1914* (New York: Penguin, 2016).

Ferguson, N., *The Cash Nexus. Money and Power in the Modern World, 1700–2000* (New York: Penguin, 2001).

Ferguson, N., *The World's Banker. The History of the House of Rothschild* (London: Weidenfeld & Nicolson, 1998).

Fijnaut, C., *Opdat de macht een toevlucht zij? Een historische studie van het politieapparaat als een politieke instelling* (Arnhem: Gouda Quint, 1979).

Fitzpatrick, B., *Catholic Royalism in the Department of the Gard, 1814–1852* (Cambridge: Cambridge University Press, 1983).

Forrest, A., K. Hagemann and J. Rendall (eds.), *Soldiers, Citizens and Civilians. Experiences and Perceptions of the Revolutionary and Napoleonic Wars, 1790–1820* (Basingstoke: Palgrave Macmillan, 2009).

Forrest, A., K. Hagemann and M. Rowe (eds.), *War, Demobilization and Memory. The Legacy of War in the Era of Atlantic Revolutions* (Basingstoke: Palgrave Macmillan, 2016).

Frary, L., *Russia and the Making of Modern Greek Identity, 1821–1844* (Oxford: Oxford University Press, 2015).

Freeman, C., *The Horses of St Mark's. A Story of Triumph in Byzantium, Paris and Venice* (London: Little, Brown, 2004).

Frevert, U., *Emotions in History. Lost and Found* (New York: Central European University Press, 2011).

Frevert, U., et al. (eds.), *Emotional Lexicons. Continuity and Change in the Vocabulary of Feeling 1700–2000* (Oxford: Oxford University Press, 2014).

Gabriëls, J., 'Cutting the Cake: The Congress of Vienna in British, French and German Political Caricature', *European Review of History*, 24:1 (2017), 131–57.

Garnett, P., 'The Wellington Testimonial', *Dublin Historical Record*, 13:2 (1952), 48–61.

Geikie, R., and I. Montgomery, *The Dutch Barrier, 1705–1719* (London: Cambridge University Press, 1930).

Gével, C., 'Mademoiselle Élisa Garnerin, aéronaute', *Revue politique et littéraire, Revue bleue* (1912), 434–9.

Ghervas, S., *Réinventer la tradition. Alexandre Stourdza et l'Europe de la Sainte-Alliance* (Paris: Honoré Champion, 2008).

Ghervas, S., 'La Sainte-Alliance: Un pacte pacifique européen comme antidote à l'Empire', in S. Aprile et al. (eds.), *Europe de Papier. Projets Européens au XIXe siècle* (Lille: Septentrion, 2015), 47–64.

Gillespie, A., *History of the Laws of War*, vol 2: *The Customs and Laws of War with Regards to Civilians in Times of Conflict* (Oxford: Bloomsbury, 2011).

Gils, R., *De versterkingen van de Wellingtonbarrière in Oost-Vlaanderen. De vesting Dendermonde, de Gentse citadel en de vesting Oudenaarde* (Gent: Dienst Monumentenzorg, 2005).

Giurescu, C., *Istoria românilor* ['A History of the Romanians'], vol. 3: *De la moartea lui Mihai Viteazul la sfârşitul epocei fanariote (1601–1821)* ['From the death of Michael the Brave to the end of the Phanariot Age'] (Bucharest: Editura All, 1944).

Goede, M. de, *European Security Culture. Preemption and Precaution in European Security* (Amsterdam: Vossius Press, 2011).

Goldstein, R., *Censorship of Political Caricature in Nineteenth-Century France* (Kent, OH: Kent State University Press, 1989).

Goujon, B., *Monarchies postrévolutionnaires 1814–1848. Histoire de la France contemporaine* (Paris: Seuil, 2012).

Graaf, B. de, 'The Allied Machine: The Conference of Ministers in Paris and the Management of Security' in B. de Graaf, I. de Haan and B. Vick (eds.), *Securing Europe after Napoleon. 1815 and the New European Security Culture* (Cambridge: Cambridge University Press, 2019), 130–49.

Graaf, B. de, 'Bringing Sense and Sensibility to the Continent. Vienna 1815 Revisited', *Journal of Modern European History*, 13:4 (2015), 447–57.

Graaf, B. de, 'Nederland en de collectieve veiligheid', in J. Pekelder, R. Raben and M. Segers (eds.), *De wereld volgens Nederland. Nederlandse buitenlandse politiek in historisch perspectief* (Amsterdam: Boom, 2015), 42–58.

Graaf, B. de, 'Second-tier Diplomacy: Hans von Gagern and William I in their Quest for an Alternative European Order, 1813–1818', *Journal of Modern European History*, 12:4 (2014), 546–66.

Graaf, B. de and M. van Leeuwen-Canneman, 'De prijs van de vrede: De Nederlandse inbreng in het Europees Concert, 1815–1818', *BMGN*, 133:1 (2018), 21–51.

Graaf, B. de and C. Zwierlein, 'Historicizing Security: Entering the Conspiracy Dispositive', *Historical Social Research*, 38:1 (2013), 46–64.

Graaf, B. de, I. de Haan and B. Vick (eds.), *Securing Europe after Napoleon. 1815 and the New European Security Culture* (Cambridge: Cambridge University Press, 2019).

Graft, C. van de, 'Kozakkendag te Utrecht', *Maandblad van Oud-Utrecht*, 41:4 (1968), 37–9.

Green, J., Edmund Burke's German Readers at the End of Enlightenment, 1790–1815 (Unpublished PhD thesis, University of Cambridge, 2017).

Green, J., '*Fiat iustitia, pereat mundus*: Immanuel Kant, Friedrich Gentz, and the Possibility of Prudential Enlightenment', *Modern Intellectual History*, 14:1 (2017), 35–65.

Greenfield, J., 'Financing a New Order: The Payment of Reparations by Restoration France, 1817–1818', *French History*, 30:3 (2016), 376–400.

Grever, M., 'Van Landsvader tot moeder des vaderlands: Oranje, gender en Nederland', *Groniek*, 158/9 (2002) 131–45.

Gruner, W., *Der Deutsche Bund 1815–1866* (Munich: C. H. Beck, 2012).

Gruner, W., 'Frankreich in der europäischen Ordnung des 19. Jahrhunderts', in W. Gruner and K.-J. Müller (eds.), *Über Frankreich nach Europa. Frankreich in Geschichte und Gegenwart* (Hamburg: Krämer, 1996), 201–74.

Gruner, W. (ed.), *Gleichgewicht in Geschichte und Gegenwart* (Hamburg: Krämer, 1989).

Gruner, W., *Grossbritannien, der Deutsche Bund und die Struktur des europäischen Friedens im frühen 19. Jahrhundert. Studien zu den britisch-deutschen*

Beziehungen in einer Periode des Umbruchs 1812–1820 (Munich: Eigenverlag, 1979).

Gruner, J., 'Gruner, Justus von', in *Allgemeine Deutsche Biographie*, vol. 10 (Leipzig: Duncker & Humblot, 1879).

Gruner, J., 'Müffling und Gruner', *Deutsche Zeitschrift für Geschichtswissenschaft*, 11:1 (1894), 364–8.

Gruner, W., 'Was There a Reformed Balance of Power System or Cooperative Great Power Hegemony?', *American Historical Review*, 97:3 (1992), 725–32.

Gruner, W., *Der Wiener Kongress 1814/15* (Stuttgart: Reclam, 2014).

Gueniffey, P., *Bonaparte, 1769–1802* (Paris: Gallimard, 2013).

Guerrin, Y., *La France après Napoléon. Invasions et occupations, 1814–1818* (Paris: L'Harmattan, 2014).

Haan, I. de and M. Lok (eds.), *The Politics of Moderation in Modern European History* (Basingstoke: Palgrave Macmillan, 2019).

Haas, E., 'The Balance of Power: Prescription, Concept, or Propaganda?', *World Politics*, 5:4 (1953), 442–77.

Hagemann, K., '"Unimaginable Horror and Misery": The Battle of Leipzig in October 1813 in Civilian Experience and Perception', in A. Forrest, K. Hagemann and J. Rendall (eds.), *Soldiers, Citizens and Civilians: Experiences and Perceptions of the Revolutionary and Napoleonic Wars, 1790–1820* (Basingstoke: Palgrave Macmillan, 2009), 157–78.

Hampson, N., *A Cultural History of the Enlightenment* (New York: Pantheon, 1968).

Hantraye, J., *Les Cosaques aux Champs-Élysées. L'occupation de la France après la chute de Napoléon* (Paris: Belin, 2005).

Härter, K., 'Security and Cross-Border Political Crime: The Formation of Transnational Security Regimes in 18th and 19th Century Europe', *Historical Social Research*, 38:1 (2013), 96–106.

Hartley, J., *Alexander I* (London: Longman, 1994).

Hartley, J., 'Patriotism in the Provinces in 1812: Volunteers and Donations', in J. Hartley, P. Keenan and D. Lieven (eds.), *Russia and the Napoleonic Wars* (Basingstoke: Palgrave Macmillan, 2015), 148–62.

Hartley, J., 'War, Economy and Utopianism: Russia after the Napoleonic Era', in A. Forrest, K. Hagemann and M. Rowe (eds.), *War, Demobilization and Memory: The Legacy of War in the Era of Atlantic Revolutions* (Basingstoke: Palgrave Macmillan, 2016), 84–99.

Haynes, C., 'Face à l'occupation étrangère de 1815–1818: Les sorties de guerre des Alsaciens', *Source(s)*, 4 (2014), 37–50.

Haynes, C., 'Making Peace: The Allied Occupation of France, 1815–1818', in A. Forrest, K. Hagemann and M. Rowe (eds.), *War, Demobilization and Memory: The Legacy of War in the Era of Atlantic Revolutions* (Basingstoke: Palgrave Macmillan, 2016), 51–67.

Haynes, C., *Our Friends the Enemies. The Occupation of France after Napoleon* (Cambridge, MA: Harvard University Press, 2018).

Head, D., 'A Different Kind of Maritime Predation: South American Privateering from Baltimore, 1816–1820', *International Journal of Naval History*, 7:2 (2008), 1–38.

Heideking, J., *Areopag der Diplomaten. Die Pariser Botschafterkonferenz der alliierten Hauptmächte und die Probleme der europäischen Politik, 1920–1931* (Husum: Mathiesen Verlag, 1979).

Helmert, H., and H.-J. Uszeck, *Der Befreiungskrieg 1813/4. Militärischer Verlauf* (Berlin: Militärverlag der DDR, 1968).

Herlihy, P., *Odessa. A History, 1794–1914* (Cambridge, MA: Harvard University Press, 1986).

Herremans, V., 'Van oorlogsbuit tot kerncollectie: Hoe het KMSKA een Rubensstempel werd', in F. Judo and S. van de Perre (eds.), *Belg en Bataaf. De wording van het Verenigd Koninkrijk* (Antwerpen: Polis, 2015), 158–73.

Heuer, J., '"No More Fears, No More Tears"? Gender, Emotion and the Aftermath of the Napoleonic Wars in France', *Gender & History*, 282:2 (2016), 438–60.

Hilton, B., *A Mad, Bad and Dangerous People? England 1783–1846* (Oxford: Oxford University Press, 2006).

Holland, R., *Blue-Water Empire. The British in the Mediterranean since 1800* (London: Allen Lane, 2012).

Holmes, R., *Wellington. The Iron Duke* (New York: Harper Collins, 2003).

Horricks, R., *Marshal Ney. The Romance and the Real* (London: Archway, 1988).

Houssaye, H., *1814* (Paris: Perrin, 1888).

Houssaye, H., *1815. La première restauration, le retour de l'île d'Elbe, les cent jours* (Paris: Perrin, 1893).

Houssaye, H., *1815. La seconde abdication – la terreur blanche* (Paris: Perrin, 1905).

Houssaye, H., 'Le retour du Roi en 1815', *Revue de Deux Monde*, 5:24 (1904), 481–509.

Houssaye, H., *Napoleon and the Campaign of 1814* (trans. R. McClintock, London: Hugh Rees, 1914).

Hoyle, M., *Mixed Courts of Egypt* (London: Graham & Trotman, 1991).

Hubatsch, W., *Die Stein-Hardenbergschen Reformen* (Darmstadt: Wissenschaftliche Buchgesellschaft, 1977).

Hunt, L., 'The French Revolution in Global Context', in D. Armitage and S. Subrahmanyam (eds.), *The Age of Revolutions in Global Context, c.1760–1840* (Basingstoke: Macmillan Education, 2010).

Hunt, L., *Inventing Human Rights. A History* (New York: Norton, 2007).

Hutchinson, E., and R. Bleiker, 'Theorizing Emotions in World Politics', *International Theory*, 6:3 (2014), 491–514.

Ikenberry, G. J., *After Victory. Institutions, Strategic Restraint and the Rebuilding of Order after Major Wars* (Princeton/Oxford: Princeton University Press, 2001).

Ilsemann, A. von, *Die Politik Frankreichs auf dem Wiener Kongress. Talleyrands aussenpolitische Strategien zwischen Erster und Zweiter Restauration* (Hamburg: Krämer, 1996).

Ingram, E., 'Bellicism as Boomerang: The Eastern Question during the Vienna System', in P. Krüger and P. Schroeder (eds.), *The Transformation of European Politics, 1763-1848'. Episode or Model in Modern History?* (Münster: LIT Verlag, 2002), 202–25.

Ionescu, S., *Bucureştii în vremea fanarioţilor* ['Bucharest in Phanariot times'] (Cluj-Napoca: Dacia, 1974).

Jarrett, M., *The Congress of Vienna and its Legacy. War and Great Power Diplomacy after Napoleon* (London: I. B. Tauris, 2013).

Jaspers, K., *The Question of German Guilt* (trans. New York: Fordham University Press, 1965).

Jaspers, K., *Die Schuldfrage* (Heidelberg: Schneider, 1946).

Jenkins, S., 'Buying Bonaparte', *Apollo*, 172 (2010), 50–5.

Jensen, L., *Celebrating Peace. The Emergence of Dutch Identity, 1648–1815* (Nijmegen: Vantilt, 2017).

Jensen, L., 'De hand van broederschap toegereikt: Nederlandse identiteiten en identiteitsbesef in 1815', in F. Judo and S. van de Perre (eds.), *Belg of Bataaf. De wording van het Verenigd Koninkrijk der Nederlanden* (Antwerp: Polis, 2015), 79–101.

Jensen, L., *Verzet tegen Napoleon* (Nijmegen: Vantilt, 2013).

Jensen, L., and B. Verheijen, 'De betekenis van 1813 voor het gewone volk: Oranje boven!', *Thema Tijdschrift*, 4:4 (2013), 10–11.

Jones, R., '1816 and the Resumption of "Ordinary History"', *Journal for Modern European History*, 14:1 (2016), 119–44.

Joor, J., *De Adelaar en het Lam. Onrust, opruiing en onwilligheid in Nederland ten tijde van het Koninkrijk Holland en de Inlijving bij het Franse Keizerrijk (1806–1813)* (Amsterdam: De Bataafsche Leeuw, 2000).

Joor, J., '"A Very Rebellious Disposition": Dutch Experience and Popular Protest under the Napoleonic Regime (1806–1813)', in A. Forrest, K. Hagemann and J. Rendall (eds.) *Soldiers, Citizens and Civilians: Experiences and Perceptions of the Revolutionary and Napoleonic Wars, 1790–1820* (Basingstoke: Palgrave Macmillan, 2009), 181–204.

Jourdan, A., *Mythes et légendes de Napoléon. Un destin d'exception, entre rêve et réalité* (Toulouse: Privat, 2004).

Julien, C.-A., *Histoire de l'Algérie contemporaine*, vol. 1: *La conquête et les débuts de la colonisation (1827–1871)* (Paris: Presses Universitaires de France, 1979).

Kaehler, S., *Wilhelm v. Humboldt und der Staat. Ein Beitrag zur Geschichte deutscher Lebensgestaltung um 1800* (Göttingen: Vandenhoeck & Ruprecht, 1963), 324–8.

Katzenstein, P. (ed.), *The Culture of National Security. Norms and Identity in World Politics* (New York: Columbia University Press, 1996).

Kaufmann, J., and H. Kaufmann, *The Forts and Fortifications of Europe, 1815–1945*, vol. 1: *The Central States*; vol. 2: *The Neutral States* (Barnsley: Pen and Sword, 2014).

Kelly, P., *Utilitarianism and Distributive Justice. Jeremy Bentham and the Civil Law* (Oxford: Clarendon Press, 1990).

Kempe, M., *Fluch der Weltmeere. Piraterie, Völkerrecht und Internationale Beziehungen* (Frankfurt: Campus, 2010).

Kennedy, C., 'From the Ballroom to the Battlefield: British Women and Waterloo', in A. Forrest, K. Hagemann and J. Rendall (eds.), *Soldiers, Citizens and Civilians: Experiences and Perceptions of the Revolutionary and Napoleonic Wars, 1790–1820* (Basingstoke: Palgrave Macmillan, 2009), 137–56.

Kennedy, P., *The Rise and Fall of the Great Powers. Economic Change and Military Conflict from 1500 to 2000* (New York: Random House, 1989).

Keohane, R., *After Hegemony. Cooperation and Discord in the World Political Economy* (Princeton: Princeton University Press, 1984).

Kielmansegg, P. von, *Stein und die Zentralverwaltung 1813/1814* (Stuttgart: Kohlhammer, 1964).

King, D., *Vienna 1814. How the Conquerors of Napoleon Made Love, War, and Peace at the Congress of Vienna* (New York: Crown Publishing, 2008).

Kirmse, G., *Der Musterpräfekt vom Donnersberg. Das Leben des Jeanbon St. André und dessen geschichtlicher Hintergrund* (Simmern: Pandion, 1998).

Kissinger, H., *Diplomacy* (New York: Simon & Schuster, 1994).

Kissinger, H., *A World Restored. The Politics of Conservatism in a Revolutionary Age* (New York: Grosset and Dunlap, 1964).

Klemann, H., 'The Central Commission for the Navigation on the Rhine, 1815–1914. Nineteenth-Century European Integration', ECHR working paper: ECHR-2013-1.

Klingaman, W., and N. Klingaman, *The Year without a Summer. 1816 and the Volcano That Darkened the World and Changed History* (New York: St. Martin's Press, 2013).

Kloes, A., *German Awakening. Protestant Renewal after the Enlightenment, 1815–1848* (Oxford: Oxford University Press).

Knaack, J., 'Wie die "Völkerschlacht" bei Leipzig 1813 zu ihren Namen kam', in S. Dietzsch and A. Ludwig (eds.), *Achim von Arnim und sein Kreis* (Berlin/ New York: De Gruyter, 2010), 269–78.

Koch, J., *Koning Willem I, 1772–1843* (Amsterdam: Boom, 2013).

Koselleck, R., *Vergangene Zukunft. Zur Semantik geschichtlicher Zeiten* (Frankfurt: Suhrkamp, 1989).

Koskenniemi, M., *The Gentle Civilizer of Nations. The Rise and Fall of International Law, 1870–1960* (Cambridge: Cambridge University Press, 2004).

Kraehe, E., 'A Bipolar Balance of Power', *American Historical Review*, 97:3 (1992), 707–15.

Kraehe, E., *Metternich's German Policy*, vol. 2: *The Congress of Vienna, 1814–1815* (Princeton, NJ: Princeton University Press, 1983).

Kraehe, E., 'Wellington and the Reconstruction of the Allied Armies during the Hundred Days', *The International History Review*, 11:1 (1989), 84–97.

Kurtz, H., *The Trial of Marshal Ney. His Last Years and Death* (New York: Knopf, 1957).

Landheer, H., 'Afrekenen met het verleden: De vereffening van de achterstallige schulden van het Koninkrijk der Nederlanden in het begin van de negentiende eeuw', in H. Boels (ed.), *Overheidsfinanciën tijdens de Republiek en het Koninkrijk, 1600–1850* (Hilversum: Verloren, 2012), 189–230.

Landheer, H., 'Arm Vlissingen: Hulpverlening en schadevergoeding', in V. Enthoven (ed.), *Een haven te ver. De Britse expeditie naar de Schelde van 1809* (Nijmegen: Vantilt, 2009), 257–77.

Lang, J., 'New Histories of Emotion', *History & Theory*, 57:1 (2018), 104–20.

Lange, E. de, Menacing Tides. Piracy, Security and Imperialism in the Nineteenth-Century Mediterranean (Unpublished PhD thesis, Utrecht University, 2019).

Laux, S., '"Errors of statesmanship" en 1815? Le Congrès de Vienne et les régions allemandes', *Austriaca*, 84 (2017), 157–76.

Laven D., and L. Riall (eds.), *Napoleon's Legacy. Problems of Government in Restoration Europe* (Oxford: Berg, 2000).

Lefebvre, G., *La Grande Peur de 1789. Suivi de Les foules révolutionnaires* (Paris: Armand Collin, 1932).

Lefèvre, C., 'Le département de l'Aisne et l'invasion de 1815 d'après les lettres contemporaines inédites', *Bulletin de la Société historique et académique de Haute-Picardie*, 18 (1847), 42–81.

Legêne, S., and M. Eickhoff, 'Postwar Europe and the Colonial Past in Photographs', in A. Rigney and C. de Cesari (eds.), *Transnational Memory. Circulation, Articulation, Scales* (Berlin: De Gruyter, 2014), 287–311.

Leggiere, M., *Napoleon and the Struggle for Germany* (Cambridge: Cambridge University Press, 2015).

Lehmann, M., *Scharnhorst*, vol. 2 (Leipzig: Hirzel, 1887).

Leighton, J., 'The Experience of Demobilization: War Veterans in the Central European Armies and Societies after 1815', in A. Forrest, K. Hagemann and M. Rowe (eds.), *War, Demobilization and Memory: The Legacy of War in the Era of Atlantic Revolutions* (Basingstoke: Palgrave Macmillan, 2016), 68–83.

Lemmens, W., 'Het ontluikend liberalisme: Franse migranten, hun netwerken en journalistieke activiteiten in de Zuidelijke Nederlanden, 1815–1830', *Revue Belge de philologie et d'histoire*, 89:3/4 (2011), 1165–91.

Lemmens, W., '"Une terre hospitalière et libre"? Franse migranten tussen restauratie en revolutie in het Brussel van Willem I, 1815–1830', *De Negentiende Eeuw*, 36:4 (2012), 263–84.

Leonhard, J., *Bellizismus und Nation. Kriegsdeutung und Nationsbestimmung in Europa und den Vereinigten Staaten 1750–1914* (Munich: Oldenbourg, 2008).

Levie, S. et al., *Het vaderlandsch gevoel. Vergeten negentiende-eeuwse schilderijen over onze geschiedenis* (Amsterdam: Rijksmuseum, 1978).

Ley, F., *Alexandre 1ᵉʳ et sa Sainte-Alliance (1811–1825). Avec des documents inedits* (Paris: Fischbacher, 1975).

Leys, R., 'The Turn to Affect: A Critique', *Critical Enquiry*, 37:3 (2011), 434–72.

Lieven, D., 'International Relations in the Napoleonic Era: The Long View', in J. Hartley, P. Keenan and D. Lieven (eds.), *Russia and the Napoleonic Wars* (Basingstoke: Palgrave Macmillan, 2015), 12–27.

Lieven, D., 'Introduction', in J. Hartley, P. Keenan and D. Lieven (eds.), *Russia and the Napoleonic Wars* (Basingstoke: Palgrave Macmillan, 2015), 1–11.

Lieven, D., *Russia against Napoleon. The Battle for Europe, 1807 to 1814* (London: Allen Lane, 2009).

Lin, P. 'Caring for the Nation's Families', in A. Forrest, K. Hagemann and J. Rendall (eds.), *Soldiers, Citizens and Civilians: Experiences and Perceptions of the Revolutionary and Napoleonic Wars, 1790–1820* (Basingstoke: Palgrave Macmillan, 2009), 99–117.

Ling, E., and A. Marquis, '1816. Prints by Turner, Goya and Cornelius', Department of Paintings, Drawings & Prints (The Fitzwilliam Museum, University of Cambridge, 2016).

Lok, M., '"Un oubli total du passé?" The Political and Social Construction of Silence in Restoration Europe (1813–1830)', *History & Memory*, 26:2 (2014), 40–75.

Lok, M., '"Renouer la chaîne des temps" ou "repartir à zéro"? Passé, présent, futur en France et aux Pays-Bas (1814–1815)', *Revue d'histoire du XIXᵉ siècle*, 49 (2014), 79–92.

Lok, M., *Windvanen. Napoleontische Bestuurders in de Nederlandse en Franse Restauratie (1813–1820)* (Amsterdam: Bert Bakker, 2009).

Lok, M., and N. Scholz, 'The Return of the Loving Father: Masculinity, Legitimacy and the French and Dutch Restoration Monarchies (1813–1815)', *BMGN-Low Countries Historical Review*, 127:1 (2012), 19–44.

Long, R. (ed.), *The Man on the Spot. Essays on British Empire History* (Westport, CT: Greenwood Press, 1995).

Luh, J., *Der kurze Traum de Freiheit. Preussen nach Napoleon* (Munich: Siedler, 2015).

Lukács, G., *The Historical Novel* (trans. H. and S. Mitchell, Lincoln: University of Nebraska Press, 1962).

Lynn, J., 'Looting/Plunder/Booty', in R. Cowley and G. Parker (eds.), *The Reader's Companion to Military History* (New York: Houghton Mifflin, 1996).

Lyons, F., *Internationalism in Europe, 1815–1914* (Leiden: Sythoff, 1963).

Macalister-Smith, P., and J. Schwietzke, *Diplomatic Conferences and Congresses. A Bibliographical Compendium of State Practice, 1642 to 1919* (Graz: Neugebauer Verlag, 2017).

Macartney, C., *The Habsburg Empire 1790–1918* (London: Faber & Faber, 1969).

MacKenzie, J., 'European Imperialism: A Zone of Cooperation Rather than Competition?', in V. Barth and R. Cvetkovski (eds.), *Imperial Cooperation and Transfer, 1870–1930. Empires and Encounters* (London: Bloomsbury, 2015), 35–56.

Macmillan, M. *Peacemakers. The Paris Conference of 1919 and its Attempt to End War* (London: John Murray, 2001).

Mai, G., *Der Alliierte Kontrollrat in Deutschland 1945–1948. Alliierte Einheit – deutsche Teilung?* (Munich: Oldenbourg, 1995).

Mallez, P., *La Restauration des finances françaises après 1814* (Paris: Dalloz, 1927).

Mandelbaum, M., *The Fate of Nations. The Search for National Security in the Nineteenth and Twentieth Centuries* (Cambridge: Cambridge University Press, 1988).

Manhart, S., *In den Feldern des Wissens. Studiengang, Fach und disziplinäre Semantik in den Geschichts- und Staatswissenschaften (1780–1860)* (Würzburg: Köningshausen & Neumann, 2011).

Mannheim, K., 'Das konservative Denken: Soziologische Beiträge zum Werden des politischen-historischen Denkens in Deutschland', *Archiv für Sozialwissenschaft und Sozialpolitik*, 57:1 (1927), 68–142.

Mansel, P., 'From Exile to the Throne: The Europeanization of Louis XVIII', in P. Mansel and T. Riotte (eds.), *Monarchy and Exile. The Politics of Legitimacy from Marie de Médicis to Wilhelm II* (Basingstoke: Palgrave Macmillan, 2011), 181–213.

Mansel, P., *Louis XVIII* (Thrupp: Sutton, 1999).

Mansel, P., 'Wellington and the French Restoration', *The International History Review*, 11:1 (1989), 76–83.

Marcowitz, R., *Grossmacht auf Bewährung. Die Interdependenz französischer Innen-und Aussenpolitik und ihre Auswirkungen auf Frankreichs Stellung im europäischen Konzert 1814/15–1851/52* (Stuttgart: Thorbecke, 2001).

Marjolin, R., 'Troubles provoqués en France par la disette de 1816–1817', *Revue d'histoire moderne*, 8: Nov.–Dec. (1933), 423–60.

Marshall, P., *Problems of Empire. Britain and India, 1757–1813*, vol. 2 (London: Routledge, 2001 [1968]).

Martin, J.-C., *Contre-Révolution, Révolution et Nation en France 1789–1799* (Paris: Seuil, 1998).

Mazower, M., *Governing the World. The History of an Idea* (London: Penguin, 2012).

McConnell, A., 'Alexander I's Hundred Days: The Politics of a Paternalist Reformer', *Slavic Review*, 28:3 (1969), 373–93.

McLynn, F., *Napoleon. A Biography* (London: Pimlico, 1998).

McNally, T., 'Das Russlandbild in der Publizistik Frankreichs zwischen 1814 und 1843', *Forschungen zur osteuropäischen Geschichte*, 6 (1958), 82–170.

Meinecke, F., *Die Entstehung des Historismus* (Munich: Oldenbourg, 1936).

Meinecke, F., *Die Idee der Staatsräson in der neueren Geschichte* (Munich: Oldenbourg, 1925).

Meinecke, F., *Weltbürgertum und Nationalstaat. Studien zur Genesis des deutschen Nationalstaates* (Munich: Oldenbourg, 1907).

Menger, P., 'Die Heilige Allianz – "La Garantie Religieuse du nouveau système Européen"?', in W. Pyta (ed.), *Das europäische Mächtekonzert. Friedens- und*

Sicherheitspolitik vom Wiener Kongress 1815 bis zum Krimkrieg 1853 (Cologne: Böhlau, 2009), 209–36.

Menger, P., *Die Heilige Allianz. Religion und Politik bei Alexander I. (1801–1825)* (Stuttgart: Steiner, 2014).

Merecy, R., 'De Antwerpsche pers onder het "Vereenigd Koninkrijk"', *De Gulden Passer*, 23 (1945), 81–95.

Michel, T., 'Time to Get Emotional: Phronetic Reflections on the Concept of Trust in International Relations', *European Journal of International Relations*, 19:4 (2013), 869–90.

Mitzen, J., *Power in Concert. The Nineteenth-Century Origins of Global Governance* (Chicago: University of Chicago Press, 2013).

Moncan, P. de, *Les jardins du baron Haussmann* (Paris: Les Éditions du Mécène, 2007).

Morgenthau, H., *Politics among Nations. The Struggle for Power and Peace* (New York: McGraw-Hill, 1992 [1948]).

Muir, R., *Wellington. The Path to Victory, 1769–1814* (New Haven/London: Yale University Press, 2013).

Muir, R., *Wellington. Waterloo and the Fortunes of Peace, 1814–1852* (New Haven/ London: Yale University Press, 2015).

Müller, H., 'Internationale Beziehungen als kommunikatives Handeln. Zur Kritik der utilitaristischen Handlungstheorien', *Zeitschrift für Internationale Beziehungen*, 1:1 (1994), 15–44.

Näf, W., *Zur Geschichte der Heiligen Allianz* (Bern: Paul Haupt, 1928).

Naimark, N., *The Russians in Germany. A History of the Soviet Zone of Occupation, 1945–1949* (London/Cambridge, MA: Belknap Press, 1997).

Nelson, C., 'The Duke of Wellington and the Barrier Fortresses after Waterloo', *Army Historical Research*, 42 (1964), 36–43.

Nicholson, H., *The Congress of Vienna. A Study in Allied Unity, 1812–1822* (New York: Grove Press, 2001 [1946]).

Nicolle, A., *Comment la France a payé après Waterloo* (Paris: Boccard, 1929).

Nicolle, A., 'The Problem of Reparations after the Hundred Days', *The Journal of Modern History*, 25:4 (1953), 343–54.

Nicolson, H., *The Congress of Vienna. A Study in Allied Unity, 1812–1822* (London: Constable, 1946).

Nipperdey, T., *Deutsche Geschichte 1800–1866. Bürgerwelt und starker Staat* (Munich: C. H. Beck, 1998).

Nübel, C., 'Auf der Suche nach Stabilität: 1813 und die Restauration der Monarchie im europäischen Vergleich', in B. Aschmann and T. Stamm-Kuhlmann (eds.), *1813 im Europäische Kontext* (Stuttgart: Steiner, 2015), 163–86.

O'Brien, M., *Mrs. Adams in Winter. A Journey in the Last Days of Napoleon* (New York: Farrar, Straus and Giroux, 2010).

Oldfield, J., *Transatlantic Abolitionism in the Age of Revolution. An International History of Anti-Slavery, c.1787–1820* (Cambridge: Cambridge University Press, 2013).

Oliver, B., *From Royal to National. The Louvre Museum and the Bibliothèque Nationale* (Lanham/New York: Lexington, 2007).

Oosterlinck, K., L. Ureche-Rangau and J.-M. Vaslin, 'Baring, Wellington and the Resurrection of French Public Finances Following Waterloo', *The Journal of Economic History*, 74:4 (2014), 1072–102.

Oppenheimer, C., 'Climatic, Environmental and Human Consequences of the Largest Known Historic Eruption: Tambora Volcano (Indonesia) 1815', *Progress in Physical Geography*, 27:2 (2003).

Opsommer, R., *Ieper en de Frans-Belgische grens (17e–18e eeuw). 300 jaar vredesverdragen van Utrecht en Rastatt* (Ypres: City Archives, 2013).

Organski, A., *World Politics* (New York: Knopf, 1958).

Ortemberg, P., 'El tedeum en el ritual político: Usos y sentidos de un dispositivo de pactos en la América española y en la revolucion de Mayo', *Anuario del Instituto de Historia Argentina*, 10 (2010), 199–226.

Osiander, A., *The States System of Europe, 1640–1990. Peacemaking and the Conditions of International Stability* (London: Oxford University Press, 1994).

Osterhammel, J., *Colonialism. A Theoretical Overview* (Princeton: Wiener, 1997).

Osterhammel, J., *The Transformation of the World. A Global History of the Nineteenth Century* (Princeton: Princeton University Press, 2014).

Oțetea, A., 'Fuga lui Caragea' ['The flight of Caradja'], in *Omagiu lui P. Constantinescu-Iași. cu prilejul împlinirii a 70 de ani* ['Tribute to P. Constantinescu-Iași on the occasion of his 70th birthday'] (Bucharest: Editura Academiei Republicii Populare Romîne, 1965).

Otto, H., *Gneisenau. Preussens unbequemer Patriot. Biographie* (Bonn: Keil, 1979).

Ozavci, O., *Dangerous Gifts. Imperialism, Security and Civil Wars in the Levant, 1798–1864* (Oxford: Oxford University Press, forthcoming).

Pakenham, E., *Tom, Ned and Kitty. An Intimate Portrait of an Irish Family* (Phoenix: W&N, 2008).

Panzac, D., *Barbary Corsairs. The End of a Legend, 1800–1820* (Leiden: Brill, 2005).

Parkinson, R., *The Hussar General. The Life of Blücher, Man of Waterloo* (London: Purnell, 1975).

Patten, R., *George Cruikshank's Life, Times and Art*, 2 vols. (London: Lutterworth Press, 1996).

Paulmann, J., *Pomp und Politik. Monarchenbegegnungen in Europa zwischen Ancien Régime und Erstem Weltkrieg* (Paderborn: F. Schöningh, 2000).

Pedersen, S. *The Guardians. The League of Nations and the Crisis of Empire* (Oxford: Oxford University Press, 2015).

Petiteau, N., *Napoleon, de la mythologie à l'histoire* (Paris: Seuil, 1999).

Petiteau, N., 'Survivors of War: French Soldiers and Veterans of the Napoleonic Armies', in A. Forrest, K. Hagemann and J. Rendall (eds.), *Soldiers, Citizens and Civilians: Experiences and Perceptions of the Revolutionary and Napoleonic Wars, 1790–1820* (Basingstoke: Palgrave Macmillan, 2009), 43–58.

Petonke, W., *Der Konflikt zwischen Preussens Staats- und Heeresleitung während der Okkupation in Frankreich, Juli bis November 1815* (Berlin: Adler, 1906).

Pfeil, T., 'Tot redding van het vaderland'. Het primaat van de Nederlandse overheidsfinanciën in de Bataafs-Franse tijd, 1795–1810 (Amsterdam: Amsterdam University Press, 1998).

Pingaud, A., 'Le projet Polignac (1829)', Revue d'histoire diplomatique, 14 (1900), 402–10.

Pink, G., The Conference of Ambassadors (Paris 1920–1931). Its History, the Theoretical Aspect of its Work, and its Place in International Organization (Geneva: Geneva Research Centre, 1942).

Pippidi, A., Hommes et idées du sud-est européen à l'aube de l'âge moderne (Bucharest: Editura Academiei Republicii Socialiste România, 1980), 295–314.

Pippidi, A., 'Notules phanariotes, II, Encore Jean Caradja à Genève', Ho Eranistes, 17 (1981), 74–85.

Pirenne, J., Geschiedenis van Europa, vol. 2 (Brussels: Renaissance du Livre, 1960).

Pittock, M. (ed.), The Reception of Sir Walter Scott in Europe (London: Continuum, 2006).

Pitts, J., A Turn to Empire. The Rise of Imperial Liberalism in Britain and France (Princeton: Princeton University Press, 2005).

Plamper, J., Geschichte und Gefühl. Grundlagen der Emotionsgeschichte (Munich: Siedler, 2012).

Platt, D., Foreign Finance in Continental Europe and the United States, 1815–1870. Quantities, Origins, Functions and Distribution (London: Allen & Unwin, 1984).

Ploux, F., 'L'imaginaire social et politique de la rumeur dans la France du XIXe siècle (1815–1870)', Revue historique, 302:2 (April-June 2000), 395–434.

Post, J., The Last Great Subsistence Crisis in the Western World (Baltimore/London: Johns Hopkins University Press, 1977).

Pöthe, Z., Perikles in Preussen. Die Politik Friedrich Wilhelms II. im Spiegel des Brandenburger Tores (Berlin: epubli, 2014).

Prescott, L., 'Voices in Britain during the Napoleonic Wars: Jane Austen', Jane Austen Studies Center, paper 1 (2009).

Price, M., Napoleon. The End of Glory (New York: Oxford University Press, 2014).

Price, M., The Perilous Crown. France between Revolutions (Basingstoke: Palgrave Macmillan, 2009).

Probst, E., Königinnen der Lüfte in Deutschland. Biografien berühmter Fliegerinnen, Ballonfahrerinnen, Luftschifferinnen und Fallschirmspringerinnen (Munich: Grin, 2010).

Pyta, W. (ed.), Das europäische Mächtekonzert. Friedens- und Sicherheitspolitik vom Wiener Kongress 1815 bis zum Krimkrieg 1853 (Cologne: Böhlau, 2009).

Raeff, M., The Well-Ordered Police State. Social and Institutional Change through Law in the Germanies and Russia, 1600–1800 (New Haven: Yale University Press, 1983).

Rain, P. L'Europe et la restauration des Bourbons 1814–1818 (Paris: Perrin, 1908).

Raphael, L., *Recht und Ordnung. Herrschaft durch Verwaltung im 19. Jahrhundert* (Frankfurt: Fischer, 2000).

Rech, W., *Enemies of Mankind. Vattel's Theory of Collective Security* (Leiden/ Boston: Martinus Nijhoff, 2013).

Reddy, W., *The Navigation of Feeling. A Framework for the History of Emotions* (Cambridge: Cambridge University Press, 2001).

Reeder, T., '"Sovereign Lords" and "Dependent Administrators": Artigan Privateers, Atlantic Borderwaters, and State Building in the Early Nineteenth Century', *Journal of American History*, 103:2 (2016), 323–46.

Reiter, H., *Politisches Asyl im 19. Jahrhundert. Die deutschen politischen Flüchtlinge des Vormärz und der Revolution von 1848/49 in Europa und den USA* (Berlin: Duncker & Humblot, 1992).

Renier, G., *Great Britain and the Establishment of the Kingdom of the Netherlands, 1813–1815. A Study in British Foreign Policy* (London: Allen & Unwin, 1930).

Resnick, D., *The White Terror and the Political Reaction after Waterloo* (Cambridge, MA: Harvard University Press, 1966).

Resnick, E., 'A Family Imbroglio: Brazil's Invasion of the Banda Oriental in 1816 and Repercussions on the Iberian Peninsula', *Revista de História*, 51:101 (1975), 179–205.

Rey, M.-P., *Alexander I. The Tsar Who Defeated Napoleon* (Illinois: NIU Press, 2012).

Reynolds, D., *Summits. Six Meetings That Shaped the Twentieth Century* (London: Allen Lane, 2007).

Rials, S., 'Essai sur le concept de monarchie limitée (autour de la charte de 1814)', in S. Rials, *Révolution et contre-révolution au 19ème siècle* (Paris: Albatros, 1987), 119–25.

Ribhegge, W., *Preußen im Westen. Kampf um den Parlamentarismus in Rheinland und Westphalen, 1789–1947* (Münster: Aschendorff Verlag, 2008).

Richardson, L., 'The Concert of Europe and Security Management in the Nineteenth Century', in H. Haftendorn, R. Keohane and C. Wallander (eds.), *Imperfect Unions. Security Institutions over Time and Space* (Oxford: Oxford University Press, 1999), 48–80.

Riemens, H., *Het Amortisatiesyndicaat. Een studie over de staatsfinanciën onder Willem I* (Amsterdam: Paris, 1935).

Riley, J., *International Government Finance and the Amsterdam Capital Market 1740–1815* (Cambridge: Marten, 1980).

Roberts, A., *Napoleon and Wellington. The Battle of Waterloo and the Great Commanders Who Fought It* (New York: Simon and Schuster, 2001).

Roberts, A., *Wellington and Napoleon. The Long Duel* (London: Weidenfeld and Nicolson, 2003).

Robijns, M., *Radicalen in Nederland, 1840–1851* (Leiden: Universitaire Pers, 1967).

Rosen, F., 'Bentham and Mill on Liberty and Justice', in G. Feaver and F. Rosen (eds.), *Lives, Liberties and the Public Good* (Basingstoke: Macmillan, 1987), 121–38.

Rössler, H., *Zwischen Revolution und Reaktion. Ein Lebensbild des Reichsfreiherrn Hans Christoph von Gagern 1766–1852* (Göttingen: Musterschmidt, 1958).

Rothenberg, G., *The Art of Warfare in the Age of Napoleon* (Bloomington: Indiana University Press, 1977).

Rowe M. (ed.), *Collaboration and Resistance in Napoleonic Europe. State-Formation in an Age of Upheaval, 1800–1815* (Basingstoke: Palgrave Macmillan, 2003).

Rowe, M., *From Reich to State. The Rhineland in the Revolutionary Age, 1780–1830* (Cambridge: Cambridge University Press, 2003).

Rythoven, E. van, 'Learning to Feel, Learning to Fear? Emotions, Imaginaries, and Limits in the Politics of Securitization', *Security Dialogue*, 46:5 (2015), 458–75.

Sargeant, L., *Harmony and Discord. Music and the Transformation of Russian Cultural Life* (Oxford: Oxford University Press, 2011).

Sas, N. van, 'From Waterloo Field to Bruges-La-Morte: Historical Imagination in the Nineteenth Century', in H. Dunthorne and M. Wintle (eds.), *The Historical Imagination in Nineteenth-Century Britain and the Low Countries* (Leiden/ Boston: Brill, 2013), 19–41.

Sas, N. van, *Onze natuurlijkste bondgenoot. Nederland, Engeland en Europa, 1713–1831* (Groningen: Wolters-Noordhoff, 1985).

Sautyn Kluit, W., 'Dagbladvervolgingen in België', *Bijdragen voor Vaderlandsche Geschiedenis en Oudheidkunde*, 3:6 (1892).

Savoy, B. (ed.) *Napoleon und Europa. Traum und Trauma. Kunst- und Ausstellungshalle der Bundesrepublik Deutschland, Bonn, 17. Dezember 2010 bis 25. April 2011* (Munich, 2010).

Savoy, B., *Patrimoine annexé. Les saisies de bien culturels pratiqués par la France en Allemagne autour de 1800*, vol. 1 (Paris: Éditions de la Maison des sciences de l'homme, 2003).

Schama, S., 'The Exigencies of War and the Politics of Taxation in the Netherlands 1795–1810', in J. de Winter (ed.), *War and Economic Development. Essays in Memory of David Joslin* (Cambridge: Cambridge University Press, 1975), 103–37.

Schechter, R., *A Genealogy of Terror in Eighteenth-Century France* (Chicago/ London: University of Chicago Press, 2018).

Schenk, J., 'The Central Commission for Navigation of the Rhine: A First Step towards European Economic Security?' in B. de Graaf, I. de Haan and B. Vick (eds.), *Securing Europe after Napoleon. 1815 and the New European Security Culture* (Cambridge: Cambridge University Press, 2019), 75–94.

Schmitt, C., *Politische Romantik* (Berlin: Duncker & Humblot, 1919).

Schofield, P., and J. Harris, 'Editorial Introduction', in P. Schofield and J. Harris (eds.), *'Legislator of the World'. Writings on Codification, Law, and Education* (Oxford: Oxford University Press, 1998).

Schroeder, P., 'Alliances, 1815–1945: Weapons of Power and Tools of Management', in K. Knorr (ed.), *Historical Dimensions of National Security Problems* (Lawrence: University Press of Kansas, 1976), 227–62.

Schroeder, P., 'Did the Vienna Settlement Rest on a Balance of Power?', *American Historical Review*, 97:3 (1992), 683–706.

Schroeder, P., 'A Mild Rejoinder', *The American Historical Review*, 97:3 (1992), 733–5.

Schroeder, P., *The Transformation of European Politics, 1763–1848* (Oxford: Clarendon, 1994).

Schulten, K., *Plein 1813. Het Nationaal Monument in Den Haag* (The Hague: Hega Offset, 2013).

Schulz, M., 'The Construction of a Culture of Peace in Post-Napoleonic Europe: Peace through Equilibrium, Law and New Forms of Communicative Interaction', *Journal of Modern European History*, 13:4 (2015), 464–74.

Schulz, M., 'Cultures of Peace and Security from the Vienna Congress to the Twenty-First Century', in B. de Graaf, I. de Haan and B. Vick (eds.), *Securing Europe after Napoleon. 1815 and the New European Security Culture* (Cambridge: Cambridge University Press, 2019), 21–39.

Schulz, M., *Normen und Praxis. Das Europäische Konzert der Großmächte als Sicherheitsrat, 1815–1860* (Munich: Oldenbourg, 2009).

Sellin, V., *Gewalt und Legitimität. Die europäische Monarchie im Zeitalter der Revolutionen* (Munich: Oldenbourg, 2011).

Severn, J., *Architects of Empire. The Duke of Wellington and his Brothers* (Oklahoma City: University of Oklahoma Press, 2007).

Siborne, W., *The Waterloo Campaign, 1815* (Westminster: Constable, 1895).

Siemann, W., *Metternich. Stratege und Visionär* (Munich: C. H. Beck, 2016).

Skeen, C., 'The Year without a Summer: A Historical View', *Journal of the Early Republic*, 1:1 (1981), 51–67.

Sluga, G., 'Economic Insecurity, "Securities" and a European Security Culture after the Napoleonic Wars', in B. de Graaf, I. de Haan and B. Vick (eds.), *Securing Europe after Napoleon. 1815 and the New European Security Culture* (Cambridge: Cambridge University Press, 2019), 288–305.

Sluga, G., 'Madame de Staël and the Transformation of European Politics, 1812–1817', *International History Review*, 37:1 (2015), 142–66.

Sluga, G., '"Who Hold the Balance of the World?" Bankers at the Congress of Vienna, and in International History', *The American Historical Review*, 122:5 (2017), 1403–30.

Sluga, G., 'Women, Diplomacy and International Politics, before and after the Congress of Vienna', in G. Sluga and C. James (eds.), *Women, Diplomacy and International Politics since 1500* (London: Routledge, 2015).

Smets, J., *Les Pays Rhénans (1794–1814). Le comportement des Rhénans face à l'occupation français* (Bern: Peter Lang, 1997).

Smith, D., *The Napoleonic Wars Data Book. Actions and Losses in Personnel, Colours, Standards and Artillery, 1792–1815* (London: Greenhill, 1998).

Sparrow, E., *Secret Service. British Agents in France 1792–1815* (Woodbridge: Boydell Press, 1999).

Sperber, J., *Revolutionary Europe, 1780–1850* (London/New York: Routledge, 2017 [2000]).

Sperber, J., *Rhineland Radicals. The Democratic Movement and the Revolution of 1848–1849* (Princeton: Princeton University Press, 1991).

Spitzer, A., *Old Hatreds and Young Hopes. The French Carbonari against the Bourbon Restoration* (Cambridge, MA: Harvard University Press, 1971).

Stauber, R., *Der Wiener Kongress* (Vienna: Böhlau, 2014).

Steiner, Z., *The Lights That Failed. European International History, 1919–1933* (Oxford: Oxford University Press, 2005), 403.

Stern, A., 'Der grosse Plan des Herzogs von Polignac vom Jahre 1829', *Historische Vierteljahresschrift*, 3 (1900), 49–77.

Stettiner, P., *Der Tugendbund* (Koningsberg: Koch, 1904).

Stirling-Maxwell, W., *Napoleon's Bequest to Cantillon. A Fragment of International History* (London: Longwood, 1858).

Stites, R., *The Four Horsemen. Riding to Liberty in Post-Napoleonic Europe* (Oxford: Oxford University Press, 2015).

Stollberg-Rilinger, B., *Maria Theresia. Die Kaiserin in ihrer Zeit. Eine Biografie* (Munich: C. H. Beck, 2017).

Stollberg-Rilinger, B., *Der Staat als Maschine. Zur politischen Metaphorik des absoluten Fürstenstaats* (Berlin: Duncker & Humblot, 1986).

Stollberg-Rilinger, B., 'State and Political History in a Culturalist Perspective', in A. Flüchter and S. Richter (eds.), *Structures on the Move* (Berlin: Springer, 2012), 43–58.

Street, J., *Artigas and the Emancipation of Uruguay* (Cambridge: Cambridge University Press, 1971 [1959]).

Stück, H., and A. Grelon, 'Die Ingenieure des Corps des Ponts et Chaussées: Von der Eroberung des nationalen Raumes zur Raumordnung', in H. Stück and A. Grelon (eds.), *Ingenieure in Frankreich, 1747–1990* (Frankfurt: Campus, 1994).

Sweet, P., *Friedrich von Gentz. Defender of the Old Order* (Madison: University of Wisconsin Press, 1935).

Todd, D., 'A French Imperial Meridian, 1814–1870', *Past & Present*, 210 (2011), 155–86.

Tosi, A., *Waiting for Pushkin. Russian Fiction in the Reign of Alexander I (1801–1825)* (Amsterdam/New York: Rodopi, 2006).

Triomphe, P., 'Des bruits qui courent aux mots qui tuent. Rumeurs et violences dans le Gard en 1815', *Revue d'Histoire du XIXe Siècle*, 36 (2008), 59–73.

Tsygankov, A., *Russia and the West from Alexander to Putin. Honor in International Relations* (Cambridge: Cambridge University Press, 2012).

Tulard, J. (ed.), *Dictionnaire Napoléon* (Paris: Fayard, 1987).

Uhm, L. van, The Moving Dead. The Politics of Mourning, Dead Bodies, and Violent Conflict (Unpublished PhD thesis, Utrecht University, forthcoming).

Uitterhoeve, W., *'Een innige vereeniging'. Naar één koninkrijk van Nederland en België in 1815* (Nijmegen: Vantilt, 2015).

Uitterhoeve, W., *Cornelis Kraijenhoff 1758–1840. Een loopbaan onder vijf regeer-vormen* (Nijmegen: Vantilt, 2009).

Urechia, V., 'Din domnia lui Ioan Caragea. Avenire la tron. Mişcări contra grecilor. Finanţe, 1812–1818' ['From Caradja's reign: his enthronement; movements against the Greeks; finances, 1812–1818'], *Analele Academiei Române*, 22:2 (1900).

Vandermeersch-Lantmeeters, E., *Uit de geschiedenis van het Geslacht Vandermeersch te Oudenaarde* (Sanderus: Oudenaarde, 1973).

Vasold, M., 'The Epidemic Typhus of 1813/14 in the Area of Lower Franconia', *Würzburger Medizinhistorische Mitteilungen*, 23 (2004), 217–32.

Vec, M., 'Verrechtlichung internationaler Streitbeilegung im 19. und 20. Jahrhundert?', in S. Dauchy and M. Vec (eds.), *Les conflits entre le peuples* (Baden-Baden: Nomos, 2011), 1–21.

Velde, H. te, *Over het begrijpen van 1813 tweehonderd jaar later* (The Hague: National Archives, 2013).

Veve, T. D., *The Duke of Wellington and the British Army of Occupation in France, 1815–1818* (Westport: Greenwood Press, 1992).

Veve, T. D., 'Wellington and the Army of Occupation in France, 1815–1818', *The International History Review*, 11:1 (1989), 98–108.

Vick, B., *The Congress of Vienna. Power and Politics after Napoleon* (Cambridge, MA: Harvard University Press, 2014).

Vick, B., 'Power, Humanitarianism, and the Global Liberal Order: Abolition and the Barbary Corsairs in the Vienna Congress System', *The International History Review*, 40:4 (2018), 939–60.

Vick, B., 'The London Ambassadors' Conferences and Beyond. Abolition, Barbary Corsairs and Multilateral Security in the Congress of Vienna System', in B. de Graaf, I. de Haan and B. Vick (eds.) *Securing Europe after Napoleon. 1815 and the New European Security Culture* (Cambridge: Cambridge University Press, 2019), 114–29.

Viel-Castel, L. de, *Histoire de la Restauration*, vol. 5 (Paris: Michel Lévy frères, 1862).

Wacker, V., *Die alliierte Besetzung Frankreichs in den Jahren 1814 bis 1818* (Hamburg: Kovac, 2001).

Waresquiel, E. de, *Le Duc de Richelieu, 1766–1822. Un sentimental en politique* (Paris: Perrin, 1990).

Waresquiel, E. de, *Fouché. Les silences de la pieuvre* (Paris: Fayard, 2014).

Waresquiel, E. de, *L'histoire à rebrousse-poil. Les élites, la Restauration, la Révolution* (Paris: Fayard, 2005).

Waresquiel, E. de, *Talleyrand. Le prince immobile* (Paris: Fayard, 2003).

Waresquiel, E. de, and B. Yvert, *Histoire de la Restauration (1814–1830). Naissance de la France moderne* (Paris: Perrin, 1996).

Webster, C., *The Congress of Vienna, 1814–1815* (Oxford: Oxford University Press, 1918).

Webster, C., *The Foreign Policy of Castlereagh, 1815–1822. Britain and the European Alliance*, vol. 2 (London: G. Bells and Sons, 1931–47).

Wemyss, A., 'L'Angleterre et la Terreur blanche de 1815 dans le Midi', *Annales du Midi*, 73:55 (1963), 287–310.

White, E., 'Making the French Pay. The Costs and Consequences of the Napoleonic Reparations', *European Review of Economic History*, 5:3 (2001), 337–65.

Wight, M., 'The Balance of Power and International Order', in M. Brands, N. van Sas and B. Tromp (eds.), *De veiligheid van Europa. Aspecten van de ontwikkeling van het Europese statenstelsel* (Rijswijk: Universitaire Pers Rotterdam, 1991), 1–25.

Williams, M., *Culture and Security. Symbolic Power and the Politics of International Security* (London: Routledge, 2007).

Wolfe, S., *The Politics of Reparations and Apologies* (New York: Springer, 2014).

Woolf, S., *Napoleon's Integration of Europe* (London/New York: Routledge, 1991).

Wüppermann, W., *De vorming van het Nederlandsche leger na de omwenteling van 1813 en het aandeel van dat leger aan den veldtocht van 1815* (Breda: KMA, 1900).

Zamoyski, A., *Phantom Terror. The Threat of Revolution and the Repression of Liberty 1789–1848* (London: Harper Collins, 2015).

Zamoyski, A., *Rites of Peace. The Fall of Napoleon and the Congress of Vienna* (London: Harper Collins, 2007).

Zanten, J. van, *Koning Willem II, 1792–1849* (Amsterdam: Boom, 2013).

Zanten, J. van, '"Met verscheidene dolkstoten afgemaakt": Moraal en politiek in de berichten over de moord op August von Kotzebue', *De Negentiende Eeuw*, 27:1 (2003), 39–49.

Zanten, J. van, *Schielijk, Winzucht, Zwaarhoofd en Bedaard. Politieke Discussie en Oppositievorming 1813–1840* (Amsterdam: Boom, 2004).

Zeisler, K., 'Justus von Gruner. Eine biographische Skizze', in W. Breunig and U. Schaper (eds.), *Berlin in Geschichte und Gegenwart* (Berlin: Gebr. Mann Verlag, 1994), 81–105.

Ziegler, P., *The Sixth Great Power. Barings, 1762–1929* (London: Knopf, 1988).

Zürn, M., *Interessen und Institutionen in der internationalen Politik. Grundlegung und Anwendungen des situationsstrukturellen Ansatzes* (Opladen: Leske & Budrich, 1992).

Zwaan, A. van der, 'Holland is vrij: Dankzij Rusland', *Thema Tijdschrift*, 4:4 (2013), 44–7.

INDEX

Adams, John Quincy, 1, 12, 441–442
Adams, Louisa, 1, 2–4, 12, 28, 135, 168
Africa, 20, 44, 129, 192
  North Africa, 32, 128, 138, 260, 430,
    436, 440, 447, 454
Alexander I, tsar of Russia, 19, 22, 27,
  34, 42, 43, 45–46, 49, 53, 55–59,
  61–65, 66–67, 71, 72, 76–77, 81,
  82, 89, 118, 123, 125, 127, 130, 132,
  145, 146, 148, 149–150, 152, 158,
  163–164, 167, 171, 173, 175, 176,
  178, 188, 195, 197, 205, 210, 221,
  229, 239, 241, 242–243, 245–251,
  255, 258, 261, 275, 282, 294, 300,
  311, 313, 364, 377, 396–398, 400,
  402–403, 406–410, 411, 413–414,
  417, 419, 434, 437, 439, 444, 448,
  451, 452, 453
Alexander the Great, 89
Algeria, 454–456
Algiers, 129
Allies, Allied
  Army of Occupation, 9, 12
  Central Administration, 48, 51, 53,
    145
  cooperation, 3, 28, 34, 75, 360, 394
  Council of Ambassadors, xii, 9–17,
    18–19, 20, 26, 28, 30, 33–35, 76, 77,
    92, 102, 105, 108, 139–140, 143,
    144, 154, 157, 158, 159, 160,
    161–167, 170, 171–172, 174–183,
    187–192, 195, 198, 201, 202–203,
    205–210, 215, 217, 224, 226, 228,
    230, 232–233, 237, 242, 244, 246,
    249–250, 252, 253–255, 257–258,
    261, 263, 267–269, 276, 277–278,
    296, 298–301, 303–304, 307–308,

309, 312, 315, 317, 319, 326–327,
  329, 330–333, 338, 343, 348–349,
  352, 354, 360–361, 364–365, 369,
  371, 373, 379–381, 385, 388,
  390–391, 394, 396, 397, 398, 401,
  404, 406, 407, 416–417, 418, 419,
  422, 427–428, 429–433, 435, 439,
  446, 448–450, 451, 453, 456–457
  machine, 11, 20, 30, 35, 50, 55, 83–84,
    92, 94–95, 105–108, 133, 135,
    159–163, 202, 240, 257, 361, 388,
    406, 417, 427, 429, 430, 435, 439,
    453
Alopeus, Frans David, Count, 51–52,
  55, 170
Alquier, Charles-Jean Marie, 266, 270
Alsace, 193, 202, 221, 363, 364
Altenstein. *See* Stein zum Altenstein
ambassadorial conference, 11
  in London (1816–23), 425, 430–432,
    440
  in Paris (1815–18), 11–15, 19, 30–31
Amis de la Patrie, 261
Amsterdam, 19, 94, 110, 264, 341, 342,
  353–354
ancien régime, 8, 11, 17, 68, 116, 122,
  127, 132, 135, 203, 235, 245, 247,
  353, 450, 452
Anderson, Benedict, 25
Angers, 78, 198
Anglès, Jules, 283, 286–287
Angoulême, 223
Anjou, 193
Anstett, Jean d', 183, 319
Antibes, 423
Antwerp, 46, 186, 290–291, 292, 293,
  358, 372, 375, 378, 382, 418, 425